Loss of the Steamer Jeannette

Loss of the Steamer Jeannette

GOVERNMENT REPRINTS PRESS
Washington, D.C.

© Ross & Perry, Inc. 2001 All rights reserved.

No claim to U.S. government work contained throughout this book.

Protected under the Berne Convention. Published 2001

Printed in The United States of America
Ross & Perry, Inc. Publishers
717 Second St., N.E., Suite 200
Washington, D.C. 20002
Telephone (202) 675-8300
Facsimile (202) 675-8400
info@RossPerry.com

SAN 253-8555

Government Reprints Press Edition 2001

Government Reprints Press is an Imprint of Ross & Perry, Inc.

Library of Congress Control Number: 2001093153

http://www.GPOreprints.com

ISBN 1-931641-43-9

♾ The paper used in this publication meets the requirements for permanence established by the American National Standard for Information Sciences "Permanence of Paper for Printed Library Materials" (ANSI Z39.48-1984).

All rights reserved. No copyrighted part of this publication may be reproduced, stored in a retrieval system, or transmitted, in any form or by any means, electronic, photocopying, recording, or otherwise, without the prior written permission of the publisher.

47TH CONGRESS, } HOUSE OF REPRESENTATIVES. { Ex. Doc.
2d Session. } { No. 108.

LOSS OF THE STEAMER JEANNETTE.

LETTER

FROM

THE SECRETARY OF THE NAVY,

RELATIVE TO

The loss of the steamer Jeannette.

MARCH 2, 1883.—Referred to the Committee on Naval Affairs and ordered to be printed.

NAVY DEPARTMENT,
Washington, March 2, 1883.

SIR: Referring to my letter of the 17th ultimo, transmitting to the House that part of the record of proceedings which contained the finding of the court of inquiry convened in pursuance of the joint resolution of Congress, approved August 8, 1882, for the purpose of investigating the circumstances of the loss in the Arctic seas of the exploring steamer Jeannette and the death of Lieutenant-Commander DeLong and others of her officers and men, I now have the honor to transmit to the House a copy of the entire record of the proceedings of the court, consisting of seven parts and an appendix.

Very respectfully,

WM. E. CHANDLER,
Secretary of the Navy.

Hon. J. WARREN KEIFER,
Speaker of the House of Representatives.

TABLE OF CONTENTS.

	Page.
ORDERS TO THE COURT:	
Order convening the court—the precept	3, 285
Appointment of judge advocate	4, 285
Secretary's letter ordering open court to be held	4, 286
Order reconvening the court	324
Relieving Capt. Joseph N. Miller from duty as a member	324
Relieving Master Samuel C. Lemly from duty as judge-advocate	325
Appointment of new judge-advocate	325
TESTIMONY OF WITNESSES:	
Commodore E. R. Colhoun, U. S. N	7–9, 14
Capt. P. C. Johnson, U. S. N	9–12
Chief Engineer E. Farmer, U. S. N	12–14
Lieut. J. W. Danenhower, U. S. N	15–73, 250–255
Chief Engineer G. W. Melville, U. S. N	75–165, 248, 255, 256
W. F. C. Nindemann, seaman	171–228
Louis P. Noros, seaman	229–234
Raymond L. Newcomb, naturalist	235–241
Charles Tong Sing, steward	242
Henry Wilson, seaman	243–246
H. W. Leach, seaman	267, 268
Frank E. Manson, seaman	268, 269
John Lauterbach, coal-heaver	269, 270
James H. Bartlett, first-class fireman	270–277
FINDING OF THE COURT	260–266, 277
EXHIBITS:	
A. Original precept	285
B. Letter transmitting precept	285
C. Judge-advocate's warrant	285
D. Secretary's letter ordering open court	286
E. Commodore Colhoun's letter appointing board of survey	286
F. Report of board of survey	286
G. Easby to Colhoun, work in Construction and Repair Department	288
H. Memorandum of work in Construction and Repair Department	288
I. English to Colhoun, repairs in Equipment and Recruiting Department	289
K. Telegram, English to Colhoun, supply coal to Jeannette	289
L. Telegram, Shock to Colhoun, repairs in Steam Engineering Department	289
M. Colhoun's letter appointing board of inspection	290
N. Report of board of inspection	290
O. Secretary to De Long (final instructions)	292
P. De Long to Secretary (final report before sailing)	293
Q. Danenhower's sketch of repairs to Jeannette ...... opposite..	293
R. De Long's letter to Danenhower, London, June 2, 1878	294
R 2. Danenhower's chart from Koltenoi Island to Cape Barkin .. opposite..	294
S. Danenhower's chart used in the retreat .... opposite..	294
T. Sketch of river, by Vashily .... opposite..	294
T 2. T Chart showing piloting of whale-boat by natives .... opposite..	294

H. Ex. 108   I

CONTENTS.

EXHIBITS: Page.
- U. Commandant's road sketch..................................opposite..   294
- V. Chart made by Danenhower in October, 1881.................opposite..   294
- W. Orders given Danenhower by Melville in October, 1881   295
- X. Orders given Melville by De Long, Bennett Island, August 5, 1881....   295
- Y. Orders given Danenhower by Melville, Bologna, November 4, 1881....   295
- Z. Orders given Danenhower by Melville to go south, January 8, 1882.... 296
- A A. Receipt from Lieutenant Harber for certain men, March 22, 1882.... 297
- B B. Receipt from Lieutenant Harber for certain articles................ 297
- C C. De Long's Ounalaska letter to Secretary, August 4, 1879............ 297
- D D. De Long's report to Secretary Navy, Saint Lawrence Bay, August 26, 1879.. 298
- E E. Chipp's report to De Long—routine on ship from September 6 to 30, 1879... 299
- F F. List of articles, boats' outfits, June 17, 1880...................... 300
- G G. Station bill for fire quarter, winters of 1880 and 1881............. 300
- H H. Note sent by Nindemann and Noros, requesting help 301
- I I. De Long's record of September 22, 1881........................... 302
- K K. De Long's record of September 26, 1881........................... 303
- L L. De Long's record of October 1, 1881.............................. 303
- M M. Melville's letter to Espravnik of Verkeransk..................... 304
- N N. Telegram, Melville to Secretary Navy, November 2, 1881........... 304
- O O. Telegram, received by Melville from Secretary at Yakutsk......... 306
- P P. Telegram, received by Melville from Hoffman, chargé.............. 306
- Q Q. Melville's chart used in the search ....opposite.. 306
- R R. De Long's record, found in Erichsen's hut........................ 306
- S S. Melville's telegram requesting permission to return to United States 307
- T T. Secretary's answer to above..................................... 307
- U U. De Long's record of September 19, 1881, found in navigation box.. 307
- V V. Letter of Nindemann and Noros to United States minister, St. Petersburg.. 308
- W W. Nindemann's chart...opposite.. 309
- X X. Melville's orders to Nindemann on leaving Yakutsk................ 309
- A B. Melville's orders to Nindemann for search........................ 309
- B C. Danenhower's request to be allowed counsel 310
- C D. Original interrogatories to George W. Much, naval constructor, United States Navy.. 310
- D E. Original answers to interrogatories by George W. Much, naval constructor, United States Navy 311
- E F. } F G. } Original plans referred to in answer of Naval Constructor Much, G H. } United States Navy, as A, B, and C, respectively ....opposite.. 313
- H I. Interrogatories put to Sir Allen Young, R. N. R., &c.............. 313
- I K. Answer to interrogatories by Sir Allen Young, R. N. R., &c 314
- K L. Chipp's report of visit to Indian village 314
- L M. Chipp's report of journey toward Herald Island.................. 315
- M N. De Long's order about ventilation................................ 316
- N O. Chipp's report on ice-thickness.................................. 317
- O P. De Long's letter to Secretary; gallant conduct of Nindemann and Sweetman.. 317
- P Q. Order naming Jeannette and Henrietta Islands................... 318
- Q R. Collins's letter to De Long...................................... 318
- R S. Order in relation to leaving and returning to ship 319
- S T. Memorandum in relation to Collins............................... 320
- T U. Rough draft of letter to Secretary of Navy in regard to Collins 322
- U V. Telegram from Ensign Hunt, announcing death of Aniguin Indian 324

The following documentary evidence, not appended, but accompanying the record, was likewise considered by the court:

Log-books of the Jeannette, four parts.
Lieutenant-Commander De Long's private journal, three parts.
Lieutenant-Commander De Long's ice journal.
Rough draft of Lieutenant-Commander De Long's report to the Hon. Secretary of the Navy.
Chief Engineer Melville's report of trip to Henrietta Island.
Mr. J. J. Collins's memorandum book, used by the court for reference (appended).
V. W. Spar and sail plan of the Jeannette.
W. X. Circumpolar chart, showing the track of Jeannette.

EXHIBITS:

	Page.
1 A. Order reconvening the court	324
1 B. Relieving Capt. J. N. Miller from duty as member	324
1 C. Relieving Master S. C. Lemly from duty as judge-advocate	325
1 D. Appointment of new judge-advocate	325
1 E. Telegram from D. F. Collins, M. D	325

RECORD

OF THE

PROCEEDINGS OF A COURT OF INQUIRY

CONVENED AT

THE NAVY DEPARTMENT, WASHINGTON, D. C., BY VIRTUE OF AN ORDER SIGNED BY THE HON. W. E. CHANDLER, SECRETARY OF THE NAVY, TO INVESTIGATE THE CIRCUMSTANCES OF THE LOSS OF THE EXPLORING STEAMER JEANNETTE.

Commodore W. G. TEMPLE, United States Navy, president; Master Samuel C. Lemly, United States Navy, judge-advocate.

Record of Proceedings of a Court of Inquiry convened at the Navy Department, Washington, D. C., by virtue of an order signed by the Hon. W. E. Chandler, Secretary of the Navy, the original of which is hereunto annexed, marked A, and which is in the words and figures following, viz:

To Commodore WILLIAM G. TEMPLE, United States Navy,
  Navy Department, Washington, D. C.:

In conformity with a joint resolution of Congress, approved August 8, 1882, a court of inquiry, of which Commodore William G. Temple is hereby appointed president, Capt. Joseph N. Miller and Commander Frederick V. McNair, members, and Master Samuel C. Lemly judge-advocate, is ordered to convene at the Navy Department, Washington, D. C., on Thursday, the 5th day of October, A. D. 1882.

The court will diligently and thoroughly investigate the circumstances of the loss in the Arctic seas of the exploring steamer Jeannette, and of the death of Lieut. Commander George W. De Long and others of her officers and men.

The court will also carefully inquire into the condition of the vessel on her departure, her management up to the time of her destruction, the provisions made and plans adopted for the several boats' crews upon their leaving the wreck, the efforts made by the various officers to insure the safety of the parties under their immediate charge and for the relief of the other parties, and into the general conduct and merits of each and all the officers and men of the expedition.

At the conclusion of the investigation, the court will report their proceedings, the testimony taken, and the facts which they deem established by the evidence adduced.

Given under my hand at the Navy Department, Washington, D. C., this 29th day of September, A. D. 1882.

WM. E. CHANDLER,
Secretary of the Navy.

FIRST DAY.

NAVY DEPARTMENT,
Washington, D. C., Thursday, October 5, 1882—12 m.

The court met pursuant to the foregoing order.

Present, Commodore William G. Temple, United States Navy, president; Capt. Joseph N. Miller, United States Navy, Commander Fred-

erick V. McNair, United States Navy, members; and Master Samuel C. Lemly, United States Navy, judge-advocate.

The court was then cleared and the judge-advocate read aloud the order convening the court, as hereinbefore set forth, and the letter from the Honorable Secretary of the Navy transmitting the order to the court, of which a certified copy is appended to this record, marked B, and also the judge-advocate's warrant of which a certified copy is appended to this record, marked C, and which is in the words and figures following, namely:

NAVY DEPARTMENT,
Washington, September 29, 1882.

SIR: A court of inquiry, of which you are appointed judge-advocate, is ordered to convene at the Navy Department, Washington, D. C., on Thursday, the 5th day of October, 1882; at which time and place you will appear and report yourself to Commodore Wm. G. Temple, United States Navy, the presiding officer of the court.

Very respectfully,

WM. E. CHANDLER,
Secretary of the Navy.

The court was then opened and the judge-advocate administered to the president, and to each of the members of the court, the oath prescribed by law, which was taken by them, and the president of the court then administered to the judge-advocate the oath prescribed by law, which was taken by him.

The president of the court then addressed a letter to the revising authority, the Honorable Secretary of the Navy, asking for instructions as to whether the sessions of the court should be held with open or closed doors.

And the court then, at 2 p. m., adjourned to meet to-morrow, the 6th day of October, 1882, at 10 a. m.

SECOND DAY.

NAVY DEPARTMENT,
Washington, D. C., Friday, October 6, 1882—10 a. m.

The court met pursuant to the adjournment of yesterday.

Present, Commodore William G. Temple, United States Navy, president; Capt. Joseph N. Miller, United States Navy, Commander Frederick V. McNair, United States Navy, members; and Master Samuel C. Lemly, United States Navy, judge-advocate.

The record of the proceedings of yesterday, October 5, 1882, the first day of the inquiry, was read and approved.

The president of the court then produced, and the judge-advocate read aloud, the following communication from the honorable Secretary of the Navy, the convening authority, a certified copy of which is appended to this record, marked D:

NAVY DEPARTMENT,
Washington, October 5, 1882.

SIR: In reply to your inquiry of this date, you are informed that the investigation by the court of inquiry of which you are president will be held in open court.

Very respectfully,

WM. E. CHANDLER,
Secretary of the Navy.

Commodore WILLIAM G. TEMPLE, U. S. N.,
President Court of Inquiry, Navy Department.

The judge-advocate then placed before the court, as evidence, the official log-books of the exploring steamer Jeannette from the 25th day of June, 1879, the day when she was commissioned at San Francisco, Cal., to the date of her loss in the Arctic seas, June 10, 1881, in four volumes, which accompany this record.

And the court then, at 10.30 a. m., adjourned to meet to-morrow, the 7th day of October, 1882, at 10 a. m.

THIRD DAY.

NAVY DEPARTMENT,
Washington, D. C., Saturday, October 7, 1882—10 a. m.

The court met pursuant to the adjournment of yesterday.

Present, Commodore William G. Temple, United States Navy, president; Capt. Joseph N. Miller, United States Navy, Commander Frederick V. McNair, United States Navy, members; and Master Samuel C. Lemly, United States Navy, judge-advocate. The record of the proceedings of yesterday, October 6, 1882, the second day of the inquiry, was read and approved.

The court was then cleared for deliberation, by request of the judge-advocate, and afterward reopened.

The judge-advocate then read aloud, and placed before the court as evidence, the acts of Congress of March 18, 1878, and February 27, 1879, under which the Secretary of the Navy was authorized to accept, for the purpose of a voyage of exploration by the way of Behring's Straits, the ship Jeannette, tendered by James Gordon Bennett for that purpose, and which acts are as follows:

[PUBLIC No. 58.]

AN ACT authorizing the Secretary of the Navy to accept, for the purposes of a voyage of exploration, by the way of Behring's Straits, the ship Jeannette, tendered by James Gordon Bennett for that purpose.

Be it enacted by the Senate and House of Representatives of the United States of America in Congress assembled, That the Secretary of the Navy be, and he is hereby authorized to accept and take charge of for the use of a North Polar Expedition, by way of Behring's Straits, the ship Jeannette, owned by James Gordon Bennett; and by him devoted to this purpose; that he may use in fitting her for her voyage of exploration, any materials he may have on hand proper for the purposes of an Arctic voyage: and that he is further authorized to enlist the necessary crew for the said vessel for "special service," their pay to be temporarily met from the pay of the Navy, and to be paid or refunded by James Gordon Bennett to the Navy Department, under the order of the Secretary of the Navy, and as he may require: The vessel to proceed on her voyage of exploration under the orders and instructions of the Navy Department: that the men so "specially enlisted" as above, shall be subject in all respects to the Articles of War, and Navy Regulations and discipline: and that all parts of the act approved March eighteenth, eighteen hundred and seventy-eight, inconsistent with the above, be, and they are hereby repealed; *Provided,* That the Government of the United States shall not be held liable for any expenditures, incurred or to be incurred on account of said exploration.

Approved February 27, 1879.

AN ACT in aid of a polar expedition designed by James Gordon Bennett.

Whereas James Gordon Bennett a citizen of the United States, has purchased in Great Britain, a vessel supposed to be specially adapted to Arctic expeditions, and proposes, at his own cost, to fit out and man said vessel, and to devote her to efforts to solve the polar problem: and whereas it is deemed desirable that said vessel, while so engaged shall carry the American flag, and be officered by American Naval officers: Therefore

Be it enacted by the Senate and House of Representatives of the United States of America, in Congress assembled, That the Secretary of the Treasury be authorized to issue an American register to said vessel, by the name of Jeannette and that the President of the United States be authorized to detail with their own consent, commissioned, warrant and petty officers of the Navy, not to exceed ten in number, to act as officers of said vessel during her first voyage to the Arctic seas. *Provided, however,* That such detail shall be made of such officers only, as the President is satisfied can be absent from their regular duties without detriment to the public service.

Approved March 18, 1878.

The judge advocate then placed in evidence the following letters taken from the files of the Navy Department, each of which was read aloud, and certified copies are appended to the record, as follows:

Letter from Commodore E. R. Colhoun, commandant at navy-yard, Mare Island, California, appointing a Board to thoroughly examine the yacht Jeannette, and report what repairs, if any, she needs to her hull, boilers, machinery, &c., to fit her for an extended cruise in the Arctic regions, dated December 31, 1878. Exhibit E.

Report of the Board recommending repairs, dated January 24, 1879. Exhibit F.

Copy of a letter from Chief Constructor J. W. Easby, of the Navy, to Commodore E. R. Colhoun, inclosing memorandum of work to be done on the Jeannette, in Construction Department, dated March 11, 1879. Exhibit G.

Copy of memorandum of work to be done inclosed with above letter. Exhibit H.

Copy of letter from Commodore Earl English, Chief of the Bureau of Equipment and Recruiting, to Commodore E. R. Colhoun, dated March 14, 1879. Exhibit I.

Copy of a telegram from Commodore English, to Commodore Colhoun, dated May 16, 1879. Exhibit K.

Copy of a telegram from W. H. Shock, Chief of the Bureau of Steam Engineering, to Commodore Colhoun, ordering repairs to be made on the Jeannette under the cognizance of the Bureau of Steam Engineering, in accordance with the recommendations of the Board of survey, dated March 10, 1879. Exhibit L.

Letter from Commodore E. R. Colhoun, appointing a Board to carefully examine and report upon the repairs and outfit of the Arctic steamer Jeannette, dated June 6, 1879. Exhibit M.

Report of Board in accordance with above order, dated June 26, 1879. Exhibit N.

And the court then, at 12.45 p. m., adjourned to meet on Monday, the 9th day of October, 1882, at 11 a. m.

FOURTH DAY.

NAVY DEPARTMENT,
Washington, D. C., Monday, October 9, 1882—10 a. m.

The court met pursuant to the adjournment of Saturday.

Present, Commodore William G. Temple, United States Navy, president; Capt. Joseph N. Miller, United States Navy, Commander Frederick V. McNair, United States Navy, members; and Master Samuel C. Lemly, United States Navy, judge-advocate.

The record of the proceedings of Saturday, October 7, 1882, the third day of the inquiry, was then read and approved.

The court was then cleared by request of the judge-advocate and afterward reopened.

The judge-advocate then read aloud and placed before the court as evidence the originals of the following letters, certified copies of which are appended to the record, as follows:

Final letter of instructions to Lieut. George W. DeLong from the Honorable Secretary of the Navy, dated June 18, 1879. Exhibit O.

Final report from Lieutenant DeLong to the Honorable Secretary of the Navy, dated July 8, 1879. Exhibit P.

And the court then, at 1.10 p. m., adjourned to meet to-morrow, the 10th day of October, 1882, at 10.30 a. m.

FIFTH DAY.

NAVY DEPARTMENT,
Washington, D. C., Tuesday, October 10, 1882—10.30 a. m.

The court met pursuant to the adjournment of yesterday.

Present, Commodore William G. Temple, United States Navy, president; Capt. Joseph N. Miller, United States Navy, Commander Frederick V. McNair, United States Navy, members; and Master Samuel C. Lemly, United States Navy, judge-advocate.

The record of the proceedings of yesterday was read and approved.

The judge-advocate then requested an adjournment to enable him to get up the documentary evidence already in, and the court accordingly adjourned at 11.50 a. m. to meet to-morrow, the 11th day of October, 1882, at 10.30 a. m.

SIXTH DAY.

NAVY DEPARTMENT,
Washington, D. C., Wednesday, October 11, 1882—10.30 a. m.

The court met pursuant to the adjournment of yesterday.

Present, Commodore William G. Temple, United States Navy, president; Capt. Joseph N. Miller, United States Navy, Commander Frederick V. McNair, United States Navy, members; and Master Samuel C. Lemly, United States Navy, judge-advocate.

The record of the proceedings of yesterday, October 10, the 5th day of the inquiry, was read and approved.

Commodore E. R. COLHOUN, United States Navy, was then called as a witness, and having been sworn according to law, by the president of the court, testified as follows:

Examination by the JUDGE-ADVOCATE:

Question by the JUDGE-ADVOCATE. Please state your name, rank, and present duty, or station.

The WITNESS. Edmund R. Colhoun, Commodore, United States Navy, waiting orders, Washington, D. C.

Question by the JUDGE-ADVOCATE. Did you perform any duty in

connection with the fitting for Arctic service of the exploring steamer Jeannette; and if yes, where and when?

The WITNESS. On the 31st of December, 1878, while commandant of the navy-yard, Mare Island, Cal., I ordered a Board, consisting of four officers, namely, Chief Engineer Fletcher, Commander Kempff, Naval Constructor Much, and Chief Engineer Kutz, to thoroughly examine the yacht Jeannette, then at the navy-yard, Mare Island, and intended for an extended cruise in the Arctic regions, to report what repairs were necessary to her hull, boilers, machinery, &c.

Question by the JUDGE-ADVOCATE. Was the duty assigned to these officers carried out, and what action if any, was taken upon their report?

The WITNESS. It was carried out, and their report was forwarded to the Department.

Question by the JUDGE-ADVOCATE. Were all instructions given by the Navy Department, or the Bureaus thereof, relative to repairs and alterations on the Jeannette, executed?

The WITNESS. They were.

Question by the JUDGE-ADVOCATE. Did you personally examine the Jeannette at any time when she was fitting for sea, or afterwards, with a view to ascertaining her fitness for the duty to which she was assigned?

The WITNESS. I examined her frequently; I was aboard of her almost every day, to see that the work was being carried on in accordance with the recommendations of the Board of Survey, and the directions of the Navy Department.

Question by the JUDGE-ADVOCATE. Did you take any further action, with a view of ascertaining the fitness of the Jeannette for Arctic service; and if yes, what was it?

The WITNESS. On the 6th of June, 1879, I ordered a Board, consisting of Capt. Philip C. Johnson, Commander Charles J. McDougal, Naval Constructor George W. Much, Chief Engineer George F. Kutz, and Chief Engineer Edward Farmer, to carefully examine and report upon the repairs and outfit of the Arctic steamer Jeannette, and whether the repairs and alterations as recommended in the survey upon that vessel had been made, and if any other work not embraced therein, but considered necessary, had been done.

Question by the JUDGE-ADVOCATE. Was this duty executed in accordance with your order?

The WITNESS. Yes, it was.

Question by the JUDGE-ADVOCATE. From your personal observation of the Jeannette while undergoing repairs, and from the official report of the Board of Survey appointed to inspect her after the repairs were made, what is your opinion of that vessel as to her general seaworthiness, and as to her special fitness for an extended cruise in the Arctic regions?

The WITNESS. I thought she was seaworthy, but I do not think I would myself have chosen her for a cruise in the Arctic regions.

Question by the JUDGE-ADVOCATE. Why would you not have chosen her for such a cruise; in what qualities was she lacking to thoroughly fit her for it?

The WITNESS. I did not think she would handle well; she was slow; I suppose she was strong enough. I do not know how she handled under sail; under steam she was slow. I think six or seven knots was the most they could get out of her in smooth water.

Question by the JUDGE-ADVOCATE. Do you consider that the Jeannette was, so far as possible, strengthened and fitted for an Arctic cruise?

The WITNESS. I think as far as practicable she was.

Question by the JUDGE-ADVOCATE. What, then, was the condition of the Jeannette before her departure from Mare Island?

The WITNESS. She was in good condition, but I thought she was very low in the water on account of having so much aboard of her.

Examination by the COURT:

Question by the COURT. Do you remember whether all the recommendations of the Board of Survey were ordered to be carried out by the various Bureaus of the Department?

The WITNESS. I do not remember.

The testimony of this witness being here concluded, was read over to him, and pronounced by him to be correct. The witness then withdrew.

Capt. P. C. JOHNSON, United States Navy, was then called as a witness, and having been sworn according to law by the president of the court, testified as follows:

Examination by the JUDGE-ADVOCATE:

Question by the JUDGE-ADVOCATE. Please state your name, rank, present duty and station.

The WITNESS. Philip C. Johnson, captain and chief signal officer of the Navy, Washington, D. C.

Question by the JUDGE-ADVOCATE. What duty, if any, did you execute in connection with the fitting of the exploring steamer Jeannette for Arctic service?

The WITNESS. I was senior member of a Board, appointed by the Commandant of Mare Island navy yard, Commodore Colhoun, to inspect and see if the recommendations in regard to repairs and alterations made by a former Board had been carried out. I do not recollect the exact wording of the order, but the idea was to see if the ship was prepared in all respects for a cruise in the Arctic.

Question by the JUDGE-ADVOCATE. Did the Board inspect the ship in obedience to orders, and if yes, what was their report as to the execution of recommendations and orders for repairs and alterations?

The WITNESS. They did. The report in general was that the recommendations of the previous Board had been carried out, but with some exceptions that were not authorized by the Bureaus, and there was also some considerable work done that had not been recommended by the previous Board. The ship was prepared as far as it was possible for a cruise in the Arctic.

The court then, at 11.50 a. m., took a recess until 1 p. m., when it reconvened with all the members and the judge-advocate present.

The witness under examination, Capt. P. C. Johnson, then came in, and his examination by the judge-advocate continued as follows:

The judge-advocate then quoted from the report of the Board of which the witness, Captain Johnson, was senior member, already in evidence as follows:

"For an extended cruise in the Arctic regions it was not possible, in our opinion, to make her particularly adapted for such service."

Question by the JUDGE-ADVOCATE. Why was it impossible, as stated, to make the Jeannette particularly adapted for Arctic service?

The WITNESS. Because it would have been necessary to rebuild her; her frames were single, very light, probably 6 by 8 inches in dimensions, and spaces between frames about 2 feet. The clamps were very light and beams light; in fact she was a lightly built vessel. This is to the best of my recollection.

The judge-advocate then again quoted from the report of the Board, as follows:

> To strengthen her in the space between the lower edge of spar-deck clamps, and upper edge of bilge strake in wake of boilers, engine, and coal bunkers, she was planked with 6-inch Oregon pine, well fastened through and through; in lieu of the four 6-inch bulkheads as recommended in the survey, beams and heavy trusswork or athwartship diagonal bracing has been substituted.

Question by the JUDGE-ADVOCATE. What effect had this deviation from the recommendations of the board of survey upon the strength of the vessel, to increase or to diminish it?

The WITNESS. In my opinion this athwartship truss work tended greatly to increase her strength, but in my opinion it would have been advisable to put in the bulkheads in addition. I think the effect produced by the truss work was not so good as it would have been had she been strengthened by the four bulkheads, as each one of them would have acted as effectively as the truss work. The truss work was made of about 8 by 10 inch timber, and the recommendation was to have four 6-inch bulkheads, which would have been much better.

The judge-advocate then again quoted from the report of the Board:

> Heavy stanchions under every beam were not put in, because they were not authorized by the Bureau.

Question by the JUDGE-ADVOCATE. What effect, if any, had this omission upon the strength of the vessel?

The WITNESS. It would have been stronger had they been put in.

The judge-advocate then again quoted from the report of the Board, as follows:

> In addition to the original iron truss hooks, and instead of the three or four heavy wooden hooks, as recommended by the survey, it was found after removing the joiner work, above the berth-deck, that hooks of the proper shape could not be obtained, so pointers and bracing were used instead.

Question by the JUDGE-ADVOCATE. What effect, if any, had this deviation from the recommendations of the Board upon the strength of the vessel?

The WITNESS. It was, in my belief, better than the plan recommended by the Board. It filled her in solid with pointers so that the butt-ends of the timbers would receive the blows instead of the sides.

The judge-advocate then further quoted from the report of the Board, as follows:

> The spars were not changed, as there was no authority from the Bureau to do so.

Question by the JUDGE-ADVOCATE. Did you deem the vessel's spars unsuited to her, particularly for a Polar expedition, and if yes, why?

The WITNESS. They were too taunt and too slight; the yards not heavy enough in the slings.

Question by the JUDGE-ADVOCATE. Were any of the deviations from the report of the Board or any of the omissions above enumerated in consequence of the recommendations of the officers detailed for the expedition?

The WITNESS. I cannot answer with certainty about that, but my impression is that the wishes of the commanding officer of the expedition were generally complied with where not in conflict with the Bureau's authority. Indeed, I know that some of the omissions were in accordance with his wishes; for example, the omission in regard to the water-tanks.

Question by the JUDGE-ADVOCATE. Did you visit the Jeannette at any time during the progress of the repairs and alterations being made upon her?

The WITNESS. Frequently.

Question by the JUDGE-ADVOCATE. From your observations of her at these visits, and your subsequent inspection of her, as a member of the Board of Survey, as stated, what is your opinion, 1st, as to her general sea-worthiness, and 2d, as to her fitness for extended Arctic exploration?

The WITNESS. Loaded as deeply as she was when she left Mare Island, I did not consider her in a condition to combat the weather she would probably meet in those high latitudes. She had very little free-board, being light framed and lightly sparred; very logy, heavy seas would, I should think, strain her so as to leak badly. For the same reasons enumerated above, I considered her as unfitted for Arctic exploration.

Examination by the COURT:

Question by the COURT. Do you know why the athwartship bulkheads were not put in as recommended by the first board of survey?

The WITNESS. I do not.

Question by the COURT. Would you have considered the Jeannette fitted to encounter the dangers of her expedition if the athwartship bulkheads and the stanchions under her beams had been added as recommended by the first Board of Survey?

The WITNESS. I should not.

Question by the COURT. Was the Jeannette's model adapted to encounter the ice of the Arctic seas?

The WITNESS. No; I think she was too sharp and had too much dead rise; she would not rise to a squeeze; she was too wedge-shaped.

Question by the COURT. Did Lieutenant DeLong at any time express to you dissatisfaction with the Jeannette or her outfit?

The WITNESS. No; on the contrary, he expressed to me entire satisfaction.

The testimony of this witness being concluded, was read over to him, and pronounced by him to be correct. The witness then withdrew.

The court then, at 2.20. p. m., adjourned to meet to-morrow, the 12th day of October, 1882, at 10.30 a. m.

SEVENTH DAY.

NAVY DEPARTMENT,
Washington, D. C., Thursday, October, 12, 1882—10.30 a. m.

The court met pursuant to the adjournment of yesterday.

Present, Commodore William G. Temple, United States Navy, president; Capt. Joseph N. Miller, United States Navy, Commander Fredrict V. McNair, United States Navy, members; and Master Samuel C. Lemly, United States Navy, judge-advocate.

The court took a recess to enable the judge-advocate to prepare the record of yesterday.

At 12 m. the court reconvened, with all the members and the judge-advocate present.

The record of the proceedings of yesterday, October 11, 1882, the sixth day of the inquiry, was then read, and, after making several corrections of clerical errors, approved.

The testimony of Chief Engineer EDWARD FARMER, United States Navy, being deemed essential to the prosecution of the inquiry, the judge-advocate, acting under the instructions of the court, issued a summons for his attendance.

Capt. P. C. JOHNSON, a former witness, was then recalled, and having been reminded by the president of the court that he was still under oath, was examined by the court, as follows:

Question by the COURT. Did you express to the Department the opinion that the Jeannette was not well adapted for the service on which she was to be sent?

The WITNESS. We expressed it indirectly, in the report of the Board, by stating that for an extended cruise in the Arctic regions it was not possible in our opinion to make her particularly adapted for such service.

The order convening the Board did not require any expression of opinion in regard to her fitness for the work for which she was destined, further than that which was expressed in the report.

As it was a private enterprise, and the ship had been purchased, and was satisfactory to those most interested in the enterprise, it was rather a delicate thing to express an unfavorable opinion of it in our official capacity. I cannot say that that was what actuated the other members of the Board, but it influenced me.

The testimony of the witness having been concluded, was read over to him, and was pronounced by him to be correct. The witness then withdrew.

The testimony of Naval Constructor George W. Much, United States Navy, being deemed essential to the prosecution of the inquiry, and he being now stationed at the navy-yard, Mare Island, California, and therefore not available as a witness before the court, the judge-advocate was directed by the court to prepare interrogatories to be sent to the said Naval Constructor George W. Much, United States Navy.

And the court then, at 12.50 p. m., adjourned to meet to-morrow, the 13th day of October, 1882, at 10.30 a. m.

EIGHTH DAY.

NAVY DEPRTMENT,
Washington, D. C., Friday, October 13, 1882—10.30 a. m.

The court met pursuant to the adjournment of yesterday.

Present, Commodore William G. Temple, United States Navy, president, Capt. Joseph N. Miller, United States Navy, Commander Frederick V. McNair, United States Navy, members, and Master Samuel C. Lemly, United States Navy, judge-advocate.

The record of the proceedings of yesterday, October 12, 1882, the seventh day of the inquiry, was then read and approved.

Chief Engineer EDWARD FARMER, United States Navy, was then called as a witness and, having been sworn according to law by the president of the court, testified as follows:

Examination by the JUDGE-ADVOCATE:

Question by the JUDGE-ADVOCATE. What is your name, rank, present duty, and station?

The WITNESS. Edward Farmer, chief engineer United States Navy, at present head of the Department of Steam Engineering at the Naval Academy.

Question by the JUDGE-ADVOCATE. Were you a member of the Board appointed by Commodore E. R. Colhoun, United States Navy, then commandant of the navy-yard, Mare Island, California, in a letter dated June 6, 1879, to carefully examine and report upon the repairs and outfit of the Arctic steamer Jeannette?

The WITNESS. Yes.

Question by the JUDGE-ADVOCATE. State fully why, in the opinion of the Board, it was not possible to make the Jeannette particularly adapted for an extended cruise in the Arctic?

The WITNESS. I think a vessel should be built new for that service, and every appliance that modern science can devise should be incorporated in her from the beginning. The Jeannette was an old vessel, and such devices as were practicable were applied, but they would not in my opinion be equal to a new vessel, with all the modern appliances and necessary arrangements.

Question by the JUDGE-ADVOCATE. State fully what, in your opinion, was the effect upon the strength of the Jeannette of the following deviation from the recommendation of the survey.

In addition to the original iron breast-hooks and instead of the three or four heavy wooden hooks as recommended by survey, it was found after removing the joiner work above the berth deck, that hooks of the proper shape could not be obtained, so pointers and bracing were used instead; but the extreme fore end of the vessel from 8 to 10 feet aft of the apron, and from the berth deck down, has been filled in solid, and all well bolted through and through.

The WITNESS. I think that that improved her strength, though taking away from her inside carrying space.

Question by the JUDGE-ADVOCATE. What, in your opinion, would have been the effect upon the strength of the vessel had the recommendations of the first Board of Survey been carried out, in regard to the four six-inch bulkheads, and, if practicable, the beams and heavy truss on athwartship diagonal bracing had also been put in so as to combine the two?

The WITNESS. I do not know whether or not the bulkheads could have been put in with the bracing. If practicable, I think that it would have added to her strength.

Question by the JUDGE-ADVOCATE. State, if you know, who was responsible for any or all of the above-enumerated deviations from the recommendation of the first board of survey?

The WITNESS. I do not know.

Question by the JUDGE-ADVOCATE. What were your opportunities for observing the Jeannette while she was undergoing repairs and alterations at the Mare Island navy-yard.

The WITNESS. She was lying under the shears, and I went aboard of her from time to time, and also saw her machinery in course of construction and repair, in the Department of Steam Engineering, between the 22d of February and the time of her going out into the stream. I never went aboard of her after the trial trip.

Question by the JUDGE-ADVOCATE. From your observation of the Jeannette while undergoing repairs and alterations what was your opinion of that vessel; first, as to her general seaworthiness; and, second, as to her fitness for extended Arctic cruising.

The WITNESS. My impression was that she was a seaworthy vessel;

a safe vessel to go to sea in. I think she was as well adapted to Arctic cruising as any old vessel, repaired, could be made.

Question by the JUDGE-ADVOCATE. Did the commanding or any other officer of the Jeannette at any time express to you dissatisfaction with that vessel; or did they express themselves as satisfied with her?

The WITNESS. I never heard any of the officers express themselves as dissatisfied with her. Captain De Long on the trial trip expressed himself as pleased with what had been done for the vessel by the authorities of the yard. Mr. Melville, with whom I was quite intimate, never complained of want of anything in his Department, that of Steam Engineering. When the Board was about leaving we asked each officer, separately, if he was satisfied with the equipment of his department, and none of them made any complaint.

Question by the JUDGE-ADVOCATE. Do you or do you not consider that the model of the Jeannette adapted her to Arctic cruising?

The WITNESS. I never noticed her when out of water. I do not think she was docked while I was there. I don't think she had much dead rise. My opinion of the dead rise is, from what I saw from the inside, she did not have as much dead rise as would be put in a new vessel for Arctic service.

Question by the JUDGE-ADVOCATE. In what manner would this effect the vessel as an Arctic cruiser?

The WITNESS. She would be less likely to get clear, when nipped in the ice, if flat.

Question by the JUDGE-ADVOCATE. What was the condition of the Jeannette when she sailed, or when you last visited her?

The WITNESS. She was very deep in the water, but so far as practicable I think she had been repaired and placed in condition for service in the Arctic Ocean.

Question by the JUDGE-ADVOCATE. Have you any further statement to make in relation to the adaptability of the Jeannette for Arctic cruising, particularly as to her strength and model? If you have, make it now.

The WITNESS. No.

Examination by the COURT:

Question by the COURT. Were the boilers and machinery of the Jeannette well adapted and adequate to the work required of them?

The WITNESS. Yes; I think they were.

The testimony of this witness being here concluded, was read over to him, and pronounced by him to be correct. The witness then withdrew.

Commodore E. R. COLHOUN, a former witness, was then recalled, and having been reminded by the president of the court that he was still under the obligation of his oath, was examined by the court as follows:

Question by the COURT. Did you express to the Department the opinion that the Jeannette was not well adapted to the service on which she was to be sent?

The WITNESS. No; to the best of my recollection I did not.

The testimony of this witness being here concluded, was read over to him, and pronounced by him to be correct. The witness then withdrew.

And the court then, at 12.20 p. m., adjourned to meet to-morrow, the 14th day of October, 1882, at 10.30 a. m.

NINTH DAY.

NAVY DEPARTMENT,
Washington, D. C., Saturday, October 14, 1882—10.30 a. m.

The court met pursuant to the adjournment of yesterday.

Present, Commodore William G. Temple, United States Navy, president; Capt. Joseph N. Miller, United States Navy, Commander Frederick V. McNair, United States Navy, members; and Master Samuel C. Lemby, United States Navy, judge-advocate.

The record of the proceedings of yesterday, October 13, 1882, the eighth day of the inquiry, was then read and approved.

Lieutenant J. W. DANENHOWER was then called as a witness, and, having been sworn, according to law, by the president of the court, testified as follows:

Question by the JUDGE-ADVOCATE. What is your name, rank, present duty, and station?

The WITNESS. John W. Danenhower, lieutenant, United States Navy; at present on waiting orders.

Question by the JUDGE-ADVOCATE. To what vessel and to what special service were you last attached?

The WITNESS. To the Arctic steamer Jeannette, during the exploring expedition in the Arctic seas.

Question by the JUDGE-ADVOCATE. Where is the Jeannette now?

The WITNESS. She is sunk in thirty-eight fathoms of water, latitude 77° 15′ N. and longitude 156° 6′ E., both approximate. Having been crushed by the ice June 12, 1881, she sunk June 13, 1881. Correct local dates for geographical position.

Question by the JUDGE-ADVOCATE. When and where did you join the Jeannette, and what service, if any, did you perform in that vessel prior to her being specially fitted for Arctic exploration?

The WITNESS. I joined the Jeannette at Havre, France, July 7, 1878, and made the voyage by way of the Straits of Magellan to San Francisco, arriving December 18 [28*], 1878.

Question by the JUDGE-ADVOCATE. Were you ordered to the Jeannette, for the Arctic Expedition, upon your own application?

The WITNESS. No; I expressed my assent to going, and at Smyrna, in June, 1878, received a telegram from Mr. James Gordon Bennett that my services were accepted; and on July 4th he telegraphed to the United States and had me ordered.

Question by the JUDGE-ADVOCATE. Was your assignment then to that vessel and service made with your consent and approval?

The WITNESS. Yes.

Question by the JUDGE-ADVOCATE. Subsequently to your arrival at San Francisco what were your further movements, in so far as they were preparatory for starting on the Arctic expedition in the Jeannette?

The WITNESS. I was detailed by the Secretary of the Navy to report to the commandant of the navy-yard at Mare Island, California, for the resumption of duties on board the Arctic expedition steamer Jeannette on the 1st of April, 1879. I was sent to report the progress of work on the Jeannette, and to disburse the funds in payment thereof. This was done at the instance of Lieutenant DeLong, who gave me written specifications relative to the repairs of the ship.

Question by the JUDGE-ADVOCATE. Have you these specifications now?

---
*Corrected by witness.

The WITNESS. No; they went down in the ship.

Question by the JUDGE-ADVOCATE. What were they, in so far as you you can recollect?

The WITNESS. The details of work of repairs on the hull, boilers, and engines of the ship were given, and also instructions relative to tallying the work, reporting progress, and paying off hands.

Question by the JUDGE-ADVOCATE. State as fully as you can what repairs and alterations were made on the Jeannette under your observation; particularly as to strengthening her hull?

The WITNESS. The old boilers were first hoisted out, and the diagonal wooden trusses in the boiler and coal-bunker spaces were removed. This space was 39 feet and 8 inches between bulkheads, which were the main bulkheads of the ship. For these trusses strakes of Oregon pine were substituted, and made a complete ceiling from the boiler-bed timbers up to the lower-deck shelf.

(The witness here produced a sketch, which had been made at the time when the repairs were in progress, which was offered by the judge-advocate and accepted by the court as evidence, and a certified copy is appended to the record marked Q.)

These strakes were from 10 to 12 inches in width and 6 inches in thickness, and from 60 to 40 feet in length, in order to shift butts on the frames. There were also two pieces of plank put in the fore hold, one of which was 26 and the other 10 feet in length and 5 inches thick, to supply old ceiling that showed some sign of decay. Heavy frame-work, forward of the bowsprit bitts, on the berth deck, was also inserted. They were of varying dimensions, the section 18 by 12 inches and the length about 10 feet. The space below the berth deck was filled in solid with Oregon pine, 10 feet abaft the stem. The ship was put on the floating dock and all the new work was fastened with through bolts. While on the dock she was calked, outside and in, and a coating of coal tar and arsenic was given to her under-water body. The wood lock from the rudder was removed, and special chain pendants were fitted, by which the rudder could be shipped and unshipped quickly. At this time work was going on with the repairs of the engines and the new [cylindrical boilers*] cylinder and boilers were constructing. The hull of the ship was thoroughly examined, and only a few insignificant traces of the work of the teredo could be found. This was done by boring, and a few marks were found on the surface, but insignificant. The ship had previously received a doubling of American elm, 5 inches in thickness, and extending from about 1 foot above the water line to below the turn of the bilge. She had also been fitted with iron plates, extending from the cut-water to near the fore chains on the bows. These plates or iron straps were about 2 inches in thickness and 5 inches in width. They were separated by about their own width. The stem of the ship was cased with iron from about one-half to three-quarters of an inch in thickness. I think this was wrought iron. The object in the distribution of the straps and the casing of the stem was to avoid superfluous weight. A new suit of sails was provided and the old sails thoroughly repaired, and storm sails also overhauled. Spare blades for the propeller were cast. The foregoing work was performed while I was the representative of Lieutenant DeLong, but about April 23, 1879, Lieutenant Chipp arrived from China, and as he was going out as executive officer of the ship he desired to go on duty at once to assist in fitting her out. About that date he received orders to join her, and I turned over everything to him except the money affairs, having received such directions from

---
*Correction by witness.

Lieutenant DeLong. In regard to the quality of the work that was performed at the Mare Island navy-yard at that time, it was A No. 1, and there were men kept aboard constantly who were looking out for our interests: Alfred Sweetman, a thorough ship-carpenter, who was lost with Lieutenant Chipp's party, and John Cole, boatswain, who returned with me from Siberia, who is now an inmate of the Government Insane Asylum. Both of these men were special employés of Mr. Bennett's, and I often availed myself of the suggestions of Mr. Sweetman. Every facility was given Mr. Chipp and myself by the commandant and the other officials at the navy-yard.

When the vessel came off the dock her boilers were hoisted in, and the repairs on her rigging were effected under the direction of Mr. Chipp. A heavy truss was placed in the main coal-bunker. The beam was 12 inches by 14 in section, and extended athwartships, and was supported by two heavy diagonals. The old iron truss that had been in the ship was placed abaft the boilers, and in contact with them. Both of these trusses were put in after the boilers were put in place. There were small details carried out with a view to the comfort of the officers and crew, such as the placing of berths in the forecastle, and in arranging the galley; also building a deck-house to be put up in winter quarters. The boats were thoroughly overhauled, being placed in the boathouse for that purpose.

Question by the JUDGE-ADVOCATE. What opinion did you form at the time of the suitability of the spars of the Jeannette for an Arctic cruiser?

The WITNESS. The spars were all right as to strength. I thought the ship should be resparred and given more canvas.

Question by the JUDGE-ADVOCATE. Why did you so think?

The WITNESS. Because she would not tack under sail alone.

Question by the JUDGE-ADVOCATE. What was the rig of the Jeannette?

The WITNESS. She was marked in the register barquentine, and she had three masts, square-rigged on the fore and main, except the mainsail, which was fore-and-aft; fore-and-aft sail on the mizzen. She carried fore and main top-gallant sails; nothing above them. The top-sails were patent rolling.

The court then, at 12 m., took a recess until 12.20 p. m., at which time it reconvened, with all the members and the judge-advocate and the witness under examination present.

The judge-advocate then continued his examination of the witness, as follows:

Question by the JUDGE-ADVOCATE. Did you from your personal observation of the Jeannette and of the repairs and alterations made in her, consider her a vessel adapted to Arctic exploration?

The WITNESS. Yes.

Question by the JUDGE-ADVOCATE. It is in evidence before this court that a Board of Survey recommended that four six-inch bulkheads be put in the Jeannette, and that beams and heavy truss-work or athwartship diagonal bracing was afterward substituted. What effect had this substitution upon the strength of the vessel?

The WITNESS. It is hard to tell; the vessel performed all the work that could be expected of a vessel, and an opinion on this point would only be problematical.

Question by the JUDGE-ADVOCATE. It is further in evidence that instead of three or four heavy wooden hooks, as recommended in survey, it was found after removing the joiner work above the berth-deck, that hooks of the proper shape could not be obtained; so pointers and bracing were used instead. What, in your opinion, was the effect of this substitution upon the strength of the vessel?

The WITNESS. No material effect; because, in the experience of January 19, 1880, had the ship been strengthened by breast-hooks the result would have been the same.

Question by the JUDGE-ADVOCATE. State fully to what you refer, as the experience of January 19, 1880?

The WITNESS. On that day the ship was subjected to a tremendous longitudinal pressure from the ice ahead, and she sprung a leak. It was afterward found that the forefoot had been twisted.

Question by the JUDGE-ADVOCATE. What, in your opinion, would have been the effect upon the strength of the vessel if the two modes of strengthening, the one by three or four heavy wooden hooks, and the other by pointers and bracing, had been adopted, so as to combine the two?

The WITNESS. The one actually used was the stronger; that by filling in solid and fastening by through bolts. The two systems could have been combined; but I do not know whether it would have been good judgment. I do not know whether a shipwright would have combined them. I understand the system adopted to be an improvement upon the plan suggested by the board, with a view of particularly adapting the ship to ramming and boring the ice.

Question by the JUDGE-ADVOCATE. Could not the four six-inch bulkheads, and the beams and heavy truss-work, or athwartship diagonal bracing, which was substituted therefor, both have been used; and what would have been the effect upon the strength of the vessel of such combination?

The WITNESS. The ship would doubtless have been stronger, but there would have been no stowage capacity. Had she been all bulkheads she could not have withstood the pressure to which she was subjected on June 12 and 13, 1881.

Question by the JUDGE-ADVOCATE. State, if you know, who was responsible for each and all of the above-enumerated deviations from the recommendations of the survey?

The WITNESS. I do not know.

Question by the JUDGE-ADVOCATE. What was the condition of the Jeannette when she sailed from San Francisco?

The WITNESS. She was a good, strong, sea-worthy vessel. She was deeply laden, but that is always the case with Arctic ships, and she was well adapted to the service she performed.

Question by the JUDGE-ADVOCATE. Did you examine the Jeannette's lines when she was in dock?

The WITNESS. Yes.

Question by the JUDGE-ADVOCATE. Did you or did you not consider that her model was such as to fit her for an Arctic cruise?

The WITNESS. I had no fault to find with the model at the time; but subsequent experience makes me think that another model may have been better.

Question by the JUDGE-ADVOCATE. State fully what this subsequent experience was, and in what manner the Jeannette's model could be improved upon for Arctic cruising.

The WITNESS. For the particular kind of work to which she was subjected, a kettle bottomed vessel, with flare-out sides, would probably be the best; because the ice would shove under her, and lift her quicker than if she was wedge-shaped.

Question by the JUDGE-ADVOCATE. With particular reference to the frames of the vessel was she lightly or strongly built?
The WITNESS. Lightly. She was a single-framed vessel.
Question by the JUDGE-ADVOCATE. Have you any further statement to make in relation to the adaptability of the Jeannette for Arctic cruising, particularly as to her strength, her fittings, and her model? If yes, make it now.
The WITNESS. No.

Examination by the COURT:

Question by the COURT. Was the Jeannette a sharp or a flat bottomed vessel?
The WITNESS. Her greatest breadth was just abaft the foremast. From that place to near the mainmast she had a very full under-water body, and then was cut away aft. She was full amidships and cut away at both ends, having a great deal of dead rise abaft the mainmast and forward of the foremast. The sides tumbled home slightly from above the water line.
Question by the COURT. Was the stern of the Jeannette protected on the outside by any iron straps or sheathing similar to that on the bows?
The WITNESS. No.

The court then, at 12.50 p. m., adjourned to meet on Monday, the 16th day of October, 1882, at 11 a. m.

TENTH DAY.

NAVY DEPARTMENT,
Washington, D. C., Monday, October 16, 1882—11 a. m.

The court met pursuant to the adjournment of Saturday.
Present, Commodore William G. Temple, United States Navy, president; Capt. Joseph N. Miller, United States Navy, Commander Frederick V. McNair, United States Navy, members; and Master Samuel C. Lemly, United States Navy, judge advocate.
The record of the proceedings of Saturday, October 14, 1882, the ninth day of the inquiry, was then read and approved.

The witness under examination, Lieut. JOHN W. DANENHOWER, then came in, and the judge-advocate placed before him the originals of plans of the Jeannette, which were furnished to the ship at Mare Island navy-yard; also a plan made by Lieut. George W. De Long, all of which were identified by the witness and accepted by the court for reference.

The examination of the witness by the court then continued as follows:

Question by the COURT. Were you satisfied with the condition of the Jeannette on her departure from San Francisco for the Arctic regions? If not, state in what particular you were dissatisfied?
The WITNESS. I was satisfied.

Examination by the JUDGE-ADVOCATE:

Question by the JUDGE-ADVOCATE. State fully the names, rank or rate, and generally the duty of each officer and man who was attached to the Jeannette when she sailed from San Francisco for the Arctic regions?
The WITNESS. George W. DeLong, lieutenant United States Navy,

commanding; Charles W. Chipp, lieutenant, United States Navy, executive officer; John W. Danenhower, master, United States Navy, navigator; George W. Melville, passed assistant engineer, United States Navy, chief engineer of the Jeannette; Dr. James M. Ambler, passed assistant surgeon, United States Navy; William Dunbar, seaman, for special service as ice-pilot; Jerome J. Collins, seaman, for special service as meteorologist; Raymond L. Newcomb, seaman, for special service as naturalist and taxidermist; Walter Lee, machinist; James H. Bartlett, first-class fireman; George W. Boyd, second-class fireman; seaman John Cole, boatswain; Alfred Sweetman, carpenter; W. F. C. Nindemann, chief quartermaster and carpenter; Louis P. Noros, H. W. Leach, Henry Wilson, C. A. Görtz, P. E. Johnson, Edward Starr, Henry D. Warren, H. H. Kaack, A. G. Kuehne, T. E. Manson, H. H. Erichsen, Adolph Dressler, Charles Tong Sing, Ah Sing, Ah Sam, and coal-heavers Walter Sharvell, Nelse Iverson, and John Lauterbach.

The witness was allowed to refer to the log-books of the Jeannette, already in evidence, for details of names, dates, and position in giving his evidence.

Question by the JUDGE-ADVOCATE. What changes, if any, were made in the list of officers and men during the cruise of the Jeannette, when and where?

The WITNESS. At St. Michael's, Alaska, August 21, 1879, Ah Sing, seaman, was discharged and provided with passage to San Francisco, and the Indians, Alexy and Aniguin, were employed as hunters and dog-drivers. No other changes were made.

Question by the JUDGE-ADVOCATE. Who had charge of the deck watches on board the Jeannette?

The WITNESS. William Dunbar, John Cole, W. F. C. Nindemann.

The court was then, by request of a member, cleared for deliberation, and afterwards reopened.

Question by the JUDGE-ADVOCATE. Give a narrative account of the voyage and management of the Jeannette from the date of her leaving San Francisco to that of her loss, referring to the log-books of that vessel, and to any notes you may yourself have taken at the times enumerated?

The WITNESS. The Jeannette left San Francisco, July 8, 1879, and arrived at Ounalaska, Alaska, August 2, by way of Akoutan Pass.

The court was here cleared by request of the judge-advocate, and afterwards reopened, the witness being present.

The judge-advocate then offered, and the court accepted for reference, the original track chart of the Jeannette, which the witness identified.

The witness then continued as follows:

She made a long passage from San Francisco to Ounalaska, owing to light head winds, and also to fog in the vicinity of Akoutan Pass. The ship was coaled at Ounalaska, and a quantity of furs and special stores received. She left Ounalaska, August 6, 1879, bound for St. Michael's, Alaska, and arrived at that port August 12, 1879, having been delayed by fogs, head winds, and currents. Her greatest speed during that passage was seven knots and six-tenths, which was made under sail and steam. We waited at St. Michael's until August 18, when the schooner Fannie A. Hyde, of San Francisco, arrived with stores and coal for our ship.

During this time we had the skin clothing made by the natives, two suits for each person on board. We also received forty-eight pairs of snow-shoes, one large and two small skin boats, and a number of minor articles, and purchased forty dogs and obtained two dog-drivers. We transferred most of the supplies from the schooner, and August 21 left St. Michael's bound to St. Lawrence Bay, arriving at that place on August 25, after experiencing a heavy northerly gale and very rough chop sea. The ship lay to on the starboard tack all day on August 24. She behaved very well, though she was heavily ladened and had a deck-load of dogs, provisions, and coal. She was under storm-sail, fore-and-aft sail, and spanker. While we were lying to, we were under sail alone. On the 23d the ship was pitching heavily, and the forward water-closets were carried away by a heavy sea. The engines were then slowed to thirty turns and the ship was easier. In the first dog-watch of August 23 banked fires, and the ship lay under storm-sails until 1.40 p. m. August 24. The schooner arrived at 5 p. m. August 26. We took the remaining stores on board. We communicated with the natives, and were informed that a steamer had passed to the southward during the previous month. From the description we judged it to be the Vega, Professor Nordenskjöld. The object in stopping at St. Lawrence Bay was to gain information on that subject. On August 27, we left St. Lawrence Bay, and towed the schooner out and sent our mail home by her. We stood north through Behring's Straits, and crossed the Arctic Circle on August 28. The weather was cloudy and misty, with moderate breezes blowing. On the evening of the 29th August we touched at Cape Serdze Kamen and anchored for the night. We interviewed the natives, and what we learned at St. Lawrence Bay about Professor Nordenskjöld was corroborated. We got under way at 6 a. m., August 30, and stood to the westward. A party of natives from a village came alongside and examined the ship, but there was no intercourse. On August 31, at daylight, we met an extensive pack of old ice, extending five miles from the land, and in an east and west direction as far as the eye could see. At 8.20 a. m. the same day we saw some skin tents near a point of land. The ship remained off the edge of the pack, while Lieutenant Chipp was sent ashore with the whale-boat, accompanied by Mr. Dunbar and myself. We visited the tents of the Tchoncktchees, a native tribe, and were taken to a place where they said the Vega had wintered. We obtained some papers, buttons, tin pans, photographs, and other evidences that the ship had been in that locality. The papers were written in Swedish and the photographs bore the name of Stockholm. At 1.10 p. m. we started ahead with the engines full speed, shaping the course for the southeast coast of Wrangel Land as it was then called.

Pending the further examination of this witness, the court, at 2.30 p. m., adjourned to meet to-morrow, the 17th day of October, 1882, at 10.30 a. m.

ELEVENTH DAY.

NAVY DEPARTMENT,
Washington, D. C., Tuesday, October 17, 1882—10.30 a. m.

The court met pursuant to the adjournment of yesterday.

Present, Commodore William G. Temple, United States Navy, president; Capt. Joseph N. Miller, United States Navy, Commander Frederick V. McNair, United States Navy, members; and Master Samuel C. Lemly, United States Navy, judge-advocate.

The record of the proceedings of Monday, October 16, 1882, was then read and approved.

The witness under examination, Lieutenant JOHN W. DANENHOWER, then came in and continued his answer to the question pending at the time of adjournment yesterday, which was repeated by the judge-advocate, as follows:

Question by the JUDGE-ADVOCATE. Give a narrative account of the voyage and management of the Jeannette, from the date of her leaving San Francisco to that of her loss, referring to the log books of that vessel, when necessary for details, and to any notes you may yourself have taken at the times enumerated ?

The WITNESS. We stood to the northward and westward until September 2d, when we had to change course to the northward and eastward, and coast the pack ice. Occasionally the ship would enter leads, and finding that they were converging or closing would come out. Leads are large cracks or lanes between floe pieces of ice, which a ship can enter. The general appearance of the ice at this time, was smooth, and from 7 to 10 feet in thickness, showing about 3 feet above the water. The floe pieces on the edge of the pack were not extensive in area. While working along the pack the captain, the ice pilot, or myself, was always in the crow's-nest. The crow's-nest of the Jeannette may be described as a large cask, having a trap-door in the bottom, through which the observer entered. It was then closed and formed a floor on which he stood. The crow's-nest was secured by iron bands to the foretop-gallant mast, above the topmast cross-trees. It was made of wood and was about 5 feet in height and 4 in diameter at the base and 3 at the top. There was a little ridge where a person could sit. There were places for putting glasses, the long glass, and the binoculars. We coasted the pack until September 6, when we entered a wide lead and commenced to work to the west-nor'-west, using steam and sail.

Herald Island was in sight on September 4th and 5th. On September 3d a whaling bark was also sighted early in the morning. The engines were slowed and we waited for her to come up, but a heavy fog came up and we lost sight of her.

The weather was foggy and misty, with very light airs, during the time that we were cruising along the pack.

We made fast a number of times to floe pieces, being unable to proceed on account of the fog. Spread fires and got under way the last time at 1 p. m. September 6 1879, and worked through the pack about one and one-half miles to the west-northwest. The captain was in the crow's nest, ice pilot Dunbar on the top-sail yard. Mr. Chipp in charge of the deck, with all hands. I was at the conn, and at times in the cabin looking out for the instruments. About 4 p. m. the weather became very thick, and the ship could proceed no farther. At 2.20 she was secured to a floe piece, with her head at W. N. W. per compass. She was secured with ice anchors at bow and quarter. Herald Island was at that time enveloped in fog and could not be seen. In the forenoon land had been seen to the sou,-sou,-west (magnetic) at an estimated distance of 75 miles. Two range poles were set upon a sou,-sou,-west (magnetic) bearing, and by them a small drift to the northwest was observed; took soundings in forty fathoms, blue mud bottom. While working through the ice Mr. Chipp and a number of the crew went out on the ice to breast some heavy pieces of ice from the ship's side.

From the motion of the ship the ice in the immediate vicinity got in motion and the party had to go up to the head of the lead to get on board. The ship forced her way by boring and ramming.

During the night of September 6 the temperature fell from $29\frac{1}{2}°$

Fahrenheit at noon to 24° Fahrenheit at midnight, and young ice formed, so that on the morning of September 7, it was impossible to move. The drift was observed on that day to be to the northwest. The custom was to observe the drift by the trend of the lead line, and also by the land when in sight.

The object of putting up the range poles was to decide at once whether there was any movement in the surrounding ice in which the ship was fixed. The ship was a fixed body in the ice, and the two poles were placed in range with the point on Herald Island. Any movement then of the ice would be shown by throwing the poles out of range. The range poles were only of service where land was in sight, and were used only when the motion was so slight that it could not be detected by the lead line, which was sometimes the case in calm weather.

The ship was put in winter quarters and secured for the winter. This was in the month of September. The deck-house was put in place forward; vestibules were placed outside of the deck-house and outside of the cabin, with storm-doors. The after awnings were housed; the rudder was unshipped and triced up; the propeller was turned, with the blades up and down; the engines were coated with tallow and white-lead, but not disconnected, and the ship was banked up with snow to keep in the warmth. Fur clothing was served out for all hands, and a winter routine was established. The crew was stationed at fire-quarters, and for abandoning the ship, sleds and boats were placed in readiness for immediate use; the stoves were gotten in place, and mode of heating and ventilation established. The crew was detailed as follows:

Captain DeLong, with six men, formed No. 1 sled party, and manned the first cutter; Lieutenant Chipp, with six men, No. 2 sled party, and manned the second cutter; Master Danenhower, with six men, No. 3 sled party, and manned the first whale-boat; Chief Engineer Melville, with five men, No. 4 sled party; Surgeon Ambler, with five men, formed No. 5 sled party. Sled parties Nos. 4 and 5 were to be distributed among the three boats. In the original detail of boats the second whale-boat was also manned and fitted out.

During my sickness I was detailed to go with Mr. Chipp, and Mr. Dunbar was to take my place in the first whale-boat. The boats were mounted on sleds, made by the seaman Nindemann, and the provision sleds were McClintock's. The boats were fitted out completely with instruments for navigation, boat compasses, and a supply box, containing necessary articles for repairing damages. This outfit was in the fall of 1879.

The ship heeled over to starboard during the ice pressure in September and October from 5° to 11°, and mast-head tackles were gotten up on the port side; the lower blocks hooked to heavy ice-anchors, and the upper hooks to straps above the eyes of the lower rigging. The ice anchors were about 60 yards off the port beam. Each person was provided with a knapsack containing spare clothing and ammunition for immediate use in case of disaster. The boats and provisions were stowed on the spar-deck for the same purpose. The ice was comparatively quiet during September and October, but early in November great crushing and ramming took place. The ice was thrown up in ridges, and numerous cracks radiated from the ship. There was a great surging stream of ice about 100 feet from the starboard quarter, and it was constantly encroaching upon her. The motion of this stream was much greater at regular intervals, as though affected by tides. The motion of the ice was greatest when the water was shoalest and about the time of full and change of the moon.

And the court then, at 12.05 p. m., took a recess until 12.30 p. m., at which time it reconvened, with all the members, the judge-advocate and the witness under examination, J. W. Danenhower, present.

The witness then continued his answer to the pending question as follows:

The shoalest water was 18 fathoms; the deepest about 40 fathoms. This was during the fall of 1879. When we were between Herald Island and Wrangel Land the motion of the ice seemed greatest, as if affected by currents, and we sometimes saw large pieces of ice covered with dirt and shells as if they had been in contact with the land. Land was frequently visible to the southwest, and especially so on the 28th and 29th of October, when high land was distinctly visible from deck, the higher point bearing S. 32° W. (true) and the extremes were S. 16° 30′ W. and S. 36° W. (both true). The land appeared to be from 30 to 50 miles distant, and was mountainous.

On October the 29th a greater extent of land was visible, the eastern extremity bore S. 20° E. and the western S. 46° W. (both true). It appeared to be a mountain with two peaks and a shallow saddle between them. All bearings were taken with the azimuth compass 20 yards from the ship, and hence free from local influence.

The winter routine commenced November 1; all hands called at 7 a. m. and fires started in the galley; breakfast, forward and aft, at 9 a. m. At 11 a. m. all hands were called out on the ice for exercise until 1 p. m., and the quarters were thrown open for ventilation, except when the temperature was more than 30° Fahrenheit below zero, when the system of ventilation was slightly modified by closing the doors before 1 p. m. Dinner forward and aft at 3 p. m., and galley fires put out at that hour; tea at 7.30 p. m. made from water obtained at the condenser, it being necessary to condense water all the time because the snow and ice were salty.

On the first of each month the medical officer examined each person on board. The watches were kept by the seamen, two hours each; while hourly observations were made by the officers of the ship.

About November 6, at 11 p. m., the ice suddenly opened in the prolongation of the ship's keel, and she was left lying on her starboard side in a half cradle and the observatory was brought on board.

From the commencement of the work a full series of meteorological observations were made, and astronomical observations as frequently as the weather and other circumstances permitted. The observatory was put up soon after the ship was beset, at about 200 yards off the starboard beam, and the thermometers were placed in a box on a hummock near the observatory, with the anemometer on a pole above them. Star observations for position were made with the artificial horizon and sextant. The transit and zenith telescopes were not mounted in the observatory on account of the uncertainty of the situation, and as our position was constantly changing.

When the ice opened, November 6, nothing was lost except a canvas out house that had been erected. This was found about fifteen months afterward, at a distance of only 4 miles from the ship. This fact shows that there was very little change in the relations of the ice in our vicinity, especially after what followed on November 25, 1879. During a southwest gale the ice wedged in under the starboard bow, and pushed the ship off the half cradle. She was heeling about $2\frac{1}{2}°$ to starboard after she was waterborne. The ship drifted to northward and eastward down the lead, which was filled with drifting ice. She was subjected to heavy pressures. The first was from the stern, and in a fore-and-aft direction; the others were athwartships, and were very heavy. The ship stood them very well, and drifted to the E. N. E. true. As soon as the ice slacked up, the ship swung all the way around the compass, and about 7 p. m. brought up in some young ice on the south side of a considerable expanse of open water. It was probably 2 or 3 miles in area, judging from the ice which formed afterward. The rudder remained triced up, because it would have been crushed had it been shipped. The fore-and-aft sails were ready for use, and the topsails were also in readiness. At this time the weather had cleared up, and the wind was light, still from the southwest. The ship was here frozen in, heeling 1° to starboard. She had drifted nine hours on November 25. It was impossible to make any progress in any given direction, as there were no connecting leads. The weather was stormy, and darkness prevailed. The ship was subjected to a considerable pressure on the 27th November, 1879, and the young ice opened on her port side, showing a narrow belt of water, which soon froze over, the ship heeling $2\frac{1}{2}$° to starboard at that time. The ice continued to accumulate, and the ship became firmly frozen in. Heavy ice-pressures were taking place in the vicinity of the ship, and were constantly felt. When she brought up in the young ice it was too thin to bear the weight of men, and she could not be secured, but when the ice opened on the port side she was secured with ice anchors on the starboard bow and quarter, the ice having become thick in the mean time.

On December 11, as stated in the log, "The ship is now in a floe of young ice, which is about 500 yards wide, 1,200 yards long, ship heading south three-fourths west, magnetic, and her bows at the south edge of the floe. Heavy floe pieces of old ice encroaching on the young ice, and in constant motion." That was the final freezing in of the ship.

The ship was again banked up with snow, and all the former arrangements and winter routine were carried out. There was nothing more of importance during the year 1879.

The court was then cleared by request of a member, and afterward reopened.

And the court then, at 1.45 p. m., pending the further examination of the witness, adjourned to meet to-morrow, the 18th day of October, 1882, at 10.30 a. m.

TWELFTH DAY.

NAVY DEPARTMENT,
Washington, D. C., Wednesday, October 18, 1882—10.30 a. m.

The court met pursuant to the adjournment of yesterday.

Present, Commodore William G. Temple, United States Navy, president; Capt. Joseph N. Miller, United States Navy, Commander Frederick V. McNair, United States Navy members, and Master Samuel C. Lemly, United States Navy, judge-advocate.

The record of the proceedings of yesterday, October 17, 1882, the eleventh day of the inquiry, was then read and approved.

The witness under examination, Lieut. J. W. Danenhower, then came in and continued his answer to the pending question, which was repeated by the judge-advocate as follows:

Question by the JUDGE ADVOCATE. Give a narrative account of the voyage and management of the Jeannette from the date of her leaving

San Francisco to that of her loss, referring to the log-books of that vessel, when necessary, for details, and to any notes you may yourself have taken at the times enumerated.

The WITNESS. Before finishing for the year 1879, I would state that in the middle of September an effort was made to reach Herald Island by a sled party composed of Lieutenant Chipp, Chief Engineer Melville, Ice Pilot Dunbar, and the Indian Alexy, with a team of dogs. The island at this time was in sight, 21 miles distant, as measured from a base line of 1,100 yards, and bore to the southward and westward of the ship. The exact details were in the navigator's work-books. The object of the expedition was to deposit records on the island. It arrived within 6 miles of the island and found open water, and was obliged to return.

The reason that the journey was not again attempted with boats, and also on other occasions when land was in sight, was that we had an uncertain base of operations (the ship) that was constantly shifting, and we could not tell what an hour would bring forth.

In relation to the diet of the crew, the ration table for the officers and men was the same. Commencing with Monday morning: for breakfast, oatmeal, canned fish; dinner, canned soup, salt beef, two kinds of canned vegetables, bread and butter, tea, and a small quantity of canned fruit. Tuesday: breakfast, bacon and hominy; dinner, canned soup, canned roast mutton, and two canned vegetables; supper, canned cold tongue and peach butter. Wednesday: breakfast, oat-meal and hash; dinner, pork and beans, one vegetable, turnips and duff for desert; supper, cold pork and quince or apple butter. Thursday: breakfast, pork hash and hominy; dinner, soup, canned roast beef and two vegetables; supper, cold roast beef. Friday: oatmeal and hash for breakfast; canned cold corn beef and two vegetables for dinner; cold corn beef and the fruit butter for supper. Saturday: breakfast, corned-beef hash and hominy; dinner, pemmican with rice and curry, and two vegetables; supper, cold pemmican and fruit butter. Sunday: breakfast, beef hash or some canned fish and either oatmeal or hominy; dinner, a soup, canned meat and two vegetables—duff for desert; supper, generally curried lobster or stewed kidneys with a canned fruit, peaches, apples, pears, &c. This diet was varied with bear and seal meat at least twice per week during most of the cruise. We had soft bread for breakfast and supper, and hard bread for dinner in the cabin. The men had the same allowance of flour as the officers, and arranged the times of eating the bread to suit themselves. The allowance of hard bread was not limited during most of the cruise. One ounce of butter per day was allowed to each person, and the Navy table of allowances was used in issuing coffee, tea, sugar, and small articles. We had coffee for breakfast and after dinner, and tea for supper. The provision estimates were made on the basis of three pounds of solid food per day per man, for thirty-three persons for three years' service. A large quantity of provisions in excess of this estimate was also taken.

It was found in October and November, 1879, that the expenditure of provisions by actual gross weight was from 6 to 7 pounds per man per day. We kept daily and weekly accounts of provisions, and the commander acted on the principle of giving everybody plenty to eat. I had charge of the issue of provisions and the accounts, having Mr. Sweetman to act as paymaster's yeoman. This was until January 1, 1880; and I wish to state to the court that I was not an eye-witness of what occurred from that date until June 12, 1881, when the ship was crushed; but was kept fully informed of what was going on by daily visits from shipmates. In

December, 1879, my eyes became affected. They first became inflamed, and writing appeared blurred. I was then writing and working on observations from 5 a. m. until 9 a. m. each day by lamp and candle light, it being during the long winter night. By the routine, I was called at 4.45 a. m. to take the meteorological observations for 5 and 6. I availed myself of the quiet time in the cabin to get up my work for the day.

About January 1, 1879, the surgeon advised me to go on the sick list, which I did; and was in a dark room for the greater part of the time until the date the ship was crushed. From January 21, 1880, to October 15 of that year, about fifteen cuttings and probings were performed on the left eye, on account of a small abscess that had formed in the iris.

Examination by the COURT:

Question by the COURT. Did the Jeannette ground or meet with any accident from the time she left San Francisco until she was beset in the ice? If so, state the circumstances and how the vessel was managed at the time.

The WITNESS. She did not ground or meet with any accident except what is mentioned in Behring's Sea, which was not serious.

Question by the COURT. Do you know whether it was intended by the commanding officer to pass the winter of 1879–'80 in the ice, before the vessel became fast in it?

The WITNESS. I do not know positively.

Question by the COURT. Did the commanding officer of the Jeannette hold a consultation with the officers of the vessel as to the propriety of entering the ice pack?

The WITNESS. No.

The witness then made the following statement:

I understood from conversations with the captain that he hoped to reach the coast of Wrangel Island, Wrangel Land as then called, during the first season; put the ship in winter quarters in a safe harbor; send exploring parties out to examine the land during the fall of 1879 and spring of 1880; and during the summer of 1880 to work to the northward in the coast water to Wrangel Land, should it prove to be an extensive land as theorists supposed. I can further state that in the captain's last communication to the Navy Department he mentioned the probability of wintering on the coast of Siberia, should he be unable to reach Wrangel Land. Furthermore, during the voyage from France, the captain, on one occasion, remarked to me that putting a ship in the pack was the last thing to do. I have thought over the subject very carefully since my return home, and I do not believe that it was his intention to pass the winter in the pack. I think the fact that two whaleships were beset at about the same time, and to the southward of the Jeannette, should also be considered.

Question by the COURT. When the vessel entered the ice was it with a view to forcing her way through to the supposed coast of Wrangel Land?

The WITNESS. Apparently with that object in view.

Question by the COURT. What was the variation of the compass in the vicinity of Herald Island, and what course (magnetic) would have been steered but for the ice encountered there?

The WITNESS. The variation was about 20° east in that vicinity. On August 31, on leaving the Vega's winter quarters, we wished to shape a course for Cape Hawaii, and did so as long as the state of the ice permitted. After falling in with heavy ice we were forced to go to the northeast, and as stated at the time to me by the captain, he regarded the lead we entered as a division between the Siberian and American packs, and it was so marked on the chart by me. A sketch of the packs was made by me at the time, the captain having indicated by pencil his ideas on the subject and the relations of the two packs. I do not know what course would have been steered if the ice had not been in the way.

Question by the COURT. Did the commanding officer of the Jeannette inform you or consult with you as to the course he intended to pursue in his endeavor to reach the North Pole? if so, state all you know on the subject, especially as to why he deviated from his original plan, as already stated by you, in getting into the ice.

The WITNESS. He told me he had something more definite and tangible in view than reaching the North Pole, and that was to explore Wrangel Land and the Siberian Ocean. The prospects for reaching a high latitude depended on the continuity of the coast-line to the northward, for having land as a basis was considered one of the first principles of Polar navigation. The captain did not consult with me on the especial subjects mentioned in the question.

I wish to state further that I had a letter, under date of June 2, 1878, from Capt. George W. De Long, in which he stated:

> It is our intention to attack the Polar regions by the way of Behring's Straits, and if our efforts are not crowned with success, we shall have made an attempt in a new direction and examined a hitherto unknown country. The vessel which we have selected and purchased was originally Her Britannic Majesty's ship Pandora, and which was sold in 1872 to Sir Allan Young, from whom Mr. Bennett bought her in January last. We have changed her name to Jeannette, and have had her thoroughly repaired and put in shape.

He stated that he wished to go to work quietly and without any splurge.

The witness here gave the judge-advocate the letter referred to, and was asked the following questions:

Question by the JUDGE-ADVOCATE. Do you believe this letter to be in the handwriting of George W. De Long?

The WITNESS. I do.

Question by the JUDGE-ADVOCATE. Do you recognize the signature as that of George W. De Long?

The WITNESS. I do.

The judge-advocate then offered, and the court accepted, the letter as evidence, and it was accordingly read aloud by the judge-advocate, and a certified copy is appended, marked R.

And the court then, at 2.20 p. m., pending the further examination of this witness, adjourned to meet to-morrow, the 19th day of October, 1882, at 10.30 a. m.

THIRTEENTH DAY.

NAVY DEPARTMENT,
Washington, D. C., Thursday, October 19, 1882—10.30 a. m.

The court met pursuant to the adjournment of yesterday.

Present, Commodore William G. Temple, United States Navy, president; Capt. Joseph N. Miller, United States Navy, Commander Frederick V. McNair, United States Navy, members; and Master Samuel C. Lemly, United States Navy, judge-advocate.

The record of the proceedings of yesterday, October 18, 1882, the twelfth day of the inquiry, was then read and approved.

Lieut. JOHN W. DANENHOWER, the witness under examination, then came in, and his examination continued as follows:

Question by the COURT. What are the chances of a vessel's being able to get out of the ice pack usually found off Wrangel Island when once she is beset in it? Please state fully the grounds on which you base your opinion.

The WITNESS. The chances are slight, judging from the experience of the whale ships, three of which were beset and lost during the first season we were there. The steam whaler North Star was beset and lost, during the summer of 1882, and since the year 1871, 56 whaling ships have been beset and lost. This is stated on the best authority, that is, the report of Captain Hooper to the Secretary of the Treasury, relating to the cruise of the Corwin, in the summer of 1880 and 1881.

Question by the COURT. Do you know of anything in the management of the vessel which subsequent experience has proved to have been prejudicial to the objects of the expedition and which could have been avoided?

The WITNESS. I would state to the court that it is a question of judgment that is called for by the question, and when I embarked in the expedition it was to abide by the judgment of the commander, and I do not wish to set my judgment against his or that of any one else, unless it is absolutely required.

The judge-advocate here called the attention of the court to Harwood, page 247, on the subject of "opinion of witnesses," and read the paragraph referred to, which is completed on page 248.

The court was then cleared by request of a member, and afterward reopened.

Whereupon the question last submitted to the witness was revised by the court and put to the witness as follows:

Question by the COURT. Are there any material facts, within your knowledge, relating to the management of the Jeannette, which you have not already stated?

The WITNESS. No.

Question by the COURT. At the time the Jeannette entered the lead in the ice pack was it, in your opinion, with a fair promise of success of forcing her way through and reaching the land?

The WITNESS. I would not give my opinion, unless I had been in the crow's nest to get a full view of the situation. When the captain came down on deck it was very foggy, and I did not go aloft. I could not form a positive opinion at the time.

Question by the COURT. In general terms, how were the crew of the Jeannette employed and amused while the vessel was beset in the pack?

The WITNESS. There was one man kept on watch on deck at all times. His duty was to pump the ship out at regular intervals; to keep the lookout. There was one man employed at the condensing apparatus, which consisted of the Baxter boiler and distiller. The general work of the ship was performed by a watch of men in the forenoon. The holds and store-rooms were broken out and re-stowed at regular intervals, and everything about the ship kept in thorough order. The men and officers were supplied with musical instruments, books, cards, and other games for amusement and recreation. The clothing of the men kept them pretty busy, as they made such alterations as best suited their taste. Each person was allowed a rifle, and was encouraged in hunting. Foot-ball was sometimes played on the ice, and foot races also took place. A team of dogs was often hitched up and short excursions made in the immediate vicinity of the ship. Minstrel and theatrical performances took place about the holiday season of each year, when a suitable change was also made in the diet for the occasion.

Question by the COURT. Were the provisions always of good quality? If not, please state the names of the contractors and manufacturers who furnished those which were found defective.

The WITNESS. No. A considerable quantity of canned goods turned out badly. A large invoice of canned beef, marked with Erie Company's brand, was bad, and had to be rejected at Mare Island. Canned goods of all descriptions proved bad at times, and had to be condemned by survey, mention of which was made in the ship's log from day to day. The flour, bread, coffee, tea, sugar, butter, and such articles were very good. The goods were furnished by J. H. Leggett & Co., of New York, and were from the various canneries of the East and West.

Question by the COURT. Was or was not the deterioration in canned provisions the result of temperature to which they were exposed?

The WITNESS. No. From the time of leaving San Francisco they were condemned from time to time.

Question by the COURT. State fully what observations, meteorological and others, were taken.

The WITNESS. During the first year in the ice the meteorological observations were taken hourly by a detail of officers, and consisted of noting the height of the barometer with thermometer attached, the wet and dry bulbs, maximum and minimum thermometers, the anemometer, the black bulb in a vacuum, the state of the clouds and movements thereof, the direction of the wind, and the general character of the weather, also the state of the ice. The astronomical observations were those of the sun, moon, and stars, by artificial horizon, for latitude, longitude, and time. The observations with the azimuth compass for variations, lunar observations, and eclipses of Jupiter's satellites, for chronometer error, soundings, and temperature of sea water by the Miller-Casella thermometer, specimens of the water examined, and specific gravity determined; surface temperature, and those at different depths, also determined. Dredge was hauled for specimens from the bottom, and of the animal life specimens from each sounding were kept, and other specimens turned over to the naturalist and taxidermist. Bears, seals, and birds were carefully examined when obtained, their stomachs especially, to gain all possible knowledge about the food obtained in that region, and their habits. The soundings were made with ordinary lines, and specimens of the bottom were brought up in the Sands cup; the specimens of the water were brought up in the Sigsbee cup, the maximum and minimum thermometers being attached to the line and fitted with a special copper guard. The temperature was generally taken at the surface, at the 15-fathom mark, and just above the lead.

Question by the COURT. Did the character of the provisions supplied to the Jeannette cause sickness at any time? If so, state all you know in reference to the matter.

The WITNESS. In May, 1881, a number of the people became affected with stomach disorders, which were attributed to tin poisoning. It had been observed that the inside of the tomato cans had turned dark, as though acted upon by acid. I was not affected. The tomatoes were marked Red Cross brand, and were excellent in quality most of the cruise. They had been subjected to two winters and two summers' exposure.

The court then, at 12.40 p. m., took a recess until 1.10 p. m., at which time it reconvened, with all the members, the judge-advocate, and the witness present.

Examination by the COURT continued:

Question by the COURT. At the time the Jeannette entered the lead in the ice-pack what was the estimated distance to the land which was then supposed to exist to the westward of you?

The WITNESS. About 100 miles.

Examination by the JUDGE-ADVOCATE:

Question by the JUDGE-ADVOCATE. You have stated in your evidence that the events which transpired between the dates of January 1, 1880, and June 12, 1881, are not within your personal knowledge by reason of your physical disability; are you personally cognizant of the events of June 12 and 13, 1881?

The WITNESS. Yes.

Question by the JUDGE-ADVOCATE. State all you know of the events of those days, on the latter of which, as you have stated, the Jeannette went down.

The WITNESS. I was convalescent at the time, and went on deck at 1 p. m., June 12, 1881, for an hour's exercise. The weather was clear and pleasant, and there was a light breeze from the northward and eastward. The ship lay secured to the ice on her starboard side and in the form that had been made when she was frozen in. As I remember, she was heading to the east of south, as the wind was near the port beam. The ice on the port side had opened on the previous day and was about 200 yards distant, with smooth water between it and the ship. There were no connected leads at the time by which the ship could have navigated, but in the vicinity there were a number of patches of water like small ponds. The men went out to hunt as usual. About 2 p. m. I I noticed the ice on the port-beam commenced to move toward the ship. It was immediately reported to the captain by the man on watch, and the captain came on deck. He ordered the hunters' recall to be hoisted at the main-truck, and they returned one by one, to the ship. The last two, coming in a little after 3 p. m., were Bartlett and Aniguin, who were dragging a seal. They came to the port side, for the ice at that time was in contact with the ship, and she was heeling from 15° to 20° to starboard, with a heavy pressure under the port bilge. The captain was on the bridge, giving orders about the boats, provisions, &c.; all hands were on deck. During the first pressures the ship was forced astern, and when the pressure slacked up she was hauled back into the orignal place. The pressures were very heavy and gave forth a hissing, crunching sound. Several times the pressures relaxed and the ship righted. About 3.40 p. m. Machinist Walter Lee reported the ice coming through the starboard coal-bunkers, and the captain gave the order "Lower away" to the men who had previously been stationed at the boat's falls. At that moment Mr. Melville came on deck and contradicted the statement, and the order to "Hold on the boats" was immediately given. Between 3.45 and 5.30 p. m. a quantity of provisions was placed on the ice to starboard of the ship. About 5.30 p. m. one watch was sent to supper and the word was passed for the officers to get tea. At that time the ship was heeling more that 20° to starboard by the cabin indicator.

And the court then, at 1.45 p. m., pending the further examination of this witness, adjourned to meet to-morrow, the 20th day of October, 1882, at 10.30 a. m.

FOURTEENTH DAY.

NAVY DEPARTMENT,
Washington, D. C., Friday, October 20, 1882—10.30 a. m.

The court met pursuant to the adjournment of yesterday.

Present, Commodore William G. Temple, United States Navy, president; Capt. Joseph N. Miller, United States Navy, Commander Frederick V. McNair, United States Navy, members; and Master Samuel C. Lemly, United States Navy, judge-advocate.

The record of the proceedings of Thursday, October 19, 1882, was then read, and after correcting several clerical errors, approved.

Lieut. JOHN W. DANENHOWER, the witness under examination. then came in, and his examination was continued, the judge-advocate repeating the pending question, as follows:

Question by the JUDGE-ADVOCATE. State all that you know of the events of those days (the 12th and 13th of June, 1881), on the latter of which, as you have stated, the Jeannette went down.

The WITNESS. About 6 p. m. on June 12 very heavy pressures were felt. I saw Mr. Dunbar step below in the wardroom and bring up his knapsack and throw it in the cabin. At that moment I met Dr. Ambler, who said loudly, "The order is to abandon ship." I then threw my knapsack over the starboard rail upon the ice, and returned to get other things, but found the water half-way up the wardroom ladder. I then went to Mr. Chipp's room and assisted in getting him out. He was sick abed at the time. His room was the forward room on the port side of the poop cabin. At this time all hands were employed, under the direction of the captain (who was on the bridge), in getting out pemmican, camp gear, ammunition, and other stores, which were principally in the deck-house, forward; but another party of men was also working in the after hold as long as the water would permit. There was also a detail of men on the ice, placing the stores in a safe situation as they came from the ship. A few minutes before this time the ensign had been hoisted at the mizzen truck. Just before supper I reported to the surgeon that I was ready for work, and requested him to recommend me the captain to do light duty at least. He said he would do so, and in the mean time requested me to assist him in looking out for the medical stores and the liquors, which I stowed in one of the boats. About 8 p. m. the order was given by the captain for everybody to leave the ship. At that time the water was up to the spar deck on the starboard side, the ship keeling about 23° to starboard. I would further state that during the pressures the ship at times seemed to lift a little, sometimes at the bow, and sometimes at the stern. This was during the pressures, before she was crushed; but when she was hove over to starboard the ice, coming above her doubling, seemed to hold her down, and the pressures were felt on the timber heads. Dr. Ambler, at the time, told me that he went down in the wardroom to get some articles, and on lifting a hatch cover found the water coming in the ship. He immediately reported to the captain, who was on the bridge at the time, and the order was given to get everything out of the ship. My object in stating this circumstance is to show at what time the ship commenced to leak. Everybody left the ship, and the order was given to camp and prepare coffee. This was after the provisions, boats, and stores had been shifted to a large floe piece about 250 yards off the starboard bow. This was done at the suggestion of Mr. Dunbar, the ice pilot, as the ice in the close vicinity of the ship was too much broken up to afford a good and safe place for camping. The sun had been above the horizon at midnight since the early part of May, and the light was strong even during cloudy weather. The snow was about 2½ feet deep, and the thermometer ranging between 25° and 30° Fahrenheit.

When the order was given to camp, Dr. Ambler relieved me from the care of the medicine, liquor, &c., and I went to work with No. 3 party, which had been assigned to me originally. We pitched the tent abreast the whale-boat, and I went to work to collect the boat's outfit for the journey. I saw four prismatic compasses in the stern sheets of the first cutter, one of them hanging over the side. I took one for the use of the whale-boat, and got everything together that belonged to her and the tent, as each party's gear had been previously marked and stowed in a state of readiness on the spar deck or in the deck-house. While waiting for coffee I went back to the ship in order to take a last look at her. I met John Cole, boatswain, and Alfred Sweetman, carpenter, and we stood for five or ten minutes examining and discussing the situation. I noticed a place on the ship's side below the after end of the fore-chains, on the port side, in the vicinity of the water line, which appeared to me to have been bulged in by the pressure, but it was then, the ship having a list of 23° to starboard, out of water. It was probably no more than 3 feet square, speaking roughly, and looked as if a tongue of ice had impinged on that part. The steam-launch at the time was on the ice, about 20 yards from the ship, abreast the port fore-chains. The captain was standing near the port quarter of the ship, and the second whale-boat was hanging at the davits near him. Mr. Sweetman suggested that we go aboard and lower the whale-boat, and asked me to speak to the captain about it. I declined, but said there were enough of us there to lower her if necessary. He then spoke to the captain, who quietly and pleasantly remarked that he had a sufficient number of boats already on the ice. I then proposed to return to the camp; so Cole, Sweetman, and I returned together, leaving the captain near the port quarter, and the only person in the vicinity of the ship. After having coffee we turned in; it must have been about 11 p. m. A few moments later a loud crack in the ice was heard, and was followed by the order "Turn out, everybody." The ice had cracked near the captain's tent, and it became necessary to shift everything to an adjoining and safer floe-piece. We turned in again about 1 a. m. on the 13th. A watch was of course set, and about 4 a. m. I was awakened by Seaman Kuehne, who was calling Fireman Bartlett, his relief. He told him to hurry up to see the ship go down. I heard a crash and various remarks from the two men as they watched her go down. That morning, after all hands were called, the spot where the ship went down was visited by a party, and a cabin chair, a signal chest, and a few pieces of wood were found.

And the court then, at 12 m., took a recess until 12.30 p. m., at which time it reconvened, with all the members, the judge-advocate, and the witness present.

The examination of the witness was then continued.

Question by the JUDGE-ADVOCATE. Describe the condition of the ice on the 12th of June, 1881. Was it broken, or in large floes, and what was its general movement?

The WITNESS. The ice was very much broken, and hove up in ridges and hummocks; the highest observed about 20 feet. The large floe in which we had been drifting for eighteen months seemed to have been broken up by hinging, as it were, on Henrietta Island, and swinging around to the northwest. The thickness was about 10 feet, which is the average winter growth in that region, but it was hove up in a very confused way, and the greatest draught of water of any piece I saw measured was 23 feet. The floe pieces were generally of small area. There were no lengthy or connected leads, but only small ponds of water here and there, and the ice was in constant motion The general motion was dependent on the wind, but the local motion depended upon the amount of surface exposed to the wind, and was very irregular, owing to the hummocks. In some cases the floe would have a sort of turning motion.

Question by the JUDGE-ADVOCATE. Was this crushing of the ship, to which you have referred as the crisis, unexpected, or was it anticipated and provided for?

The WITNESS. It was anticipated and provided for.

Question by the JUDGE-ADVOCATE. What was the condition of the Jeannette on the 12th day of June, 1881, particularly as to her strength, prior to the heavy pressures to which she was then subjected?

The WITNESS. She was a very strong ship, and in the same condition as when she left San Francisco, except having the fore-foot twisted, and on that day Seaman Nindermann pointed out to me the fore-foot, which could be seen under water and twisted a little to port, as I remember it, having been done on the 19th of January, 1880, but was not in sight until the time specified, about June 12, 1881, owing to the ship being imbedded in ice. She had been leaking since January 19, 1880. After the ship floated she leaked less than when she was gripped in the ice. A large quantity of provisions, coal, and stores having been expended, she floated lighter. I think it was also due to her natural trim, the bows going up when she was freed from the ice.

Question by the JUDGE-ADVOCATE. Do you then attribute the loss of the ship to frequent and severe strains, or solely to the heavy pressures to which she was subjected on June 12 and 13, 1881?

The WITNESS. To the actual pressures on June 12 and 13, 1881; and on that day she stood the pressure for over three hours before commencing to leak.

Question by the JUDGE-ADVOCATE. If, then, she had been able on the 12th of June to get clear of the surrounding ice by connecting leads, do you or do you not believe that she would have proven a seaworthy ship, and one capable of continuing Arctic exploration?

The WITNESS. She would have been a seaworthy ship, but it would have depended upon the actual experience she would encounter as to her capability for Arctic work.

Question by the JUDGE-ADVOCATE. Knowing her condition at that time, would you, if in command of the expedition, have deemed it expedient to continue the Arctic exploration?

The WITNESS. No; for she had been fitted out for three years, and the supply of provisions, clothing, &c., would not warrant another year in the ice. The supply of coal, also, would have been insufficient for the coming winter, and the crew had already been exposed for two years to the rigors of the Arctic climate. Furthermore it is the custom, when a ship is fitted out for three years for Arctic work, to return at the end of the third summer.

Question by the JUDGE-ADVOCATE. Was it, then, owing solely to the reasons enumerated in your last answer, and in no degree to defective strength of the vessel, that you would have deemed further exploration in her inexpedient?

The WITNESS. Yes.

Question by the JUDGE-ADVOCATE. You have stated that between

5 and 6 p. m. the officers went to tea. Did any one of them remain on deck; and, if so, which of them?

The WITNESS. The captain remained on the bridge. Mr. Melville, Mr. Dunbar, and the doctor were on the alert, attending to their duties, and one watch of men was also at work.

Question by the JUDGE-ADVOCATE. In reference to the heavy pressures testified to on the 12th June, what part of the ship was principally subjected to them?

The WITNESS. It seemed that the heaviest pressure came on the timber-heads [of the*] starboard frames after the ship was hove over by the ice; and also the heavy pressures were felt on the port side, on the bilges of the ship.

Question by the JUDGE-ADVOCATE. Where, if you know, did she first give way?

The WITNESS. I do not know.

Question by the JUDGE-ADVOCATE. You have stated that the captain, when asked for permission to lower the second whale-boat, replied that the boats already down were sufficient. Did subsequent experience prove this to be the case?

The court was here cleared, by request of a member, and afterwards reopened, the witness being present.

The judge-advocate then stated that he withdrew for the present the last question, to be put to the witness at a further stage of the proceedings.

Question by the JUDGE-ADVOCATE. Were all of the officers and men of the expedition landed safely and without accident on the ice?

The WITNESS. Yes.

Question by the JUDGE-ADVOCATE. Referring to the log-book, date of June 10, local date 11, 1881, do you recognize the handwriting in which the events of that day are recorded?

The WITNESS. I recognize it as the handwriting of the late Lieutenant-Commander George W. De Long, United States Navy, commanding the Jeannette at that date.

Question by the JUDGE-ADVOCATE. Do you believe it to be the handwriting of the late Lieutenant-Commander George W. De Long?

The WITNESS. I do.

The judge-advocate then proceeded to read from the log-book the record of the day in question, which was the last entry therein, and which is as follows:

FRIDAY, *June* 10, 1881. (SATURDAY, *June* 11, 1881.)

At 12.10 a. m. the ice suddenly opened alongside, and the ship righted to an even keel. Called all hands at once, and brought in the few remaining things on the ice. The ship settled down to her proper bearings nearly, the draught being 8 feet 11 inches forward and 12 feet 5 inches aft. A large block of ice could be seen remaining under her keel.

At the first alarm the gate in the water-tight bulkheads forward was closed; but the amount of water coming into the ship was found to decrease, a small stream trickling aft being all that could be seen.

There being many large spaces of water near us, and the ice having a generally broken appearance, it was concluded to ship the rudder, to be ready for an emergency involving the moving of the ship.

After some trouble in removing accumulations of ice around the gudgeons, the rudder was shipped, and everything cleared away in the wake of the booms and yards for making sail.

As well as could be judged by looking down through the water under the counters, there was no injury whatever to the after body of the ship. As soon as possible a bow line and quarter line had been got out, and the ship secured temporarily to the ice, which remained on the starboard side, as nearly in the same berth as she could

---

* Correction by witness.

be placed. By looking down through the water alongside the stem, on the port side, one of the iron straps near her fore foot was seen to be sprung off; but otherwise no damage could be detected. It was assumed by me that the heavy ice, which all day bore heavily against the stem, had held the plank end open at the garboards, and that as soon as the ship was able to move from this heavy ice the wood ends came together again, closing much of the opening and reducing the leak. The water line, or rather the water level, being below the berth-deck, no difficulty was anticipated in keeping the ship afloat, and navigating her to some port, should she ever be liberated from the pack-ice of the Arctic Ocean.

Sounded in 33 fathoms; bottom, mud; rapid drift W. S. W.

GEORGE W. DE LONG,
Lieutenant, United States Navy, Commanding.

[This entry was written in pencil, and was very indistinct, some of the words being scarcely legible.—S. C. L., J. A.]

And the court then, at 2 p. m., pending the further examination of this witness, adjourned to meet to-morrow, the 21st day of October, 1882, at 10.30 a. m.

FIFTEENTH DAY.

NAVY DEPARTMENT,
Washington, D. C., Saturday, October 21, 1882—10.30 a. m.

The court met pursuant to the adjournment of yesterday.

Present, Commodore William G. Temple, United States Navy, president; Capt. Joseph N. Miller, United States Navy, Commander Frederick V. McNair, United States Navy, members; and Master Samuel C. Lemly, United States Navy, judge-advocate.

The record of the proceedings of yesterday, October 20, 1882, the fourteenth day of the inquiry, was then read and approved.

Lieutenant JOHN W. DANENHOWER, the witness under examination, then came in, and his examination by the judge-advocate was continued, as follows:

Question by the JUDGE-ADVOCATE. Was the abandonment of the ship anticipated and prepared for at any time prior to June 12 and 13, 1881; and if yes, what were the preparations made?

The WITNESS. Yes; sudden disaster was anticipated, and, as I have previously stated, preparations were made when the ship first entered the pack.

Question by the JUDGE-ADVOCATE. What was the physical condition of the officers and men of the Jeannette when landed on the ice, June 12, 1881 (local date)?

The WITNESS. The physical condition was good, with the following exceptions, viz: Lieutenant Chipp was disabled and prostrated by what was supposed to be tin-poisoning. I was disabled by the condition of my eyes, and unable to perform the duties of navigator, but able to do other work. The Indian, Alexy, was affected with an ulceration in one of his legs. A number of the men, among whom were Seaman Kuehne, coal-heaver Lauterbach, and the steward, Charles Tong Sing, were also affected by the tin-poisoning, and were prostrated a few days later.

The witness was then examined by the COURT as follows:

Question by the COURT. On the 12th and 13th of June, 1881 (local dates), was the pressure perceptibly more severe than had been previously experienced, before that fact became evident from the vessel's yielding to it?

The WITNESS. It was perfectly evident before she yielded to them that the pressures were heavier than she had experienced before.

Question by the COURT. Was everything done that was possible to avoid the loss of the Jeannette? If not, state what was neglected to insure her safety.

The WITNESS. Everything that circumstances would permit was done.

Question by the COURT. In your opinion, could any vessel have been practically constructed so as to have lived through the pressure that the Jeannette was subjected to on June 12 and 13, 1881 (local dates)?

The WITNESS. The ice pressures are so different, and cannot be foreseen, that a vessel could not be built and fully insured, so to speak, to go through such an ordeal successfully. For example, whatever the model of the ship, and however well it may be adapted to rise under theoretical pressures, when it comes to practice, a tongue of ice may destroy her, as we frequently saw such projecting tongues under water. The force was sufficient to crush any ship if held in the same position as the Jeannette.

Question by the COURT. You have stated in your testimony the immediate cause of the destruction of the Jeannette; looking back, to what do you now attribute, primarily, the cause of the loss of that vessel?

The WITNESS. To the fact that she was beset in the Polar pack.

Question by the COURT. Can you state when and where the two whaling vessels already mentioned in your testimony were beset in the ice in the autumn of 1879; also when and where they were finally lost?

The WITNESS. I can state only what I have heard read on the subject in the accounts of the cruises of the Corwin and the Rodgers.

The court was here cleared, by request of a member, and afterwards reopened, the witness being present.

The witness then continued his answer to the pending question, as follows:

The whalers Mount Wollaston and Vigilant were beset in the autumn of 1879 to the southward of where the Jeannette entered the pack. The crews stood by their ships. In the summer of 1881, I think, a sled party from the Corwin learned from the natives at Cape Yaken that a ship had been seen in the offing and had been visited. I think it was about the middle of September when they were beset. I know nothing definitely of the position.

The court was then cleared, by request of a member, and afterwards reopened, the witness being present.

Examination by the COURT continued:

Question by the COURT. At what time of the year do Arctic cruisers usually consider it necessary to leave the vicinity of Wrangel Island in order to avoid being beset in the ice?

The WITNESS. As I understand it, they seldom get in the vicinity of Wrangel Island, but cruise off the floe edge, between Point Barrow and the vicinity of Herald Island. Of late years they leave the whaling ground in the month of October, generally before the 10th.

Question by the COURT. In order to make Arctic explorations, is it or is it not necessary to enter the pack ice? If yea, state the time of year most favorable for following a lead opening into the pack ice.

The WITNESS. It is necessary, and is frequently done in some localities; the Greenland Seas, for example. The summer season during calm weather; in the middle of summer. To make explorations northwest of Herald Island it is necessary to enter the pack, for that part of the ocean is seldom free from ice. Vessels enter the pack boldly off the west coast of Greenland in forcing their way to the northward, because if they are beset they drift southward and get free.

Question by the COURT. Previous to the 12th of June, 1881 (local date), was it at any time supposed that the necessity for abandoning the ship had became imminent or advisable?

The WITNESS. The necessity had not become imminent, but as to the advisability, that was simply a matter of judgment. I do not think it would have been advisable for an exploring expedition to abandon its ship, but for a whaler it would have been.

Question by the COURT. Can you state approximately how far to the southward of the Jeannette the two whalers already referred to were at the time they were beset in the ice?

The WITNESS. No.

Question by the COURT. You have stated that the position of the Jeannette when she sank was, latitude 77° 15′ N., longitude 150° 6′ E.; how were these determined?

The WITNESS. Determined by observation by the commanding officer.

Question by the COURT. Had the ship's company been regularly drilled at abondoning the vessel during the cruise? If so, what was the character of that exercise?

The WITNESS. They were stationed, but never drilled.

Question by the COURT. At the time the Jeannette entered the pack-ice, in 1879, would you, if in command, have navigated the ship differently? If so, state what you would have done under the circumstances.

The WITNESS. I should have tried to have gotten out on the evening of September 6th.

Question by the COURT. What would have been the prospects of your succeeding in getting clear of the ice at that time?

The WITNESS. Good.

Re-examination by the JUDGE-ADVOCATE:

Question by the JUDGE-ADVOCATE. You have stated that, in your opinion, it would not have been advisable for the crew of the Jeannette, an exploring vessel, to abandon the ship prior to the time that vessel was crushed; but for a whaler it would have been advisable. Why do you make this difference?

The court was then cleared, by request of a member, and afterwards reopened, the witness being present.

The witness then answered the pending question as follows:

The WITNESS. The mission of an exploring ship is to explore; and, in doing so, extraordinary risks are undertaken, and it would not be creditable to abandon ship, however imminent the danger, unless it became a necessity to do so. Time is the important element for whalers, and they could not afford to remain two or three years in the pack. Thirty-three out of fifty-six whalers, therefore, abandoned their ships to the ice since 1871, as stated on the authority previously mentioned.

And the court then, at 1.30 p. m., pending the further examination of this witness, adjourned to meet on Monday the 23d day of October, 1882, at 10.30 a. m.

SIXTEENTH DAY.

NAVY DEPARTMENT,
Washington, D. C., Monday, October 23, 1882—10.30. a. m.

The court met pursuant to the adjournment of Saturday.

Present, Commodore William G. Temple, United States Navy, president; Capt. Joseph N. Miller, United States Navy, Commander Frederick V. McNair, United States Navy, members; and Master Samuel C. Lemly, United States Navy, judge-advocate.

The record of the proceedings of Saturday, October 21, 1882, the fifteenth day of the inquiry, was then read and approved.

The witness under examination, Lieut. JOHN W. DANENHOWER, then came in and continued his testimony, as follows:

Question by the JUDGE-ADVOCATE. State fully, in narrative form, what provisions were made and what plans adopted for the several boats' crews upon their leaving the wreck.

The WITNESS. On June 14, 1881, the assortment of the provisions and clothing recovered from the ship was commenced, also the outfit and preparation of the boats for the journey. There were five boats saved from the wreck, namely, the first cutter, second cutter, whaleboat, iron dinghy, and wooden dinghy. Each person had a knapsack and sleeping bag, of deerskin or sealskin. In most cases the sleeping bags were single, in others they were double. Each single bag was made of seal or deer skin, and was large enough for a person to slip into and lie at full length. The fur was inside, and the bag was covered with tanned sealskin, a cotton drilling on the outside, so that the snow could be readily brushed off. A half blanket was allowed to each person. For each tent there was a macintosh to cover the entire floor space, which was 9 feet by 6, and to be occupied by seven persons in their sleeping bags. There were five tents and an office tent: No. 1, Captain De Long and six others; No. 2, Lieutenant Chipp and six others; No. 3, Lieutenant Danenhower and six others; No. 4, Chief Engineer Melville and five others; No. 5, Dr. Ambler and five others. The office tent was occupied at night by a portion of No. 1 party. Each tent was provided with a fire-pot, which contained a large copper kettle of about three gallons capacity, and a stewpan above it. Below it was a large alcohol lamp, with a circular asbestos wick about five inches in diameter. The mess gear, when not in use, was stowed in the big kettle, and consisted of a tin cup and a tin pan and spoon for each person. Each knapsack contained one undershirt, one pair drawers, one pair woolen stockings, two pairs of blanket nips, that are worn outside the stockings, one pair of sealskin boots, one spare cup, one pair of spare gloves, one comforter, one wind-guard, which was a broad piece of leather to be placed on the weather side of the face in case of necessity, one pair snow-goggles, one pipe and one plug of tobacco, two hundred safety matches, and twenty-five wind matches, thread, needles, and soap at discretion, and twenty rounds of Remington ammunition. Another pair of sealskin boots was allowed to be carried in his sleeping bag; thus allowing each person three pairs of boots. Each person was allowed one suit of clothes, those he stood in, which was to be skin or other kind at discretion. The spare clothing was gathered together, and each person was allowed to make such selections as he considered improvement on what he possessed. The object was to leave the poorest articles behind, for we could not carry all.

The provisions saved consisted of about 1,200 pounds of hard bread, about 3,500 pounds of pemmican in canisters of 45 pounds each, a large quantity of tea, a small quantity of sugar and coffee, a large quantity of Liebig's extract of beef, some canned turkey and chicken, a few cans of ham, tongues, and pigs' feet, a large quantity of chocolate, and a large quantity of alcohol for fuel. On June 14 the provisions were assorted, the bread, sugar, tea, and coffee stowed in bags, some of them black ship's bags and others made from oil-skin clothing.

The five provision sleds were then stowed as follows: A tier of alcohol cans in the middle, with a tier of pemmican tins on either side, with thin planks intervening to prevent crushing the alcohol cans. This lower tier was firmly lashed, and bags of bread and other provisions placed on top and also firmly lashed. The sleds, when loaded complete, weighed about as follows: No. 1 sled, a ship-made sled, with heavy oak runners, was about 1,500 pounds; No. 2, 1,300; No. 3, 1,200; No. 4, 1,300; and No. 5, 1,300. A considerable quantity of the provisions could not be stowed on the sleds, and it was arranged to transport them, and also the medical stores, by means of two St. Michael's sleds and dogs, we having twenty-three dogs remaining. The camp equipages of No. 1 and No. 4 parties were stowed in the first cutter, that of No. 2 in the second cutter, and that of Nos. 3 and 5 in the whale-boat. Each boat was mounted on a ship-made sled, and the total weight of the sled and boat, with complete outfit, was about as follows: First cutter, 3,000 pounds; second cutter, 2,200; whale-boat, 2,500. The outfit of the whale-boat, which was made under my direction, was as follows: One set of four oars, one mast and lug sail, one rudder and yoke, two boat-hooks, two boarding pikes, and two small paddles with ice-chisels on the end (the object of the boarding pikes was to push drift ice from the boats, and of the paddles to paddle the boat across leads without getting out the oars from under the boat cover), one cotton canvas boat-cover, one long manila painter, one small hemp luff tackle, one supply box, containing marlin-spike, palm and needle, sail twine, and cotton twine, flint and steel and tinder box, also matches in tin boxes, and three candles, a can of tallow, two can-openers, fish-hooks and lines, forty rounds of ammunition, one saw and one hatchet, sheet lead and copper tacks. We also had some spare canvas and spare rope, some of the light running rigging of the ship that had been saved; two Remington rifles, .45 gauge, were assigned to the whale-boat, and Mr. Newcomb, of that boat, was allowed to carry his shotgun, with from twenty-five to fifty rounds of ammunition. The steering oar, the anchor, and the grapnel were intentionally left behind on account of their weight. The first and second cutters were fitted out in about the same way as the whale-boat.

The court then, at 12 m., took a recess until 12.30 p. m., at which time it reconvened, with all the members, the judge-advocate, and the witness under examination present.

The witness then continued his answer to the pending question, as follows:

The whale-boat was furnished with one prismatic compass and a pocket chronometer. The second cutter had the same and a Bowditch Navigator; the first cutter a sextant and artificial horizon, a box chronometer, a pocket chronometer, a comparing watch, a Nautical Almanac for 1881, a Lunar Distance, a Bowditch table of logarithms, and a pair of binoculars; Mr. Chipp also had a private pair of binoculars. At that time there were no charts, but a copy of the captain's chart was subsequently furnished to Mr. Melville, and I made a chart in order to keep the run of our positions on the retreat.

The witness here submitted the chart made by him to the court, and a correct copy thereof is appended to the record, marked R^2. The witness then continued his testimony as follows:

The first cutter was a clinker-built, square-sterned boat, 20 feet 4 inches in length, 6 feet greatest beam; depth from top of gunwale to top of keel, 2 feet 2 inches. She had an inner lining and was fitted with one mast and a shifting lug-sail. The boat was double banked, and pulled eight oars. She was fitted with a heavy keel-piece of oak, to strengthen her in hauling out upon the ice, and launching.

The second cutter was a clinker-built, square-sterned boat; length 16 feet 3 inches, extreme breadth 5 feet 1 inch; depth from top of gunwale to top of keel, 2 feet. She was fitted with one mast and shifting lug-sail and with a heavy oak keel-piece. I think she was double banked and fitted with six oars, though four were generally pulled.

The whale-boat was clinker-built, 25 feet 4 inches in extreme length, 5 feet 6 inches beam, and 2 feet 2 inches in depth from top of gunwale to top of keel. She had one mast and a shifting lug-sail, was single banked and fitted for five oars. She had an oaken keel-piece also. The boats were English built, and purchased with the ship.

From June 14 until the 18th preparations were made for the journey. The provision sleds were overhauled, relashed, and provisions stowed upon them. The boat sleds were refitted, relashed, and boats mounted and equipped. The clothing of the men was put in good order, the sleeping bags overhauled and refitted, and a lot of spare foot nips made. During this time the party lived on the canned goods that were not intended for the journey. A delay was also made on account of the sick men. On the evening of the 17th the commanding officer read to all hands the programme for the retreat, which was to commence on the following day at 6 p. m. All hands to be called at 4.30 p. m.; breakfast to be cooked, camp to be struck and work to commence at 6 p. m.; halt at midnight for one half hour for dinner; halt at 6 a. m. for supper and sleep; pipe down generally at 9 a. m. This was done in order to save the eyes of the party from the glare of the noonday sun. The plan of moving the sleds forward was also stated, but subject to such modifications as the commanding officer should find necessary. The diet scale was also established, as follows: Breakfast, per man: Four ounces of pemmican, one ounce of ham, one-fourth pound bread, two ounces of coffee, two-thirds of an ounce of sugar. Dinner: Eight ounces pemmican, one ounce Liebig's extract, half an ounce of tea, two-thirds of an ounce of sugar. Supper: Four ounces of pemmican, one ounce tongue, half an ounce of tea, two-thirds of an ounce of sugar, quarter of a pound of bread, one ounce of lime-juice, a large quantity of that article having been saved. This diet scale was modified, the ham and tongue not being served out, and a smaller quantity of tea being served. The lime-juice was taken after breakfast, all hands being mustered, each tent in its turn, for that purpose.

A cook for each tent was to be detailed for each week; an assistant appointed, whose duty it was to get snow from the highest hummocks for melting purposes for water, and also to draw the provisions from the yeoman, they being generally served out at each meal. A ration of alcohol was also served out at the same time with the provisions, one pint for each tent, for fuel. This was sufficient to cook the tea or coffee and the beef tea.

And the court then, at 1.25 p. m., pending the further examination of this witness, adjourned to meet to-morrow, the 24th day of October, 1882, at 10.30 a. m.

SEVENTEENTH DAY.

NAVY DEPARTMENT,
Washington, D. C., Tuesday, October 24, 1882—10.30 a. m.

The court met pursuant to the adjournment of yesterday.

Present, Commodore William G. Temple, United States Navy, president; Capt. Joseph N. Miller, United States Navy, Commander Frederick V. McNair, United States Navy, members; and Master Samuel C. Lemly, United States Navy, judge-advocate.

The record of the proceedings of yesterday, Monday, October 23, 1882, the sixteenth day of the inquiry, was then read and approved.

The witness under examination, Lieut. JOHN W. DANENHOWER, then came in and continued his answer to the pending question, which was repeated by the judge-advocate as follows:

Question by the JUDGE-ADVOCATE. State fully, in narrative form, what provisions were made and what plans adopted for the several boats' crews upon their leaving the wreck?

The WITNESS. The course stated in the captain's order was south 17° east, magnetic, which was south (true), there being 17° of easterly variation.

Mr. Dunbar, the ice pilot, was detailed to go ahead, select a road, and plant black flags to show the line of march; and the proposed arrangement was to advance the boats and provision sleds by short stages, and as many of them at a time as practicable.

The court was then cleared, by request of a member, and afterwards reopened, the witness being present.

Question by the JUDGE-ADVOCATE. Was there a detail made of officers and men to the various boats before commencing the retreat?

The WITNESS. There was a detail made in September, 1879, as previously stated, and the final detail was made at Bennett Island, August 6, 1881.

Question by the JUDGE-ADVOCATE. What disposition was made of the men's knapsacks and personal accoutrements on the retreat?

The WITNESS. They were stowed in the boats.

Question by the JUDGE-ADVOCATE. Were the provisions saved from the wreck and provided for the retreat all that it was possible to transport?

The WITNESS. Yes; and some had to be left behind to prevent encumbering the party too much.

Question by the JUDGE-ADVOCATE. You have stated that five boats were saved from the wreck, namely, two cutters, a whale-boat, and two dinghys, and that three only, the cutters and whale-boat, were equipped for the retreat. What became of the remaining boats?

The WITNESS. The iron dinghy was left at the first camp, and the wooden dinghy was carried with the party for quick use in picking up seals or carrying out lines in warping across leads. She was carried on a small McClintock sled, dragged by dogs, and was eventually cut up for fuel.

Question by the JUDGE-ADVOCATE. You have stated that the boats were all clinker-built. Is this deemed the best description of boat for Arctic service, and why?

The WITNESS. Yes; on account of their lightness. They were all clinker-built and copper fastened, except the iron dinghy.

Question by the JUDGE-ADVOCATE. You have stated that on the day before the ship went down it was proposed to the captain to lower the second whale-boat, and that he replied to the effect that the boats already down were sufficient; did subsequent experience prove this to be the case?

The WITNESS. The stowage capacity of the boats was sufficient for the thirty-three people and their effects. The boats had to be crowded, and when we reached the coast water, fourteen persons were in the first cutter, eleven in the whale-boat, and eight in the second cutter. While traveling over the ice the second cutter was considered the favorite boat and fully adapted to the service she was intended to perform. She was short and handy, and was not subjected to the racking strains and heavy thumps that the other boats got. The captain evidently meant that all the boats the party could carry were on the ice; and that it was not necessary to take more risk and trouble in lowering the second whale-boat after the ship had been abandoned.

Question by the JUDGE-ADVOCATE. If it had been decided to use the second whale-boat on the retreat, would there have been sufficient force to transport this additional boat, with her necessary equipment?

The WITNESS. I think not, as an additional boat.

Question by the JUDGE-ADVOCATE. Was any one of the boats used considered deficient in strength or as a sea-boat; and, if yea, which of them?

The WITNESS. There was no boat, at the time of commencing the retreat, that was considered deficient in strength or badly adapted to what was expected of it, except the whale-boat, she being long, and necessarily subjected to rough usage in transporting over hummocks. She had her garboards stove, and all her fastenings were loose, and was unfit to put in the water when we reached Bennett Island, where she was overhauled and repaired by Carpenter Sweetman.

And the court then, at 12.15 p. m., took a recess until 12.25 p. m., at which time it reconvened, with all the members, the judge-advocate, and the witness under examination present.

The witness then made the following statement in relation to the last question: When the boats were fitted out it was with the expectation of a protracted journey over the ice and through the leads, but not through a belt of 100 miles of coast water.

Examination by the COURT:

Question by the COURT. Was there a boat-sledge already constructed at the time of the wreck for the transportation of the second whale-boat, if it had been desired to make use of her in the retreat?

The WITNESS. I think there was, though I am not positive. She was fitted out like the other boats and her gear was all marked "Second whale-boat" and kept in readiness.

Question by the COURT. If there was no such boat-sledge already constructed at that time, could one have been prepared after the wreck?

The WITNESS. No; but the ship-made provision sled could have been substituted, as it was built like the other boat-sleds. There was no material saved which was suitable for making another boat-sled.

Question by the COURT. If the provision sledge had been used for the second whale-boat, how would the provisions have been transported?

The WITNESS. On the other provision sleds and by means of the St. Michael's dog-sled. The same amount of provisions could not have been carried in the same time.

Question by the COURT. After the preparations for the retreat by sledges had been completed, for what length of time was it estimated that the fuel, provisions, and stores would last?

The WITNESS. I understood that the sleds were to carry sixty days' provisions, including alcohol for fuel, and a large surplus was to be brought forward by the dog teams. More than eighty-five days provisions were thus actually transported.

Question by the COURT. Were any provisions or stores overlooked and left in the ship which, on fitting out the sledges for the retreat, were deemed important for the safety of the parties?

The WITNESS. I think not.

Question by the COURT. Was it your opinion, at the time, that the plans adopted upon leaving the wreck to insure the safety of the Jeannette's crew were as efficient as circumstances would permit? If nay, state in what particulars the plans were insufficient, with your reasons for so thinking.

The WITNESS. In my judgment, at the time, too much was carried, both in provisions and clothing. I thought, at the time, it was best to reduce everything to a minimum of weight; to carry sixty days' provisions, and strike due south as rapidly as possible for the Asiatic coast waters.

Question by the COURT. With the exception already stated, was it your opinion, at the time, that the plans adapted to insure the safety of the Jeannette's crew were adequate?

The WITNESS. No; each boat should have been provided for the case of separation in the way of compass, sextant, almanac, and logarithm tables.

Question by the COURT. Were the articles just named in the Jeannette? If so, was their absence inadvertent or intentional?

The WITNESS. The articles were in the Jeannette, and in October, 1879, a box was fitted out for each boat, to contain a full set of everything that was required for navigation. This was done, with a list of the articles specified by the captain. The boxes and the boat compasses were stowed in the starboard chart-room, ready for immediate use. I do not know that the articles were intentionally left in the ship on that afternoon of June 12. The prismatic compasses were always kept hanging in the chart-room ready for immediate use, and were taken on that day.

Question by the COURT. How did the provisions actually taken hold out?

The WITNESS. They held out for more than eighty-five days on the ration established, and at times the pemmican ration was increased to $1\frac{1}{2}$ pounds per day after the bread supply had given out.

Question by the COURT. After the sinking of the ship, and when the preparations had been completed, what weight was it estimated that each man would have to drag?

The WITNESS. A close estimate was not, to my knowledge, made, and would not have been of practical value; but after the provision sleds were loaded, it was found (excepting one or two cases) that they could not be advanced over the rough ice by their special crews alone. No. 3 sled had been used on the trip to Henrietta Island and was considered the weakest and loaded with about 1,200 pounds. It could be managed by seven men. A weight of 240 pounds per man is the estimate in Arctic traveling when the ice is not very rough. In our experience the ice was also covered with snow, and the entire force had to be employed in dragging each boat until the snow disappeared.

And the court then, at 1.30 p. m., pending the further examination of this witness, adjourned to meet to-morrow, the 25th day of October, 1882, at 10.30 a. m.

EIGHTEENTH DAY.

NAVY DEPARTMENT,
Washington, D. C., Wednesday, October 25, 1882—10.30 a. m.

The court met pursuant to the adjournment of yesterday.

Present, Commodore William G. Temple, United States Navy, president; Capt. Joseph N. Miller, United States Navy, Commander Frederick V. McNair, United States Navy, members; and Master Samuel C. Lemly, United States Navy judge-advocate.

The record of the proceedings of yesterday, Tuesday, October 24, 1882, the seventeenth day of the inquiry, was then read and approved.

The court was then cleared by request of the judge-advocate, and afterwards reopened.

Lieut. JOHN W. DANENHOWER, the witness under examination, then came in and his examination by the court continued as follows:

Question by the COURT. At the time the Jeannette was abandoned, what boats would you have fitted out for the retreat, had you been in command?

The WITNESS. The first cutter and the two whale-boats.

Question by the COURT. Why would you have chosen these boats in preference to the ones fitted?

The WITNESS. I considered the second whale-boat a better and more seaworthy boat than the second cutter.

Question by the COURT. Had the second whale-boat as much carrying capacity as the second cutter?

The WITNESS. Yes, more; she was the counterpart of the first whale-boat.

Question by the COURT. Did you express to the commanding officer your opinion that it would be better to lighten the sledge loads?

The WITNESS. No.

Question by the JUDGE-ADVOCATE. Which of the two boats, the second cutter or the second whale-boat, was the more readily transported over the ice.

The WITNESS. The second cutter.

Question by the JUDGE-ADVOCATE. Was not this an important desideratum in the selection of boats for the retreat?

The WITNESS. It was a very important consideration.

Question by the JUDGE-ADVOCATE. Was not the whale-boat, on account of its greater length, much more liable to be injured in transporting than the cutter?

The WITNESS. It was much more liable and was much more injured.

Question by the JUDGE-ADVOCATE. Considering everything, then, the greater difficulty of transporting the whale-boat and its liability to be more seriously damaged, do you not think that the selection of the lighter boat was a wise measure?

The WITNESS. I do not think so.

Question by the JUDGE-ADVOCATE. Give a full and detailed narrative of the retreat after the loss of the vessel.

The WITNESS. On June 18 the order was given for the camp to turn in at noon, in order to rest and sleep before the work that was to continue all night. All hands were called at 4.30 p. m. Camp struck and the march commenced at 6 p. m. The drag-rope of the first cutter was manned by most of the working party under charge of Mr. Melville; each person had been provided with a harness which consisted of a broad canvas band that crossed one shoulder diagonally, and to it was attached a lanyard with a button at the end or a diamond knot. About twelve of the party hitched to the drag-rope, and about eight to the thwarts on either side of the boat to lift her over rough ice and keep her from capsizing. I was at the starboard quarter, Dr. Ambler at the port quarter, and Mr. Collins at the stern pushing her along. We advanced slowly and steadily; the snow was more than knee-deep, and often had to be shoveled out from under the bow in crossing hollows where the boat would get stuck. She was advanced about a mile, and then the party turned back, taking up the other boats and sleds. In the mean time, Mr. Chipp, Seamen Kuehne, the Indian Alexy, with dogs, were to advance the hospital sled. Just before reaching the stopping-place with the first cutter, Machinist Walter Lee fell down with cramps in his legs, and on our return to the camp a call was made for the doctor, that Mr. Chipp had fainted. The dogs not having proved useful in dragging the sleds on rough ice, Mr. Chipp had overexerted himself in lifting. The captain, in the mean time, with a few men, had moved forward No. 1 sled and the whale-boat. The latter was launched in a crack about 15 yards wide, and in hauling out, the after beam of the sled was broken. No. 1 sled was stuck in the snow, and in hauling her out, the starboard runner turned inward. By this time the working party had got back, and then advanced the second cutter and the other sleds. A nice movement had taken place and broken up the first road that we went over. When the drag-rope of the first cutter was manned, it was with three cheers and enthusiasm, being homeward bound. About 6 a. m. on the 19th we camped abreast the second cutter and most of the sleds, about half a mile from the first camp; the first cutter being about half a mile in advance, and a portion of the goods being in the first camp. On the night of the 19th we went to work repairing sleds and bringing up the remaining goods to the second camp, to the second cutter. It being found that the weights on the sleds were too heavy for the state of the ice on the roads, they were lightened by removing the goods from above the tier of pemmican and alcohol. The smallest McClintock sled was rejected as a provision sled and afterwards used for transporting the wooden dinghy. We then had four provision sleds and three boats on sleds, which were to be advanced by the main working force; the remaining goods were to be advanced by the two St. Michael's sleds, each with a detail of two men and a team of dogs; the dinghy to be advanced by the road-makers and a team of dogs. It was to carry also pick-axes, shovels, and some light lines. The line of march was resumed on the 20th, and the whole camp-equipage carried to the position of the first cutter, which was a mile and a half from the first camp, instead of a mile, as stated a few moments ago, from memory alone, but by reference to notes made at the time I see that it was a mile and a half. While the snow lasted the party was able to advance one piece at a time, and thus had to make seven trips with the loads and six empty-handed. The progress made during the first week was from one-half to one mile a day. During that time it rained several times, the snow began to melt and form large pools on the ice. The wind was from the southward and eastward, and light. We judged that the ice was drifting to the northward, and westward at times. The regular routine was carried out. In the second camp, just before starting, the captain called me to his tent and ordered me to go with the hospital sled. The custom at that time was to load up a St. Michael's sled with the medical stores and a tent, advance the first stage, pitch the tent for the sick, and then the dog sled continued its regular work until another advance of the hospital tent was necessary. At this time, Mr. Chipp, Coal-heaver Lauterbach, and Indian Alexy were the sick. About July 17 Lauterbach and Alexy were returned to duty, and a change was made in the programme, by which tents in the first camp were left standing until the first fleet was made. They were then struck and brought forward by the dog teams. This was done to lighten the boats, the tents and camp stores having been stowed in them at first, and afterward carried by the dog sled. At all meals the cook or other detailed men in each tent divided the food out, equally serving it. The traveling improved some about July 4, and about 2 miles by the road was made during the day. On the 6th there was a great movement of ice, and traveling became very bad. On the 7th a number of gulls and seals were seen. On the 8th a snow-storm occurred, and on the 9th the ice was open and much broken in places. A great deal of time was lost in crossing leads, ferrying on pieces of ice; there were no leads going to the southward. On the 11th land was seen to the southward and westward. We sounded in 23 fathoms, and there was a slight drift to the northward. On the 13th of July the captain announced that we had made 27 miles to south by east during the past week, against 13 during the previous one. This was by observation, and during that time there was some drift to the southward. The ice on this day was loose and shifting.

And the court then, at 12.20 p. m., took a recess until 12.40 p. m., at which time it reconvened, with all the members, the judge-advocate, and the witness present.

The witness then continued his answer to the pending question, as follows:

The course had been south, true, until June 30, when it was changed to south-southwest, true. On July 16 the land bore southwest by west one-half west (magnetic), and the course was directed to it. Mr. Collins killed a seal that day, and it furnished a meal for the whole party. On July 17 he killed a seal, and Mr. Newcomb shot a sea hen. Walrus were also seen, and more birds were seen than usual. The party advanced toward the island as rapidly as possible, and at that time it was enabled to move more rapidly, advancing two pieces at a time. By a piece I mean either a provision sled or a boat. This necessitated going over the road four times with loads, and three times empty-handed. On July 24 soundings were taken in $20\frac{1}{2}$ fathoms, and the drift was toward the middle of the island, which extended from north-northwest [magnetic.*] It was from 6 to 8 miles distant, and from 400 to 500 feet in height. Wild geese were seen on that day. On the 25th Mr. Collins killed two seals and got one, and Seaman Görtz killed a bear. On the 26th our camp was between two points of the island which bore east and west, magnetic, from each other. We were between the Southeast Cape and the south point of the island, and about 2 miles from the land. The weather was cloudy and misty, gentle breeze from eastward, and numerous birds in sight. During the night of the 27th the wind shifted to the northward and blew in fresh squalls, accompanied by rain, ice drifting along the land. Called at 8 p. m., and the word was passed that we would not move until after meridian. Remained all day in camp. Weather cleared during the afternoon, and considerable open water seen; fresh northeast breeze. Thursday, July 28, foggy, with fresh squalls of wind; ice drifting; wind moderated after meridian. At 7 p. m. weather cleared, and land was plainly visible. Shifted to an im-

---

* Correction by witness.

mense floe piece, and advanced 1½ miles landward toward an inlet marked by a castellated mountain about 1,200 feet high. Camped at 11 p. m., Friday, July 29. Overcast and misty, with fresh breeze from northeast. Called at 6 a. m., and advanced; birds very numerous; crossed large floe, and encamped for dinner at noon. Started at 1 p. m.; ice in rapid motion, drifting to southwest. At 2 p. m. a mountain suddenly appeared, towering above the fog. I think it bore about west. The party moved over rough ice that was in motion, and got everything on a floe piece on the side nearest the land. This floe piece was moving to the southward and westward, and when it struck the grounded ice near the island the whole party made a rally and jumped the sleds and boats upon the grounded ice, and the floe piece immediately drifted away. After two hours' work the party got the sleds and boats to some flat pieces that were inside of the outer line of grounded pieces, and camped for supper. This was at the foot of the island. The land was so steep as not to afford a camping place. The tents were pitched on several different pieces, some of which rose and fell with the tide. The greatest rise and fall of the tide here, as afterward determined by a series of regular tidal observations, which commenced July 30, was about 3 feet. The moon was in its first quarter August 4, so the observations were made about the time of change of the moon. About 7 p. m. the day we landed the captain visited the island with all hands, hoisted the American ensign, and took possession in the name of the President of the United States, calling it Bennett Island, and telling Mr. Chipp to give the party all the liberty they wished on American soil. The next day parties were sent out to get birds, large quantities of which were obtained and distributed equally among the tents.

On July 31 Mr. Dunbar and the two Indians were sent out to explore the southeast face of the island. Divine service was also held. On August 1, Mr. Chipp with a party in the second cutter started out on a three days' trip, to explore the southwestern face of the island. On August 2, Mr. Dunbar and the Indians returned, having gone from 12 to 15 miles along the southeast face of the island. They found birds and drift-wood plenty in a few places, and Mr. Dunbar established a cairn on the southeast face of the island on August 5. The weather was very foggy, misty, and raw, and the ice to the eastward and southward of the island was in rapid motion most of the time. The movement seemed to depend on the ebb and flow of the tide. A considerable number of the party were sick with bad diarrhea from eating birds.

On August 5, the whale-boat was repaired by refastening and pouring grease inside along her keel for the leaks to take up the grease and dirt. Some white lead was also used both in patching the boat and filling the seams. The repairs were made by Carpenter Sweetman, Bartlett, and Leach. Twelve dogs were shot on that day, they being in a crippled condition, and not fit to be usefully employed. The dogs had been allowed one pound of pemmican per day, per dog, for food. They were buried in the water.

And the court then, at 1.40 p. m., pending the further examination of this witness, adjourned to meet to-morrow, the 25th day of October, 10.30 a. m.

NINETEENTH DAY.

NAVY DEPARTMENT,
Washington, D. C., Thursday, October 25, 1882—10.30 a. m.

The court met pursuant to the adjournment of yesterday.

Present, Commodore William G. Temple, United States Navy, president; Capt. Joseph N. Miller, United States Navy, Commander Frederick V. McNair, United States Navy, members; and Master Samuel C. Lemly, United States Navy, judge-advocate.

The record of the proceedings of yesterday, Wednesday, October 25, 1882, the eighteenth day of the inquiry, was then read, and, after correcting several clerical errors, approved.

The court then, at 11 a. m., having to vacate the court-room for the use of the Naval Examining Board, took a recess until 1 p. m., at which time it reconvened, with all the members and the judge-advocate present.

Lieut. J. W. DANENHOWER, the witness under examination, then came in and continued his answer to the pending question, which was repeated by the judge-advocate, as follows:

Give a full and detailed narrative of the retreat, after the loss of the vessel.

The WITNESS. On the morning of August 6, we left Bennett Island, embarking in the boats, crossing a wide lead, and about noon hauled up on some ice for dinner. Just before embarking, the executive officer, Lieutenant Chipp, gave me the captain's order to go in the whale-boat as a passenger, and he told me further that I was so detailed to assist in emergencies, if necessary. Chief Engineer Melville was transferred from the captain's boat, and placed in charge of the whale-boat, and Dr. Ambler was transferred to the captain's boat. During the afternoon the boats and stores had to be transported across a large floe piece.

On August 7 the provision sleds were abandoned and all the provisions stowed in the boats. The provision sled Walrus was retained, because it would answer for a boat sled, if needed. On this day the crew was rearranged in messes, thirteen men in the first cutter forming two messes, and ten men in the whale-boat and ten in the second cutter each forming one mess. We advanced that day through leads, and had a great deal of trouble with the dogs, as they wished to jump out and run away on the ice.

On the 8th of August, which was my first opportunity, I spoke to the captain and again asked to be put on duty, but he stated that, as long as the surgeon recommended, I should be kept on the sick-list. On the 9th all but two of the dogs jumped and ran away.

On the 10th we made about 15 miles to the southward and westward, and Mr. Collins killed two seals. On the 11th Dr. Ambler promised to discharge me from the sick-list, when clear of the ice. He stated that he feared one or two days of sunshine would injure my eyes very much while in the ice. The doctor did not fully promise to discharge me, but stated that I might hope to be discharged as soon as we were clear of the ice. From that time until the 19th the boats were working through leads, sometimes to the southwest, sometimes to the southeast, and sometimes northeast. It was often necessary to haul out and cross floe pieces several times a day. The boats were dragged across on the oaken keel pieces already referred to, and the provisions and baggage were carried on the backs of the party. The extent of the floe pieces was various, and from 200 yards to 1,000 yards in width across. Considerable game was seen, walrus and seal, of which one species was very numerous, especially Thong seal, commonly called the "Orgook." Birds were numerous. On the 19th of August the ice was very slack, and was of a different character from what we had just left. It was not as thick, and the surface was smoother, not being thrown up in hummocks. Long lanes of water were seen in all directions, and a heavy water-sky to the southeast. About 11.30 p. m. the captain ordered the boats to stop and fill up everything with snow from the highest pieces of ice that could be found. It was evidently with the expectation of reaching open water very soon. The boats then stood to the southward and westward under sail, and about 12.30 p. m. the ice suddenly came together and nipped the second cutter, she being the last boat of the three. The first cutter usually led, and was followed by the whale-boat and second cutter. In a number of instances previous to that day the second cutter had barely escaped such an accident. A hole was stove in her bow, which was temporarily repaired, and she was transported over the ice about a half a mile, where the other two boats were awaiting her. The three got under way, and stood on until about 6 p. m., when it was found impracticable to proceed further, as the ice had closed in by a shift of wind which occurred a few hours before. A piece large enough for the camp was found, and the party went into camp.

On the 20th, broke up the sleds for fuel, and divided the stores among the three boats. The last bread was consumed the day before.

On the 21st three of the men were very sick. About this time land was in sight bearing from south to west-northwest (true), and estimated to be 20 miles distant. The ice in the vicinity of the camp was very much broken, so that a boat could not be transported over it or navigated in the water. Soundings in 8 fathoms were taken, with rock and sand bottom. The drift of the pack was very slight to the southward. On the 23d the ration was reduced to $1\frac{1}{4}$ pounds of pemmican per man. Nindemann killed a small seal on that day. On the 24th we were in 8 fathoms, with muddy bottom. Several seals were killed on the following day, and on the 29th we left the "Ten Day" camp, as it was called, because we were detained there ten days, got under way at about 2 p. m., and at dark hauled upon a drifting ice floe. We were now out of the region of the midnight sun at that time of the year, and had from six to eight hours of darkness. Sounded in 6 fathoms, muddy bottom. In the ten-day camp the weather was generally foggy, but land was occasionally seen. On the night of the 29th the ice drifted rapidly to the southward down the strait between New Siberia and Fadejowski Island.

On the 30th there was a headland bearing west by south (true), and land could be seen as far as west-northwest (true). No land to the eastward, and very little ice in sight. We embarked at 4 a. m., pulled around the headland and coasted the island until about 4 p. m., when we effected a landing with some difficulty, owing to the shallow water, and camped on the mossy plain above the beach. Large parties were sent out hunting. Numerous deer tracks were seen, and an old deserted hut was found. Human footprints were also reported, made by a civilized boot. The next morning we got under way at 6 a. m., and tried to land about 7 p. m., but the water was too shallow, and we stood off to the south-southwest, with a shoal under our lee. Passed a very rough night, there being a fresh easterly breeze, and the boats constantly getting aground in the shallow water. About midnight we stood off on the port tack to the southward and eastward, and at daylight, on September 1, the second cutter was not in sight. The first cutter and whale-boat parties camped on a small piece of ice to await the second cutter to come up. A few minutes later the captain's tent was washed out by a sea breaking over the ice, and we again manned our boats. At that moment we sighted the second cutter, and when she came up Mr. Chipp reported that everything was all right, but they had had a very rough night. The three boats then stood to the southward, and about 1 p. m. came to a large water-hole, across which we were not able to see the ice on the other side. The wind was about northeast, blowing with a force of from 4 to 5. We stood across the water space, and the whale-boat was nearly swamped. When we reached the ice on the opposite side I judged that the water space was about 4 miles wide. The first cutter rounded to, and got a sounding; she then stood in the leads between the ice, and the whale-boat followed. The second cutter was out of sight astern. About an hour later the first cutter and whale-boat parties went into camp, and had supper. Remained in camp September 2; fresh breeze and heavy squalls from the southward and eastward, ice drifting to the northwest and packing. Sounded in 10¾ fathoms at noon, and at 2 p. m. in 7 fathoms, and land was reported, and about 6 p. m. a black flag was hoisted on a boat's mast as a signal for the second cutter. On September 3, the weather was overcast and misty, and there was a light breeze from the eastward. The ice was closely packed against the land, which was in sight at times to the westward. Sounded in 22 feet of water at noon. No drift observed.

At 5 p. m. a boat sail was sighted to the northward and westward, and the second cutter was seen approaching the broken ice about 1¼ miles distant. Mr. Chipp and Seaman Kuehne were next seen coming on the ice to our camp. They first went to the captain's tent and then came to our tent, and told us their experience. Mr. Chipp said that on the afternoon of the 1st September, in crossing the water space, his boat made very bad weather, and he had to haul up on a piece of drifting ice. The party were so benumbed and exhausted that Seaman Edward Starr was the only man who was able to jump out of the boat and haul her up by the painter when they reached the lee side of the ice. Some of the party had to be lifted out of the boat. They remained on the ice the night of the 1st and all day of the 2d. On the morning of the 3d he was able to get under way and stand toward the southeast end of Kotelnoi Island, which the captain had recommended as a place to touch. On September 4, Mr. Chipp brought his party to assist in getting the first cutter and whale-boat to the water. The ice was very rough and in motion, principally in small pieces, and three or four trips had to be made with the provisions and outfit on the backs of the men, and finally the two empty boats were transported to the position of the second cutter. A number of people got overboard in this work. We then embarked and reached the southeast point of Kotelnoi that evening. Camped on a low spit, and remained there until 5 a. m., September 6. Parties were sent out hunting, but the reindeer had all run to the mountains, though their tracks were everywhere seen. There was a deserted Russian hut with traces of the ivory hunters about a mile from the camp. On the 6th we coasted the island, and about noon had to make a portage, in order to get clear of some grounded ice. While making it Mr. Dunbar fell down with a stroke of heart disease. That night we camped near the south end of Kotelnoi, on some high bluffs. The next morning, September 7, we got under way at 7 and coasted the island until 9, when we took our departure from the south point, steering so as to pass Stolbovoi. On the morning of the 7th a large quantity of ice was in sight, but during the afternoon we crossed a large water-space. The wind was fresh from the northward and eastward, and there was a long following sea. The boats made heavy weather, everybody wet all the time. We stood on during the night, and I judge that we made 40 miles to the west-south-west before dark, which was about 8 p. m. About 1 a. m. on the 8th we again met drift ice, and the first cutter became embayed in the ice, but eventually got clear.

We stood on all day of the 8th, and passed the island of Stolbovoi, having it in sight at times to the southward and eastward, but very distant. At dark we camped on a [floating]* piece. September 9 was clear and beautiful, with a light breeze, and we started under oars at 6, and pulled all day to the southward and westward. On September 9 we camped on a large piece of ice in 7 feet of water. The weather was very foggy and misty. On September 10 Semenov Island was in sight, about 3 miles distant. We rounded the northern end of it and stood to the southward along its western coast. About noon we hauled in to get dinner and rest the men, who had been pulling all the morning. The captain and others went ashore and found a number of deer tracks going to the southward. A party of hunters was then sent ashore to move to the southward end of the island, to form a skirmish line, as it were, in order to intercept the deer. A number skirted the mud hills for that purpose. The boats in the mean time proceeded to the south end of the island to pick up the hunters. A deer was shot, and the boats returned, made a landing, and camped. The deer was served out to the party. We remained at Semenov Island until 5 a. m. September 12, and at that place all three boats were prepared for the voyage across the coast water, as it was evident that but little more ice would be encountered. Weather cloths were made from the boat covers, and stanchions placed along the gunwale. I have not yet stated that, on September 4, two men were transferred from Lieutenant Chipp's boat, namely, Frank E. Manson, seaman, to the whale-boat, and Ah Sam, ship's cook, to the first cutter. While at Semenov Island the weather was stormy from the eastward. We were camped on a mossy plain.

The court was then cleared by request of the judge-advocate and afterward opened, the witness being present. And the court then, at 3 p. m., adjourned to meet to-morrow, the 27th day of October, 1882, at 10.30 a. m.

TWENTIETH DAY.

NAVY DEPARTMENT,
Washington, D. C., Friday, October 27, 1882—10.30 a. m.

The court met pursuant to the adjournment of yesterday.

Present, Commodore William G. Temple, United States Navy, president; Capt. Joseph N. Miller, United States Navy, Commander Frederick V. McNair, United States Navy, members; and Master Samuel C. Lemly, United States Navy, judge-advocate.

The record of the proceedings of yesterday, Thursday, October 26, 1882, the nineteenth day of the inquiry, was then read and approved.

Lieut. J. W. DANENHOWER, the witness under examination, then came in, and continued his answer to the pending question, which was repeated by the judge-advocate, as follows:

Give a full and detailed narrative of the retreat after the loss of the vessel.

---

* Correction by witness.

The WITNESS. On Monday, September 12, we left Semenov Island at 7.15 a. m., and stood to the southward along the west coast of Vassiliev Island, the first cutter leading, the whale-boat next, with orders to keep within hail, and the second cutter bringing up the rear.

The following was the detail in the different boats: First cutter—Lieutenant Commander George W. De Long; doctor, James M. Ambler; meteorologist, J. J. Collins; machinist, Walter Lee; seamen, W. F. C. Nindemann, L. P. Noros, H. H. Ericksen, H. H. Kaack, C. A. Görtz, A. Dressler; second-class fireman, G. W. Boyd; coal-heaver, Nelse Iverson; cook, Ah Sam; dog driver, Alexy. Second cutter—Lieutenant Charles W. Chipp; ice pilot, William Dunbar; carpenter, Alfred Sweetman; seamen, H. D. Warren, P. E. Johnson, Edward Starr, A. G. Kuchne; coal-heaver, Walter Sharvel. Whale-boat—Chief Engineer George W. Melville; Lieut. John W. Danenhower; naturalist and taxidermist, R. L. Newcomb; boatswain, John Cole; first-class fireman, J. H. Bartlett; seamen, H. W. Leach, Henry Wilson, F. E. Manson; steward, Charles Tong Sing; coal-heaver, John Lauterbach; dog driver, Aniguin. There were, therefore, fourteen in the first cutter, eight in the second cutter, and eleven in the whale-boat.

The wind was fresh from the northeast at times, and there was very little ice in sight. About 11.30, in running through a chain of drift ice, the whale-boat was stove, and commenced to fill rapidly. We hauled her bow up on a piece of ice and patched her. The whole party took dinner. That was the last piece of ice we saw. During the afternoon the wind and sea increased; the boats were standing about south-southwest, with the wind about two points on the port quarter, and we were under close-reefed sail. The whale-boat being the fastest sailer, we often lowered our sail to keep in position, and had great difficulty in keeping the sea from breaking over the boat. About 5 p. m. we were out of position, being about a thousand yards off the weather quarter of the captain's boat.

Question by the JUDGE-ADVOCATE. Have you any chart or plan made or used at the time which shows the position of the boats, or any of them, during the retreat after the final embarkation? If yes, produce it.

The WITNESS. Yes; this is the chart which I made in the ten-days camp, it being a copy of Mr. Melville's, and he giving me the original while we were in the boat, after September 12, during the voyage to the Asiatic coast.

The witness here produced the chart in question, which the judge-advocate submitted and the court accepted as evidence, and a true copy is appended to the record, marked S.

The witness then continued his narrative, as follows:

Mr. Melville asked my opinion about getting into position. I said we could do so by jibing carefully twice. He told me to go ahead, so I took charge, got out oars to keep up the boat's headway before the sea, lowered the sail and jibed the boat; stood down to the captain's wake, and jibed again, and soon came in position. At that time I suggested that Seaman Leach take the helm, Mr. Cole having been there from the start in the morning. The boat ranged ahead and to windward of the first cutter, and we were afraid to lower the sail on account of the seas boarding her. As we passed the first cutter the captain hailed and said he wished the second cutter to come within hail. About that time the second cutter was well up to windward and abaft the beam of the first cutter. About 1 p. m. our boat was off the weather bow of the first cutter, and the men reported that the captain was standing up in the boat and waving his hand as if for a signal to separate. It was also stated that the second cutter was lowering her sail, as if rounding to. Owing to the strength of wind and sea, it would have been impossible for one boat to have helped the other at that time. It was then growing dark; Mr. Melville asked my opinion, and I stated that we should haul up to the southward, and run with the wind and sea about four points on the quarter, until we could prepare a drag, and at dark we should round to and lay to a drag, in order to avoid being smashed by ice, if we should meet any during the darkness. He commenced to give the order, and the boat was hauled up to the southward. He then told me to go ahead. I directed Boatswain Cole and Seaman Manson to take three of the hickory tent poles, lash them in a triangle, and lace in a piece of cotton canvas that we had in the boat. I measured off a bridle of three parts, each about nine feet in length, using the painter and a spare piece of rope for that purpose. The tent poles were between six and seven feet in length, and each had a heavy brass nib at the bottom. The luff-tackle fall was unrove to be used for a drag rope. I examined the drag thoroughly, had it placed forward of the mast, and the drag rope coiled down upon it, then had the end of the drag rope made fast, and the fall coiled down clear for running. I then stationed Bartlett n the bows to launch the drag, Cole at the halliards to lower the sail, Aniguin and the steward to gather it in, the two seamen, Wilson and Manson, at the midship oars, keeping them peaked high above the sea, and Seaman Leach at the helm. Each of the others in the boat had a tin pan, for a bailer, in hand. I cautioned everybody that at the order "Lower away" the sail should be lowered, the helm put hard a-starboard, give away hard with the starboard oar, and back the port one, if possible, in the sea-way. I watched for a chance, for I felt that our lives depended on the success of the evolution. When the proper time came I ordered "Lower away," and everybody did his duty. The boat came round head to sea with a tremendous dive, a large volume of water coming over the bows, which was quickly bailed out. We then eased the oars, and launched the drag and veered out the line. It watched at first on the port bow, and the port oar was kept backing to keep her head to sea. We then sent down the spare fire-pot and boat bucket by putting beckets on the bales. Mr. Cole suggested sending down an empty black-bag, which was done. The boat now lay head to sea, and we laid in the port oar and hauled up the weather cloths [snug*], parceled the drag-rope where it was liable to chafe, and made everything as snug as possible for the night. A number of the party turned in under the canvas forward, and Seamen Leach and Wilson took turns in the coxswain's box, with a short paddle. The upper gudgeon of the rudder carried away soon after rounding to, and the rudder was taken in-board. I remained up all night in charge, and watching the boat. The next morning at daylight nothing was in sight, and the storm was still raging. We had lost sight of the two other boats when darkness came on the night before, and I have never seen them since.

The court then, at 12 m., took a recess until 12.30 p. m., at which time it reconvened with all the members, the judge-advocate, and the witness under examination present; and the witness continued his answer to the pending question, as follows:

About 10 a. m. on the 13th I noticed a new sea was making, and I judged the wind had veered to the southeast. About 1 p. m. we got a glimpse of the sun, which at that time bore about south by west, and from it I found the wind was southeast. Mr. Melville's watch had to be

---

* Strike out the word "snug"; correction by witness.

wound two or three times a day, and was very incorrect. I carried it with the two charts. I had tried to use the pocket prismatic compass during the morning, but found it useless in the boat.

During the morning the sea broke over the port quarter, for the boat was trimmed by the stern. We tried to shift the sleeping-bags forward, but they had become so much swollen after being wet, that they jammed between, so we rigged the mackintosh on the port quarter to keep the water out. All the fresh water in the boat had become salty. During the afternoon the weather moderated, and after rigging a jury gudgeon and shipping the rudder, I called Mr. Melville and proposed getting under way and standing to the westward until the sea went down and gradually haul up to south-southwest. He said, "All right," and I got the boat under way and stood to the westward. The drag was placed forward of the mast, and was not unrigged until the following day, thinking that we might have to use it again during the night. About 8 p. m. we were enabled to haul by the wind on the port tack, and stood south-southwest until 6 a. m. on the morning of the 14th, when the boat struck in two feet of water with no land in sight. There was said to be a thin skim of ice in sight that looked like fresh-water ice, and the water alongside was only brackish. We then had a consultation, and I proposed standing to the eastward until we got deep water, and then to stand due south for the high land on the coast to the eastward of the Lena Delta. I stated my belief that there was nothing but shoal water to the westward.

We stood to the eastward, and occasionally felt our way south, but always found shallow water. About 10 a. m. Bartlett thought he saw land, but on taking another look he changed his mind and thought it only a smooth patch of water among the shoals, but subsequent experience and learning the character of the land made us think that we were then very near a low, swampy beach.

On Wednesday, the 14th, we had light airs from the south-southeast, and we stood all day to the eastward under sail, and oars at times. At midnight we were in ten fathoms of water, and at daylight on the 15th we decided to shape a southwest course. We had noticed that there was a considerable easterly set. We steered southwest all day and night on the 15th, and the course was set from the sun's bearing. I reckoned that at that time of the year the sun was on the prime vertical, and bore west at about 5.50 p. m., and that the change of azimuth during the day averaged 14° per hour. I first noted the time and the bearing to correspond to that time, and then the direction of the wind, and shaped the course accordingly. At night the moon was shining, and I took the highest altitude, as near as I could judge, for south, in order to check the course.

At 6 a. m. on the 16th we sounded in ten feet of water, and no land in sight. About 7 we sighted a low sand beach, and stood in and tried to land, but could not get within half a mile of the beach on account of shoal water. We pulled out and had a consultation. I thought from the fact that the land trended north and south, and from the run that we had made to the eastward of the delta, but what distance south of Barkin I could not tell. The dead reckoning put us about forty miles south, but the easterly current was a very uncertain element in the calculation. Mr. Melville proposed to go up the coast to Barkin, evidently with the view of meeting the other boats, for the captain had recommended touching at Barkin, which was stated on the chart to be winter huts in which the seal hunters lived all the year round. The captain hoped to get a pilot there and proceed westward to a place marked Sagastyr, which was marked on the chart as a permanent village. There was also a signal tower marked on the chart, which was to have been erected for the guidance of Professor Nordenskjöld's party in the summer of 1878. I stated that we might be able to reach Barkin from the southeast, and we had a fair wind for running up the coast, but that if a gale came on the boat would probably be swamped in the shoal water.

We stood up the coast to the northward, and in about a half an hour saw two low points of beach at the mouth of a river. The wind was about east, and increasing after dawn. We then stood up the river to the west-northwest and tried several times to effect a landing in order to dry our clothing and effects. We could not get within a mile of the beach on either side, the river being at least three miles wide, with a swift current and five fathoms of water in the middle, and shoaling rapidly toward either side. The atmospheric effect was very peculiar at the time, and it was hard to judge accurately of distance. We decided to stand up the river until noon, and if not able to land, to have a consultation and decide our next movement at that time. Noon came, and Mr. Melville and I had a consultation. I said that we would have to beat out, but that we had a fair current with us, and after getting clear of the point we would have a fair wind up the coast. We decided to return, and I was about to haul on the wind when Bartlett spoke up from the bows, where he was stationed with a sounding pole, and said that he believed we were in the coast branch of the Lena; that he had been at the mouth of the Mississippi, and that this river had a greater volume of water than it. I said that the trend of the river was right for the east coast, but that we should have high land to our left hand if it were the coast branch; also that if we found a small island about thirty miles up the stream it would indicate that it was the coast branch. Mr. Melville and I then had another consultation, and decided to continue up the river in hope of making a landing before dark. We had a fresh breeze, which was fair, but the current against us was very strong, and we were troubled very frequently, the boat getting aground in shallow water.

About 7 p. m. we succeeded in reaching a hut situated on a point of land about ten feet above the water. The party was very much exhausted, having been in the boat for one hundred and eight hours, wet all the time, very little food, and no fresh water after the first day. A number of the party had their feet and legs badly swollen. In some cases the skin was broken and part of the feet black. We camped in a hut, built a fire, and cooked tea. There were numerous traces of recent inhabitants; foot-prints and fish-bones were numerous, and a small piece of black bread was found. We slept with our feet toward the fire, and the next day the disabled men were a great deal worse, after having spent a sleepless night. We started next morning, and hoped to reach the main branch of the river, if it should be the coast outlet that we were in at the time. About 11.30 our way was barred by mud flats. We stopped, and sent Bartlett out ahead to see what there was beyond a point of land that was near by. Seeing that he was limping badly I ran after him and sent him back to the boat. I went to the point of land and found that there was an immense swamp river coming from the northwest, with numerous mud flats in it. I returned to the boat and suggested getting dinner while Manson and I would make an extended scout. We went beyond the point of land some distance, and saw a line of higher land to the southwest. I asked Manson if he could trace a passage over to it, and he thought he could, all except in one small place, where we might have to wade and drag the boat over. We returned with that report, and a few minutes after dinner retraced our steps a short distance so as to clear a mud flat, and then shaped the course for the high land. That afternoon we made a splendid run to the west-northwest, and also passed a small island; so we began to think that Bartlett was right in his judgment, and we hoped to reach the turning point in the river that night. About 8 p. m. we reached a point of land sixty feet high, and camped on a small sand-beach. This was called Mud Hill Camp, as it was adjoining high mud hills. We pitched both tents, and Bartlett, Newcomb, Manson, and I climbed the hills and found a hunter's hut, in which we remained that night. The sleeping-bags were so wet that some of us would not use them. At 4 a. m. on the 18th Bartlett and I took a scout. I wanted to see the region before sunrise, to get the clearest view. We saw broad streams making to the northward and northwestward, and before us was one coming from the southward, which we thought was the main branch of the river, though we did not feel sure of it. The wind during the night had shifted to the west and was blowing very fresh. I called the camp at 6 a. m., and we had breakfast, consisting of tea and pemmican. We went on half rations immediately after the separation, and the tea had been wet with salt water in the gale. A few of us loaded the boat, and when all was ready we struck the tent and helped the sick people down.

After a great deal of difficulty we got the boat off the lee shore, close-reefed the sail, and stood about south under the lee of a mud flat. I took the helm, and Bartlett the sounding pole at the bow. We saw a herd of seven reindeer, which fled when they saw us. About 11 a. m. we arrived at two large summer huts, and decided to land and dry out everything, as the day was bright and sunshiny. We remained there for the rest of the day, and dried all our clothing and sleeping-gear. We also erected a staff, bearing a black flag, made from the flap of a knapsack, and to the staff was secured a paper stating that the whale-boat had been there that day.

On Monday, September 19, we called at early daylight and got under way at 6 a. m. We decided to stand up the west bank of the river, and we hoped to reach a settlement that night. We used sail and oars. The crew was divided into two watches of four each. I was at the helm, and Bartlett at the bow, sounding with a tent-pole. We proceeded very well until about 11, when we came to mud flats extending from the westward shore and forcing us to the eastward.

About 1 p. m. we noticed a strong current from the southwest, and also a ridge of land that seemed higher than any in the vicinity. After a hard pull we effected a landing, about 3 p. m., and the cook started to get dinner. I set up the compass to get bearings and the time of day. At this time we saw three natives, each in a canoe, shoot out from near the point and approach us. We immediately embarked in order to meet them. They pulled by us rapidly, and occasionally glanced over their shoulders in a furtive sort of way, as though afraid of us. We held up some pemmican, and a young man approached cautiously with his boat, and the other two soon followed. The entire party, including the natives, then returned to the landing place, and we had quite a festival. They gave us a goose and one fish, all they had at the time, and we gave them tea and pemmican. We became very friendly and talked as best we could by signs, indicating that we wanted a place to sleep, and that we wanted them to go south with us. We again embarked, and they took us around the point, and into what seemed to be a branch of the main river. They hauled their boats out on the beach very quickly, and, coming to our assistance, helped the disabled people up to a house on a steep hill, while the rest of the party unloaded and hauled up the whale-boat. On climbing the hill I found there were four houses and a number of storehouses in sight. One house was in good condition, and the other three were very dilapidated. There was a graveyard about one-fourth of a mile distant from the houses, with a lot of large wooden crosses. Afterwards I learned from the commandant at Bulun that the place was called Borkhia.

We slept there that night, and the natives hauled their nets and gave us a good supply of fish and some deer meat. We noticed that one of the natives left the party, and from that imagined that other natives were in the vicinity.

And the court then, at 2 p. m., pending the further examination of this witness, adjourned to meet to-morrow, the 28th day of October, 1882, at 10.30 a. m.

TWENTY-FIRST DAY.

NAVY DEPARTMENT,
Washington, D. C., Saturday, October 28, 1882—10.30 a. m.

The court met pursuant to the adjournment of yesterday.

Present, Commodore William G. Temple, United States Navy, president; Capt. Joseph N. Miller, United States Navy, Commander Frederick V. McNair, United States Navy, members; and Master Samuel C. Lemly, United States Navy, judge-advocate.

The record of the proceedings of yesterday, Friday, October 27, 1882, the twentieth day of the inquiry, was then read, and on the correction of several clerical errors approved; and the convening authority having authorized the employment of a stenographer, the judge-advocate requested that E. W. Grant might be sworn to act in that capacity, and the said E. W. Grant was accordingly duly sworn by the judge-advocate of the court.

Lieut. J. W. DANENHOWER, the witness under examination, then came in and continued his answer to the pending question, which was repeated by the judge-advocate, as follows:

Give a full and detailed narrative of the retreat after the loss of the vessel.

The WITNESS. That evening the young native who had the most intelligence of the party told us that we were going wrong, and drew a diagram on the sand, representing that Bulun was seven sleeps distant by placing his hand on the side of his face and snoring. The next morning we turned out early, and I took the compass and went to an adjoining hill to get the bearings of the sun and points of land. The party in the mean time loaded the boat, and on my return Mr. Melville asked me to hurry up. I asked where the natives were, and he said they would not come with us; so I asked him to wait awhile, while I went up to the hut to see them. I found it empty, and was about to go away, when I saw the young man on the top of the house. I called him down and tried to get him to go with us. He seemed very much troubled and bewildered and would not come. I shook hands, good-bye, with him, and gave him a silk handkerchief, to leave a good impression, for I expected to return. We then started out in the boat and worked to the eastward among the mud flats all day. We were trying to find a channel south. We worked under oars and sail at times. About 5 p. m. Bartlett stood up in the bow and said it looked like the open sea to the eastward. We then decided to turn back and find the natives if possible. Bartlett piloted the boat back. There was a shift of wind, and a snow-storm came on. I had been at the helm all day and was very tired. I found that I was steering badly, and asked Herbert Leach to relieve me. He did so. We made fast to tent-poles driven in the mud, under the lee of a mud flat, and remained all night.

At daylight Bartlett and Wilson stood up in the boat, and Wilson thought he recognized the same land that we had left the day before. This was on Wednesday the 21st. Bartlett thought it was not, but said we could reach it with a fair wind if we could get to windward of the mud flat in sight. We close-reefed the sail, and I took the helm and headed the boat to windward of the mud flat and then ran in with a fair wind. It was then snowing very hard. We encamped on the muddy beach and spread the Mackintosh for shelter, while the cook prepared tea. Mr. Newcomb shot some sea-gulls. They were cooked for breakfast. After breakfast Wilson and Manson started out to look for the houses we had left the day before. In about fifteen minutes they returned with the information that the houses were round the point. We immediately embarked, and on reaching the beach near the houses saw an old man and three others approaching. They took off their hats and said "drastie drastie," which meant "how do you do?" They assisted the sick to the house and helped us unload the boat. On seeing one of the sea-gulls that had been shot, they threw it down and said it was bad, and brought us some venison in place of it. They treated us very kindly. Mr. Melville was sick, and requested me to speak with the old native about piloting us to Bulun. He made me understand that Bulun was six days' journey, and that there were priests and traders there, and that he would pilot us willingly. He also measured the draft of the boat, and I got him to make a sketch of the river, which I will present to the court as evidence.

The witness here produced the sketch referred to, which the judge-advocate placed before the court, and a certified copy, marked T, is appended to the record.

The witness then produced and the judge-advocate placed before the court a plan showing how the boats were piloted by the three native canoes, and a certified copy, marked T 2, is appended to the record.

The witness then continued as follows:

I heard Bartlett speak to Mr. Melville about going ahead, and I understood a proposition was on foot to send somebody in the advance, so I told Mr. Melville that I thought if any one was sent that I should be the person, because I would have more force with the Russian officials, and might meet some one who spoke French and Spanish. He did not think it practicable at the time to send any one, and I agreed with him that it was not. The next day we started with the old native (who was known as Vashily Coolgiyork—"Cut-eared" Vashily) and two other pilots. This was on the 22d. Vashily went ahead, and the other two on either beam, sounding with their paddles as they advanced. We started out in the same direction we had taken Tuesday, two days previous, and about noon Vashily found a passage between the mud flats, and we went south. After ten hours' work we encamped on a low beach, and the natives brought us fish for supper. The next morning, the 23d, we started at daylight, and proceeded up a broad river, and then through a narrow cut-off, as it were, and reached two native empty huts, at which we remained for the night. On the next day, which was Friday, we got under way early and stood up a broad river. About 11.30 two natives were sent in advance, and about 12 we came to a village of about six empty houses, in excellent condition, and having a number of store houses attached. The store houses were locked, and there were cooking utensils in the houses. We occupied one of the houses, and during the afternoon a large boat was seen approaching. It contained two men and two women. They landed and went to another house. On that afternoon Mr. Newcomb shot a number of ptarmigan. Soon after the arrival of the party, Vashily took Mr. Melville and me to the house occupied by the native, and we had a long conversation with Spiridon, who was the chief of that village. They seemed to understand our shipwreck, and the three boats, and they said something about a person whom they called the "Commada." We did not clearly understand it. Spiridon gave us a large goose that was boned and stuffed, with seven others, which he said we should use the next day, after sleeping. We remained at the village during the night, and the next morning Vashily indicated that he wished us to embark. This was Saturday, the 24th. Vashily showed us a gunshot wound in one of his legs, and informed us that he could not proceed farther, but that Carannie and Kapucan and Theodore would accompany us. They were three young men. We started, and worked all day to the southward and westward, and that night encamped in a deserted hut. Got under way the next morning, Sunday, the 25th, and by noon arrived at another village, and were received by about a dozen men, women, and children. The party had been working, watch and watch, with four oars in each watch, for the past three days, and I was steering the entire time. The sick people were carried up to the huts, and Mr. Melville and I were taken to the "Commada," as he was called. His name was Nikolai Shagra, and he was chief of the village of Geeomovialocke, which consisted of five houses, a church, and a number of storehouses. We explained to him about the shipwreck and the missing boats, and he seemed to understand. That night we were quartered in his house, and they gave us a hearty supper of fish and goose. He told us that it would take fifteen days to reach Bulun, and expressed his assent to take us there.

I find by reference to notes made at the time that it was on Monday, September 26, that we arrived at this village. The next morning it was blowing very fresh. Nikolai Shagra came and told us that we could not start that day, but by 9 a. m. he again came and wanted us to hurry up to embark. He seemed in a great hurry. We embarked as quickly as possible, and he gave us sixty fish for the journey. The three native pilots went home, and I, with the Russian exile Yopheme Kopalloff, and Gabrillo Passhin, started out. The latter lived at the village and was dependent on the natives.

We pulled to the eastward until about noon, when the pilots suddenly turned around and beckoned to us to return to the village, which we did, and were taken to the house of Gabrillo Passhin, where we were quartered for the night. The condition of the party at this time was very bad. Mr. Melville was carried on a sled from the boat to the house, and Leach and Lauterbach had not been able to stand for several days, but they had taken their regular tricks at the oars. The whole boat party was disembarked and quartered in Gabrillo's house.

The next day, Wednesday, September 28, Nikolai Shagara came to our house and asked for a document in writing, for what he called the "Paraiya," and which I understood to be the priest at Bulun. I wrote a letter in English and one in French. Lauterbach translated one in German, and Wilson one in Swedish; for we thought it probable that some of Professor Nordenskjöld's people might be in the vicinity. Mr. Newcomb furnished a picture of the ship in the ice, a picture of the

American flag, and some postage-stamps. I took all of these papers and sewed them up in an oil-skin, and with Mr. Melville went to Nikolai's house. Mr. Melville gave them to Nikolai, who was in very high spirits and seemed to wish us to understand that we should soon go to Bulun. On that day Yopheme and Gabrillo came to our hut and beckoned to me to come out. I went out, and they took me to a hut at the end of the village, where there were some old women at work cleaning it up. They indicated that they wished the whole party to move there; so I informed Mr. Melville, and with two or three others prepared the house, and then moved the whole party to it. On that day Mr. Melville announced to the whole party that he and I thought the scurvy was among us. He recommended cleanliness and cheerfulness, and stated that during his sickness I should have charge of the police and the administration of the party. At this time we were getting eight fish per day from the natives. They kept the account, and at the end of the week presented the bill for sixty fish, for which receipts were given. The Russian, Yopheme Kopalloff, was very useful to us in making the natives give us good fish. The natives at this time were kind and friendly, and each day Nikolai Shagra would call and see us, and indicate how thick the ice was and the chances of getting away. He was a very wily and plausible fellow. We thought that the natives would get rid of us as soon as possible, because there seemed to be a scarcity of fish at that time; but one day when I was going to give Gabrillo an extra pair of foot-nips that I had, Yopheme called me aside and told me to hold on to them, for by and by we would have to trade them for food. That was the only cause that I ever had to mistrust the natives and not thoroughly believe them.

On October 12 *[2] Mr. Melville gave me the captain's written orders to him, and requested me to copy them, which I did at the time, he saying that the original might be lost.

On October 8 we were surprised to see a Russian in the village, and he was invited to our house by Mr. Newcomb. I acted as interpreter at the time, as well as I could, having formed a vocabulary from what I had learned from Yopheme. I told Kusmah the story of the wreck and the missing boats, and he seemed to understand. Kusmah was the name of the Russian, and I afterwards learned that Kusmah's name was also Jeremihoff, the custom of the country being to call by the first name only. I proposed that Kusmah should take me to his house, for I wanted to learn his resources and what I could about the country. Mr. Melville consented, and I started with Kusmah on a team of dogs, taking also Yopheme. About 1 p. m., in about two hours, after traveling ten versts to the southwest, we reached his house, which was about the same as that of the natives, excepting that it was cleanly, and that his resources in tea and flour were rather greater. I went over my vocabulary with him, and over the charts. Also I told him that the captain had a big paper, a ukase from the Emperor, commanding all Russian subjects to assist us. He asked the name of the Emperor, and I told him Alexander Nicholas, whereupon he said that Alexander Nicholas was "*pomerie*," and placed his hands across his breast. By that he meant that he was dead, and he further said that he had been blown up in the previous March. He seemed to understand thoroughly the nature of the paper. During the evening Kusmah's wife gave me a small bag of flour, a bag of salt, some tobacco, about four pounds of tea, and a little sugar. The next morning Kusmah showed me a deer, and asked me if it was all right; and when I expressed my approval he had

---

* Correction by witness.

it killed and placed upon a sled. That was on Sunday, October 9. He said he gave money for the deer, and I told him that as soon as we telegraphed to the United States we would give him plenty of money. Just before starting Kusmah turned to me and said that next Sunday he and I would start for Bulun. I asked him how many Tuṅgoos (meaning the natives) would go with us, and he said the Tungoos were bad; none should go, but two Russians. I told him to come over and speak with Mr. Melville, and he said he would go on the following Wednesday. I then returned with the provisions, and Mr. Melville expressed great satisfaction with the result of the visit.

On Wednesday Kusmah came. We first took him down to the boat, which was hauled up on the beach.

I have neglected to state that after the boat was hauled up Mr. Melville was better, and had resumed charge of the party. The condition of the party had very much improved. The day after reaching the village, John Cole, the Indian Aniguin, and myself were the only people able to go out and get wood and water for the party. Wilson was able to hobble about and do the cooking. One by one the people got better and able to work.

October 3 Mr. Melville resumed charge informally. We turned the boat over and let Kusmah examine it. Mr. Melville, Kusmah, and I then went into an empty summer-house and had an interview. I acted as interpreter. The first question was, how many days would it take Kusmah and Mr. Melville, or I, to go to Bulun and return. Kusmah answered, five. The next question was, how many days would it take him to go alone and return. And he also said, five. Mr. Melville then decided that he should go alone, for, in his judgment, he thought he could go and get back quicker than if he had any one with him. Kusmah was told that he should have the whale-boat and five hundred rubles as a reward, but the whale-boat should be kept subject to the condition that we might use her during the spring and summer following. The arrangement seemed satisfactory to Kusmah, and he went home that night to start for Bulun on Sunday, and if possible on Saturday. The next day we were very much surprised to hear that Nikolai Shagra was going with Kusmah, at the latter's request, on Friday morning. I went to Mr. Melville and suggested that before Kusmah started it should be impressed upon his mind that he should spread the news about the two missing boats everywhere he went and offer a large reward for any traces that were found. He assented, and I went to Nikolai to get a dog team, when, seeing old Spiridon approaching with a team from his village, I got him to take me to Kusmah's house. I explained to him what I had come for, and he seemed to understand it fully. We again went over the charts, and he told me that Barkenstein, as he called Barkin, was only fifty versts to the northeast. I went back to our village and told Mr. Melville that I thought I could get Spiridon to take me to Barkin, and might find traces of the missing boats. He finally agreed, and that night I went ten versts to the northward, to Spiridon's village, and had a conversation with Spiridon and Carannie. They said it was impossible to go, on account of the ice being too thin, and then there were no people to the north of them. I then went to see old Vashily, and he agreed to take me to Conhouma, which Kapucan indicated was to the northwest of Arii, which was the name of Spiridon's village. Saturday, October 15, this interview occurred.

On the morning of the 16th I started out with Vashily and Kapucan to go to Conhouma, which I supposed was to the northwest. They first went down a small river to the southeast, and the ice broke in many places. They then swung round to the westward and brought up at Kusmah's house, Conhouma being the native name for Kusmah, and I then had another talk with Kusmah, and he again stated positively that Barkin was fifty versts northeast. I set up the compass, and he not only pointed northeast, but also said "Searavastoke," he having taught me the names of the cardinal points in his language. He got Vashily to agree to take me there on the following morning. After that I arrived at another small village, and on the morning of the 17th I started out with three natives and two sleds to go to Barkin. Kusmah had told me that we would first have to go southeast, and then make up to the northward. We started in that way and traveled all day. Camped in a small hut near a point of land, about two miles distant to the southeast. The natives called that Myak, and indicated that the steamer Lena had entered there, and that traces of the party might be found on that island. The next morning we started for the island, and found the ice black and treacherous, so that the natives positively refused to go farther, and it was evident they were right; and we then tried to go around the point to the northward, but the natives refused positively, on account of the young ice not being strong enough to hold the dogs and sledge. They then insisted on returning to Kusmah's house, which we did, having found only that the natives' statement was true, that it was impossible to travel over the ice at that time of the season.

The court then, at 12.15 p. m., took a recess until 12.35 p. m., at which time it reconvened, with all the members, the judge-advocate, and the witness under examination present.

The witness then continued his narrative in answer to the pending question as follows:

The WITNESS. I will here submit the chart of Pilot Vashily, made at my request, and also the chart made by me in October, 1881, on information derived from Kusmah Jeremihoff.

The judge-advocate then submitted, and the court accepted as evidence, these charts; and certified copies, marked respectively U and V, are appended to the record.

The witness then continued his narrative as follows:

We returned to Geeomovialocke on Monday, October 17, on Kusmah's tracks, he having left his village for Bulun on that day. I reported the unsuccess of our trip to Mr. Melville. About the time Kusmah was to return his wife came over and said that he had been detained by the death of the Cossack commandant of Bulun, but she expected him in a day or two. Kusmah returned on Saturday, October 29, and immediately presented a short note signed by the seamen Nindemann and Noros. It stated that the captain's party was starving and needed immediate assistance. Kusmah stated that he had met the two men at a place called Seven Houses, and that they had given him the note. Kusmah also brought us some provisions and a note from the commandant at Bulun. He stated that he would come to us on November 1. Mr. Melville then sent over to the village of Arii for old Vashily. He came the next day with a dog team, and Mr. Melville turned the charge of the party over to me and started for Bulun. At the time I said to him that I was ready to start immediately in search of the other party. I was well, but had been sick for about a week, some days previously, from dysentery and my stomach refusing food. Mr. Melville started the next morning for Bulun.

The witness here produced the original order given to him by Passed Assistant Engineer George W. Melville, dated October 29, 1881, at Tongoos village, with an appended copy of the order given to Passed

Assistant Engineer Melville by Lieut. George W. De Long, dated August 5, 1881, at Cape Emma, Bennett Island. The court was then cleared, by request of a member, and afterwards reopened, the witness being present.

And the judge-advocate then read aloud these two documents, and certified copies of them are appended to the record and marked, respectively, W and X.

The witness then continued his answer to the pending question, as follows:

The WITNESS. On November 1 the commandant of Bulun arrived at our village about 10 a. m. He took breakfast with the chief, and came to our hut at 11 a. m., and presented a long written document signed by Nindemann and Noros. That document and the one previously referred to as received from Kusmah Jeremihoff were brought home from Siberia by me and turned over to the Navy Department.

After reading it and seeing that the location of the captain's party was not definitely stated, I determined to send it immediately to Mr. Melville, then on his way to Bulun, and also to inform him that we were all right. I immediately told James H. Bartlett to prepare to start, and then I informed the commandant of the contents of this document, which was addressed to the American minister at St. Petersburg. This statement refers to the document that the commandant brought, which is signed by Nindemann and Noros. The commandant said that the deer were very tired and must have rest, and the man could not be sent. I insisted, and he finally agreed to send him at 5 p. m. with written documents for a subordinate at Bulun. This was done. The commandant would not state definitely how soon we should start, and the next morning, November 2, I was awakened by the exile Yopheme getting ready to start somewhere. He told me that he was going with the commandant to Arü, and I told him to bring the commandant there right away. He did so, and I told the commandant that if he did not start the next morning with us that I would report him to General Schernieff, who, I had learned, was the governor of the province of Yakutsk; but if he did get us started he should be well rewarded. The next morning we started from the village with twelve teams of dogs and under the guidance of the commandant. Kusmah visited us, and I asked for his name on paper, and he told me that he would give me a big paper, which he wished me to have translated on my reaching civilization. He did so, and I had it translated at Verkeransk, and the Espravnik of that place had an official copy made. It was a declaration from Kusmah, stating that the Tungoos had wrongfully detained us among them. That night, the 2d, we arrived at a povarina, an uninhabited log house, having made 110 versts with the dog teams. The next day, the 3d, we passed Tas Ari, as the commandant told me, and reached Ku Mark Surk at 7 p. m. Here was the village that Kusmah had called the "Seven Honses," and was the place at which Nindeman, met Kusmah. In hopes of finding some of the natives who had brought the two men there, I proposed to start a search from that place, but he said that we would see Mr. Melville in a few hours, and as he had been in communication with the two men, I though it best to wait and see him. We started early in the morning of the 4th, crossed a river, and reached a deer station, which the commandant called Ku Mark Serail. The proper name of this place is Bavulack. We found Mr. Melville there awaiting us, and had a consultation with him and the commandant.

It proved that in the written order sent by the commandant to his subordinate he gave him directions to fit out Mr. Melville with sleds, in order to meet him (the commandant) at Bulun. Mr. Melville then told him his plans for going north with the natives, and to make a search for the men of the captain's party. He told me that I would find written orders at Bulun for me to proceed south. He also stated verbally that he wished me to leave James H. Bartlett at Bulun, to communicate with him if necessary. We parted about 3 p. m., he with the intention of going to Ku Mark Surk and my party to Bulun. We traveled all night by deer team, and reached Bulun early on the morning of the 5th, where we found Bartlett, Nindemann, and Noros. Nindemann was very sick and confined to his bed. Noros was on his feet and apparently in a fair condition. Bartlett was perfectly well. I found there this order, which I will submit in evidence.

The witness here produced, and the judge-advocate submitted to the court, the original order from Passed Assistant Engineer Melville to Lieutenant Danenhower, dated Bologun, November 4, which was read aloud by the judge-advocate, and a certified copy, marked Y, is appended to the record.

The witness then continued his answer to the pending question:

The commandant at Bulun furnished us with black bread, deer meat, and butter; also sugar and tea, and some delicacies for the sick men. The men were quartered in a new log house, and the second night after our arrival I was invited to the commandant's house, which was near by, and I lived with him during the few remaining days. We had plenty of everything that the village afforded, and were making a great inroad upon their winter stores, for our party consumed as much as thirty-five pounds of bread a day and large quantities of meat, owing to our long fast. The commandant agreed to forward six of the people to Verkeransk on the following Saturday. There not being sufficient transportation for the whole party, I selected the six weakest and most disabled of the party, and prepared for the journey. I left written orders with Bartlett, whom Mr. Melville had requested to have left in charge, and a regular ration established by the commandant; also ordered Bartlett that if Mr. Melville did not return by November 20 to start the party north and at the same time a courier south to me. I had the same understanding with the commandant, whose name was Gregory Miketereff Bryeshoff. He was a non-commissioned officer of Cossacks.

I started from Balun on Saturday, November 12, with the following men: R. L. Newcomb, naturalist and taxidermist; John Cole, boatswain; Herbert Leach, seaman; Henry Wilson, seaman; and Charles Tong Sing, steward. These were the weakest men of the party, and it was thought that Leach's foot might have to be amputated, as mortification appeared to have set in at the toes. The condition of John Cole at that time was getting very bad, he being under mental aberration. All the men left at Bulun were in good condition, except Nindemann, and he stated that he would prefer to remain and build up before starting south. I also considered it a good plan to leave both him and Noros to furnish further information to Mr. Melville, should he require it. At Bulun I had obtained a large quantity of provisions and clothing, and had the commandant make bills for the amount, which bills I carried to Yakutsk.

We traveled fifteen days by deer teams across the mountains, and reached Verkeransk, which was distant 900 versts, on Sunday, November 27, and missed meeting the sub-Espravnik of Verkeransk, who had been sent to Bulun with medical stores and provisions for our relief. We remained at Verkeransk three days, and the doctor of the place stated that it was necessary to amputate one of Leach's great toes, and that we should hasten to Yakutsk. I obtained an amount of clothing and provisions here, and started for Yakutsk on November 30. Made a journey of 960 versts with deer teams, oxen, and horses, and reached Yakutsk Saturday, December 17. We received a cordial reception from the governor-general, Tcherneiff, who quartered us well and offered to forward the party immediately to Irkutsk; but I told him my orders were to await the return of Mr. Melville, which occurred on December 30. The remainder of the party, under Bartlett, arrived about January 3, and the thirteen survivors of the Jeannette were then all present at Yakutsk.

Mr. Melville was in communication with the Department, and he gave me the following written orders to proceed south, which I will submit in the evidence if it please the court.

The witness then produced the orders in question, which were read aloud by the judge-advocate, and a certified copy, marked Z, is appended to the record.

The witness likewise produced and offered as evidence a receipt from Lieut. Giles B. Harber, United States Navy, for certain articles delivered to him by the witness at Nishnendinsk March 21, 1882.

The judge-advocate objected to the admission of the paper, as being irrelevant.

The witness then made the following statement:

I will also state that other articles mentioned in Mr. Melville's order were turned over to the Navy Department on January [June*] 2, 1882, and that five men were turned over to Lieutenant Harber at Nishnendinsk, Siberia, March 22, 1882, for which the following order will be a receipt:

The witness here produced the order in question, dated March 22, 1882, at Nishnendinsk, Siberia, which the judge-advocate read aloud, and a certified copy, marked A A, is appended to the record.

A member here moved that the receipt which the witness had produced for certain articles named in this letter be admitted in evidence, if the witness so desired.

The court was then cleared, upon the motion of the member, and decided that if the witness desired, the paper in question shall be admitted. The doors were accordingly reopened, and the witness being present, the decision of the court was announced. The witness then produced the receipt previously offered, which the judge-advocate read aloud, and a certified copy, marked B B, is appended to the record.

The witness, continuing, said:

I would further state that at Irkutsk, about March 10, I received a telegram from the Secretary of the Navy, and through the chargé d'affaires at St. Petersburg, which directed me to allow the seaman L. P. Noros to accompany the special Herald correspondent to the Lena Delta, which order was obeyed.

Upon arriving at New York, Seaman John Cole was turned over to the custody of Lieut. W. H. Jacques and Assistant Surgeon Percy. R. L. Newcomb returned to his home in Salem, Mass., and Charles Tong Sing, steward, accompanied me to Washington, and was discharged by the Department at a subsequent date.

And the court then, at 3 p. m., pending the further examination of this witness, adjourned to meet on Monday, the 30th day of October, 1882, at 11 a. m.

---

* Correction by witness.

TWENTY-SECOND DAY.

NAVY DEPARTMENT,
Washington, D. C., Monday, October 30, 1882—11 a. m.

The court met pursuant to the adjournment of Saturday.

Present, Commodore William G. Temple, United States Navy, president; Capt. Joseph N. Miller, United States Navy, Commander Frederick V. McNair, United States Navy, members; and Master Samuel C. Lemly, United States Navy, judge-advocate.

The record of the proceedings of Saturday, October 18, 1882, the twenty-first day of the inquiry, was then read, and after making several corrections of clerical errors, approved.

The judge-advocate then stated to the court that testimony of Sir Allen Young, of London, England, is important to the furtherance of the inquiry, particularly as to the strength of the vessel and her fitness for Arctic service. And the court then directed the judge-advocate to prepare interrogatories to be sent to Sir Allen Young. The court was then closed by the request of the judge-advocate and afterwards reopened.

The judge-advocate then requested that an adjournment be taken until Wednesday next, to enable him to prepare the interrogatories in question.

And the court accordingly, at 12.15 p. m., pending the further examination of Lieutenant Danenhower, adjourned to meet on Wednesday, November 1, 1882, at 10.30 a. m.

TWENTY-THIRD DAY.

NAVY DEPARTMENT,
Washington, D. C., Wednesday, November 1, 1882—10.30 a. m.

The court met pursuant to the adjournment of Monday, October 30.

Present, Commodore William G. Temple, United States Navy, president; Capt. Joseph N. Miller, United States Navy, Commander Frederick V. McNair, United States Navy, members; and Master Sameel C. Lemly, United States Navy, judge-advocate.

The record of the proceedings of Monday, October 30, 1882, the twenty-second day of the inquiry, was then read and approved.

The court was then, by the request of the judge-advocate, cleared for deliberation, and afterwards reopened.

Lieutenant J. W. DANENHOWER, the witness under examination, then came in, and his examination by the judge-advocate was continued, as follows:

Question by the JUDGE-ADVOCATE. Before quitting the wreck of the Jeannette did you expect to encounter a hundred miles of open water before reaching the coast? If yea, upon what did you ground your expectations?

The WITNESS. Before quitting the Jeannette I expected to encounter from fifty to sixty miles of open water. The impression was derived from what I had heard and what I had read.

Question by the JUDGE-ADVOCATE. How much did you actually encounter?

The WITNESS. About 90 miles; that is, the nearest point of the delta is about 90 miles from Semenov Island.

Question by the JUDGE-ADVOCATE. What was the physical condition of the ship's company on leaving Semenov Island?

The WITNESS. The physical condition of the whale-boat party was good; also that of the remainder of the people, with the following exceptions: Mr. Dunbar had been sick, and was said to be subject to heart disease. The seaman Peter Johnson was sick the day before we left. My left eye was disabled and the right one covered with a dark glass. The others were in fair condition.

Question by the JUDGE-ADVOCATE. Where and when was the wooden dinghy abandoned, and why?

The WITNESS. The wooden dinghy had been used by the road-makers until before reaching Bennett Island. I think she was leaking very badly and was considered of no further use, so she was cut up and equally divided among the tents for fuel, to save the alcohol that remained. This was done, as I remember, about the 20th of July.

Question by the JUDGE-ADVOCATE. Give the latitude and longitude of any point established on Bennett Island?

The WITNESS. The latitude and longitude of Cape Emma, the southeast point of the island, was established by the commanding officer, and stated in order of August 5, given to Mr. Melville, as latitude 76° 38′ N. and longitude 148° 20′ E.

Question by the JUDGE-ADVOCATE. How many days' rations were on hand on the 21st day of August, when the provisions were divided up among the boats?

The WITNESS. About twenty days' provisions on the ration of a pound and a half of pemmican per day per man. There was tea for twenty-five days. There was also a can of ham, and in our boat one quart of whisky and one quart of brandy, as medical stores, which were consumed during the gale, and gave two drinks, of two ounces, to each man.

Question by the JUDGE-ADVOCATE. How many days' rations were on board when you took your departure from Fadejowski Island?

The WITNESS. On August 31, when I left Fadejowski Island, we had but ten days' provisions, diminished rations.

Question by the JUDGE-ADVOCATE. How many days' provisions had you on board when the whale-boat landed, September 16?

The WITNESS. About four days' provisions, on the ration established immediately after the separation, which I think was three-quarters of a pound of pemmican per day per man.

Question by the JUDGE-ADVOCATE. From what date was Passed Assistant Enginer Melville so sick as to be unable to do duty, and when did he convalesce sufficiently to resume duty?

The WITNESS. On Wednesday, September 28, Mr. Melville addressed the party, stating that he and I thought the scurvy was among us. He recommended cheerfulness and cleanliness, and stated that I would be in charge of the police and administration during his sickness. On October 3, the condition of the party had improved, and I suggested turning over the whale-boat and securing her for the winter, at which he said he would go down. He went down and took charge, and I assisted in turning over the boat with the men. From the time of leaving "Mud Hill" camp, on Saturday, September 17, he was very much disabled, but I always acknowledged him in command of the party. I had charge in loading and unloading the boat, in steering her, and managing her under sail and oars.

Question by the JUDGE-ADVOCATE. From what day and place do you date the commencement of the active search for the parties in the first and second cutters?

The WITNESS. The first active search was commenced on Friday, October 14, when I went to Kusmah's house to request him to spread the news on his way to Bulun, and when I returned with Spiridon to the village of Arii, to make arrangements to get to Barkin, which was stated to be fifty versts northeast of Kusmah's house. On October 16 and 17 I went with a native to an island they call Myok, at which place they expected to find traces of the party. We were unable to reach the island on account of the thin ice, and we were unable to proceed to to the northward for the same reason, as the ice at the mouths of the streams was broken and too thin for sledding. The native would not go north, saying, that there were no houses and no people there, and that the young ice was too thin for sledding. Previous to this active effort the natives were all informed as clearly as possible of the two missing crews, and in fact from the very first day we met them.

Question by the JUDGE-ADVOCATE. You have stated that on the evening of September 12, it was reported to you that Lieutenant De Long was making a signal, as if he desired the boats to separate. What do you suppose his object to be in desiring a separation?

The WITNESS. The state of the weather at the time, and all the circumstances demanded that each boat should look out for itself, as in reducing sail and manœuvering to keep together it would very much endanger the safety of the boats, and I understood his signaling to be, "Make the best of your way," which, under the circumstances, would have been natural.

Question by the JUDGE-ADVOCATE. What kind of weather were the two cutters making when you last saw them?

The WITNESS. During the afternoon it was remarked in our boat that the second cutter seemed to be doing better than the whale-boat. The second cutter was well fitted with weather cloths. The first cutter was sailing almost dead before the wind, and several times during the afternoon the sail jibed over; but she seemed to be doing as well as the whale-boat, because the latter was very much trimmed by the stern, and was constantly shipping seas over the port quarter.

Question by the JUDGE-ADVOCATE. Was it possible, then, for the boats to relieve or assist each other?

The WITNESS. In my judgment, it would have been exceedingly dangerous to have attempted anything of the kind, but in case of such a disaster it would have been our duty to have tried it, even at such a risk, had we seen one of the other boats swamping.

Question by the JUDGE-ADVOCATE. If you had taken sixty days' rations when you left the ship, how would you, with your knowledge at that time, have conducted the retreat?

The WITNESS. I should have reached the coast water as quickly as possible, and then decided my movements according to the state of the weather and the condition of the party. If the weather were good, as it is during the months of July and August in that region, I should have gone to Behring's Straits to meet a whaler, or a relief ship, which was expected during that year.

Question by the JUDGE-ADVOCATE. Have you any charge to lay or special commendation to offer concerning any officer or man connected with the Jeannette expedition—first, as to the condition of the vessel on your departure from San Francisco; second, her management up to the time of her loss; third, her loss; fourth, the provisions made and plans adopted for the several boats' crews after leaving the wreck; fifth, the efforts made by the various officers to insure the safety of the parties under their charge, and for the relief of the other parties; sixth, the general conduct and merits of each and all the officers and men of the expedition?

The WITNESS. I have no charge to make against any officer or any person connected with the expedition. I believe that every person did his best. As far as special commendation, I would mention Seamen Nindemann and Noros, also Seaman Herbert Leach and first-class fireman James H. Bartlett, as well as Seamen Henry D. Warren and John Cole. The above-named were the leading men during the retreat.

Examination by the COURT:

Question by the COURT. Did the doctor discharge you from the sick list when you first asked him to do so, on the day of the wreck?

The WITNESS. No sir; I first asked the doctor to put me on light duty, in the month of March, 1881, and again the day the ship was crushed. The next morning he told me that the captain had consented, and I replied that I had done some work in anticipation of it. I was not discharged from the the sick list, as the doctor, considered it necessary to examine my eyes twice a day particularly, and apply counter-irritants; this was continued until the date of the separation.

Question by the COURT. What was the condition of your eyes from the time of the separation of the boats until you started for home?

The WITNESS. During the gale and the time we resided at the village of Geeomovialocke my eyes did very well, and I could protect the right one with a dark glass, the left being bandaged. They continued to do well untill the latter part of December, when I was unable to wear a glass. On the journey between Verkeransk and Yakutsk I was obliged to go without a glass, on account of the breath freezing on them constantly, but the right eye did not break down until my arrival at Irkutsk, January 27, 1882. I had caught a severe cold on the journey there while sleeping in the sled. At Irkutsk I overtaxed my eyes by writing in answer to dispatches received from this country, and was confined sixteen days in a dark room before being able to travel. When I answered the telegram and asked to go back in the steamer Lena, the oculist reported that my eyes would be well in a few days.

Question by the COURT. Was the subject of your ability to resume duty again discussed between yourself and the commanding officer after the 8th of August?

The WITNESS. Yes, sir; once in the "Ten Day" camp; I had a long interview with the captain in his tent, and he said as long as the surgeon recommended me to remain on the sick list that I should stay there.

Question by the COURT. How was fresh water obtained for use in the boats?

The WITNESS. Working in the ice, we always stopped for meals, and took snow from the highest places. About the 15th of August it became the custom to fill the cooking utensils with snow on first breaking camp, for we might be in large ponds of water, and unable to get snow at meal hours. That was also the custom on leaving the islands, to fill up every thing with snow; but it required five or six buckets of snow to make one bucket of water, and during the gale the snow became salty from the water that dashed into the boat, so we were without fresh water a few hours after leaving Semenov Island, and the two drinks of liquor were given in lieu of it, until we reached the brackish water of the delta.

Question by the COURT. You have stated that the island of Kotelnoi was recommended by the commanding officer as a point for touching at. How was it, then, that he steered to the southward when you came to open water?

The WITNESS. There is a large shoal between Kotelnoi and Fadejowski. It was necessary to steer to the southwest to get around the shoal, and the statement about the rendezvous recommended by the captain is based upon what Mr. Chipp stated as his reason for standing that way for Kotelnoi Island. Mr. Chipp further stated that he passed very close to a shoal that was thickly covered with heavy driftwood.

Question by the COURT. Did Mr. Melville desire you to take charge of the boat on the evening of September 12? If so, how long did you retain charge of her?

The WITNESS. He did tell me to go ahead and lay the boat to, and I was the only person in the boat who gave an order until 4.40 p. m. on September 13, when, after shipping the rudder, I called Mr. Melville and suggested that we get under way, stand to the westward, and haul up to the south-southwest when the sea went down. He told me to go ahead, and I got the boat under way and conned her until she reached the shore. I always consulted with him in particular matters and always acknowledged him in command of the party by authority of the captain's order. I carried the watch and the two charts and shaped every course.

Question by the COURT. Were any dates or localities given in the communications received from Noros and Nindemann?

The WITNESS. There were none in the first communication, except dates. In the second communication there are a number of places given. They were strange to us, as they were not named on our charts. I learned from the natives that they had met Kusmah at the "Seven Houses" on Ku Mark Surk, which they said was 140 versts from his house and 90 versts from Bulun. The locality of the captain's party was not clearly mentioned in their paper, and I considered it best at the time to get in communication with the two men and start the relief from Bulun, which was nearer to the location of the captain's party and at which there were abundant resources.

Question by the COURT. Where were the twelve teams of dogs procured from with which your party was provided on the 3d of November, and could they have been provided sooner than they were?

The WITNESS. They were provided from the villages of Mensehurkoff, Geeomovialocke, and Arii; and, also, there were some strangers, whom I had never seen before, but who came from the immediate vicinity of Geeomovialocke. I think the sleds could have been provided some days before had there been a Russian officer to order them, for about the 20th of October there were natives who came to our village from other places, and before Kusmah returned from Bulun several parties had come, thus showing that the sledding season was good at that time.

Question by the COURT. State in what spirits the officers and men were at the various times during the cruise.

The WITNESS. The spirits of the officers and men were generally very good, with a few exceptions. At times some would show signs of very low spirits, but they were generally in good spirits, and hopeful. After the ship was crushed the men worked steadily and well, and at times the camp was very cheerful, although at the time of leaving Fadejowski Island some were looking anxiously to the future few days; for we knew that the young ice might form at any time and bar our progress to the Lena River. Particular enthusiasm was manifested the day we commenced the retreat; also on Bennett Island, when the captain addressed the party and named the discovery. It was followed by three cheers, and then another three cheers and a tiger for the captain.

Question by the COURT. During the gale on September 13, 1881, what would have been the probable result had you not rounded to and ridden by the drag which you constructed?

The WITNESS. If the boat had been able to stand all night with the wind and sea on the port quarter head about south, she would have probably fetched in to the eastward of the delta, but in my judgment she could not have been steered successfully through the gale. We had the usual whaleboat-rudder, and had decided not to take the steering-oar on account of its weight, and specially from the fact that it would have been impossible for a man to have stood in the stern sheets and steer, because they were crowded with passengers. Before leaving the steering oar I consulted with Mr. Dunbar, who was a whaleman of thirty years' experience, and he agreed with me that it was best to leave the steering-oar and to take the rudder, because the steering-oar could not be used in such a crowded boat, and the chances were that we would have no use for it. I think the boat would not have lived through the gale except riding head to sea to a drag.

Question by the COURT. When navigating in the boats were you able to make signals to each other, and, if so, what means were used?

The WITNESS. On September 1, when we crossed the large water-hole, and were losing sight of Lieutenant Chipp's boat, I asked Mr. Melville if there was any system adopted by which we could communicate with the captain, because I wanted to ask if we could wait for the second cutter before entering the lead. Mr. Melville said that there was no such system, and to the best of my knowledge none was subsequently adopted.

And the court then, at 12.10 p. m., took a recess until 12.40 p. m., at which time it reconvened, with all the members, the judge-advocate, and the witness under examination, present.

The examination by the court was then continued as follows:

Question by the COURT. What was the temperature, generally, during the retreat? State fully the ranges of the thermometer.

The WITNESS. The temperature ranged, I should judge, from 28° to 40° Fahrenheit. The weather was generally cold, as the melting process was going on all the time, except at night, when the young ice sometimes formed.

Question by the COURT. Before starting on the retreat, after the loss of the vessel, was there any consultation of the officers held as to the course to be pursued?

The WITNESS. To the best of my knowledge there was no consultation held until we reached Bennett Island. During our stay there I was informed that a consultation was held between Captain De Long (Lieutenant De Long), Lieutenant Chipp, and Chief-Engineer Melville.

Question by the COURT. Do you know of any instructions given by the commanding officer providing for the separation of the boats, beyond the copy of his order which was furnished to you by Mr. Melville.

The WITNESS. It was stated at the time that the intention was to reach Barkin, which was marked with winter huts of seal-hunters. It was thought we would get a pilot there, and proceed to Sagastyr, at the north mouth of the river. Sagastyr had winter huts marked also, and the place marked "signal stone" or "signal station" was also marked on the charts as near Sagastyr.

Question by the COURT. After the sinking of the ship, did you at any time think there was unnecessary delay in endeavoring to reach the land? If so, state fully the time and circumstances.

The WITNESS. I thought at the time we should have pushed more rapidly south, and that the delay at Bennett Island and at Semenov Island was not advisable; also, that our visit to Fadejowski and Kotelnoi Islands was not advisable.

Question by the COURT. Were not the delays you mention necessary to the recuperation of the parties and repairs to the boats?

The WITNESS. No, sir; the boats could be repaired on the ice, and the party was in very good condition on arriving at Bennett Island—better than when they left.

Question by the COURT. You have stated that if you had been in command on the 13th of September you would have tried to get out at once. If you had succeeded, what would have been your course afterward?

The WITNESS. Put the ship in winter quarters on the coast of Siberia, as nearly south of Wrangel Island as possible; to have explored the Siberian coast to the westward, and, if the circumstances would have permitted, to have sent out parties to the northward to reach Wrangel Island, which was a little more than 100 miles from the nearest point of the coast. I understood that the captain had expressed the intention of returning to the Siberian coast to winter.

The judge-advocate then put the following question:

Question by the JUDGE-ADVOCATE. How do you so understand?

The WITNESS. I was told that it was in the last communication sent to the Secretary of the Navy.

(The judge-advocate objected to this testimony as heresay.)

The WITNESS. I have no further knowledge of the matter.

Neither the court nor the judge-advocate desired further to examine this witness, and there being no further questions to ask him, the judge-advocate proceeded to read to him his testimony.

At 1.30 p. m., the court, pending the further reading of the testimony of the witness, adjourned to meet to-morrow, the 2d day of November, at 10 a. m.

TWENTY-FOURTH DAY.

NAVY DEPARTMENT,
Washington, D. C., Thursday, November 2, 1882—10.30 a. m.

The court met pursuant to the adjournment of yesterday.

Present, Commodore William G. Temple, United States Navy, president; Capt. Joseph N. Miller, United States Navy, Commander Frederick V. McNair, United States Navy, members; and Master Samuel C. Lemly, United States Navy, judge-advocate.

The judge-advocate then stated that the record of the proceedings of yesterday, Wednesday, November 1, 1882, the twenty-third day of the inquiry, was not yet ready, and asked to have its reading deferred, which request the court granted.

Lieut. J. W. DANENHOWER came in, and the judge-advocate proceeded with the reading of his testimony until 12 m., when the court took a recess until 12.30 p. m., and then reconvened, with all the members, the judge-advocate, and the witness, present.

The reading of the testimony of the witness then continued until 2 p. m., when the court adjourned to meet to morrow, November 3, 1882, at 10 a. m.

TWENTY-FIFTH DAY.

NAVY DEPARTMENT,
Washington, D. C., Friday, November 3, 1882—10 a. m.

The court met pursuant to the adjournment of yesterday.

Present, Commodore William G. Temple, United States Navy, president; Capt. Joseph N. Miller, United States Navy, Commander Frederick V. McNair, United States Navy, members; and Master Samuel C. Lemly, United States Navy, judge-advocate.

The witness, Lieut. JOHN W. DANENHOWER, then came in, and the judge-advocate completed the reading of his testimony for correction.

.The record of the proceedings of Wednesday, November 1, and Thursday, November 2, the twenty-third and twenty-fourth days of the inquiry, was read and approved by the court, and the witness, having then had all his testimony read to him, desired to make the following corrections, viz:

On page 15, line 32, change "December 18" to "December 28, 1878."
On page 16, line 34, change the words "new cylinder and boilers" to "new cylindrical boilers."
On page 35, line 10, insert the words "of the" between the words "timber heads" and the word "starboard."
On page 47, line 40, after the word "west," add the word "magnetic."
On page 52, line 9, insert the words "floating" before the word "piece."
On page 54, line 39, strike out the word "snug."
On page 61, line 28, change October 12 to October 2.
On page 66, line 25, change the word "January" to the word "June."*

With these corrections made, the witness pronounced his testimony to be correct.

The president of the court then, at the request of the judge-advocate, instructed the witness to consider himself subject to recall in the event of developments in the inquiry which should make it necessary. The witness then withdrew.

The court then, at 12 m., took a recess until 12.30 p. m., and on reconvening at that time, with all the members and the judge-advocate present, adjourned to meet to-morrow, the 4th day of November, 1882, at 10.30 a. m.

TWENTY-SIXTH DAY.

NAVY DEPARTMENT,
Washington, D. C., Saturday, November 4, 1882—10.30 a. m.

The court met pursuant to the adjournment of yesterday.

Present, Commodore William G. Temple, United States Navy, president; Capt. Joseph N. Miller, United States Navy, Commander Frederick V. McNair, United States Navy, members; and Master Samuel C. Lemly, United States Navy, judge-advocate.

The record of the proceedings of yesterday, Friday, November 3, 1882, the twenty-fifth day of the inquiry, was read, and, after making corrections of clerical errors, approved.

The judge-advocate then offered, and the court accepted, as evidence

---

* These corrections were, by direction of the judge-advocate, made in the places indicated in red ink, and are here inserted in brackets.

the following original letters and documents, each of which was read aloud, and certified copies thereof were appended to the record, as follows:

Lieut. George W. De Long's report to the Hon. R. W. Thompson, Secretary of the Navy, dated August 4, 1879, at Ounalashka Alaska, (Exhibit C C).

Lieut. George W. De Long's report to the Hon. R. W. Thompson, Secretary of the Navy, dated August 26, 1879, at St. Lawrence Bay, Siberia (Exhibit D D).

Lieut. Charles W. Chipp's report to Lieutenant De Long of the general routine from the 6th to the 30th of September, 1879 (Exhibit E E).

List of articles of boat outfit June 17, 1880 (Exhibit F F).

Station Bill, in case of fire or accident to ship, winter of 1880–'81 (Exhibit G G).

And the court then, 11.50 a. m., adjourned to meet on Monday, the 6th day of November, 1882, at 10.30 a. m.

TWENTY-SEVENTH DAY.

NAVY DEPARTMENT,
Washington, D. C., Monday, November 6, 1882—10.30 a. m.

The court met pursuant to the adjournment of Saturday.

Present, Commodore William G. Temple, United States Navy, president; Capt. Joseph N. Miller, United States Navy, Commander Frederick V. McNair, United States Navy, members; and Master Samuel C. Lemly, United States Navy, judge-advocate.

The record of the proceedings of Saturday, November 4, 1882, the twenty-sixth day of the inquiry, was then read and approved.

Chief Engineer GEORGE W. MELVILLE, United States Navy, was then called as a witness, and having been sworn according to law by the president of the court, testified as follows:

Examination by the JUDGE-ADVOCATE:

Question by the JUDGE-ADVOCATE. Please state your name and rank.

The WITNESS. Name, George Wallace Melville; chief engineer, United States Navy.

Question by the JUDGE-ADVOCATE. To what vessel and to what special service were you last attached?

The WITNESS. The Arctic steamer Jeannette, on a cruise to the Arctic Ocean.

Question by the JUDGE-ADVOCATE. When and where did you join the Jeannette, and what service, if any, did you perform in that vessel prior to her being specially fitted out for an Arctic expedition?

The WITNESS. I joined the ship at Mare Island, California, in the latter part of April, under the Department's order of April 4, 1879. I have lost the order and indorsement, and do not know the exact date.

Question by the JUDGE-ADVOCATE. Was your assignment to that vessel made with your consent?

The WITNESS. Yes, sir.

Question by the JUDGE-ADVOCATE. What duty, if any, did you perform in connection with the fitting out of the Jeannette for that service at Mare Island navy-yard?

The WITNESS. I attended to the fitting of the engines and the supplying of her stores in the engineer department.

Question by the JUDGE-ADVOCATE. State in detail what alterations and repairs were made in the engineer department under your supervision.

The WITNESS. The completion of a pair of boilers, the general overhauling of the engines, the fitting of two new steam-valves to the main engine, a new auxiliary pump, and fitting of a distilling apparatus.

Question by the JUDGE-ADVOCATE. Was everything done in the way of repairs and alterations and all stores provided for the engineer department that were necessary to make the ship, as far as possible, adapted to Arctic exploration?

The WITNESS. Yes, sir. In mentioning the amount of work that I had done there, I omitted to state that there were four additional composition propeller blades cast and fitted on the ship.

Question by the JUDGE-ADVOCATE. Did you express yourself to any one as dissatisfied with the general fittings and strength of the ship, or did you express yourself as satisfied with them?

The WITNESS. I expressed myself as satisfied with all her fittings and her strength.

Question by the JUDGE-ADVOCATE. Give a narrative account of the voyage and management of the Jeannette from the day of her leaving San Francisco to that of her loss, referring to the log-books of that vessel for the dates, and to any notes you may yourself have made at the times enumerated.

The WITNESS. We left San Francisco on the 8th of July, 1879, the ship and her appurtenances operating well, meeting with no accident. We anchored, owing to a fog, to the southward of the Aleutian Islands. After the fog cleared away, we got under way again, and arrived at the port of Ounalashka, in the island of Ounalashka, without accident. At Ounalashka we coaled the ship and took aboard a lot of skin clothing, or skins to make clothing. After coaling the ship and receiving the stores, we sailed from Ounalashka and arrived at the harbor of St. Michael's on August 12, and there awaited the arrival of the schooner Fanny A. Hyde, which was to bring us additional coal and supplies. The Fanny A. Hyde arrived on Monday, August 18, and the same day we commenced to remove the coal and supplies to the Jeannette. We sent a lot of our skins on shore at St. Michael's and had them made into clothing. On August 21 we received as much of the coal and stores as we could conveniently carry. The ship was got under way, bound to St. Lawrence Bay. During the passage we had a gale of wind that lasted from Saturday, August 23, about noontime, until 8 a. m. in the morning of the 24th, about. The ship was loaded pretty deep, and behaved very well, after the engines were slowed down. Before the engines were slowed down, she took considerable sea on board.

We arrived at St. Lawrence Bay on the afternoon of August 25. The schooner Fanny A. Hyde arrived, with the remainder of the supplies and coal, August 26, at St. Lawrence Bay. August 27, we commenced discharging schooner's stores, supplies, and coal into the Jeannette; that same evening we went to sea and towed the schooner to sea with us, and outside the bay cast her adrift. After separating from the schooner the ship stood to the northward, through the straits. After passing through the straits we stood westward, along the coast, until we came up with a native village, on the afternoon of August 29. We came to anchor the same evening, and the commanding officer went on shore to make inquiries with regard to the whereabouts of Nordenskjöld's ship.

He returned the same evening, and brought a party of natives with him. On the morning of August 30 we got under way, and stood to the westward. We stopped off a settlement, Koljutschin, on August 31. Lieutenant Chipp was sent on shore, in charge of a boat, to inquire into the whereabouts of Nordenskjöld's ship. He returned that same day, having found that Nordenskjöld's ship had wintered in the immediate vicinity of the place where he landed. This is where we first came up with the ice. The ice was loose and scattered at this time. We skirted on the edge the pack to the westward and northward, the ice becoming more dense and heavier, and headed us off more to the northward and eastward. We skirted along the ice until Herald Island bore to the westward of us. This was about September 1. The ship was worked through the ice in a number of lanes of water, trying to make to the northward and westward as far as the ice would permit. The ice about this time was very heavy, being full of lanes and open leads, leading in every direction, but the pack proper extended from the southwest toward the northeast. About September 5, the ship was forced into the ice as far as she could go to the westward, and anchored to the floe that night. We passed through open lanes of water and some young ice that had made. The ship forced her way through the young ice. The pack was all in motion at this time, to the eastward of us, and as we passed through it closed behind us. There were open holes and leads of water to the westward, which we were endeavoring to reach.

On September 6, the young ice commenced to make around us, and freeze fast to the old pack that had been loose, cementing the whole mass, so that it was impossible to move the ship. Lieutenant De Long said to me at this time that he would put the ship to the westward, in hopes of boring through the ice and making the east coast of Wrangel Land. Wrangel Land, by this time, was in sight. He also stated that it was his intention to work along the coast-water of Wrangel Land to the northward; in case we could not get the ship further northward, to attempt sledding along the land, when the sledding season set in, if Wrangel Land was a continent, as he had been led to suppose. At this time the general routine of the ship was carried on from day to day. As soon as the ice set hard enough around the ship, the people kicked foot-ball, raised a bear or two, and had a bear hunt. All things were cheerful and happy about the ship. I think about this time we found that the ship was drifting to the northwest. Between the 7th and 9th of September there was a good deal of motion of the ice in the immediate vicinity of the ship, under-running the main floe, and coming in contact with the body of the ship, which made a list to starboard. About September 9, the ship was pretty severely nipped, making her groan and strain considerably, but showing no damage in the way of leaks. She was pressed so badly as to start the oakum and pitch out of her deck-seams. A bucket of water standing on the ship's deck would be jarred and disturbed so as to make the water run over the top of the bucket onto the deck. About the 10th or 11th the ice was so much in motion that we found it necessary to unship the rudder to save its being wrenched and carried away. Masthead tackles were got to the masthead to try and right the ship, which was so firmly held by the ice that we found it impossible to bring her back again to an even keel. On September the 13th Lieutenant Chipp was sent in charge of a sled party to try to make a landing at Herald Island; the party consisted of Lieutenant Chipp, myself, Mr. Dunbar, the ice pilot, and the Indian Alexy, the team of eight dogs, and ten day's provisions. The island, at that time, was estimated from 15 to 25 miles distant. We started in the morning about 8 o'clock, the Indian running ahead, leading the dogs, and continued all day long at a dog trot until dark in the evening.

We came up with another [an*] open lead of water, from 700 to 1,000 yards wide, encircling the island. Not having a boat it was impossible to cross the water. We turned about and returned toward the ship. We camped that night, after returning some 3 or 4 miles, on our way toward the ship. The object in getting to Herald Island, I was told, was for the purpose of leaving a record by building a cairn, and to see if there was any possibility of finding a place to winter the ship in. I read Mr. Chipp's orders, and I think this was his orders. I know the first part was, and I think the second part, in regard to finding a place to winter the ship in, in case we drifted down on the island, was also. We arrived at the ship the next morning, Sunday, September 14. During the time that we were absent from the ship, the ice was drifting very rapidly to the northwest. It was not considered safe to make a second attempt to land on the island by carrying a boat on a sled for the purpose of crossing the water. On the morning of the 14th of September there was a bear sighted, and a lot of the people left the ship to hunt the bear.

It being Sunday morning, all the men expected to be mustered. Some of the people, not coming back in time, were spoken to by the commanding officer for leaving the ship without leave. Among these was Mr. Collins, Nindemann, and others, I do not remember at this time. On the 14th or 15th there was a general order issued that no person should leave the ship without proper authority, that is, the leave of the commanding officer, or the leave of the executive officer. During the whole of this time the ship was still drifting to the northwest on to the northward and westward of us, or, in other words, we nearly drifted across what appeared to be the north face of Wrangel Land.

November 1, the winter routine was set up with regard to time for meals, exercise on the ice, the temperature of the apartments to be maintained, and the keeping of watches.

On or about November 3, the commanding officer directed the medical officer of the ship to make a thorough examination of every officer and man attached to the ship with regard to his physical condition. The examination continued during the winter months only. It took place once a week.

About November 6 the ice commenced to work [break*] up near the ship, grinding as it passed on, passing the ship. Early on the morning of November 6, we had to remove the observatory very hurriedly on board the ship, with all the instruments, and carry it on the ship. During the whole of this time, up to November 14, the ice was very much in motion, grinding, crowding, and, at times, in all directions. On November 14, the ice split in halves at the ship, and under her keel. One half of it drifting away from the ship, left the other half of the ship imbedded in the side of the other in the some [same*] manner, as though imbedded in a mold. The ice on the front side of the ship drifted off about 1,000 yards. This lead of water was filled with small pieces of drift ice. On the 17th and 18th of November the ice closed in this lead that was open on our port side, and on the 18th of November the ship was very severely nipped. The ice piled up on the port side as high as the deckhouse sides. The ship was held [heeled*] over to the starboard at this time by the pressure of the mass. The ship was severely strained,

---

* Correction by witness.

scratched [screeching *], and groaning in the timbers, and seemed to be spewing in the openings of the deck-seams [the calking out of the seams *]. It shook down a good deal of loose matter inside of the ship and the bunkers, but the ship sustained no material damage, and showed no signs of leaks. I will here state that during a portion of this time I was directed by the commanding officer to observe the condition of the inside of the ship in the coal-bunkers, and in the vicinity of the engines, and to watch the bilges to see if the ship made any water.

And the court then, at 12 m., took a recess until 12.30 p. m., at which time it reconvened, with all the members, the judge-advocate, and the witness under examination, present.

The witness then continued his narrative, in answer to the pending question, as follows:

The WITNESS. November 24, young ice commenced to run down the open lead of water and pile up under the bows of the ship, exerting pressure between the main floe and the starboard bow of the ship, which forced her out of the mold or bed in which she lay. The ship was now free from ice, and righted on an even keel to within one or two degrees. The ship drifted up the lead, making a complete turn on her center before she brought up with her head toward the floe to the southward and eastward. At this time there were large spots of open water in sight, but no possible means of getting the ship out of the lead in which she lay into any communicating lead. The young ice commenced to form about the ship immediately where she lay in this open lead of water. On the morning of the 26th November the young ice had made around the ship sufficiently strong for the people to run over it, the main floe crowding the young ice together, overlapping or telescoping the young ice, and piling it up on the side of the ship, but was doing no material damage. This is the last time the ship was free from the grasp of the ice before she went down. Before this time, the 24th of September, arrangements had been made by Lieutenant De Long for the preparations to abandon the ship, in case of accident, and each party was assigned a sled, with proper provisions set on the sleds, placed in position on the poop-deck ready for arranging [launching *] on the ice. Proper stations had been given the different officers, and the proper members of the crew with them, in case of fire or of abandoning the ship. I believe I had six men assigned to me, in which order I was directed to make the men fully acquainted with all the duties in extinguishing fire, getting at the sleds or boats, cooking-stoves, tents, rifles, and ammunition, in case the order was given to abandon the ship. When sufficient snow had accumulated on the floe, the ship was banked in snow, and the carpenter and his gang, after fitting up the deck-house, felted it on the inside to make it as warm and comfortable as possible. The galley on deck, in which the cook and steward slept, was felted in the same manner. December 11, the young ice, in which the ship was imbedded, worked under her bows in an east and west direction; the floe-piece in which the ship was embedded apparently standing still, the opposite floe-piece running at right angles to the keel of the ship, the floe in motion, running under the bows, the projecting pieces continually hammering at the stem-piece and the fore-foot, jarring the ship considerably, but doing her no material damage at this time.

Christmas time we had a good dinner, and then had the minstrel show in the deck-house; everybody apparently comfortable and happy. Morning of the "New Year" was ushered in by the ringing of the bell by

---

* Correction by witness.

some of the ship's crew. The men came aft, and, I believe, got something to drink. Had a minstrel entertainment New Year's night. I would state that from time to time the men's bedding was aired in the deck-house, and that during the winter routine all hands were required to go on the ice for exercise from 11 o'clock in the morning until 1 o'clock in the afternoon. During this time the doors, sky-lights, and, generally, windows or hatches were all thrown open for the purpose of thoroughly ventilating the ship, meaning the quarters, not the ship's hold. During these hours all the officers and crew were required to remain on the ice for two hours, amusing themselves in any manner they saw fit. The sick alone were excused. The commanding officer inspected the ship fore and aft, and all the officers' quarters, and quarters occupied by the men, on Sunday morning, the medical officer being directed to inspect them as often as he saw fit. The executive officer inspected the forecastle every morning. In the mean time sleeping-bags had been made, fur clothing had been issued to the officers and crew, and we were all occupied in fitting our clothing to suit ourselves, the men making new moccasins of the seal skins they captured from time to time; also, general clothing, jackets, or trowsers, as they saw fit to make.

Between January 10 and 15 there was a great deal of motion in the ice, leads making in nearly all directions, and the ice telescoping and shoving up with a loud, groaning noise, the ice indicating a great motion in the pack. This continued until the 19th or 20th of January. At this time the ship was frozen in a drift [solid*] bed of ice, the bottom of the ship being continually struck and hammered by the ice running underneath, where, looking over the surface of the floe, everything looked quiescent, and, but for the noise heard in the distance, I would hardly have known where the ice was coming from, or what caused the thumping at the bottom of the ship. This was caused by the interlacing [overlapping*] or telescoping of the ice.

On the morning of the 19th of January the ice commenced to be thrown up in immense masses in all directions, and apparently gradually approaching the ship, as if to overwhelm her. The ship was in the center of a large floe-piece, and it appeared to be coming in all directions, almost in a circle, entirely around the ship. About 2 o'clock in the morning water was found running in at the bottom of the ship. Previous to this she had received several very severe jars, apparently in a fore-and-aft direction. Examination was made immediately after the thumps or jars, but no damage was discovered until the people went below to get out the coal for the day's supply. As soon as we discovered it coming into the ship all hands were called to man the pumps, and I was directed to get steam on the ship as quickly as possible. The fore hold was broken out, and all the provisions removed without any material damage, except to some flour, which was slightly damaged on the surface only, the water not extending to any distance inside the barrel-staves. As soon as we had steam on the boilers the pumps were got in operation. We found that the water did not fall rapidly enough to keep the forward part of the ship free from the water, the deck hand-pump being worked during the whole time. A steam pump was improvised from the Baxter boiler, and one of the "Sewell" pumps taken from the engine-room. The Baxter boiler not being of sufficient capacity, steam was let from the main boilers to supply the pump then erected in the fore-hold. The water was reduced to such an extent that the carpenters could go to work abaft the peak to build a

---

* Correction by witness.

bulkhead to shut off the water and confine it to the peak. At this time the water was going through the ends of the solid fillings that had been put in the eyes of the ship for strengthening. In addition to coming through the timber that had been put in for this purpose, the water would find its way around the frames, between the inner and outer skin, passing beyond the bulkheads that had been built to confine the water to the fore peak. It had become necessary to get [cut*] the inner ceiling or planking of the ship in places, and to fill the space between the frames with plaster of paris, ashes, tallow, oakum, or such stuff as would make a water-tight place between the frames. This work continued for the space of ten days. During all this time the steam-pumps, both fore and aft, continued in motion. I said at this time that the ship was securely frozen in her bed, and the damage done to the fore-foot that caused the leak was caused by the underrunning ice; that is, the ice in which the ship was embedded was not in motion. The ship lay fast in her bed, and the running ice rammed her.

From the time that we commenced to fill the water-spaces between the frames the leak continually decreased. At this time it was not possible to put a sail or thrum-mat or any such contrivance under the bows of the ship to prevent the flow of water. The weather was very cold at this time, the ice making rapidly, and as soon as possible an effort was made to excavate a dock in the ice down toward the fore-foot. This was continued day after day, a little at a time, to admit of the ice making underneath, as the work advanced downward through the ice.

About January 31, the leak was stopped to such an extent that the ship could be kept free by the Sewell pumping engines, instead of the main one. The boiler and engine of the steam cutter were adapted to working the bilge-pump attached to the main engine. While this work was going on a second pump in engine-room was kept running all day long at a rate of thirty-five strokes per minute. On the trial of the steam cutter's engine and boiler it was found that the main engine bilge-pump was too large, and a small pump made to suit the size of the steam cutter's engine and boiler. By February 9, the leak had decreased to such an extent that the ship was kept free by running the Sewell pump about fifteen minutes during each hour. I would here state that the gates in the water-tight bulkhead had been kept closed, and the Sewell pump was used to remove the leakage that passed through the water-tight bulkheads, the Baxter boiler and pump keeping the ship free forward in the fore-hold. The gates in the water-tight bulkhead. [Therefore it was discovered that there was a leak in the gate which was not properly down on its seat. The obstruction was cleared and the gates made tight, and when the water arose to a certain height then the water found its way through the bulkhead.*] It was discovered that there was a leak through the bulkhead. On February 13, the Sewell pump and boiler got into condition, so as to keep the ship free from water, and the fire was hauled from the main boiler. I will here state that at first the fire was started in both furnaces of the main boiler, afterwards reduced to but one furnace, and then but a half furnace fire in the main boiler. The pumping was now done entirely by the Baxter boiler and pump. The engine attached to the hand bilge-pump, afterward by means of the steam cutter's launch and boiler attached to the improvised pump in the engine-room. During this time the coal was trimmed out of the bunkers. The spare provisions that had been taken out of the hold were put in the bunkers. Provisions that could not be fitly stored in the bunkers were stored in the deck-

---

* Correction by witness.

house on deck. After November 30, all the water used in the ship was distilled, part of the time by means of the Baxter boiler and part of the time by means of the steam cutter's boiler. During this time it was impossible to get snow and get [ice to make *] water sufficiently fresh for drinking purposes.

The court was then, by request of the judge-advocate, cleared for deliberation and afterwards reopened.

And the court then, at 1.45 p. m., pending the further examination of the witness, adjourned to meet to-morrow, the 7th day of November, 1882, at 10.30 a. m.

TWENTY-EIGHTH DAY.

NAVY DEPARTMENT,
Washington, D. C., Tuesday, November 7, 1882—10.30 a. m.

The court met pursuant to the adjournment of yesterday.

Present, Commodore Wm. G. Temple, United States Navy, president; Capt. Joseph N. Miller, United States Navy, Commander Frederick V. McNair, United States Navy, members; and Master Samuel C. Lemly, United States Navy, judge-advocate.

The judge-advocate then requested that more time be allowed the clerk to complete the record of yesterday, which request being granted by the court, its reading was deferred.

Chief Engineer GEORGE W. MELVILLE, United States Navy, the witness under examination, then came in and continued his testimony, in answer to the pending question, which was repeated by the judge-advocate, as follows:

Give a narrative account of the voyage and management of the Jeannette from the date of her leaving San Francisco to that of her loss, referring to the log-books of that vessel, when necessary, for dates, and to any notes you may yourself have taken at the times enumerated.

The WITNESS (continuing). The winter passed quietly and comfortably with all hands, and there was nothing of importance occurred during the winter more than the usual monotony of the life on board ship, besides the usual duties performed, such as taking the hourly observations. The people who could, read most of the time; the officers, in particular, read nearly all the time when off duty. After dinner and after supper there was the usual conversation among the officers in regard to politics, religion, and general conversation. The manner and tone of the mess, as is customary in most men-of-war officers' messes, of a pleasant character throughout. In fact, there was less disagreement among the officers in the Jeannette's mess than in many messes I have served in during twenty-one years' service in the Navy. On Sunday afternoon, when we had a better dinner than usual, it seemed to be the desire of the commanding officer, who messed with us, to bring on a general conversation and to discuss almost anything that would come uppermost in our thoughts.

In the first part of the cruise, the captain, the doctor, Mr. Collins, and Mr. Dunbar, and occasionally Mr. Chipp, would play cards for amusement. I never played cards; never knew how, and don't know now. During the day-time any person, officer or man, could take their guns, rifles or shot-guns, and hunt over the floe for any distance, the only

---

* Correction by witness.

restriction being to be on board ship at sundown or at the dropping of the ball from the mast-head. During the winter time the hunters shot a number of bears. I believe Mr. Dunbar was accredited with getting the greatest number of bears. Fireman Bartlett and Seaman Nindemann, being the most persistent hunters, I believe, were accredited with getting the greatest number of seals and walrus. The most of the seal and walrus, however, were gotten in the spring and fall. When spring time approached, between the first and middle of March, the sun commenced to get pretty strong; the snow was removed from the ship's side, and a trench dug all the way around the ship to ease her in case she should attempt to rise. From the use of the coal and provisions out of the ship during the winter, if the ship was afloat, she would float lighter, and the ice was removed to give her an opportunity to rise in the water as she would do naturally. In addition to this, in case the ice came in on the ship, this trench would admit the ice underrunning her and lifting her up instead of crushing in her sides. We found as spring approached and the ship loosened in her bed she invariably rose in the water. This was accounted for by the lightening up of the ship by the use of the coal and provisions during the winter. About the 18th of March the ship had set so far back to the southward and eastward as to bring the mountain peaks of Wrangel Land in sight. I mention this fact to show that the drift was not continuously to the northwest; that at odd times the whole floe was found to be drifting at various times to all points of the compass; at times apparently governed by the wind, at other times, when calm, we supposed governed by the current.

During the month of March, 1880, the weather was disagreeable, with a great deal of fog. After April 1, the spring and summer routine was put in force, such as changing the meal hours, and the compulsory exercise on the ice was discontinued. The weather being fine, it was natural to suppose that people would take sufficient exercise to maintain good bodily health. In the spring time the store-rooms were broken out and all accumulations of ice removed. During the first part of April, 1880, the hand bilge-pump was removed from forward and placed in the fire-room hatch aft; the ship being by the stern, the water ran aft and was more readily removed by the after pump, the flood-gates being left open for the purpose. What little water had accumulated in the forward part of the ship was pumped out by the bilge-pump that remained forward. About this time the forward deck-house was removed and many of the stores that had been removed from the forehold the previous winter, at the time the ship sprung a leak, were re-stowed below.

I will here state that I had orders from the commanding officer to attend the heating of the quarters of the officers and men, and the order of the commanding officer was, during the winter time, to maintain a temperature of 60° Fahrenheit as steadily as possible. In order to save coal and relieve the crew of as much labor as possible, during the month of April we made a wind-mill, 12 feet in diameter, which was mounted on the bridge, and when the wind blew at the rate of 4 or 5 miles an hour it kept the ship free, the flood-gates being open forward to admit all the water running aft.

Toward the latter part of May the fires in all the stoves, both in the forecastle and in the cabin, were discontinued between the hours of 9 a. m. aad 6. p. m. To avoid the expenditure of coal in the galley the tea water was heated at the cabin and forecastle stoves. Toward the 1st of June the decks were cleared up, the ship was painted, the running-gear attended to, and the ship gotten ready for sea.

Toward the 1st of July, 1880, long lanes of water commenced to make in all directions, but none leading directly in to the ship. It was impossible to travel more than a mile in any direction without the use of a boat, or, as the hunters managed it, by paddling across the leads of water on a piece of ice. About this time Mr. Chipp and the commanding officer discussed the possibility of blasting the ice between the ship and the nearest lead in which the ship could be worked.

And the court then, at 12 m., took a recess until 12.30 p. m., at which time it reconvened, with all the members, the judge-advocate, and the witness under examination present.

And the witness continued his answer to the pending question, as follows:

I was present at this discussion, although I did not take part in the discussion, and the conclusion they came to was that there was not sufficient powder in the ship to effect this; Mr. Chipp jocularly remarking that it would take a ship load of powder. Mr. Chipp was directed to make torpedos of small kegs. He improvised fuses and insulated wire for torpedo purposes, to be used with what powder we had, provided the leads made closer to the ship. Later in the season the ice thawed astern of us, making a short lead nearly at right angles to the line of the ship, but not leading into any of the main leads. The ship's forefoot was resting on a large sunken floe piece, which it was supposed at the time might strain the ship and open the old wound in her forefoot. An effort was made to heave the ship astern into the open water, recourse being made to saws and other devices to remove the ice from around the body of the ship, on both beams and under her counters. Immense masses of ice were moved in this manner, the people working up to their waists in water. Finally the ship was hove astern a short distance, the large floe piece rising under her bows. The ship settled down nearly to an even keel, and the leak in the bow was watched closely and found to increase considerably. As there was still a piece of ice under her forefoot, it was considered best to let the ship lay as she was. During the summer time the carpenter's force altered the shape of the deck-house, fitting it over the forecastle hatch and skylight for the purpose of making it warmer and drier. The doctor took the psychrometer a number of times during the day. During the first winter, when the ship leaked badly, the forecastle was very wet, because in filling in the space between the frames and fitting in the watertight bulkhead, the forecastle deck being below the water line, the water found its own level above the forecastle deck, and at times ran along over the deck, but as soon as the leak was sufficiently stopped the water was allowed to flow aft to the pumps and this relieved the forecastle of a great deal of its moisture. At all times there was a regular record kept by the surgeon of the ship during the whole of the cruise, also the tests for carbonic acid gas in the living apartments of officers and men. She was damp in proportion to ordinary ships, but from what I have read of other Arctic ships I think she could be considered very dry.

Toward the latter part of August, when the stern of the ship was freed from ice, the propeller was raised and examined and returned to its place, and all preparations made with ship and engines to get under way in case the floe broke up. About the 15th of September the deck-house was erected over the forward part of the ship and covered with sails and awnings for the winter, and the pemmican removed from the lower hold and stowed in the deck-house for emergencies. The crew's knapsacks and spare clothing, the tents, the cook-stoves, and all the small gear intended for the retreat in case of fire or disaster to the ship were always kept on deck, or in a convenient place to be passed over the ship's side onto the ice; the alcohol alone being stowed below under the main hatch for safety. At times some of the alcohol was stowed on the spar deck and covered with a tarpaulin, but as soon as some of the cans were found to be punctured and leaking they were stowed under the main hatch.

November 1, the winter routine was put in force, including the customary exercise on the ice and the examination of the officers and crew by the medical officer. During this winter, as the previous winter, the people amused themselves as they saw best during the two hours' exercise on the ice, kicking foot-ball, walking or hunting, as they chose. During this winter the officers read more than the previous winter, and there appeared to be less playing of games among them, none of the officers seeming to be in as good spirits as the winter before.

The life was dull and monotonous during the winter, even the capture of a fox being considered something of interest. There was not much movement of the ice during the fall and winter of 1880; except the starting of the metal fastenings and noises from shrinkage, and distant grinding of the ice, the ship lay comparatively quiet.

On New Year's eve the crew gave a minstrel entertainment in the deck-house, at the termination of which the commanding officer made them an address, commending their good behavior and cheering them on to do as well in the future as they had done heretofore. He told them that there had been no trouble among them, no man had been punished, and he hoped that the next New Year we would all be at our homes.

And the court then, at 1.35 p. m., pending the further examination of this witness, adjourned to meet to-morrow, the 8th day of November, 1882, at 10 a. m.

TWENTY-NINTH DAY.

NAVY DEPARTMENT,
Washington, D. C., Wednesday, November 8, 1882—10 a. m.

The court met pursuant to the adjournment of yesterday.

Present, Commodore William G. Temple, United States Navy, president; Capt. Joseph N. Miller, United States Navy, Commander Frederick V. McNair, United States Navy, members; and Master Samuel C. Lemly, United States Navy, judge-advocate.

The record of the proceedings of Monday, November 6, and Tuesday, November 7, 1882, the twenty-seventh and twenty-eighth days of the inquiry, were read, and, after correcting clerical errors, approved.

Chief Engineer GEORGE W. MELVILLE, the witness under examination, then came in and continued his answer to the pending question, which was repeated by the judge-advocate, as follows:

Give a narrative account of the voyage and managment of the Jeannette from the day of her leaving San Francisco to that of her loss, referring to the log-books of that vessel for the dates and to any notes you may yourself have made at the times enumerated.

The WITNESS. The ship lay perfectly quiet during the remainder of the winter, the ice surrounding the ship remained solid. Toward the latter part of April and beginning of May the ice commenced to break up, lanes of water leading in toward the ship and continual thumping and jarring with the breaking up of the floe. May 16, or 17, land was sighted from the north [from the crow's nest to the northward and westward*] by Mr Dunbar, the ice pilot. There had been indications of land for some time to the westward, and the breaking up of the floe caused us to look out for land or obstructions from shoals or from other causes in the direction in which we were drifting. Mr. Dunbar had been a steady occupant of the crow's nest for several days previous to the day on which the land was sighted. At this time we were drifting rapidly by the island, to the northwest. The island was so far distant, the pack drifting so rapidly, and the ice so broken, that the captain did not think it prudent to attempt to make a landing on this first island. There were several sketches made of the land by different parties from the crow's nest, giving the estimated distance and bearings by the compass. These sketches are to be found in the private journal of Captain De Long. While in sight of this island the ship was continually thumped and jarred by the moving ice.

On May 24 and 25 another island was sighted, the drift of the ship continuing into the northwest floe [full*] upon this second island; in other words, I thought we were going to strike it.

About May 30, the commanding officer sent for me, and asked me if I thought I was strong enough to reach the island. He then stated that he had estimated the distance to be about 15 or 20 miles. This was the second island; we drifted by the first island. At this time the executive officer was very sick from lead poisoning. Mr. Danenhower had been sick for some time with his eyes. There were several other persons sick on board the ship from lead poisoning about the same time. On the morning of May 31, or June 1, Lieutenant De Long gave me written orders to take charge of a sled party with dogs and boat and seven days' provisions—sixteen dogs—accompanied by Mr. Dunbar, the ice master, Seaman Nindemann [Seaman Erichsen*], First-class Fireman James Bartlett, Coal-heaver Walter Sharvell, with orders to make as rapid an advance to the island as possible; to effect a landing; to build a cairn on any prominent point; to erect a beacon staff, which he gave me for the purpose, and inclosed a record in a prepared cylinder, supplied for the purpose; to display our colors, and to name the island "Henrietta" Island, and claim it in the name of the United States as a portion of the territory of the United States. The sled and boat was fully equipped. A supply of provisions, rifles, shot-guns and ammunition, the tents, sleeping bags, a keg of fresh water, a cook-stove, alcohol for cooking purposes, a medicine chest, and a certain amount of lime juice, and written instructions from the surgeon to use such medicines as might be required on the journey. The party landed on the island on the 2d day of June, or, by the corrected date, June 3. I carried out my instructions and made a hurried survey of a portion of the island. I had orders not to remain on the island more than twenty-four hours. I remained there what I suppose was about twelve hours. I made the necessary sketches of the principal headland, mountain range, hills, and hummocks, making them in my own book and taking the bearings, Seamen Erichsen holding [reading*] the compass and I

---

* Correction by witness.

myself writing the notes, from which I constructed a small chart, which will be found in the ship's records.

On June 5 and 6, corrected date, I returned to the ship. During this trip the eyes of Mr. Dunbar were badly affected by snow blindness; Erichsen, seaman, and Nindemann, seaman, were badly affected with cramps. This at the time was supposed to have been caused by the lead poisoning, from which the other members of the ship's company were suffering on board the ship. The ice in the vicinity of the ship, impinging on these islands, was broken down in immense masses, the whole pack being alive, as it is termed in ice phrase. Lanes of water leading in all directions, but continually closing again, a lead at no time remaining open for any length of time, at least not for sufficient time to work a ship. Any vessel being in such a moving mass would be ground to powder.

About May 5 or 6, there was a general order issued on board the ship naming the first island "Jeannette" Island, and the second island, the one on which we landed, was named "Henrietta" Island, the approximate latitude and longitude of each island being posted at the time and recorded in the log-book. The ice was becoming broken to such an extent in the immediate vicinity of the ship that all small articles were removed from the ice and set on board. Every preparation was made that could be made for the safety of all the equipments and crew to make a retreat in case the ship was crushed. During this time the ship was imbedded in a small island of ice, which protected us from the direct crushing or jamming of the ice on our sides, but there was a continual hammering and thumping of the underrunning ice at the ship's bottom.

On June 11, corrected date, just after 12 o'clock midnight, it was my watch to read the thermometer and instruments at the observatory; I passed over the gangway for this purpose. The ice floe split in half in the direction of the ship's keel or on a line with the ship's keel. In less than a minute's time the ship was set free, the floe slowly separated, leaving the observatory and instruments on one part of the floe, the ship drifting in alongside the opposite side. The ship righting suddenly started all hands from their beds, and in a few minutes all persons were on deck. The instruments and such small articles as remained on the ice were gotten on board. The ship was moved to one side of the floe; the dogs and the remaining articles on the opposite floe were transferred to the floe on the side of which we were. The lead opened to a distance of 500 to 700 yards and then slowly commenced to come together again. Toward 8 or 9 o'clock in the morning of the 11th, corrected date, the ice commenced coming on the side of the ship and she was hauled ahead into a hole, where it was supposed the ice coming together would impinge on itself instead of on the ship. It was a little place like a dock.

And the court then, at 12 m., took a recess until 12.30 p. m., at which time it reconvened with all the members, the judge-advocate and the witness under examination, present.

And the judge-advocate continued his examination of the witness, as follows:

Question by the JUDGE-ADVOCATE. Did the boilers and engines of the ship prove equal to the work required of them?

The WITNESS. Yes, sir; the boilers were made a little smaller than was originally designed for the Jeannette when she was originally built, for this reason, that by substituting compound boilers of the American design we managed to stow 47 per cent. more coal than the ship did originally.

Question by the JUDGE-ADVOCATE. When the ship entered the pack, as you state, about the 5th of September, 1879, give in detail the appearance of the ice in the vicinity.

The WITNESS. The ice to the eastward was very much scattered and broken. We passed through lanes of open water until we came up to the edge of the main pack to the westward of us. Beyond us was still some open lanes of water and ponds; but as the ship passed through the ice the pack to the eastward of us was apparently all in motion, because at times we had these open leads and lanes of water, and shortly after they would be entirely closed, so that as the ship passed in to the westward the ice closed in behind us.

Question by JUDGE-ADVOCATE. You have stated that during the winter season there was a physical examination, of both officers and men, made each month by the doctor; were all alike subjected to examination, and what was it?

The WITNESS. Yes, sir. The commanding officer was the first man examined. Previous to the examination there had been some question raised among the officers about the propriety of being examined. Lieutenant De Long sent for me and asked me if I had any objections to subjecting to a medical examination. He remarked at the time that I was the oldest commissioned officer in the ship and that if I had no objection he did not see why younger officers should object to a physical examination. I said to him I had no objection whatever, that it was a medical necessity in an expedition of this kind, and that I was willing to submit to anything in reason, and the next day the physical examination took place, Lieutenant De Long being the first man examined. The examination took place in private in Lieutenant De Long's private apartment, and the examination consisted in the medical officer inquiring of each officer, or of me in particular, whether I was in good physical condition, whether my appetite was good, whether my general health was good, if I had any spots or sores on my body. I was then stripped to my waist and a cursory examination was made of the upper part of my body by the surgeon. He counted my pulse and counted the beats of my stomach by placing his hand on my stomach, and I was then discharged.

Question by the JUDGE-ADVOCATE. In preparing the ship for the winter season, was anything neglected which was possible to be done that was necessary to insure the comfort of the officers and men and the safety of the ship?

The WITNESS. Everything was done to the best of my knowledge and belief, and I heard no adverse criticisms from any one.

Question by the JUDGE-ADVOCATE. State fully the condition of the officers and the men as to health and spirits while the vessel was in the ice-pack.

The WITNESS. During the first winter everybody was comparatively cheerful and happy; but the second year, I do not think the people were as well, and the people were not as cheerful as they were the previous winter. I do not think any one was despondent at any time with regard to the safety of ourselves or the ship.

Question by the JUDGE-ADVOCATE. How do you account for the depressed spirits of the men during the second as compared with the first winter in the pack? Was it due wholly to natural dissatisfaction at the prolonged imprisonment in the ice, or to some other cause?

The WITNESS. I think it was owing to their prolonged imprisonment in the ice. We all had probably got tired of each other; the stories and jokes had got stale, and people imprisoned as closely as we were, that at first would be comparatively happy, but a year or a year and a half of confinement would be very uncomfortable.

Question by the JUDGE-ADVOCATE. You stated that during the first winter in the pack the officers played cards for amusement, but that during the second winter this amusement ceased; why was this?

The WITNESS. For the reason that the people had got tired of each other and there was not the same cordiality of feeling in playing games; and people are more apt to make selections of comrades with each other, to walk and to talk or amuse themselves, as best they might, separately instead of in a mass, as we did when we first went to sea.

Question by the JUDGE-ADVOCATE. About what date did it appear certain that you would be compelled to spend a second winter in the pack?

The WITNESS. During the month of August.

Question by the JUDGE-ADVOCATE. What Divine services, if any, were held on board the Jeannette, and by whom?

The WITNESS. Prayers were read every Sunday by the commanding officer, on board of the ship and on the ice, from the time we left San Francisco until we separated in the boats.

Question by the JUDGE-ADVOCATE. Please state what amount of coal was on hand when the ship entered the ice pack, how much was consumed daily for working, heating, and distilling purposes, and how much remained on hand on the day the ship went down.

The WITNESS. When we entered the pack there was 115 tons on hand. During the winter time the expenditure ran along about 350 pounds per day for heating, distilling, and cooking. During the summer, about 110 pounds per day. There was on hand about $15\frac{1}{2}$ tons when the ship went down, by the log-book and by a close estimate; a few days before there was nearly 25 tons in the ship, for I measured it with a tape-line and estimated the quantity, by order of the commanding officer.

Question by the JUDGE-ADVOCATE. Have you any further statement to make in connection with the voyage of the ship from the day of her leaving San Francisco to that of her loss? If yea, make it now.

The WITNESS. When the ship was put into the ice toward the westward, about the 5th of September, 1879, the commanding officer told me that he had overheard an adverse criticism, which was the reason why he desired to tell me that the ship was put into the pack for the purpose of reaching Wrangel Land; that the season was still early, and that there was every probability of the fall gales breaking up the pack and scattering the ice, so that we would have no difficulty in making Wrangel Land, and that it was impossible to get anywhere with the ship in the Arctic Ocean unless we encountered ice.

Examination by the COURT:

Question by the COURT. Had you any other conversation with the commanding officer relative to getting beset in the ice, either before the occurrence, as to his intentions, or after it, as to his views of the situation? If so, please state the substance of such conversations.

The WITNESS. I never had any conversation with the commanding officer, before the ship was beset in the pack, on this subject, but after the ship was beset in the pack we had many conversations in regard to the possibilities and probabilities of being freed in the spring time by the spring gales and by the melting of the ice during the summer time, and at one time he was quite hopeful that the ship would be caught in the counter-eddy that sets along the coast of Siberia to the westward, and so be set free in the spring time. I do not remember having had any conversation with him in regard to his reason for having put the ship into the pack; neither do I remember his having expressed any opinion whether he would have put the ship in the same place again.

Question by the COURT. When you entered the ice on September 5, 1879, was there apparently a fair prospect of being able to force her through to Wrangel Land?

The WITNESS. Wrangel Land was too far distant to form any estimate of the possibilities of reaching Wrangel Land, but there were ponds and lanes of water open to the westward, and in working through a pack you can only work from pack [pond*] to pack [pond*] and from lane to lane, taking advantage of these ponds and lanes, if there is any movement of the pack.

Question by the COURT. Previous to September, 1879, when the chase after the bear occurred which you have related, was it customary to start off in a hurry, without special permission, in pursuit of game?

The WITNESS. No, sir; it was not. The people used to ramble over the floe within a short distance of the ship. I invariably got the permission of the commanding officer to leave the ship for any length of time.

Question by the COURT. Was there any prospect of getting the vessel free of the ice at any time during the summer of 1880, beyond what you have already stated?

The WITNESS. No, sir.

Question by the COURT. What caused the lead poisoning from which so many suffered in the spring of 1881?

The WITNESS. In the manufacture of tin-plate for commerce there are different qualities of tin-plate manufactured. All that is coated with pure tin is much more expensive than that coated with a mixture of tin and lead. Dealers in canned goods, or the people who prepare them, for greater profit, are apt to use an inferior quality of tin-plate coated with a coating of tin and lead. Provisions put up in this manner, to be used in a short time after being put up, in all probability no harm would come from the use of such canned goods, but where vegetables, meats, and particularly acid fruits are put up in inferior tin-plates of this description, the acid attacks the lead and causes lead poisoning.

Question by the COURT. Could the Jeannette have gotten clear of the pack on September 6, 1879?

The WITNESS. I do not think so; I do not believe she could.

Question by the COURT. Who composed the officers' mess on board of the Jeannette?

The WITNESS. The commanding officer, Lieutenant Chipp, Mr. Dannenhower, Passed Assistant Surgeon Ambler, Mr. Collins, the meteorologist, Mr. Newcomb, the naturalist, Mr. Dunbar, the ice pilot, and myself, making eight persons.

Question by the COURT. What caused the ice to be so much alive in May and June, 1881?

The WITNESS. A strong current making in for the northwest, carrying the pack on the islands which stood in the path of the moving pack.

And the court then, at 1.20 p. m., pending the further examination of this witness, adjourned to meet to-morrow, the 9th day of November, 1882, at 10.30 a. m.

---

* Corrections by witness.

THIRTIETH DAY.

NAVY DEPARTMENT,
Washington, D. C., Thursday, November 9, 1882—10.30 a. m.

The court met pursuant to the adjournment of yesterday.

Present, Commodore William G. Temple, United States Navy, president; Capt. Joseph N. Miller, United States Navy, Commander Frederick V. McNair, United States Navy, members; and Master Samuel C. Lemly, United States Navy, judge-advocate.

The record of the proceedings of Wednesday, November 8, 1882, the twenty-ninth day of the inquiry, was read, and, after correcting clerical errors, approved.

Chief Engineer G. W. MELVILLE, the witness under examination, then came in, and his examination by the judge-advocate was continued, as follows:

Question by the JUDGE-ADVOCATE. Give a detailed narrative of all the events within your knowledge connected with the crushing and loss of the Arctic exploring steamer Jeannette.

The WITNESS. On the 12th of June, 1881, the ice commenced to come in on our port side. In addition to coming in on that side it took a fore-and-aft direction. The ship was moored, and the ice on the port side, in addition to coming alongside, ran aft along the ship's side. This commenced early in the morning, after breakfast. The ice crowding under the port bow, commenced to raise the ship's head, and at the same time depress her starboard quarter. The pressure on the ship's side at the same time was very great, making the ship's timbers screech and groan. All hands were called and ran on deck. Captain De Long was on the bridge sometimes, up and down from the bridge to the poop deck, in fact all around the spar deck of the ship. Up to noon time the ship was pretty badly squeezed, but no serious damage had yet shown. The ice did not come on steadily; it would squeeze up the ship for a spell, and then stop, apparently of its own volition, or ease off a little. After noon time the ice commenced again, much stronger than it had during the forenoon, and threw the ship's bows way up, out of the ice, depressing her starboard quarter still more. At this time the ramming and thumping on the ice on the ship's sides and under her bottom was very great. Theere were two men in the fire room attending to the distilling of the water, Boyd, and Lee, the machinist. About this time Lee, in a very excited manner, ran up on deck and shouted that the ice was coming through the ship's side. The captain spoke to him about causing an alarm and said that he should not have shouted in the manner that he did, and thought that a man of his years and experience would have known better than to create an alarm on board the ship. I was on the deck at the time, and the captain told me to go below and take a look through the bunkers and watch if the ship was making any water. I went below and went through the bunkers, on both sides of the boilers, and made inquiries if there was any water coming into the ship. We always kept the sounding rod in the engine room for measuring the height of water in the bilge; a couple of floor plates were kept up, so as to observe the water in the bilge, if there was any. I asked Lee, what had alarmed him so. He said that the thumping of the ice on the ship's side had sprung her timbers in so that he thought the ship's side was coming in. He said that the ramming of the ice was making the dust fly. I went all over the bunkers and found that the seams in the inner skin were burst open some, but there was no water coming into the ship at this time. As soon as the pressure was off, the ship's timbers sprung back and the seams closed. There was a good deal of iron work around the bunkers and boilers, which created a great deal of cracking and snapping, and started a great many of the rivets from the bunker plates, but up to this time no material damage had occurred to the hull of the ship. I went on deck and reported these facts to the commanding officer. From about noon time until about 4 o'clock in the afternoon the ice was comparatively quiet. There was no confusion on board of the ship. The captain came about the ship's decks in the same manner as though we were in no danger whatever. He seemed to try and have the officers and men feel as cool and collected as he was at the time.

About 4 o'clock in the afternoon the ship was lying perfectly quiet, but her bows were thrown up so high in the air, and the ship listed to starboard so that looking down through the water the injury could be seen that occurred to her forefoot in the winter of 1879–'80. At this time the captain told me to get out the camera and try and get a picture of the ship as she lay. I will state at this time that during the winter of 1879–'80 the photographic apparatus, with all its equipments, was put in my charge, and at this time I was the photographer. I set up the camera and exposed a plate, carried the instrument back to the ship, and went into the dark-room to develop and fix the plate. I will here state that during the whole time that we were in the ice, that after the photographs were taken, the plates were developed and fixed, but no paper prints made at any time on board of the ship, the temperature being too cold to have the chemicals work well. While I was in the dark-room developing the plate, the ice commenced to crowd the ship again, and the order was passed to prepare to abandon the ship. I closed the dark-room door and left the photographic apparatus where it was. My station on abandoning the ship was to see to getting out the chronometers, the rifles and ammunition, the chart case, the navigation box, the compasses, the cooking stoves, and after the specific articles, which I was directed to put on the ice, I was to assist in getting the provisions and stores over the ship's side on the ice. I assisted in carrying them back on the floe to a place of safety. The captain ordered the boats lowered, designating which, and the crew ran them back to a safe place on the ice. The first cutter was lowered, the second cutter, and the first whale-boat. There were two dinghys—a small wooden dinghy and a metallic dinghy—but I do not remember whether they were lowered or already on the ice. The pemmican was in the deck house, the sleeping bags, the men's knapsacks, clothing, provisions of all kinds, were passed rapidly over the ship's side and carried to a place of safety. Dr. Ambler looked after getting out his medical stores and supplies. I do not know who was assigned to assist him. Mr. Chipp was very sick, was in bed, but he was notified. He got up and dressed himself, and I think Dr. Ambler and some other person assisted him over the ship's side on to the ice. Each person who had anything to do, so far as I know, attended to their duty; Captain De Long apparently being everywhere, and seeing that all things went on smoothly and quietly, without the least haste or consternation among the people. In fact, as the men passed the stuff over the side, they were singing merchant-ship songs.

The ice continued to grind on the side of the ship, and Dr. Ambler came below into the officers' quarters to get some additional medical supplies; hurried on deck and reported that the lower hold was filling with water. I heard the captain say, "I know it," and kept the men still at work getting the stores on the ice. The water rose very rapidly in the ship when it commenced to come in, and it was the general opinion of the officers, the captain and the carpenter included, that the ship had been seized and held so firmly by the ice at the water line that the ice underrunning the ship either pushed the keel out of its place or pressed her garboard strakes open, as the water rose right up from the bottom of the ship. There was ample time for all persons to get out their personal effects. The alcohol, the whole or part of which was set in the lower hold, had to be removed from the water. There was more difficulty in getting out a barrel of lime-juice from the forward storeroom, Seaman Starr getting in there, swimming in the water, at the risk of his life, to get out this barrel of lime-juice, which we believed was so necessary for our health on our march, to prevent the scurvy. I remember of Captain De Long's speaking of this matter in the most commendable terms.

Toward six or seven o'clock in the evening tea was prepared for those who wished it. Some of the officers were in the [cabin*] captain's room partaking of supper, and the crew were to have their supper one watch at a time. Captain De Long, myself, and the doctor, I do not believe had any supper. We were out around the decks all the time. When the water rose in the ship's hold the ship was thrown over so far on her beam ends that it was impossible to stand on the deck without crawling on our hands and knees. The captain told everybody to leave the ship. Just before this time, while the water was in the lower hold, I went below and got my knapsack and threw it out on the ice, and was returning to get a pillow case that I had there with woolen clothing and foot-nips; the water rose so rapidly that I was obliged to leave them. I then went into the captain's room and assisted in passing out clothing from a bureau and drawers. Some of the officers assisted Mr. Chipp in getting out such articles as he desired. At that time the captain gave the order for all hands to leave the ship. Her water ways were broken in, the decks bulged up and broken, the iron work around the smoke-pipe also buckled up, and the rivets sheared off and started the smoke-stack, which stood supported by its guys. It must have been about eleven o'clock at night when all hands left the ship, and we commenced and made our camp on the floe. We had all been set off in regular messes and tents, the whole party of thirty-three people being distributed in five tents, some tents composing six persons, others seven. Some time after midnight, after we had all turned in, the floe commenced to break up in the camp. We turned out quickly and moved all of our supplies farther away to [from*] the edge of the floe and to a place of safety.

About four o'clock in the morning, when the watch was being called, I heard some of the men say "There she goes; hurry up and have a look, the last sight you will have of the old Jeannette." While the ice held together, the ship was kept there; but as soon as the ice parted she went down, stripping her yards upwards, as she passed through the floe. She sank in about 38 fathoms of water. The next morning I accompanied Lieutenant De Long, in one of the small boats, along the lead where the ship went down, to see if any portion of the wreck remained. We found one of the old signal chests, a box of succotash, and a piece of one of our top-gallant masts, or a piece of one of our yards, I do not remember which. We gathered up all we had in the vicinity of the wreck, the evening before, and on this morning gathered up what empty barrels or drift wood lay about, to be used for fuel in cooking,

---

*Correction by witness.

while we remained in camp in the vicinity of the wreck. Captain De Long ordered all the clothing that the people did not have on their bodies, to be thrown into one common heap, to be distributed equally among all hands, before we started on the retreat. [The proper allowance that each person was directed to carry was selected from this heap.*] This order was passed from tent to tent, and was generally complied with. In the mean time arrangements were made to make up a lot of bags to bag off the bread. The bread was stowed in casks; we could not afford to carry the weight of the casks. We used what bags we had and made additional bags of all the skin clothing that had been thrown out on the ice. There was a package of black painted bags intended for this purpose, that was thrown over on the ice, but by some mishap was thrown into the water, or covered by the ice running up over it, but I know that a lot of bags had been set aside for this purpose. The alcohol had been secured in tin boxes; they were all covered with wooden boxes and it was necessary to remove all this weight to lighten our loads in traveling. The sleds had been kept lashed all the winter and required relashing, and the boats that had been mounted on the sleds, their fittings were not considered as good as they might be, as the chocks stood athwartships. The chocks made in this manner, in attempting to haul the sleds through the snow, piled up immense piles of snow in front of the sleds; for this reason this was changed and fore-and-aft chocks fitted along to boat's bilges, the ends being sharpened off, like the bow of a boat, to let them pass freely through the snow. Captain De Long then issued a written order, designating what each person should carry in their knapsacks. This order was passed from tent to tent and the officer of each tent opened the men's and their own knapsacks and arranged said knapsacks according to the order. The order about clothing was that each officer and man should carry but one suit of clothing, that which he stood in—making his own selection, whether it be woolen or fur; all hands being cautioned at the time to remember that after making their selection they must stand by it. The people were then called by tents to come to the clothing pile to make such selections of clothing as they desired, limiting themselves, however, in the quantity to that designated in the captain's order. I was assigned the duty of seeing this order carried out, and so far as I know, unless some person surreptitiously carried more clothing than the captain ordered, that is all that was carried. It took five or six days to complete the arrangements for stowing the sleds, preparing the provisions and getting properly organized for the march to the southward. I remember there were plenty of guns and ammunition put upon the ice and more clothing than we could use. Many of the provisions that were put out were not originally intended as a part of the retreat provisions, such as pemmican [strike out words "such as pemmican" *]. That is, there was a great lot of general provisions, such as cheese and canned meats of all kinds, that was thrown out and used by us while we were in camp and on the first few days of our retreat. It was at first supposed that each tent party could haul their own sleds. After the sleds were loaded, and a day or two before we got ready for the march each tent party tried to haul their sleds. The snow was so deep it was impossible to move them without additional help, or two sled parties to a single sled. The snow at this time was not only soft but very soggy, that is it would ball up. In the winter time the snow generally beats down so hard by the wind, that you might sled right over the top of it [especially after

---

* Correction by witness.

pressed in snow floes*], but in the early spring the snow becomes soggy and wet and balls up, which was the reason why we found the sleds with their loads so difficult to haul. Had the ice been free of the snow there would have been no difficulty at all about hauling our sleds.

Question by the JUDGE-ADVOCATE. How large was the open water space around the ship when the ice commenced to approach her on the 12th day of June, 1881, local date, and in what direction did it extend relatively to the position of the ship?

The WITNESS. It was a varying width. The ice was continually in motion, sometimes approaching, sometimes leaving the ship. I suppose the greatest width it ever amounted to was about 500 yards. The opening was in a fore-and-aft line with the keel of the ship, but varying in all directions, mostly when away from the ship. The lead ran fore and aft with the keel of the ship and the ship was moored with her starboard side to the floe. The open water space ran along by our [port†] side.

Question by the JUDGE-ADVOCATE. How thick was the ice?

The WITNESS. The ship was first frozen in in still water, and the greatest thickness of the ice was about 9 feet, but as the ship and floe had shifted positions it was impossible to say how thick the ice was there without measuring it, because many times during the winter when the floe split or was pressed upon, by using the grapnel, the ice was measured in many places and found to vary from 10 to 20 feet.

Question by the JUDGE-ADVOCATE. You have enumerated certain articles which you were detailed to get out on the ice when deserting the ship; did you carry out your orders in this respect, or was any article assigned you left on board?

The WITNESS. There was no article left that I was ordered to place upon the ice, that was left behind by me or the party in my charge. I would like to state that the boat equipments, the boat box and such articles as had been designated and prepared under the orders of the captain of the ship, during the first winter, and I believe a modification of the same order was issued during the second winter, and the navigation box that had been prepared for each boat, were intentionally left behind owing to their weight. In starting out from where the ship was crushed, we having a longer march before us than ever was known to have been attempted in the Arctic Ocean before, every ounce in weight, that could be dispensed with, with good judgment, was left behind. I have seen the men compare a jack-knife with a sheath-knife, and throw the heavier away in preference to carrying it.

And the court then, at 12 m., took a recess until 12.30 p. m., at which time it reconvened with all the members, the judge-advocate, and the witness under examination present, and the examination of the witness was then continued as follows:

Question by the JUDGE-ADVOCATE. Can you now recall to mind anything which was left behind when deserting the ship, the want of which was afterward essentially felt on the retreat?

The WITNESS. No, sir; I recall nothing.

Question by the JUDGE-ADVOCATE. Who assisted Lieutenant Chipp himself, and with his effects, when deserting the ship?

The WITNESS. Well, several persons did. I cannot say precisely who; I did, and other persons. I remember seeing Captain De Long in the room, and speaking to him, and asked him if he could help him out of his room. His room was on the spar deck, and I saw several of the

---
* Strike out these words. Correction by witness. † Corrected by witness.

sailors pass out of his room for the purpose of assisting him with his effects

Question by the JUDGE-ADVOCATE. To what do you now attribute the loss of the Jeannette; to the gradual weakening of the ship from the effects of repeated strains, or to the crush of June 12 and 13, 1881?

The WITNESS. No doubt the ship was weakened and strained by the two winters' action of the ice, but she was lost at the moment by the crushing strains brought upon her during the 12th and 13th days of June, and it is doubtful in my mind, from the direction in which the strains came, the ship's bow being lifted up and the stern being depressed, that any ship could have stood the crushing strain of the ice at that time. The strains brought upon the ship at that time could hardly be measured in tons, the pressure being in square miles of ice piled up against her. I do not believe any ship that was hollow could stand the strain of the ice in the Arctic Ocean at all times.

Question by the JUDGE-ADVOCATE. Had she been liberated from the ice on the 12th of June, 1881, instead of being crushed, do you believe she would have been capable of continuing her voyage of Arctic exploration?

The WITNESS. Nobody would send a ship on an Arctic cruise in the condition that the Jeannette's fore-foot was at this time; but, on the other hand, if she had been released from the ice, she could be safely navigated to a port of safety.

Question by the JUDGE-ADVOCATE. Have you any further statement to make in relation to the loss of the ship? If yea, make it now.

The WITNESS. I neglected to state that all the books and papers and small gear that was intended to be carried in the boats, was kept prepared in the starboard chart-room. That all the ship's books and papers and everything intended to be carried was put on the ice. At the time when we abandoned the ship, the books and papers having been placed in tin boxes prepared for this purpose the previous winter, Captain De Long asked me if I had any private papers that I desired to carry. I told him no; that the steam log-books were not of sufficient importance to be carried, as all matters important contained in the steam log-books are always copied into the ship's logs; the amount of coal and oil used, the meteorological information, is obtained from the ship's log. All of my private papers were contained in a box that went down with the ship. There were several persons in the cabin whose things were gathered there. Anybody that wished had ample time to gather all their books, papers, and clothing into the upper cabin. The reason why I did not get my additional clothing is because I was careless.

Examination by the COURT:

Question by the COURT. How was the wind and weather on the 12th day of June, 1881?

The WITNESS. There was very little wind and the weather was fair.

Question by the COURT. Did you recognize the fact that the movement of the ice on that day was more violent than it had been previously, before it was made evident by the crushing in of the vessel? If so, can you assign any reason for it?

The WITNESS. Yes, sir; for days previous we saw the ice very much in commotion. I do not think it was more violent on that day than on previous days, but the ship was not then in a position where the violence would affect her as in this case. When she was in a solid floe of ice, with ice around that protected her from the crushing of the ice in the vicinity.

Question by the COURT. Was the order given to lower the boats when Lee first gave the alarm?

The WITNESS. There was no hurry about lowering the boats at all; we had plenty of time.

Question by the COURT. Name the persons who were on the sick list at the time of the loss of the Jeannette.

The WITNESS. Lieutenant Chipp and Mr. Danenhower. I do not know whether these men whose names I will give were on the sick list, but I know they were being treated for lead poisoning: Mr. Newcomb, the steward Charles Tong Sing, and Kuehne the seaman, and Lauterback, coal-heaver, [also Alexy*]. I think that was all.

Question by the COURT. You have stated that the boat boxes, with instruments for navigation, &c., were purposely left on board the vessel; was this done by order of the commanding officer?

The WITNESS. Yes, sir; I had instructions not to carry them out with the other articles. They were too heavy to be carried.

Question by the COURT. Was not the want of compasses felt during the retreat?

The WITNESS. We had a prismatic compass [prismatic compasses*] during the whole retreat, and in the boats during the time of the gale. The prismatic compass did not work quickly. That was the only time, that I know of, when there was any difficulty about compasses.

Question by the COURT. You have stated that Lieutenant De Long's order, to make a common pile of the clothing, was generally complied with; did any one fail to carry out this order? If so, state who did so fail, and all you know about the subject.

The WITNESS. I do not know who failed to comply with the order, but had I known of any person failing to comply, I would have informed the commanding officer; but after we were on the retreat Captain De Long directed some person to throw away a coat that was in excess of the quantity allowed. I think that was Mr. Collins, but I am not sure. I would like to state that Mr. Chipp was allowed to carry his large ulster, because he was sick and he was wrapped up [in it*], but when he went on duty he threw this coat away, and it was made into a pair of trowsers for one of his messmates.

And the court then, at 1 p. m., pending the further examination of this witness, adjourned to meet to-morrow, the 10th day of November, 1882, at 10.30 a. m.

THIRTY-FIRST DAY.

NAVY DEPARTMENT,
Washington, D. C., Friday, November 10, 1882—10.30 a. m.

The court met pursuant to the adjournment of yesterday.

Present, Commodore William G. Temple, United States Navy, president; Capt. Joseph N. Miller, United States Navy, Commander Frederick V. McNair, United States Navy, members; and Master Samuel C. Lemly, United States Navy, judge-advocate.

The record of the proceedings of yesterday, November 9, 1882, the thirtieth day of the inquiry, was then read and approved.

Chief Engineer GEORGE W. MELVILLE, United States Navy, the

---

* Correction by witness.

witness under examination, then came in, and his examination by the judge-advocate was continued as follows:

Question by the JUDGE-ADVOCATE. Give a detailed narrative of the retreat after the loss of the ship.

The WITNESS. The retreat was commenced on the evening of about the 18th of June, and the day before starting Captain De Long and the ice master ran out a line of flags toward the southward at a distance of about a mile and a half from the camp. I was sent with a sled load of provisions as far as I supposed was the farthest flag. The farthest flag had been knocked down or had fallen. We commenced to march during the night instead of the day, so as to avoid the glare of the sun as much as possible during the march, and sleep warm during the day. When we made the start, the commanding officer directed me to take charge of the working party and to carry the first cutter as far as the farthest flag. About twenty of the people started to haul the first cutter to the front, all hands having working harness and canvas belts going over the shoulder and under the opposite arm, and a lashing attached nearly a fathom in length. The snow was very deep and soggy. We made very slow progress with the boat; she would bury at times way above the depth of the runners so that the bottom and bilges of the boat would burrow in the snow. It then required standing hauling, and the force of all the hands to lift the boat and haul at the same time. When I got the first cutter as far as the place where I had deposited the provisions the day before, I stopped with the intention of returning to the camp to bring up the other boats and sleds. Mr. Dunbar, the ice master, then informed me that the farthest flag was more than half a mile to the front; my orders being to carry the boat to the farthest flag. I then hitched on a second time, and continued the march until we deposited the boat at the farther flag. This took us the best part of the working time, getting back to the first camp, after considerable delay. When I returned to the camp, we found that the ice had opened between the floe where the camp was and where we had carried the first cutter.

Captain De Long, with a few men with him, was trying to get the boats and sleds across the lead. I think he had launched the whale-boat and got across the open water; the second cutter also. The most of the sleds were on the floe on the side of the lead, nearest the camp. The ice was now moving quite rapidly, and so to keep our material together it was necessary to work quickly, and so all hands took a hold of the sleds and boats, one piece at a time, and roused them over the lead as quickly as possible. In doing this, some of the sled-runners were turned under, the lashings being fresh and wet with water and slushy snow they stretched. I will here remark that the lashings were made of raw hide. We succeeded in this day's work in getting all of our sleds and remaining boats up as far as the first depot, that had been made of the provisions. We then found it necessary to dismount the boats and provisions from most of the sleds, relash the runners and the cross-piece. In the mean time the people were sent back to the original camp to bring up a lot of loose provisions, that is, canned provisions. The pemmican was all hauled throught on sleds. They also brought up a lot of wood from the original camp to serve as fuel for cooking purposes, to save the alcohol.

Before leaving the first camp Lieutenant De Long had prepared a cask or a water breaker, in which he placed a lot of papers stating the time and place of the wreck and directing any person who might find it to send the cask or the contents to the Government at Washington. The outside of the cask was marked directing any person who might find it to look within. The iron dinghy, a lot of old arms and clothing and other stuff, of no value, was left behind on the ice. As long as we remained in the second camp, all the provisions were brought up from the first camp. The first day's work everybody except the sick assisted in moving the boats and sleds.

After the sleds had been relashed and the boats remounted we started to make the next march as far as the first cutter. On this morning, before starting, the captain sent for Mr. Danenhower and said to him that he should remain with the sick people. I heard Captain De Long call Mr. Danenhower to his tent. After Mr. Danenhower returned from the captain's tent, he told me that he had been relieved from duty or directed to go with the sick people. On this day's march, in addition to the sick who were already on the list, Mr. Collins was taken with cramps and Machinist Lee was also taken with cramps. That day we succeeded in moving all of our weights as far as the first cutter. The ice at this time was very much broken and many leads of water ran in all directions, requiring a rapid movement of the pieces of baggage from floe piece to floe piece. We endeavored to keep all our stuff together, and to do this and move rapidly it was necessary that the working party should move but one piece of baggage at a time. The snow was so deep that it was impossible to haul two pieces at the same time unless it happened to be at a place where the snow was not so deep, and two of the lightest pieces would be hauled at once, such as the bread sled and one of the pemmican sleds. The whole of the working force at this time had to pass back and forth across the floes about thirteen times to make one distance good; that is, if we had a mile to advance, the whole party would have to advance about thirteen miles on a direct line to make one mile good. There was a dog sled fitted under the charge of the doctor, and one of the natives, I think, to assist him in hauling forward the medical tent and medical supplies, was assigned him. As soon as an advance was made with one of the sleds or boats the medical tent was moved to that position, the tent set up and the sick people were cared for at the medical tent, remaining there until another advance was made. The ice was [always*] in motion, and we seldom had a half a mile straight going without having to launch the boats in the water and hauling them out on the opposite side or through miles of ice into the opening between the floes, making a bridge to jump the sleds over. During all this time the men were wet, at least up to their knees, very often plunging in up to their shoulders. In making the bridges the first sled or two might pass safely over without wetting anybody, but the weight of the sleds moving across rapidly would jar and start the ice in such a manner that when the third or fourth piece of baggage went over, it was almost certain that some of the people would tumble in. Our supply of clothing, of necessity, was limited; we had one suit of clothing on our bodies, and every man was supposed to have one suit of underclothing in his knapsack. When opportunity was offered the clothing was changed. In the first cutter there was one suit or possibly two suits of trousers or jackets for general service, to relieve any man who might tumble in and get wet. In addition to the working party that was hauling the boats and sleds, two men were detailed to [drive*] *direct* the two dog sleds, carrying forward what loose provisions we still had with us, to carry the cooking stoves and tents that were also put on the dog sleds to relieve the weight in the boats. Carrying the knapsacks and sleeping bags in the boats made

---
*Correction by witness.

them top-heavy and tumble over and wet all our gear. The doctor, in addition to his duties as surgeon, was detailed as roadmaker. He had a small McClintock dinghy on a sled, and four or five dogs to haul it with Lee, who was a poor traveler, and I think Mr. Newcomb and Mr. Collins assisted in making the roads to prevent the boats taking the hummocks, and making as straight a way as possible for the sleds and boats in their advance. During the first few days, we took [used*] the loose provisions, altogether, until they were entirely consumed. These stores and provisions consisted of canned chicken, mutton broth, pigs' feet, cheese, and other general stores in cars. These supplies might have been supplemented by a small amount of pemmican; I am not sure that pemmican was issued along with these small stores. On starting I understood that we had sixty days' supply of bread. I took the weights on the barrels and bagged it off in bags, giving the weights to the commanding officer. On starting, we were allowed, in addition to our meat provisions, a half pound of bread per day, or biscuit, running about twelve biscuits to the pound; that would be six whole biscuits a day or two biscuits at a meal. When the bread became very much broken up it was necessary to weigh it, and the issue was made daily by the carpenter. In my tent, that a fair division of the provisions should be made, I directed Seaman Görtz to divide the pemmican into six equal parts at each meal, to divide the bread in the same manner, putting the broken bread in the pan and setting all the pans in the center of the tent, when each man took his pan of bread and pemmican. By this means every person seemed satisfied, and I know each person got his share of the provisions. I do not know whether this system was carried out in all the other tents or not. As the summer advanced and the sun got strong, the snow rapidly left the ice. The march became much easier, that is, as regarded our weights, reducing the number of passages across the ice to eleven times, and finally to nine or seven times passing across the floe. It was impossible to march in any direction in a straight line. The flags were set up by the compass, by the ice master and the commanding officer, the ice master going ahead and the commanding officer conning him to certain hummocks, and then between them they made the most direct and the best road among the hummocks. We could not always find roads between the hummocks. It often became necessary to cut our way directly through the hummocks or partially leveling the hummocks or to make an inclined plane, hauling the boat up one side and lowering it slowly down the inclined plane on the opposite side. They often got away from us, damaging the sleds and boats; the whale-boat in particular was so long and extended so far forward and abaft the sled that she kept continually hammering with her bow or stern on the ice hummocks so that eventually she burst her stern open. If open water were in our course, which was not too deep, no more than knee deep, in preference to hauling the boats through the snow and over the hummocks, making a circuitous detour, we generally marched right through the water. We avoided this all we could with the bread sled, often making the detour with it to prevent the wetting of the bread, but very often in steering the course, a pond of water might not be very deep to begin with, but before we got across we would have to rush the bread-sled through, which wet considerable of our bread; but this did us little harm, as we ate it as we went along. During this march we understood that we were making for the New Siberian Islands. Before the ship was lost, it was well known by all hands

---

* Correction by witness.

that that was the nearest point to the ship. After we had been on the march about ten days the captain got an observation of the sun, although he had been getting observations all along, but at this particular time he told me that he was very much surprised to find that we had drifted way up into the northwest. He said to me that he had worked a couple of Sumners, and at first he thought it was hardly possible, but his observations agreed so well with his Sumners that he was sure that was the case. Mr. Chipp was very sick at this time, hardly able to stagger along. He told me not to tell Mr. Chipp what he had told me, nor to tell any other person, as he did not want to discourage the sick or the people. Dr. Ambler was present at the time he spoke to me about this. All hands at this time were bright and cheerful, the men singing as they launched the boats and sleds, the two leading men at the bows of the boats, and at the bows of the sleds singing and giving the word to haul as the occasion required it. When the sledding got better, they generally started out two of the light sleds, using the lightest, a bread sled, to break the way through the snow, the heavier sled following. In the same manner we took the light sled and the lightest boat, the second cutter. At first it required all hands to haul the first cutter or the whale-boat, one at a time; the second cutter being a much lighter boat, was hauled with great facility, and being short sat well on the sled, and took no damage. The whale-boat was considered the worst boat of the three to haul. The men always complained more of the hauling of this boat than even the first cutter, which was a much larger boat. After awhile the sledding became sufficiently good to haul the first cutter and the whale-boat at one time, dividing the working party in the proportion of ten to twelve or eleven to thirteen, I think; that is, ten or eleven men on the whale-boat, and twelve or thirteen on the first cutter; and in doing this, the men used to complain to me that it was not a fair division of the work; that the whale-boat was a harder boat to haul than the first cutter; but I, knowing the first cutter to be a heavier boat than the whale-boat, continued that division of the men in hauling their respective boats, as I was in charge of the working gang at the time. Very often one of these boats would get mired in the snow, or the largest provision sled, which the sailors named the Walrus, would get mired. It then became necessary to work [break off*] all hands from any piece of baggage we were hauling, and fist on to her and haul her through.

And the court then, at 12.05 p. m., took a recess until 12.30 p. m., at which time it reconvened, with all the members, the judge-advocate and the witness under examination, present, and the witness then continued his answer to the pending question, as follows:

At times, when the water leads were too wide apart to bridge across, they generally found a large floe piece of ice that we would float down, haul alongside of the main floe, and put on it all our traps. We used the dinghy for running a line across the leads to haul this ferry-boat or raft over. Sometimes a piece of ice would be so small that we could carry but one or two pieces of baggage; at other times we would get a piece large enough to put all hands on, boats, sleds, dogs and people, then run a line across it by means of the dinghy and haul the raft or floe piece over. At other times it was more convenient to make a bridge for the sleds and launch the boats across the leads. We always worked in the most advantageous manner in transporting our sleds across the leads or bridges. At times, after a road had been laid out and a bridge

---

* Correction by witness.

built, the whole ice would move and the labor was lost, but that was no fault of the party who laid out the road or had the bridge built—it was simply an action of the ice, over which we had no control. After we had been for some time on the march, the commanding officer directed Mr. Collins not to do any more work.

I will now have to go back until some time in March, to state that owing to a conversation between Lieutenant De Long and Mr. Collins, in regard to disobedience of orders on the part of Mr. Collins, the commanding officer relieved Mr. Collins from duty; that is, he suspended him from duty, but did not place him in arrest. Mr. Collins at all times was free to come and go, as the other officers of the mess were; to take his gun and hunt over the floe in the same manner as any other officer would hunt, simply by getting the permission of the executive officer or the commanding officer of the ship. The reason why he was directed to perform no further duty, at this time, I do not know. Mr. Collins spoke to me of it at the time, and said to me that he had been directed not to perform any duty. At this time I think Mr. Collins was working on the roads along with Lee and Mr. Newcomb, the doctor being in charge of the road party. While the march continued, the people living on pemmican and bread rapidly recovered—I mean those that were sick; I supposed it was owing to the absence of lead-poisoning. Mr. Chipp was still very sick, and at one time for a short distance, when he was delaying the advance of the party, Lieutenant De Long directed him to get on the sled and be carried. The poor fellow, at this time, was entirely broken down; he rolled over on his face, on the sled, and said, "You had better leave me behind." Captain De Long at the time remarked that no man would be left behind while another man was left to haul him. About this time Mr. Chipp appeared to get better quite rapidly, and about the 20th day of August he reported himself ready for duty, and took charge of the working gang. Before this time we had raised a strange land. At first we supposed it might be New Siberia, as we had been heading for the New Siberian Islands during the whole of our march; but the captain, knowing our position, said it was possible but not probable; that distances in the Arctic Ocean were very deceptive. Land raised sometimes by refraction is seen at great distances; but he said to me that it was a strange island, and if so he would haul up the course and land on the island—the island at that time being nearly but not quite on our course—and "I will kill two birds with one stone. We will land on the island, and at the same time have a rest and repair our boats." As we approached the island, the ice was very much more broken up, more open water, the ice whirling in all directions, sometimes carried east or west as the tide seemed to set in these regions. After a great deal of labor and several ineffectual attempts to land, we effected a landing about the last day of July. After making a landing the ice-master with a party was sent to explore northern side of the island to the westward, and Lieutenant Chipp, with a boat and party, explored the southern part of the island to the westward. A tide gauge was set up, and the record of the tides made while we were there. On the evening of our landing on the edge of the ice a procession was formed, and Captain De Long formally took possession of the island in the name of the United States, and named it Bennett Island. While we were there, all the people were directed to roam over the island, in any direction they chose, only being cautioned to be tack in the evening by supper time. The sailors killed guillemots, bea birds, with rocks, and brought them into the camp and equally dissributed them among the messes as fresh food.

The carpenter set to work to repair the stern of the whale-boat, which had been burst open by the thumping of the boat on the floe ice, and removed the loggerhead from forward. There was so much water in the vicinity of the island that the captain made up his mind at this time to shoot the remainder of the dogs and to take to the boats. Accordingly all the dogs were shot except seven, which were retained, as we might have some sledding to do.

About the 6th of August, everything being in readiness, we broke camp, and by means of the boats started from the edge of the ice floe, which was probably a mile or a mile and a half off. Before starting, the commanding officer sent for me and said to me that I was to take charge of the whale-boat, and gave me a written order to that effect.

The witness produced and the judge-advocate read aloud, and placed before the court as evidence, the original order referred to, and a certified copy, marked X, is appended to the record.

The witness then continued his narrative as follows:

The three boats were launched and loaded as deeply as they would float, with the sleds, dogs, and all of our gear, which was landed on the edge of the floe; some of the boats making two trips to accomplish this. We were landed at the edge of the floe; one party of the ship's company was directed to haul the sleds to the southward on our course, the three boats being beaten around the point of the floe where we expected to meet the sleds. Lieutenant De Long, with one or two people, sailed the first cutter, myself, Mr. Danenhower, and Mr. Newcomb working the whale-boat; I do not know who worked the second cutter.

Captain De Long directed that they should get in the boat and should assist me in handling the sails. I will state at this time that while we were on the march, before reaching Bennett Island, that owing to some controversy between Mr. Danenhower and Mr. Newcomb, Mr. Newcomb was suspended from duty by the commanding officer. Before pushing off in my boat, Mr. Newcomb being designated to take passage in my boat, I inquired of the commanding officer what the status of Mr. Newcomb was. He told me that he was under suspension, but that he should perform such duties as I found necessary for him to perform while in the boat. In beating up around the point, Captain De Long was making much better headway with the first cutter than I was with the whale-boat. I thought that Mr. Newcomb did not work the sail fast enough. At this time I was steering the boat and Mr. Danenhower was attending to the sheet. I asked Mr. Danenhower to take the tiller and Mr. Newcomb to take the sheet and I would go forward and work the sail as I was much stronger and could probably work it quicker.

We beat by Lieutenant De Long's boat and got under the edge of the ice all right. Upon landing, Lieutenant De Long asked me whether Mr. Danenhower had assumed the charge of the boat; asked why it was I permitted him to sail the boat. I stated the case as it was; that I did not like to see the first cutter beating the whale-boat; that Mr. Newcomb did not work the sail well, and that I requested Mr. Danenhower to take the tiller; that I would work the sail much quicker. Captain DeLong said that was all right, but that I must know that he did not intend that Mr. Danenhower while on the sick-list should perform any duty. I told Mr. Danenhower of this, and he said he was able to do duty and would prefer to do duty. I said that it was the captain's order, but that if he did not like that, I would go back to Lieutenant De Long and ask to have him removed from my boat and some other person put in his place. He said that he did not wish it. He remarked at the time that he had rather be on my boat than on any other boat. I then said to him that we had been the best of friends and there was no reason why we should not be best of friends hereafter; that as long as he was on the whale-boat that I would neither do nor say anything that would be hurtful to his feelings as a commissioned officer.

This same day we left the small sleds behind, taking the boat sleds, which were heavy oaken sleds, and put them in our boats from the edge of the floe, working through the leads to the southward, taking the nearest leads as they presented themselves going toward the south. The boats were very deeply loaded and we had great difficulty about keeping the dogs in the boats. There was no particular quantity of the provisions put into each boat at this time. The boats were all loaded to the capacity at which they were supposed to safely float. There was more room in the first cutter and the whale-boat than in the second cutter, and the dogs were carried in these two boats. The boats were being rowed at this time, and the dogs were very much in the way; the punching of the oars and the men's elbows against the dogs made them jump out of the boats on the floe, and the first day we lost the most of them. In a day or two all the dogs were gone, except two favorite dogs that the sailors tied fast in the boat, Snoozer in the first cutter and Kasmatka in the whale-boat. After journeying for a day or two there was another arrangement made about the tenting of the people: two tents were assigned to the whale-boat, and the owner of Kasmatka, Görtz, in charge of Kasmatka, was transferred to the first cutter; he took his dog with him. At this time there were ten people on the whale-boat, thirteen people on the first cutter, and ten people on the second cutter. When we landed at Bennett Island the water was running from all parts of the island from the melting snow and ice. Before we left there it ceased to melt and was freezing. There was little or no running water. When there were light falls of snow and the island was becoming whitened with the falling snow; while the loose pack remained loose, that is, not cemented together by young ice, we got on very rapidly. You could watch the floe pieces, part them, and get on very well with the boats, but the cold weather set in almost immediately and the young ice commenced to make among the loose pack, cementing them together. During the whole advance it was necessary to work the way through the young ice, where a couple of men over [were*] on the bows of the first cutter opened the way [breaking the way with their feet*], the first cutter taking the lead.

I will here state that ice a quarter of an inch thick could not be rowed through by any of our boats; it was necessary to break the way. We followed the leads as long as they continued to the southward, and when we came up with a floe piece we hauled the boats out, mounted them on the sleds and hauled them across the floe, whatever the distance might be, and launching them on [from*] the floe side toward the southward. We were having a good deal of wind at this time, which sometimes massed the loose pack together so that it was impossible to navigate through it. During one of these blows we were caught in a snow-storm, and we were obliged to camp for about twenty-four hours owing to the broken condition of the pack and the young ice not being strong enough to travel over it. As soon as the snow-storm stopped we got under way again, hauling the boats across the broken pack, plunged into the water as we came to any open lead, and finally made the opposite side of the floe.

And the court then, at 1.30 p. m., pending the further examination of this witness, adjourned to meet to-morrow, the 11th day of November, 1882, at 10.30 a. m.

---

* Correction by witness.

THIRTY-SECOND DAY.

NAVY DEPARTMENT,
Washington, D. C., Saturday, November 11, 1882—10.30 a. m.

The court met pursuant to the adjournment of yesterday.

Present, Commodore William G. Temple, United States Navy, president; Capt. Joseph N. Miller, United States Navy, Commander Frederick V. McNair, United States Navy, members; and Master Samuel C. Lemly, United States Navy, judge-advocate.

The record of the proceedings of yesterday, Friday, November 10, 1882, the thirty-first day of the inquiry, was then read, and, after the correction of clerical errors, approved.

Chief Engineer G. W. MELVILLE, United States Navy, the witness under examination, then came in and continued his answer to the pending question, which was repeated by the judge-advocate as follows:

Give a detailed statement of the retreat, after the loss of the vessel.

The WITNESS. About this time the weather had set in pretty cold; the young ice was making in open leads, so that it was necessary to break the way for the boats. There were two men continually over the bows of the first cutter, breaking the way with pike poles, and looms of the oars, and often breaking the way with their feet and legs; but up to this time none of the party had suffered any from cold. The weather was sufficiently temperate, with the clothing we had on, and the labor that we were performing kept us sufficiently warm, and the sleeping bags were warm enough to sleep in at night. The severest part of the work, that most laborious, was performed while hauling on the floe, before we reached Bennett Island. There was so much soft snow and water on the surface of the ice that it softened the soles of the moccasins, which were made of raw-hide, that is hoopjook; leather not answering for this purpose because it gets hard in cold weather. The soles of the moccasins would take in water if not made of raw-hide, and when the men were hauling, if their feet slipped, it would tear the bottoms out of their moccasins.

In the start each person was told to carry three pairs of moccasins; in cold or dry weather this would have been plenty. But the water on the surface of the ice and the sharp, needled surface ice cut out the moccasins so rapidly that we were soon very badly off for foot gear. All the hoopjook skin that was in the ship was thrown out on the ice and carried with us for repairing shoes. The sailors made thrum-mats to cover the ball of the foot, while others made little mats of rope to cover the heel of the foot; they unspun the rope and laid it up in sennit to make mats to cover their heels and the balls of their feet, sewing these mats to the wrecked [ragged*] portion of their moccasins. The men also made soles for their shoes of canvas, rags, and the leather of the looms of the oars, the knapsack straps, and some of them made soles of wood.

After Mr. Chipp took charge of the working party, I was set at work on the roads with the road party. Dr. Ambler, who had been at work on the roads, in addition to caring for the sick, volunteered to work along with the men in the harness, but as we were getting on very rapidly at the time, it was not considered necessary. After we shoved off in the boats the labor was not as severe as it was when we were on the sledge, but we suffered more from cold sitting still in the boats.

---

* Correction by witness.

While working through the leads we generally hauled in alongside of a floe piece at the noon-time for our dinner, and at night we hauled out and made camp for the night near the edge of the floe, in a convenient place to launch our boats. Very often as the boats passed through the opening, one following the other in regular order, the first cutter would pass through, she would cause sufficient motion in the ice to start the pack in motion in the immediate vicinity, and the passage that had been open to the boat that had already passed through would probably be closed to the next boat coming along. Sometimes it would nip and catch the whale-boat; at other times it would catch the second cutter, which was the rear boat, sometimes cutting off their passage entirely. The other boats would have to stop and haul the other boat over the floe or she would take a circuitous route through the leads. As the season advanced the winds became stronger and the ice in the vicinity of the New Siberian Islands commenced to be more broken up, and there was more open water, so that while we had open water to sail in we got along quite rapidly. At this time we were carrying our boat sleds on the top of the boat and carrying our provisions inside of the boats.

An equal distribution of the provisions had not been made up to this time, the greater part of the pemmican being carried in the first cutter and the whale-boat, the pemmican being used from the boat which contained the largest amount at the time being.

In transporting the boats over the floe, where a lead, we generally hauled the boat out, discharging her provisions, and we would then haul her out, mount the boat on the sled, and haul the boat up to the opposite edge of the floe, then return with the sled and mount our provisions, tents, and camp equipage and haul it to the other side of the floe, each boat's crew taking care of and hauling its own gear. In this way we got on quite rapidly, owing to the pleasant rivalry between the boats' crews as to who would first get across the floe.

When the boats were sailing in open water I was ordered to keep within hail at all times of the commanding officer; Mr. Chipp, in the second cutter, always bringing up the rear. When the assignment was made of the officers and crews to the boats, Jack Cole, boatswain, was assigned to my boat, Captain De Long informing me at the time that Cole was the best fore-and-aft sailor out of New York; that he had sailed the Dreadnaught across the Atlantic, and had served as a watch officer in all the ocean races. He acted as coxswain of the whale-boat most of the time. On the day that we expected to reach or sight the New Siberian Islands there was a good deal of open water, considerable wind, and the boats were running very rapidly. Before shoving off in the morning from the floe the captain directed us to fill all our kettles, pots, and pans with snow for use as drinking water and for making tea. He also directed us to make our tea in the boats, on this day for the first time; that if the open water continued he would run all day, in hopes of reaching the islands that night. About noon-time he passed the word to my boat, directing me to issue the proper amount of pemmican and to make our tea in the boat. The second cutter being astern of me, he also directed me to pass the word astern to Mr. Chipp. We lit the fire in the cooking stoves and proceeded to melt the snow and make the tea, but during dinner time Mr. Chipp's boat fell a long way astern. There was a good deal of wind, and the ice was in rapid motion, whirling in all directions. The first cutter ran through a lead; I was close aboard the first cutter, and followed quickly after, but before Mr. Chipp could come through the opening, the ice closed on him. We continued on for about an hour, and the second cutter not appearing, Captain De Long ran his boat in alongside a floe and I ran the whale-boat in alongside of him. We waited for a little while to see if the second cutter would come up. The captain then directed the most of the people to go on the floe in the direction in which the second cutter was last seen, to assist in getting the second cutter through. After the hands had started from the first cutter and the whale-boat, the crew of the second cutter was seen coming over the floe, carrying their gear and making a deposit of it and returning for their boat. I think before our party got to Chipp's relief he managed to get his boat clear of the ice and launched again. He then joined company with the other two boats, and explained that his boat had got nipped in the ice and was stove. It was necessary to put a patch on her. The delay in putting on the patch gave the ice a chance to close in, which caused his delay in joining the other two boats. By this mishap, we considered that we had lost about three hours. The wind was freshening all the time, and carrying our sleds on the rail of our boats made them very top-heavy. They were large oaken sleds, and were laid along the boats athwartships just forward of the masts. We got under way and continued to run in the direction of the New Siberian Islands, expecting to make them at any moment. The sea was so heavy, the boats being overloaded and top-heavy from the weight of the sleds, that they commenced to make very bad weather. The first cutter and whale-boat were doing pretty well, but both boats were taking in considerable water. The second cutter was behaving very badly. When the second cutter came within hail of the captain's boat, Lieutenant Chipp said he would have to haul out or heave his sled overboard, as he was in danger of swamping. All three boats tried to weather a point of ice beyond which was a cut-off [cove*], and from which we could readily haul out; but failing in this, we hauled out on the left [weather*] edge of the pack. There was a good steady sea rolling in then, which made this maneuver difficult and dangerous. A little while after we hauled out the boats the whole of the pack had driven in together, so that there was little or no water to be seen. The New Siberian Islands were in sight at this time. Several people in the whale-boat said they saw the land. I believed I saw the land, and after hauling out I heard other persons in each of the boats say that they had seen the land; it bore to the southward of us.

We camped that night and we were directed to cut up our sleds for fuel in order to save the alcohol. There was so much wind, and the ice was in such rapid motion, that we expected to be able to launch the boats on the morrow. On the next morning the pack was driven close together, the wind apparently having set the pack down on to the land. The land in the morning was in plain sight, estimated anywheres from ten to fifteen miles distant; it might be more, it might be less. The captain said it was the island of Fadejowski. His observations had been good, and he hoped to make the channel leading between the island of New Siberia and the island of Fadejowski.

When the bread had given out, some time previous to this, and the ration of pemmican had been raised from a pound and a quarter to a pound and a half and as high as one and three-quarter pounds of pemmican per day, the whole of the working gang was found to have fallen down in flesh, although they were strong and vigorous; the men were trained down light, but what remained of them was hard as iron. The

---

* Correction by witness.

captain supplied them with an extra allowance of pemmican in the boats [for the purpose of*] building them up, as it appeared the people were running down too thin.

While on the march across the floe, we got a very small amount of game to what might have been expected of the summer season. We got a very few seals, one walrus and one bear, the whole of the march. I do not know the number of seals. Mr. Collins was the principal hunter while on the march. He carried his repeating Winchester rifle nearly the whole of the time, and got the majority of the seals shot on the march. At the time we were to the northward of the New Siberian Islands we caught a few seals, but, as I remember, I do not believe there was sufficient game procured to supply the party for two days.

Owing to the ice setting down on the islands it was impossible to move across the pack, and we were detained there about ten days. During this time a constant watch was kept, night and day, with orders throughout the camp for any person if they saw an opening in the ice to notify the commanding officer, that a start might be made if possible. While we were at this camp, Captain De Long sent for Lieutenant Chipp and myself to come to his tent. He asked Mr. Chipp if he thought it was possible to take the boats across the broken pack to the land. Mr. Chipp replied that he did not think it could be done with safety. The pack was all alive and in motion. There was not sufficient footing for the people to hold on to in transporting the boats, and we could not carry our provisions in the boats without staving their bottoms. He asked me my opinion, and asked me if I thought the pack was worse than when I had landed at Henrietta Island. I told him that the pack was equally bad, and I did not think it was possible to get the boats to the island in safety; that no doubt we could take the boats ashore, but when we got them there they would be worthless. He remarked that [in that case*] there would be no use in taking them there. At the same time it would have been unwise to have attempted to carry our provisions loosely over the floe, as the pemmican and the cans were awkward to hold, and in falling overboard would be apt to be lost. He also sent for Seaman Starr, who spoke and read German. The captain at this time had a small German pamphlet, known as one of Petermann's publications, that contained all the information that we possessed in regard to the New Siberian Islands and the approaches to the Lena River. Starr translated the pamphlet, Mr. Chipp, Captain De Long, and myself going over the chart, De Long tracking the line as Starr made the translation. At this time De Long laid out the course down through the channel between the New Siberian Island and Fadejowski Island, pointing out the prominent points where we would make camps in the evening, allowing for a good day's work; or, in case of separation, as a rendezvous. He also discussed freely the best mode of advancing from New Siberia Island to the Siberian coast, going from point to point and from island to island, to avoid as much as possible any long sea passage.

And the court then, at 12.05 p. m., took a recess until 12.30 p. m., at which time it reconvened, with all the members, the judge-advocate, and the witness under examination, present, and the witness then continued his answer to the pending question as follows:

There was no different [difference of*] opinion in regard to the course to be taken toward the Lena Delta, Cape Barkin being decided on as the best point to reach. Captain De Long at this time expressed himself as being confident that we would find natives near this point win-

---

* Correction by witness.

ter or summer. On the chart were marked winter huts, which further led us to suppose that we would find natives there during the winter season. I suggested at this time that in case we made Cape Barkin it would be better to try to make an entrance to the river through one of its eastern branches, because there were many branches making out to the eastward and but two or three to the northward. I also mentioned at the time that the steamer Lena had remained off the north mouths of the river for three weeks, and eventually was obliged to make an eastern entrance. Mr. Chipp said, "Never mind, Melville; she was a big ship; we are only small boats, so we will have no difficulty about getting in." De Long remarked at the same time, "You will have no difficulty in your navigation, in case you shall become separated, because the coast line to the northward runs east and west near Barkin, and north and south on the east side of the delta, and in case you strike the coast running east and west you will know that you are to the westward of Barkin, then work along the coast to the eastward until you make Barkin, when you will be sure to find natives. You will there undoubtedly find a native pilot who will pilot you into the main river. In case you strike the east side of the delta, in the line running north and south, you will know well enough that you are on the east side of the delta; then you can work up to the northward to Barkin and find a native pilot. "However," he said, "you keep within sight of me, and it will be all right." I think that was all that transpired at the council in the tent. During the time that we lay there for ten days, we did what little fitting we could to our boats. We puttied up the seams with tallow from the pemmican and calked them with pieces of rag and lampwick—anything we could use for the purpose. Mr. Chipp looked after the fittings of his boat, and I looked after the fittings of mine.

Nindemann, who had charge of all the small fittings around the boats, was looking after the fittings of the first cutter. We fastened the boat covers down over the forward part of the boat [cover*], and made a mast coat on the boat capable [for the purpose*] of holding the cover up on the mast, but the captain cautioned me at this time against cutting the boat cover of the whale-boat. All small fittings of this kind were prepared in all three boats while we lay at the "Ten-Day" camp. I think washboards or little pieces of weather cloths were fitted on the second cutter at this time. I am not sure about the first cutter. At this time I did not have the weather cloths to the whale-boat.

By the latter part of August, or after remaining there about ten days, the ice commenced to open, or drift down through the channel between New Siberia and Fadejowski. As soon as this was observed we hauled the boats about a half a mile over the pack and landed [launched*] them, and worked our way to the southward or toward the land. A few days previous to this time land was sighted away to the eastward of us, which we knew could be no other than New Siberian Island. De Long was pleased with his navigation, as he said to me the old chronometer had been upset from the sled and tumbled upside down on all the journey, and yet it was running as true as it was when we left San Francisco. He told me that he had struck his longitude almost exactly; that it was just to the northward of Fadejowski Island.

Toward evening of the first day after we got under way from the "Ten-Day" camp, the ice closed in upon us and we were obliged to haul out; the watch was set, looking out for a movement of the ice, and very early the next day all hands were called and launched the boats. We

---

* Correction by witness.

worked that day to the southward, between the islands, sighting land on the starboard side only, that is, not seeing the land on the New Siberian side of the boat. Before night we were entirely clear of ice in this channel. Beyond was an ice blink to the southward. We thought at times we could see the ice itself to the southward. An ice blink is a white or a light mark in the heavens, that shows over a line or pack of ice, just the reverse of a blue spot that shows in the heavens over water in an ice pack. We ran along the coast on the southern side of Fadejowski, looking for a place to land. The water was very shoal, and we made some [several*] ineffectual attempts to get ashore. Toward 6 or 7 o'clock in the evening we pulled in towards the beach near an ice foot at the head passes [one of the headlands*] of the island. The captain directed me to put the most of my people into his boat, his boat being grounded, and go in with the whale-boat to try and make a landing. I also put out all my gear and pemmican into the first cutter. After trying two or three places, I found a place where the water was bold enough to get the whale-boat in, and jumped ashore. We then used the whale-boat as a ferry-boat to land all the people and all the supplies, and then hauled the three boats up on the beach. This was really our first camp on the land, from the time that we joined the ship. While we were at Bennett Island we camped on the ice foot, the island on that side being too steep to set up our tents. We camped there that night, and turned in. The people ran around the island in every direction, and they had to be cautioned not to go too far. Hunting parties were out with their guns, and found traces of reindeer, but none were sighted. Mr. Newcomb, with his shot-gun, shot a few ducks, probably half a dozen; no other game was procured at this time. Some of the people found a deserted ivory hunter's hut, made near the banks of a small river, which De Long found marked on his Peterman chart. The next morning we started to work on to the westward to try to make a run to the first headland on the island of Kotelnoi. We worked all day to the westward. There is a shoal making out to the southward that lay in our course. The wind again commenced to blow, and we tried to make a landing. The whale-boat was detailed, as on the evening previous, to find a landing. We found the nearest we could approach to the beach was from five hundred to seven hundred yards. The bottom was soft mud, and it was considered best to stand on. The night looked bad, and it was coming on to blow. The captain was anxious to land to avoid a bad night on the shoals. This seemed impossible; so we worked on and off the shoals all night; sometimes the boats grounding, and all hands had to get them off. The captain said that the shoal had increased very much to the southward from its former position as laid down on the chart. Toward morning it was blowing pretty fresh, and the second cutter got separated from us. We had a very bad night, and we ran for the nearest floe-piece, where we hauled out for breakfast, and after remaining there for a few hours the sea commenced to break over the floe-piece that we were on, and washed us out. By this time the second cutter hove in sight, and the three boats joined company and stood on to the southward and westward far enough to take them clear of the shoal. It was blowing pretty fresh at this time, and the captain headed his boat into the lead in the ice to get out of sea. I had no difficulty in following him, the whale-boat being a fast sailer; but the second cutter was much slower than either the first cutter or the whale-boat. For this reason she dropped astern; at the same time

---

* Correction by witness.

she was making very bad weather—that is she was taking in considerable water. The ice was all in motion at this time, the leads opening and closing. Toward 5 o'clock in the afternoon we lost sight of the second cutter altogether, but supposed that she would work down through different leads after us. About 6 or 7 o'clock in the evening we hauled out on a solid portion of the floe, but the ice shoving up, we were obliged to shift from our position and haul over to another place.

The same evening the ice set in around us solid. The boats were moored in two little holes of water. I do not think we hauled the boats out at this time. We set up the tents, and the birds that had been shot at the island were distributed between the two boats' crews, the first cutter, and the whale-boat. We ate these for supper, or for breakfast. The next morning Captain De Long had a large black flag made of a piece of tarpaulin or black oil-cloth of some kind, and hoisted at his mast-head, as a signal to attract the attention of Lieutenant Chipp in the second cutter. A lookout was kept at all times on one of the high masses of ice for the approach of the second cutter. The weather was very stormy here all day, and we were all very miserable, but from the fatigue of the previous night on the shoals and the cold, the sleep and the rest were very acceptable. On the second or third day the man on the lookout reported Lieutenant Chipp's boat in sight. I think Aniguin, the Indian, was on watch at the time, and if he was not the man on the lookout I think he was the man who saw the boat. We watched the boat as she ran along the edge of the ice. She hauled out on the floe, and after a while we saw two people approaching us. They reached our camp that evening, and proved to be Lieutenant Chipp and Seaman Kuchne. We were all very glad to see him, because we knew that he had heavy weather, and feared some accident might have happened to his boat. He made his report to the commanding officer, and paid a visit to the two tents in which I was located. He sat down, and we had a talk, and he told me all about his troubles, and of the evening of bad weather, which, he stated, as he was making toward the ice the sea came tumbling into his boat so rapidly that she nearly swamped; that they pulled [bailed*] all the time [and were*] very wet and frozen. He said that when the boat struck the ice there was only one man in the boat who was able to jump out of the boat with a painter and hold on to it. I think he said that this was Seaman Star; that himself and Mr. Dunbar, sitting up cramped in the boat, were so badly used up that they had to be lifted out of the boat. Mr. Dunbar before this time had been very sick on the retreat on the ice. It was his business to track out a road for the advancing of our parties after the captain had laid the course. He traversed the floe to such an extent that every evening he was actually used up. Captain De Long cautioned him not to do this; that he was working himself down, and told him never to put a harness on to assist in hauling any of the boats, as he had shown symptoms of heart disease or giddiness of the head. But he used to traverse over the floe like a pointer dog, and in this manner used himself up. During the time that they were in the boat Mr. Dunbar and Lieutenant Chipp, while in smooth water, used to take turns in steering; but when it was bad weather Mr. Chipp never allowed any one to steer the boat but himself. For this reason he was very much exhausted when he joined company. The next day Lieutenant De Long ordered an advance of boats over the pack to where the second cutter lay in the open water. This was a very difficult task, as the pack was all loose and more or less

---

* Correction by witness.

in motion; yet we carried all our provisions, also our light gear, as far over as the second cutter, Nindemann and Bartlett going ahead staking the road for the boats to follow along. Toward the afternoon we arrived with all our gear safe at the open water where the second cutter was. This was probably a distance of a mile to a mile and a quarter, to a wide lead. After getting ready to start, the captain fell overboard in getting into his boat. Somebody hauled him in over the stern. He went clear down out of sight, and of course was wet to the skin.

The island of Kotelnoi was in sight, but we could not have stopped at this time, and so pitched camp, and the same evening got into a bight of water formed by the ice and an opening in the land. It was blowing pretty fresh. The boats were running pretty rapidly. We hauled up at the edge of the ice, the captain takeing most of the men out of my boat; but soon he sent me in to sound the way to the cape, and, if possible, round the cape. As soon as he saw me approaching the land, and turn our boat round and return, the other two boats advanced, the second cutter taking the lead, rounded the cape and hauled out in a little cove or bay, the hills and mountains of Kotelnoi to the northward and westward of us. I went alongside of the first cutter and received the remainder of my crew. Following the first cutter all three boats hauled out on the island of Kotelnoi.

And the court then, at 1.30 p. m., pending the further examination of this witness, adjourned to meet on Monday, the 13th day November, 1882, at 10.30 a. m.

THIRTY-THIRD DAY.

NAVY DEPARTMENT,
Washington, D. C., Monday, November 13, 1882—10.30 a. m.

The court met pursuant to the adjournment of Saturday, November 11, 1882.

Present, Commodore William G. Temple, United States Navy, president; Captain Joseph N. Miller, United States Navy, Commander Frederick V. McNair, United States Navy, members; and Master Samuel C. Lemly, United States Navy, judge-advocate.

The record of the proceedings of Saturday, November 11, 1882, the thirty-second day of the inquiry, was then read, and, after correcting clerical errors, approved.

Chief-Engineer GEORGE W. MELVILLE, the witness under examination, then came in and continued his testimony, in answer to the pending question, which was repeated by the judge-advocate, as follows:

Give a detailed statement of the retreat after the loss of the vessel.

The WITNESS. We set up the tents. The people gathered large quantities of drift-wood that they found on the low sand-spit, and built large fires to dry our clothing and warm ourselves. Before we left the island [ice*] the previous day Captain De Long detached two men from the second cutter, and sent Seaman Manson to the whale-boat, and the cook, Ah Sam, to the first cutter. While at the "Ten-Day" camp the provisions had been equally divided, except one can of pemmican, that the first cutter was still carrying for the second cutter. We remained at the camp on the island of Kotelnoi, one night. The next day all hands started out to see if they could find game. Many reindeer tracks

---

* Correction by witness.

were found, but no reindeer were seen by anybody. While running on the south side of the island, before making this harbor or this camp, Mr. Newcomb shot a number of ducks from the bow of the whale-boat. They were equally distributed among the messes, and ate at the camp at Kotelnoi. The next morning we sailed the boats around the point, and tried to work along the water-leads between the grounded ice and the shore. We proceeded this way for about half a day, when the ice had shoved up on to the land so that the boats had to be hauled out on their keels for a distance of more than a mile on the sand [snow*]. Wherever there were sand patches the boats were hauled across the sand patches. All the small gear and camp equipment was carried on the people's backs to lighten the boats. I think every person that was able to carry anything to assist at this time did carry the gear. Each boat's crew handled its own boat and carried its own gear. While making this approach, Mr. Dunbar was struck with faintness or giddiness, which the doctor thought to be heart disease. He dropped down while assisting in hauling the boat. He was told to desist from doing any further work, and early in the afternoon we got our boats floating again, and made a good run along the south side of the islands, until night fell. The boats were hauled out. We camped. The next day launched the boats, and kept on in the boats, pulling most of the time, but sailing whenever the wind served. This evening we camped on the southernmost point of Kotelnoi. It was about the 6th of September we shoved off from Kotelnoi, intending to make the run to the next and nearest island, Stolbovoi. Before shoving off we filled our pans and pots and kettles with snow, to be used for drinking-water. The wind was quite fresh, and we had considerable to do in keeping the boats clear of the ice. We were under way with the sails all day, all three boats keeping pretty close together. Toward night it came on to blow very hard; the boats were making very bad weather. The whale-boat jibed and broached to and once filled with water. We lowered the sail and bailed her out and kept her head to the sea with the oars, and caught up with the other boats again. We were under way all night this night, running into the loose pack and broken ice, at times losing sight of each other, but coming [running*] in the same direction. We got into the loose ice, where the sea did not have much effect on us, and the three boats hauled up at a large floe-piece in the morning, where we made tea and had breakfast. It had been pretty cold the night before; all hands were very wet and most of us pretty badly used up. The sun came out fine that day, and after working on toward the island of Stolbovoi, which was in sight to the eastward of us, we hauled out on a floe-piece, pitched our tents, and lay there until the next morning, when we got under way and stood to the westward. The ice was considerably scattered, and we rowed and poled the boats through the loose pack. During this day we camped on the ice. About the 9th of September we sighted the island of Semenowski, and worked until late that night to try and make the land, to camp on the island. Darkness and fog set in, and we hauled out on a large floe-piece that was grounded near the island. On the morning of the 10th we found ourselves within a mile or a mile and a half of the island. We got the boats under way and pulled around the northern end of the island, turned to the southward and continued along the west side of the island to the southward until noontime. A convenient place offering to land and have our dinner presenting itself, the boats were hauled into a little cove, and we

---
* Correction by witness.

went ashore and got water and made the tea and ate our dinner. The people who went after the tea-water reported to the captain that they had found the tracks of a bear and the tracks of reindeer. After dinner we started to proceed to the southward with the boats, and a hunting party was detailed from each boat to spread themselves across the island and march to the southward, to intercept any game that might be on the island. The hunting party came across a doe and her fawn. The doe was killed by the hunting party; the fawn escaped. The hunting party hailed the boats; the reindeer was tumbled down the banks and put in the second cutter, and De Long directed us all to land. By this time it had got toward evening; we set up the tents, dressed the deer, and cooked portions of it for supper. In the mean time hunting parties were sent out to try and capture the fawn. At the same time Mr. Newcomb, with a shot-gun, shot a number of ptarmigan and a couple of geese. The hunt for the fawn was not successful. We had two suppers that night of the reindeer meat. Although the weather was cold, it was wet and raw. We consumed the deer, as it would be likely to spoil if we attempted to carry the fresh meat in our boats. The next day was Sunday. A hunt was again instituted for the fawn, which was unsuccessful, and we lay in camp all day Sunday. While we lay there on Sunday, Nindemann fitted new wash-boards or cloths to the first cutter. I cut the boat cover from the stern up as far as the foremost [mast*] and had Bartlett and Mr. Cole fit stanchions inside of the boat; the lower ends rested on the ribbons, the upper ends sixteen or eighteen inches above the rail, and bored holes in the gunwale of the boat to lash the stanchions fast. We tacked the canvas around on the outside and sewed a piece of canvas across the forward part of the boat cover to keep the water out and high enough to go [to prevent water coming*] over the forecastle [from tumbling*] into the cockpit of the boat. This gave us weather-cloths eighteen inches high, and the cloths were long enough or wide enough to hold up on the men's backs to the windward when they sat in the boat. All the boats had some fitting of this kind at the island of Semenov (Semenowski). About 8 o'clock on Monday morning the boats were shoved off, standing to the southward, Lieutenant De Long informing us that it was about ninety miles southwest to Barkin, the point of our destination. We stopped at the island of Vashily, and one of the boats I think left a record. I did not see the record go ashore, but I understood it was left there; but the island was visited for some purpose. We ran on until about noontime. The wind was freshening at the time, the boats making pretty good weather. We hauled out about noontime at the edge of the ice-floe and had our dinner. It was this day, before noontime, on the day before we arrived at the island of Semenov, that in running through the loose ice the plug of the whale-boat was forced out; at the same time she struck heavily on some loose pieces of ice. I thought she was stove, and hailed the captain and told him the difficulty. He ordered me to take her out to the nearest floe and haul her out, the other boats hauling up at the same time and having their dinner. I found the bottom of the boat stove a little at one of the joints; put on a leather [lead*] patch, sawed off the bottom of the boat plug, so that it should not be pushed out hereafter. That same afternoon in following the first cutter through a narrow lead in the ice, I struck the starboard side of the whale-boat against the sharp ice and stove her in; this was patched by a piece of wood with copper tacks. After leaving the edge of the ice-floe, we

---

* Correction by witness.

ran on, making pretty good weather, but the wind freshening all the time. While on the ice I asked Mr. Chipp if he had received the remainder of his pemmican. He said he had not, but he supposed he would get it this day as we were toward the end of the ice. I do not know whether he should have had a whole can or a portion of a can of pemmican from the first cutter. I had none belonging to any one else except to my own boat's crew. Toward o'clock it was blowing so fresh that the boats reefed down. The whale-boat had a double-reefed sail at this time While we were in the pack and in the loose leads, I had Mr. Cole act as coxswain all the time. As we generally hauled out at night everybody could rest. The crew was divided into two watches working at the oars, but necessarily two hours each. But when we got in the open water, after the first night's gale, it became necessary to put the other three seamen in the watches at steering, as there was little or no rowing done when we were in the open water. Mr. Cole was pretty old, and the cold weather and sleeplessness appeared to make him stupid, so that I directed that Leach, Manson, and Wilson should take tricks at steering. About 7 o'clock in the evening it was blowing a whole gale of wind, and the boats were making considerable water. At this time the wind was about northeast, and we were running dead before it, keeping the sail out by a boat-hook to prevent its jibing. I had orders to keep astern of the first cutter, but the sea was running so that every time I would lower the sail a little to slacken the boat's speed and have the men gather in the belly of the sail, the sea would come in on us over the stern. The sea was so heavy and running before the wind that it was impossible to work the boat well with tiller and sail to deaden her speed. About 7 o'clock in the evening some person in the whale-boat told me that the captain was making signals to me. At this time I was on his weather bow, to windward and ahead of him. I looked and saw him wave his hand at me or toward the boat. I then told the man at the halliards to lower the sail very carefully and have a hand or two gather in the sail at the foot from the water, to slacken the speed of the boat, and drift down toward the first cutter. This slackening the speed of the boat caused the sea to come tumbling in over the stern, but we drifted down so as to be almost within hail of the first cutter. At this time the captain, seeing the condition my boat was in, shook his head and waved his arm, as much as to say—I understood it to mean—"Go on;" or that he did not want to speak to me. At the same time he turned around and waved his arm toward the second cutter. I supposed at this time that he wanted the second cutter to come within hail, either for instructions or to put the pemmican in Chipp's boat, in case it had not been done before we left the edge of the ice. I do not know whether Lieutenant Chipp got the remainder of his pemmican or not. I understood the signal "to run and take care of ourselves," although I had orders to keep in sight of the commanding officer at all times; but the sea was so heavy and the boat was taking in so much water that I felt the necessity of running to keep before it. I then directed the boat to be hauled a point or two further to the southward, so as to bring the wind on the quarter to prevent the jibing of the sail and make better weather. In a few minutes I was out of sight of the other two boats. In fact this is the last I saw of the second cutter and her people, and I saw nothing more of the first cutter and her people until I found them dead in the Lena Delta [except Nindemann and Noros, whom I met at Bulun about November 2*].

When the boat was hauled on the wind a little she made much better

---

* Correction by witness.

weather. I then told Mr. Danenhower, who was sitting by me in the stern-sheets, that if this weather continued, unless we could come up with the ice, it would be necessary to heave the boat to. He said, "Yes, Melville, you should have hove her to before." We then set about making the drag. The different articles in the boat being discussed which would best answer the purpose, Mr. Danenhower proposed to use the oars and other light gear we had in the boat to use as a drag. I said that would not do, for we might lose them, and we would have to hold on to our oars. After some discussion I concluded to use tent-poles lashed together and covered by a piece of canvas, giving us about six square feet of surface. The ends of the tent-poles were tipped with brass, which answered for the purpose of sinking it, but was not considered quite enough. We unrove a small watch-tackle we had in the boat to use as an anchor, and the additional weight of the blocks to be used in assisting in sinking the drag. When all things were ready, Mr. Danenhower said, "Melville, will you let me heave her to?" I did not answer for a moment, but thought if there was any advantage in making use of a professional man's ability it was my duty to permit him to perform the evolution. I told him to go ahead. When all things were in readiness, the oars prepared, and the sails lowered, Mr. Danenhower giving the orders, the boat was first brought nearly round, head to the sea, but she shipped considerable water, nearly swamping. Then the boat was put off again and steadied in the water, until a quiet spell came, when a second time she was brought round fairly, and the drag hove out. At first the drag kept rising to the surface and drifting home on us. We had two fire-pots in the boat or cooking-stoves. I directed the copper one to be run down over the drag-rope to assist in burying the drag. This kept the drag below the surface all right, and now all did pretty well.

In dragging the boat over the ice the lower gudgeon of the rudder had become broken, and I had temporarily repaired it many times. But on this occasion the iron work could not be repaired, so that for that moment the boat was steered by a steering oar or paddle at times—sometimes the steering-oar, sometimes the paddle. We cleared the stern-sheets to make room for the man with the steering-oar. The boat kept taking in water during the night, and all hands remained under the shelter of the weather-cloth or covered themselves with the waterproof blankets we had in the boat, and kept down out of the force of the gale. I directed the three seamen to take the watches, to keep the boats's head up to the sea, the rest of the people being employed all night long in bailing. This continued until the evening of the 13th of September. I should have said that the gale occurred on the 12th of September. About evening of the 13th, about 5 o'clock, the wind and sea had gone down so that it was perfectly safe to run. We hauled in the drag, got the boat under way, and stood first to the westward and then to the southwest off [for*] the coast of the Lena Delta. When we heaved the boat to I considered that we had run about forty miles, and that the boat was hove to about fifty miles from the Lena Delta. During the whole of the gale the wind was about northeast. This would give us a southwest drift, without allowing for the current, and would draw [have driven*] us down in the direction in which I was ordered to go; but when I got the boat under way my intention was to stand to the southwest. On the morning of the 14th the boat grounded on a shoal, out of sight of land, the young ice making along the coast.

---

* Correction by witness.

And the court then, at 12 m., took a recess until 12.30 p. m., and then reconvened, with all the members, the judge-advocate, and the witness under examination present; and the witness then continued his testimony, in answer to the pending question, as follows:

Several of the people stood up in the boat, looking in the direction in which we supposed we saw what looked like land, but were not certain. I tried to work to the southward, but always brought up in shoal water. I worked to the eastward, taking some time trying [trying from time to time*] to work to the southward again to the land, in hopes of making Cape Barkin, as my orders directed. I worked on to the eastward all day long and tried to work to the southward, but would always bring up in shoal water. Toward six o'clock in the evening the weather looked bad, and I was in shoal water; so feared if a blow came on the boat would be rolled over in the surf on the shoals; so I worked as rapidly as possible toward the eastward, until I found the water deepening, and then I laid the course southeast, for I was now standing, as I supposed, into the bay of Maloi. The next morning at 6 o'clock I put the boat about and stood off to the southwest, in hopes of striking the north and south coast of the delta. The current running out of the rivers to the eastward gave me so much of an easterly set that I did not make the coast-line on the eastern side of the delta until the morning of the 16th. As we approached the coast we saw the mountains to the southward. Mr. Danenhower advised me to go to the southward to where we saw the mountains, but my orders told me to go to Barkin. Remembering my instructions, after I struck the east coast of the delta, standing north and south, I should follow up the coast-line to the northward to Barkin. At this time I cannot state how far I was to the southward of Barkin on the east coast, but about six o'clock on the morning of the 16th we raised two low sand-spits or headlands forming the mouth of a large river. The water was muddy, and upon tasting it we found the water was brackish. The people had not had anything to drink since the noon of the 12th, and were all anxious to drink the water, which we found was brackish only. I stood in between the two headlands, and as we approached we found the water getting sweeter. I tried to make a landing at one of the headlands at the mouth of the river, but the shoal made so far off and the swell rolling in, nearly capsized the boat. We managed to get her off and stood up the muddy river between the two headlands. We soon found that the water was perfectly fresh, and from this I concluded I was in one of the eastern branches of the river. I had a small chart in pencil that was copied from De Long's chart while we were on the march. This showed many entrances on the eastern side of the delta. The river that I made was very wide at its mouth, the headlands being barely discernible from one side of the river to the other, and the river discharges its water very rapidly. The wind was from the eastward. We worked on up the river; the channel was so crooked that we were continually grounding. The river was full of shoals and sand-spits. Sometimes we would be in three or four fathoms of water, and at times the boat would be aground. We kept a man sounding all the time with a seven-foot tent-pole. In sounding on the north coast of the delta, as well as to the eastward of the delta, I got soundings with the tent-pole. My orders directed me to go to Barkin, where I would find a pilot, but I had got into the river and was loath to turn back. I did not know how far I was from Barkin at the time, and in talking the matter over with

---

* Correction by witness.

the people in the boat I made up my mind that if the river did not show evidence of being a narrow and deeper channel at noon-time that I would turn round and go out of the river and try to make Barkin in accordance with my orders. I had been trying all the morning to make a landing. We were all very badly cramped, cold, and wet by sitting quiet in the boat during the gale. At 12 o'clock I stopped the boat and was about to pull her up [put her about*] to go out of the river again to try to work my way up to Barkin, when Bartlett, hearing our conversation, said, "Why, Mr. Melville, this river is as big as the Mississippi at New Orleans, and instead of being a narrow swamp [river*] as you suppose it is, it must be one of the main branches of the river." From what I had heard and seen, and from what the commanding officer of the ship had said, I understood, or was made to believe, that there were many natives all over the Lena Delta; many hunting lodges and huts and permanent huts, marked winter huts on the chart, in which I supposed natives lived all the year round. After my experience of the four days previous in the gale, and after the gale at sea, I did not want to go to sea again, and thought it better to try and find the natives anywhere in the vicinity of the river. I simply headed the boat up stream, kept working the boat up the river toward its source or head. Toward evening of the first day, after making many attempts to land, we sighted a hut on the bank, and that evening hauled out above it. The hut was deserted, but there was evidence of people having been there but a short time before. We hauled our boat up, got all our gear out of the boat, built a fire in the hut, and set about drying our clothes and making tea for supper.

On the evening of the 12th of September, when we dropped company with the first cutter, I thought it prudent to put everybody on half rations, that is, a half of a pound and a half of pemmican a day, or three-quarters of a pound of pemmican per man per day. By so doing our five days' provisions was made to stand out for about ten days. When we got out of the boat to go to the hut we were all so badly used up with the cramps in our legs, feet, and hands, which were so badly swollen from the cold, that the majority of us were barely able to walk. We had paddled round in the icy waters of the river, our moccasins all open, but [and*] I supposed that the ice-water would draw the frost out of our feet and legs; but after we made a fire and crawled in the hut our feet and legs began to thaw out; the pains were terrible; nobody slept that night; and in the morning our feet and legs were worse off than they were the day before.

We shoved off the boat in the morning and continued up the river against the stream, the river all the time making to the northward of west, sometimes as high as northwest. On the little chart that I had was an island laid down in the mid-channel of the river, and the river was very broad. This led me to suppose that I was in the main branch of the river, near Cape Bukoff. We worked along all day, and finally turned a headland to the southward; I thought it was the main branch of the river itself. It was a large range [long reach*] of water, making due north and south to the northward of the camp and the southward. I made the camp on a sand-spit at the foot of a headland forty or fifty feet high. We called this Mud Camp, owing to the muddy condition of the beach on which we camped. Mr. Danenhower, Bartlett, and some one else went off the on top of a hill to sleep in some hunter's lodge that we saw on top of the hill. In the morning got ready to shove off. All

---

* Correction by witness.

hands in the boat, with but one or two exceptions, were pretty badly crippled from frozen feet and legs. We gathered up all our gear, and getting it in the boat, got ready to start. Mr. Danenhower said: "Melville, if you like, I will be your coxswain for to-day." I said: "All right; tumble in, everybody." We pushed the boat off, standing to the southward an hour and a half or two hours. On this day I think the wind was from the westward; however, we stood to the southward, and the wind was abeam. The people were pretty badly crippled; the boat was taking in considerable water, and after being under way for an hour and a half or two hours, we came up with a couple of nice-looking houses on the west bank of the river, looking as though intended for a permanent dwelling-place of the natives. We landed here and unloaded the boat and carried all our gear up to the houses to dry them out. Our two previous attempts at camping not giving us any rest or sleep, we staid at this place all day and all night. We found the huts well supplied with wood and evidences that the people had left there but a short time before; fresh offal of fish and reindeer and stuff of that kind was lying about there.

On the 19th, as I supposed, in the main river, keeping the west bank of the river aboard, and after running a little while we passed from the river into a great bay, fifteen or twenty miles across, on which the land could not be seen on the opposite side. Then I found myself in a bay, a labyrinth of sand-spits and shoals, but still kept trying to work to the southward. Finally we raised a headland to the southward that showed some houses on it. I made toward these houses, in hopes of reaching them by noon-time, where we could cook our tea and take our dinner, but the channel was so intricate that we could not haul [go a mile*] in any one direction; it was continually bringing up on a sand-spit. About 1 o'clock in the afternoon, we finally effected a landing to to the eastward of the huts which I was trying to make. We went on shore and had our dinner, at this time a quarter of a pound of pemmican and tea. We soon saw the evidences of this having been a thriving fishing station, and got ready to shore off again to work our way toward the huts. We saw three natives approaching us in their canoes; we pulled up toward them, beckoning. The natives came alongside; they appeared a little alarmed at first, and kept away from us; a young fellow, more venturesome than his two companions, came alongside, and I told one of the men to offer him a piece of pemmican to eat; told him first to eat a bite of it himself. This brought him alongside, and he took the pemmican. I then told one of the men to seize his canoe and hold on to it. This alarmed him a little at first. We then showed him our guns and hatchets, and other gear we had in the boat, and made him understand by signs that we were friendly toward him. In the meantime the other two men, with their canoes, had drifted with the stream and hauled out on the beach, and we hauled out the whale-boat by the canoes. We made some tea and put a little alcohol in it to please the natives; the alcohol was put only in that given to the three natives, about a table-spoonful of alcohol in each. They gave us some fish and a goose and a piece of venison. Our people chopped them up and put them in the kettle and made a stew, and all hands partook of it. In the mean time we got on very comfortable terms with the natives, and by means of pencil sketches we made them understand that we wanted them to take us to Bulun. They made me understand that it was impossible, stamping on the ground and talking of the "booze." At this time we supposed the "booze" meant the ground; afterward we found

---
*Correction by witness.

it meant the ice in the river. When I insisted on their conducting me to Bulun one of the young men in pantomime laid down on the ground, and by pantomime made us understand that we would all die, saying, "Pomerie, pomerie," which we afterwards learned meant that we would die. We in turn made them understand by pantomime that we must go to a place to get something to eat and a place to sleep. I made them a sketch, putting one canoe ahead of another, one man paddling, the whale-boat as she looked, and the other two canoes following. I made them understand that they must take me to that place to sleep; they understood me very readily. As soon as we finished our meal we started off, and they conducted us to the place where the houses were, on the headland, to which we were trying to get them to go along [I had been trying to get all day long*]. On arriving there we found that they had been fishing there. They had their nets and fishing gear there; in the settlement there were two or three habitable huts and storehouses, and a grave-yard. This place I afterward found to be called Little Cape Borkhia. We staid there that night, the natives staying there with us and catching us fish. In the morning they got ready to go. I then tried to induce them to conduct us to Bulun, or to go with us as a pilot. In the morning we found that one of the three natives had left. He said the evening before that he was going to get us something to eat. When we got ready to shove off, the young man not desiring to go with us, I tried to force him into the boat. At this he became very much excited and went through the motions of dying, stamping on the ground, seized the gunwale of the boat as in the act of hauling her along the land, crying, "Pomerie, pomerie booze pomerie," which I afterward found out meant that we would have to haul the boat over the ice in the river; that in attempting to get to Bulun we would die.

And the court then, at 1 p. m., pending the further examination of this witness, adjourned to meet to-morrow, the 14th day of November, 1882, at 10.30 a. m.

THIRTY-FOURTH DAY.

NAVY DEPARTMENT,
Washington, D. C., Tuesday, November 14, 1882—10.30 a. m.

The court met pursuant to the adjournment of yesterday.

Present, Commodore William G. Temple, United States Navy, president; Capt. Joseph N. Miller, United States Navy, Commander Frederick V. McNair, United States Navy, members; and Master Samuel C. Lemly, United States Navy, judge-advocate.

The record of the proceedings of yesterday, November 13, 1882, the thirty-third day of the inquiry, was then read, and, after correcting clerical errors, approved.

Chief Engineer GEORGE W. MELVILLE, the witness under examination, then came in and continued his testimony in answer to the pending question, which was repeated by the judge-advocate, as follows:

Question. Give a detailed statement of the retreat after the loss of the vessel.

The WITNESS. The natives would not go along with us to pilot us. I pushed off the boat and tried to work my own way up the river, following along the west bank. The water was so shoal along the bank of

----
* Correction by witness.

the river that I was obliged to beat [push*] out into the bay, following the channel and sounding with tent-poles. I always tried to work to the southward. The bay was so full of shoals and sand-spits that we could not go in any particular direction—just kept over the deep water by missing the sand-spits. We worked all day in the boat until about 5 o'clock in the evening, when it seemed impossible to go anywhere except to the eastward, which was entirely out of the course. Toward evening the weather looked bad, and the wind blew so that about 5 o'clock in the evening we put the boat about, intending to return to the hut where the natives were. It began to hail and snow. As the darkness extended, the channel being so tortuous, it was impossible to run directly back to the place from which we started. After dark we found the boat in the lee of a shoal, which kept the sea from breaking over us, and then drove three tent-poles into the sand or mud, not having an anchor. I made the boat fast to the tent-poles by slipping the end of the painter, on which was a bowline, so that it might sink down to the surface of the earth and not pull the poles out. The night was very cold; wind and snow and hail; all hands were very uncomfortable. As soon as daylight came, got under way again and stood back to where we left the natives in the hut at Cape Borkhia. By this time we found that the people who had not been pretty badly frozen before were now very badly frozen. It was my intention to return to the huts, to induce the natives to pilot me through to Bulun, or to one of their villages, either to remain by them or make them prisoners—make them go with me. Toward 1 o'clock we were in the vicinity of the huts, but not quite sure of our position. We went ashore and made tea and had our dinner. While we were getting the dinner some of the men who had an argument jumped up on the bank and ran along in the direction in which the huts were supposed to be. They returned in a few minutes and said they could see the huts at Borkhia, and had been as far as the first place that we had taken dinner the day before. We then shoved off and came up to the huts at Cape Borkhia early in the evening. On our arrival there we found that there were four natives. The young man who had met us, who had worked and assisted us in getting our boat ashore and helped to carry a portion of our gear up to their huts was [not*] here. We then found that the young man had gone after the Starosti or head man of the village. He brought some venison with him and they got some more [fish†]. We got supper at the huts and slept there that night. The next morning we made the Starosti understand that I wanted to go to Bulun. He at first demurred about going to Bulun, but finally consented. He measured the draft of the water of the boat on his paddle. I made him understand that his boat drew about 6 inches of water, while mine drew about 2 feet. He appeared to understand that all right and we shoved off. Instead of going in the direction of Bulun, however, he went down the stream to the southward and eastward, and after knocking about in the shoals all day, finally landed in the evening on the beach, made a fire, and we camped on the beach that night. We got under way the next morning and reefed the sail of the boat, an he took us through a small river, and that night we camped in two or three deserted huts. The pilot made us understand that there was so little water in the bay that he could not go directly down to the village to which he was taking us. For that reason he would take us out of one of the small rivers to the sea, then back again, and then around an

---

*Correction by witness; strike out.   †Correction by witness.

island in the main river, and eventually to a deserted village called Arii. We arrived there about the 25th day of September. The pilot then told us that his arm was so weak that it was impossible for him to conduct us any further. We remained at Arii. Here the pilot sent one of the young men who had accompanied us in the canoe to ask the Starosti of the village of Arii to assist us. He arrived in a boat with two women and a young man, and the young man was immediately detailed as a pilot to take us to Geeomovialocke. They gave me a goose that had been boned and three or four geese stuffed into it as provisions to last us to reach the next village. We started from Arii and arrived at Geeomovialocke under the guidance of the three young men pilots, arriving on the evening of September 26. As we approched the island there were several canoes shoved out to pilot us into the deep water at the edge of the banks. This was the first inhabited village that we came up with. It was situated on an island on one of the outer ranges of sand-spits to the eastward of a range of mountains that forms the eastern banks of the Lena River proper. We discharged our boat and hauled her to the bank. That night the Starosti of the village gave us the use of his house to sleep in. At this time the majority of the people in the boat were so badly frozen as to be barely able to do any work whatever; but two or three, at the most four, were able to do any work whatever. The natives assisted us in discharging our boat, and the women brought the sled down with two or three dogs attached, and hauled me up to the nearest house, about 75 or 100 yards. Leach and Lauterbach were very badly crippled; the sled went back for them. I don't know whether they walked up with sticks or whether they were hauled up on the sleds. The Starosti gave us boiled goose for dinner. In the afternoon all went to sleep, and about 9 or 10 o'clock at night he woke us up and gave us a supper of boiled fish. We turned in again and slept until the next morning. In the mean time I had made the Starosti understand that he must take me to Bulun. When we turned out in the morning it was blowing pretty fresh. The natives said that it was too stormy, and they could not go, but by 10 o'clock the wind went down. The Starosti came in and said that he would make a start. Our provisions were about expended at this time, even with the reduced rations, and I depended on the natives for supplies. They made me understand that it took sixteen days to go from Geeomovialocke to Bulun. They put sixty fish into a sack that was put in the whale-boat, and they took their nets with them, with the intention of gathering food. I made them understand that sixty fish was not sufficient for a sixteen-day's journey. By this time our party had increased from eleven men in the whale-boat by the addition of the pilots to fourteen or fifteen men. They assured me that they could catch fish in their nets and they pushed off. They turned across the bay to the westward, with the intention of skirting the land around by way of Cape Borkhia and Cape Rodono [Ordono*] into the Lena River proper, but after working until 2 or 3 o'clock in the afternoon, the wind blowing considerably, the boat got aground. We failed to weather the point of land or shoals, continually touching the ground. The men had been very much crippled from the frosts [being frozen*]. It seemed impossible to pull the canoes around the point. During the whole of this time there was a good deal of ice drifting in the river; the ice was an inch or an inch and a half thick, all broken and drifting. The natives were very much afraid of the ice, but appeared to understand that if our boat was frozen in, the party was not in a condition to make a march across the country.

---

* Correction by witness.

Finally the pilots said they could go no farther in the canoes, and made me understand that we must return to the village. We put the boat about and ran back to the village in a very short time. When we arrived there I crawled out of the boat and sat on the bank until the boat was discharged, the natives making me understand that they must haul the boat up. I did not want to haul the boat up, because the bank was so steep that I was afraid they would break the boat's back. It was blowing a good deal at the time. I supposed that they understood the weather and the wind, and supposed this was the reason why they wanted to haul out the boat. By this time the women had brought down the dog-sled again and two or three of us got on the dog-sled and rode up to the hut. I told Mr. Danenhower to see that the natives did not break the boat in hauling her out. He remained there with the remainder of our people who were able to walk and the boat was hauled up on the bank. The natives lent us a hut to live in, and we gathered all of our people in this hut, with all of our cooking gear and everything from the boat that would be likely to be carried away. That was about the 27th of September, 1881.

Question by the JUDGE-ADVOCATE. What, if you know, was the particular or overt act for which Mr. Collins was, as you say, suspended from duty some time in March, 1880?

The WITNESS. Of my own knowledge I do not know, as I was not present in the cabin at the time.

Question by the JUDGE-ADVOCATE. In what spirits were the officers and men when they started on the retreat? Were they at any time despondent?

The WITNESS. They were all in the best of spirits, as far as I know, when they started on the retreat; and if there was any despondency, that our people looked more serious and stuck closer together, it was when they were in the "Ten-Day" camp, to the westward of the New Siberian Islands, at the prospect of being detained there by the ice. If they were despondent at any time, it was about that time.

Question by the JUDGE-ADVOCATE. Was there a fair division of labor made among all the members of the expedition on the retreat?

The WITNESS. Yes, sir, with the exception of those that were on the sick-list or suspended from duty.

Question by the JUDGE-ADVOCATE. You have stated that Mr. Collins was told by the commanding officer to do no more duty while on the retreat. Was Mr. Collins then fully able to work?

The WITNESS. I think he was.

Question by the JUDGE-ADVOCATE. How much out of the set course was Bennett Island when the party headed for it?

The WITNESS. I cannot state exactly, sir; but I know it was something out of the course, as we held more to the westward; possibly a point or two of the compass.

Question by the JUDGE-ADVOCATE. Was the delay at Bennett Island necessary for the repair of the boats and the recuperation of the men, and was it of no longer duration than was requisite for those purposes?

The WITNESS. The men were in very good condition at that time, and rest undoubtedly was for the advantage of the people. The labor had been very severe, and although the boats might have been repaired upon the ice with the same tools that we used on the island, still I do not believe that the boats could have been repaired as readily on the ice or with the same advantage as on the island, for this reason, that the ice was continually in motion, and we might be carried in any direction by the drifting ice while the repairs were going on on the boats; and we remained there no longer than was necessary to effect the repairs and make the new organization to take to the boats. After this time there was no regular sledding done.

Question by the JUDGE-ADVOCATE. Were there any unnecessary delays on the retreat, either before or after the separation of the boats?

The WITNESS. No, sir; I do not believe there were.

Question by the JUDGE-ADVOCATE. Did the boats selected for the retreat prove themselves to be the best possible of those available for the requisite service, as to the facilty with which they were transported over the ice; as to their capacities for accommodating their crews, and as to their qualities as sea boats, or taking into consideration all three of these points?

Pending an answer to this question, the court, at 12.10 p.,m., took a recess until 12.30 p. m., at which time it reconvened, with all the members, the judge-advocate, and the witness under examination present; and the witness then answered the pending question as follows:

The WITNESS. Yes, sir; they were. The three boats, as regards their transportation over the ice, varied in this respect: the whale-boat, which was considered the best sea boat, was regarded as the worst to haul; the second cutter was considered the best of all the boats while on the march; Mr. Chipp and his boat's crew always said that they had the best boat when each boat's crew were hauling their own boat and gear. As to their capacity for accommodating their crews, as was the capacity of the boat so was her proportion of the crew. To my mind, I think that the second cutter had the advantage in having the fewest number of men; she floated much lighter than either the whale-boat or the first cutter. As regards their qualities as sea boats, the second cutter being much shorter than the whale-boat or the first cutter, I do not think that she could be considered as good a sea boat, but I do not believe that either the first cutter or the whale-boat would have reached the coast of Siberia but for the immense weather-cloths that were fitted to these two boats; in particular, the weather-cloths on the first cutter, which were at least a foot high, and I have seen the water roll along the whole length of the first cutter and still roll in. Had her weather-cloths been but 8 or 6 inches high the sea would have been tumbling into her all the time. The whale-boat in the same way; her weather-cloths were 16 or 18 inches high, and the water used to break over her all the time with that weather-cloth. The weather-cloths and weather-boards on the second cutter were not more than 6 inches high, and had she had as high weather-cloths as on the other boats, I think it would have kept some of the water out of the boat; but taking all things into consideration from the time the ship was crushed, the hauling of the boats, the weight of them, and damage occurring to the boats, I think the selection of the three boats for the thirty-three people was as good as could have been made to accommodate the whole of them. With three boats as awkward to haul as the whale-boat, it is doubtful if the party would have reached open water at all.

Question by the JUDGE-ADVOCATE. Under whose direction, with reference to each of those boats, were the weather-cloths fitted?

The WITNESS. I fitted mine in regard to height and all about it. I presume Mr. Chipp did the same, though I do not know. I was present when Nindemann was fitting the weather-cloths to the first cutter at New Siberian [Semenowski*] Island. I recollect the commanding officer talking about their weather-cloths to Nindemann, but whether he gave directions as to the height I do not know, only that Nindemann fitted them.

---

* Correction by witness.

Question by the JUDGE-ADVOCATE. What, if you know, was the controversy between Lieutenant Danenhower and Mr. Newcomb, for which the latter was suspended from duty just before leaving Bennett Island?

The WITNESS. I only know from the talk in the camp; I was not a witness.

Question by the JUDGE-ADVOCATE. You have stated that he (Newcomb) was still permitted to do some work in the boat; was he at all times allowed to assist when his services were needed?

The WITNESS. Yes, sir; I had orders for him to perform all duties or any duty that I might assign to him.

Question by the JUDGE-ADVOCATE. What arrangements, if any, were made for communicating between the boats by signals?

The WITNESS. None that I know of.

Question by the JUDGE-ADVOCATE. You have stated that the ice one-fourth of an inch thick could not be rowed through with the boats which you had; was this owing to any defect in those particular boats, or would the same difficulty have existed with any boats?

The WITNESS. It would have existed with any boat that was not a steamboat, with power enough behind it to drive it. Ice a quarter of an inch thick will stop any boat.

Question by the JUDGE-ADVOCATE. How many days' provisions did Lieutenant Chipp have in the second cutter when the party left Semenov Island, September 12, 1881?

The WITNESS. I think I had five or six days' provisions. Lieutenant Chipp must have had one or two days less, if he had not received his pemmican at the edge of the ice floe. I do not know how much provisions Lieutenant Chipp had in his boat.

Question by the JUDGE-ADVOCATE. Did Lieutenant Danenhower assist either in the manual labor of making the drag or with his advice?

The WITNESS. Both.

Question by the JUDGE-ADVOCATE. Did you regard the evolution of rounding to and putting out the drag in the gale of September 12, 1881, highly important and the time of performing it a critical one?

The WITNESS. I considered it an evolution of importance, but not particularly critical.

Question by the JUDGE-ADVOCATE. In what manner was the evolution performed under the direction of Lieutenant Danenhower?

The WITNESS. All right.

Question by the JUDGE-ADVOCATE. Have you any further statement to make in relation to the retreat? If yea, make it now.

The WITNESS. I do not remember anything else that I care to refer to.

Examination by the COURT:

Question by the COURT. Do you know whether it was the intention of the commanding officer, at the time of leaving the wreck, to make for the New Siberian Islands, and thence to the Lena River, or did he intend at that time to make a due south course towards the Siberian coast, and modify this plan after finding that the current had carried the party to the northwest?

The WITNESS. Before the ship was crushed, it was very well understood among the senior officers of the ship that the course was to be laid to the New Siberian Islands in case the ship was lost. De Long was always free in communicating matters of this kind to the executive officer, myself, and the doctor. After we commenced our retreat, the course was laid south true; after marching for some time, owing to the current setting us so far into the northwest, De Long made a diagram in his ice journal and explained to me why he thought it best to haul the course up some to the westward of the course, in order to cross the ice at right angles to its drift. While on board of the ship and in the vicinity of the New Siberian Islands, that is, when at the nearest point to them, De Long always said that it would be the line of retreat. While we were on the march he never said that we were going to take any other course, although I understood that the line of retreat was the nearest land, which was the New Siberian Island. Yes, sir; the intention was to go to the Lena River. Our conversation for weeks, before the ship was lost, always in regard to our line of retreat being the Lena River. We understood that the steamboat Lena ran the whole length of the Lena River down to its mouth, and we often spoke about going up the Lena River on the steamboat Lena. For this reason I believe that the course was intended by way of the New Siberian Islands to the Lena, and up the Lena River through Russia home.

Question by the COURT. What was the amount of pemmican in each package?

The WITNESS. Forty-five pounds net.

Question by the COURT. How many days' provisions, full rations, did you have on commencing the retreat?

The WITNESS. That I do not know. I did know at the time, but I do not remember now.

Question by the COURT. Would or would not the retreat have been more judiciously conducted had you started with lighter loads, so that you could have retreated with more rapidity?

The WITNESS. The loads were as light as it was possible for them to be, with the exception of the provisions, and had we been shorter of provisions I doubt if we would have pulled through.

Question by the COURT. Was open water made as quickly as possible, under the circumstances, after the loss of the Jeannette?

The WITNESS. So far as any person knew, we reached the open water as rapidly as possible on our line of retreat, though signs of the open water did show to the eastward of our line of march; but whether we would have ever got to open water sooner by going to the eastward is something that could only be known by going there and trying it over [on*].

Question by the COURT. Would the delay which occurred at the "Ten Days" camp have been avoided if the boat-sledges had not been destroyed?

The WITNESS. No, sir; the destruction of the sleds at the time had little or nothing to do with the transportation of the boats through the running pack that lay between us and the New Siberian Islands. The whole pack was in motion. It would be impossible to move the boats without having something to stand on. We could not lead out the painter to haul the boat by; neither could the men get around the gunwale of the boat close enough to haul the boat along by her gunwale, because the ice was so broken that there was not standing room for the people. Sleds or no sleds, the boats could not have been landed on Semenov [Fadejowski*] Island without endangering the sea qualities of the boats entirely; that is, there was greater possibility of staving the boats to pieces than there was of getting them ashore.

Question by the COURT. When and where was the change made from traveling by night to traveling by day?

The WITNESS. I think it was at Bennett Island.

---

* Correction by witness.

Question by the COURT. When you last saw the second cutter, did you consider her overloaded, and did she carry more proportionally than either of the other boats?

The WITNESS. No, sir; I think that both her men and equipment were less than that of either the first cutter or whale-boat—the least weight for the greatest capacity.

Question by the COURT. Had Mr. Collins been restored to duty after his first suspension and before starting on his retreat over the ice?

The WITNESS. No, sir; I believe not.

Question by the COURT. In your opinion, were the services of those persons who were suspended from duty needed for the advance of the parties, and did or did not their suspension add to the labors of the other members of the party?

The WITNESS. There is no doubt that we required all the working force we could get, and had the parties that were suspended from duty been used, it would have lightened the burdens of those who were doing the work.

Question by the COURT. How long did Mr. Collins remain suspended from duty?

The WITNESS. From the time that he was suspended on board of the ship to the time when the boats separated he remained under suspension. When he worked on the drag-rope or on the roads, I understood that he worked of his own volition.

The court was then, by request of a member, cleared for deliberation, and afterward reopened, and the examination of the witness by the court was continued as follows:

Question by the COURT. After the whale-boat became separated from the other boats, on September 12, 1881, did Lieutenant Danenhower express to you, at any time, that he was either able, willing, or desirous of assuming command?

The WITNESS. No, sir.

Question by the COURT. From September 12, 1881, was Mr. Danenhower able to perform duty?

The WITNESS. He was able to perform some duty, but not all duty that would pertain to an officer in either of our positions.

And the court then, at 1.15 p. m., pending the further examination of this witness, adjourned to meet to-morrow, the 15th day of November, 1882, at 10.30 a. m.

THIRTY-FIFTH DAY.

NAVY DEPARTMENT,
Washington, D. C., Wednesday, November 15, 1882—10.30 a. m.

The court met pursuant to the adjournment of yesterday.

Present, Commodore William G. Temple, United States Navy, president; Capt. Joseph N. Miller, United States Navy, Commander Frederick V. McNair, United States Navy, members; and Master Samuel C. Lemly, United States Navy, judge-advocate.

The record of the proceedings of yesterday, November 14, 1882, the thirty-fourth day of the inquiry was read, and, after making clerical corrections, approved.

Chief Engineer GEORGE W. MELVILLE, the witness under examination, then came in, and his examination by the judge-advocate was resumed, as follows:

Question by the JUDGE-ADVOCATE. State in detail what efforts were made or attempted by yourself, or any of the officers or men of the party under your command, to further insure the safety of that party or for the relief of other parties.

The WITNESS. On the morning of the 28th of September the ice had nearly covered the bay between the islands where we were situated and the mainland. There were spots of water in the bay, but in the middle of the bay, where the current ran, it was still open. I had prepared a telegram to the Secretary of the Navy and to the minister resident at St. Petersburg, also a letter to the Russian authorities, stating who we were and where we came from. I, in company with Mr. Danenhower, walked over as far as the house of the Starosti of the village. These papers were done up in a piece of oil-skin and the Starosti made to understand that they were to be sent at the first possible convenience. The Starosti made us understand that they would go as soon as the river froze over. He also made us understand that it would be impossible to go away from the island of Geeomovialocke before fifteen days; that the wind blowing in the bay would drive the ice out of the bay, and it would not be possible to cross the bay to the mainland, as that was the direction in which they had to go and cross the mountains about 280 versts to the nearest Russian or Cossack settlement at Bulun. On our way back from the house of the Starosti to the hut in which the people were located—I was very lame, my feet and legs being badly frozen—Mr. Danenhower said, "Melville, you are pretty badly used up, and if you would just as lief as not, I will attend to the details of the house or hut and see that the men get wood and water." I said, "All right," and when we got in the hut I told the men that we were in a bad way; that we had not gotten out of the woods by any means. We were very short of provisions; the sixty fish that the Starosti had given us the day before for the journey had been carried away again by the Starosti, and we were allowed but four fish morning and evening, each fish weighing about four pounds.

At this time an exile had been put to live with us, making twelve men in our hut. We had no bread for about forty days; we had no anti-scorbutics of any kind, no salt to use with our food, and the geese which we were supplied with were in a very bad state of decay, so much so that when we would hang them up their intestines would drop out. I told the men that they must be as cheerful as they could; entertain and amuse themselves every way they could; make a point of burning plenty of wood; keep themselves as warm as they could; anyway get plenty of wood, so as to exercise all hands. I was very anxious at this time, owing to our short supply of provisions and the kind we were living on, fearing that the decayed geese would cause typhoid fever, from the fact that we had no anti-scorbutics; in case we staid there, I felt there was great probability of the whole party dying of scurvy.

I will state at this time that when I gave Mr. Danenhower the directions to look after the hauling of wood and water and the general policing of the hut, that I did not turn over the command to him, not at any time, neither before this time nor after this time, until I gave him orders to proceed south. The men were cheerful and happy under the circumstances, no one being despondent, and the people rapidly recovered from the numbness of their limbs caused by the frost. Many of the people were pretty badly frozen, their legs were badly blistered and were sore, but in a few days nearly all the people were running about. In the mean time I had made the people of the village understand where we came from and pretty well who we were, as the exile who was living with us had been to Vladivostok and knew the American flag that we made in pencil, so that he immediately remarked, "Americansk," so that the people understood who we were.

The ice made pretty rapidly on the shoal [along the shore*], but the wind kept the bay open. This continued along until about the 10th day of October, when the exile came into my hut, saying that a Russian had arrived in the village. He came in and saw us. We inquired his name. He was friendly and gave us a box of salt; he told us his name was Kusmah and that he lived about 10 versts across the bay. He said he had very little or no provisions at his house, but the little he had he would supply us with. I then made him understand that I was very anxious to get our party to Bulun, to a place of safety. I made him understand the manner we were living; that it was close quarters, and that the short supply of fish and decayed geese would make the people sick; that it was necessary we should get to a settlement as soon as possible. I did not consider that myself and party had yet arrived at a place of safety as long as the danger of scurvy setting in among the party existed. He told me that it was impossible to go to Bulun; that the bay was not frozen over; that he picked his way across the bay with great difficulty, and that the bay was still open, and that if it should come on to blow any person being caught in the ice on the bay might be carried off to sea; but he promised to return in three or four days, which would make just about the time that the natives said to me it would be fifteen days before the river or bay would be safe to travel on. He made the natives understand that their fish supply was too small for so many men, and that the geese were not fit for dogs. After his visit the Starosti increased our supply of fish.

When we first landed at Geeomovialocke, there were very few fish in the village, and the natives were catching very few, and there were not more than twelve or fifteen adult persons in the village. When I landed eleven men on these people, they were alarmed at the inroads we were making on their supplies. This is probably the reason why they supplied us with so small a quantity of fish and insisted on our using the decayed geese.

When Kusmah returned to his hut across the bay, Mr. Danenhower said he would like to go [along*] and get any supplies that Kusmah might give us. I told him, "All right," and he accompanied Kusmah to Kusmah's hut across the bay. He remained all night and returned the next day, Kusmah having supplied him with some tobacco for the sailors, some tea, about four or five pounds of rye flour, and about five or six pounds of salt [also a reindeer dressed, weighing 94 pounds.*] He also told me that Kusmah would be back on the following Thursday. That would be about the 14th of October. Kusmah returned according to promise. I then made an agreement with him to give him the whaleboat and 500 rubles if he would go to Bulun and see the commandant and bring us the necessary food and clothing and the reindeer teams to the party to Bulun. He consented to this, and said he would leave in a day or two. I insisted on his going right away. Mr. Danenhower expressed the desire of going with him; but as Kusmah did not have a full team of dogs of his own and obliged to borrow dogs to make up a team, he could not carry and go rapidly the food and supplies for two men instead of one; that is, one man and his supplies would amount to about 400 pounds for a journey, and two men would nearly double that; and as the man had a short team of dogs, although a good team, I considered

* Correction by witness.

it best to send Kusmah alone, as he would make better time. Kusmah thought he could go and return in five days. After Kusmah went away that evening, promising to leave on the morrow, Mr. Danenhower said, "Melville, you forgot a very important point in your conversation of the day before with Kusmah. You forgot to tell Kusmah to spread the news as he went along the road of the other and the [two*] missing parties." He said, "I will get a dog team in the village, of three or four dogs, as many as will carry me, and carry the message to Kusmah. I said, "All right"; and he got a team and went over to Kusmah's hut. He told him to spread the news as he went along of the other two missing boats. Before this, and at all times when in company with the natives, by signs and pictures and by making models of men and ships and boats, I made the natives at Geeomovilocke thoroughly understand that there were two boats and their people missing. Mr. Danenhower returned the next morning. He said that while at Kusmah's house he had heard that there was a hut somewhere about 40 or 50 versts to the northeast of where we were. He said that Kusmah told him this was a hut at Barkin, and that if I had no objection he would go there. At this time the bay was open, the ice still running in the bay. I told him I did not consider it safe for a person to attempt to cross the ice, because if he should venture across, if a gale of wind came on and drove the ice out of the bay or mouth of the bay, it would be impossible for him to get back or anybody to come to his assistance. We had some further conversation about the matter, and finally I said to him that he might go, but not to remain away more than four days at the longest, as I expected Kusmah back about that time, and in no case to venture across the bay where the ice was broken and where he would be liable to be cut off. He got a team of dogs from Arii (Arrhu), a village 10 versts to the northward, and was carried to Kusmah's house to obtain further information. Upon his arrival there Mr. Danenhower learned that the Starosti of the village was going to Bulun along with Kusmah, and on his return reported this matter to me. It seems that the Starosti is the head man at the village, and is responsible for the keeping of the criminal exiles in a particular locality. For this reason Kusmah was afraid to go to Bulun without authority. At this time I had no knowledge of Kusmah being a criminal exile, the exile who was living in the hut at Geeomovialocke having stated to me that they were soldiers. On Mr. Danenhower's return to Geeomovialocke, the dog-sled driver I found that he had engaged would not go with him any further. In the morning Mr. Danenhower returned to the hut at Geeomovialocke with a new dog driver and another team of dogs, and related to me the circumstance of Spiridon taking his pay of tea and tobacco and refusing to go any further, but said he had engaged this new man, who said he would take him to the hut in question. They started in the morning about eight or nine o'clock, but instead of going to the northeast to Barkin, they carried him down to a different hut, called Darrahoo, about 60 or 80 versts to the southeast. He remained at this hut over night, and returned the next morning, and he then reported to me where he had been; that the natives said that the ice was so badly broken that they could not go up to the northeast, where he wanted to go, and that he attempted to go from the main spit of Darrahoo to a little outlying island, but the ice was so black and treacherous that they were obliged to return. I had seen [could see*] nothing for us to do but await the arrival of the commandant from Bulun with deer teams to convey us to Bulun. I expected Kusmah's return. I was not at first very much troubled; but as

*Correction by witness.

the days grew on and he did not return for five or six days, I then commenced to be troubled and proposed to take a couple of the sleds in the village and lay in what fish was necessary, and to have [march*] the whole force the 280 versts from Geeomovialocke to Bulun. I talked the matter over fully with both Mr. Danenhower and Bartlett in particular, who said he could march the distance without any difficulty at all. We were all in pretty good condition at this time [except Leach, who would have had to be hauled on a sled;*] but the winter had set in, and it was pretty cold, with a good deal of wind and snow. We had very little clothing, in fact, no proper clothing in which to take a march in the Arctic region. During our march across the floe we were very lightly clad to begin with, and what clothing we had at first was worn out, and much of our clothing not adapted to such a march. We had nothing for food, and the natives had little or nothing to give us; so that the strongest argument against the attempt to make the march was the want of clothing and the want of a pilot. It was impossible to attempt a march of this kind across the mountains without a guide. There was no guide in the village or none that we could use; so I proposed, as nothing else would do, to wait the return of Kusmah with the necessary clothing and the reindeer sleds to carry us to Bulun. Kusmah returned on the evening of the 29th day of October. He had been absent thirteen days. He brought about 40 pounds of bread, a ball of butter, about 6 or 8 pounds, and tobacco, tea, and salt. He brought two letters, one from the commandant, who was a Cossack sergeant of Bulun, and another letter from the young priest of the village of Bulun. He also brought a short note, written in pencil, that he told me he had received from two Americans that he met somewhere near Ku Mark Surk. The note was written by Nindemann and signed by Nindemann and Noros, in which they said that they wanted assistance to go for Captain De Long, Dr. Ambler, and nine other men who were starving to death to the northward.

Question by the JUDGE-ADVOCATE. Would you recognize now the pencil note given you by Kusmah?

The WITNESS. Yes, sir.

The judge-advocate here handed to the witness the note signed by William C. Nindemann and Louis P Noros, seamen, United States Navy.

The WITNESS. That is the note.

The judge-advocate then read aloud and placed before the court the note in question, and a certified copy, marked HH, is appended to the record.

The witness then continued his narrative, as follows:

I see by reading the note that it did not state that De Long and his people were to the northward. I wish to correct that part of my statement. I learned that later and from another source. I had the exile read the two Russian letters I had received from Bulun, as no person in the camp of our people could read Russian. The exile read the letters in Russian, and notwithstanding [I did not understand*] his language, he made me understand that the commandant would be at Geeomovialocke on the day after to-morrow. The letter from the young priest was only a friendly letter. Kusmah explained that he could not bring the clothing and the reindeer necessary to carry the party away from Geeomovialocke, neither had he any means of procuring them, but that the commandant who had charge of everything in that section of the country would provide the necessary food and clothing and the deer teams. I

---

* Correction by witness.

inquired of Kusmah and his companion the reason why he was gone so long—thirteen days instead of five. He explained to me that when he had crossed the mountains and reached the main river Lena, that the ice in the river, although it had been frozen, had broken and run out, and that the ice in the river was still open; that he had great difficulty in reaching the place called Burroloch, not being able to cross the river, and was detained there at Burroloch until the river was frozen. They explained that they had carried all their material on their backs in crossing the river, and that this was the cause of their delay. That immediately upon their arrival at Bulun the commandant sent them back with a small amount of food; that he supplied them with instructions and letters to inform me that he would leave the day after to-morrow.

When I read the note that had been written by Nindemann and Noros, that was the first intimation I had of the whereabouts or any knowledge of the first cutter's people having landed. In all conversations during the whole of our time at Geeomovialocke we considered the first cutter and second cutter as having foundered at sea. I think it was a surprise to every one when we heard of the safety of these two men. In fact, we were discussing the probabilities or possibilities of either of the boats having landed when Kusmah returned and brought us the letters. As soon as I received Nindemann's letter, I told Kusmah that he must put the food and supplies on one of the sleds, and that same night, with the same dog team, go to Bulun to find Nindemann and Noros. Kusmah told me that he met Nindemann and Noros on the evening of the 27th of October when at or near Ku Mark Surk. He said that they were in the hands of some natives who had them on deer sleds and were conducting them to Bulun. It was necessary for me to go to Bulun to see Nindemann and Noros and find in what direction they had come and where they had left the captain and his party, as there was no other means of finding this out. Kusmah and the natives said that the dog team could not go; that they had been thirteen days on foot; that their feet were sore; were cut from running on the ice, and that they seldom worked more than one or two days in succession; that they had nothing to eat, and it was necessary to feed them for a couple of days before starting them on another journey. I then said to them that they must go to Arii the same night and get a fresh team of dogs from Spiridon, who lived at Arii, about 10 versts to the northward. [They*] started off that night [and returned in the morning with a fresh team of dogs*] and saw the hut in the morning, there being three of us. I was not properly clad for a journey of 280 versts in the winter time, not having but our skin clothing; but I had a half blanket that had been carried during the march, and started in the morning, arriving at Kusmah's house in the afternoon. I traded the half blanket for a reindeer-skin blouse. The next day I arrived at the mountain gorge; stopped there that night, and in the morning there was a great deal of snow drifting. The native did not care to move on; but as the wind was behind us, I insisted on his going. That evening we arrived at Ku Mark Surk. The dogs were so badly used up that they could not carry me as far as Burroloch, where I was told I would get reindeer sleds. We stopped at Ku Mark Surk, and they sent out and got reindeer that carried us to Burroloch; started from there that night, and the next morning started, and arrived at Bulun after dark in the evening. This was about the 2d day of November that we arrived at Bulun. The native told me where Nindemann and Noros were quartered, in a hut, which was the public waiting place for natives and travelers who were traveling through that portion of the country. When I entered the room it was dark. I saw

---

* Correction by witness.

Nindemann, who was reclining on a little settle or bedstead. Noros was standing up behind the table. He did not recognize me when I entered the room, but I spoke to Noros. He said, "My God, Mr. Melville, are you alive? We thought that the whale-boat's were all dead." I told him that I had tried to communicate with Bulun for more than twenty days; that all the whale-boat's were well. They then told me they were supplied with a poor kind of food; that they were both very sick with their bowels, from the effects of eating a lot of decayed fish they found in a hut where the natives had picked them up. Nindemann was so sick as hardly to be able to stand. Noros complained of the weakness of his bowels, but he was not in as bad a condition as Nindemann was. I then found that there was a vacant house in the village and plenty of fresh reindeer meat and flour. The commandant, when he left, had not made any proper provision for these people. At the time they were in his house he treated them well, and fed them out of his own provisions; there appeared to be no one in authority in the village. The Starosti was there, but refused to do anything. I then found the young priest, and told him that I must have a house for the people to live in; that he must supply them with reindeer meat and food that would be strengthening. They must have bread or flour to make bread. He told me that he had no authority in the village; that he did not dare to enter a house that he did not own. Noros and myself hunted up a house that was vacant, selecting one of the proper size, and I opened the door and told the priest that he must supply all the wood the men could burn to keep them warm, and get a house to hold them, which would enable them to live to themselves; and that if he had no authority, that I had the authority and would use it to obtain anything there was in the village for the use of myself or the people; that my government would repay. I slept with the people at the native hut the first evening, and the second evening Bartlett arrived at Bulun from Geeomovialocke. When I left Geeomovialocke I was in hopes of meeting the commandant on his road from Bulun to Geeomovialocke; but as I traveled with dogs and the commandant with reindeer, we took two different roads; they were nearly parallel to each other, but far enough apart for us to miss meeting.

The judge-advocate then announced that, with the permission of the court, he would now introduce, as evidence, the private journal of Lieut. Commander George W. De Long, and explained, as his reasons for so doing, that the convening authority had expressed a desire to have the original of these journals for transmission to the widow of the late Lieutenant-Commander De Long. The judge-advocate further stated that a copy of the journals from the files of the department was at the disposal of the court. No objections being made, the judge-advocate proceeded as follows:

Question by the JUDGE-ADVOCATE. Would you now recognize the private journal of Lieutenant-Commander De Long?

The WITNESS. Yes, sir.

The judge-advocate then handed the witness the original book in question.

The WITNESS. That is the book.

The judge-advocate then placed before the court, as evidence, the private journal in question, which commences with the record of July 8, 1879, and ends with that of June 9, 1881.

Question by the JUDGE-ADVOCATE. Would you now recognize the ice journal kept by Lieutenant-Commander De Long?

The WITNESS. Yes.

The judge-advocate then handed to the witness the journals in question, two volumes.

The WITNESS. Those are the books.

The judge-advocate then placed before the court the ice journals of Lieutenant-Commander De Long, commenced with the record of June 11, 1881, and ending with an entry made October 30, 1881.

The witness then continued his narrative as follows:

When I left Geeomovialocke to go to Bulun I was in hopes of meeting the commandant on the road, but as he traveled by deer and I by dog, there were two roads, which, although running nearly parallel to each other, were far enough apart that we missed meeting each other. It was my intention if meeting the commandant with the reindeer teams to turn him back to Bulun to get Nindemann and Noros and go north at once with the reindeer teams with the necessary supplies for the relief of De Long, but failing to meet him, I was obliged to go on to Bulun. When I saw Nindemann and Noros they related to me all their story of the landing and of the march to the southward, all of which I wrote down as instructions to me to follow in my search to the northward. They told me that they had left De Long on or about the 9th day of October; that when they had left him, that the party had nothing to eat for two days and had been subsisting on two or three ounces of alcohol per day. Nindemann said he thought they had landed on the island [the shore*] of the Arctic Ocean, and had to go south, striking the main branch of the Lena River. They probably held a little to the westward, struck a bend or bight of the river. That before leaving the Arctic Ocean they carried their stuff ashore from the boat a mile or a mile and a half from the shore. They had made a cache of their log-books, chronometers, and navigation box, all of the sleeping bags and old clothing. They had erected a tall flag-staff alongside of the cache before they started south. The first day's travel they passed two or three old huts, and finally brought up at a hut or huts where they stopped over night. In this hut a record had been left of their advance. They continued along the bank of the river, and they stopped at a second hut. They slept there over night where another paper had been left, and so on down, until they came to a hut on the bank of the river with another river making into it to the eastward. The river was open, and it was impossible to cross it, and they remained there three or four days. On this march they managed to kill two or three reindeer, and that afternoon, following the river as far as they could, they crossed the river to the westward. They related to me all the circumstances attending the difficulties of their march, having to haul Erichsen on a sled, and that after crossing the river to the westward they followed the main branch of the river to the westward from 15 to 20 miles, more or less, and finally took refuge in a hut where Erichsen died. This they described as being on the west bank of the main branch of the river, and they described the hut and said that I would know it by the epitaph board they had placed over the hut. They also believed this place to be the island of Tas Arii. The men were too sick to go with me on a journey at this season of the year, and it was difficult to supply either dog teams or food for such a journey. Therefore I made as close an investigation, and wrote down carefully what Nindemann said to me, to use these instructions for my first search for De Long and his party. On the evening of the 3d of November, Bartlett arrived from Geeomovialocke bringing a letter written in Russian by the Cossack commandant who

---

*Correction by witness.

had arrived at Geeomovialocke. As soon as Nindemann had arrived at Bulun, he had written a telegram intended to be sent to the American Minister at St. Petersburg; but the commandant, instead of sending it on its journey, carried it over to Geeomovialocke to give to me, at the same time he brought the letter from the commandant written in Russian, directing the Starosti of the village to supply me with a deer team to Burrolock, where he would meet me in a day or two, while conveying the whale-boat party to Bulun. At this place I could get two teams of dogs that he used to carry the whale-boat party from Geeomovialocke to Burroloch. The commandant on his journey found that there was not snow enough in the country [mountains*] for the reindeer to haul the party, so he sent all the reindeer back to Burvoloch and carried the party by dog sleds.

I arrived at Burroloch on the evening of November 4; the next day, about eleven o'clock, the commandant and the whale-boat party arrived. Before I left Geeomovialocke, I gave Mr. Danenhower orders, as soon as the commandant and the reindeer sleds arrived, to come to Bulun as quickly as possible. When I met the people at Burroloch, I then gave him written orders to go as far as Yakutsk and to carry all the people with him except Bartlett. After we had dinner at Burroloch I started the two dog teams with two native drivers and ten days' supplies of fish for the men and dogs. That evening I arrived at Ku Mark Surk, remaining there over night, and the next morning started out for the hut known as Bulcour. This was the hut that Nindemann described to me as being the one where they were found by the natives. We arrived there and found the huts where the people had slept there over night. This was from 50 to 55 versts from the Ku Mark Surk to Bulcour. The next morning it was stormy and blowing, so that the natives would not move; the storm was so fierce that we all would have perished. My feet being tender from the previous freezing, I froze my feet pretty badly on the journey from Bulun to Burroloch, and was obliged to lie aside this one day. The next morning it cleared up. I followed the west bank of the river, as Nindemann had gone on and explained to me that when he came away from De Long he said to him, "Keep the west bank of the river," and that "De Long and his party will follow in your footsteps." Therefore my intention was to follow Nindemann's track to the northward, and if De Long were following in their footsteps, as he said he would do, I would come upon them. This day I found the place known as "the place of the sleds," and evidence to show that Nindemann and Noros had remained there a night, and where the sleds had to be burned for fuel, and from that point I continued on my journey, making 60 versts, and making a hole in the snow and camping that night.

The next morning got under way again and continued along the western bank of the river, looking out for the place known as the "Two Crosses." Nindemann explained this place to me as being the first huts in which they slept after leaving De Long. They described it so that I had no difficulty in finding the place. I examined the huts where Nindemann and Noros had found the fish [fishing places*] they spoke of, but found no signs of De Long or his people. Nindemann had described to me the shoal around the Island of Stolbvoi; said that they had been near this large, rocky island [on this night I had reached a shelter*], and had reached a shelter one night, at what the natives told me was the nearest hut, called Mat Vay ; that we had better run to the place for shelter,

---

* Correction by witness.

and as it was on the west bank of the river it was in the line of march. So we took refuge in the hut at Mat Vay this night.

The court was then cleared by request of the judge-advocate and afterward reopened, and the court at 1.20 p. m., pending the further examination of this witness, adjourned to meet to-morrow, the 16th day of November, 1882, at 10 a. m.

THIRTY-SIXTH DAY.

NAVY DEPARTMENT,
Washington, D. C., Thursday, November 16, 1882—10 a. m.

The court met pursuant to the adjournment of yesterday.

Present, Commodore W. G. Temple, United States Navy, president; Capt. Joseph N. Miller, United States Navy, Commander Frederick V. McNair, United States Navy, members; and Master Samuel C. Lemly, United States Navy, judge-advocate.

The court having to vacate the room to the use of the Naval Examining Board, took a recess until 1 p. m.

At 1 p. m. the court reconvened with all the members and the judge-advocate present.

The record of the proceedings of yesterday, the thirty-fifth day of the inquiry, was then read and, after correcting clerical errors, was approved.

And the court then, at 2.30 p. m., having to give up the rooms for two days to the Naval Examining Board, adjourned to meet on Monday, the 20th day of November, 1882, at 10.30 a. m.

THIRTY-SEVENTH DAY.

NAVY DEPARTMENT,
Washington, D. C., Monday, November 20, 1882—10.30 a. m.

The court met pursuant to the adjournment of Thursday, November 16, 1882.

Present, Commodore Wm. G. Temple, United States Navy, president; Capt. Joseph. N. Miller, United States Navy, Commander Frederick V. McNair, United States Navy, members, and Master Samuel C. Lemly, United States Navy, judge-advocate.

The record of the proceedings of, Thursday November 16, 1882, the thirty-sixth day of the inquiry, was then read and approved.

Chief Engineer GEORGE W. MELVILLE, the witness under examination, then came in and continued his answer to the pending question, which was repeated to him by the judge-advocate, as follows:

Question by the JUDGE-ADVOCATE. State in detail what efforts were made or attempted, by yourself or any of the officers or men of the party under your command, to further insure the safety of the party or for the relief of the other parties.

The WITNESS. Upon entering the hut, I found the beds as usually arranged in the Yakutsk huts were changed; that the sticks had been arranged to make a bed with the feet toward the fire. I inquired of the natives if the Yakutsks ever made their beds in huts that way. They said, "No; it must be the Americans had been there." Nindemann and Noros had described to me the hut at Mat Vay, [the two crosses*] and when I arrived at the hut of Mat Vay [the two crosses*] the door was banked up with snow, which had been done with shovels, but the opening in the roof had been left open, and whoever had been in there had dropped down through the hole in the roof. It was quite evident some of De Long's party had been there. We slept there during this night. On the next morning got ready to start. One of the natives picked up a waist belt. By examining the buckle, I knew it had been made in the fire-room on the Jeannette. Nindemann and Noros had their waist belts on when they were at Bulun. This made me suppose that some of De Long's party had been in this particular hut. I searched the hut, but found no [further*] trace of any of the party having been there. This was about the 10th day of November. We got ready to start, and I told the natives that we must follow along the west bank of the river. I suppose that probably Alexy, the Indian hunter, had been sent on in advance, as Nindemann and Noros had been sent, and in all probability he had slept in this hut, and that he had arranged the bed sticks with his feet toward the fire, as was the custom of the North American Indians, Alexy being from the northwest and the Alaskan Territory.

I told the natives to get ready to move on again. We loaded the sleds, and, very much to my surprise, they said they could not go any farther; that they had no provisions. The Cossack commandant told me he would put ten days' provisions on the sleds for the dogs and men, and yet while I had been but five days on my journey the provisions had given out, and the natives said they must return; that they had nothing for themselves or their dogs to eat. I then inquired how far it was to the nearest village; they said about 150 or 170 versts into the northwest, but as they did not have provisions, they did not even want to go there. They said we would all perish on the journey from the cold and for the want of food. We had twenty-two dogs, and I said that the natives must go on, and that if necessary we would eat the dogs, and when the dogs gave out I would eat them, but they must continue on toward the northwest to the village. They got under way that day and followed the west bank of the river, and found many huts as we followed along the main branch, first to the westward and then to the northwest. In many of these huts we found scraps of reindeer meat, fish heads, and offal of all kinds, that we gathered up and carried with us for our own use and that of the dogs. The next night we arrived at a hunting station called Cass Carta, where we found a goodly quantity of reindeer scraps and offal of that kind left in the huts. As all this material was good for food in an emergency, I concluded that De Long and his people had not come down that way, although it was the main branch of the river leading to the northward, which I had understood from Nindemann's description to be the river along which they had come from the northward.

The next day I arrived at Cass Carta early in the morning, and sometime after midnight we arrived at the village of North Bulun or Tomat. It was terribly stormy and cold weather during this trip. I was so badly frozen when I arrived at Tomat, that I was carried into the hut. After being there a little while, the natives commenced to swarm into the hut from the surrounding villages. One of the natives brought me a paper which, by reading, I found was one of the records left by Lieutenant De Long on the banks of the river. I asked the native where

---

*Correction by witness.

he got it, and he said at a place 50 versts to the eastward at a deserted hunting station, called Balloch. He also said there were two other papers in the neighborhood, and a gun, and if I would wait until to-morrow they would bring the other two papers and the gun to me. The weather was very stormy at this time, and there was some delay about the natives getting the other papers and the gun; but during the day they brought me the two papers, which, upon reading, I found were records left by Lieutenant De Long in two other huts along the river by which they came from the northward. The first paper stated where they had landed and how they had come along to the first hut, and enumerating the people who had landed, and stating what they had done with their books and papers and how they might be found. The second paper told us where they had stopped at a second hut or a couple of huts. After leaving that place they continued to the southward. Finally the third paper stated where they had stopped at a place which, upon inquiry about of the natives, they said was called Usterda, where the gun was found. This last paper stated that they had been obliged to remain there three or four days, I do not remember which.

Question by the JUDGE-ADVOCATE. Can you identify these three records referred to? (The judge-advocate here handed the witness three papers.)

The WITNESS. I do; these are they; the first one, of the 22d of September, is the paper that was found by the natives at the place called Balloch, and delivered to me on the evening of my arrival at the native village of North Bulun or Tomat. The second one, dated September 26, is the second paper, and was found at a deserted hunting station called Osoctoc, and delivered to me the day following the night of my arrival at the village of Tomat. The third paper, dated October 1, 1881, was the paper that was delivered to me at the same time with the Winchester repeating rifle, and was found by the natives at the hunting station called Usterda.

The judge-advocate then read aloud these three papers and placed them before the court, and certified copies thereof marked, respectively, II, KK, and LL, are appended to the record.

The witness then continued his testimony as follows:

Having examined and read these records, they gave me definite information how to follow the search. The teams we had carried from Burroloch at that time were worn out and had to be renewed by fresh teams at North Bulun. I secured fresh teams at North Bulun and directed them to put on the sleds ten days' food for myself and dogs, at the rate of a fish a day for each dog and a fish a day for each man. The natives were reluctant to put on this amount, but counted out the fish ready for the teams, and I returned to the hut to put on my fur clothing to proceed on my journey. At this time my feet and legs were so badly frozen that I could not wear moccasins, but the women of the hut made a pair of deer-skin mufflers or mittens for me to wear in lieu of moccasins. I afterward found that while I was at the hut getting on my feet covers, the natives stole most of the fish off the sleds and put them back in the store-house. However, I started and went to the hut called Balloch, where the first record was found. The natives said that was 50 or 55 versts distant. I arrived there in the evening and slept in the hut that night. There was no door to the hut. The hut had drifted full of snow, so that no other articles were found having anything to do with the expedition. The next morning we started along the east bank of the river and followed the river until I struck the Arctic Ocean. I turned to the eastward and followed along the shore until I came up with a flag-staff, marking the place where the articles of the boat were cached. The ice had forced itself well up on the beach toward the cache, and before digging out the cache I ran back and forth north and south [east and west*] along the beach for a mile or two, in the dog sleds, to see if I could find anything of the boat—the first cutter. Not seeing anything of the boat, I dug out the cache and found the log-books, the chronometer, the navigation box, a lot of pots and pans and kettles, five stoves, a lot of old sleeping bags and old clothing that they had used to cover up the instruments. I loaded the two sleds with everything worth carrying away and a great deal not worth anything, so as to avoid misleading any person who might go there afterward on a similar search. I returned to the hut at Balloch the same evening; the night was again stormy. The next morning the storm continued snowing and blowing, and as I understood Osoctoc was 40 versts to the southward, I wanted the natives to descend to the southward these 40 versts. They told me that they had no provisions; that they had taken them off their sleds and put them in the store-houses.

There was a famine in that portion of the country, and they said that eighty of their dogs had died from starvation, and that it was impossible to supply me with more than enough food for myself during the time I staid there.

From this point to Ku Mark Surk was about 300 versts, and it was impossible for me to travel that distance without supplies. This compelled me to return to North Bulun to renew the supply of fish. That same day I arrived at the village of Tomat or North Bulun. I then overhauled the stuff I had picked up at the cache, and gave the old clothing and sleeping bags and worthless stuff away. I at first told them to burn them, that they might not mislead any other person. I left all the old stuff in this village, at the house where I stopped. I took care of everything in the way of books and papers, instruments, or anything of importance either to the expedition or the Government.

The next day it stormed so badly the natives would not move. The day following I managed to get two good teams of dogs and a short team of seven dogs, loaded up all the stuff that I had concluded to carry away, and started for the hut called Osoctoc. That was the second hut where they had stopped on their way to the southward. It was stormy, and snowing terribly during this time. That afternoon I arrived at the hut Osoctoc. I found nothing there, the huts being filled with snow. I continued down the river to the hut called Usterda. This was the hut where De Long said in his record that he had crossed [would cross*] the river to the westward and descend on the west bank to the southward in hopes of reaching some settlement. This is in his third record. This hut was filled with snow. Seeing a hut about a mile further to the southward, called Mesja, I went to the hut Mesja and slept there that night. The next morning I returned to the hut Usterda and crossed the river where De Long did. I could see the track of the sled in the ice, where it cut a groove in the soft slush or ice a month or so before. I followed down the west bank of the river to the southward in hopes of meeting or finding the hut in which Erichsen died, Nindemann having described to me that the hut was on the west bank of the river and somewhere between 15 and 20 or maybe 25 miles from where they had stopped after crossing the river at the hut of Usterda. I made the natives understand thoroughly what I wanted. They said "Yes"; they knew where there was a hut on the west bank, 20 miles to the

---

*Correction by witness.

southward. They took me to a hut answering the description, but it proved not to be the hut of which I was in search. I inquired if there was any other hut in the neighborhood. They replied, "Yes," but not on the west bank, but on the east bank, about 8 or 10, maybe 15 versts further to the southward. Knowing that the people were sick, miserable, and frozen, and that perhaps they had forgotten whether they were on the west or east bank, I proceeded down until I found it; I searched it, but found nothing of the people. Nindemann had told me that I would know it by an epitaph board they had inscribed to Erichsen where he died, and placed it over the door of the hut. I inquired if there were other huts in the neighborhood; they said nothing nearer than the hunting lodge known as Sister Ganak.

It was blowing and storming terribly the whole of this time, so much so that we could barely find our way. The snow was very deep. The dogs were poor and hungry. We had but two or three days' provisions to see me down as far as the native village of Ku Mark Surk. We got into the hut of Sister Ganak in the evening, out of the storm, and there found considerable offal of all kinds from deer and fish, which we gathered up to assist in eking out the few provisions we had on hand, to descend to the southward as far as Mat Vay, in which vicinity I expected to find De Long and the people. The next morning it was storming as badly as ever; the natives did not want to move on, but as it was but 40 versts to go they finally consented, and toward the evening of that day we arrived at the hunting station or lodge known by the name Qu Vina. In this hut we found more offal and scraps of reindeer meat, all of which evidence went to show that the first cutter's party did not go down that branch of the river, although it is one of the largest and is the main branch leading from the northward to the southward as far as Mat Vay.

I arrived there on Saturday, and on the next day, Sunday, it was still storming and blowing. The natives again did not want to move on, saying that it was Sunday and they preferred to be idle; that probably on the morrow the storm would abate. This was about the 21st day of November. The next morning the weather cleared up and was comparatively fine. I started at three or four o'clock in the morning to follow the river bank down as far as the hut Mat Vay. This is where I was doubling on my own track. It was now thirty or thirty-two days after the time that Nindemann and Noros had left them there poorly clad, but I had made up my mind by this time, that after thirty days' starvation they were all probably dead or frozen to death; that in the mean time, if they had found the natives or if the natives had found them, they were as safe as our party were, but if they had not found the natives, they would surely be dead. I then made up my mind to make as quick time as I could by way of the hut Mat Vay back to Bulun. Now that the weather was fine, I intended to run by the hut, as it was but 40 versts, even if it stormed. I concluded to stop at Mat Vay as short a time as possible, as we were out of provisions except the offal that I had picked up in the huts. After leaving Qu Vina about two hours the natives stopped their teams and dug up a cache of venison bones, that they had buried the summer before. They added this to our load and we sledded along, passing Mat Vay in the afternoon. About seven o'clock in the evening, in entering a mountain gorge where the river debouched into the bay, the storm blew from the southward so that we were compelled to camp down. It is impossible to move when it storms and blows, because the dogs cannot be made to face the wind. They simply lie down and howl; and beat them as you may you cannot make them move. The natives dug a hole in the snow about 6 feet square, 3 or 4 feet deep, turned the sleds up to the windward of the hole and got into their sleeping bags in the snow bank. The storm continued to blow during the whole of that night; the next day and the next night it was impossible to move, until the next day morning, when it cleared up a little, but in the mean time we had nothing to eat. It was too stormy to make a fire to make tea, and the venison bones that the natives had dug out were full of maggots. We chopped this up in little cubes and swallowed it whole, which made me so sick after it warmed up in my stomach that I vomited it all out again.

About seven o'clock in the morning got ready to start the teams to the southward, turning the short team back again to go home. The short team of dogs had something like 250 versts to go northwest and no supplies but two dried fish and a quarter of a pound of tea. I put all the loads from the three sleds on to two sleds and started for Bulcour, the nearest place where I could make a fire. I arrived at Bulcour about eleven or twelve o'clock at night. It stormed so during this day, the wind had carried dogs and sleds whither it would. Owing to the manner in which the sleds were made in traveling over the snow [sand*] banks, it wore away the runners, so that the lashings kept coming [cutting*] out, and the sleds continued breaking down. Arrived at Bulcour and set to work repairing the sleds and the next morning started for the native village known as Ku Mark Surk, about 50 or 55 versts from Bulcour. On my journey to the northward, this 50 versts I had traversed in about seven hours, but on my return it was so stormy and the snow so deep that it took about fourteen hours. The dogs were so exhausted from starvation that they could only drag the sleds along. I was frozen so badly that I could not walk. The natives were not frozen, but were so tired from hauling the sleds, that when they got within 8 versts of the village they proposed not to go any farther but wait until the next day and camp in the snow. When the natives stopped, the dogs howling like wolves, the dogs in the village hearing the dogs attached to the sleds howling, answered the call, and the dogs made a fresh start and got in all right that night out of the storm. I arrived at Ku Mark Surk on the 24th of November.

And the court then, at 12 m., took a recess until 12.30 p. m., at which time it reconvened with all the members, the judge-advocate, and the witness under examination present, and the witness then continued his answer to the pending question as follows:

I remained there all night and the next morning started the dog teams and arrived at Burroloch over night, and the next morning started for Bulun, a distance of 80 versts. The snow at this time was so deep and the weather so bad that it required a train of six [sixteen*] reindeer to carry myself and one dog driver and the articles recovered at the cache; and these eighty versts, the ordinary time is eight hours, and I have made it in seven hours before. On this occasion it required fourteen hours to make it, being obliged to stop at a native village called Ajaket, the natives having lost their way on the river and bringing up at this place to warm up. I arrived at Bulun on the morning of the 27th of November, having been absent twenty-three days. Upon my arrival at Bulun I found that there had not been sufficient transportation for the people, on the road, and that Mr. Danenhower had taken away five of the sickest people on his way to Yakutsk, leaving six people behind for me. The cause of this is, that ordinarily, traveling through this section of the country seldom extends to more than two or three traveling together, unless with their own deer trains. The mail-route people at stations must keep

---

* Correction by witness.

transportation but for three people bound for or arriving at Bulun. I also learned that the assistant espravnik of Verkeransk had been sent to the Lena delta to inquire into the landing of the people there, as they had never learned or knew anything about the Jeannette having sailed from the United States. The assistant espravnik was named Epatchieff. When he left Bulun, Bartlett having orders that if I did not return within twenty days he should send somebody to look for me, gave Epatchieff 40 pounds of bread to carry with him to me for my use in case he found me. Epatchieff instead of following in the track that I went on, was carried by his business across the county to Geeomovialocke. Upon his arrival at Geeomovialocke, he learned from my dog drivers that I had sent home from North Bulun, that I had been to North Bulun, had gone to the Arctic Ocean to get the books and papers, and was probably on my return to Bulun. Epatchieff went from Geeomovialocke to North Bulun, and having learned that I had left on my way to Bulun, he followed my track and arrived at Bulun about the 28th day of November. The clothing that had been supplied to the whale-boat party to conduct them from Geeomovialocke to Bulun was only borrowed and had to be returned to the natives who loaned it. Upon the arrival of the people at Bulun, the Cossack commandant set about having new clothing made for the people to enable them to travel from Bulun to Yakutsk by the way of Verkeransk. Upon my return to Bulun, I found that it was not possible to fit out an expedition from Bulun to renew the search until spring time, the commandant complaining that the sailors had eaten more bread during the time that they were there than all his people put together. He said he had no authority to supply me with anything but transportation accompanied by the assistant espravnik of the district as far as Verkeransk. I then made arrangements that the men should be supplied with the necessary fur clothing and that food be supplied them on the journey from Bulun to Verkeransk.

All through this section of country to Verkeransk even to Irkutsk it is necessary to carry with you the bread and beef or venison or fish that you are going to live on, and use teams sufficient to transport your material, as you cannot be supplied with any of the necessary articles on the road.

About the last day of November I left Bulun in company with the assistant espravnik of Verkeransk, having made arrangements with the commandant to supply the party with the necessary food and clothing. I traveled with the assistant espravink in order to prepare the reindeer sled and teams on the road, and arrived at Verkeransk about the 6th day of December, 960 versts from Bulun.

Bartlett and the remainder of the whale-boat party arrived three or four days after I had arrived. At Verkeransk I had bread baked and prepared for the people to travel from Verkeransk to Yakutsk, and supplied the people with the fur clothing found necessary for their travel from Bulun to Verkeransk.

Before leaving Bulun I made the Cossack commandant understand that I desired him to aid in regard to finding or searching for the bodies of the dead, promising him a thousand roubles if he found them, with all the books and papers and any of the people. I also explained to him, in case he found the bodies of the dead, how I wanted him to put them in a hut, bank it up properly with snow, and prevent the entrance of any animals, or anything which would destroy the bodies; and also that when I arrived at Verkeransk, where the espravnik was, I would have written instructions sent to him, having learned that there was an exile in Verkeransk who spoke English and who could make a translation for that purpose.

Upon my arrival at Verkeransk I had the exile, Leon, make a translation of a letter that I wrote in English to the espravnik of the district, who was named Kastaroffski.

The witness here produced a letter, and said "This is a copy of the letter to the espravnik of the district of Verkeransk, inculding instructions for him to send the same to the Cossack commandant at Bulun, directing him to continue the search for the bodies of the dead and the books and papers, during my absence at Yakutsk to get the authority of the governor of Eastern Siberia to fit out an expedition for the spring search."

The judge-advocate then proceeded to read aloud the letter in question, a certified copy of which is appended to the record, marked M M.

The witness continued his narrative as follows:

After the arrival of the whale-boat party from Bulun, in charge of Fireman Bartlett, I started with one of the secretaries of Governor Tcherneiff, a day in advance of the party, for the purpose of preparing teams on the road for the transportation of the party that were behind me, and to see the governor as soon as possible to arrange for a summer search. I arrived at Yakutsk about the 27th day of December, and immediately waited upon the governor and inquired if an answer had come to my original telegram to the Navy Department.

The witness here produced a paper and said, "This is a copy of the original telegram sent by me from Bulun by special courier to Irkutsk, the terminus of the telegraph wires, three copies of which were made, one copy to the Secretary of the Navy, one to the American minister at St. Petersburg, and one to Mr. James Gordon Bennett. These were sent about the 2d day of November."

The judge-advocate then read aloud and placed before the court the telegram, and a certified copy, marked NN, is appended to the record.

The witness then produced the original telegram received by him at Yakutsk, which the judge-advocate read aloud and placed before the court, and a certified copy, marked O O, is appended to the record.

The WITNESS. This was received by me about the 5th day of January [referring to the first telegram], and this [producing another telegram] was received on the same day. And the witness here presented the original telegram from Hoffman, chargé at St. Petersburg, which the judge-advocate read aloud and placed before the court; and a certified copy, marked P P, is appended to the record.

The WITNESS. At this time I would like to correct (having since examined my notes), by changing the date of our arrival at Yakutsk from the 27th day of December to the 30th day of December.

The witness continued his answer to the pending question as follows:

No telegram had arrived up to this date. I told the governor that I desired transportation for myself and people as far as Irkutsk; that I wanted his assistance in fitting out an expedition to go north in the spring time to search for the missing boats' crews. He informed me that he could only provide transportation for myself and party to the governor-general at Irkutsk. He said a letter [mail*] would probably arrive in three or four days; that he would recommend me to wait until I received by mail a letter in answer to my telegram. In the mean time he supplied me with five thousand roubles for the expenses of the road journey to Irkutsk. I had made all the preparations for procuring the

---

* Correction by witness.

provisions and clothing necessary to transport the party to Irkutsk. I was also informed that but six people could travel at a time. I awaited the arrival of the telegram, which arrived about the 5th of January.

About the ninth or tenth day I started Mr. Danenhower and the remainder of the people, except Nindemann, and Bartlett, to go to Irkutsk and thence to the Atlantic seaboard. I retained Nindemann and Bartlett as the two best men in the party to assist me in the search, intending to make three search parties with an interpreter in each one. More people could not be used successfully in a search such as I had before me, owing to the scarcity of the provisions and dog-teams at the Arctic Ocean where the search was to take place.

After Mr. Danenhower had left, and the remainder of the party, I set to work to prepare the expedition as rapidly as possible, to commence the search in the early spring. Upon my presentation of the telegram from the Secretary of the Navy to Governor Tchernieff, he told me that there was no limit to the demands of money, provisions, or the people; that the telegram was an offical telegram from the American Government, and that the whole force of Russia at his command was at my service. It was necessary to have tobacco, food, and clothing supplied from Yakutsk and transported over the mountains in midwinter on packhorses and reindeer sleds and dog sleds to the Lena Delta. This is a distance by the post road of over 2,360 versts to the Arctic Ocean. I set Bartlett and Nindemann at work to buy up such small articles as might in their judgment seem best, an made an arrangement with Governor Tchernieff to supply me with six months' supplies for ten people, all of which was to be sent immediately from Yakutsk to Bulun, and then to any point on the delta where required; also to duplicate the order in the month of June if the order was not countermanded in the meantime, in tending that the provisions should reach Bulun for the Lena Delta in the month of July or August. This was for a reserve in case I might be detained there during the fall or until the sledding would commence and return to Yakutsk in the fall time. I engaged three interpreters, one for myself, one for Nindemann, and one for Bartlett, all three of them speaking the Russian language and some Yakutsk. One of them was the captain of the steamboat Lena, who understood the river Lena very well, having plied in that river on the steamboat Lena; another was an ex officer of cavalry, in the employ of the Russian Government, and the third was a Cossack sergeant in Governor Tchernieff's service, in which he had traveled all over this section of country. Owing to the scarcity of teams on the road it was necessary that we should go forth in three separate parties, and I got Nindemann and his interpreter away about the 19th of January, giving them orders to wait at Bulun for my arrival. I got Bartlett with the provision train and his interpreter started about January 23 with orders to take care of the provisions and provision train, to go as far as Bulun and await my arrival. The provision train required so many horses and reindeer to transport the provisions that it was necessary that I should give them time to advance them on their journey and return. For this reason I remained behind, and after signing the necessary vouchers for General Tchernieff I left Yakutsk for Bulun, by way of Verkeransk, about the 27th day of January. I arrived at Verkeransk about the 4th day of February, overtaking the provision train, started on the night of the 4th of February, on the morning of the 5th of February, and remained at Verkeransk until the 10th of February, to give the provision train the right of way, and to await the return of the animals for the transportation of myself and party, which at this time consisted of myself, Captain Greenbeck, and the espravanik of the district, Epatchieff. I had orders from the Governor for the espravanik of the district to go with me to enforce all contracts with Russian and native travelers, and all others, to assist in such manner as the circumstances might demand. The mountain divide was very stormy, and the traveling very difficult. I overtook Bartlett with the provision train on the route to within one hundred or a hundred and fifty versts of Bulun. He was snowed in, and killed six or more of his reindeer trying to get them through the snow-drifts. He told me that Nindemann in advancing had killed several of his reindeer. Bartlett and the party with the provision train was unable to advance at the time. They had plenty of dead reindeer for subsistence. I gave them what fresh reindeer I had and took what reindeer he had to spare that were able to work, and went on to Bulun, arriving at Bulun on the evening of February 17. Bartlett and the provision train arrived on the evening of February 18; myself and provisions the previous day, with the exception of salt and dried beef that were being prepared at Verkeransk and was not yet at Bulun.

And the court then at 2 p. m., pending the further examination of this witness, adjourned to meet to-morrow, the 21st day of November, 1882, at 10.30 a. m.

THIRTY-EIGHTH DAY.

NAVY DEPARTMENT,
Washington, D. C., Tuesday, November 21, 1882—10.30 a. m.

The court met pursuant to the adjournment of yesterday.

Present, Commodore Wm. G. Temple, United States Navy, president; Capt. Joseph N. Miller, United States Navy, Commander Frederick V. McNair, United States Navy, members; and Master Samuel C. Lemly, United States Navy, judge-advocate.

The record of the proceedings of yesterday, November 20, 1882, the thirty-seventh day of the inquiry, was then read, and after correcting clerical errors, approved.

Chief Engineer GEORGE W. MELVILLE, United States Navy, the witness under examination, then came in, and continued his answer to the pending question, which was repeated by the judge-advocate, as follows:

State in detail what efforts were made or attempted by yourself or any of the officers or men under your command to further insure the safety of that party, and for the relief of the other parties.

The WITNESS. Before leaving Yakutsk I had prepared three charts, copies of Peterman's chart, corrected by Nordenskjöld. This is the chart that I used myself, and made copies for Nindemann and Bartlett. They worked on copies the same as this chart. All the distances marked on this chart and the official distances established by the Russian authorities for the payment of tax or toll in the transportation of merchant supplies.

The witness here produced the chart referred to and the judge-advocate placed it before the court, and a certified copy, marked Q Q, is appended to the record.

The witness then continued his narrative, as follows:

The chart in its coast lines is apparently correct, but there are many rivers in the delta and islands that are not laid down on the chart at all. For instance, on the chart, between the village of North Bulun and a place known as Ballock, on the River Osoctoc, one of the main branches running to the northward, I crossed eleven good sized rivers in passing from the village to the river, and on the chart you will find none laid down. I mention this to show the unreliability of the charts. After the arrival of myself and party at Bulun it was necessary to get the dogs and the dog teams to commence the search at once. Reindeer teams generally carried freight or travelers as far as Ku Mark Surk. Beyond this there are no regular stations or depots for the transportation of travelers or goods of any kind; the travelers and merchants supplying their own teams. The dog teams could only be procured at Geeomovialocke or at North Bulun, or on the islands up to the westward at a village called Turak on Long Island.

I found it necessary to employ in the mountain from three to five teams of dogs, numbering fifteen dogs to a team; and for hauling supplies, five or even ten teams at times, to keep up the supply of fish for the subsistence of the dogs, as every dog while working required a fish a day, weighing from four and a half to five and six pounds each.

The espravanik of the district was with me, and he sent a messenger to collect all the dogs in the district at Cass Carta, which was to be the principal depot of supplies, as soon as possible. The Russians [Russian traders *], knowing that I would require a large amount of fish, had bought up all the fish that were in the district, and fish that could be bought recently for three kopeks, a kopek being the hundredth part of a rouble, they wanted ten to fifteen roubles for. This made it necessary for me to cross the mountain range over to Geeomovialocke. I left Bulun for the purpose of going to Geeomovialocke about the 23d day f February, carrying an interpreter and the espravanik of the district with me. I arrived at Geeomovialocke about the 25th or 26th of February. I had purchased seventeen head of reindeer on the hoof for food. These I put in charge of Nindemann and Bartlett, who were in charge of the provision train, with their interpreters and the Cossack sergeant; also a man and a woman that I had hired as cook and wood and water carrier for the camp. I gave Bartlett orders to proceed as far as Ku Mark Surk; that is as far as he could go with reindeer, and wait the arrival of the dog teams that I would send him from Geeomovialocke to carry him and his party up the river as far as Mat Vay, where I had promised to have a depot of fish for him and his party and for the dogs that were carrying them from there. He had orders to go as far as Cass Carta; if he got there before I did, he would wait my arrival. When I arrived at Geeomovialocke, I learned that no person had been able to pass between Geeomovialocke and Bulun for three months, owing to the stormy state of the weather, the snow-storms and wind. I secured six thousand fish at Geeomovialocke, the espravanik of the district breaking all the contracts that the merchants had made where the money had not been paid and turned the fish over for my use. The day following my arrival at Geeomovialocke, I fitted seven dog teams with fish and supplies, to go as far as Ku Mark Surk, to carry Bartlett and the provision train to the northward, up the main branch of the Lena. The natives started off in a snow storm. It set in to snow and stormed and stormed there, so that after an absence of five or six days the dog teams returned in a terrible state; the hands and faces and legs of the drivers were frozen so that they were hardly able to move. Four of their dogs had died in harness and some had escaped. They were obliged to leave the fish and return to Geeomovialocke. In the mean time I had started

---

* Correction by witness.

the provision train and fish to Mat Vay, the first depot of supplies, to have the fish there in readiness for Bartlett and the provision train. These teams had orders, in addition to delivering their fish at Mat Vay, to remain there [go on*] and assist in hauling Bartlett and the provision train there. The snow storm detained them in the huts at Borkhia, Stolbovoi, and Terganak, and by the time they arrived at Mat Vay they had consumed nearly all of their fish, but proceeded according to their orders as far as Ku Mark Surk to assist in bringing the provision train there. As soon as the weather cleared up at Geeomovialocke, I started fresh teams with half loads to increase the number of teams. I told them they must go over [through*] to Ku Mark Surk, stormy weather or no; to eat the fish if necessary to go on to Ku Mark Surk. I sent a letter by the dog teams, instructing Bartlett, if necessary, to kill the reindeer to feed the dogs, and to go through to the depot at Mat Vay and Cass Carta. At the second attempt the dogs got through to Ku Mark Surk. Immediately after sending the second series of dogs I started by way of Arii, Stolbovoi, Terganak, and Ordono for Cass Carta. The huts are the summer habitations of the natives, but after the end of winter time the weather had been so stormy the natives were loath to go unless by way of a line of huts to have shelter. On this journey we slept at the hut at Stolbovoi. The next morning, as we approached the huts at Terganak, very much to our surprise, as we expected to find the hut vacant on our arrival there, the dog drivers attempted to enter the huts, and came out saying, "Somebody was dead in there." Upon inquiry we found that nobody was dead in there, but that there was an old man and an old woman and a young man and a young woman and five children in this place, nearly starved to death; that they had started to go from the village of Turak, on Long Island, and owing to a famine in that section were on their way down to the southeast, to Geeomovialocke, to get something to eat. They were caught in the snow storm I have described, lost their way, but in close proximity to the huts, and three of their youngest children had frozen to death and were buried in a snow bank outside the huts. The other people in the huts were so badly frozen that they were hardly able to crawl. They had eaten all the lashings from their sleds and were burning the inside of their hut to keep themselves warm. I gave them what tea and fish I had to spare. I told them the teams would return in three or four days and carry them to Geeomovialocke.

About the evening of the 12th of March I arrived at Cass Carta, passing in sight of the hunting station known as Qu Vina. While at Geeomovialocke I had my interpreter with me and the espravnik of the district. I made inquiries in regard to the cause of the delay of Kusmah in passing from Geeomovialocke to Bulun and back. I also had the espravnik of the district make official inquiry into the contract of the Starosti of the village in supplying us with rotten geese instead of fish. He sent for Kusmah and all the people in the vicinity. Kusmah and Nikolai Shagra stated that the cause of the delay was the breaking up of the Lena River after they had crossed the first range of mountains, and the reason they had not left Geeomovialocke before they did was because of the open water in the bay and in the river beyond; it was impossible for Kusmah or Nikolai or any other person to leave Geeomovialocke before they did. That he went as soon as he could go, and returned as rapidly as possible.

While I was at Geeomovialocke I paid all the bills that the natives

---

* Correction by witness.

had against me for supplies for myself and the whale-boat party while I was there before. I also paid Kusmah for carrying the message to the commandant, but as he did not supply the reindeer teams and the clothing according to his contract, I paid him three hundred rubles instead of five hundred rubles, because the additional charges of the commandant amounted to two hundred rubles. A day or two after my arrival at Cass Carta, Bartlett and Nindemann, with the provision train, arrived. I had made an arrangement while at Geeomovialocke to have the dog teams continue hauling the fish to Mat Vay and Cass Carta. The espravnik had ordered all the dogs collected in the vicinity of Cass Carta, and I immediately set to work to organize the teams for the search. The search was intended to have been carried on in three separate parties, myself and interpreter as one party, Nindemann and his interpreter as a second, and Bartlett and the Cossack sergeant as the third party. There were many dogs employed in hauling the fish, though I could not hire the dogs for the search party until about the 16th of March. On the 16th I had two good teams of dogs, fifteen dogs in a team, and while waiting the arrival of the additional dogs for the other teams I started, in company with Nindemann and the interpreters, up the main branch leading to the northward, toward a hut called Usterda. This is where De Long crossed the river to the westward, and where his record said he followed the west bank of the river to the southward. We arrived there late in the evening, and as soon as we came in sight of the hut Nindemann recognized the place immediately, saying: "That is the hut, and there is the river making up to the northeast, and the other hut to the southward, that De Long and his people could not get to because of the stream of water to the eastward." This hut to the southward was the hut called Mesja. We slept in the hut that night, and the next morning crossed the river to the westward, as the record said De Long was going to, and as I had done the season before." Here the river takes a great bend to the westward. Nindemann then said he thought that after they had crossed the river to the westward it proceeded to the southward about a mile or a mile and half, and turned so far to the westward that Captain De Long had an idea that this branch ran off into the northwest, which would carry him off to sea or up into the northwest, where he did not want to go, as his course lay to the southward. For this reason Lieutenant De Long recrossed the river to the eastward, and followed a dry branch of the river down into the southeast. This accounts for my loss of De Long's track the previous fall. Nindemann recognized the point at which they camped the first night after leaving Usterda and recrossing the river. We hunted for the fire at every place they had been, but the bank was snowed in so deep that nothing could be found. I inquired of the dog-drivers that I had engaged specially for this part of this search, as men who hunted and trapped in this district, if they knew of a small hut, and described it to them as being on the bank of a good-sized river, and about fifteen or twenty, or may be twenty-five, versts distant from the place where we then were, into the southward or eastward. They said yes; they knew where there were two. We then followed up the dry bed of the stream, which Nindemann recognized as having been on their march, and finally coming up with a hut on the right bank of the stream, but it was not the right one; that is, it was not the hut in which Erichsen had died. I was anxious to find the hut in which Erichsen had died, because after finding this hut it would shorten my march fifteen, twenty, or twenty-five versts, whatever it might be, and give me less ground to search over. This not being the hut I wanted, I returned to the starting point, and started a second time, going more to the southward and in to the eastward, to find the second hut the native spoke of. It came on to snow and blow, and got pretty well toward evening. I inquired how far it was to Sister Ganak hunting station. They said thirty or forty versts; that we would camp there that night. Arrived there late in the evening. The storm continued the next day. I concluded to leave the fish there and return with the dog-sleds to Cass Carta. It was still storming and blowing, but the storm was behind us, and we had no difficulty in traveling. Arrived at Cass Carta on the evening of that day, and the next day it continued to blow; but the day following it cleared up, so as to enable us to make another start. In the mean time more dogs had arrived, and Bartlett was fitted with his search party, dog-teams, and drivers. I then directed Bartlett to go with his dog-team as far as Mat Vay, the other depot of supplies. Nindemann having informed me that they had come down some branch of the river that made out from the great bay, on the southward of which is the hut Mat Vay, I told Bartlett to start from Mat Vay and work from Mat Vay to the northward on the largest branch of the river that he might find; that myself, along with Nindemann and his teams, would work from the northward to the southward, in hopes of finding Erichsen's hut and recover the record, gun, and ammunition, and other articles that were in the hut; that in case he found my tracks ran across him he was to double on my tracks and follow me to the southward, eventually bringing up at Mat Vay, working from the northward to the southward. Bartlett and I started at the same time from Cass Carta, as I had instructed him to do. He arrived at Mat Vay the same evening that he left Cass Carta. It was coming on to storm and blow, and he remained there all night, Nindemann and myself camping down in the snow. The next morning it continued to blow so hard from a southward direction, in which we wanted to go to reach Mat Vay, that the dog drivers could not proceed; neither men nor dogs will face a gale of wind on snow. The hut Qu Vina was about twenty or thirty versts to the westward. I ran for the hut of Qu Vina. It continued to storm, and during the day three or four of the dog teams loaded with fish took refuge in the same hut. Bartlett in the mean time had started out from Mat Vay, was caught in the snow-storm, and camped down and remained in camp all day, not being able to move. I left Qu Vina, however, in the storm, and ran down to Mat Vay, having made up my mind that as Nindemann had advised, it would be better to try to search from the southward to the northward, as he though he would be able to recognize the river on which he and Noros had come. The storm continued. Bartlett remained at Qu Vina. Nindemann and myself remained one night and one day at Mat Vay, owing to the storm; the day following it cleared up. Nindemann not being sure which of the rivers it was he had marched along, I had made up my mind to start from the hut Mat Vay, going to the westward, from headland to headland, as far as the mouth of each river. At the time when I made an examination of the headlands I went all along round the bay from the westward to the northward, and so along to the eastward, until I had examined every headland and river that was on the bay, until I found a large river with the ice very much piled up in it, as Nindemann had described it, the water being open and running the season before. On my passage from Geeomovialocke to Cass Carta I crossed a very large river, the ice there being in immense masses, which answered to the description of the river that Nindemann had described to me. This I learned to be the river Vogoastock or Duropean. We followed the bay until late in the evening, having visited all the headlands; finally came up to the large river with the broken ice. I jumped up on the headland or point of land making down in the bay and found where an immense fire had been made. The fire-bed was probably six feet in diameter, large drift-logs hove into it, and a large fire made, such as a signal-fire. There were many foot-prints and marks around the fire. I then hailed Nindemann and the natives, saying, "Here they are." They thought that I had found the place where the De Long party had been. Nindemann came up on the point of land and said that neither he nor Noros had made a fire of that kind, only a small fire in the cleft of a bank; but he was sure that this was the point of land they had turned going to the westward, and that this was the river along which he and Noros had come. I asked them if the Yakutsks made a fire like that, and they said no; that they only make small fires. I then concluded that De Long and his party had been here, but supposed they had turned, as Nindemann and Noros had, down to the westward, and expected to find them somewhere to the westward. Nindemann had described an old flat-boat that lay on the bank of the river a short distance up this same river. If we found the flat-boat, that would show this to be the river on which Erichsen's hut was located. I then started up the river with the intention of going as far as Erichsen's hut, getting the relics there known to be in the hut, and to return to the point of land and continue the search between the point where the fire had been and Mat Vay. Nindemann started with his dog-team in advance some four or five hundred yards, and while running along sighted the flat-boat. I followed after him, sitting on the sled, facing the bank. The bank here was twenty-five or thirty feet high above the bank of the river, and the snow filled in with a natural slop to the height of the bank, and passing probably forty or fifty feet out to the river; but the wind blew so fiercely in this section that very little snow lies on the highlands or Tundras. The snow was blown into the valleys, forming banks equal in depth to the depth of the natural bank of the river. It is the custom in making a search to go facing the bank of the river, and when they see anything to attract them, drop off the sled and examine it or pick it up and go on. In this manner about five hundred yards from the point where the fire had been, I saw the points of four sticks standing up out of the snow about eighteen inches, and lashed together with a piece of rope. Seeing this, I dropped off the sled, and going up to the place on the snow bank, I found a Remington rifle slung across the points of the sticks, and the muzzle about eight inches out of the snow. The dog driver seeing I had found something, came back with the sled, and I sent him to Nindemann to tell him to come back, he having gone as far up the river as the flat-boat. When they returned I started the natives to digging out the snow bank underneath the tent poles. I supposed that the party had got tired of carrying their books and papers, and had made a deposit of them at this place, and erected these poles over the papers and books as a land-mark, that they might return and secure them in case they arrived at a place of safety. Nindemann and myself stood around a little while, got upon the bank, and took a look at the river. Nindemann said he would go to the northward and see if he could find anything of the track and find the way to Erichsen's hut. I took the compass and proceeding to the southward to get the bearings of Stolbovoi and Mat Vay, so that I might return there that night, in case it came on to blow. In proceeding to a point to set up the compass, I saw a tea-kettle partially buried in the snow. One of the natives had followed me, and I pointed out to him the kettle, and advancing to pick up the tea-kettle, I came upon the bodies of three men, partially buried in the snow, one hand reaching out, with his left arm raised way above the surface of the snow—his whole left arm. I immediately recognized them as Captain De Long, Dr. Ambler, and Ah Sam, the cook. The captain and the doctor were lying with their heads to the northward, face to the west, and Ah Sam was lying at right angles to the other two, with his head about the doctor's middle and feet in the fire, or where the fire had been. This fire-place was surrounded by driftwood, immense trunks of trees, and they had their fire in the crotch of a large tree. They had carried the tea-kettle up there and got a lot of Arctic willow they used for tea, and some ice to make water for their tea, and had a fire. They apparently had attempted to carry their books and papers up on this high point, because they carried the chart case up there, and I suppose the fatigue of going up on the highland prevented their returning to get the rest of their books and papers. No doubt they saw that if they died on the river bed, where the water runs, the spring freshets would carry them off to sea. I gathered up all the small articles lying around in the vicinity of the dead. I found the ice journal about three or four feet in the rear of De Long; that is, it looked as though he had been lying down and with his left hand tossed the book over his shoulder to the rear or to the eastward of him. I referred to the last pages of the journal and saw where the last man had died after Erichsen. The first man that died after Erichsen was Alexy, the Indian hunter. The journal stated that he had died in the flat-boat; that was about five hundred yards from where we then were. Referring to the journal, I found that the whole of the people were now in the lee of the bank, in a distance of about five hundred yards. In the mean time the native that had gone for Nindemann had brought him back. Nindemann and myself pried the bodies up from the ground. They were frozen into the soft slush and snow, and it was necessary to take a stick and put it underneath them to pry them up. We covered them with a piece of old tent cloth. In rolling them over, I found that the pistol that had been carried by De Long during the march was in possession of Dr. Ambler; that is, it was apparently in his right hand, and laid under his body when we rolled him over. This made me suppose that Captain De Long had died before Ambler did, and that Ambler had taken the pistol to shoot a fox or any animal that might come near to interfere with the bodies, or possibly to shoot anything that might come along, to get something to eat. The natives continued to dig underneath the tent poles, at the edge of the bank, and after awhile struck the earth and found nothing. In the mean time it came on to snow and blow. I told the natives to dig away for a spell, and just before night set in we found the head of one man and the feet of another underneath the snow bank. The natives being frightened, jumped out of the hole quickly. I told them to dig a little longer; that they may have their books there; and after digging for a spell they threw out a box of books, and exposed the shoulders of a third person. It was about twenty versts across the bay to Mat Vay, where our camp was. We stuck a stick of timber in the hole where we were digging, gathered up some traps we found, and returned to Mat Vay. That night, on my arrival at Mat Vay, I learned that Bartlett had been to Qu Vina, and on my track to the northward, and had returned to Mat Vay the same evening. I started a messenger to Cass Carta. He brought all my force down to assist in digging the next day. The next morning Nindemann and Bartlett, with all the natives, with snow shovels, started over to the point of land to dig out the people. I remained behind with the interpreter. I prepared the letters and telegrams to the Secretary of the Navy, and the interpreter making translations for the use of the Russian Government, as I had instructions from General Tchernieff that the Russian Government must be informed of all my movements; and I also made a copy of the last thirty pages of De Long's journal, which I transmitted to the Secretary of the Navy. When Nindemann and Bartlett left Mat Vay, I told them when they returned in the evening to bring in the three bodies that we found on the highlands and the three bodies that we discovered in the snow bank, and continue digging until they reached the inner edge of the bank; but in the evening bring home all the bodies that they had found; to be careful of everything that they found in the way of books and papers or anything that was on the persons of the dead. After the first day's work they brought in six people, De Long, Ambler, Ah Sam, Görtz, and two others. These were carried to the hut at Mat Vay, covered well up with an old tent cloth. We buried them in the snow to prevent the dogs and foxes from getting at them.

The next day they started out again, myself and the interpreter remaining behind to try and finish the letters. The smoke in these huts was so bad that it was almost impossible to write or to see at all, for which reason it took so long to write the letters. The next evening, I think, they brought in two more of the dead from the snow-bank, making eight persons so far. They returned to the search the next day; returned in the evening with some small articles, but no more of the dead. De Long's journal stated that he had buried Alexy in the river from the flat-boat. It also stated that the next two men who died, who I think were Kaack and Lee, the party were too weak to carry the bodies out on the ice, and for that reason they had carried them round the corner when his eyes closed. I did not understand what he could mean by "round the corner," as it was comparatively a straight bank, except fissures or holes in the bank that had been washed away by the water. But the next day I went over with the digging party and examined the river where the dead were, and came to the conclusion, as to the others, that Alexy had been buried in the ice of the river. It was comparatively early in the fall, and the ice had fallen in when it ceased to be supported by the water, and the ice had run out by this natural action of the rivers. They sometimes froze up two or three times; as the water falls away the ice tumbles in and runs out; it is frozen over again, and falls in again as the water goes out. I concluded it was useless to search any further for Alexy, but as some idlers were about the camp, that is Yakutske, I offered a reward if they would hunt for Alexy on the river. I concluded that Captain De Long meant that he carried the bodies of the two men around the corner of his tent, and as that was set up to the southward of the tent poles, I started to look for them to the southward, where the tents stood. I started the digging party to dig just to the southward, and I returned to Mat Vay to finish the letters. That evening, when Nindemann and Bartlett returned to the camp, they brought in the last of the dead and the remainder of the small articles we had been looking for, including the flag that was on the flag-staff, covered with a piece of yellow oilskin, and a small mahogany medical case. It then became necessary to find a place to bury them. The whole of the territory to the northward of where I was, and the headland where De Long and Ambler had died, was sometimes covered with 10 or 15 feet of water. The whole of that portion of the delta is covered at some seasons of the year with ice and snow, and is carried away by the floods that come down the river. When the snows melt up the river the floods come down the river, rush over and on the ice like an ocean bore, and carry everything before it away. The nearest place of safety was the foot-hills to northward of the mountains that form the banks of the Lena River proper. About 10 versts to the southward of Mat Vay there was a little whale-back rock between three and four hundred feet high. I selected a flat spot on the top of that mountain and started the hands at work to dig a hole in the rock in whch to set up a cross. Nindemann and Bartlett were set at work with a loit of the natives to break up the old flat-boat to get timber to make a box. The planks of the flat-boat were about 7 inches thick and 2 feet wide. We got out two pieces long enough to make the sides 25 feet long, and sufficient timber from the bottom of the boat to make a cover to the box. The box we completed had inside dimensions of 22 feet by 7 feet, and about 2 feet deep. We hauled all this timber from the flat-boat over to Mat Vay, and on the shoals I found a spruce spar about 13 inches in diameter and 50 feet long, and hauled that to Mat Vay with which to make a cross. I cut the piece 25 feet long off the spar, and another piece of 12 feet, out of which to make the cross-arms. We made the cross-arms and squared one face of it, Nindemann doing the work. Bartlett, in the mean time, carried the box up on the mountain after Nindemann had finished it. After Nindemann had finished the work of hewing out the cross, myself and the interpreter worked the end of it into the hut and cut the inscription. I started Nindemann off with the dog team to follow up the river to find the hut where Erichsen had died. The first time he failed, but the second time he was gone two days and returned with the gun, record, epitaph board, and some ammunition.

And the court then, at 1 p. m., pending the further examination of this witness, adjourned to meet to-morrow, the 22d day of November, 1882, at 10.30 a. m.

THIRTY-NINTH DAY.

NAVY DEPARTMENT,
Washington, D. C., Wednesday, November 22, 1882—10.30 a. m.

The court met pursuant to the adjournment of yesterday.

Present, Commodore William G. Temple, United States Navy, president; Capt. Joseph N. Miller, United States Navy, Commander Frederick V. McNair, United States Navy, members; and Master Samuel C. Lemly, United States Navy, judge-advocate.

The judge-advocate then stated that the record of yesterday had not been completed, and requested that its reading might be deferred, which request the court granted.

Chief Engineer George W. MELVILLE, United States Navy, the witness under examination, then came in, and his examination by the judge-advocate was continued.

Question by the JUDGE-ADVOCATE. Can you now identify the record found at the hut in which Erichsen died?

(The judge-advocate here handed the witness a paper.)

The WITNESS. Yes, sir; this is the record that Nindemann found at Erichsen's hut and gave to me, along with a Winchester rifle and some ammunition. He also brought the epitaph board, from the hut, that was erected to Erichsen.

The judge-advocate then read and placed before the court the record in question, and a certified copy is appended to this record, marked R R.

The judge-advocate then repeated the question which was pending at the time of adjournment yesterday.

Question by the JUDGE-ADVOCATE. State in detail what efforts were made or attempted by yourself or any of the officers and men of the party under your command to further insure the safety of that party and for the relief of the other party.

The WITNESS. When I found the bodies of Lieutenant De Long, Dr. Ambler, and Ah Sam, I did not make a further search of these three bodies, but removed a chronometer watch that was around Lieutenant De Long's neck. When Bartlett and Nindemann started to carry them to the hut the following day, they removed everything they could from about their persons, the persons of Lieutenant De Long, Dr. Ambler, and Ah Sam. They tied them up in separate packages, and delivered them to me on the night they were brought to the hut. The day following they found the bodies of Görtz, Boyd, and Mr. Collins. Nindemann and Bartlett searched these people, and brought all the articles found on these persons tied up in a separate package and delivered them to me at the hut. I was not present at the digging out of the bodies after I had discovered the three bodies under the tent poles in the snow. This work was done actually under the direction of Nindemann and Bartlett. After the bodies had been carried to Mat Vay, and I had prepared the tomb, I told Nindemann and Bartlett to again search the bodies to make sure that there was nothing left about them. This occurred at the back of the hut at Mat Vay, where I had deposited them in the snow bank, myself and Captain Greenbeck, the interpreter, being present. Nindemann and Bartlett searched the bodies again, cutting through their pockets with jack-knives, and searching all around their persons where it is likely books, papers, and relics of any kind might be stowed. Nothing additional was found except a spoon or a jack-knife in the pockets of coal-heaver Iverson. In searching Mr. Collins' body they put his clothing down as far as the breast, and exposed a large bronze crucifix, three or four inches long. Either Nindemann or Bartlett held the object up and asked whether they should remove it. I was a little undecided at first, and said that in all probability his friends would like to have it, but I supposed it was a part of his religion, and therefore we would bury him with the crucifix on his body. I then told him to tuck it in the bosom of his shirt, and to the best of my knowledge and belief the man was buried with the crucifix on his person. I then carried all the bodies over the mountain to the southward of Mat Vay, where I had prepared the tomb. I arranged the bodies side by side, Lieutenant De Long first to the southward, head to the west, feet to the east; laid Dr. Ambler alongside of him, then Mr. Collins, then Lee, and so on in regular rotation, placing the bodies as the names were cut on a vertical portion of the cross, the cook Ah Sam being the furthest to the northward. I covered the bodies with old tent cloth and pieces of rag that we had, and covered the tomb or box proper with seven-inch plank for its whole length. I hauled some large round timber and laid it around the base of the box, and shored the cross with diagonal braces from the edge of the box to the cross. I also erected a ridge pole, and jogging it into the vertical portion of the cross, in order to build up a regular pyramid. From the shoals I hauled some round timber from 4 to 7 inches in diameter, and built up a regular pyramid over the tomb. I then hauled [quarried*] out sufficient stones

---

* Correction by witness.

to cover the whole tomb in with stone, rough stone, pieces from 150 to 200 pounds at the base, with small pieces at the top and sides. I then hoisted the cross-arm up into its place, and Nindemann keyed it with a large wooden key to keep it in place. This finished the burial. This was about the 7th day of April. I then withdrew the whole of my force up to Cass Carta. I still had provisions and dogs and some supplies there, and it was the best point for me to make the search on the coast line for the second cutter, Lieutenant Chipp's party. I had secured dog drivers and guides that were well acquainted with the east coast of the Lena delta. Two men were in the habit of hunting and trapping on [from*] that coast; also two guides and dog drivers that were in the habit of hunting and trapping along the north coast. I secured dog drivers that were acquainted as far west as the river Olinac. I threw out two depots of supplies in the northwest, of fish, for my own use on the return trip on the river Olinac, the distance being too great to carry fish with me on the whole journey. I started Nindemann and Bartlett, and gave them four dog-sleds and drivers, and put ten days' supplies on for their use and dog feed, and directed them to follow up the main river, which runs up to the northeast to Cape Barkin, on the river Kogoastock or Duropean. I gave them both written instructions on arriving at Cape Barkin to part company; Bartlett to take southern track, the east coast of the Lena delta, visiting all the headlands, and running as far into the mouths of the rivers as the provisions would permit him, and continue along down the coast until he arrived at Geeomovialocke. Nindemann's instructions were after he parted company with Bartlett at Cape Barkin to follow along the north coast of the delta, examining all headlands and coast lines, going as far into the mouths of the rivers as he conveniently could until he got as far as the river Osoctoc. In case his provisions ran short he was to go down the river as far as the station known as Balloch. From Balloch, if he was short of provisions, he could run over to North Bulun and get fresh supples. If his provisions held out he was to continue along the coast as far as the river Ketak; he was to descend the river to a village of that name, located on the same river, in the vicinity of North Bulun, after which he was to follow his way down by way of the two small villages, and finally arrive at Cass Carta, and there await my arrival.

A day or two after they started I started to the northward and westward, as far as the village of North Borkhia then to the westward across the short island to Long Island, where there were numerous deserted huts and a number of people still living. I slept at the village of Turak, on the western end of Long Island, and from there I went to the southward and westward until I struck the coast and visited the village of Jaillock and made inquiries there concerning the boats of our party. The people who had this station had not heard of any of our people having been in the delta. They did not know that I had been there or that searching parties were searching for the lost. From Jaillock I followed the coast line around all the promontories as far as the deserted village called Chanker. I then crossed the peninsula into the river Olinac, and followed down the Olinac to the mouth of the river to the main village, which is located there of this name. The river for the whole of its length on which I traveled was pretty thickly populated; that is, there was a village every ten or fifteen versts, with four or five, or as many as twenty people in a village. The people in this vicinity were suffering from a famine, many of their people dying from eating

---

* Correction by witness.

fish with the intestines, which poisoned the people. While at this village, by request of General Tchernaieff, I searched for and found the place where a Russian officer, his wife, and whole Cossack force had died of scurvy. A Russian officer having been sent there for the purpose of finding this out failed to do so, and was so chagrined at his failure that on his return to St. Petersburg he committed suicide. I mention this as showing the difficulty of finding at times exactly what they are hunting for in this section of the country; also the probability of a civilized force dying of scurvy, even when in company with the natives. I then followed along the north coast to the eastward until I doubled on my own track near Turak, at an island, and then followed the coast around to the northward and eastward, following out and in all the bays and indentations of the coast, until I arrived at the river Ketak, that is, down the river Ketak, by way of North Borkhia, then to Cass Carta.

I found Nindemann on my arrival, he having made the search along the coast, and found nothing of Lieutenant Chipp's boat or party, but found the first cutter, Lieutenant De Long's boat, where she had been left in the ice, off shore, the bows and stern above the surface of the ice, the body of the boat sunk [snowed*] in. This was about the 21st of April. I then withdrew the whole of my force to Geeomovialocke, where I made a list of all the supplies that had been sent there for my use to the keeping of the Starosti of the village. This completed the search for Chipp's boat on the coast line as far as Geeomovialocke.

I at this time learned that Lieutenant Harber and a party had been sent out from the United States to renew the search, or to continue the search. I also heard that he was about to charter the steamboat Lena. Knowing that it was impossible to get in sight of the coast with a steamer that drew as much water as the Lena, I made up my mind to go as far in my search as the Jana River, and then go up to Yakutsk and confer with Mr. Harber in regard to the steamer. I then started in company with Nindemann and Bartlett across the bay of Maloy, and so on into the river Jana, and arrived at Oceansk about the 1st of May. By this time the sledding season was over. I had used up all the dogs and their feed to work them. I used so many fish of the natives that many of them were almost in a starving condition. In one place they were grinding up wood and pounding fish and mixing it with snow to eat.

I used so many dogs and required so much fish for them to eat that it created a famine in the Lena delta. After leaving Oceansk I arrived at Verkeransk on my way south about the 6th of May. I left Verkeransk the next day on my way to Yakutsk. I arrived at the mountain divide between Verkeransk and Yakutsk about the 14th day of May. Owing to the snow in the mountains and the floods in the river and everywhere, I was detained there until the 24th day of May. While at this station, Kangarack, Lieutenant Berry overtook me, in company with Ensign Hunt and a Cossack. He had followed me from Oceansk by way of Verkeransk, and overtook me in the mountains. We had a consultation, talked over what had been done. I showed them a track chart, and we concluded that it was not worth while to return to the Lena delta; that I had done everything that could be done during this season of the year. In the month of June it is necessary for the people to leave the whole of the Lena delta and go out on the highlands and foot-hills until after the floods pass away, and if bodies or relics or portions of a boat are not found in the early springtime or during the

---

* Correction by witness.

winter, the spring floods coming down the river carry everything off to sea. There was no reason why I should remain in that vicinity any longer, but was proper that I should hasten on to confer with Mr. Harber, who was somewhere up the river, I believe at Yakutsk. I had had no official information of his whereabouts whatever. I arrived at Yakutsk about the 8th of June, and expected to find Mr. Harber and his party there, but not hearing from him by letter, the governor informed me that he was building a couple of small vessels at a small place called Vittin, about a thousand versts distant. I left Yakutsk about the 11th of June, in a steamer, in hopes of catching Mr. Harber at Vittin. I told the captain of the steamboat that if he saw any other steamer coming down the river, or the small boats belonging to the other American party, that in case of so meeting them during the run he would stop them and let me know, but during the night of the 15th some of the people aboard the steamer said that a steamboat had passed us with a small sloop and a whale-boat in tow. This afterward proved to be Lieutenant Harber and his party. The steamer stopped to get wood at a place called Olekma. Lieutenant Harber had stopped at Olekma and had left a note with the espravnik, requesting me, if we passed, to return to Yakutsk, as he was anxious to see me. This I did not think necessary. Lieutenant Berry had concluded to send Ensign Hunt back to join Mr. Harber, Mr. Hunt having volunteered for the service. At the same time he recommended me to send back one of the two men with me. Bartlett having volunteered to go with Mr. Hunt, requested me to let him go. I gave him orders to report to Mr. Hunt for duty; supplied him with money for his traveling, made a track chart of my whereabouts and researches on the Lena delta, and sent to Mr. Harber a letter containing all the information I could think of that would be of use to him. I gave him the list of provisions and stores, and where they would be found. Nindemann volunteered to go back at the same time that I sent Bartlett, but I did not know how well Mr. Harber was fixed with provisions, and did not know about adding two or three people to his party, how it might inconvenience him for food and supplies. As Bartlett was well acquainted with all my actions in the delta, and he being the first to request permission to go, I selected him. They left Olekma about the 17th of June. I was on my way to Irkutsk about the 5th day of July, and I telegraphed the Secretary of the Navy my arrival, and asked permission to return to the United States. He telegraphed his answer.

The witness, producing a paper, said: "This is a copy of the Telegram that I sent to the Secretary of the Navy requesting his permission to return to the United States. This is the answer of the Secretary of the Navy, permitting me to return to the United States."

The judge-advocate read aloud and placed before the court these two papers; and certified copies, marked SS and TT, are appended to the record.

The witness then continued his narrative as follows:

When I arrived at Irkutsk I discharged the interpreter, Captain Greenbeck, the other people being discharged at the Lena delta before I left there, and the two interpreters employed at Yakutsk were discharged on my return to Yakutsk. While at Irkutsk, Mr. Jackson, the correspondent of the New York Herald, turned Seaman Noros over to me, having gotten through with his services, and about the 12th of July I started to the United States, and arrived in New York on the 13th day of September, and reported my arrival at the Navy Department on the 25th day of September.

Question by the JUDGE-ADVOCATE. During the progress of your search did you find any other records of the first cutter's party than those already mentioned? If yea, when and where?

The WITNESS. Yes, sir; I found one, in the navigation-box. It shows the time and place De Long and his party landed, in the month of September, 1881; that is the first record written.

Question by the JUDGE-ADVOCATE. Can you identify that record now?

(The judge-advocate here handed the witness a paper.)

The WITNESS. That is the one.

The judge-advocate then read aloud and placed before the court the record in question; and a certified copy, marked UU, is appended to this record.

Question by the JUDGE-ADVOCATE. When and from what place did you or any of the party under your command first commence your efforts for the relief of the other parties?

The WITNESS. It was about the 20th day of October, 1881, that Lieutenant Danenhower went with a sled party down to the southeast to the Island of Tarrahoo, but immediately upon my arrival at Geeomovialocke we made the people understand that the other boats were missing, and had the natives look out for any signs of them in their huts and villages.

Question by the JUDGE-ADVOCATE. Was it or was it not possible to initiate the search for these people at an earlier date, and why?

The WITNESS. No, sir; it was not, for the following reasons: We were on an island from which it was impossible to get away; the boat could not be worked through the rough running ice, and the ice had not made sufficiently strong for persons to pass over it. The first messenger that it was possible to send was sent to Bulun for the relief of my own party. Before I had found the Russian exile, Kusmah, the starosti of the village, Nikolai Shagra, and all of his people said it was impossible to go until the ice made sufficiently hard for transportation. The whole of the Lena delta is a series of islands and river channels, over which it is impossible to cross except in boats in the summer time or sleds in the winter time, after the ice has made sufficiently strong to bear the people. It was about the 20th day of October when Mr. Danenhower and the dog-sleds attempted to go to the northeast to Barkin, and went southeast to Tarrahoo, and then was always stopped by the unsafe condition of the ice. From where we were located, at Geeomovialocke, on the island, you could see open patches of water across it, but as late as this date every time it came on to blow with any force the ice broke up in some portions of the bay and drifted out. None of our people were properly clad at the time to make a search in the month of October, and they were supplied only with clothing that remained by us after our summer's march. Even the clothing that was supplied us to travel in from Geeomovialocke to Bulun was borrowed clothing, and returned to the natives after our arrival at Bulun. I was dependent upon the natives for food and clothing wherewith to pay for the use of provender or use of a dog-sled. The first messenger that it was possible to send from Geeomovialocke, which I did not consider a place of safety, was sent to Bulun to the commandant. The delay and the difference between the five days and the thirteen days has already been explained, that is, the breaking up of the ice in the river.

Question by the JUDGE-ADVOCATE. Judging from the condition and position of the bodies at the time when you found them, with all the surrounding circumstances within your knowledge, to what cause do you attribute the death of Lieutenant-Commander George W. De Long and his comrades of the first cutter's party?

The WITNESS. They died of hunger and cold.

Question by the JUDGE-ADVOCATE. Did you deem it necessary to adopt any measures for the subsequent identification of the bodies; and if yea, what were they?

The WITNESS. When I discovered the bodies they were perfectly recognizable. I then gave directions to bury the men in the box, putting the commanding officer to the southward, the next in rank next to him, Dr. Ambler, the next officer, Mr. Collins, then the petty officers following, Mr. Lee, and so on, and inscribing their names on the vertical portion of the cross, and making a record in my note-book, stating how each body would be known. Thus, commencing with De Long to the southward, the others in the order named, and the last being Ah Sam, the cook, the farthest to the northward.

Question by the JUDGE-ADVOCATE. In describing the names on the cross, how were the different persons designated?

The WITNESS. Lieutenant George W. De Long (the "U. S. N." was not [done*] put down at this time when it was put up, but after the cross was erected), Doctor J. M. Ambler, J. J. Collins, W. Lee, and so on down the stanchions of the cross.

Question by the JUDGE-ADVOCATE. Have you any further statement to make in relation to the efforts made or attempted by yourself, or any of your party, to insure the safety of that party or for the relief of the other parties? If yea, make it now.

The WITNESS. While we were detained at the Island of Geeomovialocke, it was almost the most extreme point, the most distant from the point where De Long and the first cutter's people landed. It was impossible to go more than two hundred miles to that point where De Long had marched down into the southeast, and to take this party there across the great bay that was running ice and open water at the time that De Long had started Nindemann and Noros to reach Ku Mark Surk. This was about one hundred and thirty miles from where I was located, by the dog roads, and a range of mountains intervening between myself and where Lieutenant De Long was. The evening of the day that I heard of De Long and his party having landed, I was then so far divided from De Long that could I have seen him from where I stood it would have been impossible for me to have reached him by any means in my power with dog-teams before he would have perished. In other words, I heard of his having landed on the night of the 29th of October, and his last record was written on the 30th day of October. I could not possibly have traveled the distance from Geeomovialocke to the point where he died in less than three days. When I heard that he had landed I had no idea whatever, neither had any other person in my party, of his whereabouts.

Question by the JUDGE-ADVOCATE. Have you any charge to lay or special commendation to offer concerning any officer or man connected with the Jeannette expedition—first, as to the condition of the vessel on her departure from San Francisco; second, her management up to the time of her loss; third, her loss; fourth, the provisions made and plans adopted for the several boats' crews on leaving the wreck; fifth, the efforts made by the various officers to insure the safety of the parties under their charge, and for the relief of the other parties; sixth, the general conduct and merits of each and all the officers and men of the expedition?

---

* Correction by witness.

The witness was here allowed to refer to his report of the trip made to Henrietta Island, dated June 6, 1881.

The WITNESS. In my report of the trip to Henrietta Island, made to the commanding officer of the Jeannette, I stated, in regard to men and equipment, that I desired nothing superior to travel any distance. This referred to Ice-master Mr. Dunbar, Seaman Nindemann, Fireman Bartlett, Seaman Erichsen, and Coal-heaver Sharvell. But two of these men remain alive, Bartlett and Nindemann. I believe that every officer and man performed his duty to the best of his ability and according to his lights. I will specially mention among the crew Nindemann and Bartlett, who were the two leading men in all the work on the floe and in the search. Nindemann, in addition to doing the duty of a seaman, was quartermaster and carpenter, fitting the oaken sleds for the carriage of the boats, and, from the beginning to the end of the cruise, was considered one of the leading men of the ship's company. I desire to state particularly of Doctor Ambler, during the whole of the time that he was attached to the ship, in addition to the ordinary duties of the surgeon, he was always careful of the sanitary condition of the ship and the ship's company, always trying to devise some means for the health and well-being of the people in regard to air, light, ventilation, and care of the drinking water, the Jeannette being the first ship that I ever knew that has passed through two winters in the Arctic Ocean free from scurvy. This was wholly due to the skill, care, and attention bestowed on the sanitary condition of the ship and her people by Dr. Ambler. Further, I will say that, in addition to his duties as surgeon in the care of the sick, he acted as road-master, working like a laborer on the road, and after his sick-list became comparatively free he volunteered to work in the drag-ropes the same as the seamen under all circumstances and at all times. There can be no more worthy man and surgeon than Dr. Ambler. In conclusion, I would say that it is difficult to make any distinction among the working force, and I can only say that I believe that every man "done his level best."

The judge-advocate then announced that, if it pleased the court, he would now proceed to cross-examine the witness in accordance with the request and suggestions of Mr. B. A. Collins and Dr. D. F. Collins, brothers of the late J. J. Collins, meteorologist of the Jeannette expedition, who was lost with the first cutter's party.

Cross-examination by the JUDGE-ADVOCATE:

Question by the JUDGE-ADVOCATE. Do you know anything further than you have stated of the alleged trouble between Lieutenant-Commander De Long and Mr. J. J. Collins?

The WITNESS. No.

Question by the JUDGE-ADVOCATE. Did De Long ever speak to you about a difficulty with him?

(The judge-advocate objected to this question, on the ground that it calls for hearsay evidence, and referred the court to Greenleaf, part 1, paragraphs 99, 124, 101, 104. The court was then cleared for the discussion of the objection of the judge-advocate, and afterwards reopened, and the president of the court then announced that the objection of the judge-advocate is sustained, and the question would not be put.)

Question by the JUDGE-ADVOCATE. Did you have any difference with Mr. Collins? And, if yea, state fully what.

The WITNESS. I never had any personal altercation with Mr. Collins, except in the line of argument, in which all, probably, or nearly all, the members of the mess took part. But one evening when all hands were at supper, we were joking about the ship's drifting in the ice, and not having much amusement in the way of hunting, Mr. Collins, who sat at the table with me, said; "Poor old Melville is getting thinner every day." I replied in a pleasant manner, not caring for what he said, "During the time I had been in the ship I had suffered from neither heat nor cold, hunger nor thirst, and that I was neither gray-headed nor bald-headed over the trouble; but that had the ship drifted in the northeast we could have had a much better time, because we would have some amusement in hunting." He seemed to get angry at what I said. He said I had become personal in referring to his gray head; that he got his gray hairs in difficulties and troubles that I knew not of. After supper this was adjusted between us. Mr. Collins was assured that I simply returned a shot that he fired into me. On another occasion, when Captain De Long and Mr. Collins were having some conversation in regard to the instruments, Mr. Collins said to the commanding officer that he wished other people would treat him with the same courtesy that he treated others. The captain asked what the trouble was, and invited him into his room to discuss the question. The next morning, while walking on the ice, the captain hailed me, and said that Mr. Collins had complained to him that Melville was making game of his countrymen; that I was singing Irish songs and making Irish jokes; and as this was disagreeable to Mr. Collins, he thought I had better not sing any more, that there might be no trouble; and from the time of that conversation I never told an Irish joke or sang an Irish song in his presence. We never had any difficulty beyond these two statements, but, on the other hand, were on the best of terms. But after he had spoken to the commanding officer in regard to my singing songs, I told him that if, instead of speaking to the commanding officer, he had spoken to me, I would have desisted, and that I did not think it was upright or manly on his part to complain to the commanding officer before speaking to me. From this time forth we never had anything to do with each other, except officially, such as passing the orders that came in the line of duty; that is all.

Question by the JUDGE-ADVOCATE. Did you ever give an order to any one of your party to bring Lieutenant Danenhower back to camp, dead or alive, when he went away?

(The judge-advocate objected to this question, on the ground that it touched upon matter not brought out in the direct examination, and reminded the court that the cross-examination should be confined to such matters as were adduced in the examination in chief.)

The court was then cleared for the discussion of the objection of the judge-advocate, and afterward reopened, and the president of the court announced that the objection of the judge-advocate was not sustained, and that the question would be put, which was accordingly done.

The WITNESS. I do not remember giving such an order at any time. Mr. Danenhower generally went as directed by me, and I can remember no reason why I should give such an order; but, had it been necessary, I would not hesitate to give such an order, under the circumstances, the time, and place in which I was placed.

Question by the JUDGE-ADVOCATE. Would you now recognize your handwriting in such an order?

The WITNESS. I would.

The judge-advocate here said, in reply to an inquiry from the court, that he had not been furnished with any order such as the one referred to, and that he did not know of the existence of such an order.

Question by the JUDGE-ADVOCATE. Have you given up all the letters which you found on Jerome J. Collins?

The WITNESS. Everything that was found on his body, except the crucifix, already referred to, and delivered into my charge by Nindemann and Bartlett, was delivered into the hands of the Secretary of the Navy. While on the way up the Lena River, Mr. Jackson, the correspondent of the New York Herald, furnished me with a copy of an original telegram, which he showed me at the time, from the Secretary of the Navy, giving him permission to overhaul the books, papers, and effects of Mr. Collins and Lieutenant De Long. On the strength of this order I gave Mr. Jackson the package containing all the effects that were found on the body of Mr. Collins. I was as careful as possible that none of the articles were filched, and, so far as I know, every article was returned in the package to me. As I stated above, I delivered every article to the Secretary of the Navy. The court will please make note that I did not examine the body of Mr. Collins when he was found, nor when he was at the back of the hut, but all the searching was done by Nindemann and Bartlett, and the articles given to me.

Question by the JUDGE-ADVOCATE. When one of your men asked you what would be done with the cross that was on Collins's neck, what did you say?

The WITNESS. I said to him that in all probability his friends would like to have it, but as I supposed it was part of his religion, we would bury it on him. I then directed either Nindemann or Bartlett to tuck it in the bosom of his shirt, and, so far as I know, to my best knowledge and belief, he was buried with this cross on his person.

The judge-advocate did not further desire to cross-examine the witness.

And the court then, at 1.30 p. m., pending the further examination of this witness, adjourned to meet to-morrow, the 23d day of November, 1882, at 10.30 a. m.

FORTIETH DAY.

NAVY DEPARTMENT,
Washington, D. C., Thursday, November 23, 1882—10.30 a. m.

The court met pursuant to the adjournment of yesterday.

Present, Commodore William G. Temple, United States Navy, president; Capt. Joseph N. Miller, United States Navy, Commander Frederick V. McNair, United States Navy, members; and Master Samuel C. Lemly, United States Navy, judge-advocate.

The records of Tuesday, November 21, 1882, and of Wednesday, November 22, 1882, the thirty-eighth and thirty-ninth days of the inquiry, were then read, and after correcting clerical errors, approved.

The court then, at 12.30 p. m., took a recess until 1 p. m., at which time it reconvened with all the members and the judge-advocate present.

Chief Engineer GEORGE W. MELVILLE, the witness under examination, then came in, and his examination by the court proceeded, as follows:

Question by the COURT. Did the members of your party attempt any hunting or fishing while at Geeomovialocke?

The WITNESS. Mr. Newcomb attempted some hunting with a shotgun. We had a net that Mr. Newcomb purchased from the natives at

Geeomovialocke. Beyond this there was no hunting or fishing, as there was no game in the neighborhood.

Question by the COURT. From your arrival at Geeomovialocke, about September 26, 1881, until your departure from that place, about October 29, 1881, state in detail the physical condition of yourself and party, their ability to prosecute a search for the first and second cutter's people, and, finally, state if you did all that was practicable to ascertain the fate of your missing comrades during that time.

The WITNESS. After the first fifteen days all except Leach were able to travel. Our feet and legs were sufficiently recovered to be able to walk. Seaman Leach's feet remained bad until after his arrival at Yakutsk. Mr. Danenhower's eyes seemed to trouble him up to the time that we parted company, as he always complained of the smoke in the hut hurting his eyes.

Question by the COURT. How did their condition affect their ability to prosecute a search for the first and second cutter's people.

The WITNESS. It was limited by the means at hand for prosecuting the search, their want of food and clothing, and the state of the ice. They were also limited in the way of guides. To the best of my knowledge and belief, everything possible to be done was done, and I think everybody did the same; I did all that was possible for me to do.

Question by the COURT. You have stated that the Cossack commandant at Bulun arrived at Geeomovialocke with reindeer teams to take your party to Ku Mark Surk, but that he afterwards found it better to use dog-teams for that purpose. Where were those dog-teams procured from, and why could they not have been procured sooner for the transportation of your party?

The WITNESS. Some were procured from the village in which we were located Geeomovialocke, some from Arii, and a part from Tamoos. In the first place, because we did not know that there were so many dogs in the neighborhood; in the second place, that the natives would not serve us in the manner that they would under the authority of the commandant; in the third place, our inability to make them understand, or to understand the people. For instance, on one occasion I wanted a team of dogs to go to Tamoos to see Kusmah about securing some provisions. I could not get the use of a team at all in the village, though the distance for which I wished it was but ten versts.

Question by the COURT. When you gave Mr. Danenhower orders to proceed south with the party, did you consider him physically capable of commanding the party?

The WITNESS. I did, for that service.

Question by the COURT. You have stated that on leaving Bulun in November, 1881, on your first search, you were under the impression that you had ten days' provisions, whereas they were nearly exhausted in five days; please explain this.

The WITNESS. The Cossack commandant, on his arrival at Bulun, told me that he would furnish me ten days' supplies, with our teams and dog-drivers. This was done at my request, as I had demanded of him ten days' supplies. He talked the matter over with the dog-drivers and with the starosti of the village, and assured me that I had ten days' supplies of food for myself and dogs. At that time, not being acquainted with the amount of food required by the dogs in that section of the country, I could not judge for myself how much supplies should have been put on the sleds.

Question by the COURT. On your first arrival at Mat Vay, could you have stopped to search in that vicinity?

The WITNESS. No, sir; I was out of supplies. It was necessary to get supplies to undertake the search.

Question by the COURT. Did you suppose at that time that the first cutter's party had been at or near Mat Vay?

The WITNESS. Only the expectation that they would follow Nindemann and Noros's footsteps. For that reason I thought they might be in the vicinity of Mat Vay.

Question by the COURT. On your first arrival at Balloch, while in search of De Long and party, why did you visit the landing-place of the first cutter and increase your sled-loads by log-books, instruments, cooking utensils, &c., when you had every reason to believe that De Long had gone in an opposite direction?

The WITNESS. I considered it important to get any record that should be there, and, as I was but a very short distance from the landing-place, believed it to be very important to secure the books and records and carry them south with me on the return trip. Continuing the search to the southward, the pots, pans, kettles, and sleeping-bogs were discarded, immediately after my return. On the southern journey I carried with me only the books, papers, and instruments.

Question by the COURT. Did you think the first cutter's party dead or alive at these time you went for these books, &c.?

The WITNESS. Common sense and my own judgment had led me to believe the people were dead. That was my belief. I will state, in addition, that while in conversation with Nindemann in regard to the search, that he said to me: "There is no use in looking for them now; we will have to wait until the spring time." I do not remember whether Noros said the same at the same time or not, but the two men were very much of the same opinion. I was morally certain the people were dead.

Question by the COURT. Did you explore the coast from Geeomovialocke to the Jana River in the same thorough manner in which you had explored the delta shore-line?

The WITNESS. No, sir; the shoals make out so far that it is almost impossible to follow the coast-line.

Question by the COURT. Do you know who, if any one, was present at the alleged difficulty between the commanding officer and Mr. Collins?

The WITNESS. On one of the days Mr. Danenhower was present.

Question by the COURT. How was Mr. Collins treated officially and socially by the officers of the Jeannette during the cruise and the retreat?

The WITNESS. He was treated exactly in the same manner that any other officer of the officers' mess was treated by each other. If people were pleasant and social in manner and deportment with others they were treated pleasantly and socially; but Mr. Collins had a notion at one time about not speaking to any member of the mess; that is, in giving the ordinary morning salutation he would not answer the captain. He had been in the habit, when keeping one of the night watches, of generally coming out a little late, but he was always out in time for breakfast. On leaving his apartment to come into the living room, he invariably made the salutation of "Good morning, gentlemen"; or to any person in the room, as, "Good morning, Melville," or "Chipp," as the case might be; but the usual morning salutation with which we answered the captain Collins would not give. He did not do this, but on the reverse was in the habit of turning his back and looking in the opposite direction. The commanding officer, Captain De Long, told me he had spoken to him about it. Every officer and civilian that was in the captain's mess stood on their own merits for sociability. I do not believe the commanding officer or any other officer attached to the ship made any distinction with regard to the social standing of any member of the mess. It was quite natural that officers who had cruised together and messed together should like to talk of old cruises and old companionships, and for this reason I suppose the regular officers of the service would monopolize a good deal of the conversation; but in the same manner Mr. Collins and Mr. Newcomb used to walk and talk together, and be more sociable with each other than they were with the regular officers of the Navy. Beyond what I have stated there was no distinction whatever made by the commanding officer between an officer or any other person.

Question by the COURT. Are there no persons deserving of special commendation among the names of the Jeannette's officers and crew other than those you have already mentioned?

The WITNESS. In the transportation of the boats the second leading party was Mr. Cole, the boatswain, and Henry Warren, a seaman, and Leach, seaman. Wilson and Manson, seamen, were the coxswains of the whaleboat, and did their duty thoroughly and well. Leach had his toes frozen, having remained at the tiller for twelve hours without relief, because of the danger of making a change which might cause the boat to broach to. The general opinion on board the ship of Mr. Chipp was that he was the best seaman on the ship, and his conduct was considered that of a thorough good officer in all respects. I did not know whether it was proper that I should pass judgment on my commanding officer, but to my mind he was as good a man as was possible to undertake any duty that might be assigned to him at any time or place; that seemed equal to any emergency that arose at all times. I think whatever he done he done with his whole soul and to the best of his lights.

And the court then, at 1.30 p. m., pending the further examination of this witness, adjourned to meet to-morrow, the 24th day of November, 1882, at 10.30 a. m.

FORTY-FIRST DAY.

NAVY DEPARTMENT,
Washington, D. C., Friday, November 24, 1882.—10 a. m.

The court met pursuant to the adjournment of yesterday.

Present, Commodore Wm. G. Temple, United States Navy, president; Capt. Joseph N. Miller, United States Navy, Commander Frederick V. McNair, United States Navy, members; and Master Samuel C. Lemly, United States Navy, judge-advocate.

The judge-advocate then requested that the reading of the record of yesterday's proceedings might be deferred, which request the court granted.

Chief Engineer GEORGE W. MELVILLE then came in, and the judge-advocate continued the reading to him of his testimony for correction. At 11.25 a. m. the court was cleared for deliberation by request of the judge-advocate, and afterwards reopened, and the reading of the testimony to the witness was resumed.

At 12.10 p. m. the court took a recess until 12.40 p. m., at which time it reconvened with all the members, the judge-advocate, and the witness present.

The reading of the testimony to the witness was then resumed, and continued until 2 p. m., at which time the court adjourned to meet tomorrow, the 25th day of November, 1882, at 10 a. m.

FORTY-SECOND DAY.

NAVY DEPARTMENT,
Washington, D. C., Saturday, November 25, 1882.—10 a. m.

The court met pursuant to the adjournment of yesterday.

Present, Commodore Wm. G. Temple, United States Navy, president; Capt. Joseph N. Miller, United States Navy, Commander Frederick V. McNair, United States Navy, members; and Master Samuel C. Lemly, United States Navy, judge-advocate.

The judge-advocate then requested that the reading of the records of Thursday, November 23, and Friday, November 24, the fortieth and forty-first days of the inquiry, might be deferred, which request the court granted.

Chief Engineer G. W. MELVILLE then came in, and the judge-advocate continued the reading of his testimony to him for correction.

At 12.10 p. m. the court adjourned to meet on Monday, the 27th day of November, 1882, at 10 a. m.

FORTY-THIRD DAY.

NAVY DEPARTMENT,
Washington, D. C., Monday, November 27, 1882.—10 a. m.

The court met pursuant to the adjournment of Saturday, November 25, 1882.

Present, Commodore Wm. G. Temple, United States Navy, president; Capt. Joseph N. Miller, United States Navy, Commander Frederick V. McNair, United States Navy, members; and Master Samuel C. Lemly, United States Navy, judge-advocate.

By request of the judge-advocate, the reading of the records of Thursday, November 23, Friday, November 24, and Saturday, November 25, 1882, the fortieth, forty-first, and forty-second days of the inquiry, was deferred.

Chief Engineer G. W. MELVILLE then came in, and the judge-advocate continued the reading to him of his testimony for correction.

At 12 m. the court took a recess until 12.30 p. m., and then reconvened with all the members, the judge-advocate, and the witness present, and the reading of the testimony was resumed and continued until 1.45 p. m., when the court adjourned to meet to-morrow, the 28th day of November, 1882, at 10 a. m.

FORTY-FOURTH DAY.

NAVY DEPARTMENT,
Washington, D. C., Tuesday, November 28, 1882.—10 a. m.

The court met pursuant to the adjournment of yesterday.

Present, Commodore Wm. G. Temple, United States Navy, president; Capt. Joseph N. Miller, United States Navy, Commander Frederick V. McNair, United States Navy, members; and Master Samuel C. Lemly, United States Navy, judge-advocate.

By request of the judge-advocate, the reading of the records of Thursday, November 23, Friday, November 24, Saturday, November 25, and Monday, November 27, 1882, the fortieth, forty-first, forty-second, and forty-third days of the inquiry, was deferred.

Chief Engineer GEORGE W. MELVILLE then came in, and the judge-advocate continued the reading of his testimony to him for correction.

At 12.15 p. m. the court took a recess until 12.45 p. m., and then reconvened with all the members, the judge-advocate, and the witness present, and the reading of the record was resumed; and the witness, having had all his testimony read to him, made the following corrections, which are recorded in the body of the record by interlineation in red ink at the proper places for the suitable application of the corrections to the evidence corrected:

On page 78, line 3, change "another" to "an."
On page 78, line 38, change the word "work" to the word "break."
On page 78, line 46, change the word "some" to the words "the same."
On page 78, line 52, change the word "held" to the word "heeled."
On page 79, line 1, change the word "scratched" to the word "scratching."
On page 79, line 2, change the words "the openings of the deck seams" to the words "the caulking out of the seams."
On page 79, line 34, change the word "arranging" to the word "launching."
On page 80, line 25, change the word "drift" to the word "solid."
On page 80, line 31, change the word "interlacing" to the word "overlapping."
On page 81, line 7, change the word "get" to the word "cut."
On page 81, line 38, strike out all after "forward" to the end of sentence, and substitute therefor "it was discovered that there was a leak in the gate, which was not properly down on its seat. The obstruction was cleared and the gates made tight, and when the water arose to a certain height, then the water found its way through to the bulkhead."
On page 82, line 4, before the word "water" insert the words "ice to make."
On page 86, line 5, read "from the crow's nest to the northward and westward" instead of "from the north."
On page 86, line 22, change the word "floe" to the word "full."
On page 86, add Seaman Erichsen to the list of men who were on the expedition to Henrietta Island.
On page 86, line 54, change the word "holding" to the word "reaching."
On page 90, line 10, change the words "from pack to pack" to the words "from pond to pond."
On page 93, line 16, change the words "captain's room" to the word "cabin."

On page 93, line 44, change the word "to" to the word "from."

On page 94, at end of sentence, line 4, add "the proper allowance that each person was directed to carry was selected from this heap."

On page 94, line 44, strike out the words "such as pemmican."

On page 94, line 54, strike out the words "especially after pressed in snow floes."

On page 95, line 15, between the words "our" and "side" insert the word "port."

On page 97, add to the list of those on the sick list when the ship went down the name "Alexy."

On page 97, line 19, for the words "a prismatic compass" substitute the words "prismatic compasses."

On page 97, line 33, after the words "wrapped up," insert the words "in it."

On page 99, line 34, change the word "already" to the word "always."

On page 99, line 51, change the word "direct" to the word "drive."

On page 100, line 8, change the word "took" to the word "used."

On page 100, line 37, change the words "work all" to the words "break off all."

On page 104, line 35, insert the word "were" before the word "over," and strike out the word "on"; and on line 36, for the words "opened the way" substitute the words "breaking the way with their feet."

On page 104, line 43, strike out the words "*on the floe side*" and insert the words "*from the floe.*"

On page 105, line 42, for word "wrecked" say "ragged."

On page 107, line 29, change words "cut-off" to "cove."

On page 107, line 30, change word "left" to word "weather."

On page 107, line 2, insert the words "for the purpose of" before word "building."

On page 108, line 29, insert the words "in that case" before word "there."

On page 108, line 51, change word "different" to "difference of."

On page 109, line 31, insert word "cover" after "boat," and change word "capable" to words "for the purpose."

On page 109, line 42, change word "landed" to word "launched."

On page 110, line 9, change word "some" to word "several."

On page 110, line 12, change the words "the head panes" to the words "one of the headlands."

On page 111, line 36, change the word "pulled" to the word "bailed" and insert the words "and were" before "very."

On page 112, line 43, change the word "island" to the word "ice."

On page 113, line 9, change the word "sand" to the word "snow."

On page 113, line 35, change the word "coming" to the word "running."

On page 114, line 23, change the word "foremast" to the word "mast."

On page 114, line 28, change the words "to go" to the words "prevent water coming"; and on line 29 insert words "from tumbling" before the word "into."

On page 114, line 49, change the word "leather" to the word "lead."

On page 115, line 53, add after the word "delta," the words "except Nindemann and Noros whom I met at Bulun about November 2."

On page 116, line 45, change the word "off" to the word "for."

On page 116, line 50, change the word "draw" to the words "have driven."

On page 117, line 8, strike out the words "taking some time trying" and insert the words "trying from time to time."

LOSS OF THE STEAMER JEANNETTE.   169

On page 118, line 7, change the words "pull her up" to the words "put her about."
On page 118, line 10, after the word "swamp" insert the word "river."
On page 118, line 35, change the word "but" to "and."
On page 118, line 47, change the words "large range" to "long reach."
On page 119, line 27, change the word "haul" to the words "go a mile."
On page 120, line 12, change the words "we were trying to get them to go along" to the words "I had been trying to get all day long."
On page 121, line 1, change "beat" to word "push."
On page 121, line 36, strike out the word "not."
On page 121, line 39, after word "more" add word "fish."
On page 122, line 45, change the word "Rodon" to the word "Ordono."
On page 122, line 49, change the words "the frosts" to the words "being frozen."
On page 124, line 52, change the words "New Siberia" to the word "Semenowski."
On page 126, line 36, change the word "over" to the word "on."
On page 126, line 49, change "Semenov" to the word "Fadejouski."
On page 129, line 4, change the words "on the shoal" to the words "along the shore."
On page 129, line 36, insert the word "along" before the word "and."
On page 129, to list of articles supplied by Kusemah add, also, "a reindeer dressed, weighing 94 pounds."
On page 130, line 6, change the words "and the" to the word "two."
On page 130, line 53, change the words "had seen" to the words "could see."
On page 131, line 3, change the word "haul" to the word "march."
On page 131, line 7, add "except Leach, who would have had to be hauled on a sled."
On page 131, line 47, after "notwithstanding" insert the words "I did not understand."
On page 132, line 37, change the word "we" to the word "they."
On page 132, line 37, strike out the words "and saw the hut in the morning, there being three of us," and substitute the words "and returned in the morning with a fresh team of dogs."
On page 134, line 23, change the words "an island" to the words "the shore."
On page 135, line 11, change the word "country" to the word "mountain."
On page 135, line 48, change the word "fish" to the words "fishing places."
On page 135, line 51, strike out the words "and had reached a shelter one night" and substitute the words "on this night I had reached a shelter."
On page 137, lines 2 and 3, change the words "Mat Vai" to the words "Two crosses."
On page 137, line 13, insert the word "further" before the word "trace."
On page 139, line 3, change the words "north and south" to the words "east and west."
On page 139, line 40, change the words "had crossed" to "would cross."
On page 141, line 18, change the word "snow" to the word "sand."

On page 141, line 19, change the word "coming" to the word "cutting."

On page 141, line 42, change the word "six" to the word "sixteen."

On page 143, line 50, change the word "letter" to the word "mail."

On page 146, line 21, change the word "Russians" to the words "Russian traders."

On page 147, line 4, change the words "remain there" to the words "go on."

On page 147, line 11, change the word "over" to the word "through."

On page 154, line 54, change the word "hauled" to the word "quarried."

On page 155, line 11, change the word "on" to the word "from."

On page 156, line 20, change the word "sunk" to the word "snowed," and strike out "it."

On page 159, line 19, change the words "put down" to the word "done."

And the witness also added to his testimony the following statement, namely: While the ship was at San Francisco it was fitted with a double-cylinder hoisting-engine, for the purpose of warping the ship through the ice and for receiving or discharging cargo. It was used for these purposes, and was considered a great relief to the people. Also:

During the first winter, at the time when the ice broke the ship's fore-foot, a thrum mat was prepared, using either a sail or an awning for the purpose, to haul under the bows, to prevent the leak, if we got into open water. The ship being frozen in, it was impossible to apply this. This was retained on board ship.

I stated in my evidence that a waist-belt was found in the hut at Mat Vai. From the information I had received from Nindemann and Noros I had supposed that they had not slept in the hut at Mat Vai. They told me that the first hut they slept in after leaving De Long was at the place of the "Two Crosses," which is away to the southward of Mat Vai. This led me to suppose that the hut at Mat Vai had been visited by some other of De Long's people, but when I returned to Bulun, Noros recognized the waist-belt as a strap that he had carried around his blanket, but did not know where or at what time he had lost the strap, but next spring when Nindemann went to Mat Vai with the provision train he remembered the hut, and remembered having slept there. This, to my mind, satisfactorily answered for my having found the belt in the hut, the people having forgotten that they had rested there. Also, after becoming fully acquainted with the Lena Delta, and the hunters and fishers who lived there, I made efforts to select dog-drivers from the persons who hunted and fished or lived in particular sections of the delta. I found that there was no person living at the delta who knew anything at all of the middle portion of the delta, lying between the river Obibuteyaisa and the island forming the easternmost coast-line of the delta. That is, the man who built the hut in which Erichsen died, had built the hut for hire for another native; that it had never been finished and had seldom been used; that the people did not know of its whereabouts until after we had found it. They then remembered its having been built but not used. That the two guides Vashiley Koolgar and Simeon Alak, who went as guides with Bartlett to and from Barkin, said that no person had lived at hut at Barkin for two years. Simeon Alak was the man who built the hut that Erichsen died in, and he told me that it had never been used; that the game did not run in the middle section, and the fishing was not good. They knew the coast line, because they had fox traps nearly the whole length of that portion of the coast from Barkin to Geeomovialocke. With these corrections and additions made the witness pronounced his testimony correct, and then withdrew.

The record of the proceedings of Thursday, November 23, Friday, November 24, Saturday, November 25, and Monday, November 27, 1882, the fortieth, forty-first, forty-second, and forty-third days of the inquiry, was read, and, after correcting clerical errors, was approved by the court.

The court was then, by request of the judge-advocate, cleared for deliberation, and afterwards reopened, and then, at 1.50 p. m., adjourned to meet on Friday, December 1, 1882, at 10.30 a. m.

FORTY-FIFTH DAY.

NAVY DEPARTMENT,
Washington, D. C., Friday, December 1, 1882—10.30 a. m.

The court met pursuant to the adjournment of Tuesday, November 28, 1882.

Present, Commodore Wm. G. Temple, United States Navy, president; Capt. Joseph N. Miller, United States Navy, Commander Frederick V. McNair, United States Navy, members; and Master Samuel C. Lemly, United States Navy, judge-advocate.

The record of the proceedings of Tuesday, November 28, 1882, the forty-fourth day of the inquiry, was then read, and, after correcting clerical errors, approved.

W. F. C. NINDEMANN was then called as a witness, and having been sworn according to law by the president of the court, testified as follows:

Examination by the JUDGE-ADVOCATE:

Question by the JUDGE-ADVOCATE. What is your name and rate?
The WITNESS. W. F. C. Nindemann; seaman.
Question by the JUDGE-ADVOCATE. To what vessel and what special service were you last attached?
The WITNESS. To the Jeannette, on an expedition to the North Pole, on special service.
Question by the JUDGE-ADVOCATE. When and where did you join the Jeannette, and what were your duties on board of that vessel?
The WITNESS. At San Francisco. I joined the Jeannette in June, 1879. My duties on board that vessel were as seaman, quartermaster, deck officer, and carpenter. That is all, sir.
Question by the JUDGE-ADVOCATE. Have you any statement to lay before this court in relation to the fitting of the Jeannette for Arctic service, and her condition when she left San Francisco?
The WITNESS. The Jeannette was well fitted before leaving San Francisco for the Arctic regions.
Question by the JUDGE-ADVOCATE. Have you any statement to lay before this court concerning the voyage of the Jeannette from the time of her leaving San Francisco to the date when she was put in the pack, on September 5, 1879?
The WITNESS. No, sir.
Question by the JUDGE-ADVOCATE. What experience, if any, had

you in the Arctic regions prior to joining the Jeannette at San Francisco?

The WITNESS. I sailed in the Polaris in 1871 on a voyage toward the North Pole, and in 1872, October 15, we were cast away with nineteen of us on an ice floe, drifting until the 30th of April, 1873. We were picked up off the straits of Belle Isle by the sealing steamer Tigress. We were fetched to St. Johns, and from there to the United States. There were fourteen people left north; the United States Government then found it necessary to buy the ship Tigress, or steamer Tigress, the same ship that picked us up, and sent her north in search of the other fourteen people. I then volunteered, with four others that were along with me on the ice floe, to go up on the Tigress again and look for our shipmates. We got up as far. as North Littleton Island without having to pass through any ice, except young ice off Cape York. On reaching Littleton Island we discovered a house ashore that was built by the Polaris men. On landing we found some natives, who told us that the Polaris men had built two boats and had started off to Cape York. We then steamed south again to Disco to hear any news of the people there. We stood across the straits on a west course, hoping to fall in with some of the whalers and find out whether they had seen anything of the people. We sighted no whalers, and the captain then thought it best to run into one of the inlets, or at least one of the bays, where we took in ballast. On leaving there we crossed on the east course up to Ivertout, to coal the ship. After leaving there, the captain intended to stand on a west course again, to fall in with the whalers. We got into a heavy gale of wind. After the weather moderated the captain determined to run into St. Johns, and in there we learned the news that the people had been picked up by a Scotch whaler and sent to England. We then were recalled to New York; that is the last of it.

Question by the JUDGE-ADVOCATE. About when did you go back to New York?

The WITNESS. About the 20th November, 1873.

The judge-advocate then stated to the court, that in view of the great experience that this witness had had in the Arctic region, prior to joining the Jeannette, he would, if the court pleased, examine him as an expert upon all matters pertaining to ice movement, the advisability of putting the ship in the pack, her management when beset in the ice, and the preparation for and actual management of the retreat.

Question by the JUDGE-ADVOCATE. Describe in detail the appearance and condition or movement of the ice on the day when the ship entered the pack, and state fully what were your opportunities for observation.

The WITNESS. On the evening of the 4th of September I had the deck; and I think the orders were, if the ship could not make a north course to let the captain know. When I found the ship could not make a north course, I went aloft in the crow's nest to see what the condition of the ice was. I found the ice was all slack in toward the westward, and also plenty of open water to the northward and eastward, and some drifting ice to the east of us. Coming down, I reported to the captain the state of the ice, and told him there was plenty of water to the northward and eastward. The captain then said: "Nindemann, we do not want to go to the northward and eastward; I want to try and make Wrangel Land, if I can." He then gave me orders to slow the ship down, and let her go around in a circle during the night, until daylight, and to report the condition of the ice at daylight to him. The next morning the ice was slack in toward the westward. We kept on, steaming along to the northward for a little while, until we struck a large lead that ran in toward Wrangel Land. It was reported to the captain. The captain then took the crow's nest, Mr. Chipp the budge, and the officer of the deck stood alongside the man at the wheel, marking down the course as she went in the lead. We kept on making our way to the westward until about four o'clock in the afternoon, when a heavy fog set in, and we were obliged to tie the ship up alongside of an ice floe. The ice at the time was very slack, and it was no trouble for the ship to work its way through it if it had not been so foggy. The fog let up for a little while, and we cast off from the floe piece and stood some distance in toward the westward. The fog shut down upon us again, and thereupon we tied up alongside of a floe piece. We lay there during that night; the next morning it was clear; the ice had closed in some, but not enough to prevent us from steaming through it. The ice kept closing in more and more, but still we kept on working our way through it, until about in the afternoon, when we got to a place where we could not force our way through. We kept working and butting the ice for some time, but found that it was no good. We tied up alongside of the floe piece. There were still large holes of open water to the westward, and if we could have forced our way through the ice for about 50 yards ahead of us we would have made more progress toward Wrangel Land. During the night of September 6 the night was cold and the young ice was making fast. The ice had closed in more during the night, and it was impossible for us to get the ship out of the pack to the east again, to the open water.

Question by the JUDGE-ADVOCATE. In your opinion, would it or would it not have been possible to get the ship clear of the ice on September 6, 1879?

The WITNESS. No, sir; there was no possibility of getting the ship out of the pack. The ice had closed together, and the young ice had formed so thick that it was impossible for a ship to steam through it, if we had gone in the young ice; that is, ice about 5 inches thick.

Question by the JUDGE-ADVOCATE. What is your opinion of the advisability of putting the ship in the pack at that time?

The WITNESS. If I had had charge of the ship at that time I should have done what Captain De Long did; that is, if I had wanted to reach Wrangel Land.

Question by the JUDGE-ADVOCATE. What, generally, for an Arctic vessel, was the condition of the Jeannette's crew during the twenty-two months the ship was beset in the pack, as to their health, their food, and their quarters?

The WITNESS. The crew of the Jeannette was as healthy a crew and as good a crew as could be selected for an Arctic voyage. The food of the men was very good in every respect; the quarters were very good up till the time she sprang a leak, when the water was raised high enough to run over the berth-deck, sometimes for a day or two, until the leak was stopped.

Question by the JUDGE-ADVOCATE. Was anything left undone that it was possible to do to insure the health and comfort of the crew?

The WITNESS. No, sir; not to my knowledge.

Question by the JUDGE-ADVOCATE. Was or was not the crew as contented as it was possible for them to be under the circumstances?

The WITNESS. To my knowledge the crew always was contented; I never saw any of them discontented.

Question by the JUDGE-ADVOCATE. Have you any further statement to lay before the court in reference to the voyage of the ship up to the time that she was crushed by the ice and went down?

The WITNESS. No, sir.

The witness was then examined by the the court, as follows:

Question by the COURT. When you entered the lead of the ice on the morning of September 5, 1879, did you think there was a fair chance of getting her through to Wrangel Land?

The WITNESS. Yes, sir.

Question by the COURT. Could the ship have been turned about and brought out again to the eastward, clear of the ice, at any time after the fog shut down on her on the afternoon of September, 5, 1879?

The WITNESS. That is very hard to tell, as the weather was not so clear and the ice was changing all the time, whether she could have been brought out or not.

Question by the COURT. At what time of the day on September 6, 1879, did the young ice form with sufficient thickness to prevent the Jeannette from steaming through it?

The WITNESS. At that time there was very little young ice around us, it was all heavy ice; there was no way to get out of it. There were many holes of young ice astern of us.

Question by the COURT. What duty were you performing during the 5th and 6th September, 1879?

The WITNESS. Deck officer; I was at the wheel sometimes, marking down the course, the course the ship was making through the ice; at other times I was out on the ice shoving the pieces of ice so she could get clear; that is about all, sir. I used to get now and then into the crow's nest to have a look at the ice, on both the 5th and 6th of September.

The court then, at 12.15 p. m., took a recess until 12.35 p. m., and then reconvened, with all the members, the judge-advocate, and the witness under examination present.

The judge-advocate then resumed his examination of the witness, as follows:

Question by the JUDGE-ADVOCATE. When the ship was crushed and deserted on the 12th of June, 1881, was everything done, that was possible to do, to insure the safety of the crew and to provide for the retreat?

The WITNESS. Yes, sir.

Question by the JUDGE-ADVOCATE. Of the boats available, were or were not those selected the best possible for transportation over the ice, for the accommodation of the crews, and as sea boats, or, finally, considering all three of these points?

The WITNESS. They were the best boats to transport over the ice, and as sea boats, and were the best boats to accommodate the crews. They were the best sea boats that could be selected.

Question by the JUDGE-ADVOCATE. Was there a fair division of labor among the people on the retreat?

The WITNESS. Yes, sir.

Question by the JUDGE-ADVOCATE. Were there any unnecessary delays on the retreat?

The WITNESS. Not to my knowledge.

Question by the JUDGE-ADVOCATE. To what boat were you assigned?

The WITNESS. The first cutter.

Question by the JUDGE-ADVOCATE. What, if you know, was Lieutenant-Commander De Long's desire when, on the 12th of September, 1881, the day on which the boats separated, he endeavored to communicate with the whaleboat and second cutter?

The WITNESS. He made signs to the whaleboat to come alongside if she could. I then told the captain that the sea was running too high, and it was impossible for her to come alongside. He then made a sign for her to keep on her course. The second cutter at the time was some distance astern of us. We had one reef in the sail, waiting for her to come up; when we found that she did not gain on us we took another. We kept on running for some time, when the boat, not having enough sail, kept on shipping seas over the stern. Seeing that the second cutter did not gain on us, we shook out the reef again and our boat behaved a little better, not taking in so many seas. What the captain's idea at the time was, I cannot say exactly, but I think he wanted to give Mr. Chipp his can of pemmican due him, if he could. That is all, sir.

Question by the JUDGE-ADVOCATE. Give a detailed narrative of the events which transpired with the first cutter from the date of the separation of the boats on September 12, 1881.

The WITNESS. We landed on Semenov Island on September 10. On the 11th of September while staying on that island I fitted a wash-board on the first cutter. The wash-board was about 18 inches high. Mr. Melville had one fitted around his whale-boat. The second cutter had hers fitted some time before. On the morning of the 12th September, before leaving the island, a hole was dug in the ground, with a record put into it and a large pole about 20 feet high set. We left the island about eight o'clock in the morning, standing to the southward. We had a fresh breeze from the northeast. After clearing the islands the wind increased and the sea was running quite high. We kept on running until noon time, when there was something the matter with the whale-boat. Mr. Melville sung out to the captain that he would have to haul his boat up on the ice; that she was leaking very bad. All three boats were hauled up on the ice, and while we were waiting for Mr. Melville to repair his boat we had our dinner. After dinner the boats were launched again; we stood to the southward. The wind kept on increasing and we ran all the time. Toward evening it was blowing a gale. We put a reef on the sail; the sea was pretty ugly; it was breaking into the boats all the time, so that we had hard work to keep free from water. Before dark the whale-boat was on the weather bow and some distance ahead of us, and the second cutter was on our port quarter some distance astern of us. Captain De Long made signs to the whale-boat to come alongside of us if she could, as he was going to tell Mr. Melville to keep as close together as we could, but the sea was running so bad that it was impossible for the whale-boat to slow down or come alongside. We put another reef into the sail to wait for the second cutter to come up, and kept on running for some time, and our boat took in so much water, that, seeing that the second cutter did not gain on us, we shook out the reef again and ran for it, the boat making a little better weather. Shortly after that it was getting dark. The whale-boat being the fastest sailing boat, was out of sight by this time. I then could see the second cutter astern, but it did not take long before I lost sight of her. By this time the wind and sea had still increased and our boat was taking in water over both sides and the stern. Erichsen at this time was at the wheel, and running so close before it that he jibed the sail a couple of times and almost swamped the boat. After running on for a little time, we jibed her again, and we carried away her mast and sail. At this time the boat took in a heavy sea at each side and over the stern. At that time we had hard work to get the water out of her, and she was full up to the thwarts. Another little sea would have swamped her at the time. As soon as the mast and sail was carried away we got it on board the boat and she hove to herself, head to the wind, within about four points. The captain then gave orders to make a drag out of a sail and a boat breaker; this was done. After the drag was made it was put overboard and the boat behaved pretty well for some time until the drag carried away, and we then had to get to work and make another one out of the boat's masts and oars, and weighted one end of the mast with a heavy pick-axe that we had. Our boat did not behave quite as well under the drag, as this drag did not hold quite as much water as the one we made out of the sail. During the midnight it seemed as if there were two seas running from different directions, which made it very bad for the boat. The sea was pretty choppy and broke into the boat over both sides and stern and it was hard work to keep the water out of her. There were three or four men bailing all the time. The next day it was still blowing; we still hove to. Toward evening the wind had moderated a little, but the sea did not go down very fast and we were obliged to lay to that night. The next morning the wind had moderated enough, and the captain asked me what I had on the boat to make a jury sail. I told him a hammock and an old sleigh cover that we could make a sail out of. Görtz and Kaack were then put to work to sew the hammock and sleigh cover together. As soon as that was done, took in our drag, repaired the step of the mast, stepped it, and set our sail and stood to the southward and westward. I think at this time our course was southsouthwest. Toward noon the sea had gone down a good deal and the wind had shifted to the westward; we sailed her on her course. Toward evening the captain's hands and feet commenced to swell so that he could not write his journal. His sleeping bag was got out, and they put him in his sleeping bag set up in the stern of the boat. When night set in the wind had hauled more to the southward, and we could not make our course and were obliged to beat. The captain gave me orders to stand off about four hours on one tack and then to go about ship on the other tack, and in case anything should happen to call him. We kept on beating during the night, and the next morning the wind hauled to the northward and westward and we could lay our course again. I took a sounding and could find but about 8 feet of water. About ten o'clock I stood up in the stern-sheets and saw some spots on the horizon that looked to me like land. This was on the 10th; I told the captain of it, but as he was sitting down in the boat he could not see it, and finally doubted my word of what was going on. At that time the doctor stood up and looked, but he said he could not see anything that looked like land to him. Standing on a little farther it didn't take long before everybody could see the land, sitting in the boat. At this time we could see young ice extending to the east and west some distance towards the land. As there was no way or lead from the sea through the young ice we rammed into it, sailing until we got stuck. We then had to take the oars to break the ice ahead of us and put four men at the oars to help the boat through the young ice. This ice was a quarter of an inch thick. After we got through it we got into quite a lead of water, having young ice on both sides of us, and it seemed as if it extended right into the land. We kept on, sailing along in the lead until we were within about 3 miles of the mouth of a river. The water had shoaled very rapidly and we only got about 2 feet of water. We still kept on working in toward the land until we got stuck.

And the court then, at 1.40 p. m., pending the further examination of this witness, adjourned to meet to-morrow, the 2d day of December, 1883, at 10 o'clock a. m.

FORTY-SIXTH DAY.

NAVY DEPARTMENT,
Washington, D. C., Saturday, December 2, 1882—10 a. m.

The court met pursuant to the adjournment of yesterday.

Present, Commodore William G. Temple, United States Navy, president; Capt. Joseph N. Miller, United States Navy, Commander Frederick V. McNair, United States Navy, members; and Master Samuel C. Lemly, United States Navy, judge-advocate.

The record of the proceedings of yesterday, December 1, 1882, the forty-fifth day of the inquiry, was then read, and, after correcting clerical errors, approved.

Seaman W. F. C. NINDEMANN, the witness under examination, then came in, and continued his answer to the pending question, which was repeated by the judge-advocate as follows:

Give a detailed narrative of the events which transpired with the first cutter's party, from the date of the separation of the boats on September 12, 1881.

The WITNESS. As soon as the captain found that we could not make the river he gave orders to push the boat around and to shove her toward the northward, expecting to get out the same way we came in; but at this time the young ice had closed in, and we had to heel the boat over on her bilge in order to shove her. We made very little headway and at last got stuck, so we could not move the boat any more. At this time we were in a hole of open water, and the captain gave orders to have everybody go over the side and get the boat in deeper water. Some of the men took off their shoes, or, at least, their boots and stockings, and the doctor happened to observe their feet, and see that most of the men's feet were badly swelled, and some of them had turned blue already. He then whispered to the captain; what it was I cannot say. The captain then gave orders for everybody to put on their boots and shoes again, and he said we would wait until the tide raised. While stopping here waiting for the tide to raise, we took our dinner. At this time we sighted some hummocks of ice to the eastward, probably 3 or 4 feet out of the water, and we thought the water was deeper there. About three o'clock in the afternoon the water had raised very little, and we made the attempt to get to these hummocks. We had very hard work breaking the ice, and shoving the boat over the mud. About five o'clock in the afternoon we managed to get alongside of the hummocks, but we found that the water was not any deeper there, and we found that there were small shoals where the young ice had shoved up three or four feet. It was getting toward evening, and everybody was getting pretty well played out. The captain determined to lay alongside of the ice until morning. After supper some of them got out their sleeping bags; but they were wet and were not fit for use, so everybody made himself as comfortable for the night as he possibly could.

The next morning, the 17th, about 6 o'clock, we started to shove the boat. We cast off and stood to the westward. I believe at this time the captain's idea was that he could get out by standing still further to the westward. We worked for some time and we made very little headway. Now and then the boat would float off for about five or ten minutes and then we would get on a shoal again. After the captain had stood up to the westward until about 10 o'clock, the captain found that he could not make any progress to the westward; he then tried to stand to the northward and eastward.

We kept on working here for some time, but made very little headway, as the water was very shoal and the boat was very often buried about a couple of inches in the mud. We would put down our oars in the mud and push the boat, move probably for a foot or two, and then by hauling the oar out of the mud we would haul her back, in about the same place that we pushed her from. At this time I think the wind was from the northward and eastward and was quite a breeze; the water was quite choppy, washing in the boat all the time, wetting everybody. The captain saw that they could not get out to the west or northeast, and made up his mind to push the boat back alongside of the push-ice where we had cast off in the morning. We had got away from the push-ice about a mile and a half. The mud was soft. It was about 12 o'clock, and the captain gave orders to have dinner made. At this time we had been about two days out of water, and we had to use the young ice to melt and make water for cooking. It was a little brackish, but our thirst was so great that we did not notice it much. While lying alongside of the ice the captain told me to put a tent pole down in the mud and to watch the water rise. He then told us after dinner that he had made up his mind to make a landing; that we could not do anything else. While lying there waiting for the water to rise, I went to work with a couple of men and made a raft out of a boat-sleigh to put some articles on to lighten the boat. About 3 o'clock in the afternoon the tide had raised only about 2½ inches. A little after that I noticed that it had fallen a little; I told the captain of it, and he then at once gave orders to cast the boat off and put her toward the shore. We made about 15 or 20 yards, and we got stuck again. The captain, seeing that there was nothing else left, had ordered everybody that was fit to get overboard and drag the boat in to the shore. Captain De Long, the doctor, Erichsen, and Boyd were the only four that stayed in the boat. At this time, I think, the wind was from the southeast, and overcast. We then set sail, and as soon as the sail was set everybody went over the side and got a hold of the painter to drag the boat in. The four people in the boat were set over on the starboard side to heel the boat over on her bilge. Dragging the boat this way we got on about 50 yards before we got stuck again. The captain then gave orders for everybody to take a load and carry it ashore. When everybody had his load we started in toward the beach, sometimes up to our knees in water, sometimes up to our waists, sinking into the mud-holes, and had hard work to get out of them. About that time, off-shore, the young ice was about half an inch thick, and not strong enough to bear us. We broke our way through it until we reached the beach. Here we found a lot of drift-wood and the land was very low and swampy. After everybody had got ashore with the load we picked out the best place that we could find and made a pile of it, and then returned to the boat. Mr. Collins and the cook stayed behind; and I asked them what the matter was, and they said they were played out. I afterwards returned to the boat; and returning to the boat the captain asked me how much further I thought we had to drag the boat. I told him that I could not tell; that in some places the water was deep, and in other places the water was shallow. He asked me where Mr. Collins and the cook were. I told him all they had told me, that they were "played out." Everybody then got a hold of the boat again, and we dragged her on a little further; but it was not long before we got stuck again. We then took another load out of her, and carried it to the shore. At this time the wind had freshened, and it was snowing. On getting ashore we found that Mr. Collins had built a fire; and that the cook, Ah Sam, had taken his sleeping bag, and crawled into it, and was fast asleep. Some of the men tried to awaken him, but they could not. I do not know whether he did not want to wake, or whether he slept so hard that he could not be awakened. We then returned to the boat again, and dragged her on a little further. But we soon got stuck again, and then took another load and carried it ashore. I think Collins had been trying to wake Ah Sam, but did not succeed. On reaching the boat again we hauled her in a little further, and got stuck again. By this time we got the boat as far as where the young ice commenced, and the water here was about a foot and a quarter deep. We could not get the boat in any nearer; I think at this time it was a mile and a half off shore. When we found we could put the boat in no nearer, the sick people had to get out and wade. It was impossible for any one to carry them through the young ice and muddy bottom. On getting ashore the captain asked me if everything was off the boat that was of value or of any use to us. I told him there was nothing else there but the sail and the McIntosh or rubber blanket. He then told me to take a couple of men and go out and take the sleigh that we had made a raft out of, to put it in the boat, to fetch anything that I thought we could use. Going out to the boat it was dark, and we could not see either the fire or the beach; but we felt our way back again through the broken, young ice. On getting ashore, supper was ready; and at this time they had a very large fire going. Everybody sat around it, with their boots and stockings off, trying to dry their clothes and warm themselves. The doctor and the captain were sitting close to the fire. The captain asked me to sit in between him and the doctor, and to dry my foot gear. I told him I did not care to get too near the fire; that I had a good place where I was. I believe it was on the 16th when the captain got the use of his hands again. After supper we sat up until about ten o'clock, around the fire, everybody trying to dry his clothing. The captain then gave orders for the tents to be pitched, and for everybody to get some small sticks to put inside of the tent to sleep on. After that was fixed the most of them turned in, and some of them sat alongside the fire still drying their clothes. I stayed up until about twelve o'clock; I think I was the last that went to sleep. On the morning of the 18th I think the wind was still from the southeast, and snow at times. The fire was started again, and everybody got around it to dry his clothes and sleeping bags. As one fire was not large enough for drying our clothes and to get around it, we built three or four large fires. In the afternoon the captain gave orders for getting everything together, and to pick out the stuff that we were going to carry. The orders were to carry the ship's log-books, papers, pemmican, rifles, and ammunition; this was done; all the load being divided between us, except the sick people, Erichsen, Boyd, and Ah Sam. Everybody was badly frozen, but these three people were the worst. After everybody had his load that he was to carry, everybody packed it to suit himself, and carried it the easiest way he could. At this time the evening had set in; the weather was still bad. Everybody sat around the fire when he was done with his work, and we then had our supper and turned in.

On September 19 Captain De Long gave orders to start on our march south. We left behind us a good many articles that we could not carry, sleeping-bags and clothes, and did not take anything else but our provisions, log-books, ship's papers, ammunition, rifles, and a little spare clothing.

After we had traveled south for some time we fell in with a lot of fresh-water ponds and ditches. We had difficulty in working around and getting across the ditches, most of the time breaking through and sinking into mud up to our knees. Erichsen, Boyd, and Ah Sam could not walk as quick as we, and we had to sit down every quarter of an hour or half an hour to wait for them to get up. Erichsen at this time was the worst off. He was complaining all the time over his feet.

At noontime we halted for dinner. The doctor then asked me whether I would not make a pair of crutches for Erichsen, as he thought he could get along on them a little faster. I made the crutches during the dinner hour. After dinner we started again and kept on until about five o'clock in the evening, when everybody was pretty well played out, as the loads we had were a little too heavy. The captain then ordered a camp to be pitched, had the fires lighted and supper made. After supper the captain told me to take back the ship's papers, at least to take back the books and the cooking stove, and to take two of the strongest men of the party. I took Iverson and Dressler, and asked the captain whether I should take all the papers. He said, "No; only the ship logs and books and the cooking stove." All the rest of the papers we took along ourselves. We started shortly after supper with the two cases, the ship's logs, the books, and a stove. We made the distance to the cache that was made on the beach that morning, and back again, in two hours. We put these log-books and the stove in the cache, also a spy-glass; the captain told me to put that in the navigation box and lock it up again. On returning to the camp we sat around the fire for a little while; then everybody turned in.

On the morning of the 20th everybody picked up his load, and we started, traveling to the south again, leaving behind us one tent. The bottom part of the tent would get so wet and iced up that two men had all they could do to carry it. That was the reason it was left behind. Here the country was still full of fresh-water ponds and creeks, and in some ponds the ice was strong enough for going across, in others the ice was not; but we had to make long sweeps to get around them. At ten o'clock we made a halt and took a rest. There was something the matter with my load. The rest of the party went ahead and I stayed back to fix my load. Erichsen started off with the other party, but soon was left behind. The rest walked away from him. After I had my load fixed I started off again. It did not take me long before I fetched up with Erichsen. Erichsen was complaining of his feet, and said to me that he could not go much further. I tried to encourage him, and told him to come along as long as he could. He kept on for a little while longer, and then said——

(The witness here broke off, evidently much moved by his recollections, and saying "I can't go on with this; I must go out," left the room.)

And the court then at 12 m. took a recess until 12.30 p. m., at which time it reconvened with all the members, the judge-advocate, and the witness under examination present, and the witness continued his testimony in answer to the pending question, as follows:

Erichsen here told me that he wished to stay behind; I tried to coax him, but he said, "Nindemann, I do not care how far you go; if you go to St. Petersburg I cannot go any further." I then tried to hail the captain, but they were too far in advance. I walked as fast as I could to fetch up with them, and when I got within hailing distance I hailed them and they stopped. On getting up to them, I told the captain what Erichsen had said, and he told me to go ahead with the rest of the party until we found a place where there was some drift-wood, and to halt until he came up again. He then went back with the doctor to Erichsen, we going ahead for some distance until we found a place where there was some firewood. We then had seen some deer tracks going to the eastward. The rest of the men stayed there; me and Alexy started to try and follow up the deer tracks. We soon got out of sight of the men, and we came up to a range of drift-wood where the deer had started to the south. We walked along on a creek that ran along a range of drift-wood. The ice here was strong enough to get along on it—now and then it would break through. At last we saw that the tracks went in here to the eastward, between the drift-wood. We looked around and Alexy said to me, "There is the deer laying down." By this time the deer had seen us. Crawling up on them between the drift-wood, we got within about 300 yards of them and they got up and started to run. We chased them for quite a distance, and Alexy started to yelling just as loud as he could halloo. I asked him what he did that for, and he said to stop the deer, that it would scare them, which it did. When they heard him yell, they stood very quietly awhile looking around in confusion. We got within about 200 yards of them; then they started running again we kept along, yelling; they would stop now and then, and then start to running again, and we saw they were getting too far ahead of us, and that there was no possibility of getting up to them and returned back to the party. The captain asked me what I had seen, and I told him that we fell in with a range of drift-wood running to the southward, in other words, a creek running along to the southward, and that the ice in most places was strong enough to walk on. He asked me if I thought it better walking on the young ice, and I told him yes; he then halted there for dinner. During the dinner hour the doctor took the bandage off Erichsen's foot. On taking it off the flesh from under the ball of his foot dropped off. The doctor said nothing to anybody; he saw how things were. He took clean bandages and bound up his foot again, and put on his boots and stockings. After the doctor was done with him I was sitting close to Erichsen and had seen in what condition his foot was. Erichsen asked me, said he, "Nindemann, do you know anything about frost-bites?" I told him "Yes; that at the first coming on the flesh would turn blue and then black." He then said, "When the doctor took off the bandage I saw something dropping from under my foot." Says I, "Erichsen, I guess you've been dreaming." He said, "No," that he was certain of it; that he had seen something drop from under his foot. After dinner the captain told me and Alexy to go ahead and take the same road that we had taken when we followed up the deer. When we got on to the creek the captain thought it was a small river, and that it was the river we wanted to get along on. We got along pretty fast on the ice; it was a good deal better walking, and not "tundra," where we used to go in almost up to our knees in the snow and soft mud. Me and Alexy kept the lead, and we saw we were getting quite a distance ahead of them; we made a halt to wait for them to come up, as the captain had given me orders not to go any further ahead than 300 or 400 yards. When the evening came we camped down between the drift-wood, and started a big fire and set the tent up for a shelter. The most of us got our feet wet during the day. We sat around the fire drying our foot-gear; we had our supper. At this time our ration was reduced, I believe, to four ounces of pemmican a meal—three or four ounces to each man a meal. After supper each man went out, or everybody went out to get in wood enough for the night. The men picked up some small sticks to put under us to lay on. As we only had one tent at this time, not large enough to shelter fourteen, it was cut in two and used for a blanket.

When we had firewood enough for that night two beds were made as near to the fire as could be. We then turned in, seven in each bed, each one rolling himself up in his blanket and covering ourselves with the two halves of the tent; one man was kept on watch to keep the fire going, two hours apiece each. The first part of the night some of us slept pretty good; then the weather was getting colder, and it was blowing pretty fresh from the northward; I think some of them then got up and lay down on a couple of sticks of wood as near the fire as they possibly could.

On the morning of the 21st the cook was called to get breakfast; after breakfast started south again on the creek; made a good many stops during the forenoon; a little before noon me and Alexy was quite a distance in advance; we stopped for the party to come up. While stopping, looking around, I saw a couple of fox traps about three-quarters of a mile to the westward. While waiting, I thought I would go and see with what the traps were baited. On going over there I found that the fox-traps were on the bank of quite a large river, and found they were baited with young goose wings or duck wings. We then went back and waited for the captain to come up; I told him the river to the west of us was quite a large one. He says, "Nindemann, that is just what we want; we are going to take a little rest here, and then we can go ahead to the river." When we got on the river bank we halted for dinner; the captain told me to go up on the bank for a good look around to see if I could see a hut; that we ought to be within 3 or 4 miles of some huts; the river here had young ice on both sides. After dinner we walked along the river bank, now and then taking a rest, as the sick people could not get along as fast as most of us, and we always had to wait some time before they came up. I wish to state here that, on the 20th, when Erichsen wanted to be left behind, that Boyd and Mr. Collins said that they were willing to be left behind to stay with Erichsen, and if we found assistance of course we would come back and get them. That was the time that Erichsen made the remark that he wished to be left behind, and if we found assistance we could come back and get him.

About 3 o'clock on the 21st me and Alexy was almost out of sight of the other people; we then walked up the river bank and saw a hut, or a couple of huts, to the southward. We then waited until the captain and party came up and told him there were a couple of huts to the southward of us, and he told me and Alexy to go ahead and when we got to the huts to stop there. When we got there we found one of them was a new hut that had probably been built during the summer, the other one was older. We found ashes on entering the huts, on the fire-place, quite fresh, and it looked as if the people had been there about eight to fourteen days before us. Me and Alexy had been there for about half an hour before the captain came up. It was getting toward five o'clock in the afternoon; the captain said he would stay here for the night. The party was divided, seven in each hut. After everybody got warmed up a little, we went out to have a look around to see what we could see. We saw to the southward and westward and on the west bank of the river a structure of wood, where Alexy thought was probably some deer meet or fresh fish hung up, as he said the natives generally built structures of this kind to hang up their fish and deer meat. The doctor, who was outside, at the same time looking around saw away to the southward and eastward what looked to him like some huts. It was reported to the captain, and the captain told me to go down to the river bank to see if I could find some means to get across the river, to see if there was any food of any kind there. He sent Alexy to the southward and eastward to find out whether they were huts that the doctor had seen. Me and Alexy started together from the hut. I started down the river bank and we kept on walking to the southward and eastward, to see by what means I could get across the river. This structure was about 2 miles south of us. On getting down I saw four small ducks, I think about fifty yards off shore. I fired at these with the Remington rifle, but did not get near enough to kill any of them, as the water in the river was a little choppy and the ducks were very small. Getting abreast of the structure, I looked around to see whether I could see anything to make a raft of to get across, but as I saw nothing hung up under the structure, I thought that it was no use to make a raft, or try to get across. The current here was running very strong to the north. I returned back to the hut and told the captain that there was no food of any kind, and that it was wholly unnecessary labor to make a raft to try to get across. He asked me whether I was certain that there was nothing over there. I told him "yes." The way the structure looked to me was like the ruins of an old hut. I asked some of the men whether Alexy had come back. They said "no." I then went and asked the captain whether I could go again. He said "yes." I started down to the southward, along the river bank, finding quite many foxtraps. In one of them I found a large ivory gull, that was in the trap; I went still farther south along the river bank. I was about five miles off from the hut when I came to a stream that ran into the eastward. At this time it was getting dark, and I looked around to see if I could see anything of Alexy. I could not see anything of him. I walked back to the hut, on my way taking the gull along, and fetched it to the steward, or at least to the cook, to cook it. Alexy at this time had not returned. The captain told the cook to pluck the ivory gull, and he started plucking it, tearing the feathers out of it, and said the bird was rotten; it was thrown away. By this time it was quite dark, and Alexy had not returned yet. I went out a couple of times to look around to see whether I could see him, and there was nothing to be seen of Alexy, and some of us then thought that he probably had fell in with some natives, visiting their huts, that we had seen in the afternoon. I think it was about nine o'clock in the evening when Alexy returned with a quarter of deer he had. He then told the captain that they were huts, but that there was nobody living there, and that most of them had tumbled in, and that he had shot two deer a little to the southward of the huts. The captain then ordered the cook to make supper for all hands out of the reindeer meat. I think everybody ate about a pound of reindeer meat, and everybody was well satisfied with it. After supper we had a little talk, and everybody seemed quite contented, and then turned in for the night.

On the morning of the 22d we had breakfast. After breakfast the captain told me to take everybody, except the sick people, and go with Alexy and get the two deer. We started off; we had to work pretty well into the southward and eastward. We struck the river and we had to feel our way across the young ice. I would like to state here that Alexy, the night before when he came back with his reindeer meat, to make the road short had to wade through the river that was open, up to his waist in water, but farther to the eastward where we went across, it was frozen, and we felt our way across the young ice. On passing the ruins of the huts I counted them and found there were seven. I think there was only one that was fit for shelter; the rest were all broken down more or less. About noon time we got up to the deer, skinned them, and cut one of them into four quarters and the other one into two. Every one of the men took a quarter each, and me and Iverson took a half one apiece. Lee was with us at that time, but he got pretty weak in walking down, and was complaining about cramps in his legs. He did not carry anything else but our two rifles. We then started back, going down the small river. Our loads were too heavy to carry on our shoulders across the river, and we were obliged to take a piece of rope and tie it to the meat and drag it about 10 yards astern of us to keep from breaking through. I was the first one going across, again taking the lead. We took the same road that we came. At this time, when I was half way over the river, I thought that the ice was strong enough to bear me in carrying the load. I picked up my load, making about 25 paces, when we broke through, on the same path that we had come when we came out. When the rest saw that they put strings to their meat and dragged it across, and got across all right without breaking through. They were going to wait for me to get the water out of my boots, and wring out my stockings and pants. I told them to go ahead and not wait for me; that I would follow them all right. I had to stop three or four times on the way before reaching the hut to take off my boots and stockings and wring the water out of them, that kept settling down in them all the time.

We arrived at the hut about 5 o'clock in the afternoon. The captain then gave orders to have all the meat cut off the bones and then the bones mashed for making soup out of them for supper. We made our supper out of deer meat and soup from the bones of reindeer on that night.

And the court then, at 1.25 p. m., pending the further examination of this witness, adjourned, to meet on Monday, the 4th day of December, 1882, at 10 a. m.

FORTY-SEVENTH DAY.

NAVY DEPARTMENT,
Washington, D. C., Monday, December 4, 1882—10 a. m.

The court met pursuant to the adjournment of Saturday, December 2, 1882.

Present, Commodore William G. Temple, United States Navy, president; Capt. Joseph N. Miller, United States Navy, Commander Frederick V. McNair, United States Navy, members; and Master Samuel C. Lemly, United States Navy, judge-advocate.

The record of the proceedings of Saturday, December 2, 1882, the forty-sixth day of the inquiry, was then read, and, after correcting clerical errors, approved.

Seaman W. F. C. NINDEMANN, the witness under examination, then came in and continued his answer to the pending question, as follows:

Question repeated by the JUDGE-ADVOCATE. Give a detailed narrative of the events which transpired with the first cutter's party from the date of the separation of the boats on September 12, 1881.

The WITNESS. On the morning of September 23, after breakfast, the deer meat was equally divided between the party. We then made a start along the river bank to the south. After traveling about four miles we had to go into the eastward across a small river. After crossing it we walked across a point of land, when we struck the river again and then followed the river bank. Halts were made three or four times waiting for the sick to come up. At noon we halted for dinner, about half an hour, and then started to the south again until night, when we found a place where there was plenty of drift-wood. The captain then gave orders to halt for the night. Fire was then started; we took our supper. After supper everybody was sent out to get up wood enough to last during the night. Everybody crowded near the fire, as near as possible, to keep himself warm and pass the night in waiting until daylight.

On the morning of the 24th, after breakfast, the captain gave orders to take the men and try to make a raft. He thought that if he could make a raft to carry all hands that we would get along faster, on account of the sick. Everybody then started to work dragging driftwood near the water; when we had driftwood enough we started to make a raft. We were obliged to launch the raft before finishing it. After we had her launched and had finished her up, we then got up poles about 15 or 20 feet long for to shove the raft along with. I think that almost everybody went on the raft except three who walked along the river bank. We then tried to push the raft off, but we found when everybody got on to it she settled pretty well down and stuck in the mud. We worked for about an hour trying to get her off, but it was no use. At the other end of the raft the water was so deep we could not reach the bottom with about a 20-foot pole. A strong current was setting in to the north. When the captain found that we could not get her afloat he gave orders for everybody to take up his load and to walk ashore. We worked to the southward for a little while and halted for dinner. After dinner we started on again to the southward along the river bank until night came and until we found a place where there was driftwood enough to last us during the night. We then had supper; a watch was set to keep the fire going, and everybody made themselves as comfortable as they could during the night.

On the morning of the 25th we started again along the river bank until noon and then halted for dinner. After dinner, started again and walked on until the afternoon, when we halted for a while to rest. Me and Alexy walked up the river bank to see what we could see. Looking to the southward it seemed to us as if there was a hut. We told the captain; the captain then gave orders to start on our march again; we struggled on until about six o'clock and we reached the hut; here we halted. The captain gave orders for everybody to go out and get up wood enough for the night. When that was done we had our supper, and after supper everybody laid down for the night. On getting to the hut we found there was quite a large river running into the eastward that was open.

On the morning of the 26th, after we had our breakfast, the captain gave me orders to take the men and to construct a raft to carry about five hands, as the distance was too long to go to the eastward and to try to work round it. We had to go about a half a mile up the river before we found driftwood enough to make a raft. Everybody then went to work to drag the lumber down to the beach. As we only had five lashings we could not do any better than lash a frame together out of four sticks and then put the cross-pieces across, fastening the line on the forward and after end of the raft and haul it as tight as we possibly could to keep the sticks from washing off. We went up to the hut, got a few boards that were there, made paddles out of them, and then launched the raft. The captain told me to take five people across. After we had shoved the raft off into the deep water we found that she sunk with us almost up to our knees, but still we managed to paddle across and to land three persons. We then got back again and took on five more, at least three more, five all told. The captain asked me whether she would not carry another. I told him that she would not, as she was pretty well loaded with five on it. But he sent on two more and told us to shove off. As soon as we shoved off and got into the deep water the raft sunk with us; a good many cross-pieces washed off, and we were obliged to put her back on the beach. The captain then asked what to do now, and I told him the only thing we could do was to haul the raft up again and to repair it. After the raft was repaired, took on five people and got across all right. We kept on crossing until we got everybody across. The most of us all got wet through. We had to stop on the other side to build a fire to get our clothes dry again. The current in the river was setting to westward here into the big river. After everybody was dry we started on our march across the point of land until we struck the main river again and started along it to the southward. Here the walking was quite good and we made quite a good day's work. By this time Boyd and Ah Sam had got a good deal better than they were when we started, but Erichsen was getting worse. When evening came we halted under the bank of the river for the night. We took our supper and everybody was sent out again to get wood for the night. Here we had very little rest; it was blowing quite fresh and the weather was very cold.

On the morning of the 27th we had our breakfast; after breakfast me and Alexy went up on the river bank to see what we could see. He sighted some deer away to the eastward. He told the captain of it; he told us to take our rifles and see whether we could get one or two. Me and Alexy started off and went towards the deer. The wind was from the southeast at this time, and we kept to leeward of them, so they could not smell us. When we got near enough to the deer and we thought they could see us, we had to crawl on our hands and knees for a couple of hundred yards. We then got onto a fresh water pond and that gave us shelter, so that the deer could not see us. It was quite a distance across it; we got over to the other side. The deer were within about 200 yards of us then. We had no shelter and were obliged then to crawl on our hands and knees again. Every time the deer would look we would stop, and when they commenced eating again then advance again until we got within about 50 yards of them. Each one then picked out the largest deer, both of us ready to fire. Alexy whispered to me to fire. He shot the deer that he aimed at. My rifle missed fire. The deer then commenced to run. There were several rounds fired after that, but they did not hit any thing. It was a large buck that he killed, and weighed about as much as the two that he shot before, as they were very small. The men had heard the firing and the captain had sent everybody out to get the deer. The deer was dragged into the camp and was equally divided between the party, and we then started out along the river bank. At noon time we halted for an hour for dinner, and then started out again until night. That night there was nothing in sight; we were obliged to camp under the river bank again, and on the morning of the 28th we struggled along until about 2 o'clock in the afternoon, when me and Alexy went up the river bank, sighting a hut to the south of us. Here we were obliged to walk on the top of the river bank; we had to walk among the moss and snow, sometimes up to our knees. It was very hard work, and we had to rest about every ten minutes waiting for the sick to come up. We got to the hut at 4 o'clock in the afternoon, and the captain ordered a halt for the night. Here we found a large river running into the eastward, all open, but very little young ice in it. Everybody was sent out to get wood for the night and to start a big signal fire at that point of the river bank. Me and Alexy took a stroll off to the eastward to see if we could see anything which would pay. We did not fall in with anything nor see any tracks of any kind. After returning to the hut we had our supper. It was getting dark. The captain gave orders to light a signal fire outside. When it was lit everybody turned in for the night.

On the morning of the 29th it was blowing quite fresh from the northwest and the snow was drifting. After we took our breakfast the captain sent everybody out to get wood for the day and enough to start another signal fire at night. He then told me, said he, "Nindemann, we have to do something here; it seems to be quite a large river, running into the eastward. We must try to cross somehow." Said he, "I want you to see whether you can find wood enough to make a raft to cross the river on." I told him there was no use for me to go to the northward along the river, as we had seen but very little drift wood up above coming down. I then went my way along the river bank to the eastward, but did not find wood enough anywhere to construct a raft. Alexy was sent at the same time before me, and I fell in with him again about 5 miles to the eastward of the hut. It then was blowing quite fresh and the snow commenced to drift pretty hard. We kept on, going to the eastward until we found a river running more to the southward and eastward, and kept on, following it for some time, when we came up to a small fishing hut that was new and built during the summer. Here we found a couple of small pieces of fish and fresh wood shavings. We staid here for a little while, and then went outside to look around, and found some deer horns lying around the hut and a piece of a kyak. At this time the weather had cleared off a little, and we could see to the southward and eastward on the river bank a lot of poles and rails. It was then about 2 o'clock in the afternoon, and it was time for me to return to the hut. The captain had told me not to stay too long or get lost, as the weather was quite bad when we started. On walking along the river we noticed in some places that the river was frozen over, but not strong enough for anybody to go across. On arriving at the hut the captain asked me whether I had found driftwood enough to make a raft. I told him all the distance I had been, but had not seen driftwood enough to make a raft; but about 3 miles to the east of us was a place where there was young fresh ice that had frozen together, and if the weather continued as cold during the night as it had been during the day we would probably be able to get across it to-morrow. It was then about evening, and we had our supper; the signal fire was started, and everybody turned in for the night.

On the morning of the 30th the wind had moderated and there was very little snow drift. We took our breakfast, and the captain sent everybody out again to get our wood for the day and for the signal fire at night. He told me and Alexy to go away to the eastward on the river bank and see whether the ice was strong enough to cross it. We started off and got to the place, tried the ice three or four times, but it broke through when we walked on it. A little further we struck a place where we got on good ice. We had to feel our way across the young ice very carefully. The ice was all full of holes. We managed to get across all right, and we got over on the river bank to look around again to see anything of importance. We then started back to the hut and told the captain that we had crossed the river and back, about 5 miles to the east of us, and I thought if everybody was very careful that we could get across without breaking through. He asked me if I had examined the ice in the river that we came along on. I told him, "No." I said that there was not any ice on the way I came along; that the ice was not strong enough to get across. He then said, "You had better go and try it." I went up a half a mile to the northward as the river was still open to the west and south of the hut, but to the north the young ice had formed right across the river. When we got there I found the ice was not strong enough. I went back and told the captain of it, and he asked me whether I thought the ice would be strong enough to-morrow. I said to him that I hardly thought it would, the ice was too thin. He then said "Nindemann, we have got to do something for Erichsen. Erichsen is getting worse every day, and by the time we get ready to start he will not be able to walk any more." He asked me if I could not find some way to make a sleigh for him, and I told him, "Yes, I would try it." I found an old plank laying outside of the hut, about 4 feet long and 6 inches thick by 12 or 13 inches wide. I had nothing else but an old dull hatchet. I started to hew the plank to about $2\frac{1}{2}$ inches thick, then split it for the two runners. I rounded off the ends, and as we had no nails nor auger to bore a hole with, I had to get to work and take a little doctor's saw to dovetail the cross pieces into the runners and then wedged them. It was about night when I had the sleigh finished, and at this time supper was ready. We had our supper and turned in for the night. Before turning in we lit the signal fire.

On the morning of October 1 the captain told me, after breakfast, he wanted me and Alexy to try the ice on the main river. We started down, feeling our way, getting on to it. We got on a little way when the ice commenced to crack, and we were obliged to return back until we found some ice that looked more strong, and we managed to feel our way across. The ice was cracking under us all the time. I got a little stick to feel our way with; by setting it down a little hard on the ice it would drop right through, so that we worked right hard in some places in the river to get across. The captain had seen us from the hut as we crossed the river. He started the men out with their loads. By this time I had got across again, and the men told me that they had orders to start across the river with their loads. I told them they had better wait until I had seen the captain. They then stopped, and I told the captain in what condition the ice was, and that I was not certain that everybody would get across without getting wet. He said, "Nindemann, we can't stay here any longer; we have got to do something. You go ahead and show the men the road, and let them follow you." I then started out again, with the men, picking out the road, and assisting them to drag their load behind them, and not get too close together, but keep some distance apart. Got across all right with the first load. As we had only taken one-half of the load that each man had to carry, and, therefore, had to go back again for the rest of it. After we got everything across, went up to the hut to get Erichson. At this time I saw some toes lying outside of the hut. Kaack was standing outside of the hut. I asked him what that was. He told me that while we had crossed the river, the doctor had cut off all of Erichsen's toes. Erichsen at this time could not walk and he had to be carried by Noros and Iverson down to the river bank. As soon as we got him down there he was put on the sleigh and the two men dragged him across. For this we had to have a long drag-rope, and the men had to be quite a distance apart so that the weight would not be all in one place. We managed to get across all right without anybody getting in the water, and we then followed along the west bank of the river to the southward. About ten o'clock we struck quite a large river running into the southwest. We crossed this river, feeling our way across it, as the ice was not very heavy or very thick, and here and there were holes of open water. When we got across we halted on a point of land to take a rest. Getting up on the river bank, looking along, we saw that it was quite a large river, to the southward and westward, and had lots of large holes of open water in the river, but we could not see any huts along the river bank. I told the captain it was quite a large river, running to the southward and westward, but he said that could not be the river because it ran too far to the westward. But looking around we sighted a hut on the east side of the river, but as we had left a hut only that morning we did not care about going over to see whether there was anything to be found or not. After we had rested for some time we started along the river to the southward again, still on the west bank of the river. At noon we halted again for half an hour and had dinner. After dinner we started again to the southward along the river bank. About 5 o'clock we got up to another river, running in to the southward and westward and crossed it. It was getting dark by this time, and we halted for the night. The captain sent every body out to get up wood enough for the night. The wind at this time was blowing quite fresh from the southeast, and we set up our pieces of tent for weather cloths as near the fire as we could, and then everybody made themselves as comfortable as they could for the night.

And the court then, at 11.55 a. m., took a recess until 12.15 p. m., and then reconvened, with all the members, the judge-advocate and the witness under examination present.

And the witness then continued his answer to the pending question, as follows:

We got very little sleep during the night, the weather was very cold and the wind blowing pretty fresh. On the morning of October 2, after breakfast, started on the march along the river bank, to the southward, and walked until about 11 o'clock. We found the river run out dry. We got upon the river bank to look around, as it looked to us, a little to the eastward, as if it was a large river. We got across to the eastward, the snow being pretty deep, and it was hard work to get through it; but we managed to make the river, finding it to be quite a large river and running somewhere near south. We kept on this river, on the west bank, until night, and camped down with no shelter, and the wind still blowing very fresh. We managed to pass the night with very little rest, and on the morning of the 3d we had our breakfast and started south again. Traveled on some distance, when we saw a lot of fox-traps on the east bank of the river. The captain gave orders to go across the river. When we got across we halted. Alexy and me went up the river bank to see what the fox-traps were baited with. We found they were baited with old fish heads, and in overhauling a couple of them we ran across some man's tracks, which looked like his being there about four or six days before us, going south. We followed up his tracks for some time, and then we lost them, and returning we told the captain what we had seen. He then gave orders to start south again along the east bank of the river. We kept along for about an hour, and we found the river turning to the eastward. There were big holes of open water. We halted here, and the captain told me to go around the point and see whether the ice was strong enough to go around. I felt my way around the point for quite a distance, but the ice was getting risky all the time. It was not safe to advance on it further. I then turned back and told the captain the condition of the ice. We started back along the west bank of the river, and going on for a short distance we found the river that we saw now was getting smaller, and by this time had almost run out to nothing. Coming over some lowland for about a couple of hundred yards we found a small river making to the south; we marched along on it; it was getting larger; we soon saw open water ahead of us. I got up on the east bank of this river about 4 o'clock in the afternoon. The river here was all open and just enough ice on the edge of it to march along on the river. Alexy and me were finding the way along. We were quite a little distance ahead at this time. It was snowing and blowing pretty fresh from the southeast. All at once we heard somebody hallooing behind us, and looking around we found Captain De Long, Mr. Collins, and Görtz up to their necks in water. A lot of people tried to get them out as quick as they could, but before they got out, they were sokaing wet through. A little before this we had halted, and going up the river bank Alexy sighted a hut to the eastward, and one to the southward on the river that we were going along on. The weather was getting so bad that the captain asked me what I thought, as to whether they were huts or not. I told him that I would not say whether they were huts or not. He then asked which I thought was the best hut to go for. I told him that I would go to the hut to the southward; that it would be better to go there, as it was on our way south. By this time they had got close up to the place where Alexy had thought he had seen a hut. The captain then told me to run ahead as quick as possible and to find out whether it was a hut that we had seen to the southward or not. I got upon the river bank; seeing the thing which we thought was a hut about four or five hundred yards ahead of me, I ran up to it and examined it. I found that it was nothing else but a round hill of earth, and in the distance it looked like a hut. I then ran back and told the captain there was no hut there. At this time the weather became so bad that we could hardly see a hundred yards. The captain then gave orders to haul wood to start a fire as quick as possible. The clothes of the men about this time were all frozen stiff, and they kept on running and stamping their feet to keep from freezing. The fire was started as quick as possible, and the wet men got around it as near as they could. It did not take long to start the fire, but we had hard work finding wood, as the wood here was all struck pretty well into the snow and set into the river bank. I think we worked about four hours before we had wood enough to last us during the night. Here we had little or no shelter at all. We tried to take our tents or half tents for a weather cloth, but it did not make any difference where we put it, we could not make it shelter us at all.

At noon-time we had our last pemmican, and we had nothing for supper. The captain gave orders to Iverson and Boyd to take the dog to some place where nobody would see it, to kill him and dress him. The supper was made out of the head, heart, kidneys, and liver. There were some men that did not care much about it. They took a little of it, but gave most of it away to somebody else. Before supper the captain had Alexy sent out to see whether that was a hut they had sighted a little before dark to the east of us. Alexy started down and found it to be a hut. On returning he told the captain so. The captain was willing to make a start to go to the hut, but the weather was so bad that Alexy was afraid he could not find his way, and we could not do anything better than to stay there during that night.

On the morning of the 4th, as soon as daylight came, we all got ready to make a start for the hut. It still was blowing and the snow was drifting very bad.

During the night Erichsen had been put up as close to the fire, lashed on his sleigh, as could be, and that morning the doctor found that he had taken off his mittens and had both his hands frozen. He put a couple of men to work, Boyd and Iverson, I think, to rub his hands, to try by that means to restore circulation in his hands; but it was no use. By this time Erichsen was quite senseless, and had for some time lost the use of his mouth, so the doctor could not make him swallow anything; nothing but a little hot tea. After the doctor found that he could not restore any circulation in Erichsen's hands, we then started across to the eastward to find a hut. We reached the hut about 10 o'clock; then everybody was sent out to get wood to last us during the day and night, as we had not had any sleep for about three nights. After we had wood enough we had our dinner, consisting of a pound of dog meat each, then everybody went to sleep, and we slept until about the next day at dinner time, one man being kept on watch to keep the fire going. We then took another meal, and some of us lay down again; others sat up and patched their clothes and boots. Just before evening everybody was sent out again to get in some wood to last us during the night. I believe that evening we had our last tea.

On the morning of the 6th the wind was still blowing from the northeast and the snow was drifting. The captain sent everybody out to get wood, and told me to stay in the hut. After everybody had left the hut the captain asked me, says he, "Nindemann, do you think you are strong enough to make a forced march of 25 miles to go to Ku Mark Surk?" I told him "yes," that "I would try." He told me I could take any man I wanted except Alexy. He then asked me who I was going to take. I told him I would take Noros. He said, why not take Iverson, as he thought he was a stronger man. I told him that he was then complaining about his feet, a couple of days ago. The doctor hearing this, he said that he thought Noros would be a stronger man to make a march.

The doctor then asked the captain whether he could go to sleep, as he had not had any sleep that night and had slept but very little for two days while in the hut. The captain told him "yes." While me and the captain were talking of the march to Ku Mark Surk, he told me that he did not have much to give me, but that he would give me a couple of pounds of dog meat, a little alcohol, ammunition, and a rifle, and for me to go ahead and do the best I could. If I did not find any assistance at Ku Mark Surk I was to go as far as Ajaket, and that was about 45 miles, I think he said, to the south of Ku Mark Surk. He then told Mr. Collins to make a copy of his chart from the place where we were as far as a little to the southward of Bulun. While we were talking about the march the doctor had woke up again. He sat up, looking at Erichsen and saying "it is all over with him." The captain then said "Nindemann, we will all go together now." He then asked me where the best place was to bury him, and I told him that as we had no implements to make a hole in the ground, and as the ground was frozen hard the best way would be to have him lie in the hut. He studied a little while and said, "The seaman's grave is the water, anyhow, and therefore we will bury him in the river." He then gave me orders to have a couple of men sew him up in canvas. I told Noros and Kaack to take the flaps of the tent, which we used for a door, to sew him up in, and to tell some other men to go and break some sods off the river bank to put in between and around his feet to weight him with. After this was done we covered him up with our flag. The captain then called everybody in and read prayers for the dead. It was then about noontime. They took Erichsen outside of the hut and took him down to the river bank on two sticks. A hole was then cut in the ice, the captain read the burial service, Erichsen was stuck in the hole, the tide taking him away under the ice. We then fired three shots over his grave and returned to the hut.

On returning to the hut we found an old board. The captain told me to cut Erichsen's name on it and the day he died, the day of the month, and the expedition that he had been on, and to fasten it up somewhere. The only place I could find to fasten it was to stick it up over the door on the outside.

We then had the last of the dog meat for dinner. After dinner the captain told me to go and have a look at the weather; that if the weather was good enough we were going to make a start south. I went out, but it was still snowing and blowing, and we could not see any distance. I told the captain how the weather was; that it was not fit to travel, as we could not see where we were going to. He then said he would wait until the weather moderated. Everybody then was sent out again to get more wood to last during the night. After we had wood enough everybody retired for the night.

And the court then, at 1 p. m., pending the further examination of this witness, adjourned to meet to-morrow, the 5th day of December, 1882, at 10.30 a. m.

FORTY-EIGHTH DAY.

NAVY DEPARTMENT,
Washington, D. C., Tuesday, December 5, 1882—10.30 a. m.

The court met pursuant to the adjournment of yesterday.

Present, Commodore William. G. Temple, United States Navy, president; Capt. Joseph N. Miller, United States Navy; Commander Frederick V. McNair, United States Navy, members; and Master Samuel C. Lemly, United States Navy, judge-advocate.

By request of the judge-advocate the reading of the record of the proceedings of yesterday, December 4, 1882, the forty-seventh day of inquiry, was deferred.

Seaman W. F. C. NINDEMANN, the witness under examination, then came in and continued his answer to the pending question, which was repeated by the judge-advocate, as follows:

Give a detailed narrative of the events which transpired with the first cutter's party from the date of the separation of the boats, September 12, 1881.

The WITNESS. On the morning of the 7th the weather was still bad, but it was clear enough to see about three or four hundred yards ahead of us. Before leaving the hut the captain left a record, which he had done in all the huts we had been in before, and one at the cache before leaving the coast. A Winchester rifle was left in the first hut we came to after leaving the coast. The captain then ordered a start to be made across the river, and we walked about 3 miles over a low sand-spit until we struck a river again that ran to the southward. We found here that everybody after getting out of the hut was smoke blind, and could see but a short distance ahead of us. After following the river for some time, the river took a turn to the eastward and almost ran dry. Here we found a lot of drift-wood that was piled up about 7 or 8 feet high. The captain ordered a halt here; the fire was started. We had some alcohol to mix with water. After we had finished our grog we started to the eastward along a dry, river bed. Walking for about an hour, we struck quite a large river again. The captain's intention was to cross this river over to the eastward, and he asked me to try the ice and see whether it was strong enough to go across. I got on to it a little ways; it broke through up to my knees. On getting out I looked around and found that the doctor and captain had followed me and both of them had broke through up to their waists. We then got ashore again; the captain ordered a fire to be made, and we camped down to get our clothes dried. Alexy went off hunting; the captain told him not to stay away hunting longer than an hour, but as Alexy did not understand him right, he staid until late in the evening. On returning to the camp he fetched with him one ptarmigan, and told us he had shot another one but just wounded him, and the bird flew over into the river where Alexy could not get him. He here told the captain that further to the southward the river was all open, and that he had seen a good many trees in the river. It was then too late to make a start. We staid there during the night, and when the morning arrived the captain ordered a start again. We walked along the west bank of the river to the southward. About 10 o'clock we struck a river that ran to the westward. It was open in some places, the water standing on the ice. I tried three or four times to get onto it, but found that I broke through all the time, and we were obliged to get away into the westward to find a place where we could cross. On crossing a good many of us got wet, but we stuck to it until noon, when we got to some drift-wood and the captain ordered us to have dinner. After we had finished our grog and had rested a little while, we started along to the southward again. After we had walked for about an hour we struck a nice, sandy beach that ran pretty well south. By this time the wind was from the southeast, and it started snowing again. Got along pretty fast over the sand spits, and about 3 o'clock in the afternoon we found that there was a small river making in between the sand-spit and the high river bank. Here we tried to wade across, but the water was too deep, and there was nothing else left for us to do but we had to go back to the northward.

Alexy and me had the lead. We found we were getting pretty well ahead, and looking around saw that the rest of the party were sitting down. Shortly after that we started off again, walking a short distance and sat down again. At this time I saw that the captain was pretty well played, and I walked back and asked him to let me carry his load, but he told me, "Nindemann, I am all right, and you go ahead and I will follow you." I started ahead again, everybody following, and got some distance. I had to rest again, finding that the others were resting; I kept on this way for about a half an hour, and I turned back again. I told the captain the same thing, but he still said "Nindemann, go ahead; I am all right." I made another start and kept along for about a half an hour, when I found the captain and the doctor quite a distance behind again. At this time it was about a mile and a half from the river bank, and I started back again and asked the captain once more to let me carry his bundle, and he said again, "Nindemann, take the rest of the men and go ahead and find a place, when you get to the high river bank, for camping during the night, and I will be up by that time." The doctor and the captain stayed together. I and the rest of the men walked ahead until we struck the river bank. On getting here to the river bank I walked to the westward and to the northward a short distance, but could not find any place where there was shelter of any kind, nor would the bank of the river here break the wind. I picked out the best place I could find. The men were started out to get drift-wood for the night, but there was very little drift-wood here, and we only could afford to start a small fire. By this time the captain and the doctor came up, and they called me to one side and asked me whether I had found a place for the night. I told them that the place we had was the best place we could find, and that we had but very little drift-wood for burning during the night. He then wanted to know how far off the place was where we had our dinner, and said there was plenty of drift-wood there. I told him it was probably a distance of five miles yet. He then said, "Well, we have got to make the best of it for to-night"; and said that he was going to send myself and Noros from him the first thing in the morning, and went on to say that he knew I would do all a man could do. We made a little hot water to mix with the alcohol, drank it, and then everybody sat as near the fire as he could. It was blowing quite hard, and the snow was drifting, and there was no way of laying down along side of the fire, nor was there room enough for everybody to get around it. The watch was kept as usual during the night. I asked the captain if Noros and I had to stand watch during the night. He said, "No; that we must get all the sleep that we could."

On the morning of October 9 the weather had moderated, and the weather was quite clear. We then had our grog; after grog we had prayers, and the captain called me to one side and said, "Nindemann, I think you have got to go only about twelve miles to a settlement called Ku Mark Surk, and I think that you and Noros can make it in three days, or, at the longest, four." I then told the captain that I had but very little hope of finding assistance. He then said, "Nindemann, do the best you can; if you find assistance come back as quick as possible, and if you do not you are as well off as we are; you see the condition we are in." He then said he was going to give me written instructions on first going off, but that he had changed his mind and thought that if I found people they would not be able to read it. He then told me to keep on the west bank of the river and not leave it if I could help it, as I would not find any drift-wood on the east side, nor natives; if there were any they ought to be on the west side. He then told me not to wade and not to let Noros wade, but to keep out of the water, and to walk around it if we could. He then called Noros and told him he was going with me, and that he was to obey any order that I might give him. We then lightened ourselves of everything we had, just the clothes we stood in. The captain gave me a rifle, 40 rounds of ammunition, and about 3 ounces of alcohol. When we were ready to start, shook hands with everybody, and, starting up the river bank, they gave us three cheers, and we started on our journey.

Question by the JUDGE-ADVOCATE. How many days' provisions had you, sufficient to sustain life on reduced rations, when you landed from the first cutter September 17, 1881?

The WITNESS. I think about 6 days.

Question by the JUDGE-ADVOCATE. Why, if you know, did Lieut. Commander De Long refuse to allow you to take Alexy with you, when you separated from the first cutter's party to attempt the forced march to Ku Mark Surk?

The WITNESS. The simple reason was that Alexy was a good hunter and the captain wanted to keep him, telling me that if there was anything to hunt that I could hunt for myself.

Question by the JUDGE-ADVOCATE. What in detail was the physical condition of the first cutter's party when you separated from it, October 9, 1881?

The WITNESS. There was not much difference between any of them except Captain De Long; his feet gave out; his health was as good as any of them. Lee was about the same.

Question by the JUDGE-ADVOCATE. Have you any further statement to make in relation to the events which transpired with the first cutter's party, from the date of the separation of the boats until you and Noros went ahead for relief on the 9th day of October, 1881? If yea, make it now.

The WITNESS. No, sir.

The court then examined the witness, as follows:

Question by the COURT. While the first cutter was running before the gale of September 12, 1881, and just before the mast carried away, how would you have regarded the evolution of rounding to—attended with danger or otherwise?

The WITNESS. I think there would have been some danger, as the sea was running very high and breaking at times.

Question by the COURT. During the gale of September 12, 1881, you have stated in effect that the first cutter shipped a good deal of water when the mast carried away. Did the water come on board when before the wind or when the sea was abeam?

The WITNESS. She shipped her water when the sea was abeam. It rolled in right over the wash-board.

Question by the COURT. Describe fully how the wash-board was fitted to the first cutter, and, if you know, what was the difference between this one and those fitted on the whale-boat and second cutter.

The WITNESS. There were sockets fitted along the gunwale of the boat, and wooden stanchions to fit the sockets. The stanchions were about 18 inches high. A piece of canvas, about 20 inches, was tacked on the outside. The top part of it was leeched with a thin line. The wash-board was so rigged that it could be put up in about three seconds and taken down in three seconds. When it was down it was stopped up on the outside of the boat with a half a dozen stops, and the stanchions were unshipped and put where they were handy. The washboard extended as far forward as the mast, abreast of the mast. The forward part of the boat was covered in with the boat cover, hauled out to the mast and stretched down to the sides of the boat, so that the water could not break into the boat. The wash-board ran not quite around the stern, as it would have been in the way of the tiller. During the night of the gale me and Erichsen hung a piece of canvas over our heads, and letting the canvas drag astern so that the sea would not break into it. This did not keep all the water out, but it kept out a good deal. I think the whale-boat's was something similar to hers, but could not be taken down as quick as the one we had on the first cutter. The second cutter had very low wash-boards, about 6 inches high. The after part of the wash-board was fitted out of boards; the forward part out of canvas. How they had the stanchions exactly fitted I cannot say, but I know they had a top-gallant forecastle about the same way as the whale-boat and the first cutter.

Question by the COURT. Did not the second cutter set higher out of the water than either of the other boats? If so, how much higher?

The WITNESS. I think the second cutter set about two inches higher in the water than the other boats.

Question by the COURT. Do you think the first cutter would hav lived through the gale if she had not been fitted with wash-boards, or if these wash-boards had been a foot lower?

The WITNESS. No, sir; the first cutter could not have lived through the gale if it had not been for the wash-boards, or if the wash-boards had been a foot lower.

Question by the COURT. When you were ordered by Lieutenant De Long, on October 6 and 9, 1881, to make a forced march, did others wish to go with you? And, if so, state all you know about the matter.

The WITNESS. Not that I know of, sir.

The court was here, by request of a member, cleared for deliberation, and afterwards reopened; and then, at 12 m., took a recess until 12.30 p. m., and then reconvened with all the members, the judge-advocate, and the witness under examination present.

The judge-advocate then resumed his examination of the witness, as follows:

Question by the JUDGE ADVOCATE. Give a detailed narrative of your journeyings in company with Noros, after leaving the first cutter's party and until you met Mr. Melville, of the whale-boat's party, at Bulun.

The WITNESS. Before starting the captain gave me a copy of a chart that he was working by, pointing out the river we were on, and stating that we only had one more river to cross before reaching Ku Mark Surk.

The witness here produced the chart in question, which the judge-advocate placed before the court, and a certified copy, marked U U 2, is appended to the record. The witness here referring to the chart pointed out to the court the place, island of Tet Ary, where Lieut. Commander De Long supposed his party to be when Nindemann and Noros were sent ahead for relief.

The WITNESS. We then started along the river bank to the westward until we found a place where we could cross. Here we had to get long poles to put on the young ice to walk on until we got quite a little distance on the river, where the ice was strong enough to bear us. On getting off on the other side it broke through, where the water was not deep enough to fill our boots. We then cut across around to the south until we struck the river about 200 yards up. We struck the river and found the ruins of two huts. Here the river was still open, and the ice was running in it. We walked along the river bank until about noon, when we saw a ptarmigan sitting on what we thought was a heavy piece of drift-wood. I fired at him and shot his tail-feathers out, but the bird flew away. On getting up and examining the place we saw that it was a kyak. It was turned bottom up. We broke it out of the snow to see whether there was anything under it, and there was nothing. We then put it back again and started south for about a half an hour, when we made a halt to make us a little grog. While we were getting fire-wood, and when we had enough, Noros started the fire, and at this time I saw eight or ten ptarmigan within about 50 yards of us. I took the rifle and crawled up to them. I got within about 25 yards, waiting till I had three or four in line. I then fired. I killed but one of them. I cooked that and we made dinner out of it. The ptarmigan are the size of a pigeon, but have not so much meat. In the winter time there is very little of them.

During the morning we looked around quite often to see whether our comrades were following us, but we could not see anything of them.

The captain had said before we started that he was going to get ready as soon as he could and follow in our footsteps. After we had finished our bird we started south again, sometimes walking along the river and sometimes the top of the river bank. The walking on top of the river bank was very hard on account of the deep snow, and the snow not being hard enough to bear us. So whenever we could we walked along below the river bank, as it was better walking.

About 3 o'clock we struck another river, in to the westward, but here we only had to go about a mile in to the west, where we found a place where we could cross. After crossing we picked up the main river again. Walking on for about an hour, we found a big flat-boat that was shoved up on the beach. There were only the ribs, two planks on each side, and the bottom planks. The rest of the planks were all taken off, probably by some natives. We halted here for a short time to take a rest, and then started off again. A little before dark I saw something to the westward that I thought at the first going off were huts. Then it looked to me as if something was moving around them. I could not make out for certain what it was, and going along a little farther we found they were deer. At this time we had got pretty well to the southward and eastward of the deer, or where the deer were, on a large, smooth plain. I then left my blanket with Noros and walked toward the deer. I got within about a thousand yards of them, and some of them stood up. They commenced to eat. I then crawled on my hands and knees within about 300 yards of them, but as the wind was from the southeast they could smell me. As soon as they smelled me they started to run. I kept firing three or four shots at them, but did not get anything. The deer started to run to the westward; I kept on watching them until they were out of sight. I then returned back to Noros, Noros saying, "Nindemann, it is too bad you did not kill anything that time." I told him "I tried hard enough." We then started to the south again until it was quite dark. The wind was quite fresh. We camped down on a point of land where a big bay made in to the westward. We got fire-wood enough to last us during the night, and started a fire. We made ourselves some warm tea, and had a boot-sole, which we soaked in water and then burnt it to a crust, and took it along with our Arctic willow tea. After that we made bags of our blankets, and then crawled into them to lay down alongside of the fire, as near as possible, and rested for the night. The fire would get low, and anybody that felt cold would get up, put more wood on the fire, then lay down again.

On the morning of the 10th we had a little Arctic willow tea and another boot-sole. After that we started to the westward, about 9 o'clock; then turned around to the southwest. It commenced blowing, and the snow was drifting so that we could not see 50 yards ahead of us sometimes. Now and then it would let up a little, so that we could see a point of land, taking our bearings as near as we could get the way we were going on; but as we went from point to point we found in between them nothing else but small rivers and sand-spits, where we had to wade to get on the river and to get off of them. Sometimes we struck a sand-spit thinking it was the last we would come to, when we would find another small river that we would have to wade, again getting off and on. This we kept up all day. I think we made a course sometimes northwest, and west until night. Before we halted it was quite dark, and it was blowing very hard at the time. We found some fire-wood and tried to start a fire, but the wind was so hard that we were unable to start a fire, and we gave it up. We then walked along to a place on the bank of the river that was pretty high, where there was a snow-drift. There was nothing else left for us than to dig a hole in the snow so as to have a little-shelter for the night. We had nothing to dig a hole with but a sheath-knife, and I think it must have been midnight before we made a hole big enough to lay the two of us. When the hole was finished both of us crawled in, closing the hole behind us to keep the snow from drifting in, rolled ourselves up in our blankets, and lay there during the night. We did not get any sleep, as both of us were wet up to the waist and had to keep warm knocking our feet together to keep from freezing. Noros now and then would fall off asleep. I let him sleep for about five minutes, then called him, telling him to knock his feet together to keep them from freezing. In this way we got through until daylight and were glad when it came. We then tried to get out of the hole, and had quite hard work to get out of it. During the night the snow had drifted at the bank, covering up the hole we had crawled into 4 or 5 feet. We dug ourselves out, filling the hole up behind us as we dug our way out of it.

On the morning of the 11th started on our way to the south. The weather was a little better this morning, and there was very little snow-drift. We walked until about 12 o'clock, and we found drift-wood enough to start a fire. Here we stopped to make ourselves a little grog from the three ounces of alcohol the captain had given us, but Noros found by feeling in his pocket that the bottle was broken. We then got us some Arctic willow and made tea out of it, and had another boot-sole. Toward evening we got up on the river bank looking around, and sighted something to the southward that looked like a hut. When we found it was a hut we crossed the river, where we had to wade to get onto the ice and then wade again getting off of it. We then got onto a sand-spit, walking along on the bank about a mile or two, when we came to another river and had to wade again. After we got across the river we only had to go about two hundred yards to get up to the hut. This must have been about 5 o'clock in the afternoon. When we got there we then got wood enough to last us during the night, and then went to the hut and started a fire. We got some Arctic willow to make ourselves some tea, and in this hut we found some deer-bones, which we threw in the fire and burned them, and then ate them. We staid up until 10 o'clock that night drying our clothes, and lay down for the night.

On the morning of the 12th it was blowing a gale from the southeast, the snow drifting, and we could not see anything, and therefore were obliged to stay that day in the hut. During the day we made some Arctic willow tea and hunted up more bones in the hut, burning them and eating them. On the morning of the 13th the weather was a little better, but still blowing; but anyhow we could not see enough to see how we were going. Here the river to the west of us was all open to the southward and westward. The river to the southward and eastward was open on the south side, with three small mountains. Working along the river bank, we noticed a hut on the west side of the river, where we were trying to go on the ice; but the ice breaking through, and the water was getting too deep for us, and we had to go back. We kept on walking until about dinner time, sitting down a good many times to rest, as the wind was very strong and we faced it.

A little time after dinner we sighted another hut on the west bank of the river. We tried to go on, but the ice again breaking through we had to go back. We kept on going until we got abreast of it, then tried the ice again to go across. We broke through and got back. We came back again to the beach, but found that we could not go anywhere else; that we had to go on the ice and cross the river. We went again; we still kept on. We broke through. Both of us got wet to our waists; and we managed to get on the ice that was strong enough to bear us. The ice was very slippy, and as we had the wind almost in our face to drive us back all the time, we looked around for a place where the ripples under water had forced themselves into the ice, which had made it a little rough, and we could hold on to it a little better. After awhile we managed to get across, getting close up to the river bank. We saw two crosses standing near the river bank. The river bank here is about 50 feet high. On going up the river bank we found that the hut that we had seen was all broken down and was almost snowed full. Noros got then to work. I was standing outside, looking around, looking to the southward, and I saw something black. When Noros was inside trying to make a place to rest during the night I went down to the southward to find out what the object was that I saw. Finally, on getting there, I found that it was a small peaked hut; it had no door, and there were fresh wood shavings laying on the ground outside of the hut. I then saw two boxes up on the hill. I went up to find out what they were. The boxes looked old and decayed, and as we wanted wood for the night I commenced to break the box open. After having the top part off, I saw there was another box inside that did not look quite so old and weather-beaten as the outside one. I broke up the covers and found there was a dead person in the box, and left it. I then went back to tell Noros what I had seen, and told him that the small hut was a better hut and was big enough for two of us, and that we had better put up there for the night. I then walked over to pick up all the drift-wood that we could find. I came across one place where there were five or six pieces of timber laying close together, frozen to the ground. I got a stick, pried them all loose, and left them as they were, pretty close to the hut, and I was going on a little further to get some more drift-wood when Noros came along to me, and seeing the wood picked it up, and found there was a hole under it; looked into the hole and saw a wooden box half filled with earth and dirt, and lifted it out and overhauled it, and found two fish and one or two fishheads. He sung out to me and told me what he had found. On going to the hut a lemming came out of his hole, which I caught. We then went into the hut and started a fire. I roasted the lemming on the ramrod, just the way he was. After roasting it I gave Noros half of it; then we had one of the fish, and we cooked them, though we had found that they were in a state of decay and almost dropped apart. But we managed to find a couple of little flat stones to fry our fish on, and then we had a little Arctic willow tea. After supper we closed the door up with a couple of boards and then lay down by the fire, drying our clothes, and sleeping until morning.

On the morning of the 14th it was blowing very hard, and we had to face the wind. We made a start, but were obliged to return back again to the hut, as at this time it was blowing so hard and the snow was drifting so that we could not see anything; and while staying here we ate our fish and the fish-heads, and may be some other articles. Toward evening both of us got out again to look out for more drift-wood, and found but very little, and had to be very careful during the night not making a big fire, so as to make the wood last until morning.

And the court then, at 1.30 p. m., pending the further examination of this witness, adjourned to meet to-morrow, the 6th day of December, 1882, at 10 a. m.

FORTY-NINTH DAY.

NAVY DEPARTMENT,
Washington, D. C., Wednesday, December 6, 1882—10 a. m.

The court met pursuant to the adjournment of yesterday.

Present, Commodore William G. Temple, United States Navy, president; Capt. Joseph W. Miller, United States Navy, Commander Frederick V. McNair, United States Navy, members; and Master Samuel C. Lemly, United States Navy, judge-advocate.

The record of the proceedings of Monday, December 4, 1882, the forty-seventh day of the inquiry, was then read, and after correcting clerical errors was approved.

By request of the judge-advocate the reading of the record of yesterday, December 5, 1882, the forty-eighth day of the inquiry, was deferred.

Seaman W. F. C. NINDEMANN, the witness under examination, then came in, and continued his answer to the pending question, which was repeated by the judge-advocate, as follows:

Give a detailed narrative of your journeyings in company with Noros after leaving the first cutter's party, and until you met Mr. Melville, of the whale-boat's party, at Bulun.

The WITNESS. On the morning of the 15th it was still blowing from the southeast, but the snow had stopped drifting. We made a start along the river bank to the southward and eastward, looking for the main river. After awhile we crossed an island, where we found signs of natives who had been there. We then got on the river again. The ice was quite smooth and the wind had increased by this time, and the snow and sand were drifting so hard that we hardly could open our eyes. We struggled along about 5 o'clock, walking along past an island, and we sighted a crack in the river bank. The weather by this time was so bad that we could not face it any longer. We examined the crack. It was about two and a half feet wide, and started from the lower bank of the river, with a small hole extending through on top of the river bank. We were going to make halt here, but finding the draught in the crack was so great we thought we could not keep ourselves warm for the night. We then started along the river bank in hopes of finding a better shelter for the night. We walked about a mile, and not finding a better place we were obliged to walk back to the crack in the river bank, and getting there we gathered wood enough to last us during the night. One of us had to get in the crack while the other passed the wood in to him. We then started a fire, went out and got some Arctic willow to make tea of. As we had nothing to eat, I had a pair of seal-skin pants, and we cut off a piece, soaking it in water and burning it to a crust, and then ate it. There was a terrible draught through the crack. We took one of our blankets to cover the crack, but the blanket was not long enough and left quite a hole on top. There was not room for both of us to set alongside below the fire, so therefore one of us had to crawl up above the fire and lay down to keep out of the smoke. But the man on top could not stand it very long, and therefore we had to keep on shifting about every twenty minutes. We could not keep ourselves very warm, and every now and then would look out and see if daylight had not broke yet. A little before daylight the wind had moderated and the snow had stopped drifting some.

As soon as daylight came and we could see the mountains to the southward and eastward we made ourselves some willow tea and ate a little more of the seal-skin pants, and then started on our march to the southward and eastward to find the main river. We crossed the river and then got onto some sand-spits where there were heavy hummocks of ice that had lodged on the sand-spits. The wind by this time had increased a little again, and the snow and sand commenced drifting again. We had tried to rest a couple of times behind the hummocks, but we found that we could not find any shelter, and the wind blowing so fresh right through our clothing. We kept struggling along till we got on a quite large sand-bank, and within about three miles of the mountains. Here I could see no river, and I was afraid that we had passed the main river, as we had crossed so many large rivers before. But as I thought we had not passed the river where the ice was not quite rough enough, I thought I would keep on until we got on the foot of the mountains; if not finding the river, to start west again until we found it. We kept on around the sand-spit to the southward and eastward, and it did not take long when we sighted the main river. A little before this, before finding the river, we saw a crow flying across through the mountains, and this was always a sign up in the Arctic that when you see a crow that somewhere near you generally find natives. My orders were not to leave the west bank of the river if I possibly could help it. But seeing that there was nothing else but sand-spits, and I had seen no traces of game, I thought it best to cross the river and to see whether we could not find game of some kind. We then started across the river, but we had to feel our way, as there were large holes of open water beyond there. We got about half ways across when Noros told me he did not feel well, and that he had been spitting blood a couple of times. I sometimes got ahead of him and would wait for him to come to assist him to come up. We were about 300 yards from the edge of the river bank, and I told Noros that I would go ahead, and wait for him as soon as I struck the foot of the mountains. When I got across I waited for about half an hour for Noros to come up. When Noros came up we rested for a little while and then started along to the southward. The foot of the mountains ran right into the river, and we were obliged sometimes to walk on the ice. The ice here was very rough, but made hard walking. We stuck to it along till night, but had not found anything that indicated signs of natives or game. By this time it was getting dark, and we were looking for a place of shelter, but could not find anything else but a small ravine that ran in between two mountains. I here found a little drift-wood. We stopped and made ourselves some hot water, as we could not find any Arctic willow here, and ate at the same time, of our seal-skin pants. After that we walked up the ravine, trying to find a place where we could get a little shelter, but we did not find any. We came to a place where there was about two feet of snow, dug a hole in it, and set up some snow-blocks around it to break the wind. We then crawled into our blanket and lay down for the night. We did not get but very little sleep, and if we could have seen to travel during the night we would have started again, but the night was dark and we could not see where we were going. We managed to pass the time here until morning of the 17th. As soon as daylight broke we started down the ravine, following along the river bank to the south. The walking was very bad and we made very little headway. At 10 o'clock we found some drift-wood, started a fire, and then made ourselves some boiling water and had another piece of the seal-skin pants. Here we staid for an hour or so, fixing the soles of our boots, which were worn out pretty well. We then made a start again for about another mile along the river, but finding the walking was very bad and there were no signs of game, and thought it was best to cross again over to the west side. It took us till about noon before we got across the river, and we then came on some sand-spits again. By this time the wind had hauled around to the southwest of the sand-spits, and it commenced to blow quite fresh. After crossing the sand-spits we got onto quite a large river again, where the ice was more thick, and where there were some big holes of open water. Here we made our way across; struck more sand-spits again. By this time it was blowing quite fresh and snowing, and the snow was drifting pretty hard. It was getting toward evening, and we got on at the same time more sand-spits. Here there were little round hills which looked like a mixture of snow and sand. As it was getting dark and we could not see much, we tried to dig a hole into one of them, but found there was ice under it. We then struggled on for some time, until we got on some low land, where there was drift-wood. We here tried to find a piece of drift-wood large enough to lay behind for a little shelter during the night. We could not find any. Before it was getting dark we saw a high river bank to the southward and westward of us. As we could not find any shelter, we kept on struggling along until we struck another large river. We got across here, and it must have been about 12 o'clock at night, about midnight, when we struck the river bank. We struck a place where there was drift-wood. We tried to start a fire, but the wind was blowing so fresh that it was impossible to start one. We then walked off about a mile along the river bank, until we found a snow-drift where we could dig a hole in it. We just dug a hole big enough for the two of us, and took some snow-blocks, piling them around the hole to break the wind. We did not get much sleep, as the weather was too cold.

On the morning of the 18th, as soon as day broke, the wind had moderated, and we started along the river bank to the southward. About 10 o'clock we found some drift-wood, halted, made a fire, and made ourselves some willow tea, and ate some of the seal-skin pants. We then struggled along on the west bank of the river, walking on the river whenever we could. Sometimes we would go on top of the river bank to see if we could see game of any kind or sight any huts. But we could walk but a short time on top of the river bank, as the moss and snow was so deep that we used to go in up to our knees. We struggled along this way until about 6 o'clock in the evening, when we got up on the river bank and sighted a hut about a mile inland or off the river bank. We then walked up to it, and found that it was a peaked hut with no door before it, and almost snowed over. About 100 yards to the south of it we saw something piled up, and going to see what it was we found that they were sleighs. We then started to dig the hut out to make room for us, for the two of us to lay down, and as there was very little drift-wood laying around we were obliged to take the sleighs, break them up, and use them for fire-wood. We then went out to get some Arctic willow to make ourselves some tea, and ate some of the seal-skin pants. By this time we were quite weak, and had not had any sleep since we left the last hut. We slept pretty well that night.

On the morning of the 19th when we woke up, we found it was daylight. We then made ourselves some tea, and then started again on our march south. We struggled along until about 3 o'clock in the afternoon, when we came to a quite high cliff, where we saw an owl flying; we stopped, waiting for the owl to sit, but she kept on flying around in a circle, and at last flew over the cliff. We kept on struggling along, resting about every five minutes. While resting at one location I told Noros that it would have been much better for us if we had stayed in the hut we left on that morning. Still we got up again, struggling on until about 4 o'clock in the afternoon, when we sighted a small river making in to the westward. On crossing it, Noros looked back, and said, "Nindemann, there are three huts on the river bank." We then started back, walking up the river bank, and got into one of the huts. Here we found a kyak, with some fish-nets and other articles in it. There was a half kyak, where there was some fish in it. Noros, who found this, took some of it up and tasted it. He wanted to know what it was. I walked up to it, tasted it, and told him that it was fish. The fish looked something like coarse sawdust. It was all blue molded, and had no taste of any kind. It was just like taking so much sawdust. We then took some of the fish and went to the peaked hut. We lighted a small fire to make ourselves something to eat. After that we went out to pick up some wood to last us for the night. We overhauled the other hut, but found nothing in it. About 9 o'clock we boiled some more of our fish, filled up the fire, and lay down alongside of it for the night.

On the morning of the 20th we had some more tea, and then went out to get more wood to last during the day. By this time both of us had the dysentery awful bad, and we were very weak. Sitting down alongside of the fire we felt ourselves pretty strong, but when we came to get up and to walk around, picking up a little drift-wood, we found that we were very weak.

On the morning of the 21st we got ready to make a start, but as we were very weak we thought best to stay another day, fix up our things, and start on the morning of the 22d. During the 21st we measured in our tin cups the fish that we had left, and we found by taking two cupfuls a day a man that we had ten days' provisions. We had nothing else but a skull-cap apiece and a pair of foot-nips. We then went to work to fill them with the fish, to sew them up, and put straps on them to carry them. In the afternoon we went out to get more drift-wood to last us during the night. On the morning of the 22d the weather was very cold, and I wanted to make a start, but Noros said, "We are pretty weak yet, and as the weather is cold we had better rest another day." By this time our dysentery was so bad that it was almost impossible for us to start, and I think that if we had started that we would have froze on the way. I then overhauled my boots and found that the soles were all gone and only held up by the strings. I tried to pull them off, but I could not. Noros he tried it, but could not get them off, and I had to take a knife and cut them off. I then sat down to fix my boots with a piece of old seal-skin pants. Noontime came; we seated ourselves alongside of the fire, making ourselves something to eat, when I heard something going outside. I looked through the crack of the door and saw it was something large and thought it was a reindeer. I took the rifle down from over my head, loaded it, walking toward the door, when the door opened. I saw it was a native, who looked at me and seeing I had the rifle in my hand pointed toward the door he fell on his knees, throwing up his hands, saying something, what it was I cannot say.

The court then, at 12 m., took a recess until 12.30 p. m., and then reconvened, with all the members and the judge-advocate present.

The record of the proceedings of Tuesday, December 5, 1882, the forty-eighth day of the inquiry, was then read and, after correcting clerical errors, approved.

And the court then, at 1.15 p. m., pending the further examination of this witness, adjourned to meet to-morrow, the 7th day of December, 1882, at 10 a. m.

FIFTIETH DAY.

NAVY DEPARTMENT,
Washington, D. C., Thursday, December 7, 1882—10 a. m.

The court met pursuant to the adjournment of yesterday.

Present, Commodore William G. Temple, United States Navy, president; Captain Joseph N. Miller, United States Navy; Commander Frederick V. McNair, United States Navy, members; and Master Samuel C. Lemly, United States Navy, judge-advocate.

The record of the proceedings of yesterday, December 6, 1882, the forty-ninth day of the inquiry, was then read and, after correcting clerical errors, approved.

Seaman W. F. C. NINDEMANN, the witness under examination, then came in and continued his answer to the pending question, which was repeated by the judge-advocate, as follows:

Give a detailed narrative of your journeyings, in company with Noros, after leaving the first cutter's party, and until you met Mr. Melville, of the whale-boat's party, at Bulun.

The WITNESS. When I saw this native I threw the rifle in one corner and beckoned him to come in. At the first going off he was a little shy, but came in after awhile. We then offered him something to eat, but he shook his head, as much as to say that it was no good that we were eating. We then went out to have a look at his sleigh and see what he had. He had nothing with him to eat. I picked up his large deer-skin coat, took it into the hut. I took off my wet flannel shirt and offered it to him if he would give me the coat, but he shook his head. I then showed him my boots. He went out to his sleigh and got me a pair of deer-skin boots. We then tried to make him understand that we were sent by the captain to get assistance, but it seemed as if we could not make him understand much. He then made signs that he wanted to go, and that he had to have his heavy deer-skin coat, as the weather was very cold. He took the deer-skin coat, went out, and fetched me in a deer-skin, and then held up three or four fingers, as much as to say that he was going to be back, either in three or four hours or three or four days, we did not know which. He took the shirt, got up on his sleigh and then started to drive to the westward along the river. It was not long before he was out of sight with his deer sleigh. Me and Noros then got to talking about the matter. I told him I was sorry that we let the man go, for I was afraid that I had scared him with the rifle, and thought he would not come back; but Noros thought that he was a good Christian and that he would return. I then told Noros that we would wait four days, and if he did not return by that time we would start on the march to the southward. We then went over into the store-house, where we found the fish. There were some sleighs there and some other articles of wood there. We took them and carried them to the hut for fire-wood, as we were too weak to go down the river bank to get drift-wood. We burned everything in the line of wood that we could find on or around the huts. We then broke up all the berths in the huts and burned them. About 6 o'clock in the evening we boiled some more fish, when we heard something outside again. Before we could get to the door the door opened and the man stepped in with two others. They came into the hut. They then tried to talk to us, and we tried to make them understand where we came from and what we wanted. One of them then went out and fetched in a frozen fish, which he skinned, sliced it up in slices, and gave it to us. Before we had half finished them they made signs that it was time to start. They then went out and fetched us in some deerskin coats and boots, and put them on us; picked up a lot of small articles that we had laying round, put us on the deer sleighs, and drove down the river and into the westward. Going along for a couple of miles they turned into the mountains, a little to the southward and westward. They kept on driving until about 12 o'clock that night, over the mountains, until we struck a ravine, where we could see a couple of tents of deer-skin. We could see the fire shining through it. It did not take us long before we got there. They then took Noros into one tent and me into another. They then offered me, or us, something to eat. In the tent that I was in I think there were five men and two women. After we went into the hut for a little while the woman she offered me some water to wash. I washed my hands, but it did not improve them much; my fingers were bent so that when I started to wash my face I was all scratched up. The woman noticed it, took pity on me, and she washed me. After that we had some more boiled deer-meat and boiled fish, and then got to talking to the people through signs and pantomimes. I tried the best way I could to make them understand what I came for, and that I was sent by the captain to get assistance. At the first going off it seemed as if they paid great attention to it, but after awhile they wanted to know everything I had on my person. I showed them a meerschaum pipe which I had. They wanted to cut it up to smoke, and I made signs to them not to do it; then took the pipe away from them and cut a piece of the stem and gave it to them. They cut it up fine and mixed it with some shavings they had to put in their pipes and smoke it. They then wanted to know whether I had money. They could not make me understand this at first—one of them took a rouble bill from his pocket and showed it to me. Then I saw what they wanted. I tried to make them understand that we had plenty of money in the ship; that it all went down, and that if they would give me assistance that they would get plenty of money given them. Whether they understood this or not I cannot say. It was then getting pretty late. Before turning in everybody stood up and crossed themselves. I kept on sitting down. One of the men came up to me and told me to stand up and go through the same motions they did. After they were through crossing themselves everybody retired for the night. The next morning, the morning of the 23d, at daylight, I woke up, and they had breakfast ready, and we had something to eat. During the breakfast hour I tried to talk to them again, to make them understand what I had been sent for. After breakfast everybody went outside to catch the deer. While they were after the deer the man that I thought was the head man sat down on a sleigh, and I got talking to him, and drawing a chart for him in the snow of the places and landmarks that I had seen and the height of different places. Sometimes it seemed to me he understood what I wanted, and at other times again it seemed as if he did not understand a word of what I wanted.

After they had caught all of the deer and harnessed them up to the sleighs I counted them; they had twenty-seven sleighs, loaded with reindeer-meat, reindeer-skins, and fish. I counted over a hundred head of reindeer. They then took down the tents and broke camp, and we started over the mountains to the southward. About noontime we halted to give the deer rest. The man that I thought was the head man in the party made signs to me to come on the mountain side. We walked up about five or six hundred yards, and he pointed out to me a prominent landmark in the Lena Delta that was about 300 feet high that me and Noros had seen for days before we passed it. He then wanted to know whether that was the place where we had left the people. I told him as near as I could and made signs that the people were fifteen or twenty miles probably to the northward of that place. He shook his head, as much as to say he felt sorry, and then started toward the sleighs again. After they had rested here, they started off again to the southward until night, when we camped for the night. Here I tried to make them understand again, but it was of no use. After we had our supper everybody turned in.

On the morning of the 24th we broke camp again, and after breakfast started to the south again. We halted several times during the day to rest the deer. Now and then, when the deer had to draw a load up the hillside, everybody had to get out of the sleighs. They would get a long distance ahead of us and sometimes had to wait a half an hour before me and Noros would fetch up with them again. About 4 o'clock in the afternoon we struck a small river, which runs a little to the southward and eastward. They kept along this for about an hour, when we struck the main river again. We then kept along the river bank until about 5 o'clock, when we sighted the huts to the southward of us, and it did not take us long to get up to them. When we got abreast of the huts we went up a little ravine to go up to the huts. There were quite many people standing on top of the river bank watching us coming. After we got to the huts a fire was at once started and the women made us something to eat—there was quite many people in the hut. We were getting on pretty good, and everybody stopped and looked at us, talking about us. Everybody wanted to know who we were and where we were from. I then tried to talk to the people to make them understand what I wanted, but I found that it was no good, as there were too many people in the huts and that they were doing nothing else but feasting. They kept it up till about 12 o'clock that night and everybody then retired. I wish to state here that Noros was in one hut and I in another. We were not together.

On the morning of the 25th—after breakfast—I then started again, talking to the people through signs and pantomimes, but it seemed as if one of them had got some idea of where we came from or what we wanted, and he talked to one of the boys, and the boy went out, and after awhile came back with a model of a Yakutsk boat, and then they all got around me and wanted to know, as near as I could make out, whether our ship was something like it. I then went to work and got some sticks and placed them in the boat, showing them that our ship had three masts, and then got more sticks, showing them that she had yards. This seemed to surprise them very much. I then made a smokestack out of wood and pointed to the fire and smoke, and then showed them the place astern where the rudder was, and had a small roll which I turned to make them understand that our ship was a steamer. I then made models of the boats, showed them how many boats the ship had. Then I told one of the men to get me a couple of pieces of ice. He went out and got me a couple of pieces of ice, and I showed them how the ice had crushed our ship. I then pointed to the northward, as much as to say the ice crushed our ship away to the northward, and that we saved three boats, putting in each little boat so many sticks to represent how many men there were in each boat. At the time there was a dog in the room. A man pointed to the dog and wanted to know whether we had any dogs. I counted on my fingers that we had about forty, and made them understand that we had shot the most of them and left some of them behind on the ice. I then showed them a chart of the ocean and the coast line, showing that we had a gale of wind, and that one boat went in here, and that we did not know what had become of the other two. I then showed them on the chart where we had landed, and made the boat on the chart a little ways off land, and then I showed them by pencil-marks that everybody had left the boat and waded ashore. Then showed them the way we walked along the river bank by so many pencil-marks, each pencil-mark was supposed to be a man, and I marked the huts where we stopped. Here we came to the place where Erichsen had died. I showed them through signs that he had died, and that we buried him in the river. Everybody shook his head, as much as to say that they felt sorry for it. I then made them understand that we had left the captain a couple of days after that, and by putting my head down and closing my eyes, to show them how many days it had been that we had left them. This seemed to affect them pretty well, but it seemed to me as if they would not give me any assistance. Sometimes it seemed to me as if they understood everything that I wanted. Then all at once it seemed that they did not understand a word. I kept talking with those people till it must have been somewhere near twelve o'clock, but they did not show any signs by this time of any intention to give me assistance or to do anything for me.

On the morning of the 26th, Noros came up to the hut after breakfast and we started with the people again; we kept at them all day, but it seemed as if they could not get any idea of what we wanted. On the morning of the 27th, after breakfast, I was sitting on my berth, thinking of everything, and I broke down. The woman in the house noticed it; she got talking to one of the men, who came up to me and talked about the commandant. By this time I had picked up a few words of their language, and I asked them to take me to Bulun, for I thought it was no use staying any longer in this place if I could not do anything with the people. He then got to talking about the commandant, holding up five or six fingers, as much as to say he was going to be here in so many hours. After that he told me he was going to take me to Bulun to-morrow. I gave myself rest, and in the evening about nine o'clock had something to eat. After supper the woman of the house came along, gave me a couple of leaves of tobacco for my pipe to smoke. I was sitting smoking my pipe when a native came up to me and told me the commandant was coming. It did not take long when the door opened and a tall Russian stepped into the hut. I got talking to him in English, but he did not understand a word. He then mentioned the ship's name—Jeannette and Americanansk. I understood this, and I told him "Yes;" that we were Americans, and that we belonged to the Jeannette. When I found that he could not talk any English, nothing else but just mentioning the ship's name and Americanansk, I thought that he must be some Russian authority, and that he probably had orders from his Government to look out for us. I then tried him in German, but he shook his head, as much as to say, "I do not understand you." I then got out a little chart that the captain had given me and pointed out the place where the captain told me that we were when we left him; but it seemed to me as if he had no idea what a chart was. He then said something about telegraphing, which he called "telegramo," and he talked about St. Petersburgh, which I understood. I thought about this time, by the way he acted, that either he or me had to telegraph to St. Petersburgh before he could give me any assistance. I thought, at this time, that if that was the case, and if the people were not dead yet, that they surely would be if I had to telegraph to St. Petersburgh first. We then sat down. At this time Noros was here, to write a note that we wrote at that time. I cannot say now what it was, as he interrupted us and got to talking again about things. While we were talking he picked the paper up and put it in his pocket. We tried to get it from him, but we could not make him understand. By this time it was about 12 o'clock at night, and he wanted to go. I asked him before he started the name of the place where we were, and he said it was Ajaket. He then wanted to go and I asked him for some tobacco. He made signs that he had no tobacco with him, but that he would fetch me some in the morning.

On the morning of the 28th, after breakfast, the man came back again and fetched me a pound of Russian leaf-tobacco. I then made signs to him, pointing to the southward and wanted to know if he was going down to Bulun himself, to which he made signs that he was. When he went out he made signs to us that we were going to Bulun shortly after him. We then went out to see which way he went. I had missed the man that I thought was the head of the party that found us, but inquired what had become of him; they made signs that he had gone with the commandant to Bulun. After I got the tobacco, I divided it between Noros and the people that found us. By this time our driver was ready to take us on our way to Bulun. The people here had given us some of their deer-skin clothing, deer-skin stockings and deer-skin boots. When we were ready the woman of the hut fetched me a couple of smoked fish to eat on the road. I then bid them "good by" starting down the river bank, going along the west side for some time, when we crossed to the east side. Following up the east bank we fell in with a good many deer teams, and at times with a dog team traveling up and down the river to different places. When evening came we struck a small ravine running in to the eastward. Here we saw a man standing talking to our driver, what it was about I cannot say, but he turned his team into the ravine and it did not take long before we came up to a hut that was lying in the woods. On going into the hut we found the hut pretty well crowded. There were two Russians, some Tongoos and three or four women. We stopped here for the night, had some boiled fish, and one of the Russians gave us a loaf of bread to take with us, but he made signs to us only to eat half the loaf and to keep the other half for our journey on the next day; but the bread tasted so well that Noros said we might as well have the good of it now, and we ate the whole loaf. After supper we took a smoke. By this time the natives, or one of the Russians had a bed prepared for us and we turned in for the night.

On the morning of the 29th, after breakfast, we made a start across the river; after arriving at the river kept on the east bank of the river to the south. The wind was blowing quite fresh and snow was drifting. It was pretty cold, and in the afternoon about 3 o'clock we crossed the river to the westward; after crossing we found a hut. By this time we were pretty hungry. We tried to make the driver understand that we wanted him to go to the hut to get something to eat. We then drove down to the hut where we found a man, a woman, and two little children. We went into the hut and the woman gave us some smoked fish. After we finished and warmed up a little, we started off again to the southward. About 6 o'clock we sighted a lot of huts and some large boats that were hauled up on the beach. The driver told us that was Bulun. It did not take long before we got up to it, and going there he took us to a hut and took off our skin clothing. We warmed ourselves; the people in the hut made some tea for us, and shortly after that a native came making signs that the commandant wanted to see us. We put on our fur clothing, the native going ahead of us and showed us the house where he, the commandant, lived, and going into his room I saw that he was not the man I had seen at Ku Mark Surk or at least Ajaket, as I thought all the time; when I thought we were at Ajaket, we were really at Ku Mark Surk and when we got to Bulcour, we thought we were at Ku Mark Surk. He then kept on saying that he was the commandant. I shook my head, as much as to say that he was not, and to make me satisfied, he showed me his uniform and sword. I then got to talking to him the best way I could, and through signs and pantomimes told him what I had come for, and by whom I was sent. I then counted off on my fingers how many people we had left to the northward, the captain and ten others. It seemed to me as if he said "that is all right." I kept on talking, making signs and pantomimes for some time and he started to talk about the telegraph. I told him "yes." About this time, it was quite late and I made signs that we wanted a pen and paper and some ink, which he got us. Noros sat down to do the writing, and I told him what to write. This took us till about 12 o'clock at night before we had finished. After we had finished our telegram we directed it to the American minister at St. Petersburg.

Question by the JUDGE-ADVOCATE. Can you identify now the letter written by Noros to the American minister at St. Petersburg, and signed by Noros and yourself?

The WITNESS. Yes, sir.

The judge-advocate here handed the witness a paper and the witness said "That is the letter."

The judge-advocate then read aloud and placed before the court the letter in question and a certified copy, marked VV, is appended to the record.

And the court then, at 11.55 a. m., took a recess until 12.25 p. m., and then reconvened, with all the members, the judge-advocate, and the witness under examination present.

The witness here produced, and the judge-advocate placed before the court, a copy of a chart constructed by him, from compass bearings taken by him and based upon his actual experience; and a certified copy, marked WW, is appended to the record.

I wish to state here that we did not mark the paper "telegraph" but the commandant told us that he was going to take it to the captain himself to-morrow. We then retired for the night.

On the morning of the 30th I did not feel well; Noros, he felt better, and he got up about 6 o'clock in the morning. When breakfast was ready the commandant wanted to know whether I would have my breakfast in bed, I told him "no; that I would get up." We then sat down, the three of us, and had our breakfast. While at breakfast I got talking about rifles, and I told him that the party had some rifles with them, and that we had left some in the huts. I had in my pocket a Winchester cartridge and showed it to him. He then went and got a rifle to fit the cartridge, but I made him understand that the cartridge belonged to another rifle that fired seven times hand running. He kind of opened his eyes and looked astonished at me. We then got to talking about the telegraph. He handed me back the cartridge; I told him to keep it. He then made signs, as much as to say he was going to give it to the captain, which I understood. I thought at this time that he meant his own captain at the telegraph station. I did not know exactly whether the telegraph station was at Yakutsk or Irkutsk. Before leaving Captain De Long I heard him talking about these two places, but he was not certain at which place the telegraph station was. It then was getting on toward noon-time and the young Pope of the village had come to the house. The commandant at this time was packing his traveling box, telling me again he was going to give it to the captain. He then got to talking to the young Pope, who made signs to us and told us, as soon as the commandant left, that he would take us up to his house. The commandant got ready and started on his journey. It was blowing quite fresh and it was very cold. The fur clothes that had been given us at Ajaket the natives had taken from us, and we had nothing else but the clothes we traveled in after leaving the captain. I did not go outside to see what direction he took. When he had left, we staid a short while longer, when the young Pope made signs to us to go with him up to his house. Dinner time came and he had got up quite a nice dinner. We sat down to the table and tried to talk to each other the best way we could. I showed him a little chart the captain had given me, and pointed out the place where the captain thought we were when we left him. After dinner one of the men that found us came up to his house. We then got to talking again and I asked the young Pope for some paper and a lead-pencil and drew a chart, as near as I could recollect, showing all the little rivers we had crossed, and the huts where we had stopped, and how many there were in each place, and the crosses we had seen on the river bank. The man that found us seemed to know all the places that I had put down on the chart. It then was getting towards the evening and the young Pope made us understand that he was going to get married in a day or two, and that he could not keep us there any longer. He kept us until supper-time and took us then to the hut that we went to when we first came to Bulun, and he gave us a little tea, some bread and sugar to take along with us. We got down to the hut. The hut was dirty and miserable. At this time both of us did not feel well, but Noros sat up; I wanted to lay down and made one of the men of the house to understand what I wanted. They got an old bedstead; put down a deer-skin on it and he gave me a pillow and a deer-skin to cover myself. After awhile the woman of the house made some tea for us and gave us some boiled fish. After supper we retired for the night.

On the morning of the 1st of November I did not feel well, but Noros got up and stood around the hut. Both of us at this time were very weak from dysentery, which we had had ever since we struck the huts where we found the fish. During the day there were a good many people coming to the house to see us. Now and then the young Pope would come in. We had our three meals a day here, and lived here on a little grub that the Pope had given us.

On the morning of the 2d, after breakfast, I got up and went outside to have a look around. Standing outside I saw one of the men that we found in the camp coming up with a load of fish. He noticed me and took ten fish off the sleigh and gave them to me, making signs to me to take them. About this time the little grub that the young Pope had given us was giving out, and the native woman was cooking the fish that the native Alexy had given me in the morning. They themselves had fresh fish, which they enjoyed every day. I made signs to them a couple of times that we would like to have some fresh fish, but it seemed as if the woman would not give it to us.

On the evening of November the 3d, I was laying in bed; Noros was sitting on the table looking toward the door; I heard the door open, and looking round I saw a man coming in the door that was dressed up in fur clothes. I did not pay any attention to it, and lay down again, when the man stepped up to the table saying, "Hello, Noros, you are alive." As soon as he spoke I recognized him as Melville, and asked him whether all of his boat's crew were alive and well. He said, "Yes;" they were all in pretty good health, except Leach, who had both his big toes frozen; and we then told him our story, how we landed, and how we had left the captain, to where we were picked up; and I told him that on the 30th I had written a telegram to the American minister at St. Petersburg, and that the commandant had taken it himself. I told him that it was a very long one and probably would cost a good deal of money. He said it did not matter how much it cost. We then told him about our grub; that they were feeding us on fish all the time. By this time the young Pope had come to the hut, and Mr. Melville wanted to know what authority there was in the place. I told him I did not know of any in the place but the young Pope, as the commandant had left on the 30th of October. Melville by this time could speak a little Russian. He told the Pope that we were to have something better to eat than old fish, and that we would have to have the best that the place could afford to give to us. I then asked him what had fetched him on to Bulun, and he said that he had sent a messenger to Bulun to get the commandant to go down where they were to fetch them up to Bulun. The messenger that he had sent, his name was Kusmah, and that we had given him a note at Ajaket, and that he had received the note, I think it was, about on the evening of the 27th of October.

The judge-advocate here checked the witness, suggesting that the record contained full information on this subject in the testimony of Chief Engineer George W. Melville, and that its repetition was unnecessary. The judge-advocate then continued the examination of the witness as follows:

Question by the JUDGE-ADVOCATE. In what condition, physically, were you and Noros when you were found by Mr. Melville at Bulun?

The WITNESS. Both of us were in a very bad condition, and we were not fit to travel at the time. I was worse than Noros.

Question by the JUDGE-ADVOCATE. Have you any further statement to make in reference to your journeyings with Noros after leaving the first cutter's party and before you encountered Mr. Melville at Bulun? If yea, make it now.

The WITNESS. No, sir; nothing sir, but that we left at the cache on the beach a broken Winchester rifle.

The court then examined the witness as follows:

Question by the COURT. When you were first found by the natives at Bulcour were you and Noros physically able to have turned back with them, if they had consented to go to the assistance of the captain and his party?

The WITNESS. I think we were not; but if they had given us assistance and clothing we would have started and would not have delayed an hour at the huts.

And the court then, at 1.10 p. m., pending the further examination of this witness, adjourned to meet to-morrow, the 8th day of December, 1882, at 10 a. m.

FIFTY-FIRST DAY.

NAVY DEPARTMENT,
Washington, D. C., Friday, December 8, 1882—10 a. m.

The court met pursuant to the adjournment of yesterday.

Present, Commodore William G. Temple, United States Navy, president; Capt. Joseph N. Miller, United States Navy; Commander Frederick V. McNair, United States Navy, members; and Master Samuel C. Lemly, United States Navy, judge-advocate.

The record of the proceedings of yesterday, Thursday, December 7, 1882, the fiftieth day of the inquiry, was then read, and, after correcting clerical errors, approved.

Seaman W. F. C. NINDEMANN, the witness under examination, then came in, and his examination was continued by the judge-advocate as follows:

Question by the JUDGE-ADVOCATE. State generally what your movements were subsequently to your meeting with Chief Engineer Melville at Bulun, November 3, 1881, and state fully what efforts were made by yourself and within your own knowledge by any other person connected with the Jeannette expedition for the relief of the first and second cutters' parties.

The WITNESS. On November 4 we moved into a hut that Mr. Melville had rented. He then sat down and wrote three telegrams, one to the Secretary of the Navy, one to the American minister at St. Petersburg, and one to Mr. Bennett. I then gave him all the details from the time we landed until the time when we were found by the natives; then he sat down and made himself a chart, and after it was finished told me to mark down the huts, as near as I could, and how many there were in each place. He then made arrangements with the young Pope to give him provisions enough to make the search for De Long and his party.

On November 4 Bartlett got to Bulun with the telegram that I had sent by the commandant on the 30th of October. It then struck me what the commandant meant when I gave him the cartridge and he said he was going to give it to the captain; I then knew the meaning when I counted off on my fingers the number of men we had left north; that he knew by that time about Melville when he started, and that at the time I counted off eleven on my fingers that he probably thought we belonged to Melville's party.

On November 5 Melville had everything ready to make a start to search for De Long and his party. He left behind him orders for Danenhower, what to do when he got to Bulun. He took with him one of the natives that seemed to know all about the huts that we had been to.

On the 6th of November Danenhower arrived with the whole party from Geeomovialocke. He staid there a day or two to make arrangements to take the whole party south, except Bartlett, who was going to be left there in case that Melville did not return in twenty days, for him to go in search of him; but Danenhower found that he could not get transportation enough for everybody.

On November 12 Mr. Danenhower had made arrangements to take five men besides himself. He asked me whether I was fit to travel. I told him "No," and he left Bartlett and me and four others. The teams were ready on that afternoon. They started on their way to akutsk. About the 24th of November we lost sight of the sun; by this time Melville had been gone about twenty days. Bartlett went over to the commandant and had a talk with him, and asked him what he thought— whether Melville was all right. He said to him that he thought he was. The next morning an officer from Verkeransk arrived, and we went to his place, and he had a talk with us. He gave us to understand that he was going further north. As soon as we found that he was going north, and as he was an officer, we thought there was no need of Bartlett or anybody else going to look for Mr. Melville. Shortly after that we gave him some provisions to give to Mr. Melville if he should fall in with him.

November 26th, about midnight, we were awakened by a native telling us that Mr. Melville had arrived. As it was late at night, we did not have much to say to each other, and retired then for the night. The next morning Mr. Melville told me that he had found the cache that we left, and that he had fetched all the valuables that he had found there, and had taken away the old clothing and stuff that was of no good and given it to the natives, as he could not carry the whole of it; and that he had found the record and rifles, but had not found the hut where Erichsen was buried; nor had he seen anything of the captain's party. Before Melville left I told him that I had no hopes that he would find the people alive, as the last drop they had to eat was eaten on the 6th of October. We told Mr. Melville about the officer, and that he had gone north. He then made up his mind that he would stay until he returned. As soon as he returned he made arrangements with him to travel to Verkeransk. Melville and the officer left about the 1st or 2d of December. We had orders to start the next day. By this time everybody had been fitted with skin clothing. We left Bulun on the evening of December 3; we arrived at Verkeransk December 15. Here we fetched up with Melville, and we had to wait a couple of days to lay in our provisions. Here Mr. Melville, with another officer that was in business there, was to go to Yakutsk. They both of them left in company for Yakutsk December 18.

On December 19 we got in our stock of provisions and left for Yakutsk that night. We arrived at Yakutsk on January 6, 1882. Here we found the whole party. Mr. Melville told Bartlett and me that he was going to keep us and send the rest of the party south, as he thought we were the strongest men in the party, and he thought that three were enough to continue the search. Upon arriving at Yakutsk, the Russians had been Christmasing, and we could do very little with them, as they would not work in Christmas. We managed to get everything ready for the party that was going south. Danenhower and his party left Yakutsk January 10. We had staid there some days longer, going round the place, buying things, and getting things ready that we had to have on our trip going back to the Lena Delta. We got everything ready about January 17, 1882. Mr. Melville then told me that he was going to send me and Baubikoff the next morning, as there was not transportation enough along the road to accommodate the whole party.

On the morning of the 18th Mr. Melville gave me my orders to leave Yakutsk in the afternoon for Verkeransk and then for Bulun, and at that place to await his arrival. These were the orders that Mr. Melville gave me on leaving Yakutsk.

(The witness here produced, and the judge-advocate read aloud and placed before the court, the orders in question and a certified copy, marked XX, is appended to the record.)

The witness then continued his narrative as follows:

We left Yakutsk in the afternoon, traveling almost day and night, until we reached Verkeransk, on the 29th day of January. Here we had to stop a couple of days to lay in a supply of provisions. We left Verkeransk about the 2d day of February for Bulun. Four hundred versts from Bulun the way was very bad and the snow was very deep, and we killed a good many of our deer before reaching Bulun. We reached a place about 15 miles south of Bulun, where we found natives that had plenty of deer. I had to leave the provision train behind me the day before, as the deer were played out so far that they had to have rest for a day. Seeing I could not get my deer any further, I offered a man some tea and tobacco to get me fresh deer to go to Bulun, which he did. Got to Bulun about February 12. Here I went into quarters. Here I reported my arrival to the commandant, then went into our same old quarters at the hut, as when we were there before. Here I waited for Mr. Melville, who came about the 15th of February. I asked him where Bartlett was, and he said that he had passed him on the road during the early morning, and that he thought he would be in before night. Bartlett got to Bulun that night, but left the provision train behind him, which arrived the next day. Mr. Melville staid here long enough to make all arrangements necessary, and gave me and Bartlett orders to leave Bulun for Cath Carta on the 27th. I think they were written orders, and that Bartlett has got them. Mr. Melville and Mr. Greenbeck, his interpreter, left Bulun the 22d for Geeomovialocke, to buy fish enough to last during the search for Captain De Long and Lieutenant Chipp. On the morning of the 27th the weather was quite bad, and we had a little difficulty with the natives as to the weight of the provisions on the sleighs, they claiming that there was a little more than they were supposed to carry; that there was a little overweight. We went to work and we had everything overhauled again, and we found that we had somewhere about 10 poods (a pood being about 40 pounds) more than they were to get pay for, and this was the reason they kicked. We told them that we had nothing to do with it; that whatever overweight there was that Mr. Melville would pay them as soon as he returned to Bulun. By this time the weather was very bad, and our drivers told us that we did not have deer enough to start, and that the weather was very bad. We went to the head man of the village, who had signed the contract, to get him to go and tell them that they ought to get deer enough to start us off. He said that the weather was too bad, and that we could not start. We told him that we did not care how bad the weather was; that our orders were to start, and that we were going to start. He said that we would get stuck in the snow and get lost. We told him we did not care. He then went off growling, saying something; what it was I don't know. After awhile he came back again with more deer, and it was about 11 o'clock when we left Bulun. We got stuck in the snow three or four times, but we managed to get out of it again and started again.

About 5 o'clock in the afternoon the weather was so bad that we could not see anything at all. By this time we were on the east side of the river bank, and sometimes found ourselves, when the wind let up a little, in the middle of the river. A good many times we had to stop until the snow would let up drifting a little and see whether we could see an object that the natives would know. We kept on this way until after 6 o'clock, when it was quite dark. Here something hallooed behind me, and I told the driver to stop. I got out of the sleigh, looked around, and couldn't see anybody. It didn't take long before a native came up with a deer team, making a request for me to go back. We went back about 10 versts, when we came up to a hut. Here I found Bartlett and the rest of the people. I asked them what the matter was that they had not followed me. He told me they had lost some of their deer teams, that they had to make a halt for to find them. He sent a driver out to look for them. They came back and told us that they could not find them. We were not satisfied with this, and sent them out again. They went out again for about a quarter of an hour, when he came back and said he had found the deer close to the hut. We then were going to start again, but our driver was afraid to start, as the weather was bad and they could not see anything. He then said that if they would get up early in the morning, no matter how bad the weather was, that we would get started again, which they all promised us they would do. The next morning the weather was still bad and we started along the eastward bank to the northward. We kept on driving till about 2 o'clock in the afternoon, and we came up with some deer teams and I recognized two of the men. One of them was one of the men that found us in the hut, and the other was one I had staid with while I was in Ku Mark Surk. We had a talk with them for a little while, and they wanted to know where we were going. We told them, and the old man that I staid with while at Ku Mark Surk changed drivers with my driver and we started along to Ku Mark Surk. We got there about 5 o'clock in the afternoon, and on arriving there I noticed that most of the people had left the village. I think there were only two families left there. Here we had to wait for the dog teams that Mr. Melville was going to send from Geeomovialocke.

And the court then, at 12 m., took a recess until 12.30 p. m., at which time it reconvened, with all the members, the judge-advocate, and the witness under examination present; and the witness then continued his narrative in answer to the pending question, as follows:

I wish to state here that the first time when we went to Verkeransk, two days before getting there, I caught a glimpse of the sun again. After arriving at Verkeransk we saw the sun every day. While at Ku Mark Surk the wind was blowing every day. The weather was not fit for anybody to travel. Here we waited until March 8, when our dog trains arrived. We got everything ready that day and left Ku Mark Surk on the morning of the 9th. The wind was blowing and the snow drifting, but not enough to stop us from traveling that day, and we got as far as Bulcour, and while going along I noticed that the coast line was very rocky and it was very bad traveling, and I thought if Noros and me had started on the morning of the 22d of October, 1881, that we never would have reached Ku Mark Surk, as this was the worst part of the way that we had seen. We staid here until the next morning and started north again. On that afternoon we fell in with a merchant, who told us that Mr. Melville had arrived at Cath Carta, and that he had run short of provisions and that he had nothing else but fish. We asked the merchant if he had plenty of fish. He said "Yes." We said as long as he had plenty of fish there is no danger of starvation, for they would not starve if they lived on fish for about a week. Bubikoff, my interpreter, wanted us to send a sleigh ahead with some provisions to reach Cath Carta before us, but we thought it was unnecessary as long as they had plenty of fish to eat. That night we did not reach any hut, and so were compelled to camp on the island that me and Noros camped on the 16th. The next morning the weather was bad; broke camp; reached Mat Vai by noon; halted, something to eat, and then started for Cath Carta. It was blowing very fresh, snow was drifting, and our dogs were getting pretty well played out. We came to a hut in the evening which the natives call Bilak, which we had to stay at for the night. The next morning got under way and reached Cath Carta in the middle of the afternoon. Here we found Mr. Melville, Greenbeck, and the ex-espravnik of Verkeransk. I wish to state here that he was sent with Mr. Melville to accompany us in the search for Mr. De Long and Mr. Chipp, and to make arrangements with the natives to help us in every way possible for him to do. Mr. Melville had orders from the governor of Yakutsk to keep the ex-espravnik as long as he thought it was necessary. Here we had to wait for some days for the fish and dogs. After the ex-espravnik had made all the arrangements with the natives and Mr. Melville, there was no need of keeping him any longer, and he let him go back to Verkeransk.

On March 16, Mr. Melville, Greenbeck, and Bartlett's interpreter and me started for Usterda, a place where we had crossed the river when I was along with Captain De Long. Before getting there Mr. Melville sighted a hut, and he asked me whether I recognized it as the hut Usterda, and as the place where we had crossed the river. I told him "Yes," but that a couple of versts to the south of us was another hut. Mr. Melville, at first going off, wanted to go to Usterda and stay there and then cross the river at the same spot where Captain De Long had crossed it. I said there was no need of going up there, as I was certain that that was the hut, and that I had seen the hut to the south of it. This was the hut that we staid at that night. The next day we went to the point of land where we rested after crossing the river, following up along the river bank for some time, and one of our drivers told us there was a hut to the southeast about 10 versts distant, and that probably was the hut where we had buried Erichsen. I told him that if it was only 10 versts distant it could not be the hut, and he said only 10 versts if a man knew the course to take, but if a man had not the course it was probably 25 or 30 versts. So Mr. Melville thought it was best to drive over there and have a look at the hut. We got to the hut and found it was the hut the natives called Mesja, and the river that ran past it the Little Mesja. As soon as we found it was not the place we went back the same way we came, and then picked up the trail till I got to the place where we camped October 1, 1881. From there we started along the little river which ran out after a while, and then came into the eastward until we struck a large river which the natives called Big River Mesja. Just a little before striking the river the weather got so bad that after we had followed the bank for a little time we were obliged to run back to Sister Ganak. Before getting to Sister Ganak the natives were talking about a hut that was close to Sister Ganak. We had great difficulty in finding it, and lost our way a couple of times before we found it. On getting there I found it was not the hut where Erichsen was buried. We then started for Sister Ganak. The next morning it was blowing so we could not do anything. As we did not have provisions enough to lay around there until the weather should settle, Mr. Melville lifted off about fifty fish that we had and ran back to Cath Carta. By this time we had fish enough and dog teams enough to start on the expedition to the southward. A couple of days after that arrangements were made for Mr. Melville and me to start once more from the north and send Bartlett down to Mat Vay to start from Mat Vay to the northward and meet afterwards if we could. The next morning Mr. Melville and me started back and picked up the way or trail. Bartlett went to Mat Vay to start the search from Mat Vay to the northward. Before Bartlett left I gave him all the information about the land and the rivers that I could. After Mr. Melville and me had struck the large rivers again we kept on going along to the southward. One of our drivers then said that there was a hut somewhere to the eastward. By this time the weather had got bad again and it was blowing quite fresh, and I told Mr. Melville that I thought we were far enough to the eastward, and if there was a hut there I did not think it was Erichsen's hut. By this time the weather was pretty bad, and we got off the river to keep on going to the southward and eastward, until evening, when the weather was so bad that we could not reach any of the huts that we knew in the vicinity, and so were obliged to camp down for the night. The next morning the weather was still bad. Mr. Melville asked one of the drivers how far we were off from Su Vina. He thought about 20 versts. He then made up his mind, as the weather was very bad, to run for Su Vina. We got there about noon-time, when the weather had let up a little. Shortly after that time some of our teams came along from Geeomovialocke, with fish, on their way to Cath Carta. We stopped them here. Mr. Melville and me had a conversation, and he asked me what I thought; was it not best to start from Mat Vay and continue the search? I said "Yes," and that I would not have any trouble in finding them from Mat Vay. By this time the weather had let up a good deal, and we started for Mat Vay, Mr. Melville giving orders for the teams of each to take them down to Mat Vay. During this time we had seen nothing of Bartlett. We got to Mat Vay about 5 o'clock in the afternoon. There we staid for the night. This was on the evening of the 22d of March.

On the morning of the 23d Mr. Melville and me started to the northward and westward, and then kept on skirting from headland to headland until we were making a course almost straight for Stolbovoi. That was to the south of us. We here stopped and had a look around. Mr. Melville asked me if I recognized the place. I told him that I did not recognize the place we were at, but a little further to the eastward there was a place that I recognized, and that, I thought, was not far away from the river, where I expected to find the people. We then cu across the land to the eastward, and in about half an hour we ran across a place where there had been a fire. We stopped here, and Mr. Melville asked me whether me and Noros had built a fire here. I told him "no." By this time I looked around and saw the river 200 or 300 yards to the east of us. I at once recognized it, and told Mr. Melville; pointed to the point where me and Noros had stopped the first night we left the captain. Around the fire-place we found the foot-tracks of the men. I was going to walk along the river bank to the northward. When we got on the river bank I looked to the northward and saw the old scow that Noros and me had passed the day that we left the captain. Mr. Melville then said, "Nindemann, you had better sit down in your sleigh and we will drive up to the scow; we shall get there quicker." Mr. Melville and me drove on for about 1,000 yards. We saw a tripod, with a rifle hanging on it, sticking up a foot out of the snow-bank. We at once recognized the place, and stopped. When I saw the lashings of the tripod I recognized it as the drag-rope that we used for the sleigh. I thought at the time that they had left the books and papers there, and that the sleigh was below in the snow and underneath the tripod. I then said to Mr. Melville that I was going down to the scow to see if they had been there; and, going along to the northward, I looked for the kyak, to see if the people had been there. During my absence Mr. Melville walked along the river bank to the southward, and going to the flat-boat I found that there had been a fire there in two places. I then got upon the river bank and walked to the northward, now and then finding footsteps, or foot-prints, in the snow. I kept on for quite a while, but did not see anything of the kyak. On my way going back to the tripod I saw Mr. Melville coming up with his dog team, and, coming up to me, he told me that he had found three people to the south of the tripod on the bank of the river, and that they were Captain De Long, the doctor, and Ah Sam. He wanted me to go on with him to break them out of the snow, as the natives were afraid of touching them. Before this we had put the natives to work—our dog-drivers to work—to dig down and find out what was under the tripod. I then returned with Mr. Melville to the place where we found the bodies. The bodies were frozen to the ground, and we had to take sticks of wood to pry them up. Mr. Melville told me that he had found the captain's note-book laying behind him; and that the first thing to attract his attention had been the cooking-pot, standing close on the river bank, and by looking around that he had seen Captain De Long's hand sticking out of the snow. I overhauled the people to find everything they had on them—all the little things they had in their pockets, papers and everything else—and took them from them. I overhauled one of Captain De Long's pockets and found five twenty-dollar gold pieces. I was surprised when I found them, and surprised that he had carried any money with him. I gave them to Mr. Melville, and asked him if he knew that Captain De Long had carried any money. He said he knew that he had carried some, but he thought he had thrown it away. Everything that was found on their persons was tied up separately in a handkerchief or piece of cloth that was found on them. After I had taken everything from the bodies, we put them close together and covered them up with a lot of rags and pieces of the tent, and left them there. About this time it commenced to blow quite fresh, and the snow commenced to drift. We went back to the tripod, and going there we found that the natives had found the two tin cases containing the ship's papers. Mr. Melville said they could go on digging a little longer. It did not take long before they laid bare two more of the dead people. We tried to find out who they were, but could not.

The weather was getting worse, and it was getting late in the afternoon, and Mr. Melville thought it best for us to return to Mat Vay. On returning we only took the cases containing the ship's papers that we had found, leaving the bodies where we had found them. We stuck up a stick in the snow, in case the hole where we had been digging should drift full, as a mark that we could recognize the place again on coming to find the spot. We found Bartlett there. He told us that he had arrived there at noon, and that he was thinking about starting after us, but as the weather was bad he thought it was best to stay and start out the next morning again. He told about his trip, and told us he had to camp out in the snow the same night we had, and that he ran to Su Vina, and that when he arrived there he found some hot coals in the fire-place, but did not know exactly who could have been there.

I wish to state here that Mr. Melville returned to Mat Vay and sent one of the dog-drivers with a letter to Cath Carta to tell Greenbeck to come down to Mat Vay.

On the morning of the 24th Mr. Melville gave Bartlett and me orders to go back to the place where the bodies were found, and as the weather was still very bad he thought it was best for as just to fetch the three bodies and return to Mat Vay. He was going to stay at Mat Vay to do some writing and to write or telegraph to the Secretary of the Navy. Me and Bartlett started out. We arrived at the place, and we started to dig up the snow where we had found Captain De Long, the doctor, and Ah Sam the day before. By digging up the snow around there, where they lay, we found a good many small articles. We then looked round on the river ice to see whether we could see a place that looked like the place where Alexy was buried, as we found out in the captain's journal that Alexy was buried in the river to the east of the flat-boat. We dug around for quite a while, but did not find anything. The weather by this time was getting worse, and we could see but a short distance. We then went back to take the bodies; put Captain De Long on my sleigh, and Ah Sam; and Bartlett took the doctor. We started back to Mat Vay. We dug a hole in the snow and put the bodies in it and covered them up with tents.

And the court then, at 1.20 p. m., pending the further examination of this witness, adjourned to meet to-morrow, the 9th day of December, 1882, at 10 a. m.

FIFTY-SECOND DAY.

NAVY DEPARTMENT,
Washington, D. C., Saturday, December 9, 1882—10 a. m.

The court met pursuant to the adjournment of yesterday.

Present, Commodore William G. Temple, United States Navy, president; Capt. Joseph N. Miller, United States Navy, Commander Frederick V. McNair, United States Navy, members; and Master Samuel C. Lemly, United States Navy, judge-advocate.

The record of the proceedings of yesterday, Friday, December 8, 1882, the fifty-first day of the inquiry, was then read, and, after correcting clerical errors, approved.

Seaman W. F. C. Nindemann, the witness under examination, then came in and continued his answer to the pending question, which was repeated by the judge-advocate, as follows :

State, generally, what your movements were subsequent to your meeting with Chief Engineer Melville at Bulun, about November 3, 1881, and, fully, what efforts were made by yourself, and within your knowledge by any other person connected with the Jeannette expedition, for the relief of the first and second cutters' parties.

The WITNESS. On the morning of March 25, Bartlett, Greenbeck, and myself were sent back to the place where the people were found. On getting there we put the natives at work to dig out the two bodies that we had discovered two days before that. On getting one of them out we found that it was Görtz; the next one was Boyd. At this time it was noon-time, and Greenbeck had orders to return to Mat Vay to translate some writing for Mr. Melville. We told him that as he was going to Mat Vay he might as well take the two bodies along to Mat Vay. After digging a while longer they laid bare another body ; this, we found, was that of Mr. Collins. We found his face was covered with a pair of red drawers. On getting him out Bartlett and me overhauled him and took everything that we could from his pockets in the line of papers, a small book, and other small articles, and tied it all up in one of his handkerchiefs. Bartlett and me took very good care that we did not lose any, and that we got every article off of him, as we always were good friends of Mr. Collins. After a couple of hours the natives had laid bare two other bodies. On getting them out we found that they were Dressler and Iverson. We also took from them whatever they had on them, tied everything up separately and took care of it. By this time it was getting toward evening, and the weather was getting a little bad. We returned with the bodies and the things that we found on them to Mat Vay. On arriving there we put the bodies along with the rest of them, and turned over to Mr. Melville everything that we had found on them. Mr. Melville sent Greenbeck to Cath Carta to send Boubikoff down to Mat Vay to carry dispatches to Bulun. Boubikoff arrived about nine o'clock that same night. On March 27, after we had our breakfast, Boubikoff was started off with the dog team and provisions to last him to Bulun, with instructions to go there as quick as possible, and return as quick as he could to Mat Vay.

Bartlett and me were sent back again to the place where the bodies were found. We kept on digging up toward the river bank, but did not find anything else that day but a doctor box and a flag. I told Bartlett that we had everything now that the people had to carry. I kept on looking for Kaack and Lee, but did not find them.

On March 28 we had a snow-storm from the southeast, and we could not leave the hut as the weather was so bad. The storm continued until the 29th. I wish to correct what I said, that on the 27th, when we found the box and the flag, that shortly after that we struck the place where Kaack and Lee were found. Here we had found Kaack and Lee. We had then found everything that belonged to the people, and had found all the people that we expected to find.

On March 30 Mr. Melville, Bartlett, and myself went back to the place to look for Alexy, and to take the boards off the old scow, and planks to make a box large enough to hold the people. On arriving there, Mr. Melville told me to take my driver and go along the river to the northward to see what I could find of Erichsen's hut. I started off, and after we had traveled for a little time, found a kyak, and I got as far that day as where Noros and me had left the captain. Here I found a saucepan that the party had left. This was about four o'clock in the afternoon. As I did not have any provisions, I returned to Mat Vay. On April 1 I was put to work to make a box large enough to hold the people. Bartlett and the natives were sent back again to get more planks. In the evening Boubikoff returned from Bulun. I was busy making the box and cross, Bartlett with the natives being busy getting planks and a large stick for making a cross of. On April 4 Mr. Melville and Bartlett went to the southward along the high land to look for a place to bury the people. That evening I got done finishing the cross, and Mr. Melville told me that they would cut the inscription, and if the weather was fine to-morrow that he was going to start me off to look for Erichsen's hut.

On April 4, after breakfast, Mr. Melville told Bartlett and me to go and overhaul the bodies again, and to see that there was nothing left on them in the line of papers or any other small articles. Iverson was supposed to have a small book of some kind on him, which Bartlett had seen a great many times on the ice. We overhauled Iverson's pockets everywhere to find this book but did not find it. We then overhauled Captain De Long again, as there was one leaf torn out of his notebook. Mr. Melville thought that the captain probably wrote a note to his wife before he died, and thought that he tore out the leaf from his book to write it on. We overhauled him again but did not find anything on him. Before this Bartlett and I had been talking about Mr.

Collins; he was supposed to have more papers on him when he was on the ice. For this reason Mr. Melville told me to overhaul him again and to see whether we could find any more papers. We overhauled him everywhere and every place where we thought papers could be placed. We did not find any. Bartlett opened his shirt and found a large bronze cross. Me and Bartlett got talking about it, whether to leave it on him or whether to take it off. We did not know exactly what to do, and I believe I went into the hut and called Mr. Melville out. I asked him what did he think about it? At first, going off, he did not know exactly what to do with it, but at last he said that it was a part of his religion, and that he thought it was best that we should bury him with the cross on. He then told Bartlett to tuck the cross into his bosom, which Bartlett did. These three were the only parties that were overhauled at that time. By this time my driver had got ready and I took with me a day's provisions, for I thought I could make the hut in a day and return the next day. I made our course from Mat Vai across land until we struck the river that Noros and me had gone along. I stopped to give the dogs a rest where the kyak was laying, and looking around I found a wooden spool, a thread spool, that showed that Captain De Long had halted there. I also found a fire-place. I then started along until I struck the place where Noros and me had parted with the captain. Still got along to the northward, and found the place where we had camped for dinner on the 8th of October. Here I shoved off to go to the westward, but I thought that I could go back to the trail again by going along the river. After I left this place, starting along the river, a snow-storm set in, and it was getting so thick that I could not see anything. The snow-storm lasted until about five o'clock that night, when it cleared off. By this time I thought I had traveled far enough, and that I was then in the vicinity of the hut where Erichsen died. I looked around, but could see nothing, except some object to the northward, which looked to me as if it was a hut. It took us quite a time to make it, as our dogs were getting a little weak and the road was bad to travel. On getting there I found that it was nothing else but a tripod and a couple of fox traps. By this time it was getting dark, and as I thought I was far enough to the northward, I camped down for the night. The next morning the weather was fine, and as I only had one day's provisions, my intention was to run back to Mat Vay to get more provisions, and pick up the trail and follow it until I reached the hut. About nine o'clock we got on our way south. I came into a dry river bank, where I noticed the driftwood that was piled up there, and where we had halted on the 7th of October at dinner time to make some tea. I then knew where I was, and turning to the northward and westward I struck the ruins of a hut which I had sighted when I was along with the captain when I journeyed south. I then kept on to the northward until I sighted a couple of fox traps on the bank of the river. I recognized these two traps, went over there, got on the top of the river bank, and saw the hut to the west of us. We then started for it; before we reached the hut a snow-storm set in and we could not see anything; but as I had got the bearings of the hut we manged to reached it all right. On getting to the hut we found that the hut was drifted full of snow. The headboard that we had set up on the ridge after he died was still over the door. As it was after dinner, and we had no provisions to stay another day, I told my driver the place where the gun, the record, and the cartridges were laying; and as we only had one snow shovel it would take us too long to take the snow out of the hut, so we went to work and got the slats off the hut on the side where the record, rifle, and ammunition were. We then worked down to the place through the snow and we found what we were hunting for—that is, the record, rifle, and cartridges. We then started for Mat Vay, setting our course as near as we could. We struck the place where the people had died about five o'clock and reached Mat Vay about six o'clock. By this time the weather was fine. On arriving at Mat Vay Mr. Melville told me that they had buried the people, and that it would very probably take another day to cover the graves with stones and to put up the cross arm.

On April 7 everybody went up the mountains to finish up the work that was undone. We put up the cross arm and finished covering the grave with stones. We got through about sundown.

On April 8 everybody went to Cath Carta. Here everything was got ready for the search for Lieutenant Chipp. Mr. Melville made all the arrangements necessary for the search for Lieutenant Chipp along the coast line of the delta.

On April 10 everything was ready, and Bartlett and me got orders to start for Barkin and there to separate, and from there Bartlett to go south and examine the coast and the mouths of the rivers as far as Geeomovialocke, and there to stay and await Mr. Melville's and my arrival. My orders were to go west from Barkin as far as the river where the first cutter had landed, and, if I had provisions enough, to keep on along the coast as far as North Bulun, and then back to Cath Carta, and there await the arrival of Mr. Melville.

Here are the written orders which I got at the time.

The witness here produced, and the judge-advocate read aloud and placed before the court, the orders in question, and a certified copy marked A B is appended to the record.

The witness then continued his testimony, as follows:

Me and Bartlett started the 10th of April, and passing Sister Ganak we took along the fifty fish which Mr. Melville and me had left there some time before. We then started again and got as far as the place called Barchuck. Here we stopped for the night. The next morning the weather was bad and it was blowing from the southeast and the snow was drifting. Our drivers did not much like starting, but we would not give them any rest until they started. By noon we got to another place, where we stopped and had dinner. After dinner the weather was so bad that we could not see 10 yards ahead of us. We then made up our minds to stay there; but when afterwards the weather let up a little, we made a start again, and about five o'clock in the afternoon we reached a hut which the natives told us was Barkin, or called "the Barkin hut." By this time the weather was quite clear and we looked around, but we could not see the ocean anywhere, and we at first thought that this could not be the place; but as the natives kept on saying it was, we believed them. We stayed there that night. The next morning the snow was drifting some and we could not see very well. Bartlett thought it was no use starting on the search as long as the snow was drifting, as we could not see anything. About ten o'clock the snow stopped drifting and it cleared. We then made a start on a river running somewhere to the northward and eastward. Bartlett took the east side and I the west side. About noontime I had lost sight of Bartlett. The land here turned to the westward and the natives told me that we were out on the ocean. I then started to follow up the coast line as near as I could, as the land here is very low and it was very hard to tell whether you were on land or on ice. Before long I made the driver stop to find out whether it was land or ice. As the driver knew the straight course for Biloch, they would try to make a straight course, making a cut-off over some points of land, but I never would let them do this. I kept on until night, when we camped down. During the day I had seen no signs of Chipp's boat or any place that would indicate where they had been. The next morning we broke camp again and followed up the coast line. Here I had to go north, sometimes northeast, and sometimes to the northward and westward, and sometimes west. About five o'clock I sighted the mast of the boat, and, shortly after that, the pole that we had set up on the beach when we landed on the 17th of September, 1881. On sighting the mast of the boat, I told the driver to drive over to it. On getting up to the boat I found that she was all snowed in except about four or five inches of her stern, and a couple of inches of her stern sticking out of the snow. I told the natives to take some of the snow out, and I found that everything was in the boat the way we had left it, and that she was very full of ice. I took out of her an old marline spike and a monkey-wrench; all the rest of the stuff that we had left in her was frozen in, and as it was getting dark we did not have time to dig out any more. I then told the natives that I would go to Biloch to stay over for that night. They then came across the land to the south until we sighted a hut, and getting up to it I saw that it was not Biloch, and as there was only one hut and it was very small, the natives wanted to know whether I was going to stay there. I told them "no"; that I wanted to go to Bilock, as it was only a short distance. They at first kicked a little and they did not like to do it. After a while we started off, and in about a half an hour we reached Bilock. There were the two huts that we had found at the place after we left the beach. One of these was snow-filled, and the entrance to the other was snowed over. We were obliged to crawl in through the smoke hole, or top of the hut. Here we stayed during the night, and the next morning I drove along the river for some time. At last the drivers kept on edging up the river and edging more and more to the westward trying to make a short cut for North Bulun. I told them about it a couple of times, but still they kept on doing it, and at last I made them stop the dogs, turn the dogs around, and made them understand that I wanted them to go back to the first cutter. After awhile they started and they hove in sight of the first cutter. I then told them that we would start to the westward now, along the coast line; that we did not want to make any short cuts across the land; got along all right. The coast line here was running pretty well west until ten o'clock, then it got to the southward and westward. About three o'clock we struck a very large tripod, which looked to me as if the natives were using this in the summer time for a tent, and one of my drivers, on talking to me, told me they did, and that sometimes there were four or five families living in it. I kept on a little longer until we struck the river. I asked the natives whether this was the river; they said "yes"; that it was the river called North Bulun, and that about 10 versts farther, to the southward and westward, we would find North Bulun. About five o'clock we passed through North Bulun, where there was nobody living. I wanted to stay in one of these huts, but the natives told me that there was another place 10 versts to the southward and westward where there were people living. I told them "all right"; to go ahead and to make for the place. We arrived at Borkhia about six o'clock in the evening. I here stayed with a native for the night that had worked with us all the time before starting out on the search for Mr. Chipp; he got sick and went home. The next morning I started for Cath Carta, and about 10 versts to the southward of Borkhia we found another place where there were natives. Here was another man living that had worked for us, and he was one of the men that found Noros and me at Bulcour. He invited me to go in and have some tea with him. After tea I started along the river, and about three o'clock in the afternoon fell in with a man who was on the river fishing, and on the west bank of the river saw a hut where there were some natives outside. Here the river was running too far to the westward, and we left it to steer as straight a course for Cath Carta as we could. We crossed a couple of small rivers running to the east and west, and then arrived at Cath Carta about five o'clock. Here there was nobody left but Greenbeck and one of our servants. Greenbeck told me that before Mr. Melville had left that he sent Boubikoff and Koliucon with everything that we had found belonging to Captain De Long and his party south as far as Yakutsk, and had sent the rest of our servants back to Bulun. I here waited a day or two, and as we were running short of fish for dog food I sent down to Mat Vay to get up the last of the fish, as we had to have them anyhow before we could start for Geeomovialocke.

And the court then, at 12 m., took a recess until 12.30 p. m., at which time it reconvened, with all the members, the judge-advocate, and the witness under examination present; and the witness then continued his narration, in answer to the pending question, as follows:

On the afternoon of the 20th Mr. Melville arrived from his trip to Alenek, at Cath Carta. We waited here a couple of days for Mr. Melville to take a rest. On April 23 everything was ready for the trip to Geeomovialocke. We left Cath Carta in the morning at three o'clock for Geeomovialocke, and on our way passed Qu Vina. About noon we struck the river where De Long and his people had been found. Here we crossed the river to the eastward. Before we got half way across a gale of wind set in and the snow started drifting, so that we lost our way a couple of times, and had to camp down on the ice. During the night Greenbeck and me, sitting in the tent, got our hands pretty badly frozen. Early the next morning the weather had let up, and the weather was getting a little better, and we broke camp, and struck a hut about nine o'clock, called Ordono. Here we halted to have something to eat. After that we started again, and kept on till four o'clock in the afternoon, till we came to a place where there were a couple of huts. Here we were going to halt for the night, but found that there were some people in the huts; these were the people that Mr. Melville had spoken about, who had three of their children frozen to death. They were still there making coffins to bury their children. We just stopped here for a little while to have tea, and then started again and kept on until we struck another place, where we halted for the night. The next day we started again across land. The land here was about 40 or 50 feet high. We continued on until late in the afternoon, when we got on to a river. Shortly after that we passed three huts. Mr. Melville told me this was the place where they stayed one night. We stopped here to melt some ice to freeze our sleigh runners. After that we started again, and it was dark when we struck Arii; here we staid to have something to eat. As it was only 10 versts to Geeomovialocke, we started and got there somewhere near midnight, or past midnight. I do not know exactly what time it was. Here we found Bartlett; we asked him whether he had found out anything about Mr. Chipp, and his party; he said "No;" that they had seen no signs of the second cutter or its party. The next morning a native came from Tamoos, telling us that there were Americans over there. We did not know at the time who it was. Mr. Melville got a dog team and went across to find out who they were. On returning he told us that it was Mr. Jackson, a Herald correspondent, and Noros, and said that they were going to be over there in an hour or two. I also should mention Mr. Larson, who was there with them. After a time they came, and we had quite a talk with them. Mr. Jackson had made up his mind to go and see the place where the people were found, and to see the place where they were buried. I believe his idea was to take either me or Bartlett, if he could obtain us, to show him the places; but Mr. Melville thought that some of our drivers that knew the places as well as we did would answer his purpose. On April 28 everything was all ready, and Mr. Melville, Bartlett, and me started on our journeying across the bay to the river Jana, to see if we could see any signs of Chipp; but we did not see any signs in crossing the bay. We arrived at a place within 30 versts of the bay. We halted for the night. The next morning we sent our dog teams back to Geeomovialocke and started from here with reindeer teams to Oceansk. We went there to see whether the people had heard anything about Mr. Chipp's party. Upon arriving there we found that they had heard nothing of them, and as it was getting toward summer, and as it was of no use for us to stay on the Lena delta, as we had done everything we could do, we thought that it was best to return to Yakutsk. Before arriving at Yakutsk we got stuck to the northward of Yakutsk, in the mountains. Here Lieutenant Berry and Master Hunt, of the ship Rodgers, Mr. Jackson, Mr. Larson, and Noros fetched up with us. Here we had to wait some days before we could cross the mountains. We arrived at Yakutsk shortly after that, and waited for a couple of days, taking a rest. We then took passage on a steamer to go south. After we had left Yakutsk, for some time, we passed a steamer early in the morning having in tow quite a large boat, which was schooner-rigged. We saw her, but were not sure whether Mr. Harber was on board or not, but we had some idea that he was, by the way the boat was rigged that was towing astern. A day or two afterwards we got to a place where we halted to wood-up. Here we found out that Mr. Harber had gone north. From this time on I was in company with Mr. Melville, and came on with him to the United States.

The judge-advocate then examined the witness as follows:

Question by the JUDGE-ADVOCATE. You have stated that a lot of ships' papers were found near the remains of the first cutter's party. What were these papers?

The WITNESS. They were Captain De Long's own private journal and observations that he had made during the cruise of the Jeannette, and other ships' papers, which I do not know what they were.

Question by the JUDGE-ADVOCATE. Was there, to your knowledge, anything left undone by any one belonging to the Jeannette expedition which it was possible to do to effect the rescue of the first and second cutters' parties?

The court was here cleared, at the request of a member, and afterwards reopened, the witness being present, and he then answered the question as follows:

The WITNESS. As far as my own knowledge is concerned, everything has been done to save them.

Question by the JUDGE-ADVOCATE. Have you any further statement to make in relation to the efforts made to secure the first and second cutters' parties? If yea, make it now.

The WITNESS. No, sir.

Question by the JUDGE-ADVOCATE. Have you any charge to lay or special commendation to offer concerning any officer or man connected with the Jeannette expedition: First, as to the condition of the vessel on her departure from San Francisco; second, her management up to the time of her loss; third, her loss; fourth, the provisions made and plans adopted for the safety of the boats' crews on their leaving the wreck; fifth, the efforts made by the various officers to insure the safety of the parties under their charge and for the relief of the other parties; sixth, the general conduct and merits of each and all the officers and men of the expedition?

The WITNESS. No, sir.

Cross-examination by the judge-advocate in behalf of the late Jerome J. Collins, meteorologist of the Jeannette expedition.

Question by the JUDGE-ADVOCATE. Was Mr. Collins regarded and spoken of as a seaman on board the Jeannette?

The WITNESS. I never heard of it.

Question by the JUDGE-ADVOCATE. What was Mr. Collins's physical condition, as compared with the other members of the party, when you and Noros left them?

The WITNESS. I think Mr. Collins was in about the same condition as the most of us; but my belief is, if Captain De Long had sent him, that he would have staid behind and not take to the water as we did; as I used to notice when we traveled on the ice that he avoided very much getting into the water.

Question by the JUDGE-ADVOCATE. Did Mr. Collins request to be permitted to go with you and Noros when you left the first cutter's party and went ahead for relief?

The WITNESS. That I am not certain of. I do not know whether he did or not. I know the evening before I left Captain De Long I had spoken to Collins that the captain was going to send me off the next morning; and I then told him I had very little hope of falling in with natives, but Mr. Collins said that he thought as we had stood so much hardship and had weathered the gale, God would not forsake us at the last stretch.

Question by the JUDGE-ADVOCATE. Is it or is it not a fact that during the retreat the party was frequently ordered to be ready for a start at 5 o'clock in the morning, and that De Long lay in his tent until 2 o'clock in the afternoon when not sick, thereby causing unnecessary delay?

The WITNESS. In the first place I do not think that we ever started at 5 o'clock in the morning. If I am not mistaken we were called at 6 o'clock in the morning, or shortly after that. No such thing ever happened.

Question by the JUDGE-ADVOCATE. Did Mr. Collins say anything to you before you left? If yea, what was it?

The judge-advocate stated that he would permit the witness to proceed with his answer to the question, though clearly hearsay, as long as it was of a general character and not calculated to reflect injuriously upon any person connected with the expedition, reserving his right in that event to object.

The WITNESS. Not that I recollect. The only one that said anything to me on leaving was the doctor. He said, "Nindemann, I will see now what kind of man you are." What he meant by that I cannot exactly say. He was the only one who spoke to me on leaving, except that the rest of the people shook hands with us and wished us to find assistance, and hoped we would be back soon, as soon as possible. That is the only thing that I know of, that was said at the time.

Question by the JUDGE-ADVOCATE. Did Bartlett say anything to you about letters that were on Collins's body?

The Judge-Advocate objected to this question as calling for hearsay evidence, and stated that Bartlett himself would, when available, be summoned to appear as a witness before the court.

The court was then cleared for deliberation upon the objection of the judge-advocate, and then reopened, the witness being present; and the president announced as the decision of the court that the objection of the judge-advocate was not sustained and that the question should be put.

The witness then answered the question as follows:

The WITNESS. Bartlett did not say anything to me at the time when we overhauled the body of Mr. Collins. As me and Bartlett were, as I stated before in my testimony, good friends of Collins, we said that we would take good care of every slip of paper and everything that we found on him, which we did; everything which was found on him was turned over to Mr. Melville, and, as to my knowledge, it is here now.

Question by the JUDGE-ADVOCATE. What papers were taken from the body of Mr. Collins?

The WITNESS. There was only a few papers; what they were I cannot say, as they were rolled up, and they were damp, and it would not have done to open them. Besides these there was a little note-book with a black cover. These are the only papers that I know of. But we thought that Mr. Collins should have had more papers, as he had, in talking to me on the ice at some occasion, told me that he had everything that occurred on board of the Jeannette down on very little paper.

Question by the JUDGE-ADVOCATE. What, as nearly as you can give them, were Melville's exact words when he was asked what should be done with the cross that was suspended from Collins's neck?

The WITNESS. I have stated that, as near as I can in my testimony, at the first going off Mr. Melville considered and then said that he thought it was a part of his religion, and that it was the best thing to do to bury him with it; that he thought that many of his relations would like to have it sent to America and given to them, but that they would probably have thought that Mr. Melville would have done wrong by doing so, as he (Collins) was a Catholic, and every Catholic wears a cross.

Question by the JUDGE-ADVOCATE. Did he, or did he not, use any profane, obscene, or improper language in that connection? If yea, what was it?

The WITNESS. No, sir; not that I know of.

The judge-advocate did not desire to further cross-examine the witness.

And the court then, pending the further examination of this witness, at 1.40 p. m., adjourned, to meet on Monday, December 11, 1882, at 10 a. m.

FIFTY-THIRD DAY.

NAVY DEPARTMENT,
Washington, D. C., Monday, December 11, 1882—10 a. m.

The court met pursuant to the adjournment of Saturday.

Present, Commodore William G. Temple, United States Navy, president; Capt. Joseph N. Miller, United States Navy, Commander Fred-

erick V. McNair, United States Navy, members; and Master Samuel C. Lemly, United States Navy, judge-advocate.

By request of the judge-advocate, the reading of the record of the proceedings of Saturday, December 9, 1882, the fifty-second day of the inquiry, was deferred.

Seaman W. F. C. NINDEMANN, the witness under examination, then came in and was examined by the court.

Question by the COURT. State, if you know, how Mr. Collins was treated by the commanding and other officers of the Jeannette.

The WITNESS. As far as I know he was always treated like a gentleman; as far as I know he was treated like an officer. He was respected by every man on board the ship as an officer.

Question by the COURT. State, if you know, how Mr. Collins treated the commanding and other officers of the Jeannette.

The WITNESS. That is a question that I cannot answer, sir. That I do not know.

Question by the COURT. Did the crew of the Jeannette treat Mr. Collins with the respect due an officer? If not, state in what manner he was treated differently.

The WITNESS. They did treat him like an officer; he was respected like an officer.

Question by the COURT. How did Mr. Collins treat the crew of the Jeannette in comparison with others in authority?

The WITNESS. He treated them with the same respect that any other officer would treat them.

Question by the COURT. Have you any personal knowledge of any difficulty at any time between Mr. Collins and any officer of the Jeannette? If so, state what you know about the matter.

The WITNESS. No, sir; I have no idea; I have never seen any trouble between them.

Question by the COURT. What is the distance from the wreck of the first cutter to the entrance of the river on which North Bulun is situated?

The WITNESS. It is about 50 versts, in a straight course, to the southward and westward.

Neither the court nor the judge-advocate desired to further examine this witness, and his testimony being here concluded, the judge-advocate proceeded to read it to him for correction.

At 12 m. the court took a recess until 12.30 p. m., and then reconvened, with all the members, the judge-advocate, and the witness present; and the reading of his testimony to the witness was then resumed and continued until 1.30 p. m., when the court adjourned, to meet tomorrow, the 12th day of December, 1882, at 10 a. m.

FIFTY-FOURTH DAY.

NAVY DEPARTMENT,
Washington, D. C., Tuesday, December 12, 1882—10 a. m.

The court met pursuant to the adjournment of Monday, December 11, 1882.

Present, Commodore William G. Temple, United States Navy, president; Capt. Joseph N. Miller, United States Navy, Commander Fred-

erick V. Mc Nair, United States Navy, members; and Master Samuel C. Lemly, United States Navy, judge-advocate.

By request of the judge-advocate the reading of the records of the proceedings of Saturday, December 9, and of Monday, December 11, 1882, the fifty-second and fifty-third days of the inquiry, was deferred.

The witness, Seaman W. F. C. NINDEMANN, then came in, and the judge-advocate continued the reading to him of his testimony for correction.

At 11.45 a. m. the court took a recess until 12.15 p. m., and then reconvened, with all the members, the judge-advocate, and the witness, Seaman W. F. C. Nindemann, present.

The reading of the testimony of the witness was then resumed, and at 1 p. m. completed.

The witness desired to add to his testimony the following statements:

I wish to state here, on making the raft on the morning of September 26, I had a little difficulty with the captain, but it did not amount to anything. He put me under arrest for about an hour, and when we were ready to start again he gave me orders to pick up my load and go ahead as usual. I wish to say here that the captain after this never showed any hard feelings toward me, nor me toward him. Also, I wish to say that as far as my experience goes in the Arctic regions that every officer and man of the expedition have done their duty from the time we left San Francisco until the time the ship was lost, traveling on the ice, and until we reached America.

With these additions he pronounced his testimony correct, and then withdrew.

The records of the proceedings of Saturday, December 9, and Monday, December 11, 1882, the fifty-second and fifty-third days of the inquiry, were read and approved.

And the court then, at 1.10 p. m., adjourned to meet to-morrow, the 13th day of December, 1882, at 10.30 a. m.

FIFTY-FIFTH DAY.

NAVY DEPARTMENT,
Washington D. C., Wednesday, December 13, 1882—10.30 a. m.

The court met pursuant to the adjournment of yesterday.

Present, Commodore William G. Temple, United States Navy, president; Capt. Joseph N. Miller, United States Navy, Commander Frederick V. McNair, United States Navy, members; and Master Samuel C. Lemly, United States Navy, judge-advocate.

The record of the proceedings of yesterday, December 12, 1882, the fifty-fourth day of the inquiry, was then read and approved.

Seaman LOUIS P. NOROS was then called as a witness, and having been sworn, according to law, by the president of the court, testified as follows:

Examination by the JUDGE-ADVOCATE:

Question by the JUDGE-ADVOCATE. What is your name and rate?
The WITNESS. My name is Louis P. Noros; am a seaman of the Arctic steamer Jeannette.

Question by the JUDGE-ADVOCATE. When and where did you join the Jeannette, and what were your duties on board that vessel?

The WITNESS. We arrived at Mare Island the 1st day of June from New York; I joined the ship then and there; I was a seaman.

Question by the JUDGE-ADVOCATE. Have you any statement to lay before the court in relation to the fitting of the Jeannette for Arctic service, and her condition when she left San Francisco?

The WITNESS. No sir.

Question by the JUDGE-ADVOCATE. Have you any statement to lay before this court in relation to the management of the Jeannette, up to the time of her loss?

The WITNESS. No sir.

Question by the JUDGE-ADVOCATE. Have you any statement to lay before this court concerning the loss of the Jeannette?

The WITNESS. None whatever, sir.

Question by the JUDGE-ADVOCATE. Have you any statement to make in relation to the provisions made and plans adopted for the several boats' crews upon their leaving the wreck?

The WITNESS. No, sir. I think that all were provided for as well as they could be.

Question by the JUDGE-ADVOCATE. Have you any statement to make in regard to the efforts made by the various officers to insure the safety of the parties under their charge and for the relief of the other parties?

The WITNESS. No, sir.

Question by the JUDGE-ADVOCATE. Give a detailed narration of your movements subsequently to your meeting with Mr. Melville at Bulun.

The WITNESS. I think it was on the 3d day of November that Mr. Melville arrived at Bulun. I wish to state that I am not certain about the dates. Soon after Mr. Melville arrived at Bulun he started north in search of Captain De Long and party. After his return, which was about the 28th day of November, we then made preparations to go to Yakutsk. We [we left Bulun on the 3d of December and *] arrived at Yakutsk, I think, about the 20th [6th *] day of December [January *]. There was in our party Bartlett, Nindemann, Manson, Aniguin, Lauterbach, and myself. On the 9th day of December, I think, we started from Irkutsk, and Mr. Danenhower. We all started together, with the exception of Mr. Melville, Nindemann, and Bartlett, who remained behind to carry on the search during the next spring. We arrived at Irkutsk on the 12th [1st *] day of February, and there remained until Mr. Jackson and Mr. Larson arrived at Irkutsk. Mr. Jackson was a Herald correspondent, sent out by Mr. Bennett, and Larson was the artist of the Illustrated London News. Mr. Jackson asked me if I would like to go north with him. I told him "Yes"; that I did not want to go home yet—not until the rest of the people were found; that is, Captain De Long and party. So he said he would telegraph to Mr. Bennett and see if he could get me to go north with him. He telegraphed, and Mr. Bennett sent him a telegram, I believe, from the Secretary of the Navy, giving permission for me to go with him. So Mr. Danenhower then turned me over to Mr. Jackson, and told me that I should be under him to do what he should tell me to do. We left Irkutsk on the 12th day of March, 1882, and arrived at Yakutsk, traveling day and night, on the 28th of March, I think it was, and remained at Yakutsk four days. We left Yakutsk about the 1st or 2d of April. After we had been about two days from Yakutsk we met a courier bringing the news of the loss of the Rodgers. We went on to Verkeransk, at which place

---
* Correction by witness.

we arrived on about the 8th of April, I think. There we learned of the finding of the bodies. Mr. Jackson did not know which way to go, after the bodies were found, but he thought he would go to Geeomovialocke, to see if he could not meet Mr. Melville. He said he wanted to see them. So we started for Geeomovialocke instead of going to Bulun. We arrived at Tamoos about the 24th of April. At Tamoos we stopped and took breakfast. After breakfast there were two dog-teams came over from Geeomovialocke, and in one team Mr. Melville came along. He then told us that Nindemann and Bartlett were over at Geeomovialocke and told us to come over. We went over to Geeomovialocke and found them there. At this time Mr. Melville was getting ready to leave. We had about an hour's talk together, and Mr. Melville, Bartlett, and Nindemann started on their homeward journey. They wanted to get home as fast as they could on account of the snow melting. We did not remain in Geeomovialocke more than an hour after they left. We then started with some dog drivers; we got dogs there, and then drove day and night. The first place we touched at was Arii, I think. From Arii we went to Bookhia, where we stopped and had something to eat. We did our sleeping in our sleds, so we did not stop to camp anywhere. After Borkhia there was a place I don't know the name of; I have forgotten it; we just touched at it, and from there, I think, we went across the river or bay, I don't know which, to the Pomerie Point, where the people were found. We saw the places where the people were dug out, and a lot of old clothing and skins that were left behind, which were of no use. We remained there for a little while, Larson taking a sketch of the place. From there we went to Mat Vay, stopped about an hour, and crossed over to the Two Crosses, where they were buried—what we used to call the Two Crosses. From there we then started home on our homeward trip, stopping on our way at Bulcour. We left Bulcour on our way for Bulun. After we left Bulcour there was a storm set in; we could not see anything; the dogs would not go ahead, so we stopped at Kusmahs, about 20 versts northward of Bulun, until the storm went down. After leaving Kusmahs we arrived at Bulun about the 1st of May. Then the snow was melting very fast, and we had great difficulty in getting deer enough to carry us to the next station. On our way to the station we killed two or three deer, the deer not being as strong in the warm weather as they are in the cold. At the next station we had no difficulty in getting deer, and carried the same deer right through, within 50 versts of Verkeransk. We then took horses, rode horseback. I think it was about May 10th that we arrived at Verkeransk. The day after arriving at Verkeransk we started for Yakutsk. While at Verkeransk we heard how that Captain Berry, Ensign Hunt, a little Russian that Captain Berry brought along with him, and a Cossack had gone on ahead of us a day and a half. We started along the road and caught up with Captain Berry three or four days after we left Verkeransk; then we traveled together. It was about the 17th or 18th when we came to Kengasak station. Here we met Mr. Melville, Bartlett, Nindemann, Greenbeck, and their drivers snowbound, the snow being so deep they could not go up the valley to the mountains. So we had to remain there at the station about ten days. I think it was about the 26th or 27th that we left this station, and arrived at Yakutsk about June 8. From there took a steamer to Irkutsk, and arrived at Irkutsk about July the 5th. After arriving at Irkutsk, Mr. Jackson turned me over to Mr. Melville. I was put under his charge from that time up to the time I landed here in Washington.

Question by the JUDGE-ADVOCATE. What was the object of this visit to the place at which the bodies were found, and to the tomb?

The WITNESS. I do not know what Mr. Jackson's object was when we went there; but after we got there they took a sketch of the tomb. Larson said he would like to have a sketch of the people. "Well," Jackson then said, "we will look at them." I told Jackson, then, if he did that, he would have to take all the responsibilities upon his own shoulders. Jackson then told me to cut "Mr." before Collins' name. I told him he would have to stand all the responsibilities. He said "That was all right." He then told the natives to open the end of the tomb. They opened he south end, and the first one we saw was Captain De Long; next to Captain De Long was Doctor Ambler; after Doctor Ambler was Mr. Collins. All three of them were taken out, and Larson took a sketch of them. Mr. Jackson looked through Mr. Collins' clothes to see if there was anything left on them. On looking through his clothes he saw a bronze cross, and Jackson then said "I think his people would like to have this," and took it off his neck. Larson, while sketching the doctor, arranged him some way so that he could get a good view of him. He found on the doctor, I think, a half dollar with one corner cut off. What was done with it I do not know. After sketching the people they placed them in the tomb, the same way as they were before they took them out, covered them with the canvas, putting everything over the box, and making the tomb as it looked before they disturbed it.

Question by the JUDGE-ADVOCATE. You have stated that a lot of old clothing and other useless articles were found at the place where the bodies of Lieut. Commander De Long and his comrades had been found. Were there any books and papers found there and then?

The WITNESS. No, sir.

Question by the JUDGE-ADVOCATE. Were any books or papers found on the bodies of Lieut. Commander De Long, Dr. Ambler, or Mr. Collins when their remains were disturbed, as stated?

The WITNESS. I do not know of any books or papers All that was found on them to my knowledge was the bronze cross on Mr. Collins and a half dollar on Dr. Ambler.

Question by the JUDGE-ADVOCATE. Was the tomb made equally as secure after the bodies were returned to it as it had been before it was disturbed?

The WITNESS. I do not think that it was as strong after they had got through as it was before they touched it.

Question by the JUDGE-ADVOCATE. Have you any charge to lay, or special commendation to offer, concerning any officer or man connected with the Jeannette expedition—first, as to the condition of the vessel on her departure from San Francisco; second, her management up to the time of her loss; third, her loss; fourth, the provisions made and plans adopted for the several boats' crews on their leaving the wreck; fifth, the efforts made by the various officers to insure the safety of the parties under their charge and for the relief of the other parties; sixth, the general conduct and merits of each and all, the officers and men of the expedition?

The WITNESS. Yes; each and all the officers and men of the expedition did their duty, as far as I know; done everything that men could do.

Cross-examination by the JUDGE-ADVOCATE in behalf of the late Jerome J. Collins:

Question by the JUDGE-ADVOCATE. Had you any conversation with

Mr. Collins before you and Nindemann separated from the first cutter's party and went ahead for relief? If yea, what was it?

The judge-advocate stated that he would permit the witness to proceed with his answer to the question, so long as his statement is of a general character, reserving the right to object to anything reflecting injuriously upon any officer or man of the expedition.

The WITNESS. I had no conversation with Mr. Collins before leaving. Before we started they all came up to us to shake us by the hand and to bid us good-bye. When Mr. Collins came up to me, he says, "Good-bye, Noros, remember me when you get to New York." They were the only words that I heard Mr. Collins say.

Question by the JUDGE-ADVOCATE. Did you hear Mr. Collins request Lieut. Commander De Long to allow him to go with you and Nindemann?

The WITNESS. No, sir [that I know of*].

Question by the JUDGE-ADVOCATE. Did he claim the right to go?

The WITNESS. Not that I know of, sir. I never heard anything of it.

Question by the JUDGE-ADVOCATE. Were you present when the bodies of Lieut. Commander De Long and his comrades were first found and searched?

The WITNESS. No, sir.

Question by the JUDGE-ADVOCATE. Did Mr. Melville refuse to allow you to return and aid in the search for De Long's party, and what reason, if any, did he give you for so doing?

The WITNESS. When Mr. Melville met us at Bulun he made preparations to go north, right away. When I saw he was making the preparations he said nothing to Nindemann or me about going with him. I then volunteered to go with him, telling him that I would go with him if he would get me sufficient clothing to wear. I told him that I was not well, but well enough to ride, and I would be able to point out some of the prominent landmarks which I knew along the road. He then told me, "No, Noros; it will take too many dogs." This is all he said, and that is all the reason he had for me not going with him.

Question by the JUDGE-ADVOCATE. Is it or is it not a fact that during the retreat the party were frequently ordered to be ready for a start at 5 o'clock in the morning, and that Lieut. Commander De Long lay in his tent until 2 o'clock in the afternoon, when not sick, thereby causing unnecessary delay?

The WITNESS. No, sir; it is not a fact.

Question by the JUDGE-ADVOCATE. What was Mr. Collins' physical condition, as compared with the other members of the party, when you and Nindemann left them and went ahead for relief?

The WITNESS. His condition, as far as I know, was much about the same as the rest of the people.

Question by the JUDGE-ADVOCATE. Have you stated since you returned, that Mr. Collins, Dr. Ambler, and Alexy were the strongest of all the party, and that Mr. Collins was as well able to get through as you were?

The court was here cleared by request of a member, and afterwards reopened, and the witness being present answered the question as follows:

The WITNESS. I have never said that they were the strongest of the party, but I have said, since my return, there were some of the people might have got through as well as I did.

---

*Correction by witness.

The judge-advocate did not desire to further cross-examine this witness.

The witness was then examined by the court, as follows:

Question by the COURT. Could Mr. Jackson or Mr. Larson have found any books, papers, or other articles, either at the place where the bodies were found or at the tomb, without your knowing it?

The WITNESS. I do not think they could, sir.

Question by the COURT. In what respect was the tomb of Lieutenant De Long and his companions less secure after the visit of Mr. Jackson?

The WITNESS. They had to cut one of the cross-pieces, to get this plank off, from over the tomb, or box; so that it was not as secure after they got through as it was before. This cross-piece was a frame to the pyramid. [I wish to state that a plank was cut also.*]

Question by the COURT. State, if you know, how Mr. Collins was treated by the commanding and other officers of the Jeannette?

The WITNESS. I never saw him treated any other way but as an officer of the vessel.

Question by the COURT. State, if you know, how Mr. Collins treated the commanding and other officers of the Jeannette?

The WITNESS. I do not know anything about that.

Question by the COURT. Did the crew of the Jeannette treat Mr. Collins with the respect due an officer? If not, state in what manner he was treated differently?

The WITNESS. They all treated him as an officer.

Question by the COURT. How did Mr. Collins treat the crew of the Jeannette, in comparison with others in authority?

The WITNESS. He treated us just the same as any other officer of the expedition.

Question by the COURT. Have you any personal knowledge of any difficulty, at any time, between Mr. Collins and any officer of the Jeannette? If so, state all you know about the matter.

The WITNESS. No, sir; I have not any personal knowledge of any difficulty.

Question by the COURT. Was there any unnecessary delay during the retreat at Bennett's Island, or elsewhere?

The WITNESS. There was no unnecessary delay that I know of.

Question by the COURT. When Mr. Melville declined to take you with him, on leaving Bulun, in search of the first cutter's party, were you not ill with dysentery?

The WITNESS. Yes, sir.

Neither the court nor the judge-advocate desiring to further examine this witness, his testimony was concluded, and the court then, at 11.50 a. m., adjourned to meet to-morrow, the 14th day of December, 1882, at 10.30 a. m.

FIFTY-SIXTH DAY.

NAVY DEPARTMENT,
Washington, D. C., Thursday, December 14, 1882, 10 a. m.

The court met, pursuant to the adjournment of yesterday, December 13, 1882.

Present, Commodore William G. Temple, United States Navy, president; Captain Joseph N. Miller, United States Navy, Commander Fred-

---

* Addition by witness.

erick V. McNair, United States Navy, members; and Master Samuel C. Lemly, United States Navy, judge-advocate.

The witness, Seaman LOUIS P. NOROS, then came in, and the judge-advocate proceeded to read to him his testimony for correction, and the entire testimony of the witness having been read to him, he desired to make the following corrections, viz:

On page 230, lines 31 and 32, correct by saying, "We left Bulun on the 3d of December, and arrived at Yakutsk about the 6th of January."

On page 230, line 38, change "12th" to "1st," for the date of arrival at Irkutsk.

On page 233, line 15, after the word "had" add the words "that I know of."

On page 234, line 13, at the end add "I wish to state that a plank was cut also."

With these corrections made, the witness pronounced his testimony to be correct, and then withdrew.

And the judge-advocate then directed that the above corrections be interlined in the body of the record with red ink, at the proper places for their suitable application to the matter corrected.

The record of the proceedings of yesterday, December 13, 1882, the fifty-fourth day of the inquiry, was likewise read and approved by the court.

RAYMOND L. NEWCOMB, naturalist and taxidermist of the Jeannette expedition was then called as a witness, and having been sworn, according to law, by the president of the court, testified as follows:

Question by the JUDGE-ADVOCATE. What is your name and rate?

The WITNESS. Raymond L. Newcomb, seaman, United States Navy.

Question by the JUDGE-ADVOCATE. To what vessel and what special service were you last attached, and what were your duties?

The WITNESS. The Arctic steamer Jeannette; naturalist and taxidermist.

Question by the JUDGE-ADVOCATE. When and where did you join the Jeannette?

The WITNESS. On the passage from Mare Island to San Francisco. I signed the ship's articles in July, 1879.

Question by the JUDGE-ADVOCATE. Have you any statement to lay before this court in relation to the fitting of the Jeannette for Arctic service, and her condition when she left San Francisco?

The WITNESS. None.

Question by the JUDGE-ADVOCATE. Have you any statement to lay before this court in relation to the management of the Jeannette up to the time of her loss?

The WITNESS. None.

Question by the JUDGE-ADVOCATE. Have you any statement to lay before this court concerning the loss of the Jeannette?

The WITNESS. Not any.

Question by the JUDGE-ADVOCATE. Have you any statement to make in relation to the provisions made and plans adopted for the several boats' crews upon their leaving the wreck?

The WITNESS. Not any.

Question by the JUDGE-ADVOCATE. Have you any statement to make in regard to the efforts made by the various officers to insure the safety of the parties under their charge and for the relief of the other parties?

The WITNESS. Not any.

Question by the JUDGE-ADVOCATE. Have you any charge to lay or special commendation to offer concerning any officer or man connected with the Jeannette expedition—first, as to the condition of the vessel on her departure from San Francisco; second, her management up to the time of her loss; third, her loss; fourth, the provisions made and plans adopted for the several boats' crews on their leaving the wreck; fifth, the efforts made by the various officers to insure the safety of the parties under their charge and for the relief of the other parties; sixth, the general conduct and merits of each and all the officers and men of the expedition?

The WITNESS. I have none.

Cross-examination by the JUDGE-ADVOCATE in behalf of the late Jerome J. Collins:

Question by the JUDGE-ADVOCATE. Do you know anything of the trouble between Lieutenant Commander De Long and Mr. Collins?

The WITNESS. I do not.

Question by the JUDGE-ADVOCATE. What did Mr. Collins say to you regarding the affair?

The judge-advocate objected to the question as calling for hearsay.

The court was then cleared for deliberation on the objection of the judge-advocate, and afterwards reopened, the witness being present, and the president of the court then announced, as the decision of the court, that the objection of the judge-advocate was sustained, and that the question will not be put.

Question by the JUDGE-ADVOCATE. You had some trouble yourself with Lieutenant Commander De Long, did you not?

The judge-advocate objected to this question as irrelevant to the cross-examination in behalf of Mr. Collins, and stated that the witness had been given full license to lay charges against the late Lieutenant Commander De Long, if he desired to do so, or felt aggrieved.

The objection of the judge-advocate was sustained, and the question was not put.

Question by the JUDGE-ADVOCATE. Do you remember the time when Mr. Collins's notes were lost?

The WITNESS. He kept a large journal in a wooden box made by the carpenter, Mr. Sweetman. That book, I think, was lost. Further than that I do not know. If this book was the one referred to, I think it was lost with the ship.

Question by the JUDGE-ADVOCATE. Was he at liberty to rescue them?

The WITNESS. In my judgment he was.

Question by the JUDGE-ADVOCATE. When you showed him your note-book, what did he tell you regarding his notes, and what he was going to do when land was reached?

The judge-advocate objected to this question on the ground that it calls for hearsay.

The court was then cleared for deliberation on the objection of the judge-advocate, and afterward reopened, the witness being present, and the president of the court then announced, as the decision of the court, that the objection of the judge-advocate was sustained, and that the question would not be put.

Question by the JUDGE-ADVOCATE. What did the party that you were in do when you reached Geeomovialocke?

The WITNESS. Sought shelter and food as soon as possible. Made an ineffectual attempt in the whale-boat to work up the river; returned, staid at the Tungoos village of Geeomovialocke some forty days. We were much troubled by vermin, subsisting on very scanty fare, recruiting impaired health. Sent messengers to Bulun; received a message from Seamen Nindemann and Noros, giving the first tidings of the whereabouts of the first cutter. Lieutenant Danenhower made a search, with some natives, for traces of the survivors. Communications having been effected, transportation facilities afforded, we left that village on the 3d of November, 1881, bound for Bulun.

Question by the JUDGE-ADVOCATE. How did you pass the time?

The WITNESS. In repairing old clothes, trying to keep warm, and recruiting our health.

Question by the JUDGE-ADVOCATE. Did you know that the native Shagra got drunk shortly after he started with the exile for Bulun?

The WITNESS. I did not.

Question by the JUDGE-ADVOCATE. Did Mr. Collins show you any of the papers he was going to secure? And, if yea, when did he show them to you?

The WITNESS. I saw his large journal on board the ship several times. Nothing else was ever shown me that I remember.

Question by the JUDGE-ADVOCATE. Had you any trouble with Chief Engineer Melville after reaching the Lena Delta?

A member objected to this question on the ground that it is irrelevant to a cross-examination in behalf of the late Mr. Collins.

The court was then closed for deliberation upon the objection of a member, and afterward reopened, the witness being present, and the president of the court then announced as the decision of the court that the objection of the member is sustained, and that the question will not be put.

Question by the JUDGE-ADVOCATE. Did Mr. Melville threaten you in any way?

A member of the court objected to this question on the same ground as stated in relation to the preceding question. The objection of the member was sustained by the court, and the question was not put.

Question by the JUDGE-ADVOCATE. Is it or is it not a fact that during the retreat the party was frequently ordered to be ready for a start at 5 o'clock in the morning, and that Lieut. Commander De Long lay in his tent until 2 o'clock in the afternoon, when not sick, thereby causing unnecessary delay?

The WITNESS. I have no knowledge of any such occurrence.

The judge-advocate did not desire further to cross-examine this witness.

The witness was then examined by the court, as follows:

Question by the COURT. Was there any unnecessary delay during the retreat over the ice?

The WITNESS. It seems to me as if the time occupied in reaching and in staying at Bennett's Island might have been used making way south.

Question by the COURT. Did you think so at the time?

The WITNESS. I did.

Question by the COURT. How was the time occupied in reaching and staying at Bennett Island?

The WITNESS. In traveling over the ice or through the water, but mostly over the ice, transporting the boats, sleds, and provisions. After reaching Bennett Island the party encamped, repaired the boats, overhauled the clothing, and got some birds, some fresh food, principally birds, erected a cairn, or pile of stones, underneath which papers or records were buried inclosed in a proper vessel. I might add, some scientific observations were also conducted, including notes on natural history and tidal observations.

Question by the COURT. Was not the delay at Bennett Island necessary for the repair of the boats, in order to make them serviceable when open water should be reached?

The WITNESS. They leaked badly and had to be pumped constantly after that, while journeying south. I do not know what else I might say, unless that I was not a judge of the condition of the boats at that time, not having inspected them.

Question by the COURT. Did you express your opinion, relative to this delay at Bennett Island, to the commanding officer?

The WITNESS. I did not.

Question by the COURT. State, if you know, what induced the commanding officer to delay the retreat, in order to land on Bennett's Island?

The WITNESS. I do not know his reason.

Question by the COURT. During the stay of the whale-boat's party at Geeomovialocke in the month of October, 1881, did you think at the time that an expedition could and should have been fitted out and sent to the northward in search of the first and second cutters' parties?

The WITNESS. No party of any size could have been sent, in my judgment, owing to the physical condition of the same—of the survivors—at Geeomovialocke at the time. Lieutenant Danenhower did make one trip. I do not know how far he got, but remember his stating that the condition of the ice prevented his exploring to the extent which he desired.

Question by the COURT. Do you know whether the resources of Geeomovialocke could have furnished the necessary means of sending out a search party to the northward sooner than was done, and was it possible to travel either by land or water, or on the ice, in that direction?

The WITNESS. I have no knowledge of the resources of that place.

To the latter portion of the question, which was submitted to the witness separately, he said, "I do not know."

Question by the COURT. While at Geeomovialocke, did you think, or express your opinion, that it was important to organize a search party for your missing comrades?

The WITNESS. I have no recollection of so doing.

Question by the JUDGE-ADVOCATE. What, if any, experience had you in the Arctic regions prior to your joining the Jeannette expedition?

The WITNESS. None at all.

Question by the JUDGE-ADVOCATE. Do you feel that you can wholly and entirely separate in your mind your impressions at the time of the delay at Bennett Island from those made on your mind by subsequent events?

The WITNESS. I do.

Question by the JUDGE-ADVOCATE. What, as compared with the commander of the expedition, were your facilities for knowing the position of the party, at any time, while traveling on the ice, the physical condition of the men, the state of repair of the boats, and the quantity of provisions on hand?

The WITNESS. I can hardly compare my opportunities with those of my commanding officers, but the opportunities which I had were the same as those which might have been afforded to any person of ordinary observation.

Question by the JUDGE-ADVOCATE. What, exactly, do you mean when you say that you can hardly compare your facilities for knowing the points enumerated in the preceding question with those possessed by the commander of the expedition?

The WITNESS. The meaning I intend to convey is, that as the naturalist of the expedition I would not be as well qualified as the commander to judge of those things.

Question by the COURT. State how Mr. Collins was treated by the commanding and other officers of the Jeannette officially and socially.

The WITNESS. My personal knowledge of the official and social treatment of Mr. Collins I can hardly state, trusting to memory to do so. I was looking out for my own affairs, and presumed that he was doing the same. If I stated more it would be hearsay.

Question by the COURT. Was Mr. Collins treated with the usual official respect and social courtesy by his messmates?

The WITNESS. Within my own personal knowledge, yes.

Question by the COURT. State, if you know, how Mr. Collins treated the commanding and other officers of the Jeannette.

The WITNESS. So far as I know, respectfully.

Question by the COURT. Did the crew of the Jeannette treat Mr. Collins with the respect due an officer? If not, state in what manner he was treated differently.

The WITNESS. They treated him with much respect. I should say they did treat him with due respect and courtesy.

Question by the COURT. How did Mr. Collins treat the crew of the Jeannette in comparison with others in authority?

The WITNESS. About the same, as far as I know.

Question by the COURT. Have you any personal knowledge of any difficulty at any time between Mr. Collins and any officer of the Jeannette? If so, state all you know about the matter.

The WITNESS. I have no personal knowledge of difficulties between the officers of the Jeannette and Mr. Collins.

Lieut. Richard Wainwright, United States Navy, personally present, here requested that he might be allowed to examine this witness in behalf of Lieut. J. W. Danenhower, and presented a letter from Lieutenant Danenhower to Commodore William G. Temple, United States Navy, the president of the court, as his authority for making the request.

The court was here closed, by request of the judge-advocate, and afterwards reopened.

Pending a decision upon the request of Lieutenant Wainwright, the court then, at 1 p. m., adjourned, to meet to-morrow, the 15th day of December, 1882, at 10.30 a. m.

FIFTY-SEVENTH DAY.

NAVY DEPARTMENT,
Washington, D. C., December 15, 1882—10.30 a. m.

The court met pursuant to the adjournment of yesterday.

Present: Commodore William G. Temple, United States Navy, president; Capt. Joseph N. Miller, United States Navy, Commander Frederick V. McNair, United States Navy, members; and Master Samuel C. Lemly, United States Navy, judge-advocate.

The reading of the record of the proceedings of yesterday, December 14, 1882, the fifty-sixth day of the inquiry, was deferred.

The court was then cleared for deliberation and afterward reopened.

The judge-advocate then read aloud the letter from Lieutenant Danenhower to the president of the court, presented yesterday by Lieutenant Wainwright, requesting that he might be allowed counsel, a certified copy of which letter is appended to the record, marked B. C. In accordance with this request, Lieutenant Wainwright was admitted as counsel for Lieutenant Danenhower and appeared before the court.

Seaman R. L. NEWCOMB, the witness under examination, then came in, and was examined by Lieutenant Wainwright, in behalf of Lieutenant Danenhower, as follows:

Question by Lieutenant WAINWRIGHT. What part of the boat did Mr. Melville occupy on the night of the gale, September 12?

The WITNESS. Both bow and stern, if I remember rightly.

Question by Lieutenant WAINWRIGHT. What part of the boat did Mr. Danenhower occupy on the night of the gale of September 12?

The WITNESS. The stern.

Question by Lieutenant WAINWRIGHT. Who was in active charge of that boat during the night of the gale of September 12?

The WITNESS. Lieutenant Danenhower.

Question by Lieutenant WAINWRIGHT. Who conned the boat and shaped all her courses until you made the land?

The WITNESS. I think Lieutenant Danenhower.

Question by Lieutenant WAINWRIGHT. Who steered the boat up the Lena River?

The WITNESS. Lieutenant Danenhower and some of the seamen.

Question by Lieutenant WAINWRIGHT. On September 28, the day after the unsuccessful attempt to get up the river, Mr. Melville gave certain directions to the men. Please give the substance of these remarks.

The WITNESS. I do not remember them. I have a general recollection of the substance—that we were obliged to return, and must keep ourselves in as good a condition as possible, in order to preserve the general health of the party.

Question by Lieutenant WAINWRIGHT. What was the condition of the party at this time, and who were the people working during the next few days?

The WITNESS. The general condition of the party was poor; a number were suffering from swollen and frost-bitten feet and legs. At the time of the landing, on the return from the unsuccessful attempt to work up the river, Mr. Melville was carried on a sled from the boat to the hut where our party stayed. A number of the others hobbled along or were assisted. Of the party who were able to work during the next few days there were, as I recollect it, Lieutenant Danenhower, John Cole, boatswain, and the Indian, Aniguin; also myself, a little; soon followed by Steward Tong Sing; he afterward got out. Those who seemed to be suffering most were Mr. Melville, Seaman Leach, Fireman Bartlett, and Coal-heaver Lauterbach.

Question by Lieutenant WAINWRIGHT. Did or did not Mr. Melville, on September 28, already alluded to, tell Mr. Danenhower to take charge of the party during his illness?

The WITNESS. I do not remember that he did.

Re-examination by the JUDGE-ADVOCATE:

Question by the JUDGE-ADVOCATE. Who commanded the Arctic exploring steamer Jeannette?

The WITNESS. Lieut. George W. De Long, United States Navy.

Question by the JUDGE-ADVOCATE. Did he in person steer the ship, loose and furl sail, start fires, &c., or did he confine himself to the general direction of such things, delegating the actual performance to other and the proper persons?

(A member objected to this question, and the court was cleared for deliberation, and afterward reopened, and the president of the court announced, as the decision of the court, that the objection of the member was sustained, the question being deemed unnecessary, and the question was not put.)

The judge-advocate did not desire to further re-examine this witness.

Question by the COURT. Did Mr. Melville steer the boat himself before Mr. Danenhower took the helm, or was this duty performed by one of the seamen before that time?

(The judge-advocate objected to the question, as unnecessary, and respectfully called the attention of the court to the ruling of the court on the preceding question. The court was then cleared for deliberation on the objection of the judge-advocate, and afterward reopened, the witness and Lieutenant Wainwright being present, and the president of the court then announced, as the decision of the court, that the objection of the judge-advocate was not sustained, and the question was accordingly put.)

The WITNESS. Mr. Melville may have taken the helm for a brief period, but that duty was mostly performed by the seamen.

Question by the COURT. Did you understand that Mr. Melville gave over the command of the boat and party to Lieutenant Danenhower on the occasion of the gale of September 12, or did he merely make use of Lieutenant Danenhower's professional abilities for the management and navigation of the boat?

The WITNESS. I should say he made use of Mr. Danenhower's professional ability to assist in navigating the boat.

Question by the COURT. Did Mr. Melville ever turn over the command of the whale-boat party to Lieutenant Danenhower?

The WITNESS. In my judgment, during the night of the last gale, Lieutenant Danenhower had charge of the boat. I do not recollect Chief Engineer Melville verbally turning over command of the boat to Lieutenant Danenhower at any time.

Question by the COURT. Did Mr. Melville or Lieutenant Danenhower ever announce to the whale-boat party that Lieutenant Danenhower was in command?

The WITNESS. If I remember correctly, during the time of Mr. Melville's confinement in the hut at the Tongoos village, Lieutenant Danenhower was in charge of the party. I am under the impression that such an announcement was made, but have no definite recollection about it. My impressions are that the announcement was made by Mr. Melville at the time of his confinement in the Tongoos hut.

Question by the COURT. Was that the only occasion on which it was announced?

The WITNESS. It is the only occasion of which I have any recollection.

Lieutenant Wainwright, counsel for Lieutenant Danenhower, then made the following statement:

If it please the court, all that Mr. Danenhower claims is, that his previous testimony before the court is correct, and he only desires to substantiate it by this witness. He did not and does not claim to have commanded the party, but that he had charge on two occasions, and that his services were ignored by Mr. Melville in his testimony.

The court was then cleared by request of a member and afterwards reopened, the witness and Lieutenant Wainwright being present.

The court did not desire to further examine this witness, and neither the judge-advocate nor Lieutenant Wainwright desired to examine him. His testimony was concluded. The reading to him of his testimony for correction was deferred, in order to give the clerk time to prepare the record from his short-hand notes. The witness then withdrew.

The court then, at 12 m., took a recess until 12.30 p. m., and then reconvened with all the members and the judge advocate present.

Lieutenant Wainwright, counsel for Lieutenant Danenhower, was not present.

CHARLES TONG SING was then called as a witness, and was interrogated by the president of the court as follows:

Question by the PRESIDENT OF THE COURT. Do you understand the nature of an oath?

The WITNESS. Yes, sir.

Question. Did you ever take an oath?

The WITNESS. Yes, sir.

The witness was then sworn according to law by the president of the court, and testified as follows:

Examined by the JUDGE-ADVOCATE:

Question by the JUDGE-ADVOCATE. What is your name?

The WITNESS. Charles Tong Sing.

Question by the JUDGE-ADVOCATE. Were you attached to the exploring steamer Jeannette on the Arctic expedition? If yes, in what capacity?

The WITNESS. I was on board of the Jeannette. I was the steward.

Question by the JUDGE-ADVOCATE. Have you any charge to lay, or special commendation to offer, concerning any officer or man of the Jeannette expedition—first, as to the condition of the vessel on her departure from San Francisco; second, her management up to the time of her loss; third, her loss; fourth, the provisions made and plans adopted for the several boats' crews on their leaving the wreck; fifth, the efforts made by the various officers to insure the safety of the parties under their charge and for the relief of the other parties; sixth, the general conduct and merits of each and all the officers and men of the expedition?

The WITNESS. I joined the Jeannette in San Francisco. Everybody treated me all right. One thing—Captain De Long—I was not satisfied. He have three Chinamen on board and cabin boy. When we leave San Francisco three weeks he got sick. He send cabin boy back to San Francisco. He promise me—I am steward and cabin boy—me get double wages when I get back. I got my own wages, and did not get cabin boy's wages too. That is all, sir.

Cross-examined by the JUDGE-ADVOCATE in behalf of the late Jerome J. Collins:

Question by the JUDGE-ADVOCATE. What, if anything, do you know of any difficulty between Chief Engineer Melville and Mr. Jerome J. Collins?

The WITNESS. I know that Mr. Collins did not like Captain De Long. Mr. Collins did not like Mr. Melville, either; that is all I know.

The judge-advocate did not further desire to examine this witness.

The court did not desire to examine him.

His testimony was then read over to him and pronounced by him correct. The witness then withdrew.

The court then, at 1 p. m., adjourned to meet to-morrow, the 16th day of December, 1882, at 10.30 a. m.

FIFTY-EIGHTH DAY.

NAVY DEPARTMENT,
Washington, D. C., Saturday, December 16, 1882—10.30 a. m.

The court met pursuant to the adjournment of yesterday, December 15, 1882.

Present, Commodore William G. Temple, United States Navy, president; Capt. Joseph N. Miller, United States Navy, Commander Frederick V. McNair, United States Navy, members; and Master Samuel C. Lemly, United States Navy, judge-advocate.

The court was then cleared by request of the judge-advocate, and afterwards reopened. Lieut. Richard Wainwright, counsel for Lieutenant Danenhower, then came in.

The witness R. L. Newcomb was also present, and his testimony was read to him for correction, and having had his entire testimony read to him, he pronounced it to be correct and then withdrew.

Seaman HENRY WILSON was then called as a witness, and, having been sworn according to law by the president of the court, testified as follows:

Examined by the JUDGE-ADVOCATE:

Question by the JUDGE-ADVOCATE. What is your name and rate?
The WITNESS. Henry Wilson, seaman.

Question by the JUDGE-ADVOCATE. To what ship and what special service were you last attached?
The WITNESS. To the United States steamer Jeannette, on an Arctic expedition.

Question by the JUDGE-ADVOCATE. When and where did you join the Jeannette, and what were your duties on board of that vessel?
The WITNESS. I joined the Jeannette in San Francisco; I think it was the 3d or 4th of July, 1879; my duties were those of a seaman.

Question by the JUDGE-ADVOCATE. Have you any statement to lay before this court in relation to the fitting out of the Jeannette for Arctic service and the condition of the ship when she sailed from San Francisco?
The WITNESS. None, sir.

Question by the JUDGE-ADVOCATE. Have you any statement to lay before this court in relation to the management of the vessel up to the time of her loss?
The WITNESS. No, sir.

Question by the JUDGE-ADVOCATE. Have you any statement to lay before this court in relation to the loss of the Jeannette?
The WITNESS. No, sir.

Question by the JUDGE-ADVOCATE. Have you any statement to lay before this court in relation to the provisions made and plans adopted for the several boats' crews upon their leaving the wreck?
The WITNESS. No, sir.

Question by the JUDGE-ADVOCATE. Have you any statement to lay before this court in relation to the efforts made by the various officers to insure the safety of the parties under their charge and for the relief of the other parties?
The WITNESS. No, sir.

Question by the JUDGE-ADVOCATE. Have you any charge to lay or special commendation to offer concerning any of the officers or men connected with the Jeannette expedition: first, as to the condition of the vessel on her departure from San Francisco; second, her management up to the time of her loss; third, her loss; fourth, the provisions made and plans adopted for the several boats' crews on their leaving the wreck; fifth, the efforts made by the various officers to insure the safety of the parties under their charge and for the relief of the other parties; sixth, the general conduct and merits of each and all the officers and men of the expedition?

The WITNESS. All I can say is, the ship was well fitted out and a strong and seaworthy ship; I think she was managed very well.

Cross-examination by the JUDGE-ADVOCATE in behalf of the late Jerome J. Collins:

Question by the JUDGE-ADVOCATE. What, if anything, do you know of any difficulty between the commanding officer of the Jeannette and the late Jerome J. Collins?

The WITNESS. I have reason to think that there was a difficulty between the captain and Mr. Collins, but I do not know any of the details. I saw that there was a difficulty between the captain and Mr. Collins; I was not present at any of it, nor heard any of it.

Cross-examination by Lieutenant WAINWRIGHT in behalf of Lieut. J. W. Danenhower:

Question by Lieutenant WAINWRIGHT. What position in the boat did Mr. Melville occupy during the night of the gale of September 12, during the time you were riding to the drag?

The WITNESS. He occupied the position in the stern of the boat alongside of Mr. Danenhower at first, but afterward he took a position in the bow of the boat.

Question by Lieutenant WAINWRIGHT. What position did Mr. Danenhower occupy during the same time?

The WITNESS. He occupied a position in the stern of the boat.

Question by Lieutenant WAINWRIGHT. Who had active charge of the boat during the gale?

The WITNESS. Lieutenant Danenhower [*had charge of and managed the boat, under the command of Mr. Melville.**]

Question by Lieutenant WAINWRIGHT. Who conned the boat and shaped the courses until you reached the land?

The WITNESS. Lieutenant Danenhower.

Question by Lieutenant WAINWRIGHT. Who steered the boat up the Lena River?

The WITNESS. Sometimes Lieutenant Danenhower and sometimes the seamen, sir.

Question by Lieutenant WAINWRIGHT. The day after the last attempt to get up the river, namely, September 28, did or did not Mr. Melville announce to the men that Mr. Danenhower would take charge during his (Melville's) sickness?

The WITNESS. No, sir; not as I remember.

Lieutenant Wainwright did not desire to further examine the witness.

Re-examination by the JUDGE-ADVOCATE:

Question by the JUDGE-ADVOCATE. You have stated that Lieutenant Danenhower had active charge of the whale-boat on the night of the gale, September 12; that he conned the boat and shaped the courses until you reached land; that he with others steered the boat up the

---

* Correction by witness.

Lena River. Did he have sole and entire charge of the boat on the night in question, and did he conn the boat and shape the courses independently, or after consultation with Chief Engineer Melville?

The WITNESS. No; I do not think that he had entire charge of the boat, without consulting with Mr. Melville what to do, and giving Mr. Melville his opinion what it was best to do, as he was professionally a sea-going officer. He conned the boat independently; he shaped the courses independently.

Question by the JUDGE-ADVOCATE. Do you know that he did not consult Mr. Melville in relation to the conning of the boat and shaping of the courses?

The WITNESS. I do, sir.

Question by the JUDGE-ADVOCATE. How do you know it?

The WITNESS. Because I never heard it, sir.

Question by the JUDGE-ADVOCATE. Could he not have consulted with Mr. Melville without your hearing it?

The WITNESS. No, sir; he could not, because it would always be heard all over the boat what was said.

Question by the JUDGE-ADVOCATE. Were you asleep at any time between the day of the gale, September 12, and the landing of the whale-boat, September 16, 1881?

(Lieutenant Wainwright objected to the question, saying:

If it please the court, I object to the question on the ground that the judge-advocate is now trying to contradict his own witness, which is contrary to the rules of evidence. The judge-advocate stated in reply that he denies the fact that the witness under examination is at this stage of the examination his witness. It is impossible in such an extended inquiry, and where the interests of so many persons are concerned, to arrange the examination by the parties interested, as is usually done. In the direct examination of this witness, the judge-advocate claims that he acted in the capacity of prosecutor, and that he is now acting as counsel for Chief Engineer George W. Melville, one of the parties to the trial, not otherwise represented by special counsel.

The judge-advocate then, by request of Lieutenant Wainwright, read paragraph 442, of chapter 3, of Greenleaf on Evidence, volume 1.

The judge-advocate then read paragraph 443 of the same chapter.

The court was here cleared for deliberation, and afterward reopened; the witness and Lieutenant Wainwright being present, and the president of the court announced, as the decision of the court, that the objection of Lieutenant Wainwright is not sustained, and the question was accordingly put.)

The WITNESS. No, sir.

Question by the JUDGE-ADVOCATE. Were Lieutenant Danenhower and Chief Engineer Melville under your direct personal observation and within your hearing at all times between the dates named?

The WITNESS. Yes, sir.

Question by the JUDGE-ADVOCATE. Can you give in detail all the conversations between these officers which occurred within the dates named?

The WITNESS. No, sir. I do not remember them.

Examination by the COURT:

Question by the COURT. You have stated that you saw there was a difficulty between Captain De Long and Mr. Collins; did you mean that you observed this yourself, or that you had gathered it from the observations of others?

The WITNESS. I observed it myself; by the two gentlemen's manners.

Question by the COURT. State, if you know, how Mr. Collins was treated by the commanding and other officers of the Jeannette.

The WITNESS. As far as I know, he was treated respectfully and as a gentleman.

Question by the COURT. State, if you know, how Mr. Collins treated the commanding and other officers of the Jeannette.

The WITNESS. To my knowledge he treated them with the same respect that he was treated by them.

Question by the COURT. Did the crew of the Jeannette treat Mr. Collins with the respect that they did the other officers of the ship? If not, state in what manner he was treated differently.

The WITNESS. He was treated by the crew as they treated any of the other officers of the ship.

Question by the COURT. How did Mr. Collins treat the crew of the Jeannette in comparison with others in authority?

The WITNESS. The same as the others.

Question by the COURT. What experience have you had in handling boats, and do you consider yourself capable of managing a boat in bad weather?

The WITNESS. I have not had any experience in handling boats.

There being no further questions to ask this witness his testimony was here concluded, and the court then at 12.30 p. m. adjourned to meet on Monday, the 18th day of December, 1882, at 10.30 a. m.

FIFTY-NINTH DAY.

NAVY DEPARTMENT,
Washington, D. C., Monday, December 18, 1882—10.30 a. m.

The court met pursuant to the adjournment of Saturday, December 16, 1882.

Present, Commodore William G. Temple, United States Navy, president; Capt. Joseph N. Miller, United States Navy, Commander Frederick V. McNair, United States Navy, members; and Master Samuel C. Lemly, United States Navy, judge-advocate.

Seaman HENRY WILSON, the witness, then came in, and the judge-advocate read to him his testimony for correction, and he desired to add to his testimony on page 244, line 33, to the words, "Mr. Danenhower," the words "had charge of and managed the boat under the command of Mr. Melville," and the same was directed by the judge-advocate to be inserted in the body of the record by interlineation in red ink at the proper place for its suitable application to the evidence corrected; and with this addition made, he pronounced his evidence correct, and then withdrew.

The record of the proceedings of Saturday, December 16, 1882, the fifty-eighth day of the inquiry, was likewise read and approved by the court.

The judge-advocate then offered, and the court accepted, as evidence the deposition of Naval Constructor George W. Much, United States Navy, made in answer to interrogatories, which interrogatories with the answers thereto were read aloud, and the originals are appended to the record, marked, respectively, C D and D E.

LOSS OF THE STEAMER JEANNETTE.   247

The plans referred to as A, B, and C in the answer to the twelfth interrogatory were likewise placed before the court and accompany this record, marked, respectively, E F, F G, and G H.

The judge-advocate offered, and the court accepted, as evidence the deposition of Sir Allen William Young, R. N. R., &c., made in answer to interrogatories, which with the answers thereto were read aloud by the judge advocate, and the originals are appended to the record, marked, respectively, H I and I K.

The court was then, by request of the judge-advocate, cleared for deliberation, and afterwards reopened, and then, at 12 m., adjourned to meet to-morrow, the 19th day of December, 1882, at 10.30 a. m.

SIXTIETH DAY.

NAVY DEPARTMENT,
Washington, D. C., Tuesday, December 19, 1882—10.30 a. m.

The court met pursuant to the adjournment of yesterday, Monday, December 18, 1882.

Present, Commodore William G. Temple, United States Navy, president; Capt. Joseph N. Miller, United States Navy, Commander Frederick V. McNair, United States Navy, members; and Master Samuel C. Lemly, United States Navy, judge-advocate.

The record of the proceedings of Monday, December 18, 1882, the fifty-ninth day of the inquiry, was then read and approved.

The court was then, by request of a member, cleared for deliberation, and afterwards reopened.

The judge-advocate then placed before the court, as evidence bearing upon the management of the expedition, the following documents taken from the files of the Navy Department, having been found with the remains of the first cutter's party, each of which was read aloud, and certified copies were appended to the record as follows:

Lieut. Charles W. Chipp's report of visit to an Indian village off Cape Serdze Kerz, Siberia, dated August 30, 1879. (Exhibit K L.)

Lieut. Charles W. Chipp's report of a journey toward "Herald" Island, dated September 14, 1879; latitude north 71° 35′, longitude west 175° 6′. (Exhibit L M.)

Lieut. George W. De Long's order about ventilation, dated September 20, 1879; latitude 72° north, longitude 176° west. (Exhibit M N.)

Lieut. Charles W. Chipp's report on ice thickness, dated July 13, 1880. (Exhibit N O.)

Rough draft of a letter to the honorable Secretary of the Navy in regard to the heroic conduct of Alfred Sweetman (seaman) and W. F. C. Nindemann (seaman), dated March 20, 1881; latitude north 75° 15′, longitude east 171° 38′. (Exhibit O P.)

Order naming Jeannette and Henrietta Islands, dated June 15, 1881, latitude north 71° 15′, longitude east 158° 12′. (Exhibit P Q.)

And the court then, at 12 m., adjourned to meet to-morrow, the 20th day of December, 1882, at 10.30 a. m.

SIXTY-FIRST DAY.

Navy Department,
Washington, D. C., Wednesday, December 20, 1882—10.30 a. m.

The court met pursuant to the adjournment of yesterday, Tuesday, December 19, 1882.

Present, Commodore William G. Temple, United States Navy, president; Capt. Joseph N. Miller, United States Navy, Commander Frederick V. McNair, United States Navy, members; and Master Samuel C. Lemly, United States Navy, judge-advocate.

The record of the proceedings of Tuesday, December 19, 1882, the sixtieth day of the inquiry, was then read and approved.

Chief Engineer GEORGE W. MELVILLE, a former witness, was then recalled, and having been reminded that he is still under the obligations of his oath previously taken, was interrogated by the judge-advocate as follows:

Question by the JUDGE-ADVOCATE. Do you recognize the handwriting in which this document is written; and if yes, as whose? (The judge-advocate here handed the witness a document.)

The WITNESS. Yes; that is Captain De Long's handwriting.

Question by the JUDGE-ADVOCATE. Do you believe it to be the handwriting of the late Captain De Long?

The WITNESS. I do, sir.

Question by the JUDGE-ADVOCATE. Have you previously seen this same document? And if yes, state fully when and where.

The WITNESS. The first time that I saw this document was in the hut at Mat-Vai, when I removed it, along with other papers, from the tin case in which it and other papers were stowed; this and other papers were removed for the purpose of drying them, after which this and all the other papers were restowed in the boxes where found. The tin box in which these papers were was found on the bed of the river Cagoastak, west bank of the river, within ten or fifteen yards (possibly less) of the camp where most of the people were found dead, probably one hundred and fifty yards to the northward of where Lieutenant De Long, Dr. Ambler, and Ah Sam were found.

There being no further questions to ask this witness, the judge-advocate read to him his testimony just given, which he pronounced to be correct, and then withdrew.

The judge-advocate then commenced the reading of this document, the rough draft of Lieutenant-Commander De Long's report to the Secretary of the Navy of the cruise of the Jeannette, and the reading was continued until 1.30 p. m., when, pending its completion, the court adjourned to meet to-morrow, the 21st day of December, 1882, at 10.30 a. m.

SIXTY-SECOND DAY.

Navy Department,
Washington, D. C., Thursday, December 21, 1882—10.30 a. m.

The court met pursuant to the adjournment of yesterday.

Present, Commodore William G. Temple, United States Navy, president; Capt. Joseph N. Miller, United States Navy, Commander Frederick V. McNair, United States Navy, members; and Master Samuel C. Lemly, United States Navy, judge-advocate.

The record of the proceedings of Wednesday, December 20, 1882, the sixty-first day of the inquiry, was then read and approved.

And the court then, at 10.35 a. m., having to vacate the room to the use of the Naval Examining Board, adjourned to meet to-morrow, the 22d day of December, 1882, at 10.30 a. m.

SIXTY-THIRD DAY.

NAVY DEPARTMENT,
Washington, D. C., Friday, December 22, 1882—10.30 a. m.

The court met pursuant to the adjournment of yesterday.

Present, Commodore William G. Temple, United States Navy, president; Capt. Joseph N. Miller, United States Navy, Commander Frederick V. McNair, United States Navy, members; and Master Samuel C. Lemly, United States Navy, judge-advocate.

The record of the proceedings of yesterday, December 21, 1882, the sixty-second day of the inquiry, was then read and approved.

The judge-advocate then resumed the reading of the rough draft of Lieutenant-Commander De Long's report to the honorable Secretary of the Navy, which reading was completed.

The original of this report accompanies this record.

And the court then, at 12.45 p. m., to enable the judge-advocate to systematize the documentary evidence for presentation to the court, adjourned to meet on Tuesday, the 26th day of December, 1882, at 10 a. m.

SIXTY-FOURTH DAY.

NAVY DEPARTMENT,
Washington, D. C., Tuesday, December 26, 1882—10 a. m.

The court met pursuant to the adjournment of Friday, December 22, 1882.

Present, Commodore William G. Temple, United States Navy, president; Capt. Joseph N. Miller, United States Navy, Commander Frederick V. McNair, United States Navy, members; and Master Samuel C. Lemly, United States Navy, judge-advocate.

The record of the proceedings of Friday, December 22, 1882, the sixty-third day of the inquiry, was then read and approved.

The court then occupied the time until 12 m. in the examination of the late Lieutenant-Commander De Long's "Ice Journal," and then adjourned to meet on Wednesday, the 27th day of December, 1882, at 10.30 a. m.

SIXTY-FIFTH DAY.

NAVY DEPARTMENT,
Washington, D. C., Wednesday, December 27, 1882—10.30 a. m.

The court met pursuant to the adjournment of yesterday.

Present, Commodore William G. Temple, United States Navy, president; Capt. Joseph N. Miller, United States Navy, Commander Fred-

erick V. McNair, United States Navy, members; Master Samuel C. Lemly, United States Navy, judge-advocate.

The record of the proceedings of yesterday, December 26, 1882, the sixty-fourth day of the inquiry, was then read and approved.

The judge-advocate then placed before the court, as evidence bearing upon the management of the expedition and the conduct and merits of the officers and men of the expedition, the report of Chief Engineer Melville's trip to Henrietta Island, with chart attached, the original of which accompanies this record, not appended.

The court then occupied the time until 12 m. in the examination of the late Lieutenant-Commander De Long's journal, already in evidence, and then adjourned to meet to-morrow, the 28th day of December, 1882, at 10.30 a. m.

SIXTY-SIXTH DAY.

NAVY DEPARTMENT,
Washington, D. C., Thursday, December 28, 1882—10.30 a. m.

The court met pursuant to the adjournment of yesterday.

Present, Commodore William G. Temple, United States Navy, president; Capt. Joseph N. Miller, United States Navy, Commander Frederick V. McNair, United States Navy, members; and Master Samuel C. Lemly, United States Navy, judge-advocate.

The record of the proceedings of yesterday, December 27, 1882, the sixty-fifth day of the inquiry, was then read and approved.

The court then occupied the time until 12 m. in examining the journal of the late Lieutenant-Commander De Long, and then adjourned to meet on Tuesday, January 2, 1883, at 10.30 a. m.

SIXTY-SEVENTH DAY.

NAVY DEPARTMENT,
Washington, D. C., Tuesday, January 2, 1883—10.30 a. m.

The court met pursuant to the adjournment of Thursday, December 28, 1882.

Present, Commodore William G. Temple, United States Navy, president; Capt. Joseph N. Miller, United States Navy, Commander Frederick V. McNair, United States Navy, members; and Master Samuel C. Lemly, United States Navy, judge-advocate.

The record of the proceedings of Thursday, December 28, 1882, the sixty-sixth day of the inquiry, was then read and approved.

Lieut. J. W. DANENHOWER, United States Navy, a former witness, was then recalled, to testify in behalf of the late Jerome J. Collins, and having been reminded by the president of the court of the obligation of his oath previously taken, was examined by the judge-advocate as follows:

Question by the JUDGE-ADVOCATE. Do you know of any trouble between the commanding officer of the Jeannette and the late Mr. Collins, meteorologist of the Jeannette expedition? If yes, what was it?

The WITNESS. Yes, there was trouble. It commenced in September, 1879, when the captain gave an order that no one should leave the ship without his permission. Mr. Collins thought it was directed specially toward him, and he made a silent protest against it by remaining on board for many months without asking for this permission. Another trouble occurred on November 1, 1879, when the order was given for a medical examination to be made on the 1st of every month. Mr. Collins, with some others, objected to stripping before the surgeon, and the captain modified the order, and during the winter of 1879–'80 there were numerous discussions going on between the captain and Mr. Collins on the subject of duty. On one occasion I heard the captain tell Mr. Collins that if he was not satisfied with the way the duty was carried on, he could report him to the Secretary of the Navy on the return of the ship, and that he, the captain, would certainly report Mr. Collins. The trouble culminated on December 2, 1880, when the captain placed Mr. Collins under suspension, directing that he should do no more duty while on the ship. That is all, sir.

Question by the JUDGE-ADVOCATE. On one occasion, when Mr. Collins and others went after a bear, what did Lieutenant De Long say when you reported them absent?

The WITNESS. It was the Sunday on which Lieutenant Chipp and party returned from Herald Island. A bear was sighted about nine o'clock, and Nindemann started in pursuit, and was followed by myself and Mr. Collins and Mr. Newcomb. The bear distanced the party, and we saw there was no chance. Nindemann was five hundred yards ahead, running in his stocking feet; Mr. Collins and Mr. Newcomb came up with me and we three concluded there was no chance for getting the bear, but that Nindemann should be supported. As it was time to prepare the ship for inspection, I went back, and at 10 o'clock reported the ship ready and that three people were absent, and explained to the captain the cause; I think he made no particular remark, except "Very well," perhaps, and that day the order was issued that nobody should leave the ship without permission.

Question by the JUDGE-ADVOCATE. If issued, what led to the order that all the seamen should be examined naked once a month?

The WITNESS. The captain and the doctor had a consultation on the subject. I suppose that that was the result. I understood at the time that such an order was issued, and that Mr. Collins and three others objected; I understood that the order referred to everybody.

Question by the JUDGE-ADVOCATE. Do you know that Mr. Collins was subjected to that examination?

The WITNESS. I do not know; but I am confident that he was not, from what he told me at the time.

Question by the JUDGE-ADVOCATE. Were any of the other officers?

The WITNESS. No; they were examined to the waist, after the order was modified—that was the modification of the order. The seamen, I understood, were naked.

Question by the JUDGE-ADVOCATE. Were you present when Lieutenant De Long placed Mr. Collins under arrest? If yes, relate all the circumstances.

The WITNESS. I was present. On the 2d day of December, 1880, when the lights were put out in the cabin, between 11 a. m. and 1 p. m., I went up from below, and about 12.10 Mr. Collins came in to record the noon observations. He lighted a candle in the port work-room and chatted with me or whistled at times. He was in very good spirits at the time. The seaman on watch first came in, put his head into the work-room, and went out without saying anything. A few moments later the captain came in and spoke to Mr. Collins to the effect that it was very strange that he, Mr. Collins, would not obey his orders to exercise on the ice. Mr. Collins stated that he was taking the noon observations, and the captain replied that it was strange that it should take twenty minutes to make an entry, to take off his coat, and smoke, and to talk with an officer while taking it. Mr. Collins replied quickly that he did not like being chased up in that way; that he did not know that his moments were counted. The captain said the matter had gone far enough. It had better be decided then. He told him to take off his coat, which in the mean time he had put on—his fur coat. I immediately went below. The conversation that followed was in very loud tones, and I suppose the most of it came to my ears, although my room was shut up as close as could be. A long discussion followed, and it finally came to a point at which a disagreement took place, and a contradiction was involved. I heard the captain say "That is enough, sir; you have done your last duty in this ship." Then he told Mr. Collins to finish up his work to date. Mr. Collins left the cabin. The captain then called me, and asked if I had heard the trouble; I told him "yes," and commenced to relate what I had heard. Then, thinking that it might give a wrong impression, I said I had rather put what I knew in writing; and that afternoon I dictated to Mr. Chipp what I knew about it, and signed it. The next day at noon-time the captain came in the cabin to record the noon observation. He again referred to the subject of the previous day, and expressed regret at such a thing taking place aboard ship. I also said that I was sorry that I was a witness to the affair, and he said that it did not make any difference; that I would not be brought up in the matter. That is all, sir. I think that covers the question.

Question by the JUDGE-ADVOCATE. Do you know when Mr. Collins' notes, photographs, sketches, &c., were lost?

The WITNESS. I do not know. I think his big book went down in the ship. It was a quarto volume of about three hundred pages, bound in sheepskin; it was a very expensive, fine book. He may have kept private notes, but that was his chief log-book.

Question by the JUDGE-ADVOCATE. Do you know whether or not he was prevented from rescuing them?

The WITNESS. I am confident he was not prevented. I know nothing special on that subject. Mr. Collins was sitting for some time in the cabin before the order was given to abandon the ship, and his movements were perfectly free as far as a looker-on could judge.

Question by the JUDGE-ADVOCATE. Was Mr. Collins treated as a prisoner; that is, was he compelled to march behind the party, disarmed?

The WITNESS. He was for a time, but after he made the request he was allowed to carry a Winchester rifle; but his status I did not fully understand at the time. I cannot say he was a prisoner, and only know that he was suspended from work. He was free in his movements, but he was ordered to stop work after having worked for some days after the retreat commenced.

Question by the JUDGE-ADVOCATE. Did Mr. Collins tell you anything about the treatment he received?

(The judge-advocate objected to this question as calling for hearsay, and the court was cleared for deliberation upon the objection and afterwards reopened, the witness being present, and the president of the court announced as the decision of the court that the objection of the judge-advocate was sustained and the question shall not be put.)

Question by the JUDGE-ADVOCATE. If you had had your eye-sight and the command of the party when you landed, would you have remained thirty-five days at Geeomovialocke while a native and an exile were looking for your shipmates?

The WITNESS. I would have been forced to have remained for twenty days by the state of the party and by the state of the weather; but I would have gone with the people, or sent some one with them if I had been unable to go myself. Kusmah, Jeremiehoff, and the native were sent as messengers to Bulun, to bring back transportation, clothing, and provisions. They were not looking for our shipmates.

Question by the JUDGE-ADVOCATE. What was Mr. Melville's treatment of the natives when your party reached Geeomovialocke?

The WITNESS. His treatment of the natives was good, but they did the treating. We simply received what they gave us and were glad to get it. Mr. Melville explained that the two boats were missing by means of pieces of wood on a table, indicating that the boats had been dispersed by the gale and that two had probably been lost. His treatment of the natives was kind and good. I was not present when the natives refused to go with him from Cape Borkhia. I was out getting some bearings for the direction of the wind and the time of day.

Question by the JUDGE-ADVOCATE. Did they refuse to render assistance because of ill treatment at his hands?

The WITNESS. No; they said it was impossible to go north on account of the push-ice in the rivers, and that there were no habitations nor people north of the village of Arii (Arrhue), which was ten versts from Geeomovialocke.

Question by the JUDGE-ADVOCATE. Did you know, while at Geeomovialocke, what was the cause of the delay of the two messengers sent to Bulun?

The WITNESS. When the time specified elapsed and Kusmah did not return, his wife came over and told us that the commandant at Bulun was dead, and that that was the cause of the delay. One by one other natives came with sleds from the direction of Bulun, and we could not understand the cause of Kusmah's delay. On his return, he claimed that he had to make many portages of the goods, and that the river ice was broken up in many places and that he had great difficulty in getting across. I have never heard before the last two months that the men were drunk, and I know that Kusmah told me that he did not drink; that he did not use tobacco. On one occasion he had vodki in his house, but he refused to drink himself. I think Nicolai Shagra was a sober man, and I do not believe the story of their drunkenness.

Question by the JUDGE-ADVOCATE. Did you start to relieve your shipmates at any time?

The WITNESS. I stated in my testimony that I made an effort to reach Barkin and was engaged about four days on the trip—parts of four days. That was while Kusmah was on the journey to Bulun. I also made a special visit to Kusmah's house to impress upon him the necessity of passing the word everywhere—spreading the news that the two boats were missing, and that he would have a thousand roubles for each boat, for intelligence from either boat. I also wrote a letter on this visit, the 14th of October, and asked him to mail it at Bulun, and he did so. That was the only document he had from the party.

Question by the JUDGE-ADVOCATE. Did you receive an order to return or was any one sent to bring you back?

The WITNESS. Mr. Melville told me to return before Kusmah got back in order not to delay the party should Kusmah arrive on time. I know of no one being sent to bring me back on that occasion. I was told——

(The judge-advocate objected, and the witness was instructed by the court to confine his testimony to that which is within his own knowledge.)

Question by the JUDGE-ADVOCATE. What did Mr. Melville and party do during the time they were at Geeomovialocke?

The WITNESS. During the first ten days, all except Aniguin, Mr. Cole, Wilson, and myself were in the berths, disabled with frozen, swollen limbs and stomach disorder. One by one they came on duty, and at the expiration of that time—ten days—most of them were able to work, except Leach, who had to spend most of his time in his berth. There was a regular detail made for getting fire-wood, drift-wood, from under the snow and cutting it up. The men were mending their clothes and making new mittens, getting things as neat as possible. In the evenings we sat around the fire and discussed the situation and prospect for marching to Bulun without the aid of the natives. It was generally supposed that the other two boats had not outlived the gale. There was a checkerboard made, or rather a piece of canvas arranged in squares, and some played checkers. Mr. Melville, however, did not play, nor did I. Some of us used to go out walking regularly, others used to remain in most of the time. The household duties kept two or three very busy, cleaning the fish and preparing it. On some occasions I hauled nets with the natives, and during the first three weeks the returns of fish were very small, but after that time there was a great run of fish in the river and they were stacked up like cord wood, in the fish houses. We always used to lend the natives a hand in hauling up their boats and we were on very good terms with them, constantly receiving and making visits. I know of no disagreeable occurrence between our party and the natives of Geeomovialocke.

Question by the JUDGE-ADVOCATE. Was there any discipline, and if so, of what kind was it?

The WITNESS. There was all the discipline requisite on such an occasion. The cook called us about half an hour before breakfast, and we all washed and swept out the place. Cleanliness and cheerfulness were always recommended and enforced.

Question by the JUDGE-ADVOCATE. What were the opinions of Nindemann and Noros, when they were met, as to the probability of saving De Long; had an effort been made during the time the party (Melville's) were at Geeomovialocke?

(The judge-advocate objected to this question as calling for hearsay, and opinions of witnesses who have already testified before the court.

The objection of the judge-advocate was sustained by the court.)

Question by the JUDGE-ADVOCATE. Did you hear either of them say it was criminal negligence on his, Melville's, part not to look out for his comrades?

(The judge-advocate objected to this question, upon the grounds heretofore stated for the preceding question, and the objection was sustained by the court.)

Question by the JUDGE-ADVOCATE. Did you see Mr. Collins writing a report at any time?

The WITNESS. I frequently saw him writing in passing his stateroom at various times of the cruise. I have seen him writing in the chart room. I understood at the time that he was keeping a full journal of the cruise as a part of his duty.

Question by the JUDGE-ADVOCATE. Was Mr. Collins spoken of or regarded as a common seaman on board the Jeannette?

The WITNESS. I never heard him spoken of as such. He was shipped as a seaman for a special service, but always spoken of as an officer.

He took his place among the officers when the Articles of War were read and on all occasions of ceremony; he had a room in the wardroom and messed in the cabin, and was always regarded as an officer in addressing him and in the general bearing of the men toward him.

The court was here cleared by request of the judge-advocate and afterward reopened, the witness being present.

The judge-advocate did not desire to further examine or to cross-examine this witness, and as the court did not desire to examine him, his testimony was concluded.

The court then, at 12.10 p. m., in order to give the stenographer time to prepare the record, adjourned to meet to-morrow, the 3d day of January, 1883, at 10.30 a. m.

SIXTY-EIGHTH DAY.

NAVY DEPARTMENT,
Washington, D. C., Wednesday, January 3, 1883—10.30 a. m.

The court met pursuant to the adjournment of yesterday.

Present, Commodore William G. Temple, United States Navy, president; Capt. Joseph N. Miller, United States Navy, Commander Frederick V. McNair, United States Navy, members; and Master Samuel C. Lemly, United States Navy, judge-advocate.

The witness, Lieut. J. W. Danenhower, then came in and the judge-advocate read to him his testimony for correction, which he pronounced to be correct and then withdrew.

The record of the proceedings of yesterday, January 2, 1883, the sixty-seventh day of the inquiry, was likewise read and approved.

And the court then, at 11.30 a. m., adjourned to meet on Monday, January 15, 1883, at 10.30 a. m.

SIXTY-NINTH DAY.

NAVY DEPARTMENT,
Washington, D. C., Monday, January 15, 1883—10.30 a. m.

The court met pursuant to the adjournment of Wednesday, January 3, 1883.

Present, Commodore William G. Temple, United States Navy, president; Capt. Joseph N. Miller, United States Navy, Commander Frederick V. McNair, United States Navy, members; and Master Samuel C. Lemly, United States Navy, judge-advocate.

The record of the proceedings of Wednesday, January 3, 1883, the sixty-eighth day of the inquiry, was then read and approved.

Chief Engineer GEORGE W. MELVILLE, United States Navy, a former witness, was then recalled, and, having been reminded of his oath previously taken, was examined by the judge-advocate as follows:

Question by the JUDGE-ADVOCATE. Are you familiar with the handwriting in which this journal and letter are written; and, if yes, whose is it? (The judge-advocate here handed the witness a small memorandum book, and also the rough draft of a letter without address or signature.)

The WITNESS. Yes; it is in the handwriting of Mr. Collins, meteorologist of the Jeannette. I looked over this book when it was taken from Mr. Collins' body, and this paper I also recognize as Mr. Collins' handwriting; but when found on his body the sizing in the paper had glued it together, so that I could read the outside only.

The judge-advocate placed before the court the memorandum book in question, which contains a record of the events of June, July, August, and September, 1881, which the court proceeded to examine. The original journal accompanies this record.

Question by the JUDGE-ADVOCATE. State, if you know, in whose handwriting these documents are written, and when and where, if at all, you have seen them before. (The judge-advocate here handed the witness three papers.)

The WITNESS. This is in Captain De Long's handwriting, and is the order that was passed around to all of the cabin officers to read for their information and to govern their action in regard to reporting leave of absence and return to ship. This letter I recognize as Captain De Long's handwriting and the memorandum. I first saw them at the hut Mat Vay, where I removed them from the tin cases in which they had been placed on board the Jeannette.

Question by the JUDGE-ADVOCATE. Did you receive from any one a report of the action of the party composed of Mr. Jackson, Mr. Larson, and Seaman Noros in disinterring the bodies of Lieutenant-Commander De Long, Dr. Ambler, and Mr. Collins?

The WITNESS. No; I did not. The first knowledge I had of the bodies having been disinterred I read in a Philadelphia paper—about the time the evidence was given before the court.

The judge-advocate did not desire to further examine this witness, and the court not desiring to examine him, his testimony was read to him and pronounced by him to be correct.

The witness then withdrew.

The judge-advocate then proceeded to read aloud to the court the documents identified by the witness, and certified copies are appended to the records as follows:

Rough draft of the letter identified by the witness as being in the handwriting of the late Jerome J. Collins, but without date, superscription, or signature. (Exhibit Q R.)

Order in relation to reporting, leaving, and returning to ship, dated October 30, 1880. (Exhibit R S.)

Memorandum in relation to affair of December 2, 1880, concerning Mr. Collins. (Exhibit S T.)

Rough draft of a letter to the honorable Secretary of the Navy in regard to Mr. J. J. Collins, dated March 20, 1881, in latitude north 75° 15', longitude east 171° 36'. (Exhibit T U.)

The court was then, by request of a member, cleared for deliberation, and afterwards reopened.

And then, at 12.20 p. m., in order to allow the judge-advocate to prepare the entire record, adjourned to meet on Monday, the 22d day of January, 1883, at 10.30 a. m.

SEVENTIETH DAY.

NAVY DEPARTMENT,
Washington, D. C., Monday, January 22, 1883—10.30 a. m.

The court met pursuant to the adjournment of Monday, January 15, 1883.

LOSS OF THE STEAMER JEANNETTE. 257

Present, Commodore William G. Temple, United States Navy, president; Capt. Joseph N. Miller, United States Navy, Commander Frederick V. McNair, United States Navy, members; and Master Samuel C. Lemly, United States Navy, judge-advocate.
The court was then cleared for deliberation, and afterwards, at 11.50 a. m., reopened.
The record of the proceedings of Monday, January 15, 1883, the sixty-ninth day of the inquiry, was then read and approved, and the court then, at 12 m., adjourned to meet to-morrow, the 23d day of January, 1883, at 10.30 a. m.

SEVENTY-FIRST DAY.

NAVY DEPARTMENT,
Washington, D. C., Tuesday, January 23, 1883—10.30 a. m.
The court met pursuant to the adjournment of yesterday.
Present, Commodore William G. Temple, United States Navy, president; Capt. Joseph N. Miller, United States Navy, Commander Frederick V. McNair, United States Navy, members; and Master Samuel C. Lemly, United States Navy, judge-advocate.
The record of the proceedings of yesterday, January 22, 1883, the seventieth day of the inquiry, was then read and approved.
The court was then cleared for deliberation, and sat with closed doors until 12.50 p. m., when it was reopened, and then adjourned to meet to-morrow the 24th day of January, 1883, at 10 a. m.

SEVENTY-SECOND DAY.

NAVY DEPARTMENT,
Washington, D. C., Wednesday, January 24, 1883—10 a. m.
The court met pursuant to the adjournment of yesterday.
Present, Commodore William G. Temple, United States Navy, president; Capt. Joseph N. Miller, United States Navy, Commander Frederick V. McNair, United States Navy, members; and Master Samuel C. Lemly, United States Navy, judge-advocate.
The record of the proceedings of yesterday, January 23, 1883, the seventy-first day of the inquiry, was then read and approved.
The court was here cleared for deliberation, and sat with closed doors until 1.35 p. m., when it was reopened, and then adjourned to meet to-morrow, the 25th day of January, 1883, at 10.30 a. m.

SEVENTY-THIRD DAY.

NAVY DEPARTMENT,
Washington, D. C., Thursday, January 25, 1883—10.30 a. m.
The court met pursuant to the adjournment of yesterday.
Present, Commodore William G. Temple, United States Navy, president; Capt. Joseph N. Miller, United States Navy, Commander Frede-

rick V. McNair, United States Navy, members; and Master Samuel C. Lemly, United States Navy, judge-advocate.

The record of the proceedings of yesterday, January 24, 1883, the seventy-second day of the inquiry, was then read and approved.

The court was then cleared for deliberation, and sat with closed doors until 12 m., when it was reopened, and then adjourned to meet to-morrow, the 26th day of January, 1883, at 10.30 a. m.

SEVENTY-FOURTH DAY.

NAVY DEPARTMENT,
Washington, D. C., Friday, January 26, 1883—10.30 a. m.

The court met pursuant to the adjournment of yesterday.

Present, Commodore Wm. G. Temple, United States Navy, president; Capt. Joseph N. Miller, United States Navy, Commander Frederick V. McNair, United States Navy, members; and Master Samuel C. Lemly, United States Navy, judge-advocate.

The record of the proceedings of yesterday, January 25, 1883, the seventy-third day of the inquiry, was then read and approved.

The court was then cleared for deliberation, and sat with closed doors until 11.30 a. m., and then, in consequence of the indisposition of a member, adjourned to meet to-morrow, the 27th day of January, 1883, at 10.30 a. m.

SEVENTY-FIFTH DAY.

NAVY DEPARTMENT,
Washington, D. C., Saturday, January 27, 1883—10.30 a. m.

The court met pursuant to the adjournment of yesterday.

Present, Commodore William G. Temple, United States Navy, president; Capt. Joseph N. Miller, United States Navy, Commander Frederick V. McNair, United States Navy, members; and Master Samuel C. Lemly, United States Navy, judge-advocate.

The record of the proceedings of yesterday, January 26, 1883, the seventy-fourth day of the inquiry, was then read and approved.

The court was then cleared for deliberation, and sat with closed doors until 12 m., when the doors were reopened and a recess was taken until 1 p. m., at which time the court reconvened with all the members and the judge-advocate present.

The court was then again cleared for deliberation, and remained in session until 1.30 p. m., when the doors were reopened and an adjournment was taken until Tuesday, February 6, 1883, at 10 a. m.

SEVENTY-SIXTH DAY.

NAVY DEPARTMENT,
Washington, D. C., Tuesday, February 6, 1883—10 a. m.

The court met pursuant to the adjournment of Saturday, January 27, 1883.

Present, Commodore William G. Temple, United States Navy, presi-

LOSS OF THE STEAMER JEANNETTE. 259

dent; Capt. Joseph N. Miller, United States Navy, Commander Frederick V. McNair, United States Navy, members; and Master Samuel C. Lemly, United States Navy, judge-advocate.

The record of the proceedings of Saturday, January 27, 1883, the seventy-fifth day of the inquiry, was then read and approved.

The court was then cleared for deliberation, and sat until 2 p. m., when the doors were opened and an adjournment was taken until tomorrow, Wednesday, February 7, 1883, at 10.30 a. m.

SEVENTY-SEVENTH DAY.

NAVY DEPARTMENT,
Washington, D. C., Wednesday, February 7, 1883—10.30 a. m.

The court met pursuant to the adjournment of yesterday.

Present, Commodore William G. Temple, United States Navy, president; Capt. Joseph N. Miller, United States Navy, Commander Frederick V. McNair, United States Navy, members; and Master Samuel C. Lemly, United States Navy, judge-advocate.

The record of the proceedings of yesterday, February 6, 1883, the seventy-sixth day of the inquiry, was then read and approved.

The court was then cleared for deliberation and sat until 1 p. m., when the doors were opened and an adjournment was taken until Friday, February 9, 1883, at 10.30 a. m.

SEVENTY-EIGHTH DAY.

NAVY DEPARTMENT,
Washington, D. C., Friday, February 9, 1883—10.30 a. m.

The court met pursuant to the adjournment of Wednesday, February 7, 1883.

Present, Commodore William G. Temple, United States Navy, president; Capt. Joseph N. Miller, United States Navy, Commander Frederick V. McNair, United States Navy, members; and Master Samuel C. Lemly, United States Navy, judge-advocate.

The record of the proceedings of Wednesday, February 7, the seventy-seventh day of the inquiry, was then read and approved.

The court was then cleared for deliberation and sat until 3.10 p. m., when the doors were reopened and an adjournment taken until to-morrow, Saturday, February 10, 1883, at 10.30 a. m.

SEVENTY-NINTH DAY.

NAVY DEPARTMENT,
Washington, D. C., Saturday, February 10, 1883—10.30 a. m.

The court met pursuant to the adjournment of yesterday.

Present, Commodore William G. Temple, United States Navy, president; Capt. Joseph N. Miller, United States Navy, Commander Frederick V. McNair, United States Navy, members; and Master Samuel C. Lemly, United States Navy, judge-advocate.

The record of the proceedings of yesterday, February 9, 1883, the seventy-eighth day of the inquiry, was then read and approved.

The court was then cleared and deliberated until 1 p. m., when the doors were reopened.

The judge-advocate read aloud and placed before the court a telegram to the honorable Secretary of the Navy, from Ensign Hunt, attached to the search party in Siberia, a certified copy of which is appended to the record, marked U V.

The judge-advocate then announced that he had at present no further evidence to lay before the court, and the court then, at 12.15 p. m., adjourned to meet on Monday, the 12th day of February, 1883, at 10.30 a. m.

EIGHTIETH DAY.

NAVY DEPARTMENT,
Washington, D. C., Monday, February 12, 1883—10.30 a. m.

The court met pursuant to the adjournment of Saturday, February 10, 1883.

Present, Commodore William G. Temple, United States Navy, president; Capt. Joseph N. Miller, United States Navy, Commander Frederick V. McNair, United States Navy, members; and Master Samuel C. Lemly, United States Navy, judge-advocate.

The record of the proceedings of Saturday, February 10, 1883, the seventy-ninth day of the inquiry, was then read and approved.

The court was then cleared for deliberation, and agreed upon the following report:

In conformity with a joint resolution of the Congress approved August 8, 1882, and in compliance with the orders of the honorable Secretary of the Navy, dated September 29, 1882, the court of inquiry has diligently and thoroughly investigated—

The circumstances of the loss in the Arctic seas of the exploring steamer Jeannette, and of the death of Lieut. George W. De Long, and others of her officers and men.

The court has also carefully inquired

Into the condition of the vessel on her departure, her management up to the time of her destruction, the provisions made and plans adopted for the several boats' crews on their leaving the wreck, the efforts made by the various officers to insure the safety of the parties under their immediate charge, and for the relief of the other parties, and into the general conduct and merits, and of each and all the officers and men of the expedition.

And the court transmits herewith its proceedings, the testimony taken, and after mature deliberation reports that the following facts are deemed established by the evidence adduced:

First. As to "the condition of the vessel on her departure."

The Jeannette was originally Her Britannic Majesty's ship Pandora, and was purchased from the British Government in April, 1875, by Sir Allen W. Young, who made two voyages in her to the Arctic regions, and who finally sold her to Mr. James Gordon Bennett in 1877.

By an act of Congress approved February 27, 1879, she was accepted under certain conditions by the United States Government for the purpose of making further explorations in the Arctic regions, and although the weight of the evidence shows that she was not especially adapted in strength or model for that kind of navigation, the fact that an experienced Arctic explorer had voluntarily made two cruises in her to the Arctic seas sustains the judgment and care shown in her selection when last purchased.

The vessel was strengthened as much as practicable at the navy-yard, Mare Island, California, and such other additions and improvements were made as were recommended by her commanding officer, and the condition of the Jeannette on her departure from the port of San Francisco was good, and satisfactory to her officers and crew, except that she was unavoidably deeply loaded, a defect which corrected itself by the consumption of coal, provisions, and stores.

Second. As to "her management up to the time of her loss."

The lateness of the season when the Jeannette sailed from San Francisco, her want of speed, and the delay occasioned by her search along the Siberian coast, under orders from the Navy Department, for the Swedish exploring steamer Vega, placed the commander at a great disadvantage on his meeting with the pack-ice early in September, in the vicinity of Herald Island. Either he had to return to some port to the southward, and pass the winter there in idleness, thus sacrificing all chance of pushing his researches to the northward until the following summer, or else he must endeavor to force the vessel through to Wrangel Island, then erroneously supposed to be a large continent, to winter there, and prosecute his explorations by sledges. The chances of accomplishing this latter alternative were sufficiently good at the time to justify him in choosing it; and, indeed, had he done otherwise, he might fairly have been thought wanting in the high qualities necessary for an explorer.

This attempt unfortunately resulted in the vessel's becoming beset in the ice-pack within less than two months after her departure from San Francisco, from which she was never released until her destruction, more than twenty-one months later.

During these weary months of forced inaction the vessel and her people were at times threatened with great dangers. Especially was her destruction imminent on January 19, 1880, when she sprung a leak from ice pressures, and for months after that date she was kept afloat only by skillful devices and arduous labor.

It may be here mentioned that throughout the expedition every opportunity was improved for gaining scientific information. Meteorological and astronomical observations, temperature and density of the sea-water, and soundings were taken and preserved; studies of the character and action of the ice were noted, specimens of the bottom and of such fauna and flora as could be procured were examined. Three islands were discovered, two of which were visited, explored, and taken possession of in the name of the United States.

The arrangements to abandon ship at a moment's warning, and to guard against fire, were all that could be desired, and the evidence shows that in the management of the Jeannette up to the time of her destruction Lieutenant-Commander De Long, by his foresight and prudence, provided measures to meet emergencies, and enforced wise regulations to maintain discipline, to preserve health, and to encourage cheerfulness among those under his command; and the physical condition of the people was good, with the exception of a few cases of lead poisoning, the result of eating canned provisions. The fact of the ship's having passed a second winter in the pack without any appearance of scurvy on board sufficiently attests the excellence of the sanitary arrangements adopted, and reflects great credit upon her medical officer,

Passed Assistant Surgeon James M. Ambler, who throughout the expedition was indefatigable in the performance of his duties.

Third. As to the circumstances of the loss in the Arctic seas of the exploring steamer Jeannette.

The Jeannette was sunk on June 13, 1881, from being crushed by the ice in latitude 77° 15' north; longitude 155° 50' east, after drifting uncontrollably in the pack ice since September 6, 1879. Any vessel in like position, no matter what her model might have been, or however strongly constructed, and subjected to the same pressures as those incurred by the Jeannette, would have been annihilated.

She was abandoned in a cool and orderly manner on the evening of June 12th, and foundered about 4 a. m. the day following, and the court attaches no blame to any officer or man for her loss.

Fourth. As to "the provisions made and plans adopted for the several boats' crews upon their leaving the wreck."

The contingency of the loss of the vessel had been foreseen and provided for, and when the emergency arose, everything was prepared to meet it.

The officers and men were divided into three parties and assigned to the boats best fitted for the anticipated work; boat and provision-sledges had been provided, and more boats, clothing, provisions, and stores were removed from the vessel than could be transported on the retreat.

The party being thus thrown upon the ice, five days were passed in arranging for the long journey to the land, and the provisions made and plans adopted for the several boats' crews upon their leaving the wreck were judicious, as the evidence shows that ninety days after the destruction of the Jeannette the officers and men were in fair condition, notwithstanding their terrible journey.

Fifth. As to "the efforts made by the various officers to insure the safety of the parties under their immediate charge, and for the relief of the other parties."

The retreat commenced on the 18th of June; and during the ensuing three months the entire ship's company remained together, under the direction of the commander, struggling against obstacles which required indomitable pluck and perseverance to overcome—compelled to drag their heavy boats and loads of provisions over broken and shifting fields of ice, at times ferrying them over the water spaces, and often carried far out of their course by the drift of the pack, delayed by storms, fogs, and snows; there seems to have been no precaution neglected which would tend to insure their safety. During this time, as well as upon other occasions, the conduct of Ice Pilot Dunbar, Boatswain Cole, and Fireman Bartlett elicited well-deserved commendations.

The original plan of retreat was to make a southerly course, presumably to reach the open water as soon as possible, and thence by way of the New Siberian Islands to the delta of the Lena, the nearest point at which it was supposed that relief could be obtained. But the commander found after a time, by observation, that the current was sweeping them so rapidly to the northward and westward that their labor was almost in vain, and that the course made good was but little to the southward of west. He wisely refrained from discouraging the party by announcing this fact, and changed his course so as to cross this current at right angles, and get beyond its influence as soon as practicable.

After twenty-three days of toil and anxiety, Bennett Island was discovered, where they landed, and occupied eight days in resting and making necessary repairs to boats. In trying to reach this island the party suffered many disappointments and encountered unexpected dangers, difficulties, and delays in overcoming a very short distance, owing to the swift currents and rapid movements of the broken ice close to the shore.

A further delay, from August 19 to August 29, was afterwards forced upon the party by the condition of the ice, which rendered progress impossible. Meantime it had been deemed expedient at Bennett Island, in order to save food for the men, that about half of the dogs should be killed, as they were no longer needed to drag the sleds, and it was considered inhuman to leave them there to starve, and afterwards all but two of them escaped on the ice; but still it was found necessary to reduce the allowance of provisions from time to time during the remainder of the journey.

On the 12th of September the three boats were separated in a gale of wind when approaching the Siberian coast, at an estimated distance of about ninety miles to the northward and eastward of the Lena delta, and no further record exists of the second cutter's party, but as Lieutenant Chipp, who was in charge of her, was noted for his seamanlike qualities, it may safely be assumed that he did all that a brave and capable man could do to weather the gale.

The first cutter and whale-boat, under the command respectively of Lieutenant-Commander De Long and Chief Engineer Melville, barely managed to live through the gale by riding to sea-anchors, and in rounding to, the first cutter carried away the stép of her mast, and the next day lost her sail, which formed a portion of her drag. During the gale the professional services of Lieutenant Danenhower, who was on the sick list, were called into requisition, and he is deserving of credit for the skill with which he managed the whale-boat, as well as for her subsequent navigation to the land.

When the weather moderated, both boats endeavored to reach Cape Barkin, the northeast point of the Lena delta, upon which the charts erroneously indicated winter huts and inhabitants.

The whale-boat, with eleven people on board, on striking shoal water out of sight of land, stood to the eastward, and hauling in for the land the next day, she was fortunate enough on September 16 to enter one of the eastern mouths of the Lena River, and three days afterwards fell in with natives, who guided them to the village of Geeomovialocke, where they arrived on the 25th, and subsisted until they were able to communicate with the commandant of Bulum.

In the mean time, the first cutter, with fourteen persons in all, had made the best of her way under a jury mast and sail towards the land; but encountering young ice and shoal water, the party on the 17th of September was forced to abandon the boat a mile and a half from the beach, and to wade ashore through the ice and mud, carrying the few remaining stores and provisions on their backs. They had the misfortune to land at the mouth of one of the northern outlets of the Lena River, where no inhabitants were to be found, although a considerable village, not indicated on their charts, and consequently unsuspected by them, lay some twenty-five miles to the westward.

They had landed frost-bitten and exhausted, with only a few days' provisions, which were eked out by a meager supply of game. They began their painful journey to the southward, hampered in their movements by those who were disabled, but encouraged from time to time by traces of recent occupancy in the huts, and footprints about the fox-traps which they encountered on the way, and they struggled on manfully, misled by their imperfect map of the country, and always imagining themselves near a place of refuge, until toward the end of October, when, after eating their remaining dog, they perished from hunger and cold, all but two—Seamen Nindemann and Noros, whom the commander had previously sent on in advance for assistance, and who, after great hardships, were found and rescued by the natives. These two men did their utmost to make the natives understand the condition of the commander's party, and to induce them to go to its relief, but without success. It seems that there was some confusion in the minds of these people between the commander's party and that under Mr. Melville at Geeomovialocke, but the two seamen knew nothing of the whale-boat's fate, and could not therefore guess at the mistake; nor is it probable that if they had returned they would have found any of the commander's party alive.

Meanwhile the whale-boat's party remained five weeks at Geeomovialocke, living upon the limited hospitality of a few poor natives, who saw their winter supplies rapidly disappearing before the hunger of this large party. They, like the first cutter's crew, had landed frost-bitten and exhausted, and being ill fed, and badly clothed and lodged, they were many days in regaining their strength.

Efforts were made from the first, but without avail, to get transportation for the party to a place of permanent safety, and also to institute a search for the other parties, which nevertheless they believed to have been lost in the gale.

Lieutenant Danenhower started on the 17th of October, with a dog team, to explore the coast for the missing boats, but was unable, from the condition of the ice, to proceed far in any direction, and returned without results. The wide river, or rather bay, which separated Geeomovialocke from the mainland was sometimes covered with young ice, too thick for the passage of boats, and too thin for the passage of sledges, and at times was filled with floating masses of old ice; while their ignorance of the language left them unable to express their wants, or to discover the resources of the vicinity in respect to reindeer or dog teams.

It was not until October 29 that Chief Engineer Melville learned that the first cutter had survived the gale, when he at once started, and, meeting and consulting with Seamen Nindemann and Noros, did all in his power to find and succor his missing comrades. He succeeded in recovering a portion of the records left behind by the commander, but after nearly sacrificing his life from hunger and cold, and feeling assured that the remainder of the first cutter's party had undoubtedly perished, he returned southward to Bulun, and then went to Yakutsk, where he at once commenced preparations for a more extended search when the season would permit, in the mean time forwarding to Irkutsk the members of his party not needed or unfitted for the search.

On March 12 Chief Engineer Melville was enabled to assemble the relief party at Cath-Carta, the appointed rendezvous, when the search for the first cutter's crew was commenced, and resulted in finding, between March 23 and 27, the remainder of the records, and the bodies of Lieutenant-Commander De Long's party, except those of Erichsen and Alexy, which had been buried in the river.

The bodies were removed and properly interred on high land near Mat-Vay, safe from the effects of the spring floods.

After this had been done, three parties were formed under the charge of Chief Engineer Melville, Seaman Nindemann, and Fireman Bartlett, respectively, and the coasts and upper portion of the Lena delta were thoroughly searched for the second cutter's party, but without finding any traces of it. The search was continued as far as the river Jana, and as by this time the sledging season was at an end, the parties returned to Yakutsk, when Chief Engineer Melville, with all but five of his men, proceeded home by order of the Navy Department. These five remained with Lieutenant Harber, who had been sent to aid in the search.

Considering, then, the condition of the survivors, the unfavorable season, the limited knowledge of the country, the want of facilities for prosecuting the search, and the great difficulty of communicating with the natives, everything possible was done for the relief of the other parties.

The following is a list of the officers and crew of the Jeannette, showing their assignment to the boats on the retreat, and their final fate or disposition:

FIRST CUTTER (14).

Lieutenant-Commander George W. De Long, United States Navy, commanding. Died in the Lena Delta.
Passed Assistant Surgeon James M. Ambler, United States Navy. Died in the Lena Delta.
Mr. Jerome J. Collins (meteorologist). Died in the Lena Delta.
Seaman W. F. C. Nindemann. Sent ahead for relief and rescued by natives; a witness before the court.
Seaman Louis P. Noros. Sent ahead for relief and rescued by natives; a witness before the court.
Seaman Heinrich H. Kaack. Died in the Lena Delta.
Seaman Carl A. Görtz. Died in the Lena Delta.
Seaman Adolph Dressler. Died in the Lena Delta.
Coppersmith Walter Lee. Died in the Lena Delta.
Seaman Hans H. Erichsen. Died in the Lena Delta.
Coal-heaver Nelse Iverson. Died in the Lena Delta.
Coal-heaver George W. Boyd. Died in the Lena Delta.
Seaman Ah Sam. Died in the Lena Delta.
Seaman Alexy (dog-driver and hunter). Died in the Lena Delta.

SECOND CUTTER (8).

Lieut. Charles W. Chipp, United States Navy, commanding.
Seaman William Dunbar (ice pilot).
Seaman Alfred Sweetman.
Seaman Henry D. Warren.
Seaman Peter E. Johnson.
Seaman Edward Star.
Seaman Albert G. Kuehne.
Coal-heaver Walter Sharvell.
Of which boat, with her crew, no record exists subsequent to the gale of September 12, 1881.

WHALE-BOAT (11).

Chief Engineer George W. Melville, United States Navy, commanding. Rescued by natives; a witness before the court.
Lieut. John W. Danenhower, United States Navy. Rescued by natives; a witness before the court.
Mr. Raymond L. Newcomb (naturalist and taxidermist). Rescued by natives; a witness before the court.
Seaman John Cole (boatswain). Rescued by natives; now an inmate of the Government Insane Asylum.

Fireman James H. Bartlett. Rescued by natives; retained in Siberia to assist Lieutenant Harber.

Seaman Herbert W. Leach. Rescued by natives; retained in Siberia to assist Lieutenant Harber.

Seaman Henry Wilson. Rescued by natives; a witness before the court.

Seaman Frank E. Manson. Rescued by natives; retained in Siberia to assist Lieutenant Harber.

Seaman Charles Tong Sing. Rescued by natives; a witness before the court.

Coal-heaver John Lauterbach. Rescued by natives; retained in Siberia to assist Lieutenant Harber.

Seaman Ainguin (dog-driver and hunter). Rescued by natives; retained in Siberia to assist Lieutenant Harber; subsequently died at Kirinsk.

Sixth. As to "the general conduct and merits of each and all the officers and men of the expedition."

There is conclusive evidence that aside from trivial difficulties, such as occur on shipboard even under the most favorable circumstances, and which had no influence in bringing about the disasters of the expedition and no pernicious effect upon its general conduct, every officer and man so conducted himself that the court finds no occasion to impute censure to any member of the party.

In view, then, of the long and dreary monotony of the cruise, the labors and privations encountered, the disappointment consequent upon a want of important results, and the uncertainty of their fate (and apart from a natural desire to tread lightly on the graves of the dead), the general conduct of the *personnel* of the expedition seems to have been a marvel of cheerfulness, good-fellowship, and mutual forbearance, while the constancy and endurance with which they met the hardships and dangers that beset them entitle them to great praise.

Beside the mention already made, however, special commendation is due to Lieutenant-Commander De Long for the high qualities displayed by him in the conduct of the expedition; to Chief Engineer Melville, for his zeal, energy, and professional aptitude, which elicited high encomiums from his commander, and for his subsequent efforts on the Lena Delta; and to Seamen Nindemann and Sweetman, for services which induced their commander to recommend them for medals of honor.

Finally, it should be stated that there are several of the survivors of the Jeannette, who have not yet returned from Siberia, and whose testimony might or might not modify the conclusions set forth in this report.

WM. G. TEMPLE,
Commodore, United States Navy, President.
SAM. C. LEMLY,
Master, United States Navy, Judge-Advocate.

And the doors having been reopened, the court then, at 4 p. m., adjourned to await the further orders of the honorable Secretary of the Navy.

WM. G. TEMPLE,
Commodore, United States Navy, President.
SAM. C. LEMLY,
Master, United States Navy, Judge-Advocate.

NAVY DEPARTMENT,
OFFICE OF THE JUDGE-ADVOCATE-GENERAL,
February 17, 1883.

Respectfully submitted, with the recommendation that the finding of the court be approved.

WM. B. REMEY,
Judge-Advocate-General.

NAVY DEPARTMENT, *February* 17, 1883.

The finding of the court is approved.

WM. E. CHANDLER,
Secretary of the Navy.

EIGHTY-FIRST DAY.

NAVY DEPARTMENT,
Washington, D. C., Friday, March 30, 1883—12 m.

The court, which adjourned Monday, February 12, 1883, reconvened pursuant to an order from the Honorable Secretary of the Navy, which was read aloud by the judge-advocate, and is hereto annexed, marked 1 A.

Present, Commodore William G. Temple, United States Navy, president; Commander Frederick V. McNair, United States Navy, member; and Lieut. Richard Wainwright, United States Navy, judge-advocate.

The judge-advocate then read aloud a letter to the president of the court from the Honorable Secretary of the Navy, informing him that Capt. Joseph N. Miller, United States Navy, had been relieved as a member of the court, which letter is hereto annexed, marked 1 B; also a letter from the Honorable Secretary of the Navy, informing the president of the court that Master Samuel C. Lemly, United States Navy, had been relieved from duty as judge-advocate of the court, which letter is hereto annexed, marked 1 C.

The judge-advocate then read aloud his letter of appointment, which is hereto annexed, marked 1 D.

The president of the court then administered to the judge-advocate the oath in such cases prescribed by law.

Seaman H. W. LEACH was then called as a witness, and, having been sworn according to law by the president of the court, testified as follows:

Examined by the JUDGE-ADVOCATE:

Question by the JUDGE-ADVOCATE. What is your name and rate?
Answer. Herbert W. Leach; seaman.

Question by the JUDGE-ADVOCATE. To what ship and to what special service were you last attached?
Answer. The Jeannette, on a voyage of discovery and exploration in the Arctic Ocean.

Question by the JUDGE-ADVOCATE. When and where did you join the Jeannette, and what were your duties on board of that vessel?
Answer. I joined the Jeannette at Mare Island navy-yard in June, 1879; seaman.

Question by the JUDGE-ADVOCATE. Have you any statement to lay before this court in relation to the fitting out of the Jeannette for Arctic service, and the condition of the ship when she sailed from San Francisco?

Answer. No, sir.

Question by the JUDGE-ADVOCATE. Have you any statement to lay before this court in relation to the management of the vessel up to the time of her loss?

Answer. No, sir.

Question by the JUDGE-ADVOCATE. Have you any statement to lay before this court in relation to the loss of the Jeannette?

Answer. No, sir.

Question by the JUDGE-ADVOCATE. Have you any statement to lay before this court in relation to the provisions made and plans adopted for the several boats' crews upon their leaving the wreck?

Answer. Everything was done that could be done.

Question by the JUDGE-ADVOCATE. Have you any statement to lay before this court in relation to the efforts made by the various officers to insure the safety of the parties under their charge and for the relief of the other parties?

Answer. Yes, sir. I would say that everything was done in the power of the men commanding that could be done.

Question by the JUDGE-ADVOCATE. Have you any charge to lay or special commendation to offer concerning any of the officers or men connected with the Jeannette expedition: first as to the condition of the vessel on her departure from San Francisco; second, her management up to the time of her loss; third, her loss; fourth, the provisions made, and plans adopted for the several boats' crews on their leaving the wreck; fifth, the efforts made by the various officers to insure the safety of the parties under their charge and for the relief of the other parties; sixth, the general conduct and merits of each and all the officers and men of the expedition?

Answer. I would like to say a word in favor of Mr. Danenhower, who was given charge of the whale-boat during the night of the gale, as probably if he hadn't had charge I would not have been here. I would like to say that he displayed good management and good judgment through the gale, and until we reached the land shaped all the courses and took charge. I have no charge to lay against any officer or man of the expedition.

The judge-advocate had no further questions to ask, the court had no questions to ask, and the testimony of the witness was read over to him and by him pronounced correct.

Seaman FRANK E. MANSON was then called as a witness, and after being duly sworn according to law by the president of the court, testified as follows:

Examined by the JUDGE-ADVOCATE:

Question by the JUDGE-ADVOCATE. What is your name and rate?

Answer. Frank Edward Manson; seaman.

Question by the JUDGE-ADVOCATE. To what ship and what special service were you last attached?

Answer. The Jeannette on Arctic expedition.

Question by the JUDGE-ADVOCATE. When and where did you join the Jeannette, and what were your duties on board of that vessel?

Answer. In Mare Island navy-yard. I think it was the 14th June, 1879. Seaman.

Question by the JUDGE-ADVOCATE. Have you any statement to lay

before this court in relation to the fitting out of the Jeannette for Arctic service and the condition of the ship when she sailed from San Francisco?
Answer. No, sir.
Question by the JUDGE-ADVOCATE. Have you any statement to lay before this court in relation to the management of the vessel up to the time of the loss?
Answer. No, sir.
Question by the JUDGE-ADVOCATE. Have you any statement to lay before this court in relation to the loss of the Jeannette?
Answer. No, sir.
Question by the JUDGE-ADVOCATE. Have you any statement to lay before this court in relation to the provisions made and plans adopted for the several boats' crews upon their leaving the wreck?
Answer. No, sir.
Question by the JUDGE-ADVOCATE. Have you any statement to lay before this court in relation to the efforts made by the various officers to insure the safety of the parties under their charge and for the relief of the other parties?
Answer. No, sir.
Question by the JUDGE-ADVOCATE. Have you any charge to lay or special commendation to offer concerning any of the officers or men connected with the Jeannette expedition: first, as to the condition of the vessel on her departure from San Francisco; second, her management up to the time of her loss; third, her loss; fourth, the provisions made and plans adopted for the several boats' crews on their leaving the wreck; fifth, the efforts made by the various officers to insure the safety of the parties under their charge and for the relief of the other parties; sixth, the general conduct and merits of each and all the officers and men of the expedition?
Answer. No, sir; I think everything was done that could be done. I would like to say a word for Mr. Danenhower, as he had charge of the whale-boat and took us safe on shore.
There being no further questions to ask the witness, his testimony was read over to him and by him pronounced correct.

Coal-heaver JOHN LAUTERBACH was then called as a witness and after being duly sworn according to law by the President of the court, testified as follows:

Examined by the JUDGE-ADVOCATE:
Question by the JUDGE-ADVOCATE. What is your name and rate?
Answer. John Lauterbach, coal-passer.
Question by the JUDGE-ADVOCATE. To what ship and what special service were you last attached?
Answer. Jeannette, on Arctic exploration.
Question by the JUDGE-ADVOCATE. When and where did you join the Jeannette, and what were your duties on board of that vessel?
Answer. On Mare Island; coal-passer; about the 21st of May, 1879.
Question by the JUDGE-ADVOCATE. Have you any statement to lay before this court in relation to the fitting out of the Jeannette for Arctic service and the condition of the ship when she sailed from San Francisco?
Answer. No, sir.
Question by the JUDGE-ADVOCATE. Have you any statement to lay before this court in relation to the loss of the Jeannette?

Answer. No, sir.

Question by the JUDGE-ADVOCATE. Have you any statement to lay before this court in relation to the management of the vessel up to the time of her loss?

Answer. No, sir.

Question by the JUDGE-ADVOCATE. Have you any statement to lay before this court in relation to the provisions made and plans adopted for the several boats' crews upon their leaving the wreck?

Answer. No, sir.

Question by the JUDGE-ADVOCATE. Have you any statement to lay before this court in relation to the efforts made by the various officers to insure the safety of the parties under their charge and for the relief of the other parties?

Answer. No, sir.

Question by the JUDGE-ADVOCATE. Have you any charge to lay or special commendation to offer concerning any of the officers or men connected with the Jeannette expedition: first, as to the condition of the vessel on her departure from San Francisco; second, her management up to the time of her loss; third, her loss; fourth, the provisions made and plans adopted for the several boats' crews on their leaving the wreck; fifth, the efforts made by the various officers to insure the safety of the parties under their charge and for the relief of the other parties; sixth, the general conduct and merits of each and all of the officers and men of the expedition?

Answer. No, sir; except Mr. Danenhower, that he brought us safe to shore; that his judgment in making a drag on the night of the gale.

There being no further questions to ask this witness, his testimony was read over to him and by him pronounced to be correct.

There being no further witnesses at present available, the court then adjourned to meet on Tuesday, April 3, at 10.30 a. m.

EIGHTY-SECOND DAY.

NAVY DEPARTMENT,
Washington, D. C., Tuesday, April 3, 1883—10.30 a. m.

The court met pursuant to the adjournment of Friday, March 30, 1883.

Present, Commodore William G. Temple, United States Navy, president; Commander Frederick V. McNair, United States Navy, member; and Lieut. Richard Wainwright, United States Navy, judge-advocate.

The record of the proceedings of March 30, 1883, the eighty-first day of the inquiry, was then read, and, after making several corrections, approved.

First-class Fireman JAMES H. BARTLETT was then called as a witness, and, having been sworn according to law by the president of the court, testified as follows:

Examination by the JUDGE-ADVOCATE:

Question by the JUDGE-ADVOCATE. What is your name and rate?

Answer. James H. Bartlett; first-class fireman.

Question by the JUDGE-ADVOCATE. To what ship and what special service were you last attached?

Answer. I was aboard the ship Jeannette on special service in the Arctic Ocean.

Question by the JUDGE-ADVOCATE. When and where did you join the Jeannette, and what were your duties on board of that vessel?

Answer. I joined the Jeannette in San Francisco in 1879, on June 16, I think; first-class fireman.

Question by the JUDGE-ADVOCATE. Have you any statement to lay before this court in relation to the fitting out of the Jeannette for Arctic service and the condition of the ship when she sailed from San Francisco?

Answer. I haven't any, sir.

Question by the JUDGE-ADVOCATE. Have you any statement to lay before this court in relation to the management of the vessel up to the time of her loss?

Answer. I have none, sir.

Question by the JUDGE-ADVOCATE. Have you any statement to lay before this court in relation to the loss of the Jeannette?

Answer. Not any.

Question by the JUDGE-ADVOCATE. Have you any statement to lay before this court in relation to the provisions made and plans adopted for the several boats' crews upon their leaving the wreck?

Answer. Have none, sir.

Question by the JUDGE-ADVOCATE. Have you any statement to lay before this court in relation to the efforts made by the various officers to insure the safety of the parties under their charge and for the relief of the other parties?

Answer. Haven't any.

Question by the JUDGE-ADVOCATE. Have you any charge to lay or special commendation to offer concerning any of the officers or men connected with the Jeannette expedition: first, as to the condition of the vessel on her departure from San Francisco; second, her management up to the time of her loss; third, her loss; fourth, the provisions made and plans adopted for the several boats' crews on their leaving the wreck; fifth, the efforts made by the various officers to insure the safety of the parties under their charge and for the relief of the other parties; sixth, the general conduct and merits of each and all of the officers and men of the expedition?

Answer. I haven't any, sir.

Question by the JUDGE-ADVOCATE. Give, in detail, the account of your trip from the time you left Mr. Melville at Cass Carta until you rejoined him again.

Answer. I left Cass Carta in company with Nindemann and traveled in a northeast direction to Point Barkin; separated company with Nindemann at Barkin; followed the east coast of the Lena Delta to the southward as far as Geeomovialocke, where I remained until Mr. Melville's arrival. We made as thorough a search as could be made under the circumstances. There was much snow and a great deal of bad weather, and it is my opinion of it that we made as good a search of it as could be made. We done all that it was possible to do.

The judge-advocate then read a telegram from D. F. Collins requesting the court to await a list of questions to be put to the witnesses now under examination, a copy of which is hereto annexed, marked 1 E.

The judge-advocate then stated to the court that he had informed Mr. B. A. Collins, on Thursday, of the reconvening of the court, and had requested him to forward any questions he might desire to have put.

He also informed the court that there was a letter in his possession from D. F. Collins stating that his brother B. A. Collins had charge of the case in the interest of the late Jerome J. Collins. In compliance with this request, the court, suspending the further examination of James H. Bartlett, adjourned to meet to-morrow, April 4, 1883, at 10.30 a. m.

EIGHTY-THIRD DAY.

NAVY DEPARTMENT,
Washington, D. C., Wednesday, April 4, 1883—10.30 a. m.

The court met pursuant to the adjournment of yesterday.

Present, Commodore William G. Temple, United States Navy, president; Commander Frederick V. McNair, United States Navy, member; and Lieut. Richard Wainwright, United States Navy, judge-advocate.

The record of the proceedings of yesterday, Tuesday, April 3, the eighty-second day of the inquiry, was then read, and, after correcting it, was approved.

The questions to be put to the witnesses by D. F. Collins not arriving, the court adjourned to meet on Friday, April 6, 1883, at 10.30 a. m.

EIGHTY-FOURTH DAY.

NAVY DEPARTMENT,
Washington, D. C., Friday, April 6, 1883—10.30 a. m.

The court met pursuant to the adjournment of Wednesday, April 4, 1883.

Present, Commodore William G. Temple, United States Navy, president; Commander Frederick V. McNair, United States Navy, member; and Lieut. Richard Wainwright, United States Navy, judge-advocate.

The record of the proceedings of Wednesday, April 4, 1883, the eighty-third day of the inquiry, was then read and approved.

The judge-advocate then stated to the court that he had received the questions from D. F. Collins, and if it pleased the court he would examine the witness, J. H. Bartlett, on the part of the late Jerome J. Collins.

The witness, first-class Fireman JAMES H. BARTLETT, whose examination was suspended on Wednesday, April 3, 1883, was then called into court and testified as follows:

Examination on the part of the late JEROME J. COLLINS.

Question by the JUDGE-ADVOCATE. What was Mr. Collins' position on board the Arctic steamer Jeannette?

Answer. As near as I know he had charge of the weather department. Well, I know from the log, having helped bind it one time when it was sent forward, that his rate was that of seaman, but he always held the position as an officer. He messed in the after part of the ship with the officers.

Question by the JUDGE-ADVOCATE. What were your relations with Mr. Collins?

Answer. I was on pleasant terms with him the same as all the other officers. I considered him an officer. I was told by Lieutenant De Long that he would act as an officer, in San Francisco.

Question by the JUDGE-ADVOCATE. Did you know of any trouble existing between Mr. Collins and Lieutenant-Commander De Long?

Answer. No, sir; I knew of no existing trouble between them; I never heard Lieutenant De Long say an unpleasant word to Mr. Collins.

Question by the JUDGE-ADVOCATE. Did Mr. Collins speak to you on the matter, and what did he say?

(To this question the judge-advocate objects as calling for hearsay evidence. The objection was sustained by the court, and the question was not put.)

Question by the JUDGE-ADVOCATE. Were you a witness to any differences between them? State what you saw or heard.

Answer. I never saw or heard any difference between them, only Mr. Collins was off duty.

Question by the JUDGE-ADVOCATE. When the Jeannette went down was Mr. Collins free to save his property, such as notes, books, &c.?

Answer. As far as I know, he was.

Question by the JUDGE-ADVOCATE. Did Mr. Collins say anything to you relative to the loss of his papers, &c., at that time?

Answer. Not at the time of losing the ship.

Question by the JUDGE-ADVOCATE. How was Mr. Collins treated during the retreat?

Answer. His treatment, as far as I know, was similar to the other officers of the expedition; by the men and officers also.

Question by the JUDGE-ADVOCATE. Did Mr. Collins speak to you about the way he felt he was treated, and what he was going to do on his return home, during the retreat?

Answer. Yes, sir; he spoke to me in regard to that.

Question by the JUDGE-ADVOCATE. Did Mr. Collins tell you about any papers that he had on his person at that time?

Answer. Yes, sir.

Question by the JUDGE-ADVOCATE. Did Mr. Collins make any request of you relative to such papers or other things?

Answer. Yes, sir.

Question by the JUDGE-ADVOCATE. On your boat reaching land, and the party finding provisions, was there any discussion relative to the probable position and condition of the other parties?

Answer. Yes, sir.

Question by the JUDGE-ADVOCATE. In your opinion was it necessary to delay thirty-five days before making any effort to get news of or go in search of the other parties?

Answer. As far as I know, it was impossible for sixteen days, I think, to the best of my memory, to travel from where we were, and at the expiration of that time Mr. Melville made arrangements with Kusmah to take dispatches to Bulun, and also return with transportation and clothing for the entire party to Bulun, with the understanding that he would arrive back with means of transportation in five days, but did not return for fifteen, as I remember it. I think we moved from there as soon as it was practicable.

Question by the JUDGE-ADVOCATE. Did you offer to go in search of news, or to the relief of the other parties?

Answer. I believe, in company with several of the party, I did, as I remember the conversation of several of the party in regard to it.

Question by the JUDGE-ADVOCATE. Were you prevented from doing so? If so, by whom?

Answer. Yes, sir; by the general opinion of the whole party. The reason of it was that we were unfamiliar with the country, had no means of transportation, and no provisions, only what was furnished by the natives we were living with.

Question 17 was separated.

Question by the JUDGE-ADVOCATE. Did Lieutenant Danenhower offer to go? If so, who prevented him?

Answer. Yes, sir, he offered to go, and did go.

Question by the JUDGE-ADVOCATE. Did you receive any orders from Chief Engineer Melville to bring Lieutenant Danenhower back dead or alive?

(To this question the judge-advocate objects, as it can only be relevant to the inquiry under the precept, if it tends to show that any search or attempted search for the other boats was prevented by this order. If it is thus relevant it is inadmissible, as not the best evidence to show that such was the case. The objection was not sustained, and the question was put.)

Answer. No, sir.

Question by the JUDGE-ADVOCATE. Do you know of any trouble or difference existing between Mr. Collins and Chief Engineer Melville? What were their relations?

Answer. No; sir I knew of no trouble existing; they were the same as between him and the other officers, as far as I know.

Question by the JUDGE-ADVOCATE. How did Melville speak of Collins to you?

(To this question the judge-advocate objects as calling for hearsay testimony. The objection was sustained and the question was not put.)

Question by the JUDGE-ADVOCATE. Had you been in command of the party, would you have waited thirty-five days without going to find out or discover the position or condition of the other parties?

Answer. I don't know to the best of my knowledge that we waited thirty days. Taking the condition of the country and our condition, I should have moved as soon as possible, which I think was about twenty days after we arrived there, and I made the proposition to move from there; that was discussed by the whole party, Manson and myself agreeing to draw Leach on a sleigh, he being unable to walk from a frost-bite. The object of the move was to get to Bulun. The conclusion arrived at by Mr. Melville and Mr. Danenhower was that it would be impracticable and impossible, Mr. Danenhower making the statement that he thought there would be 25 per cent. of the party taken into Bulun on sleighs or dead.

Question by the JUDGE-ADVOCATE. In your opinion was it possible to have sooner commenced the search for the De Long party?

Answer. No, sir, not the proper search for them. As stated before, I thought we could have moved from Geeomovialocve in about twenty days from the time we landed there.

Question by the JUDGE-ADVOCATE. From your conversations with Mr. Collins have you any reason to suppose that Mr. Collins had papers other than a small note book on his person?

(To this question the judge-advocate objects as calling for hearsay testimony. The objection was sustained and the question was not put.)

Question by the JUDGE-ADVOCATE. Did he (Mr. Collins) tell you of his having letters addressed to persons in New York? State all he said.

(To this question the judge-advocate makes the same objection as to a former question. The objection was sustained and the question was not put.)

Question by the JUDGE-ADVOCATE. Did he request you during the retreat that in case any accident should happen him, or that he should die, that you would take care of his papers?

Answer. Yes, sir.

Question by the JUDGE-ADVOCATE. State as fully as possible the different conversations you had with Mr. Collins relative to his treatment, the loss of his note-books, and all other matters?

(To this question the judge-advocate objects as calling for hearsay testimony. The objection was sustained, and the question was not put.)

Question by the JUDGE-ADVOCATE. Were you present when Mr. Collins's body was found?

Answer. Yes, sir.

Question by the JUDGE-ADVOCATE. State all particulars relative to the same.

Answer. I was present at the finding of all the party with the exception of Lieutenant De Long, Doctor Ambler, and the cook, Ah Sam. They had been found by Mr. Melville and Nindemann, and their effects taken from them by them. But the taking out from under the snow of Mr. Collins was done under the directions of myself and Nindemann, having been sent by Mr. Melville while he was otherwise engaged at Mat Vay, and we searched the remains of Mr. Collins, and everything that he had was put into a handkerchief and turned over to Mr. Melville that evening.

Question by the JUDGE-ADVOCATE. What did you find on the body?

Answer. The articles consisted of one small note-book and a few packages of crumpled written matter that had been carried in the pocket, wet several times—I don't know the contents of it—a number of beads, a few nails, and some cartridges, and two or three pocket handkerchiefs, and I think a small money-purse. It was open written matter or paper, similar to this (showing legalcap). I think it was foolscap; I am not positive about that. To the best of my knowledge I don't think there was over ten sheets; there might have been less.

Question by the JUDGE-ADVOCATE. Did it strike you at this time that any of Mr. Collins' papers were missing?

Answer. Well, I expected that he had more; that was in regard to this conversation I had with him about them; from that, I supposed that he had more.

Question by the JUDGE-ADVOCATE. How do the papers, &c., found on his body compare with the account made of the same by Melville to the Navy Department?

(To this question the judge-advocate objects, as the court can judge for themselves from matter already in evidence, and the answer to previous question. The objection was not sustained and the question was put.)

Answer. I have never seen Mr. Melville's statement in regard to what he turned over to the Department.

Question by the JUDGE-ADVOCATE. Were you present when Melville examined, or caused to be examined, Mr. Collins' body in his presence? What did he say on the finding of a cross on Mr. Collins' neck? Who found the cross?

Answer. Yes, sir; I was present. The remark was made that we didn't know whether to leave it on him or put it with his other effects and send it to the Department, Mr. Melville saying that he did not know whether to bury it with him, or to send it home, but thought it was part of his religion, and he would bury it with him. I did, sir.

Question by the JUDGE-ADVOCATE. Did you have any conversations with Mr. Melville relative to such matters, since your return home?

(To which the judge-advocate objects as irrelevant. The objection was not sustained and the question was put.)

Answer. I have had no conversation with Mr. Melville in regard to that point at all. I have had a general conversation with him, the same as other people whom I have met since I arrived. In our conversation we have never touched on the subject, only in a general way. There never has been any particular points talked over between us at all.

Question by the JUDGE-ADVOCATE. What were your relations with Mr. Melville when in Siberia?

Answer. I was in a position of an enlisted man, and he as an officer of the United States Navy. Our relations were generally friendly.

Question by the JUDGE-ADVOCATE. In your opinion was everything done that was possible for the rescue of De Long's party?

Answer. Yes, sir.

Question by the JUDGE-ADVOCATE. If an earlier and more urgent attempt for his relief was made in the beginning, what would have been the chances?

Answer. I think there were no chances to assist him.

Question by the JUDGE-ADVOCATE. If Lieutenant Danenhower had been permitted to go on his search and was aided, in your opinion could De Long's party have been saved?

Answer. No, sir.

Question by the JUDGE-ADVOCATE. In your conversations with parties in Siberia, other than the survivors, have you expressed the same views and made the same statements as before this court?

Answer. I have never made any statements to any one in Siberia different from what I have made before this court.

Re-examined by the JUDGE-ADVOCATE:

Question by the JUDGE-ADVOCATE. Do you know of any papers Mr. Collins had during the retreat other than those found on his person?

Answer. No, sir.

Question by the JUDGE-ADVOCATE. From all your experience up to the present time, do you now think it would have been practicable to have started for Bulun sooner than was done?

Answer. I think it could have been made; the result of it, of course, I can't tell; there would have been a great deal of hardship and suffering in connection with it.

Question by the JUDGE-ADVOCATE. Was any one prevented from making a search for the other boats other than on the occasion which you have already mentioned and for which you volunteered?

Answer. I desire to state that my volunteering was in regard to going to Bulun, but not for the search for Lieutenant De Long. Not that I know of, only in the general way that I spoke of; we talked of the other parties and their probable condition, and I think that every one in the party had at some time volunteered to make a search; that was in our every-day conversation that we used to have in the house. Lieutenant Danenhower did volunteer to commence a search and did make a search of two or three days' duration; I don't remember which.

The judge-advocate had no further questions to ask.

Examined by the COURT:

Question by the COURT. Do you know whether any papers or other articles belonging to Mr. Collins were destroyed or concealed by any person or persons?

Answer. No, sir.

There being no further questions to ask this witness, his testimony was read over to him, and by him pronounced to be correct. There being nothing further to lay before the court, the court adjourned to meet to-morrow, April 7, 1883, at 10.30 a. m.

EIGHTY-FIFTH DAY.

NAVY DEPARTMENT,
Washington, D. C., Saturday, April 7, 1883—10.30 a. m.

The court met pursuant to the adjournment of yesterday.

Present, Commodore William G. Temple, United States Navy, president; Commander Frederick V. McNair, United States Navy, member; and Lieutenant Richard Wainwright, United States Navy, judge-advocate.

The record of the proceedings of Friday, April 6, 1883, the eighty-fourth day of the inquiry, was then read, and, after correcting clerical errors, was approved.

The court was then cleared for deliberation, and agreed upon the following report:

In obedience to the order of the Honorable Secretary of the Navy, dated March 29, 1883, the court of inquiry of which Commodore William G. Temple, United States Navy, is president, reassembled at the Navy Department, at 12 o'clock m. on Friday, the 30th instant, for the purpose of completing the investigation of circumstances of the loss in the Arctic seas of the exploring steamer Jeannette, and the death of Lieutenant Commander De Long and others of the officers and men, &c.

Having concluded the examination of the survivors of that vessel who have recently returned from Siberia, the court have the honor herewith to report its further proceedings, with the testimony, and, after mature consideration of the evidence adduced, find that no modification is requisite in their conclusions reported February 12, 1883.

WILLIAM G. TEMPLE,
Commodore, United States Navy, President.
RICHARD WAINWRIGHT,
Lieutenant, United States Navy, Judge-Advocate.

And the doors being reopened, the court then, at 11.50 a. m., adjourned to await the further orders of the honorable Secretary of the Navy.

WILLIAM G. TEMPLE,
Commodore, United States Navy, President.
RICHARD WAINWRIGHT,
Lieutenant, United States Navy, Judge-Advocate.

NAVY DEPARTMENT,
OFFICE OF THE JUDGE-ADVOCATE-GENERAL,
April 23, 1883.

Respectfully submitted, with the recommendation that the finding of the court be approved.

WM. B. REMEY,
Judge-Advocate-General.

NAVY DEPARTMENT,
April 23, 1883.

The finding of the court is approved.

WM. E. CHANDLER,
Secretary of the Navy.

THE LAST RECORD OF THE PARTY,

COVERING THE TIME FROM THE DATE ON WHICH NINDEMANN AND NOROS WERE SENT AHEAD FOR RELIEF, OCTOBER 9 TO OCTOBER 30, 1881, NOT INCLUDED IN THE TESTIMONY OF THE WITNESSES.

[Extract from the ice journal of Lieutenant-Commander Geo. W. De Long.]

Sunday, October 9th, 119*th day.*—All hands at 4.30. 1 oz. alcohol. Read divine service. Send Nindemann and Noros ahead for relief. They carry their blankets, 1 rifle, 40 rounds ammunition, 2 oz. alcohol. Orders to keep W. bank of river until they reach settlement. They started at 7; cheered them. Underway at 8. Crossed creek; broke through ice; all wet up to knees. Stopped and built fires. Dried clothes. Under way again at 10.30. Lee breaking down. At 1 strike river bank; halt for dinner—1 oz. alcohol. Alexy shot 3 ptarmigan. Made soup. We are following Nindemann's track, though he is long since out of sight. Under way at 3.30. High bluff. Ice running rapidly to nd. in river. Halt at 4.40, upon coming to wood. Find canoe. Lay our heads on it and go to sleep; ½ oz. alcohol, supper.
Monday, October 10th, 120 *day.*—Last ½ oz. alcohol at 5.30. At 6.30 send Alexey off to look for ptarmigan. Eat deer-skin scraps. Yesterday morning ate my deer-skin foot nips. Light S. S. E. airs; not very cold. Under way at 8. In crossing creek 3 of us got wet. Built fire and dried out. Ahead again until 11. Used up. Built fire, made a drink out of the tea leaves from alcohol bottle; on again at noon. Fresh S. S. W. wind; drifting snow, very hard going. Lee begging to be left. Some little beach, and then some long stretches of high bank. Ptarmigan tracks plentiful. Following Nindemann's tracks. At 3 halted, used up. Crawled into a hole on the bank. Collected wood and built fire. Alexy away in quest of game. Nothing for supper except a spoonful of glycerine. All hands weak and feeble, but cheerful. God help us.
Tuesday, October 11th, 121*st day.*—S. W. gale, with snow. Unable to move. No game; 1 spoonful glycerine and hot water for food; no more wood in our vicinity.
Wednesday, October 12th, 122*nd day.*—Breakfast; last spoonful glycerine, and hot water. For dinner we tried a couple of handfulls of Arctic willow in a pot of water, and drank the infusion. Everybody getting weaker and weaker. Hardly strength to get firewood. SW. gale, with snow.
Thursday, October 13th, 123*rd day.*—Willow tea. Strong S. W. wind. No news from Nindemann. We are in the hands of God, and unless He intervenes are lost. We cannot move against the wind, and staying here means starvation. Afternoon went ahead for a mile, crossing either another river or a bend in the big one. After crossing missed Lee. Went down in a hole in the bank and camped. Sent back for Lee. He had turned back, lain down, and was waiting to die. All united in saying Lord's prayer and creed after supper. Snowing. Gale of wind. Horrible night.
Friday, October 14th, 124*th day.*—Breakfast, willow tea. Dinner ½ teaspoonful sweet-oil and willow tea. Alexy shot 1 ptarmigan. Had soup. S. W, wind; moderating.
Saturday, October 15th, 125*th day.*—Breakfast, willow tea, and 2 old boots. Concluded to move on at sunrise. Alexy breaks down; also Lee. Come to empty grain raft. Halt and camp. Signs of smoke at twilight to southward.
Sunday, October 16th, 126 *day.*—Alexy broken down. Divine service.
Monday, October 17th, 127*th day.*—Alexey dying. Doctor baptized him. Read prayers for sick. Mr. Collins' birthday; 40 years old. About sunset Alexy died; exhaustion from starvation. Covered him with ensign and laid him in the crib.
Tuesday, October 18th, 128*th day.*—Calm and mild; snow falling. Buried Alexy in the afternoon. Laid him on the ice of the river and covered him over with slabs of ice.
Wednesday, October 19th, 129*th day.*—Cutting up tent to make foot gear. Doctor went ahead to find new camp. Shifted by dark.
Thursday, October 20th, 130*th day.*—Bright and sunny, but very cold. Lee and Kaack done up.
Friday October 21st, 131*st day.*—Kaack was found dead about midnight, between the Doctor and myself. Lee died about noon. Read prayers for sick when we found he was going.
Saturday, October 22nd, 132*nd day.*—Too weak to carry the bodies of Lee and Kaack out on the ice. The Doctor, Collins, and I carried them around the corner out of sight, when my eye closed up.

Sunday, October 23rd, 133rd day.—Everybody pretty weak. Slept or rested all day, and then managed to get enough wood in before dark. Read part of divine service. Suffering in our feet. No foot gear.
Monday, October 24th, 134th day.—A hard night.
Tuesday, October 25th, 135th day.
Wednesday October 26th, 136 day.
Thursday, October 27th, 137th day.—Iveson broken down.
Friday, October 28th, 138th day.—Iveson died during early morning.
Saturday, October 29th, 139th day.—Dressler died during night.
Sunday, October 30th, 140th day.—Boyd and Görtz died during night. Mr. Collins dying.

APPENDIXES.

INDEX TO EXHIBITS.

Exhibit.	Subject.	Page.
A	Original precept	285
B	Letter transmitting precept	285
C	Judge-advocate's warrant	285
D	Secretary's letter ordering open court	286
E	Commodore Colhoun's letter appointing board of survey	286
F	Report of board of survey	286
G	Easby to Colhoun, work in Construction and Repair Department	288
H	Memorandum of work in Construction and Repair Department	288
I	English to Colhoun, repairs in Equipment and Recruiting Department	289
K	Telegram, English to Colhoun, supply coal to Jeannette	289
L	Telegram, Shock to Colhoun, repairs in Steam Engineering Department	289
M	Colhoun's letter appointing board of inspection	290
N	Report of board of inspection	290
O	Secretary to De Long (final instructions)	292
P	De Long to Secretary (final report before sailing)	293
Q	Danenhower's sketch of repairs to Jeannette..........opposite	293
R	De Long's letter to Danenhower, London, June 2, 1878	294
R 2	Danenhower's chart from Koltenoi Island to Cape Barkin..........opposite	294
S	Danenhower's chart used in the retreat..........opposite	294
T	Sketch of river, by Bashili..........opposite	294
T 2	Chart showing piloting of whale-boat by natives..........opposite	294
U	Commandant's road sketch..........opposite	294
V	Chart made by Danenhower in October, 1881..........opposite	294
W	Orders given Danenhower by Melville in October, 1881	295
X	Orders given Melville by De Long, Bennett Island, August 5, 1881	295
Y	Orders given Danenhower by Melville, Bologna, November 4, 1881	295
Z	Orders given Danenhower by Melville to go south, January 8, 1882	296
A A	Receipt from Lieutenant Harber for certain men, March 22, 1882	297
B B	Receipt from Lieutenant Harber for certain articles	297
C C	De Long's Ounalaska letter to Secretary, August 4, 1879	297
D D	De Long's report to Secretary Navy, Saint Lawrence Bay, August 26, 1879	298
E E	Chipp's report to De Long—routine on ship from September 6 to 30, 1879	299
F F	List of articles, boats' outfits, June 17, 1880	300
G G	Station bill for fire quarter, winters of 1880 and 1881	300
H H	Note sent by Nindemann and Noros, requesting help	301
I I	De Long's record of September 22, 1881	302
K K	De Long's record of September 26, 1881	303
L L	De Long's record of October 1, 1881	303
M M	Melville's letter to Espravnik of Verkeransk	304
N N	Telegram, Melville to Secretary Navy, November 2, 1881	304
O O	Telegram, received by Melville from Secretary at Yakutsk	306
P P	Telegram, received by Melville from Hoffman, chargé	306
Q Q	Melville's chart used in the search..........opposite	306
R R	De Long's record, found in Erichsen's hut	306
S S	Melville's telegram requesting permission to return to United States	307
T T	Secretary's answer to above	307
U U	De Long's record of September 19, 1881, found in navigation box	307
V V	Letter of Nindemann and Noros to United States minister, St. Petersburg	308
W W	Nindemann's chart..........opposite	309
X X	Melville's orders to Nindemann on leaving Yakutsk	309
A B	Melville's orders to Nindemann for search	309
B C	Danenhower's request to be allowed counsel	310
C D	Original interrogatories to George W. Much, naval constructor, United States Navy	310
D E	Original answers to interrogatories by George W. Much, naval constructor, United States Navy	311
E F F G G H	Original plans referred to in answer of Naval Constructor Much, United States Navy, as A, B, and C, respectively..........opposite	313
H I	Interrogatories put to Sir Allen Young, R. N. R., &c	313
I K	Answer to interrogatories by Sir Allen Young, R. N. R., &c	314
K L	Chipp's report of visit to Indian village	314
L M	Chipp's report of journey toward Herald Island	315
M N	De Long's order about ventilation	316
N O	Chipp's report on ice-thickness	317
O P	De Long's letter to Secretary; gallant conduct of Nindemann and Sweetman	317
P Q	Order naming Jeannette and Henrietta Islands	318
Q R	Collins's letter to De Long	318
R S	Order in relation to leaving and returning to ship	319
S T	Memorandum in relation to Collins	320
T U	Rough draft of letter to Secretary of Navy in regard to Collins	322
U V	Telegram from Ensign Hunt, announcing death of Aniguin Indian	324

The following documentary evidence, not appended, but accompanying the record was likewise considered by the court:

Log-books of the Jeannette, four parts.
Lieutenant-Commander De Long's private journal, three parts.
Lieutenant-Commander De Long's ice journal.
Rough draft of Lieutenant-Commander De Long's report to the Hon. Secretary of the Navy.
Chief Engineer Melville's report of trip to Henrietta Island.
Mr. J. J. Collins's memorandum book, used by the court for reference (appended).
V W. Spar and sail plan of the Jeannette.
W X. Circumpolar chart, showing the track of Jeannette.

APPENDIX I.

Exhibit A.

To Commodore WILLIAM G. TEMPLE, U. S. N.,
Navy Department, Washington, D. C.:

In conformity with a joint resolution of Congress, approved August 8, 1882, a court of inquiry, of which Commodore William G. Temple is hereby appointed president, Captain Joseph N. Miller and Commander Frederick V. McNair, members, and Master Samuel C. Lemly, judge-advocate, is ordered to convene at the Navy Department, Washington, D. C., on Thursday, the fifth day of October, A. D. eighteen hundred and eighty-two.

The court will diligently and thoroughly investigate the circumstances of the loss in the Arctic seas of the exploring steamer Jeannette, and of the death of Lieutenant-Commander George W. De Long and others of her officers and men. The court will also carefully inquire into the condition of the vessel on her departure, her management up to the time of her destruction, the provisions made and plans adopted for the several boats' crews upon their leaving the wreck, the efforts made by the various officers to insure the safety of the parties under their immediate charge, and for the relief of the other parties, and into the general conduct and merits of each and all the officers and men of the expedition.

At the conclusion of the investigation the court will report their proceedings, the testimony taken, and the facts which they deem established by the evidence adduced.

Given under my hand at the Navy Department, Washington, D. C., this twenty-ninth day of September, A. D. 1882.

               W. E. CHANDLER,
                 Secretary of the Navy.

Original document.

                SAM. C. LEMLY,
             Master U. S. Navy & Judge Advocate.

Exhibit B.

                NAVY DEPARTMENT,
              Washington, September 29, 1882.

Commodore WM. G. TEMPLE, U. S. Navy,
 Navy Department, Washington, D. C.:

SIR: I transmit herewith a precept addressed to you as president of a court of inquiry ordered to convene at the Navy Department, Washington, D. C., on Thursday the 5th proximo.

  Respectfully,

                WM. E. CHANDLER,
                 Secretary of the Navy.

A true copy.

                SAM. C. LEMLY,
            Master U. S. N. & Judge Advocate.

Exhibit C.

                NAVY DEPARTMENT,
               Washington, Sept. 29th, 1882.

SIR: A court of inquiry, of which you are appointed judge advocate, is ordered to convene at the Navy Department, Washington, D. C., on Thursday the 5th day of Oc-

tober, 1882, at which time and place you will appear and report yourself to Commodore Wm. G. Temple, U. S. N., the presiding officer of the court.
Very respectfully,

W. E. CHANDLER,
Secretary of the Navy.

Master SAMUEL C. LEMLY, U. S. N.,
Navy Department, Washington, D. C.

Reported October 5th, 1882.

WM. G. TEMPLE,
Commo. U. S. Navy and President of Court.

A true copy.

SAM. C. LEMLY,
Master U. S. Navy & Judge Advocate.

EXHIBIT D.

NAVY DEPARTMENT,
Washington, October 5th, 1882.

SIR: In reply to your inquiry of this date, you are informed that the investigation by the court of inquiry of which you are president will be held in open court.
Very respectfully,

WM. E. CHANDLER,
Secretary of the Navy.

Commodore WM. G. TEMPLE, U. S. Navy,
President Court of Inquiry, Navy Department, Washington, D C.

A true copy.

SAM. C. LEMLY,
Master U. S. Navy & Judge Advocate.

EXHIBIT E.

COMMANDANT'S OFFICE, UNITED STATES NAVY-YARD,
Mare Island, California, December 31st, 1878.

GENTLEMEN: You will form a board to thoroughly examine the yacht Jeannette, now at this navy-yard, intended for an extended cruise in the Arctic regions, and report to me in duplicate what repairs, if any, she needs to her hull, boilers, and machinery, etc., together with an estimate of their probable cost.
By direction of the Navy Department.
Very respectfully,

ED. R. COLHOUN,
Commandant.

Chief Engineer M. FLETCHER, U. S. N.
Commander LOUIS KEMPFF, U. S. N.
Naval Constructor GEO. W. MUCH, U. S. N.
Chief Engineer GEORGE F. KUTZ, U. S. N.

A true copy.

SAM. C. LEMLY,
Master U. S. N. & Judge Advocate.

EXHIBIT F.

U. S. NAVY-YARD, MARE ISLAND,
January 24th, 1879.

SIR: In obedience to your order of the 31st ultimo, we have thoroughly examined the yacht Jeannette, and respectfully submit the following report:

HULL AND SPARS.

Vessel requires docking; bottom, outside, and deck to be recalked; deck over boilers to be removed, for the purpose of taking out old boilers, and replaced with new planking; a new and wider bridge to replace the one now in use; water-closets, pumps, and side lights require overhauling and repairs. The diagonal or truss braces between the lower edge of spar-deck clamps and bilge strakes are, particularly in the coal bunkers, defective, and should be replaced with new; also the defective lining over frames, and between them. The wheel-ropes should lead under the deck, and not on top and through the cabin as now arranged. Slight repairs required to hatches, and other work of minor importance. The vessel should be painted throughout. To complete the repairs as enumerated above will, it is estimated, cost for labor and material seven thousand five hundred dollars ($7,500).

The above repairs are considered necessary to place the vessel in good condition for ordinary service; but for an extended cruise in the Arctic regions we are of the opinion that the vessel requires very extensive alterations, to make her if possible particularly adapted for such service. We find the vessel in fair condition so far as soundness is concerned, but in our opinion of rather light construction for the purpose. The space between the lower edge of spar-deck clamps and upper edge of bilge strakes is not ceiled; but in lieu thereof are placed truss or diagonal braces, about ten (10) feet asunder. To strengthen her in this particular part, these braces should be taken out and the opening planked with six (6) inch Oregon pine, or oak. To accomplish this work will require the partial removal of all athwartship bulk-heads fore and aft.

This vessel forward and aft of boilers and engine space is divided into almost innumerable compartments, adding no strength to the structure, but occupying space that could be appropriated to valuable store-room. These removals, therefore, would be of importance if the additional planking referred to was not required. In place of the bulk-heads, forming so many subdivisions, we would suggest that four substantials bulk-heads, six (6) inches in thickness, extending from the skin to the spar-deck, well bolted to beams and skin, and made water-tight, be substituted; also good heavy stanchions under every beam, well secured.

In addition to the iron breasthooks now in the vessel, there should be three or four heavy wooden hooks, well fastened through and through. The extreme fore end of the vessel, from eight (8) to ten (10) feet aft of apron, and from the spar-deck down, should be filled in solid with light material and calked.

The spars, in our opinion, are not well adapted for an extended cruise in the Arctic regions. The lower masts and topmasts, including top-gallant masts, are too long, and not of sufficient diameter; and the yards too small in the sling. We would therefore recommend new lower masts, topmasts, and yards.

The above alterations will cost, it is estimated, about twelve to fifteen thousand dollars ($12,000) to ($15,000) for labor and material.

It has been suggested by the commanding officer of the vessel that for the health and comfort of the crew in winter she be provided with a house on deck thirty-six (36) feet in length and twenty-one (21) feet in width, fitted with sash or dead-lights, and fitted all around; the house to be put up in sections, that it may be readily removed and replaced when required. Also to the main cabin, or forward end of poop, there should be built an entering room, or porch, seven (7) feet high, extending in the whole width of the vessel, with one door, or entrance, and felted all around. That additional shelves in chart room and after-cabin be put up. It is also suggested that all exposed iron-work throughout the vessel be felted. To comply with these suggestions, which are approved by the board, will necessitate an additional expenditure of some twelve hundred dollars ($1,200).

RIGGING, SAILS, &C.

The vessel requires one complete suit of sails, a complete set of running rigging, a cover for poop-deck, five (5) heating stoves, and two hundred (200) tons anthracite coal: the estimated cost of which, for labor and material, is five thousand eight hundred and sixty-nine dollar and fifty-four cents ($5,869.54).

ENGINES.

The vessel is furnished with two (2) back-acting engines, with a diameter of cylinder of thirty-two (32) inches and length of stroke eighteen (18) inches; has a jet condenser and a two (2) bladed screw of thirteen (13) feet pitch and a diameter of nine (9) feet. The screw can be hoisted clear of the water. The blades are fitted into the globular hub, and can be removed and replaced when necessary. The machinery should be thoroughly overhauled. We recommend an alteration in the gear for raising the screw; the present arrangement is faulty in some respects, and can be greatly improved at a small expense. Two (2) extra or spare propeller-blades should be furnished. An alteration in the lead of the main steam-pipe is recommended, by which additional bunker space can be obtained.

BOILERS.

The boilers have been in use about fourteen years and are worn out. We recommend their removal and the substitution of new boilers of different design. The service upon which this vessel is to be employed will not require the development of the full power of the engines. It is recommended, therefore, that boilers of less power be used, and the space thus economized added to the bunkers. An outline drawing is herewith transmitted, showing an arrangement of boilers and bunkers, the adoption of which, in our opinion, would add much to the efficiency of the vessel for the duty to be performed, giving an increase of bunker capacity of forty-seven and one-half (47½) per cent.

The total cost of new boilers and fittings, and the repairs and alterations necessary, we estimate at thirteen thousand dollars ($13,000).

There are boilers at this navy-yard nearly completed, intended for the U. S. S. Mohican, which, although heavier than necessary, could be used to advantage on the Jeannette.

The total estimated cost of the foregoing repairs and alterations is forty-two thousand five hundred and sixty-nine dollars and fifty-four cents ($42,569.52).

Respectfully submitted.

M. FLETCHER,
Chief Eng'r U. S. Navy.
LOUIS KEMPFF,
Comdr. U. S. N.
GEO. W. MUCH,
Naval Constr. U. S. N.
GEO. F. KUTZ,
Chief Eng'r. U. S. N.

Commodore E. R. COLHOUN, U. S. N.,
Commandant Navy-Yard, Mare Island.

Respectfully forwarded.

EDMD. R. COLHOUN,
Commandant.

A true copy.

SAM. C. LEMLY,
Master U. S. Navy & Judge Adevocate.

EXHIBIT G.

MARCH 11*th*, 1879.

Commodore E. R. COLHOUN:

Enclosed herewith you will find memorandum of work to be done on the yacht Jeannette as required by Lieut. G. W. De Long.

In doing the work you will please direct that a careful account of the materials used be kept and charged against that vessel. With regard to the labor required to do the work, it will not be included in construction pay-roll; but a proper account of it will be kept, to be paid by the owner of the yacht or his agent.

J. W. EASBY.

A true copy.

SAM. C. LEMLY,
Master U. S. Navy & Judge Advocate.

EXHIBIT H.

Memorandum of work to be done on the yacht Jeannette, March 11*th*, 1879.

The vessel will be docked and her bottom, wales, and deck recalked. The deck over boilers will be removed for the purpose of taking out old boilers and replaced with new planking. The bridge, water-closets, pump, and side lights will be overhauled and repaired. The diagonal or truss-braces between the lower edge of spar-deck clamps and bilge strakes in the space occupied by coal bunkers, engine, and boilers will be removed; also the defective lining over frames and between them. The space between the lower edge of spar-deck clamps and upper edge of bilge strakes in the wake of the boilers, engine-room, and coal bunkers will be planked in, part with two (2) strakes of six (6) inch

Oregon pine or oak, and in part with 2½ inch Oregon pine. There will be two (2) iron box beams introduced, one abaft and the other forward of the boilers, to strengthen the sides of the vessel in these parts. In addition to the iron breast-hooks now in the vessel there will be three or four heavy wooden hooks, well fastened through and through. The extreme fore end of the vessel, from eight (8) to ten (10) feet aft of the apron, and from the spar-deck down, will be filled in solid with light material and calked. Slight repairs to hatches and other work of minor importance to be done. Vessel to be painted throughout. She will be provided with a house on deck thirty-six (36) feet in length and twenty-one (21) feet in width, fitted with sash or air ports, and felted all around. The house to be put up in sections, that it may be readily removed and replaced when required. Also to the main cabin, or forward end of poop, there will be built an entering room, or porch, seven (7) feet high, extending in the whole width of the vessel, with one door or entrance, and felted all around. Additional shelves in chart-room or after cabin will be put up. All exposed iron work throughout the vessel will be felted.

A true copy.

SAM. C. LEMLY,
Master U. S. Navy & Judge Advocate

EXHIBIT I.

MARCH 14, 1879.

The Bureau encloses herewith estimate of cost of material and labor required to make the sails required for the Jeannette; also an estimate for sundry fittings of her rigging. Please have the sails made and the rigging fitted accordingly as economically as possible.

You are also authorized to supply that vessel with any other articles of equipment she may need from the stock on hand.

Please keep a separate account of the expenditures for that vessel.

Very respectfully,

EARL ENGLISH,
Chief of Bureau.

Commo. E. R. COLHOUN,
 Comdt. Navy Yard, Mare Island, California.

A true copy.

SAM. C. LEMLY,
Master U. S. Navy & Judge Advocate.

EXHIBIT K.

MAY 16, 1879.

SIR: You will be pleased to furnish such a quantity of anthracite coal as may be desired to fit the Arctic steamer Jeannette for her contemplated cruise.

Very respectfully,

EARL ENGLISH,
Chief of Bureau.

P. S.—A separate account is to be kept of that vessel's outfit.

To Commodore E. R. COLHOUN,
 t. Navy Yard, Mare Island, Cal.

A true copy.

SAM. C. LEMLY,
Master U. S. Navy & Judge Advocate.

EXHIBIT L.

MARCH 10*th*, 1879.

COLHOUN, Commodore E. R.,
 Comdt. Navy Yard, Mare Island, Cal.:

Proceed with all possible despatch to fit out steamer Jeannette for sea in engineering department (recommendations of Board approved as regards steam-engineering). Finish two boilers (nearest ready) intended for Mohican with two furnaces each, and place them in the ship, using second-hand tubes referred to in your despatch of seventh instant. Concentrate all force necessary to furnish ship by June first.

A separate account of labor and material to be carefully kept.

W. H. SHOCK,
Chief of Bureau.

Above order sent in obedience to the verbal directions of the Secretary of the Navy this date.

MARCH 10th, 1879.

W. H. SHOCK,
Chief of Bureau.

A true copy.

SAM. C. LEMLY,
Master U. S. Navy & Judge Advocate.

EXHIBIT M.

COMMANDANT'S OFFICE, NAVY YARD,
Mare Island, Cal., June 6th, 1

GENTLEMEN: You are hereby appointed a board to carefully examine and report upon the repairs and outfits of the Arctic steamer Jeannette. You will please state if the repairs and alterations as recommended in the survey upon that vessel have been made, or if any other work not embraced therein, but considered necessary, has been done, and if in your opinion she has been, so far as practicable, repaired and placed in condition for service in the Arctic Ocean.

Please make your report in duplicate.

Very respectfully,

EDMD. R. COLHOUN,
Comdt.

Captain P. C. JOHNSON, U. S. N.
Commander C. J. McDOUGAL, U. S. N.
Naval Constr. GEO. W. MUCH, "
Chf. Engr. GEO. F. KUTZ, U. S. N.
Chf. Engr. EDW. FARMER, "

A true copy.

SAM. C. LEMLY,
Master U. S. Navy & Judge Adv.

EXHIBIT N.

NAVY-YARD, MARE ISLAND, CALIFORNIA,
June 26, 1879.

COMMODORE: In accordance with your order of the 6th instant, hereto annexed, we have made a careful examination of the repairs and outfits of the Arctic steamer Jeannette and respectfully report as follows:

In regard to the repairs and alterations as recommended in the survey upon that vessel—she has been docked; her bottom outside, and deck recalked; deck over boilers renewed; a new and wider bridge made; water-closets, pumps, and side-lights overhauled and repaired; the diagonal or truss braces for some fifty feet amidships have been removed, as also the defective lining over the frame timbers in that locality. The lead of the wheel-ropes was not changed, because the officers of the vessel preferred the present arrangements. The necessary repairs were made on hatches and other work of minor importance done. The vessel has been painted throughout. For an extended cruise in the Arctic regions it was not possible, in our opinion, to make her particularly adapted for such service. To strengthen her in the space between the lower edge of spar-deck clamps and upper edge of bilge strake, in wake of boilers, engine, and coal bunkers, she was flanked with six (6) inch Oregon pine, well fastened through and through; and in lieu of the four six (6) inch bulk-heads, as recommended in survey, beams and heavy truss work, or thwartship diagonal bracing, has been substituted. Heavy stanchions under every beam were not put in because they were not authorized by the Bureau. In addition to the original iron breast-hooks, and instead of the three or four heavy wooden hooks as recommended by survey, it was found after removing the joiner work above the berth deck that hooks of the proper shape could not be obtained, so pointers and bracing were used instead; but the extreme fore-end of the vessel, from eight to ten feet of apron, and from the berth deck down has been filled in solid, and all well bolted through and through. The spars were not changed, as there was no authority from the Bureau to do so. The suggestions made by the commanding officer of the vessel have been carried out. She has been provided with a house on deck, fitted to be put up in sections when required. Felt has been provided for felting such parts of the ship as may be desired by her commanding officer. The entering room or porch to cabin has not been put up, but material for it has been supplied as Lieut. De Long preferred to do the work with his own men.

RIGGING, SAILS, ETC.

The Jeannette has been provided with one complete suit of sails, a complete set of running rigging, a cover for poop-deck, five heating stoves, and 135 tons anthracite coal, that being all her bunkers would stow.

ENGINES.

The machinery has been thoroughly overhauled, alterations made in the gear for raising the screw and in the lead of the main steam pipe, as recommended by survey.

BOILERS.

The Board of Survey having condemned the old boilers as being worn out, new boilers of different design, less power, but occupying less space, which has been added to the bunkers, have been put into the ship. The boilers and bunkers have been arranged very nearly as shown in the outline drawing accompanying the report of the Board that recommended the changes. Other work has been done not embraced in the recommendation of survey but considered necessary, which consists as follows: A No. 4 Sewell and Cameron pump has been furnished and connected with boilers, distilling apparatus, and bilge. A pair of steam-launch engines have been fitted with gearing drums, etc., for hoisting and warping. Four extra propeller blades have been furnished (the survey recommended but two); it having been deemed advisable to increase the surface and pitch, three blades were cast from new pattern and one off the old blade. Two new main steam slide-valves have been put in, it being desired to work the engine more expansively. The old valves remain on board as extra ones. A new smokepipe has been furnished, the old one having been found not worth repairing. The distilling apparatus has been removed from forward and placed in the engine-room, and the proper connections made. The proper number of pieces of spare machinery are on board ship; the tools, outfits, and stores are good in quantity and quality, with the exception of the oil, which is of inferior quality, but there is no other kind in store. Whatever was required in the way of outfits and stores has been supplied by the different departments, so far as the stock on hand would admit. The commanding officer proposes to furnish in San Francisco whatever else he may require.

In our opinion the vessel should carry more drinking water, as she has but one tank of about 400 gallons; but Lieutenant De Long is of the opinion that with the distilling apparatus the one tank is sufficient, that being all she carried on her trip out here, and as her stowage room is contracted.

In order to complete our examination a steam trial was made after she had received her coal, stores, and provisions. The fires were lighted at 9.55 a. m. and steam found at 11.45 a. m. At 2.05 p. m. started engines ahead. Up to this time 2,600 lbs. of coal had been put into the furnaces. Steamed down Mare Island Straits into San Pablo against a fresh breeze and a strong tide averaging 58 revolutions per minute. The speed of vessel, as shown by log was $4\frac{1}{2}$ knots, the screw showing a slip of $43\frac{3}{4}$ per cent. Upon the return, with wind aft and tide favorable, the log showed $5\frac{1}{4}$ knots, engines making 60 revolutions per minute. The boilers steamed freely, and no difficulty was experienced in holding the steam pressure for 58 and 60 revolutions. The coal used was very hard anthracite, of inferior quality, containing considerable slate. The firemen were entirely inexperienced, having but recently shipped as coal-heavers. The run was not of sufficient duration to necessitate blowing the boilers (the engines have a jet condenser) nor to clean fires. The engines were stopped 5.22 p. m. During the time they were in operation 1,000 lbs. of coal were put in the furnaces. This trial was not of sufficient length to enable the Board to determine the consumption of fuel, nor cost of horse-power, but sufficient to show the satisfactory working of the engines and evaporation efficiency of the boilers. The vacuum in condenser varied from $25\frac{3}{4}$ inches to $23\frac{3}{4}$ inches; there were several leaks noticeable, which, when made tight, will give an improved vacuum. We are of the opinion that the excessive slip of the screw is attributable to the great draught of the vessel, the diameter and area of the screw being at present disproportionate to the displacement or immersed section. The drag of the propeller-well was apparent, the water being thrown against, and a current set in motion to the stem-port. The slip of the screw will be diminished as the vessel lightens. We would state in this connection that the dimensions of the propeller-well prevent the use of a screw with greater surface.

So far as practicable, we are of the opinion that she has been repaired, and placed in condition for service in the Arctic Ocean.

Very respectfully submitted.

      P. C. JOHNSON, *Captain U. S. N.*
      CHAS. J. McDOUGAL, *Commander U. S. N.*
      GEO. W. MUCH, *Naval Const., U. S. N.*
      GEO. F. KUTZ, *Chief Engr. U. S. N.*
      EDWARD FARMER, *Chief Engr. U. S. N.*

Commodore E. R. COLHOUN, U. S. N.,
 Commandant Navy Yard, Mare Island.

      COMMANDANT'S OFFICE,
    Navy Yard, Mare Island, California.

Approved June 28, 1879.

      EDMUND R. COLHOUN,
        Commandant.

A true copy.

      SAM. C. LEMLY,
    Master U. S. N. & Judge Advocate.

EXHIBIT O.

      NAVY DEPARTMENT,
    Washington, 18th June, 1879.

SIR: The act of Congress in aid of a polar expedition, designed by James Gordon Bennett, approved March 18th, 1878, enacts that—

"Whereas James Gordon Bennett, a citizen of the United States, has purchased in Great Britain a vessel supposed to be specially adapted to Arctic expeditions, and proposes, at his own cost, to fit out and man said vessel, and to devote her to efforts to solve the polar problem; and

"Whereas it is deemed advisable that said vessel, while so engaged, shall carry the American flag, and be officered by American naval officers: Therefore,

"*Be it enacted, &c.*, That the Secretary of the Treasury be authorized to issue an American register to said vessel by the name of Jeannette, and that the President of the United States be authorized to detail, with their own consent, commissioned, warrant, and petty officers of the Navy, not to exceed ten in number, to act as officers of said vessel during her first voyage to the Arctic seas: *Provided, however,* That such detail shall be made of such officers only as the President is satisfied can be absent from their regular duties without detriment to the public service."

The act authorising the Secretary of the Navy to accept for the purposes of a voyage of exploration by the way of Behring's Straits the ship Jeannette, tendered by James Gordon Bennett for the purpose, approved February 27th, 1879, provides that "the Secretary of the Navy be, and he is hereby, authorized to accept and take charge of, for the use of a North Polar expedition, by way of Behring's Straits, the ship Jeannette, owned by James Gordon Bennett, and by him devoted to this purpose; that he may use in fitting her for her voyage of exploration any material he may have on hand proper for the purposes of an Arctic voyage; and that he is further authorized to enlist the necessary crew for the said vessel, for special service, their pay to be temporarily met from the pay of the Navy, and to be paid or refunded by James Gordon Bennett to the Navy Department under the order of the Secretary of the Navy, and as he may require; the vessel to proceed on her voyage of exploration under the orders and instructions of the Navy Department; that the men so specially enlisted as above shall be subject in all respects to the Articles of War and Navy Regulations and discipline; and that all parts of the act approved March the eighteenth, eighteen hundred and seventy-eight, inconsistent with the above be, and they are hereby, repealed: *Provided,* That the Government of the United States shall not be held liable for any expenditure incurred or to be incurred on account of said exploration."

Under the authority conferred by these acts of Congress, the Jeannette has been accepted, fitted out, officered, and manned under the orders of this Department, and you have been ordered to the command of the voyage of exploration.

As soon as the Jeannette, under your command, is in all respects ready for sea, you will proceed with her to Behring's Straits to execute the important and hazardous service entrusted to you. In the execution of this service the Department must leave the details

LOSS OF THE STEAMER JEANNETTE.   293

to your experience, discretion, and judgment. It has full confidence in your ability in all matters connected with the safety and discipline of the ship, the health and comfort of the officers and crew, and the faithful prosecution of the object of the voyage.

On reaching Behring's Straits you will make diligent inquiry at such points where you deem it likely that information can be obtained concerning the fate of Professor Nordenskjöld, as the Department has been unable to have positive confirmation of the reports of his safety. If you have good and sufficient reasons for believing that he is safe, you will proceed on your voyage towards the North Pole. If otherwise, you will pursue such course as in your judgment is necessary for his aid and relief.

You will, as opportunity offers, advise the Department of your whereabouts, and of such matters of interest connected with the voyage as you may desire to communicate.

Wishing you a prosperous voyage, and commending you, the officers, and crew, and the object of your expedition, to the protecting care of Almighty God,

I am, very respectfully, yours,

R. W. THOMPSON,
Secretary of the Navy.

Lieutenant GEORGE W. DE LONG,
United States Navy, commanding voyage of exploration, by way of Behring's Straits, U. S. S. Jeannette, Navy Yard, Mare Island, California.

A true copy.

SAM. C. LEMLY,
Master U. S. Navy, Judge Advocate.

EXHIBIT P.

ARCTIC STEAMER JEANNETTE,
San Francisco, California, July 8th, 1879.

Hon. R. W. THOMPSON, Secretary of the Navy:

SIR: I have the honor to inform you that the Jeanette, being in all respects ready for sea, will sail at three o'clock this afternoon on her cruise to the Arctic regions.

Upon the receipt of the Department's telegram of June 27th informing me that no naval vessel could be detailed to carry provisions and coal for our use, I chartered the Schooner Fanny A. Hyde, Captain Jesperson, loaded her with such of our provisions as were not already embarked in the Jeanette, and one hundred tons anthracite coal, received at the Mare Island navy-yard. This schooner will sail to-day for St. Michael's Alaska, with orders to await our arrival there, and in case of our not arriving within fifteen days of her reaching that port to deposit the provisions and coal in the storehouses of the Alaska Commercial Company, for our possible subsequent use.

I have also the honor to acknowledge the receipt of your orders of the 18th June in relation to the movements of the Arctic expedition under my command; and while I appreciate the grave responsibilities entrusted to my care, I beg leave to assure you that I will endeavor to perform this important duty in a manner calculated to reflect credit upon the ship, the Navy, and the country at large.

I beg leave to return thanks for the confidence expressed in my ability to satisfactorily conduct such a hazardous expedition, and I desire to place upon record my conviction that nothing has been left unprovided which the enterprise and liberality of Mr. James Gordon Bennett and the experiences of our Arctic predecessors could suggest.

In carrying out that portion of my instructions which pertains to the search for tidings of Professor Nordenskjöld, I have to state in brief my proposed plan of operations.

Sailing from San Francisco, I shall proceed with all despatch to the Island of Ounalashka, whence, after coaling, I shall proceed to the Island of St. Paul's, in Behring's Sea. From this point I shall continue on to St. Michael's, in Alaska. At this point some tidings may be had (if intercourse has been maintained during the past winter with the tribes of Northeastern Siberia) of Professor Nordenskjöld and his party. Should nothing, however, be known in that respect, after receiving on board the provisions and coal carried up by the Fanny A. Hyde, I shall proceed to St. Lawrence Bay, in Siberia, in further quest. If Professor Nordenskjöld is, as was reported, in the neighborhood of East Cape, something must have been heard of him by the native tribes, or by the American whalers which cruise in that neighborhood. Should nothing be learned, I will proceed through Behring Straits, and, skirting the coast of Siberia, continue as far to the westward as the circumstances of navigation will permit. I will send to the Department at every opportunity detailed accounts of our progress and whatever information may be collected.

I would also acknowledge the receipt of the letters issued by the Imperial Russian Ministry of the Interior to the Siberian authorities, and I am confident that they will secure us the assistance and co-operation of all subjects of the Russian Government.

I have the honor to be, sir, very respectfully, your obedient servant,

GEORGE W. DE LONG,
Lieutenant United States Navy, Commanding Arctic Steamer Jeannette.

A true copy.

SAM. C. LEMLY,
Master U. S. Navy & Judge Advocate.

EXHIBIT R.

LONDON, *June* 2, 1878.

MY DEAR MR. DANENHOWER: Your letter of May 23d reached me yesterday. I also received a telegram from you the day before to the effect that you wished to go to San Francisco in the Jeannette, and requesting an answer. This I cannot give you immediately, as I have written to Mr. Bennett on the subject and shall await his answer. When Mr. Bennett spoke to me about you, and showed me the letter which General Grant had written, I was only too glad to have associated with me in an arduous undertaking a gentleman so worthy as yourself, and I so expressed myself. I should have been very glad to have known of your wishes several months earlier, and have secured your assistance in the repair and fitting out of the vessel which are now, however, quite complete. I expect to sail from here in four days for Havre, from which place I shall sail on June 25th for San Francisco direct. It is our intention to attack the Polar regions by way of Behring's Strait, and if our efforts are not crowned with success we shall have made an attempt in a new direction and examined a hitherto unknown country, viz, Kellett Land. The vessel which we have selected and purchased was originally Her Britanic Majesty's ship Pandora, and which was sold in 1872 to Sir Allen Young, from whom Mr. Bennet bought her in January last. We have changed her name to Jeannette, and have had her thoroughly repaired and put in shape. She is of 420 tons (builder's tonnage), 142 feet long, 25 feet beam, and draws, when loaded with complete Arctic outfit, about 13 feet; barque rigged, rolling topsails, and trices up her screw. Steams or sails about 6 knots, and is a neat, tidy little ship.

The expedition will leave San Francisco in June, 1879, and will number, all told, 33 persons. There will be but 3 line officers, Lieut. Chipp, yourself, and myself; and, with a surgeon, naturalist, photographer, engineer, and one other person yet undetermined, will constitute the officers' part, while the remaining 25 will be shipped men.

It is very difficult for me to tell you more, though in conversation I might go on for an hour. I have shipped a crew of two mates, carpenter, engineers, & others, in all 18 men to work the ship to San Francisco, where I hope to arrive before Christmas, at which time I shall commence to gather together my people and outfit.

There is really no occasion for your making any move until your cruise is up in January. There is really nothing to do now that the ship is repaired and about to start, and you would only be drifting around without an object. Were you to get your detachment now, I would suggest to your consideration the study of anything you can get on the subject of Arctic exploration, and particularly magnetism and the use of the pendulum in gravity experiments, together with astronomical observations of planets and stars.

Though there is nothing strictly private in this letter, there is no occasion to read it at general muster nor copy it in the log-book. We wish to make no splurge and no show, no boasting or promises to achieve wonders. We have plenty of hard work ahead of us, and no romance; and while we may be gone three years, we may be gone for eternity.

My address until June 25 is in care U. S. consul, Havre, France.

Give my best regards to Caldwell, and believe me,

Very truly, yours,

GEORGE W. DE LONG.

A true copy.

SAM. C. LEMLY,
Master U. S. Navy & Judge Advocate.

EXHIBIT W.

TUNGUS VILLAGE, LENA RIVER,
October 29th, 1881.

SIR: I would respectfully call your attention to the written order of Lieutenant Geo. W. De Long, comd'g Arctic steamer Jeannette, dated August 5, 1881 (a copy of which is hereby attached), by virtue of which you are hereby ordered to take charge of the party of nine (9) enlisted men which is now at this place, and proceed to Belun as soon as you can obtain transportation.

Very respectfully,

GEO. W. MELVILLE,
P. A. Engr. U. S. N.

To JNO. W. DANENHOWER,
Master U. S. Navy.

A true copy.

SAM. C. LEMLY,
U. S. N. & Judge Advocate.

Ordered received Oct. 29th, '81, from Geo. W. Melville, P. A. Engineer U. S. N.

JNO. W. DANENHOWER,
Master U. S. N.

1 inclosure.

EXHIBIT X.

U. S. ARCTIC EXPEDITION, CAPE EMMA, BENNETT ISLAND,
Lat. 76° 38' *N., Long.* 148° 20' *E., August 5th*, 1881.

P. A. Eng. GEORGE W. MELVILLE, *U. S. Navy:*

SIR: We shall leave this island to-morrow, steering a course (over the ice or through the water as the case may be) south (magnetic). In the event of our embarking at any time, in our boats, after the start, you are hereby ordered to take command of the whale-boat until such time as I relieve you from that duty or assign you to some other. Every person under my command at this time who may be embarked in that boat at any time is under your charge and subject to your orders, and you are to exercise all care and diligence for their preservation and the safety of the boat. You will under all circumstances keep close to the boat in which I shall embark; but if, unfortunately, we become separated you will make the best of your way south, until you make the coast of Siberia and follow it along to the westward as far as the Lena River. This river is the destination of our party, and without delay you will in case of separation ascend the Lena to a Russian settlement, from which you can communicate or be forwarded with your party to some place of security and easy access. If the boat in which I am embarked is separated from the two other boats, you will at once place yourself under the orders of Lieut. C. W. Chipp, and so long as you remain in his company obey such orders as he may give you.

Very respectfully,

GEO. W. DE LONG,
Lieutenant U. S. N. Comd'g Arctic Expedition.

The above is a true copy.

GEO. W. MELVILLE,
P. A. Engr. U. S. N.

Compared with original, in possession of Chief Engineer Melville. A true copy.

SAM. C. LEMLY,
Master U. S. Navy & Judge Advocate.

EXHIBIT Y.

BOLOEUGA, *Nov. 4th.*

Lieut. DANENHOWER: Your note received by hand of Bartlett; courier brought commandant's note to the priest. I leave this a. m. to go search for the 1st cutter party. I meet the commandant at Comork Surk, who supplies teams for the journey. Am to have 1 Russian, 1 Yakut or Tungoose, as guides. I have a pretty good chart to search for the missing. If time and weather permits I will go to North coast for ship's papers, chronometer, &c. I may be gone a month; fear not for my safety; I will see that the natives take care of me.

As soon as you arrive at Boloeuga get the commandant to clothe the men for our journey to Yakutz, and as soon as possible after due preparation get the commandant to forward you and *all* of our people to Yakutz, where I have no doubt General Tchernieff will see you through. I will rejoin you at Yakutz as soon as possible. I directed the telegrams from the U. S. and London to catch me at Yakutz. It would be well to collect our bills as you go along, so as to pay our score as soon as money arrives. I find money would be very useful at Boloeuga. See that *Eh Pheme gets his shirt*. Good sense and sound judgment will see you through.

Yours, faithfully,

GEO. W. MELVILLE.

I sent telegrams to minister, to Secretary of Navy, and to 43 Fleet st., London. Slight modification of originals, adding the 1st cutters & 2 men, the others missing, search being made, and to be continued until found. Nindemann or Noros can repeat the telegram to you, I have no copy. I did not say any one was dead, but there was danger of starvation.

Yours, &c.,

G. W. M.

A true copy.

SAM. C. LEMLY,
Master U. S. Navy and Judge Advocate.

EXHIBIT Z.

YAKUTZ, SIBERIA,
January 8, 1882.

Master JNO. W. DANENHOWER,
U. S. Navy, Yakutz, Siberia:

SIR: You are hereby ordered to take charge of a party of eight (8) enlisted men, viz: L. P. Noros (sea), John Cole (sea), Herbert Leach (sea), Chas. Manson (sea), Henry Wilson (sea), R. L. Newcomb (sea, for special service), John Lauterbach (C. H.), Chas. Tong Sing (steward); also Aniguin (Indian), and will proceed to Irkutsk, and thence to the Atlantic sea-board.

You will take especial care of seaman John Cole, who is at present suffering from mental aberration. You will from time to time communicate your progress to the Hon. Secretary of the Navy as your judgment may dictate, and on your arrival at an Atlantic port, or prior to that time, will doubtless receive instructions from him.

You will take charge of the following-named articles, recovered by me from the effects of the party of Lieutenant George W. De Long, U. S. N., and will deliver them to the Hon. Secretary of the Navy on your arrival in the United States, viz: 4 log-books of the U. S. Arctic steamer Jeannette; 4 records of Lieut. De Long's party; 1 Winchester rifle (main-spring broken); 1 Winchester rifle (stock broken); 1 box containing specimens from Bennett Island; 1 box containing sextant; 1 Nautical Almanac; 1 table logarithms; 1 lunar distance; 1 surgical case; 1 binocular; 1 artificial horizon; 1 box chronometer.

Very respectfully,

GEO. W. MELVILLE,
P. A. Engr., U. S. Navy, Comd'g shipwrecked party U. S. Arctic Steamer Jeannette.

A true copy.

SAM. C. LEMLY,
Master U. S. Navy & Judge Advocate.

Received, January 8th, 1882.

JNO. W. DANENHOWER,
Master U. S. N.

EXHIBIT A A.

NIZHNENDINSK, SIBERIA,
March 22, 1882.

Lieutenant JOHN W. DANENHOWER,
U. S. Navy, present:

SIR: Having received instructions from the Hon. Secretary of the Navy to take five men, now under your command, with me to assist in the search for the missing officers and men of the late Arctic steamer Jeannette, I desire to have them join me as quickly as possible. You will therefore direct the following men, now in Krasnajarsk, Siberia, to report to me in Irkutsk, Siberia, without delay: Herbert Leach (sea), Henry Wilson (sea), Frank E. Manson (sea), John Lauterbach (fireman), and Aniguin (hunter.) Three hundred (300) roubles (paper) is herewith supplied for their transportation to Irkutsk.

Very respectfully,

GILES B. HARBER,
Lieut. U. S. Navy.

A true copy.

SAM. C. LEMLY,
Master U. S. Navy & Judge Advocate

EXHIBIT B B.

NISHNENDINSK, SIBERIA,
March 21st, 1882.

Received from Lieut. Danenhower, U. S. N., the following: One box chronometer, one pr. binocular glasses, one sextant, one artificial horizon, one Nautical Almanac (1881), one Chauvenet's lunar dist., one table logarithms, one surgical box, two tourniquets.

G. B. HARBER,
Lieut. U. S. N.

A true copy.

SAM. C. LEMLY,
Master U. S. Navy & Judge Advocate.

EXHIBIT C C.

ARCTIC STEAMER JEANNETTE,
Ounalashka Island, Aug. 4, 1879.

Hon. R. W. THOMPSON,
Secretary of the Navy, Washington, D. C.:

SIR: I have the honor to report the arrival on the 2d inst. at this place of the ship under my command, and the continued good health of the officers and crew I found at anchor here the United States revenue steamer Rush, the steamer St. Paul, and the schooner St. George, the last two named belonging to the Alaska Commercial Company, of San Francisco. This letter is carried to San Francisco by the said steamer St. Paul. I learned upon arrival of the wreck of the brig Timandra, belonging to J. C. Merrill & Co., of San Francisco, on Nounivak Island, about four hundred and twenty miles to the northward of this place. The second mate and three seamen of said brig reached here on the 30th July, bringing tidings of the disaster occurring to that vessel on May 25th. The vessel they report as being a total wreck, although no lives were lost and the cargo nearly all saved. The crew built a boat from a portion of the wreck, eighteen feet in length, six feet in beam, and partly decked over, and the four men above mentioned, having volunteered to come here in search of assistance, left Nounivak on Saturday, the 26th July, and reached here at 1 p. m. on the 30th. The revenue cutter Rush sailed to-day at 11 a. m. to rescue and remove the balance of the crew, eight in number. The steamship St. Paul arrived from St. Paul's Island at 11 a. m. on August 1st, bringing with her the entire collection of furs from the seal islands and the northern settlements, numbering about one hundred thousand skins, and will leave here to-morrow morning at daylight for San Francisco direct.

The revenue cutter Rush during her visit to St. Michael's and her cruise to the northward passed through Behring Straits to some twenty miles to the northward and eastward of East Cape, in Siberia, without having encountered any ice whatever. Supposing that

Professor Nordenskjöld had already passed south, no communication was had by the Rush with St. Lawrence Bay. No communication from St. Lawrence Bay had been received at St. Michael's at the date of the sailing of the Rush on the 23rd July, and consequently there was no knowledge of the safety or movements of Professor Nordenskjöld's party. It was my intention originally, as communicated to you in my letter of July 8th, to stop at St. Paul's Island after leaving this place, but as the fur clothing which I was to have received at that place can be furnished here I have concluded to proceed directly to St. Michael's, in Alaska, leaving here on Wednesday morning, the 6th August. From all the intelligence received from the northward it appears that the last winter has been an exceptionally mild one and that no obstruction to navigation in the shape of ice has been encountered. I can but deplore that the necessity of loading this ship so deeply at San Francisco has made our progress thus far so slow, owing also to head winds and swell, as to make it doubtful whether we shall be able or not to profit by the open water in the Arctic Sea in our efforts to gain a high latitude this season. If upon our arrival at St. Michael's nothing has been heard of the party under the command of Professor Nordenskjöld I shall proceed to St. Lawrence Bay, in Siberia, to obtain tidings of them, and shall proceed subsequently in accordance with the general plan delineated in my letter of July 8th. We have been made the recipients of the most unbounded courtesy and assistance of the Alaska Commercial Company, through its agent at this place. The coal belonging to the Navy Department, and of which there was originally I believe some seven or eight hundred tons, has become reduced by the requisitions of the revenue cutter to about eighty tons, which, owing to exposure and spontaneous combustion, has become of indifferent value. The commanding officer of the Rush having expressed to me his desire to have the remaining quantity reserved for his use in proceeding to San Francisco in the coming fall, I have accepted the offer of the Alaska Commercial Company to furnish one hundred and fifty tons bituminous coal for the use of the expedition. This matter will form the subject of a private arrangement between Mr. James Gordon Bennett and the Alaska Commercial Company, and has no relation to an official transaction. We have also been furnished with fur garments and twelve thousand pounds of dried fish for dog food, both of which have been sent here by the Alaska Commercial Company for our use from Kodiak. The balance of our clothing, forty dogs, more dog food, sledges, and dog-drivers will be furnished at St. Michael's.

I would respectfully call your attention to the fact that the charts of this region are very meager. The most reliable is one published by the Imperial Russian Hydrographic Office, in 1849, which chart was furnished me in San Francisco. The prevalence of fogs and the rapidity and uncertainty of prevailing tides makes an approach to any of the passes between the Aleutian Islands hazardous in the extreme.

Very respectfully,

GEO. W. DE LONG,
Lieutenant United States Navy, Comd'g Arctic Expedition.

A true copy.

SAM. C. LEMLY,
Master U. S. Navy & Judge Advocate.

EXHIBIT D D.

ARCTIC STEAMER JEANNETTE,
St. Lawrence Bay, Siberia, August 26, 1879.

Hon. R. W. THOMPSON,
Secretary of the Navy, Washington, D. C.:

SIR: I have the honor to report the arrival of this vessel at this place yesterday afternoon, and the continued good health of the officers and men under my command.

We reached St. Michael's, in Alaska, on the 12th inst., after a passage of six days from Ounalaska. At St. Michael's we were forced to await the arrival of the schooner Fanny A. Hyde, which vessel had been chartered by me to carry some provisions and one hundred tons of coal from Mare Island. She arrived on the 18th, and having received on board all the stores we could carry, we sailed from St. Michael's on the 21st inst. for this place, encountering a gale from the north of thirty hours' duration, obliging us to lie to and drifting us about eighty miles to the southward and westward. No tidings having been received at St. Michael's concerning Professor Nordenskjöld I ordered the schooner Fanny A. Hyde to follow us to this place, in order that I might be enabled to send back to the United States any information obtainable of the Swedish expedition. Upon our arrival here I communicated with the natives, and saw a chief who says that last winter he saw a ship frozen in Koliutchin Bay, which is about one hundred and fifty miles from East Cape; and (though it is exceedingly difficult to get satisfactory information from these people, owing to our ignorance of their language and their slight acquaintance with ours) I understood him to say he had gone on board of her at that time. At all events he is quite positive that three months ago that same ship anchored off the entrance to this bay, and he again boarded her during the twenty-four hours she remained here. He describes her as a steamer smaller than the Jeannette; the "captain" was an old man, with a white beard, and did not speak English; there were two officers on board who did speak English. There was one officer on board named "Horpish" (Lieutenant Nordquish, Russian Navy?) who was a Russian, and spoke the Tchouktchi language like a native; that there were twenty-five people, all told, on board; that she was a Swiss (Swedish?) ship, and the officers said they were going home. I showed the chief a chart, which he seemed to thoroughly understand, pointing out East Cape and Koliutchin Bay without hesitation, and also the Diomede Islands. He said the ship steamed away from here to go to the Diomede Islands, and thence home by way of the Kamtschatka coast; that the officers on board had no fur clothing nor had the crew; and that whenever they came on deck they shivered with the cold. He was positive the vessel was no trader, and that she was the same one he had seen during the winter in Koliutchin Bay. Repeated attempts at inquiry could bring nothing further, and each time the same story was told.

It would seem from this that Professor Nordenskjöld has passed through Behring's Strait, bound south. But if it is three months since he left here, he should have reached civilization in time for the telegraph to have transmitted the news of his arrival previous to our departure from San Francisco, on the 8th July. It may have happened that Professor Nordenskjöld having no coal to spare has had to sail nearly all the distance from here, in which case he might not have reached Japan in time for news of his arrival to reach the United States before we sailed.

I have decided to proceed from here on the 28th inst., to Cape Serdze Kamen, at which place Nordenskjöld is last officially heard from (according to the letter from the Hon. Wm. M. Evarts, addressed to you under date of June 13th, 1879, and of which letter you have furnished me a copy). If he was at that place in May I will learn of it from the natives at that place, and shape my action accordingly. If he left there in good condition I shall assume the story told me here to be correct, and shall proceed toward Wrangel Land; and if I learn nothing shall proceed to Koliutchin Bay, where he is said to have passed the winter. I cannot say how much longer the Arctic will remain navigable even in this low latitude. The general experience of whalers in these waters has been that some good weather is experienced in September, and if we have it this year we shall do our best to make the most of it. I still have hopes of reaching Wrangel Land before going into winter quarters; but if we fail in so doing we may have to winter in Siberia and risk everything in a dash next spring and summer.

The officers and men seem animated with the same zeal and enthusiasm as ever, and are determined to acquit themselves of the task committed to their care in a manner to bring no reproach to their profession and professional brethren.

Very respectfully,

GEORGE W. DE LONG,
Lieutenant U. S. N., Commanding.

EXHIBIT E E.

ARCTIC STEAMER JEANNETTE,
1st October, 1879.

SIR: The following has been the routine since the 6th September:

From 6th to 21st September, inclusive, 4 a. m., call ship's cook; 6 a. m., all hands coffee; 6.30 a. m., turn to, clean deck, wash clothes, break ice in fire-hold, and execute morning orders; 7.30 a. m., one watch, breakfast; 8 a. m., other watch, breakfast; 8.30 a. m., turn to, all hands on deck when there was any particular work to be done; if not, one watch only; 10 a. m., forecastle reported ready for inspection. During forenoon the watch provided the ice or snow for making water, and attended to work about ship; 12 m., watch below, dinner; 12.30 p. m., relieve watches and other watch to dinner; 11.30, soundings, water temperature every 15 hrs., sea density; 11.45, put over dredge; 1 p. m., turn to and go ahead with any work; all hands, if necessary, otherwise with watch; 4 p. m., haul up dredge, relieve watch; 5.30 p. m., watch below, supper; 6 p. m., relieve watches, other watch supper. From 6 to 8 p. m. watch on deck, peal vegetables, and collect all buckets and put them on quarter deck, near fire-hole. At 8 p. m. galley fires out, boatswain and carpenter report, set anchor watch of one man, watch lasting two hours. At 9 p. m. put out forecastle lamp.

From 22nd to 30th September, inclusive, the routine has been the same, with the exceptions that all hands were called at 7 a. m., the ship's cook being called at 5 a. m. One watch did the morning work. The galley fires put out at 6.30, or as soon as cabin supper was served, and that the boatswain and carpenter reported their departments at 7 p. m. Since the 22nd two men have been standing deck watch, so that the night anchor watches have been divided among nine men.

Very respectfully,

CHAS. W. CHIPP,
Lieut. & Exec. Officer.

Lieut. GEORGE W. DE LONG, U. S. N.,
Commanding Arctic Steamer Jeannette.

A true copy.

SAM. C. LEMLY,
Master U. S. Navy & Judge Advocate.

EXHIBIT F F.

ARCTIC STEAMER JEANNETTE,
Beset and drifting in the pack ice,
Lat. N. 73° 34′, long. 177° 27′ E.

JUNE 17TH, 1880.

The 1st and 2nd cutters, 1st and 2nd whale-boats are each provided with the following articles of equipment, and the same are kept stowed in the said boats: 1 set masts and spars, 1 set sails, 1 set oars, 1 set spare oars for one thwart, 3 boat-hooks, 1 set boarding pikes, 3 in each cutter, 4 each whale-boat; 1 bucket, 1 water breaker, 1 hand grapnel, 1 anchor, 15 fms. rope for anchor, 1 painter, 1 small tackle, 1 handsaw, 1 bunch walrus hide, 1 boat box containing 2 snow knives, 1 hatchet, 1 dipper, 1 marline-spike, 1 can-opener, 2 square feet sheet lead, 2 lbs. nails, 1 box tacks, 1 lb. marline, 2 yds. canvas (sewed around the box), 2 balls cotton twine, 2 skeins twine, 3 sail needles, 1 palm, 1 piece wax, 1 lb. tallow, 2 fishing lines, 1 doz. fish-hooks, 3 candles, 1 paper harness needles, 2 spools linen thread, 2 tins table salt, 100 wind matches, 1 pckge. common matches, 1 tinder box flint and steel, 40 rounds rifle ammunition, 1 monkey-wrench (in 1st cutter only).

A true copy.

SAM. C. LEMLY
Master U. S. Navy & Judge Advocate.

EXHIBIT G G.

FIRE BILL FOR THE WINTER 1880–1881.

In case of fire on board ship, the man on watch will at once call the captain and executive officer, and then, if ordered, ring the fire alarm. Each officer and man will at once go to his station, as follows, viz:

The executive officer will proceed to the locality of the fire.

The chief engineer will collect the pocket chronometers, instrument box, log-books, rifles, and ammunition in the cabin ready to be passed on the ice.

The surgeon will remove to a place of safety inflammable medicines, have medicine chest ready for removal, and remove the helpless sick to a place of safety.

Mr. Collins will collect the ship's books and papers ready for removal, and then assist the surgeon with the sick.

Mr. Newcomb will remove to a place of safety any dangerous inflammable material in his charge, and then assist the surgeon with the sick.

Mr. Dunbar will get the fire extinguisher from the cabin and proceed to the locality of the fire.

Nos. 19 and 20 will remove sled stores to the ice and then report to the chief engineer.

Messrs. Cole and Nindemann will each get an axe and proceed to the locality of the fire.

Mr. Sweetman will see hatches covered in the neighborhood of the fire, and then report to the executive officer.

LOSS OF THE STEAMER JEANNETTE. 301

Alexy and Aniguin will collect the dog harnesses, and then assist to pass water.

No. 1 will get the keys of store-rooms and magazine and report to executive officer.

The rest of the ship's company will draw and pass water, forming a line from the fire hole to the fire in the following order, viz: Nos. 2, 4, 6, 8, 10, 12, 14, 16, 18, 17, 15, 13, 11, 9, 7, 5, 3.

If ordered to pass provisions and stores out of the ship, either on account of fire or the ship being in danger from ice pressure, each officer and man will bring his knapsack on deck and proceed to his station as follows:

The executive officer will take the deck.

The chief engineer will collect the pocket chronometers, instrument-box, log-books, rifles, and ammunition; and, assisted by Nos. 19 and 20, will pass them out of the ship, and then superintend the removal of stores, etc., from alongside to a place of safety on the ice.

The surgeon will remove to the ice the helpless sick and the medicine chest.

Mr. Newcomb will assist the surgeon.

Mr. Collins will remove the ship's books and papers to the ice, and then assist the surgeon with the sick.

Mr. Dunbar, with Sweetman and Nindemann, will pass the sleds that are on top of the deck-house to the ice, and then remove stores, &c., from alongside.

Mr. Cole and the starboard watch not otherwise stationed will pass tents, knapsacks, and provisions that are forward on the ice.

Nos. 1 and 2 will open steerage hatch and pass up the sleeping bags.

The port watch not especially stationed will work aft, passing sleeping bags, alcohol, provisions, dog food, and snow-shoes on the ice.

Nos. 19 and 20 will pass the sled stores on the ice, and then report to the chief engineer.

Alexy and Aniguin will pass the dog harness on the ice, then assist in getting the sleds on the ice and in removing provisions.

If the order be given to lower any of the boats the following numbers will perform that duty: Lower 1st cutter, Nos. 2, 8, 14; lower 2nd cutter, Nos. 1, 9, 13; lower 1st whale-boat, Nos. 5, 10, 16; lower 2nd whale-boat, Nos. 4, 6, 11; lower metallic dinghey, Nos. 3, 7, 12.

If ordered to abandon the ship everybody will at once leave her, and when sleds, boats, stores, provisions, etc., have been removed to a place of safety, will assemble by sled crews according to the following detail, viz:

Crew No. 1—Lieut. De Long, Mr. Collins, W. F. C. Nindemann, H. H. Erichsen, H. H. Kaack, G. W. Boyd, Alexy.

Crew No. 2—Lieut. Chipp, Mr. Danenhower, A. Sweetman, E. Star, A. G. Kuchne, Walter Sharvell, Ah Sam.

Crew No. 3—Mr. Dunbar, Mr. Newcomb, J. H. Bartlett, H. W. Leach, Henry Wilson, J. Lauterbach, Aniguin.

Crew No. 4—Chf. Eng. Melville, Walter Lee, L. P. Noros, Adolph Dressler, C. A. Görtz, Nelse Iversen.

Crew No. 5—Surgeon Ambler, John Cole, F. H. Manson, H. D. Warren, P. E. Johnson, C. Tong Sing.

Approved.

GEORGE W. DE LONG,
Lieutenant U. S. Navy, Commanding.

A true copy.

SAM. C. LEMLY,
Master U. S. Navy & Judge Advocate.

EXHIBIT H H.

Arctic steamer Jeannette lost on the 11th June; landed on Siberia 25th September or thereabouts; want assistance to go for the CAPTAIN and DOCTOR and nine (9) other men.

WILLIAM F. C. NINDEMANN,
LOUIS P. NOROS,
Seamen U. S. N.

Reply in haste; want food and clothing.

A true copy.

SAM. C. LEMLY,
Master U. S. Navy & Judge Advocate.

Exhibit I I.

Arctic Exploring Steamer Jeannette.

At a hut on the Lena Delta, believed to be near Tch-ol-bogoje, Lat. ——, Lon. ——.

Thursday, 22d of *Sept.*, 1881.

Whoever finds this paper is requested to forward it to the Secretary of the Navy, with a note of the time and place at which it was found.*

The following-named persons, 14 of the officers and crew of the Jeannette, reached this place yesterday afternoon on foot from the Arctic Ocean:

George W. De Long, lieutenant U. S. Navy, commander of expedition.
P. A. Surgeon J. M. Ambler.
Mr. J. J. Collins.
Walter Lee.
W. F. Nindemann.
H. H. Erichsen.
A. Görtz.
G. W. Boyd.
Nelse Iverson.
Adolph Dressler.
H. H. Kaack.
L. P. Noros.
Ah Sam.
Alexy.

The Jeannette was crushed and sunk by the ice on the 12th of June, 1881, in lat. N. 77° 15′, long. E. 155° 0′, after having drifted 22 months in the tremendous pack ice of this ocean. The entire 33 persons composing her officers and crew dragged 3 boats and provisions on the ice to lat. N. 76° 38′, long. 150° 30′ E., where we landed upon a new island, Bennett Island, on the 29th July. From thence we proceeded, sometimes in boats, sometimes dragging over ice, until the 10th September, when we reached Semenowski Island, about 90 miles NE. of this delta. We sailed from there in company on the 12th Sept., but that same night were separated in a gale of wind, and I have seen nothing since of the two other boats or their people. They were divided as follows:

2nd cutter.	Whale-boat.
Lieut. Chipp.	P. A. Engr. Melville.
Mr. Dunbar.	Master Danenhower.
A. Sweetman.	Mr. Newcomb.
W. Sharvell.	J. Cole.
E. Star.	J. H. Bartlett.
H. D. Warren.	H. Wilson.
A. G. Kuchne.	J. Lauterbach.
P. Johnson.	F. Manson.
	Charles Tong Sing.
	Aniguin.
	H. W. Leach.

Each officer in charge of a boat had written orders to proceed in case of separation to the Lena River, and not to wait for anybody short of a settlement large enough to feed and shelter his men.

The provisions, arms, and clothing had been fairly divided, we were all in good health, and had no doubt of reaching the Lena in a few days, when we were parted by this gale of wind.

My boat having weathered the gale, made the land on the morning of the 16th inst., and after trying to get in shore for two days, and being prevented by shoal water, we abandoned her and waded to the beach, carrying our arms, provisions, and records, at a point about 12 miles to the nd. a ed. of this place. We had all suffered somewhat from cold, wet, and exposure, and three of our men were badly lamed; but having only 4 days' provisions left, reduced rations, we were forced to proceed to the sd.

On Monday, Sept. 19, we left a pile of our effects near the beach, erecting a long pole. There will be found navigating instruments, chronometer, ship's log-books for 2 years, tent, medicines, &c., which we were absolutely unable to carry. It took us 48

---

* Note.—With the same notice in French, German, and Spanish, and the same or a similar one in Swedish, Dutch, and Russian.

SAM. C. LEMLY,
Judge Advocate of Court.

hours to make these 12 miles, owing to our disabled men, and the two huts seemed to me a good place to stop while I pushed forward the surgeon and Nindemann to get relief for us. But last night we shot 2 reindeer, which gives us abundance of food for the present, and we have seen so many more that anxiety for the future is relieved. As soon as our 3 sick men can walk we shall resume our search for a settlement on the Lena River.

Saturday, September 24th, 8 a. m.—Our three lame men being now able to walk, we are about to resume our journey with 2 days' rations deer meat and 2 days' rations pemmican and 3 lbs. tea.

GEORGE W. DE LONG,
Lieutenant, Commanding.

A true copy.

SAM. C. LEMLY,
Master U. S. Navy & Judge Advocate.

Exhibit K K.

At a Hut, Lena Delta,
About 12 miles from head of Delta.

Monday, *September 26th,* 1881.

Fourteen of the officers and men of the U. S. Arctic steamer Jeannette reached this place last evening, and are proceeding to the sd. this morning.

A more complete record will be found in a tinder case hung up in a hut 15 miles further up the right bank of the larger stream.

GEORGE W. DE LONG,
Lieut. Commanding.

P. A. Surgeon J. M. Ambler	N. Iverson
Mr. J. J. Collins	A. Görtz
W. F. Nindemann	A. Dressler
H. H. Erichsen	Ah Sam
H. H. Kaack	Alexy
G. W. Boyd	L. P. Noros
W. Lee.	

A true copy.

SAM. C. LEMLY,
Master U. S. Navy & Judge Advocate.

Exhibit L L.

Saturday, *October 1st,* 1881.

Fourteen of the officers and men of the U. S. Arctic steamer Jeannette reached this hut on Wednesday, September 28th, and having been forced to await for the river to freeze over, are proceeding to cross over to the west side this a. m., on their journey to reach some settlement on the Lena River. We have two days' provisions, but having been fortunate enough thus far to get game in our pressing needs, we have no fear for the future.

Our party are all well, except one man, Erichsen, whose toes have been amputated in consequence of frost bite. Other records will be found in several huts on the east side of this river, along which we have come from the nd.

GEORGE W. DE LONG,
Lieutenant U. S. Navy, Commanding Expedition.

P. A. Surgeon Ambler.	G. W. Boyd.
Mr. J. J. Collins.	A. Dressler.
W. F. Nindemann.	H. H. Kaack.
H. H. Erichsen.	N. Iverson.
A. Görtz.	Ah Sam.
W. Lee.	Alexy.
L. P. Noros.	

A true copy.

SAM. C. LEMLY,
Master U. S. Navy & Judge Advocate.

Exhibit M M.

VERKERANSK, *December 7th*, 1881.

EASE SPRAVNIK, &c.:

SIR: It is my desire and the wishes of the Government of the United States of America and of the projector of the American expedition that a diligent and constant search be made for my missing comrades of both boats. Lieutenant DeLong and his party, consisting of twelve persons, will be found near the bank of the Lena River, west side of the river. They are south of the small hunting station known among the Yakouts as Qu Vina. They could not possibly have marched as far south as Bulcom; therefore, be they dead or alive they are between Bulcour and Qu Vina. I have already travelled over this ground, but followed the river bank; therefore it is necessary that a more careful search be made on the high ground back from the river for a short distance as well as along the river bank. I examined many huts and small houses but could not possibly examine all of them; therefore it is necessary that all—every house and hut, large and small, must be examined for books, papers, or the persons of the party. Men without food and but little clothing would naturally seek shelter in huts along the line of their march, and if exhausted might die in one of them. They would leave their books and papers in a hut if unable to carry them farther. If they carried their books and papers south of that section of country between Mat Vay and Bulcour, their books and papers will be found piled up in a heap and some prominent object erected near them to attract attention of searching parties; a mast of wood or pile of wood would be erected near them if not on them. In case books or papers are found they are to be sent to the American minister resident at St. Petersburg. If they are found and can be forwarded to me before I leave Russia I will take them to America with me.

If the persons of my comrades are found dead I desire that all books and papers be taken from their clothing and forwarded to the American minister at St. Petersburg, or to me if in time to reach me before leaving Russia. The persons of the dead I wish to have carried to a central position most convenient of access from Bulun, all placed inside of a small hut, arranged side by side for future recognition, the hut then securely closed and banked up with snow or earth, and remain so until a proper person arrives from America to make final disposition of the bodies. In banking up the hut have it done in such manner that animals cannot get in and destroy the bodies.

Search for the small boat, containing eight persons, should be made from the west mouth of the Lena River to and beyond the east mouth of the Jana River. Since the separation of the three boats no information has been received concerning the small boat, but as all three boats were destined to Barkin and then to go to a Lena mouth, it is natural to suppose that Lieutenant Chipp directed his boat to Barkin if he managed to weather the gale; but if from any cause he could not reach a Lena mouth Lieut. Chipp would continue along the coast from Barkin, west, for a north mouth of the Lena or south, for an eastern mouth of the Lena River. If still unsuccessful in getting into the Lena River, he might from stress of weather, or other cause, be forced along the coast toward the Jana River.

Diligent and constant search is to commence now, in December, and to continue until the people, books, and papers are found, care being taken that a vigilant and careful examination of that section of the country where Lieutenant De Long and his party are known to be is made in early spring-time, when the snow begins to leave the ground and before the spring floods commence to overflow the river bank. One or more American officers will in all probability be in Bulun in time to assist in the search, but the search mentioned in these instructions is to be carried on independently of any other party and to be entirely under the control of the competent authority of Russia.

[Copy of a letter addressed to the Spravnik of Verkeransk, M. Kasharoffski, by Chief Engineer Melville, directing him to promulgate the same to the commandant of Bulun.]

A true copy.

SAM. C. LEMLY,
Master U. S. Navy & Judge Advocate.

Exhibit N N.

IRKUTSK. (Received at Washn., D. C., *Dec.* 21, 1881.)

To the Honorable Secretary of the Navy at Washington, D. C., U. S. of America:

The steamer Jeannette was crushed in the ice June 11th, 1881, latitude 77 degrees 15 north, longitude 157 east. With sledges and boats made good to fifty miles northwest of the mouth of the Lena River where the three boats were separated in a gale. The whale boat, in charge of Engineer Melville, entered the east mouth of the Lena River on September 17th; stopped by ice in the river. Found a native village, and as soon as the river closed put myself in communication with commandant at Boloenga. On October 29 heard that the 1st cutter, containing Lieutenant De Long, Dr. Ambler, and 12 others, landed at the north mouth of the Lena. The commandant at Boloenga sent instant relief to whale-boat party, who are all well. Nindemann and Noros arrived at Boloenga on October 29 for relief for the first cutter, all of whom are in a sad condition and in danger of starvation, all badly frozen. Commandant at Boloenga has sent native scouts to look for them; will urge vigorous and constant search until found. The second cutter not yet heard from. List of people in boats: First cutter—Lieutenant De Long, Dr. Ambler, Collins, Nindemann, Noros, Erichsen, Kaack, Dressler, Görtz, Lee, Iverson, Boyd, Alexy, Ah Sam. Second cutter—Lieutenant Chipp, Dunbar, Sweetman, Warren, Johnson, Star, Sharvell, Kuchne. Whale boat—Engineer Melville, Lieutenant Danenhower, Cole, Bartlett, Newcomb, Leach, Lauterbach, Wilson, Manson, Aneguin, Tong Sing.

GEORGE MELVILLE,
Engineer.

A true copy.

SAM. C. LEMLY,
Master U. S. Navy & Judge Advocate.

Exhibit N N 2.

To his Excellency the Minister of United States at St. Petersburg, Russia:

The American steamer "Jeannette" was crushed by ice on the 11th of June, 1881, 77° 15′ lat. N., 157° east long. By boats and sleds made good a retreat until 50 miles N W. from Lena mouth, where our three boats were separated by a gale. The whale boat, under charge of Chief Engineer Melville, entered, on the 17th of September, the eastern mouth of Lena River, and was stopped there by ice; found a native village, and as soon as the river closed communicated with the commandant at Bulun. The 29th of October learned that the 1st cutter, including Lieut. De Long, Dr. Ambler, and 12 others, landed at the northern mouth of Lena River. The commandant of Bulun immediately sent assistance to the whale boat, on which all are well. Nindemann and Noros arrived at Bulun the 29th of October to get assistance for the first cutters, all of which are badly frozen and in danger of starvation. The commandant of Bulun sent natives to search for them. I will insist on vigorous and constant search until found. The second cutter not yet heard from.

THE LIST.

1st Cutter.	2nd Cutter.	The Whale Boat.
Lt. De Long.	Lt. Chipp.	(Blank.)
Dr. Ambler.	Dunbar.	
Collins.	Sweetman.	
Nindemann.	Warren.	
Noros.	Johnson.	
Erichsen.	Star.	
Kaack.	Sharvell.	
Dressler.	Kuchne.	
Görtz.		
Lee.		
Iverson.		
Boyd.		
Alexy.		
Ah Sam.		

Telegraph money immediately through Irkutsk and Yakutsk.

Referred to by witness Melville as copy of exhibit NN (see page 636 of record), sent to U. S. minister at St. Petersburg.

A true copy.

SAM. C. LEMLY,
Master U. S. Navy & Judge Advocate.

EXHIBIT O O.

[Telegram.]

WASHINGTON.

Omit no effort, spare no expense in securing safety of men in second cutter. Let the sick and the frozen of those already rescued have every attention, and as soon as practicable have them transferred to milder climate. Department will supply necessary funds.

HUNT, *Secretary*.

MELVILLE,
    Ingénieur U. S. Navy, Irkutsk.

A true copy.

SAM. C. LEMLY,
Master U. S. Navy & Judge Advocate.

EXHIBIT PP.

[Telegram.]

Received telegram; reported to Washington. Instructed to provide everything needed; seen Minister of Interior. Russian Government will provide everything necessary to Petersburgh, also search for 2nd cutter; can you suggest anything our Government can do to aid in search?

HOFFMAN, *Chargé*.

Irkutsk. Ship Engineer Mellville of steamer Jeannette.

A true copy.

SAM. C. LEMLY,
Master U. S. Navy & Judge Advocate.

EXHIBIT R R.

FRIDAY, *October 7th*, 1881.

The undermentioned officers and men of the late U. S. steamer Jeannette are leaving here this morning to make a forced march to Kumak Surka or some other settlement on the Lena River. We reached here on Tuesday, October 4th, with a disabled comrade, H. H. Erichsen (seaman), who died yesterday morning and was burried in the river at noon. His death resulted from frost bite and exhaustion, due to consequent exposure.

The rest of us are well but have no provisions left, having eaten our last this morning.

GEORGE W. DE LONG,
Lieut. Comdg.
P. A. Surgeon AMBLER.
Mr. J. J. COLLINS.
W. F. NINDEMANN.
G. W. BOYD.
H. H. KAACK.
W. LEE.
N. IVERSON.
AH SAM.
ALEXY.
A. GÖRTZ.
A. DRESSLER.
L. P. NOROS.

A true copy.

SAM. C. LEMLY,
Master U. S. Navy & Judge Advocate.

Exhibit S S.

[Telegram.]

JULY 7TH, 1882. IRKUTSK.

SECRETARY OF THE NAVY,
    Washington, D. C., U. S. of America:
Arrived Irkutsk with Nindemann, Noros, and relics. Missed Harber on Lena; sent Bartlett to join him.
Want permission to return home.

MELVILLE.

A true copy.

SAM. C. LEMLY,
Master U. S. Navy & Judge Advocate.

Exhibit T T.

Irkutsk. Washington.

WASHINGTON, *July* 8.

May return home with party.

CHANDLER,
Secretary.

MELVILLE,
    Irkutsk, Siberia.

A true copy.

SAM. C. LEMLY,
Master U. S. Navy & Judge Advocate.

Exhibit U U.

ARCTIC EXPLORING STEAMER JEANNETTE,
Lena Delta, Lat. —, Long. —,
Monday, 19*th of September,* 1881.

☞ Whoever finds this paper is requested to forward it to the Secretary of the Navy, with a note of the time and place at which it was found.*

The following-named 14 persons belonging to the Jeannette (which was sunk by the ice on June 12th, 1881, in lat. N. 77° 15′, long. E. 155°) landed here on the evening of the 17th inst., and will proceed on foot this afternoon to try to reach a settlement on the Lena River:

Commander George W. De Long, Lieutenant, Commanding.
1. Lieut. De Long.
2. Surgeon Ambler.
3. Mr. Collins.
4. W. F. C. Nindemann.
5. A. Görtz.
6. Ah Sam.
7. Alexy.
8. H. H. Erichsen.
9. H. H. Kaack.
10. G. W. Boyd.
11. W. Lee.
12. N. Iverson.
13. L. P. Noros.
14. A. Dressler.

A record was left about ½ mile north of the southern end of Semenowski Island, buried under a stake. The 33 persons composing the officers and crew of the Jeannette left that island in 3 boats on the morning of the 12th instant (one week ago). That same night

---

*NOTE.—With the same notice in French, German, and Spanish, and the same or a similar one in Sweedish, Dutch, and Russian.

SAM. C. LEMLY,
Judge Advocate of Court.

we were separated in a gale of wind, and I have seen nothing of them since. Orders had been given, in event of such an accident, for each boat to make the best of its way to a settlement on the Lena River before waiting for anybody. My boat made the land in the morning of the 16th inst., and I suppose we are at the Lena Delta. I have had no chance to get sights for position since I left Semenowski Island. After trying for two days to get inshore without grounding, or to reach one of the river mouths, I abandoned my boat and waded 1½ miles, carrying our provisions and outfits with us. We must now try, with God's help, to walk to a settlement, the nearest of which I believe to be 95 miles distant. We are all well, have 4 days' provisions, arms and ammunition, and are carrying with us only ship's books and papers, with blankets, tent, and some medicines; therefore our chances of getting through seem good.

GEORGE W. DE LONG,
Lieutenant U. S. Navy, Commanding.

A true copy.

SAM. C. LEMLY,
Master U. S. Navy & Judge Advocate.

EXHIBIT V V.

BULUN, October 29, 1881.

To the American Minister, St. Petersburg:

Please inform the Secretary of the U. S. Navy of the loss of the Jeannette. Arctic steamer Jeannette crushed in the ice June 11th, 1881, in lat. 77° 20′ N., long. 157° 55′ E. or thereabouts; saved three boats, also from three to four months' provisions; with sleds traveled SW. to reach the new Siberian Islands; travelled two weeks or thereabouts, then sighted an island. The captain determined to reach it and landed in about two weeks on the southern end and planted the American flag, and called it Bennet Island; Lieut. Chipp was sent on the west side to determine the size, with a boat's crew; Ice Pilot Dunbar, with the two natives, on the east side. Returned in three days; remained one week on the island, took to the boats and started south, made the new Siberian Islands and encamped on a couple of them; set our course from the most southern island to strike the north coast of Siberia, to enter one of the small rivers to the Lena; on our passage a gale of wind set in, a sea running; lost sight of the boats, one in charge of Lieutenant Chipp, the other Engr. Melville; know not what has become of them; our boat almost swamped; carried away the mast; lost the sail; lay hove to under a drag one night and a day, shipping seas all the time; pumps and bailers going night and day. All hands' feet frost-bitten; when the gale was over the captain had lost the use of his feet and hands; made the coast; struck one of the small rivers, not finding water enough to enter; the ice making; beating around for two days, the captain determined to make the land; the boat struck two miles off shore; the captain made everybody that was able to stand on his feet to get overboard to lighten the boat and tow her in. We towed her one mile; could not get her any farther; took out the ship's papers and provisions; the captain then had got the use of his hands and feet a little on evening of the 25th of September. Names of boat's crew: Captain *De Long*, Surgeon *Ambler*, Mr. *Collins*, W. F. C. *Nindermann*, Louis P. *Noros*, H. H. *Erichsen*, H. H. *Kaack*, G. W. *Boyd*, A. *Gortz*, A. *Dressler*, W. *Lee*, N. *Iverson*, *Alexy*, *Ah Sam*, and *one dog*. Remained a few days on the sea-coast on account of some of the men's feet being badly frost-bitten, leaving behind the ship's log and other articles, not being able to carry them; started to travel south with five days' provisions; Erichsen walking on crutches; a few days after made a sled to drag him; came to a hut on the 5th of October; on the morning of the 6th the doctor cut off all his toes; the captain asked me if I had strength to go to one of the settlements with one of the men to get assistance, as he was going to stay by Erichson; while talking about it Erichson *died;* we buried him in the river. The captain said we will all go together; name of place, *Ow Tit Ary;* lat. 71° 55′ north, long. not known; Oct. 7 eat our last dog meat; started to travel south with about one quart of alcohol and two tin cases of ship's papers, two rifles and little ammunition; travelled until the 9th. Nothing to eat; drank three ounces of alcohol a day per man; the captain and the rest of them got weak and gave out travelling; he then sent me and L. P. *Noros*, with three ounces of alcohol and one rifle and 40 rounds of ammunition, on ahead to a place called *Kumak Surka,* distance about 12 miles, to find natives; if not finding any to travel south until we did; took us five days to walk to *Kumak Surka;* found two fish; took one day's rest; started south again; nothing to eat; travelled until the 19th; getting weaker every day; gave up in despair; sat down, rested, then walked one mile; found two huts and a storehouse where there was about fifteen pounds of *blue moulded fish;* stopped three days to regain strength, both being too weak to travel; on the afternoon of the 23rd or thereabouts, a *native* came to the hut; we tried to make him understand that there was eleven more men north; could not make him understand; he took us to his camp, where there was six more, also a lot of sleighs and reindeer, they travelling at the time south; next morning broke camp, came to a settlement on the 25th called *Ajaket;* then tried again to make the people understand there was more people north; did not succeed. Ayaket, lat. 70° 55′ north, long. not known, as the chart is a copy; sent for the governor to *Bulun;* came 27th; he knew the ship's name and knew about Nordenskjöld, but could not talk English; we tried to make him understand that the captain was in a starving condition, or probably dead, and that we wanted natives, reindeer, and food to get them, as I thought that we could make it in five or six days to save them from starvation, but the governor made signs that he had to telegraph to St. Petersburg; he then sent us on to *Bulun;* we stand in need of food and clothing; at present our health is in a bad condition. Hoping to be well soon, we remain your humble servants,

        WILLIAM F. C. NINDEMANN,
        LOUIS P. NOROS,
       Seamen of the U. S. Navy, Steamer Jeannette.

This document was brought to me by the Bulun commandant on November 1st, 1881. I immediately despatched it by special courier James H. Bartlett, 1 c. f., to Mr. Melville who was on his way to Bulun by the dog road and had missed seeing the commandant who had travelled by the deer road. The courier travelled by the deer road and reached Bulun a few hours after Mr. Melville.

        JNO. W. DANENHOWER,
         Lieutenant U. S. N.

Received Nov. 1, 1881, from Comdt. of Bulun.

A true copy.

        SAM. C. LEMLY,
      Master U. S. Navy, Judge Advocate.

Exhibit X X.

       YAKUTSK, EASTERN SIBERIA, *Jany.* 18, 1882.

WM. C. F. NINDEMANN:

SIR: You will leave this place to-day, taking with you Mr. C. Bulokoff and provisions to supply all your wants as far as Verkeransk; at Verkeransk you will replenish your supply of bread and fresh beef, or other small articles you may stand in need of. Leave Verkeransk as soon as you possibly can and get to Bulun. There you will go into quarters and await my arrival.

The commandant at Bulun will supply all your wants. You will be careful of all the property placed in your charge.

  Very respectfully,

        GEO W. MELVILLE,
        P. A. Engr., U. S. N.

A true copy.

        SAM. C. LEMLY,
     Master U. S. Navy & Judge Advocate.

Exhibit A B.

        CATH CARTA, *April* 10*th,* 1882.

WM. C. F. NINDEMANN:

SIR: You will leave this place to-day and make the best of your way to Barkin, the NE. point of the Lena Delta; arrived there you will commence your western journey to North Bulun. The object of your journey is to search the coast line, the bays, and river mouths for indications of the second cutter or the party of Lieutenant Chipp. You will be furnished with two sleds and dog teams and two experienced guides, Simeon Tomat and Starry Nicolai, a tent and ten days' provisions for yourself and guide, and fish for the dogs; more provisions cannot be carried for so long a journey without overloading the teams. Therefore you will travel at your best rate of speed, camping only long enough to give the dogs sufficient rest to prevent their breaking down. Upon your arrival at N. Bulun take a rest for a day or two if necessary and your provisions will permit or can be procured at that place, then return to Cath Carta. If indications point to the probable landing of Lieutenant Chipp's party follow the trail until some positive indications are found, then make the best of your way to Cath Carta and inform me. That the whole force may be employed for the object in view, James H. Bartlett and his party will accompany you as far as Barkin.

Very respectfully,

GEO. W. MELVILLE,
P. A. Engineer U. S. N.

A true copy.

SAM. C. LEMLY,
Master U. S. N., Judge Advocate.

EXHIBIT B C.

CHADD'S FORD, PENNA., *Nov. 4th,* 1882.

Commo. WM. G. TEMPLE,
Pres. Jeannette Board of Inquiry, Washington, D. C.:

SIR: In view of the importance of the subject under investigation I would respectfully ask to be represented by a counsel before the board of inquiry of which you are the presiding officer. My absence is caused by having made important business engagements before the resolution of Congress was passed or contemplated. I wish to fulfill the engagement if possible, and think it is my duty to do so. I therefore respectfully request that Lieut. Richard Wainwright, U. S. Navy, be permitted to represent me before the board of inquiry and in case his other duties prevent his being present that he be allowed to appoint a deputy.

I am, sir, very respectfully,

JNO. W. DANENHOWER,
Lieut. U. S. N.

A true copy.

SAM. C. LEMLY,
Master U. S. Navy & Judge Advocate.

EXHIBIT C D.

Interrogatories addressed to Naval Constructor George W. Much, U. S. Navy, by a court of inquiry convened at the Navy Department, Washington, D. C., by the order of the honorable Secretary Navy, to investigate the circumstances of the loss in the Arctic seas of the exploring steamer Jeannette.

1st interrogatory. What is your name, rank, present duty, and station?

2nd interrogatory. Did you perform any duty in connection with the fitting out of the exploring steamer Jeannette for Arctic service? If yea, state fully what that duty was, where, and when performed.

3d interrogatory. Were you a member of the board appointed by Commodore E. R. Colhoun, U. S. N., then commandant of the navy-yard at Mare Island, California, in a letter dated June 6, 1879, to carefully examine and report upon the repairs and outfits of the Arctic steamer Jeannette, to state if the repairs and alterations as recommended in the survey upon that vessel had been made, or if any other work not embraced therein but considered necessary had been done, and if in the opinion of the Board she had been so far as practicable repaired and placed in condition for service in the Arctic Ocean?

4th interrogatory. If your answer be yea to the 3d interrogatory, state fully why in the opinion of the board it was not possible to make the Jeannette particularly adapted for an extended cruise in the Arctic regions.

5th interrogatory. If your answer be yea to the 3d interrogatory, state fully what in your opinion was the effect upon the strength of the Jeannette of the following deviations from the recommendation of the board of survey:

a. In lieu of the four six-inch bulkheads, as recommended in survey, beams and heavy truss work or thwartship diagonal bracing has been substituted.

b. In addition to the original iron breast-hooks and in lieu of three or four heavy wooden hooks (as recommended in survey), it was found after removing the joiner work above the berth deck that hooks of the proper shape could not be obtained, so pointers and bracing were used instead.

c. The neglect to place good heavy stanchions under every beam well secured, as recommended by survey.

6th interrogatory. If your answer be yea to the 3rd interrogatory, state what in your opinion would have been the effect upon the strength of the vessel had the recommendation of the survey been carried out in regard to the four six-inch bulkheads, and, if practicable, the beams and heavy truss work at thwartships, diagonal bracing had also been put in so as to combine the two modes of strengthening.

7th interrogatory. State, if you know, who was responsible for each and all of the above enumerated deviations from the recommendations of the survey.

8th interrogatory. What were your opportunities for observing the Jeannette while undergoing repairs and alterations at the Mare Island navy-yard?

9th interrogatory. From your observation of the Jeannette while undergoing repairs and alterations at the Mare Island navy-yard, and your inspection if that vessel prior to her departure from San Francisco, what was your opinion of that vessel, first as to her general seaworthiness, and second as to her fitness for extended Arctic exploration?

10th interrogatory. State fully upon what grounds you base your opinion as given in your answer to the 8th interrogatory.

11th interrogatory. Did the commanding or any other officer of the Jeannette expedition express to you dissatisfaction with the fitting of the vessel just prior to her departure from San Francisco, or did they express themselves as satisfied?

12th interrogatory. Did you, or did you not, at the time of her sailing from San Francisco, consider that the model and construction of the Jeannette was such as to fit her for Arctic cruising, and upon what grounds did you base your opinion?

13th interrogatory. Have you any plans of the Jeannette in your possession which will throw any light upon her construction? If yea, furnish this court with duly authenticated copies of such plans.

14th interrogatory. State fully, in narrative form, anything further within your knowledge bearing upon the subject under investigation.

Original paper.

SAM. C. LEMLY,
Master U. S. Navy & Judge Advocate.

EXHIBIT D E.

EXPLORING STEAMER JEANNETTE, RELATIVE TO THE LOSS THEREOF.

Deposition of George W. Much, Naval Constructor, U. S. N., Navy Yard, Mare Island, California.

STATE OF CALIFORNIA,
  County of Solano, *ss*:

The deposition of George W. Much, naval constructor, U. S. Navy, in the county of Solano, State of California, taken at my office in said county and State on the fourth day of November, A. D. 1882, between the hours of ten and twelve (meridian) of the same day, to be used in evidence in the investigation of the circumstances of the loss in the Arctic seas of the exploring steamer Jeannette, before a court of inquiry of which Commodore William G. Temple, U. S. N., is president.

[SEAL]

WM. R. COX, JR.,
Notary Public.

Answer to 1st interrogatory. Geo. W. Much, naval constructor, U. S. N., having general superintendance and charge of the construction and repair of vessels at the U. S. navy-yard, Mare Island, California.

Answer to 2d interrogatory. I did. My duty was, in connection with other duty, to superintend the repairs on that vessel, under the direction of the commandant of the yard, at the U. S. navy-yard, Mare Island, California, during the time of her repairs, from February, 1879, to the July following.

Answer to 3d interrogatory. I was.

Answer to 4th interrogatory. It was the opinion of the Board that the model or form of the "Jeannette" was not adapted for ice navigation.

Answer to 5th interrogatory. *a* The effect upon the strength would be, in my opinion, to make her less liable to withstand a crushing strain. *b* The pointers and bracing, and the manner in which they were secured, made equally as strong and substantial work as if the hooks recommended by the Board could have been procured and put in the vessel. *c* In my opinion, the neglect to place good heavy stanchions under every beam did not detract from the general strength of the Jeannette, so far as sustaining the deck and beams over ward-room and forward berth-deck was concerned, as they, the beams, were supported by bulkheads running both fore and aft, with nearly corresponding bulkheads below.

Answer to 6th interrogatory. The effect would have been to give additional strength, but it would not, in my opinion, have been practicable to combine the heavy athwartship diagonal bracing with, or in addition to the four six-inch bulk-heads, without interfering to a great extent with the stowage of the vessel.

Answer to 7th interrogatory. The Bureau of Construction and Repair was responsible for the deviation from the recommendations of the Board, relative to the four six-inch bulk-heads. For the pointers, in lieu of the regular breast-hooks recommended, the naval constructor of this yard is responsible.

Answer to 8th interrogatory. My opportunities were good, as I visited the vessel at least once each day while she was undergoing repairs at this yard.

Answer to 9th interrogatory. With the repairs made she was, in my opinion, seaworthy, though I did not consider her fit for an extended Arctic exploration.

Answer to 10th interrogatory. I base my opinion upon the grounds that the Jeannette was an old vessel, of poor model; constructed of materials of sizes and general arrangement more suitable for a yacht than for an ordinary built merchant vessel of the same displacement.

Answer to 11th interrogatory. He did not, nor did any other officer, express to me dissatisfaction, but on the contrary expressed themselves satisfied with the fitting out of the vessel, so far as the Bureau of Construction and Repair was concerned.

Answer to 12th interrogatory. I did not, and for the following reasons:

First. The midship section, though having a rise of about 15°, had short bilge with straight sides, commencing to tumble home, eight (8) feet from base line; consequently the greatest beam is nearly four (4) feet below the load line; a shape, in my opinion, in no way adapted for lifting in the ice.

Second. The vessel was narrow and very sharp forward and aft.

Third. She had not sufficient displacement with proper freeboard to hold the provision and coal supply for an extended cruise in the Arctic Ocean.

Fourth. The vessel, not being originally built for such service, was not sufficiently strong; her frames were light and single, the timbers composing the frames not being closely jointed but having an opening between them of about four (4) inches. All frame timbers were more or less badly cut and split by the fastenings, and being inside strapped it was not practicable to remove them all.

Fifth. The hold was divided by a number of transverse and longitudinal bulk-heads into small apartments originally intended for magazines, shell, and store-rooms, none being water-tight or arranged to give the vessel additional strength, and occupying space that should have been appropriated for other purposes. The berth deck was small, containing only about 2,772 cubic feet, including galley-room, two state-rooms, and pantry.

Answer to 13th interrogatory. I have no plans that would throw any satisfactory light upon her construction. I have a plan of her midship section, also a plan of her spar and berth decks, taken by actual measurement, as also the whole internal arrangement of bulk-heads, store-rooms, &c., including additions made at this yard while undergoing repairs, copies of which, duly authenticated, are herewith inclosed, marked A, B, and C, also the dimensions as near as could be obtained.

Answer to 14th interrogatory. *Narrative.*—Soon after the arrival of the Jeannette at this yard, December 28th, 1878, Lieutenant De Long called at my office and gave me the history of the vessel he had purchased for the North Pole expedition, stating that before purchasing he obtained the opinion of acknowledged experts in ship-building, who had pronounced her strong and in every way adapted for service in the Arctic Ocean, and in his (De Long's) opinion she required but little in the way of repairs to make her all he could desire. Upon being ordered to make an examination of the vessel I found that to make her efficient for ordinary service would require repairs at an estimated cost of some seven thousand ($7,000) dollars, and for an extended cruise in the Arctic Ocean she was not, in my opinion, adapted with all the repairs, &c., that could be put upon her. Upon giving this opinion to De Long he exhibited indications of great disappointment, and expressed himself as willing, with some little additions, so far as construction was concerned, such as an entering porch to cabin, house on deck, berths for the crew, exposed iron below deck covered, docking, calking, and a spare rudder fitted, to start on the expedition. He appeared to be greatly exercised at the estimated cost of repairs, changes, and alterations recommended, and suggested that the work be done as cheaply as possible. Propositions from time to time were made to Lt. De Long with a view of rendering the vessel more efficient for the purpose. His replies usually were in substance, though he approved of everything recommended for the strength and efficiency of the Jeannette, he felt a delicacy about such an expenditure of money after so much had been expended in the purchase of the vessel and her repairs in England, and was fearful that the result would be the probable abandonment of the expedition. Lt. De Long was, in my opinion, not only badly imposed upon by the purchase of such a v ssel, but in her subsequent repairs in England. The repairs made there were, for the m t part, superficial, of poor workmanship, and of inferior material; so much so that it wa ound necessary to remove and replace with better material.

I conclusion, I am pleased to say that not only the commandant but all other officers of the yard did all that could be done under the circumstances to render the Jeannette efficient for the contemplated expedition, and whatever opinions may have existed in reference to her fitness, she proved herself able for over twelve months to withstand the heavy floes and crushing ice of the Arctic Ocean, and in all probability no vessel, however strongly built, could withstand such a continued strain.

GEO. W. MUCH,
Naval Const. U. S. N.

STATE OF CALIFORNIA,
County of Solano, ss:

On this 4th day of November, A. D. 1882, personally appeared before me, the above-named George W. Much, the deponent, and being first duly cautioned and sworn to speak the truth, the whole truth, and nothing but the truth relating to the cause for which the foregoing deposition is taken, the said deposition was by me carefully read in his presence and hearing, and then by him subscribed in my presence.

In witness whereof I have hereunto set my hand and appended my notarial seal of office, the day and year aforesaid.

[SEAL.]

WM. R. COX, JR.,
Notary Public.

Original paper.

SAM. C. LEMLY,
Master U. S. Navy & Judge Advocate.

EXHIBIT H I.

Interrogatories addressed to Sir Allen Young, R. N. R., F. R. G. S., F. R. A. S., of London, England, by a court of inquiry, of which Commodore Wm. G. Temple, U. S. Navy, is president, convened at the Navy Department, Washington, D. C., United States of America, by order of the honorable Secretary of the Navy, to investigate the circumstances of the loss, in the Arctic Seas, of the exploring steamer Jeannette.

1st interrogatory. Please state your name, position, and residence?
2d interrogatory. Were you ever at any time owner of the Arctic exploring steamer Jeannette, formerly Her Britannic Majesty's ship Pandora?
3d interrogatory. If your answer be yea to the 2d interrogatory, please state when and for what length of time you owned the vessel in question, and when and to whom you disposed of her?
4th interrogatory. Please state your opinion of the fitness of the vessel in question for Arctic service, having particular reference to her strength and model?
5th interrogatory. Please give in full the ground upon which you base your opinion, as stated in your answer to the 4th interrogatory, whether upon actual experience at sea in that vessel, within or without the Arctic regions, or experience within the Arctic regions in any other vessel, or both?

Original paper.

SAM. C. LEMLY,
Master U. S. Navy & Judge Advocate.

EXHIBIT I K.

On this twenty-second day of November, in the year one thousand eight hundred and eighty-two, before me, William J. Hoppin, secretary of the legation of the United States in Great Britain, personally appeared the above-named Sir Allen William Young, and made answer to the foregoing interrogatories, as follows:

First. To the first interrogatory he says: My name is Allen William Young; I am a lieutenant in the Royal Naval Reserve, and my residence is at No. 5 Saint James street, London.

Second. To the second interrogatory he says: I was the owner at one time of the Arctic exploring steamer Jeannette, formerly Her Britannic Majesty's ship Pandora.

Third. To the third interrogatory he says: I purchased the vessel from Her Majesty's Government on or about April, eighteen hundred and seventy-five, and I owned her until I sold her in the year eighteen hundred and seventy-seven to Mr. James Gordan Bennett.

Fourth. To the fourth interrogatory he says: I considered the vessel in question to be fit for Arctic service both as regards strength and model.

Fifth. To the fifth interrogatory he says: I base my opinion of the fitness of the ship for Arctic service upon my actual experience in that vessel at sea both within and without the Arctic regions. Having had the experience of serving in another vessel, the Fox, in the Arctic regions, and having made two voyages in the Pandora in the same regions, I consider the latter vessel far superior to the Fox, and in every way fit for such service both as regards strength and model.

ALLEN W. YOUNG.

The above depositions were subscribed and sworn to before me by the above-named Sir Allen W. Young, on this twenty-second day of November, in the year one thousand eight hundred and eighty-two.

In testimony whereof I have hereto signed my name and affixed the seal of this Legation the day and year last above written.

[SEAL.]

W. J. HOPPIN.

Original paper.

SAM. C. LEMLY,
Master U. S. Navy & Judge Advocate.

No. 894.

UNITED STATES OF AMERICA,
Department of State:

To all to whom these presents shall come, greeting:

I certify that William J. Hoppin, whose name is subscribed to the paper hereunto annexed, is now, and was at the time of subscribing the same, secretary of legation of the United States in Great Britain, duly commissioned, and that full faith and confidence are due to his acts as such.

In testimony whereof, I, Frederick T. Frelinghuysen, Secretary of State of the United States, have hereunto subscribed my name and caused the seal of the Department of State to be affixed.

Done at the city of Washington, this 6th day of December, A. D. 1882, and of the independence of the United States of America the one hundred and seventh.

[SEAL.]

FREDK. T. FRELINGHUYSEN.

EXHIBIT K L.

U. S. ARCTIC STEAMER JEANNETTE,
Off Cape Serdz Kerz, Siberia, 30 *August,* 1879.

SIR: I have the honor to report that in obedience to your verbal order of the 29th August, 1879, at about 3.30 a. m. to-day I landed at the Indian village that is situated about seven miles to the sd. and ed. off Cape Serdz Kerz. I was accompanied by Messrs. Collins and Dunbar and Alexy, the Indian dog driver. We proceeded to the chief's igloo and woke him, but after much talking were unable to understand him or his people nor to make them understand us until an old squaw was brought who could understand and speak the same dialect as Alexy. Through her and Alexy the chief informed me that a steam vessel spent last winter on this side of Koliutchin Bay; that she left there some time ago and stopped off his village one night and then went to the eastward. We could get no definite answer as to when she was at his village.

The captain was an old man with a grey beard, wore a coat and not fur clothing, and on his cap some sort of ornament. The chief touched the gold cord on my naval cap when describing the ornament. There were a number of people on board the steamer, described by the interpreter as "plenty man," but he could not give a definite number.

The chief and some of his people visited the steamer on sledges last winter when she was at Koliutchin Bay. In and about the igloos I saw a piece of cast-iron, the bowl of a soup ladle, two small round wooden boxes, and a small fish net made of flat twine, but could find no marks that could give intelligence as to the place of their manufacture. Mr. Collins also saw an iron axe with a wooden handle. There was nothing to indicate that white men had spent a long time at the settlement. The squaw said that one of the officers of the steamer could talk with the natives, and upon the name "Nordquish" being suggested by Mr. Collins, the squaw, chief, and another Indian repeated "orpish," as if the name were familiar, but I cannot say whether or not it was a person named "Orpish" who spoke to them.

I delivered your letter and the package of mail matter to the chief, and believe that he understood what was to be done with them, and through the interpreter and by motions he assured me that he would dispose of them as directed.

Very respectfully, your obedient servant,

CHAS. W. CHIPP,
Lieutenant U. S. Navy.

Lieutenant GEORGE W. DE LONG, U. S. Navy,
Comdg. Arctic Steamer Jeannette.

A true copy.

SAM. C. LEMLY,
Master U. S. Navy & Judge Advocate.

EXHIBIT L M.

ARCTIC STEAMER JEANNETTE IN THE PACK,
Lat. N. 71° 35′, long. W. 175° 06′, 14 September, 1879.

SIR: I have the honor to report that in obedience to your order of the 12 September, 1879, at 8.15 a. m. of the 13th inst., I left the ship accompanied by Passed Assistant Engineer Melville, Mr. Dunbar, and Alexy, with a sledge and eight dogs, to attempt to reach Herald Island. The party was equipped and provisioned as directed in your order. When about seven miles from the ship we found the ice much lighter than that about the ship, and consisted of floe pieces cemented together with young ice, which in many places was just strong enough to bear the weight of the sledge and party. At 10.30 a. m. it commenced snowing, and shut in the island, which was seen only occasionally the remainder of the day. At 11.30 sighted open water extending in a broad lead in an east and west direction as far as the eye could reach. From this lead extended branches in the S. E., S., and S. W. directions. The nature of the ice again changed, and showed evidence of having recently been subjected to heavy pressure. The old floe pieces were closer together, and the young ice was broken and forced up into ridges from eight to twelve feet high, giving it the appearance of a plain, divided into irregularly shaped lots by ice walls. I followed along the open water to the westward for some distance, until the west end of Herald Island bore S. 17° E. (magnetic), where the principal lead trended off to the N. W., and we came to ice which was soft and rotten, over which it was impossible to pass. The ice immediately about Herald Island appeared to be rotten and cut up with leads, and the new ice forced up into ridges as if lately it had been subjected to pressure. At 12.40 p. m., being unable to proceed farther towards Herald Island, we stopped and had dinner. I estimated that we had come fifteen miles from the ship in the four hours and twenty-five minutes that we had been under way. At 2 p. m. it stopped snowing for a few minutes, and we got a fair view of the island, which I estimated to be distant five miles. The east end of it bore magnetic S. 40° E., and the west end S. 17° E. The shore was high and rocky, apparently cut in deep ridges running down the face of nearly perpendicular sides. On the east end was a projection like a small steeple. About one-third the length of the island from the east end there is a cleft in the outline of the island which appears to extend across it in a N. E. and S. W. direction.

The west end of the island slopes irregularly to the water and appears to terminate in a point. The north side of the island is slightly concave, but I saw no place that would offer any protection from the ice to a ship. As it was impossible to proceed farther towards the island, and we had crossed some poor ice on our way out, I did not think it prudent to remain where we were overnight, as a northerly wind would probably open a lead between us and the ship, so at 2.30 p. m. we started on our return, and at 5.30 p. m., having come to good ice and finding a convenient place for the tent, we camped down for the night. During our return we found the water on top of the young ice in many places.

At 7.40 a. m. this morning we again started for the ship, and arrived on board at 9.25 a. m. During our absence we saw no drift-wood. We passed many bear tracks and saw one raven and one young seal, which latter Alexy shot within a few hundred yards of the ship.

Very respectfully, your obedient servant,

CHAS. W. CHIPP,
Lieutenant U. S. Navy.

Lieutenant GEORGE W. DE LONG, U. S. Navy,
Commanding Arctic Steamer Jeannette.

EXHIBIT M N.

ORDER.

ARCTIC STEAMER JEANNETTE,
Beset in the pack,
Latitude 72° N., long. 176° W.

SEPTEMBER 20, 1879.

In order to secure a more improved ventilation of the living quarters of the officers and men of this ship the following will be carried into effect:

In all fine dry weather the skylight over the forward part of the berth deck will be kept open at all times, day and night. In rainy or snowy weather, when the tenting of a tarpaulin will not be sufficient to prevent the rain or snow from going below, the galvanized iron ventilator made for the skylight will be put on and kept on until the tarpaulin can be again used or the skylight can be uncovered.

The doors leading from the berth deck to the old galley room are to be kept open at all times, day or night.

The weather side of the fore hatch is to be kept open at all times in dry weather. In wet weather the weather side will be closed and the lee one opened. The officers of the deck will, by frequent inspection between 8 p. m. and 8 a. m., observe whether this order is complied with in reference to the berth deck, reporting any violation of it to the executive officer at the earliest opportunity. The skylight over the cabin will be kept half open in fine weather. When, by reason of rain or snow, the opening must be covered, the galvanized iron cover made for it will be used, and will be kept on as long as the weather prevents, having a partially opened skylight.

The glass deck lights of the spar-deck inside the cabin bulkhead over the rooms occupied by Mr. Danenhower and Mr. Collins, and over the rooms occupied by Mr. Dunbar and Mr. Newcomb, will be removed, and in their places there will be let in the deck blocks of wood which are to have as many half-inch auger holes as possible bored in them.

As soon as it can be done conveniently with more pressing work about the ship, the doors leading from the cabin to the chart room and dispensary will be removed and shipped between the propeller-well and side bulkheads, shutting off the after part of the cabin. As soon as this is done, and until it becomes necessary to wear fur clothing, all officers living in the wardroom will hang all fur garment and oiled clothing in the space thus set apart.

The executive officer will see this order carried into effect with the least possible delay.

GEORGE W. DE LONG,
Lieutenant, U. S. Navy, Commanding.

A true copy.

SAM. C. LEMLY,
Master U. S. Navy & Judge Advocate.

EXHIBIT N O.

ARCTIC STEAMER JEANNETTE,
13th July, 1880.

SIR: In obedience to your order of last evening I to-day had five holes bored through the ice. First hole under stern of ship, bottom of ice 5′ 4″ below surface of water; 2nd hole 50 feet astern of ship, bottom of ice 4′ 3″ below surface of water; 3rd hole 100 feet astern of ship, bottom of ice 5′ below surface of water; 4th hole 150 feet astern of ship, bottom of ice 5′ below surface of water; 5th hole about 250 yards off starboard quarter of ship, bottom of ice 5′ below surface. All these holes were bored through ice formed since 30th November, 1879.

Very respectfully,

CHAS. W. CHIPP,
Lieut. U. S. N., Ex. Off.

Lieut. GEORGE W. DE LONG, U. S. N.,
Commading Arctic Steamer Jeannette.

A true copy.

SAM. C. LEMLY,
Master U. S. Navy & Judge Advocate.

EXHIBIT O P.

U. S. ARCTIC STEAMER JEANNETTE,
Lat. N. 75° 15′, long. E. 171° 38′.
ARCTIC OCEAN, *March 20th*, 1881.

Hon. SECRETARY OF THE NAVY,
Washington, D. C.:

SIR: I have the honor to report to you the heroic conduct of Alfred Sweetman (seaman) and of William F. C. Nindemann (seaman) and to recommend them as worthy of Medals of Honor.

Upon the 19th January, 1880, this vessel beset and drifting in the pack ice of the Arctic Ocean, was, in consequence of severe pressure and straining in a disruption and upheaval of the ice fields, seriously injured and caused to leak, water pouring into her, forward, at the rate of four thousand gallons per hour. Such a disaster threatened our being forced to abandon the ship, and suffer exposure to a temperature of minus 50° in an attempt to reach the main land of Siberia, then [blank] miles distant. These two men for sixteen days labored in the fore peak, standing in water frequently above their knees and at a freezing temperature, stuffing oakum, tallow, plaster, cement, and ashes among the frames, building an extra water-tight bulkhead to stop the rush of the incoming water, and in every other way endeavoring to lessen the leak. During the whole of this time these men were almost without any rest, and often were unable to take their regular meals. Commonly they continued at work all day and half the night, and frequently passed even a greater portion of the twenty-four hours in their exhausting and hazardous employment. Circumstances prevented their being replaced by others as a partial relief, and their own zeal and devotion to duty were such that they would not give up until their task was crowned with success. Without this self-sacrificing labor we would have been forced to continue steam-pumping on a large scale, which would soon have consumed our fuel, or to resort to hand-pumping, which would have exhausted the crew. But thanks to the efforts of these two men the leak was so decreased that we were able during the [blank] that elapsed before our being set free from our imprisonment to keep it under control by a limited expenditure of fuel and the employment of a small amount of hand-pumping.

That this exposure and toil did not result in the permanent breaking down of health is a matter of wonder and also of thankfulness; and I feel I am doing but simple justice to Alfred Sweetman and William F. C. Nindemann in bringing the foregoing facts to your knowledge and requesting the recognition they so eminently deserve.

Very respectfully,

GEORGE W. DE LONG,
Lieutenant U. S. Navy, Commanding.

A true copy.

SAM. C. LEMLY,
Master U. S. Navy & Judge Advocate.

EXHIBIT P Q.

ORDER.

ARCTIC STEAMER JEANNETTE,
Beset and drifting in the pack ice,
Lat. N. 77° 13′, long. E. 158° 12′.

JUNE 15th, 1881.

This island, discovered by us on May 16, and which is in lat. N. 76° 47′, long. E. 158° 56′, has been named

JEANNETTE ISLAND.

This island, discovered by us on the 24th May, and which is in lat. N. 77° 8′, long. E. 157° 43′, has been named

HENRIETTA ISLAND.

Upon Henrietta Island P. A. Engineer G. W. Melville and his party have landed and hoisted there our colors, and taken possession of these new lands in the name of the United States of America.

GEORGE W. DE LONG,
Lieutenant U. S. Navy, Commanding.

[The date of this order seems to be wrong, as the ship went down June 13th, 1881.]

A true copy.

SAM. C. LEMLY,
Master U. S. Navy & Judge Advocate.

EXHIBIT Q R.

DR. SIR: I return herewith the slip on which you require the numbers of thermometers, duly marked. A maximum must be supplied from one of the pocket cases, as the one I had was broken during the storm on our voyage from St. Michael's to St. Lawrence Bay. A "black bulb in air" (max.) we have not. Permit me to express some surprise that the occupant of the position of meteorologist on this expedition does not come under the operation of your strict rule of "official courtesy," a respect for which, in all transactions, you requested with so much emphasis a little while ago. The contemptuous disregard for my personal feeling as a member of the expedition exhibited in several ways and from time to time by yourself and your fellow-officers I can well afford to pass as unworthy of notice, but in my capacity as an employé of Mr. Bennett, and a recognized entity of the official personnel of the expedition by the Hon. the Secretary of the Navy, I regard every act of discourtesy, official and personal, as an infringement on my rights, expressed or implied, by the fact of my appointment.

As a new year of work is about to begin for me, it is of vital importance to me, in many ways, that I should understand the position I am to occupy in relation to that work, to you and to the other gentlemen associated with you. I have been aware from the commencement that the standing you were willing to accord any civilian appointed to take part in the scientific work of the expedition as "a mere accessory," to use the expression you employed to the reporter of the Washington "Post" in April, 1879, when interviewed by him. This was the way in which you endeavored to give place to the statement that all scientific work required would be done by the officers of the Navy. Mr. Bennett, when asked about this, said you must have been *mis-reported*. Mr. Connery remarked with some indignation that you never used such language. On these assurances from gentlemen who knew you, as they believed, I decided to come on the expedition, fully expecting to feel at home with a number of men who were said to be incapable of selfishness and injustice.

When at San Francisco it was easy for you to tell me that you intended to do thus and so regarding the particular work I was sent to do, and which came under the general head of *physics*. A competent man was employed to take charge of the collection, &c., of natural history and ethnological specimens. I was introduced by yourself and others of the officers to people in San Francisco as a person specially devoted to researches in physical science for the expedition. At the Academy of Sciences I made some rambling remarks, which I based on the supposition that I was something more than a "mere accessory." Nothing in your conversation gave me any grounds for believing otherwise, although you had ample opportunity to enlighten me, until during a general conversation held in your rooms at the Palace Hotel, in the course of which "interviewing" by reporters came up for discussion, you endorsed a lady's statement that the "Washington Post" interview was most faithfully and accurately reported, and that your very words were used, although the reporter did not appear to take any notes. In a moment I saw I was in a trap. Not one set by you, for you did not want anybody but Navy people with you, as your manner of acting plainly showed from the start, aye, from the first day I met you at the Herald Office. The trap was set by circumstances which will deceive any man who, trusting unreservedly to the good nature of others, devotes himself to an enterprise in which he hopes for honor or profit, or both. I hoped for honor in coming to the Arctic and also profitable information. I volunteered to come, leaving behind me a happy home, kind and true friends and companions, and many of the things that make life worth living. I volunteered on what was believed to be an enterprise full of danger, and herein lies the big tooth of the trap. I could not under any circumstances, for any cause almost, retreat from my post without incurring the slur of cowardice, which you know would be only too readily cast on any one who backed out at the last moment. Although I foresaw from the start that I was betrayed into a false position by my inconsiderate acceptance of assurances, given almost without consideration, that I would not be treated as a "mere accessory," I could not retreat. Had you told me the day before we sailed that I was to live in the forecastle, and have the work of an ordinary seaman, if I could do it, instead of being treated as a member of the cabin mess, I doubt if I could have gone back. You had and have it in your power to heap or permit to be heaped any amount of disrespect on me, socially or officially, and I was and am as a man with his hands tied. Under the circumstances I cannot retaliate; I can only resent by silence. Three several times you have threatened me with an exaction of obedience, "if it took every man on the ship," in the discussion of purely suppositious cases of discipline. When I laid before you the facts of one or two cases in which I felt aggrieved by others, you became at once the apologist of one party and did not wish to hear anything about the other. Lately things have been going on rushingly. In my official capacity I am to infer by the withdrawal of several instruments from time to time that I have either neglected or do not possess the ability to use them. First, the magnetic instruments, one by one; then photographic apparatus, which was specially given in my charge and to which all had free access by the exercise of your important "official courtesy." Then I was ordered to have four Six's thermometers ready for use. I got these ready, and requested of you that when they were to be used I would be present, as fixing them was a slow and difficult job. You said, "Certainly, Mr. Collins." But in some time after, and long after, you gave me through Mr. Chipp to understand that the deep-water tests, suspended last fall by your order, would be resumed. You told me to turn over to you the salinometer, &c., as you wanted to make some experiments with the sea water. I found next day that you had resumed the water tests and that I was wholly ignored in connection with them, notwithstanding your "Certainly, Mr. Collins." I was directed to give Dr. Ambler the Damets hygrometer, which I did. I don't believe he has used it since. No such explanation such as a kindly courtesy would suggest has been given to me, no more than if I was a lamp-trimmer in the fire-room. Yet if I wanted a little hot water to make tea for my luxurious breakfast during the midwatch, official courtesy demands that I must go to Mr. Melville about it. Don't you suppose I am as sensitive as yourself or Melville or anybody else when I am treated with official discourtesy? You think you can do with me as you please now, and laugh at the future. You are making a mistake common to men of your disposition and habits of self-complacency.

A true copy.

SAM. C. LEMLY,
Master U. S. Navy & Judge Advocate.

EXHIBIT R S.

ARCTIC STEAMER JEANETTE,
Beset and drifting in the pack.

ARCTIC OCEAN, October 30th, 1880.

ORDER.

For the purpose of correcting a seeming misunderstanding in regard to reports in connection with leaving the ship and returning on board, attention is called to the following:

Naval Regulations require all officers junior in rank to the executive to report to him their leave to be absent from the ship, and also their return on board. My verbal order directing all other members of the cabin mess to obtain my permission to leave the immediate vicinity of the vessel and to report their return to me is not to be considered as dispensing with reports to the executive of such permission and return, and these reports consequently are hereafter to be made.

Very respectfully,

GEORGE W. DE LONG,
Lieutenant U. S. Navy, Commanding.

A true copy.

SAM. C. LEMLY,
Master U. S. Navy & Judge Advocate.

EXHIBIT S T.

ARCTIC STEAMER JEANNETTE,
Beset and drifting in the pack.

DECEMBER 2nd, 1880.

MEMORANDUM.

The following is the statement of an occurrence this day, in which Mr. Collins treated me with such disrespect as to cause me to relieve him from all duty in the ship, and to inform him that upon the return of the vessel to the United States I would report him to the Secretary of the Navy. My order in relation to daily exercise requires everybody (except sick and the man on watch) to leave the ship at eleven a. m., and remain out of her on the ice until 1 p. m.; of course it has been understood that Mr. Collins should come on board at noon to make and record in the slate the meteorological observations for that hour, but I have observed on several occasions of late that he seemed to remain on board much longer than such duty required.

I had considerable trouble last winter in getting Mr. Collins to comply with the order in regard to daily exercise, his delay in getting out of bed, his requiring time for his breakfast, when up and dressed, &c., making it 11.30 a. m. before he made his appearance on the ice. I pointed out to him then his failure to obey my order, remonstrated with him on his repeating the offense, insisted on my order being obeyed, and finally secured a literal compliance with it, although, as he informed me, he had his own opinion of the wisdom or necessity for such an order, or words to that effect.

To-day, at 12.10 p. m., I went into the cabin to see why he remained so long, and at the same time to close my air-port, and found he had removed his coat, had lighted and was smoking his pipe, and while writing in the port chart room was carrying on a conversation with Mr. Danenhower. I said nothing, and returned to the ice. At 12.20 p. m., as he had not yet come out, I went again to the cabin, and found him at the stove adjusting his gloves and continuing the conversation before referred to. The following is the substance of an ensuing talk:

I asked Mr. Collins, "Has it required all this time to make and record the 12 o'clock observations?"

He replied "Well, sir, I hardly know the meaning of your question."

I said "The meaning of my question is this: Is it necessary for you, in order to make and record the 12 o'clock observations, to remove your coat, light your pipe, engage in conversation with Mr. Danenhower, and remain in the cabin until 12.20 p. m.?"

He answered, curtly, "Well, perhaps I might have done it quicker, but I did not know my minutes were counted for me."

I said, in substance, "I have seen fit to issue an order that everybody should go on the ice from 11 to 1, and your coming in the cabin and remaining until 12.20 is a violation of my order that I will neither submit to nor permit you to continue. I have noticed for several days that you were longer than necessary in taking the noon observations, and to-day I satisfied myself on the subject "

He replied. "Oh, very well; if you are satisfied, of course I have nothing to say. I was not aware (or "I did not know") it was necessary to follow me up."

I asked, "What do you mean by that?"

He said, "I mean that in taking me to task as you do, you are doing me a great injustice."

I said, "As this matter has gone so far, it must go further. Be good enough to remove your coat and sit down." When seated I continued, "Mr. Collins, a representation to me of injustice has only to be made in proper language to secure you all the justice you want. But I do not like your manner or bearing in talking with me. You seem to assume that you are to receive no correction, direction, or dictation from me; that your view of an occurrence is always to be taken; and that if I differ from you it is my misfortune, but of no importance to the result."

He commenced, "I came here supposing——"

I interrupted, "Never mind that part of it. You *are* here, in fact, and we will deal with the fact."

He resumed, "I do not like the tone or manner in which you speak to *me*, and the way in which I am taken to task."

I replied, "I have a perfect right to say what I say to you."

He said, "I acknowledge only the rights given you by Naval Regulations."

I inquired, "Do you mean to imply that I am doing contrary to Naval Regulations?"

He said, "I mean to say that you have no right to talk to me as you do."

I replied, "You should not have disobeyed my orders" (1).

He said, "I will not admit such an assertion. I have always carried out your instructions" (2).

I inquired, "Do you undertake to contradict me, Mr. Collins, and to say that I am asserting what is not so?"

He replied, (3) "I mean to say, my dear sir, that I have not disobeyed (or "violated") your order" (4).

I said, "But, Mr. Collins, I say you *have* disobeyed (or "violated") my order" (5).

He promptly and emphatically replied, "I say I have not" (6).

I said, "Great allowance has been made for your ignorance of Naval Regulations, your position in the ship, and your being so situated for the first time. But you must remember that the commanding officer is to be spoken to in a respectful manner and with respectful language, and you do not seem to attend to either particular."

He replied, "I treat the commanding officer of this ship with all the respect due to him as the head of the expedition, but when he charges me with violating an order (7) I say I have *not*" (8).

I said, "Do you suppose you will be permitted to talk to me in that way? Are you beside yourself?"

He replied, "Not at all. I am perfectly calm and collected, and know what I say."

I said, "And you contradict me flatly in that way? Have you lost your senses?"

He replied, "No, I have not lost my senses; I know what I say."

I went on, "When I say that by remaining in the cabin as you did to-day you violated my orders, you continue to contradict me."

He answered, "When you say (9) I have violated an order, I say I have *not*."

I then rose, saying, "That is quite enough. Circumstanced as we are, the matter cannot be conveniently delt with here; but upon the return of the vessel to the United States, or her reaching some point of communication, I shall report you to the Secretary of the Navy. Meanwhile you will perform no duty in the ship beyond completing the work called for in my written order of September first."

Throughout the whole interview Mr. Collins was curt, contemptuous, and disrespectful in both language and bearing, the manner of his answering being more offensive even than the words used. Instead of making suitable replies to my questions, and proper explanations of the violation of my order, he arraigned me for the manner in which the questions were put, and contradicted me flatly when I said he had violated my order (10).

Mr. Danenhower, who left the cabin at my first question, was in his room, necessarily in a position to hear the conversation and I notified him that I should refer to him as a witness. He volunteered his willingness to have a written statement of the occurrence made for his signature, while it was fresh in his memory, and I therefore requested Lieut. Chipp to write such a statement from dictation, as Mr. Danenhower's eyes of course prevented him from doing so himself.

GEORGE W. DE LONG,
Lieut. U. S. Navy, Commanding.

DECEMBER 4th, 1880.

Upon reflection, and recalling as far as possible what was said, I have to make the following additions to the foregoing memorandum in the places designated by the Nos. 1, 2, 3, &c. As to the exactness of the places I am not certain, and there may be some little doubt as to the sequence of the words. But as to the language being employed (or similar terms so closely allied as not to affect the meaning by the smallest trifle), I am absolutely certain.

(1). "I consider that by coming into the cabin as you did to-day, removing your coat, lighting your pipe, and carrying on a conversation with Mr. Danenhower, you took advantage of the 12 o'clock observations to disregard my order in relation to the exercise."

(2.) "And when you say I took advantage of the 12 o'clock observations to disregard your order I say it is *not so*."
(3.) "Wait a moment; I will not have you put words in my mouth."
4. "And when you say I take (or "took") advantage of the 12 o'clock observations to disregard your order, I say it is not so."
(5.) "And that your remaining in the cabin as you did to-day *is* taking advantage of the 12 o'clock observation to disregard my order."
6. This should read, "And I say it is *not*."
(7.) Or "taking advantage of the 12 o'clock observations to disregard it."
(8.) This should read, "I say it is not so."
(9.) This should read, "And I say I have not," (10) or rather when I said his remaining in the cabin in the manner he did this morning was taking advantage of the 12 o'clock observations to disregard my order.

GEORGE W. DE LONG,
Lieutenant Commanding.

A true copy.

SAM. C. LEMLY,
Master U. S. Navy & Judge Advocate.

Exhibit T U.

U. S. Arctic Steamer Jeannette,
Lat. N. 75° 15′, long. E. 171° 36′.

Arctic Ocean, *March 20th*, 1881.

Hon. Secretary of the Navy,
  Washington, D. C.:

Sir: I have to report to you Mr. Jerome J. Collins, shipped as seaman U. S. Navy, in accordance with the suggestion of your predecessor, attached to this vessel, and for the purpose of an Arctic expedition, known and by me entitled Meteorologist, for disrespectful language and deportment, and insubordinate conduct while in the Arctic Ocean, in this vessel under my command. Upon the disappearance of the sun on the 16th day of November, 1879, I judged it wise and proper, as conducive to health, to require every officer and man not on the sick-list, and excepting the seaman in charge of the deck, to leave the ship for the purpose of exercise on the ice, by walking or otherwise, from 11 a. m. to 1 p. m. daily, so long as the temperature was above 30° Fahrenheit, unless stormy weather or other sufficient circumstance caused me to suspend the enforced exercise for a day. This was enforced until the reappearance of the sun on the 25th day of January, 1880, and again during our second winter in the ice, while the sun was absent, from November 6, 1880, to the 5th day of February, 1881.

From the earliest date Mr. Collins showed a disposition to disregard this order, and attempted to render it inoperative in his case in various ways, such as failing to get out of bed in time to leave the ship at 11 a. m., necessitating the sending of some one to his room to call him when his absence was remarked, next delaying his appearance, though called in advance by a servant, upon the ground that he was ready to leave the ship but must get something in the shape of breakfast, and finally remaining in the cabin an unnecessary time in making and recording the noon meteorological observations.

At first he was merely reminded by me of his failure to obey my order, and requested to be more careful in future; then his continued failure was more seriously commented on, and he was made to understand that obedience would be enforced; and finally, after long endurance, he was reprimanded for thus repeatedly evading and disregarding my order, upon which he became both impertinent and disrespectful, saying that he took more exercise than any other person in the ship, that he had his own opinion about the wisdom or necessity of my order, and that I spoke to him as I would not dare to speak to an officer of the ship. In fine, instead of explaining or offering excuses for his conduct, expressing his contempt for my regulations and attempting to arraign me for enforcing them. Upon the resumption of the enforced exercise in the second winter, Mr. Collins again showed an evasion of and failure to comply with the order in relation thereto, by consuming so much time in the cabin to make and record the noon meteorological observations as to considerably shorten his exposure to the open air and daylight during the two hours set apart for that purpose. On the 3rd of December, 1880, he so far disobeyed my order as to remain in the cabin until 12.20 p. m., and meanwhile to light and smoke a pipe, do some writing, and carry on a conversation with an officer on the sick-lists then present, until I interrupted him and called for an explanation. Mr. Collins attempted to parry my questions, but failing in this assumed a disrespectful and insubordinate manner, and used disrespectful and insubordinate language, saying that he did not know his minutes were counted for him; that he was not aware it was necessary to follow him up; that I was doing him great injustice; that I had no right to talk to him as I did; that he would not admit my assertions; that he would not have me put words in his mouth; and, finally, when I repeatedly told him he had disobeyed my order he positively and as repeatedly contradicted me, saying "I have not; and when you charge me with disobeying an order, I say it is not so." I called his attention to the fact that I must be treated with respect, both as to language and deportment, and that he failed in both particulars; but he replied that "he treated me with all the respect due me, and acknowledged only such rights as were conferred on me by Naval Regulations; but that I had no right to charge him with evading or disobeying an order; and when I did so charge him, he would continue to say "it is not so." I asked him if he was beside himself, and had lost his senses, to thus continue to contradict me, but he assured me that he was perfectly calm, and knew what he was about. Upon this I informed him that he would be reported to you upon our return to the United States, or upon reaching some port of communication, and that pending such action he could perform no more duty in the ship.

I would state that many allowances have been made for this gentleman's seeming ignorance of the requirements of naval discipline, and great consideration and forbearance have been shown him by me in view of his position on board ship. He has been informed of his errors and remonstrated with on their repetition, but all to no purpose. He has manifested an unwillingness to be directed or controlled, and has resented such action so disrespectfully and impertinently as to make ignorance doubly inexcusable. He has been treated with consideration due to the commissioned officers, and has been subjected to such regulations as govern them. But he complained at having to obtain my permission to leave the ship as a restriction upon the liberty of his movements which he was not accustomed to and could not bear; and that in carrying out what he came here to perform such a restriction was very objectionable. When, in order to provide for a continuance of good health and to secure a perfect sanitary condition in our exceptionally trying circumstances, I ordered the surgeon to make each month such physical examination of officers and men, myself included, as would enable him to report to me in writing their condition, Mr. Collins protested against being examined, claiming that he would decide for himself when he wanted medical treatment, and that meanwhile he did not propose to submit his person to experiments, or to contribute to medical statistics; though upon his error being pointed out, he asked and was permitted to withdraw his letter of protest, asserting afterwards that I had announced that these examinations were for experimental purposes.

This gentleman seemed to assume that regulations were made and orders issued to give him personal annoyance and discomfort and that his obedience was exacted because he was borne upon the muster-roll as a seaman, and his remarks in connection therewith were usually extremely offensive. (It may be unnecessary, but I would here state that this gentleman was never spoken of or referred to in any way as a seaman; that he lived and messed with me in the cabin, as did the officers of the Navy; that he had a room assigned him in the ward room, and that in every manner he received from the crew the respect paid to an officer.) He complained that he was not considered head of a department, and, until corrected, added the title of "scientific observer" to the name "meteorologist," by which he was known and designated—assuming generally such an independence of authority and control as could not be tolerated in any vessel belonging to the Navy of the United States.

Situated as we were, drifting about in the ice, and liable at any moment to a disaster involving abandonment of the ship, suitable punishment for this gentleman's offenses was neither prudent nor advisable. Any adequate punishment, whether inflicted by my order or in pursuance of the sentence of a summary court-martial, would have necessitated a confinement of greater or less duration, which would have been seriously detrimental to health. I had already sufficient anxiety and difficulty in contemplating the possible dragging of one officer on a sled several hundred miles, the doubt of several others being strong enough to stand the exposure and the imminence of danger and disaster extending then over fifteen months, and I was not inclined to further add to the invalid list and further diminish my already crippled resources. So long as no overt act of violent insubordination presented itself my only remedy seemed to report the facts upon my return to the United States, and to ask that they receive such attention as to you appears right and proper.

Very respectfully,

GEORGE W. DE LONG,
Lieutenant U. S. Navy, Commanding.

The foregoing is a rough draft of a report to be made by me upon my return to the United States. In the event of any accident to me I desire this paper, as it is, shall be forwarded to the Navy Department.

GEORGE W. DE LONG,
Lieut. Commanding.

A true copy.

SAM. C. LEMLY,
Master U. S. Navy and Judge Advocate.

EXHIBIT U V.

IRKUTSK, *Jan'y* 18, 1883.

To SECRETARY OF THE NAVY,
   Washington:

KIRIUSK, *January* 5.

Aniguin died, two a. m. Small-pox. I await mail from Irkutsk. Party well.

HUNT.

A true copy.

SAM. C. LEMLY,
Master U. S. Navy & Judge Advocate.

EXHIBIT A 1.

NAVY DEPARTMENT,
Washington, March 29, 1883.

SIR: The court of inquiry, of which you are president, will reassemble at the Navy Department at 12 o'clock m., on Friday, the 30th inst., for the purpose of completing the investigation of the circumstances of the loss in the Arctic seas of the exploring steamer Jeanette, and the death of Lieutenant-Commander De Long and others of her officers and men, &c., and will proceed with the examination of the survivors of that vessel who have recently returned from Siberia, and who will be directed to report to you upon their arrival in Washington.

At the conclusion of the examination of the witnesses referred to, the court will report to the Department its further proceedings, with the testimony taken, and such modifications, if any, of the conclusions reported in its finding, 12th of February last, as may appear to be required by the evidence adduced.

Very respectfully,

WM. E. CHANDLER,
Secretary of the Navy.

Commodore WM. G. TEMPLE, U. S. N.,
  President Court of Inquiry, Navy Department,
     Washington, D. C.

EXHIBIT 1 B.

NAVY DEPARTMENT,
Washington, March 29*th,* 1883.

SIR: Captain Joseph N. Miller, U. S. Navy, has been relieved from duty as a member of the court of inquiry of which you are president.

Very respectfully,

WM. E. CHANDLER,
Secretary of the Navy.

Commodore WM. G. TEMPLE, U. S. N.,
  President Court of Inquiry, Navy Department,
     Washington, D. C.

EXHIBIT 1 C.

NAVY DEPARTMENT,
Washington, March 27, 1883.

SIR: Lieutenant Richard Wainwright, U. S. N., has been appointed judge advocate of the court of inquiry of which you are president in place of Master Samuel C. Lemly, relieved, and he has been ordered to report to you on Thursday, the 29th instant, for that duty.

Very respectfully,

WM. E. CHANDLER,
Secretary of the Navy.

Commodore WM. G. TEMPLE, U. S. N.,
President Court of Inquiry, Navy Department.

EXHIBIT 1 D.

NAVY DEPARTMENT,
Washington, March 27, 1883.

SIR: You are hereby appointed judge-advocate of the court of inquiry of which Commodore Wm. G. Temple is president, and you will report to him at the Navy Department on Thursday, the 29th instant, for that duty.

This employment on shore duty is required by the public interests, and such service will continue until May 15th, 1883, unless it is otherwise ordered.

Very respectfully,

WM. E. CHANDLER,
Secretary of the Navy.

Lieutenant RICHARD WAINWRIGHT, U. S. N.,
Bureau of Navigation, Navy Department.

Forwarded.

J. G. WALKER,
Chief of Bureau.

Reported March 29th, 1883.

WM. G. TEMPLE,
Commodore, U. S. N., and President of the Court.

Received Thursday, March 29, 1883.

EXHIBIT 1 E.

MINNEAPOLIS, MINN., *April* 2, 1883.

JUDGE-ADVOCATE, JEANNETTE COURT,
Navy Dept., Washington, D. C.:

Have received no notification of Bartlett's coming examination. Have mailed a list of questions. Please adjourn examination until received. We insist on a full opportunity to examine witness. Answer.

D. F. COLLINS, M. D.

A true copy.

RICHARD WAINWRIGHT,
Lieutenant, U. S. Navy, and Judge-Advocate.

APPENDIX II.
ROUGH DRAFT OF LIEUTENANT-COMMANDER GEORGE W. DE LONG'S REPORT TO THE HONORABLE SECRETARY OF THE NAVY.

[FROM AUGUST 26, 1879, TO DECEMBER 31, 1880.]

Hon. SECRETARY OF THE NAVY,
    Washington, D. C.:

SIR: I have the honor to submit a detailed report of the Arctic expedition under my command. At the date of my last communication to the Department, August 26th, 1879, we were at St. Lawrence Bay, Siberia, expecting to sail the next day. In that communication, I had given information of the proceedings of the ship to that time, and also had transmitted the intelligence received from the natives of St. Lawrence Bay in regard to the arrival there in June of a vessel, which had wintered in Koliutchin Bay and which I believed corresponded to some extent with the description of the Vega, Prof. Nordenskjöld's ship. Not feeling perfectly satisfied, however, and unwilling to leave the slightest doubt in connection with the missing ship, I informed the Department that I should proceed with the Jeannette to Koliutchin Bay, via Cape Serdz Kamen.

At 7.35 p. m., August 27th, we got under way, and stood out of St. Lawrence Bay, towing the chartered schooner Fannie A. Hyde to an offing, parting company with her at 9.30 p. m., and while she bore away to the Sd. on her return to San Francisco we headed up for Behring's Strait. We passed through the strait at noon on the 28th against a strong wind, which would have neutralized any moderate surface current, if any had existed, setting north, though our water temperatures, taken hourly from Ounalaska onward, had failed to show any such current north of the Aleutian Islands. We arrived at Serdze Kamen on August 29th, having no difficulty in recognizing the place by a curious formation in the cliffs on the east side of the bay, which formation resemble a cloven heart, and from which the place takes its name. Groups of skin tents were observed on the east and south sides of the bay, of which Cape Serdze Kamen is the northeast headland, and the ship was anchored at 5 p. m. as near to the south shore as was prudent. The bay has a general north and south direction, is about 4 miles in depth, and 7 miles in width at its entrance; is marked by prominent rocky cliffs on either hand, of which the one called Serdze Kamen is sufficiently distinguished by the resemblance before mentioned, and terminates at a sandy beach, back of which stands a native village of perhaps a dozen tents. The bottom, as we sounded steadily on the way in, is hard, sandy, and frequently rocky, and shoals rapidly to $8\frac{1}{4}$ fathoms at a mile from the south beach. At the date of our visit, the entire bay was fringed with an ice foot of old formation, broken blocks of which bobbed around in the swell caused by a stiff inblowing breeze, and made a surf seemingly impassable.

After waiting a short time, to see if our arrival would induce the natives to visit us, and none seeming disposed to come through the surf and broken ice, a whale-boat was manned, and, accompanied by several officers and the Alaskans as interpreters, I attempted to land. After pulling around for a half hour or more, seeking in vain for a place to get the boat through, the natives on shore shouting all kinds of unintelligible directions to us, we observed a party trying to carry out and launch a skin boat (or baidera). With much labor they succeeded, but on coming out to us we were unable to make each understand the other, although we tried our Alaskans to their utmost. Hoping to get some information by signs, we induced the natives to accompany us to the ship. The chief was of the party, and seated imposingly in the centre of the baidera, wearing a bright red tunic and a decorated cloth cap, issued his orders to his paddlers in grand style. Upon arriving on board ship nothing could make this chief or his people understand what we wanted to know; and after an hour's effort, backed by charts and various pantomimic essays, the matter had to be abandoned for the night, and the natives invited to depart. The chief seemed to be conversant with the amenities of life, for he mildly inquired "Schnapps?" and shook his head sadly when none were forthcoming.

The following morning at 3 o'clock I sent Lieut. Chipp in charge of a boat to make an effort to land and seek for some one to whom our wants might be made known. He succeeded in reaching the shore and visited the chief, who, by a happy inspiration, had an old woman brought in who spoke a language which he (the chief) knew nothing about, and hence might be a general interpreter. This woman was originally of King's Island, or its neighborhood, and our Alaskan, Alexy, could make out enough of her meaning to convey intelligible ideas to us. The story heard in St. Lawrence Bay was repeated substantially. The steamer had stopped in there one day and then gone home. The name of "Hospish" was as frequently mentioned as in St. Lawrence Bay, and no other name seemed familiar. The woman added that the ship stayed all winter on the east side of Koliutchin Bay, had built a house (an observatory), which she took down and carried away when she left.

Had Prof. Nordenskjöld left any kind of written paper at St. Lawrence Bay or at this place there would have been no doubt as to his movements and safety, but as he knew nothing of the anxiety in Europe and America on his account, his not doing so is explained; but keeping in remembrance that if he had passed south three months previous, as stated, news of his arrival at some port ought to have reached the United States before our sailing on July 8th; that, strictly speaking, the native stories would apply to any steamer, if not to any ship; that our information was obtained in very crude and easily mistaken language; and, beyond all, that if a mistake had been made it might involve a question of life; I did not feel justified in assuming that further proof was unnecessary, and I decided, therefore, to proceed further to the westward to Koliutchin Bay.

In order that there should remain no doubt of our having visited Cape Serdze Kamen I had drawn up a notice addressed to the captain of any arriving ship describing the nature of the information received, and requesting that it be transmitted to the Department; and I gave the chief a sailor cap with the ship's name in gilt letters on the ribbon, which cap I knew he would be sufficiently proud of to display to all strangers; and that there might be no question of the manner in which he had come in possession, I caused a notice describing our visit to be written and securely pasted inside of the cap, and succeeded in impressing him with the importance of exhibiting it to any arriving vessel. These measures taken, we got under way at 6 a. m., August 30th.

Arriving at the meridian of Koliutchin Bay at 5 a. m., August 31st, we here sighted a point of land which we supposed to be at the entrance of the bay proper, and a low beach beyond it to the southward. Heavy pack ice clung to the land and extended to the northward for a distance of five miles, and as far to the eastward and westward as the eye could reach. A small funnel-shaped opening seemed to present a means of getting nearer the beach, and as the chart showed a river emptying into Kalintchin Bay I assumed that this funnel-shaped opening in the ice might be caused by the discharging waters of this river, and consequently steamed into it.

The imperfect charts and meagre sailing directions for this part of the world make navigation a very groping and uncertain business. Places are sought for that are supposed to be peopled. The skin lodges of the native settlements, however, are so small and so nearly resemble in color the land behind them, that they cannot be distinguished a little distance from the shore, while the uncertainty of the positions assigned by the charts and the generally unknown condition of depths and bottom, added to the presence of drifting ice, make a near approach exceedingly difficult and dangerous. On this occasion we were frequently troubled with snow squalls, which hid everything completely from our view. By 7 a. m. we had penetrated the ice sufficiently far to observe from the crow's-nest some houses (?) on the eastern shore of the bay, and at 8 a. m. having carried the ship as close as the ice would permit, Lieut. Chipp was dispatched with a boat to thread his way into the beach. This was a tedious and difficult operation, but was finally accomplished by alternately poleing the boat and dragging her over intervening floes. At 1 p. m. Lieut. Chipp returned with the boat and brought with him the first unmistakeable evidences we had received of the Vega's position last winter. The interview with the natives was carried on entirely by signs, English being of no avail, and our Alaskan hunter having no more comprehension of the language of the natives here than they had of his own. Going through the houses, Lieut. Chipp saw various photographs, colored pictures of birds, and loose scraps of notes relating to natural history, which were undoubtedly distributed by the officers of the Vega during her stay or upon leaving. These, as well as some empty meat cans, the natives willingly exchanged for Mr. Chipp's uniform buttons, which he cut off and used as currency as occasion required. The clearest evidence obtained was in the shape of three uniform buttons, of the Swedish, Danish, and Russian navy respectively; for there had been no other ship than the Vega carrying officers of these three nations to this part of the world.

By this time the natives had become impressed with the fact that our visit had something to do with another ship, and they led Mr. Chipp to a spot about 2 miles to the

S. W. of their settlement, making it understood that a ship had remained there all winter, and had sailed to the eastward two or three months before.

Upon the return of the boat we steamed out from among the loose ice, and in four hours reached water, enabling us to shape a course.

We were now fairly at the beginning of our Arctic work, and the lateness of the season made it extremely questionable whether or not we had any chance of accomplishing anything before the winter set in. The length of the voyage to Ounalashka from San Francisco with our deeply laden ship, the delay incident to the arrival of the chartered schooner at St. Michael's and transfer of her cargo, and the subsequent various calls along the Siberian coast in search of reliable tidings of Professor Nardenskjöld had consumed so much time that we could have no choice of starting points or trails in various directions in quest of the most promising route. As the commander of the Polar expedition, my chief desire was to get north, and I had already come so far to the westward in carrying out the Department's orders that the sooner I started in a northerly direction seemed the better for the object in view. Additional time would be lost were I to attempt to get a more easterly position before heading to the northward, particularly as from the experience of American whalers and the ships of the English Franklin relief expedition there was nothing to indicate there a better chance of progress. On the other hand, we were within 220 miles of Wrangel Land, which, though seen, had never been landed on, and which, after the sighting of land even farther north by Capt. Kellett, in H. M. S. Herald, in 1849, had been assumed by some geographers to be a continent, or at least an extensive archipelago, and by others to be a second Greenland, if not even the continuation of the original across the Pole.

With a new land so near us offering a chance of exploration, and a winter harbor from which a higher latitude might be attained by sledges, and perhaps presenting what was naturally to be expected, land-water along its eastern coast, in which case a good northing might be made by the ship herself before any exploration or sledge journey might be undertaken, I concluded that I was exercising good judgment in considering that land as a kind of support for the first winter's campaign, and I accordingly shaped a course N. x W. true, proceeding with all speed. From 1 p. m., August 31st, to 8 a. m., September 30th, we therefore proceeded to the northward, inclining a little to the westward when circumstances would permit, going through occasional loose streams of ice, and at other times skirting the edge of the pack. At the last-named time we had reached a point lat. 70° 30′ N., long. 174° 30′ W. (about 90 miles E. x S. true) of Cape Hawaii, the eastern extremity of Wrangel's Land, and had no open water in sight, except to the SE. and S. A promising looking lead in the pack to the NW. was entered and followed until 3 p. m., when, a thick fog preventing farther progress, the ship was anchored to a convenient floe, where we remained until the next day, taking advantage of the fog lifting for an hour to advance a few miles further north.

Before the weather became sufficiently clear to proceed, on the 4th of September we had an opportunity of observing the kind of ice surrounding us. The pack seemed to have a uniform thickness of 7 feet (2 feet being above the water), while thickly studded with hummocks 6 and 7 feet in height. This would give an average thickness to the whole mass of 13 or 14 feet. New ice formed around us during the night of the 3d–4th, of ½ inch in thickness, the temperature of the air as shown by the deck thermometer having stood at 29° Fah. up to 8 a. m.

At 2 p. m., Sept. 4th, the fog clearing up, we again got under way and worked to the northward, availing ourselves of any narrow lane which offered itself to make any material advance; but being soon confronted by impenetrable ice, we were forced to bear away to the eastward again, and fight our way to the edge of the pack. At 4.30 p. m. we sighted Herald Island, bearing WNW. true, and according to our reckoning about 40 miles distant.

At this point, lat. 71° 10′, long. 174° W., we had ice to the westward of us, and to the northward as well, the latter stretching east as far as eye could reach from our mastheads. Two hundred and forty miles had been accomplished from Koliutchin Bay, on a course a little to the eastward of north, and we found ourselves at what seemed to be the edge of a solid ice barrier, no lane or opening appearing of any kind in it. The ice to the westward seemed to offer better chances for penetration, one very likely-looking opening attracting our attention before nightfall. Believing, as I did, that the best chance for an advance would be by land-water extending along the eastern coast of Wrangel's Land, and hoping that this promising lead to the westward would conduct us to it, I concluded to enter it as soon as there was sufficient daylight the next morning. The ship was accordingly hove to for the night, and at 4 a. m., September 5th, we again steamed into the ice pack on a general WNW. course, true. For nearly five hours we proceeded without great difficulty (though at times we were plowing through young ice of two inches in thickness, which was sufficiently tough to offer considerable resistance and score our doubling in many places), and were then brought up by the solid floe of 10 or 15 feet thickness.

Just previous to securing the ship to the floe with an ice anchor, and subsequently also, we distinctly saw land to the WNW. and SW. of Herald Island. I was at first inclined to think that we were deceived by mirage, or by some distortion by refraction of ice hills, but as the weather was bright and clear, our horizon perfectly defined, and the land to the SW. was in the form of sugar-loaf, *snow-topped* mountains, I am convinced that it really existed. Of its distance, however, we could form no idea. We had found looking across the ice to be a wonderful disturbance to the correctness of estimated distances. We had assumed Herald Island to be originally 40 miles distant in the morning, and yet, having steamed 20 miles toward it, it seemed to us as distant as ever. On the same terms this other land might have been estimated at from 50 to 70 miles distant, or from 30 to 50 miles beyond Herald Island. This will serve to verify the report by Capt. Kellett of having seen such land in 1849, while cruising here in H. M. S. Herald, and will account for a portion of the Kellett Land marked on English charts, the remainder, as our subsequent experience proved, having no existence. At that time, however, I hoped we were destined to reach this land. Though our lead had abruptly terminated at a wall of ice, the surface of the floes was cut up here and there by ponds and small lakes, which any movement of the ice might unite into a lane of navigable water. Waiting, therefore, with what patience we had, we succeeded during the afternoon in advancing another mile or two, and we worked away for three hours through thin ice, and between slightly separated floe pieces, and finally secured the ship with an ice anchor at 4 p. m.

'The next morning, September 6th, we had nothing but ice in sight, being to all appearance as firmly lodged within it as if we had been cast into it in the same mould. The temperature of the air had ranged between 23° and 25° Fahrenheit from midnight to 9 a. m., and all the small lanes and ponds in our neighborhood had become frozen over, while a thick fog prevented us from seeing any distance beyond.

At 1 p. m. the weather cleared, and we saw a chance to make a mile or so nearer to Herald Island, which we at once availed ourselves of, by twisting in and around all sorts of corners, ramming moderate obstructions, and squeezing through narrow lanes, but were finally brought to at 4.20 p. m. to floes too thick to ram and too compact for penetration.

Unless something, like a gale of wind, occurred to break up this mass of ice and by making water spaces allow us to proceed farther, our advance was no longer to be guided or controlled by any power from within the ship. We had gone as far to the northward as the heavy pack ice had permitted, and we had followed up the only water lane presenting itself, and had come to the end of that. My choice of plans was limited by the surroundings. To advance was impossible; to retreat was disagreeable, even if a chance existed of doing so, though in fact we could not have gone more than a mile; and holding our present location meant wintering in the pack and drifting we knew not where. The land-water of Kellett Land was now as unattainable as the land-water of Greenland, so far as any power of our own could be effective. The ocean we had left behind was as much out of our reach as if a continent had intervened, and there seemed nothing left but making a virtue of necessity and staying where we were. The opening in one of the heavy floes made a sort of dock, into which we hauled the ship, with her head at N. W. true, in lat. 71° 19′, long. 174° 57′ W., and hauled the fires under the boilers. As I had resolved to winter in the pack should no favorable opportunity occur for advancing, the necessity of saving our coal was evident; though, if an opportunity for advancing did come, it would be well to be ready for it at the moment, it was clearly out of the question to keep banked fires for an occasion which might not happen for months, if at all.

Between 8 p. m. and midnight of the next day the ship sustained some pressure by the seeming closing in of the sides of the ice dock, which forced her keel up on a projecting tongue of ice under water, and caused her to heel 5° to starboard. (Our lead line, which was put over and carefully watched, indicated that we were drifting to the N. N. W. true.) She righted again at 1.30 a. m., September 8th, and, sustaining another pressure in the evening, heeled 9° to starboard, jamming her rudder hard over and causing us some anxiety as to the effect on the pintles and gudgeons. It will probably be asked why I did not unship the rudder immediately, also trice up the propeller before allowing them to be endangered, and I may well explain here my reasons for not doing either. Our rudder was unusually strong and heavy, in weight something like two tons, and though a simple matter to unhang it, would be an exceedingly difficult matter to get it in place unless we had plenty of water free from ice around the stern. Though the propeller was similarly easy to trice up, ice would surely form in the spaces left and prevent lowering to its place. If I had been confident that we should remain in the ice all winter these reasons would have less weight. But as I had some hope of the September gales breaking up the ice, I wanted the ship to be in a condition to be moved without delay, and for the present, therefore, decided to leave both rudder and propeller in their places.

We now began to fear that we should experience a trouble which the statements of our predecessors in Arctic navigation had not led us to anticipate. The popular belief is that salt water in freezing ejects the salt and that in a frozen ocean no difficulty will be experienced in obtaining water for drinking and cooking. Also that when there is such an abundant supply as the Arctic regions generally affords it is a simple matter to do so, taking due care to exercise a little judgment in selecting those pieces which from age, percolation, or the presence of refrozen pools of surface melting are the likeliest to be free from salt. Without going into the subject in detail just here, reserving its discussion for a more appropriate place in my report, I will merely say that we could find no ice that would yield palatable water. No great quantity of snow was found on the surface of the floes, and such as we collected and melted contained too much salt for use. In this dilemma we saw no alternative but distilling water for our daily wants, and this would involve a great expenditure of fuel, if one of the main boilers was used. Fortunately we had a small Baxter boiler, procured for generating power to drive an electric machine for giving light, and also the boiler belonging to our steam cutter, and our chief engineer, Mr. Melville (of whose ingenuity, practicability, and untiring zeal I shall have more than one occasion to speak), set himself to work to adapt either or both of these boilers to the demand with the most economical results. Suffice it to add at this moment that he was eminently successful, and that, with brief exceptions, hereafter to be mentioned, all the water we used while drifting in the ice was distilled on board ship.*

On the 9th of September our position was determined by observation, lat. 71° 35' N., long. 175° 6' W., and the magnetic variation 23° E., showing that we had drifted, since our besetment on the 6th inst., 16¼ miles to the N. by W. At the same time, the eastern end of Herald Island bearing S. W. true, we again saw the previously sighted land beyond it, between the bearings of S. W. and W. by S., both true. That portion of it further to the westward was a low table land, with a range of peaks to its southward terminating in a low, seemingly flat rock. Distances were of course unknown, but from the positions indicated on the chart of the Hydrographic Office we were fifteen miles from Herald Island, 40 miles from the northernmost point of the new land, and 75 miles from its southernmost point, or Cape Hawaii.

The next two days passed uneventfully. No openings occurred in the ice, and we saw that we were being drifted by it to the NW. We thoroughly examined the icy dock in which the ship had been placed, and in which she lay heeled 9° to starboard, and found that we were between two floes 15 feet in thickness, with projecting tongues beneath our keel. One of these projecting tongues had driven our rudder hard over, and by the strain produced had commenced to "broom" up the rudder-post and rudder casing, and if not relieved might occasion serious damage. Accordingly the rudder was unhung and triced up to its davits across the stern. The propeller now remained to cause uneasiness, but I coincided with the opinion of the chief engineer that the probable damage to it would not be irreparable, and I decided to leave it in place, as well for its readiness for use as for its strengthening support to an otherwise unprotected rudder post.

On the 12th of September, seeing no chance for any progress, I concluded to send a party on a reconnaisance toward Herald Island, to examine the condition of the ice in that direction, and if successful in reaching the island to examine it for any drift wood that might have lodged there, with a view to our endeavoring to collect a quantity for our winter use. Accordingly at 8 the following morning Lieut. Chipp, accompanied by Mr. Melville, Mr. Dunbar, and the native Alexy, started with a sled drawn by eight dogs and equipped for an absence of [blank] days. Although my instructions to incur no unusual risk did not contemplate an absence of more than 48 hours, at 9 a. m. of the 14th the party returned to the ship without having been able to reach the island. Seven miles from the ship they had come to much thinner ice than that surrounding us, this thinner ice being broken up in floes and united by new ice of hardly sufficient thickness to bear their weight. At 10 miles from the ship they came to a lane of water ½ mile wide extending east and west, with smaller lanes running out of it to the south, southeast, and southwest. Following along its edge, to the westward, the lane, after a mile or so, curved back to N. W. At this point the party was about 5 miles from Herald Island, and could observe that the ice between them and the island was much cut up by leads, and presented such a generally rotten appearance as to justify that could the ship have been moved over the 15 miles intervening thick ice she might have been carried in to the island itself. This last, from its seemingly precipitous sides, would have afforded no protection to a vessel, although several large clefts on the northeast side, which I had studied with a glass from the ship, had led me to suppose they might have surrounded small bays, which would have served our purpose.

---

*Note by the author.

Observations for position showed that we were still drifting to the N.W., at the rate of 2½ miles a day. On the 16th September we sighted land distinctly between W.xS. and S., both true; and as it covered more points of the compass than heretofore we began to hope that we might be able to arrive by drifting where we had failed to carry our vessel. At about this time (the 18th and 19th) a strong S. E. wind brought such a marked change in the temperature as to occasion numerous small pools on the surface of our ice-field, and led me to hope for a breaking up of the ice sufficient for a resumption of navigation. Rain fell and increased the wasting of the hummocks, and our drift to the N. W. continued with considerable regularity. In anticipation of some movement I had purposely delayed making our preparations for the winter, such as erecting our deck house and stretching our tent awnings; but I was again disappointed. Numerous small lanes did indeed open in our immediate neighborhood, but of no great length and entirely unconnected, and we were therefore not inclined to break out from our solid bed merely to enter a small lane not many yards removed.

On the 21st September observations placed us in lat. 72° 10′ N., long. 175° 26′ W., indicating a drift to the nd. of about 5 miles a day. Herald Island was but a small patch on our horizon, and as we were progressing in a satisfactory direction we did not regret having failed to reach it. At this time we did not have the knowledge (which came only with subsequent experience) of how closely allied were the drifts with the winds, and I erroneously attributed the steady drift to the N. W. or N. as due to some prevailing current, which was to carry us still forward to perhaps large water spaces beyond. But I began to be shaken in my belief, and was also considerably puzzled for a reasonable explanation. The drift did not then seemingly depend upon the wind, for it was in different directions with the same wind at different times. Again, light winds seemed to occasion motion and pressure equal to those of fresh winds. About a mile from the ship in all directions the ice was constantly assuming new shapes. We seemed to be held within a solid floe, against which lighter floes were continually crowding and piling up ice-tables six inches thick, and in confused masses to heights varying from six to twenty feet. Occasionally we would be in the centre of an island of ice two miles in diameter, with a water lane a hundred yards in width surrounding it. In a night the lane would be closed by the advance of the surrounding field, and in the morning we would find our floe enclosed by a confused fence of sometimes six, sometimes twelve, and sometimes twenty feet high, from the top of which we could see nothing but one mass of ice.

By Sept. 25th, in lat. 72° 8′, long. 174° 54′ W., all sign of bird life seemed to be gone. While the pools had lasted on the surface of the floes an occasional gull had been sighted, but the pools had now become solid ice. On the 29th, seeing no chance for any further navigation, we set to work to prepare for the winter, accepting the certainty of wintering in the pack with as much care for our comfort during cold weather as if we were in a secure harbor. Our deck-house was erected, our steam cutter was moved to the ice, and our observatory placed at sufficient distance from the ship for the proper observation of meteorological subjects. The engines and boilers had been some time previously overhauled, cleaned, and protected from injury, while keeping all parts in readiness for service.

On the 3rd of October we again, and somewhat unexpectedly, sighted Herald Island, bearing S. S. E., true, and distant 30 miles. Our drift had now described the third side of a triangle, and had thoroughly dispelled all belief in any steady current in any direction which was likely to benefit us. We therefore addressed ourselves to the carrying out of our daily duties. Regular meteorological observations were taken, soundings made daily, temperature of water at different depths taken by Mr. C., with determinations of specific gravity of water brought from those depths by Sigsbee's cups, and astronomical observations made whenever possible, to determine our position. The dredge was lowered each day, and after being towed if we were drifting, or left on the bottom if no drift was perceptible, was hauled in after an hour's interval, and its contents examined and preserved. A daily routine had been established, providing for the various kinds of work and their performance, and also a fire bill for our peculiar situation with the possible emergency. Hunting parties were despatched daily in quest of game (3 bears and numerous seals having already been added to our provision list) and short excursions were made with sleds and dog teams by officers and men, with the advantage of getting some idea of the peculiarities of our surroundings.

On the 9th October we had a west gale blowing 30 miles an hour, temp. falls 31° to 6½°, and on the 11th a S. E. gale, blowing for some time at the rate of 40 miles an hour, during which the barometer fell to 28″.77, and the temperature rose to 33° Fahr., leading me to hope for a liberation for the ship by the combined action of wind and heat. But no such event took place.

On the 21st October the temperature reached zero for the first time in the voyage, and fell to —11° before the end of the day. To those of us who were new to Arctic experiences this seemed sufficiently cold, but we afterward learned to look upon this figure as indicating a very mild and genial condition of things. Our liquid compasses (Ritchie 7½ inch) were found to be frozen, and were removed from the binnacles and stowed away, protected from the weather. On the 26th October we had our first ice opening, a crack a foot wide being found 500 yards ahead (E.N.E.) of the ship, and extending in a semi-circular direction for about ½ mile; and another 500 yards beyond that, six feet wide, and extending in a curve for about the same distance as the first. In both instances the rent was a fresh one through ice varying from 12 to 14 feet in thickness, the water rising within 18 inches of the surface, though at the temperature prevailing ($-10°$ to $-17°$) promptly freezing. The next day, in order to be prepared for any emergency not then to be forseen, our party was told off into five sledge crews, commanded respectively by the five commissioned officers attached to the ship, and upon five sledges were packed forty days' rations for men and dogs. A detail was made of duties to be performed by each individual in event of disaster bringing about an abandonment of the ship; our sleeping-bags, tents, and other travelling gear overhauled and made ready for use; and the loaded sledges on the poop deck arranged with reference to the most convenient manner for getting them to the ice. All these preparations completed we could merely await the future, satisfied of our powerlessness to do more.

A heavy bank of snow had been built all around the ship and reaching up to her rail to prevent the radiation and loss of heat from within, and the sloping sides of this bank would serve as a ramp to get our sledges down unless the ice broke up all around us.

In order that I might have from time to time a correct knowledge of the physical condition of all persons under my command, to be able by observation and information to regulate or remove any source of evil, whether arising from lack of variety or quantity of food, insufficient ventilation, excess of labor, exposure to cold, or other circumstances—in short to avoid by prevention what might be difficult to cure, I now directed the surgeon to make upon the first day of each succeeding month such an examination of each officer and man as would enable him to report to me in writing our actual physical condition, and any effect which might be produced by our residence within the Arctic Circle under such uncomfortable terms as our wintering in the pack. This was regularly carried out, with an occasional intermission, and the results of such examinations, with the surgeon's reports to me, are transmitted herewith for your information.

On the 3d of November another crack was found in the ice about 200 yards NW. of the ship, running in an irregular direction for a quarter of a mile and having an average width of 20 feet. These signs of ice rupture were unpleasant because our so-called dock seemed to be threatened; for though we had laid rigidly fixed heretofore the ship now shook and trembled in high wind and we could not tell how soon we might be in a place whose openings and closings would subject us to the confused jamming and upheavals elsewhere witnessed. On the 6th of November we had a more serious experience. At 9 a. m. we were disagreeably surprised at finding a large crack in the ice about 100 yards on our starboard quarter, as well as cracks ahead and astern of us, and the unpleasant suspicion was forced on us that our dock was no more to be relied on than the thinner ice in its vicinity. At 4 p. m. the crack on our starboard quarter (and which ran WSW., ENE., in this general direction with reference to the ship), opened to a width of 4 feet, barely missing our observatory which was left on the nearest shore. After removing our instruments to a place of safety the lane of water was found to have increased to a width of 20 yards. Ice commenced forming immediately on its surface, the temperature of the air being zero. Our soundings gave 18 fathoms, muddy bottom, drift ENE. During the following night we had numerous groans and snaps of the ice in our neighborhood, but being sufficiently occupied in watching for any change in our immediate surroundings no excursions to any distance were undertaken until daylight of the 7th. We then found that the lane had closed, the ice coming together with seemingly great pressure, for great heaps of broken floe pieces were piled up. As the floe immediately surrounding the ship was the stronger the advancing ice coming in contact broke off its edges against the unyielding mass. When I mention that the thickness of these pieces was found to be 7 feet 10 inches, and our own floe was known to be 13 feet thick, some idea can be formed of the immense force which was being exerted at the line of contact and which piled up these mounds with no more difficulty than a plane turns up shavings. As these pressures were going on at only a hundred yards from us it was difficult to imagine what might happen from hour to hour; we therefore watched this conflict between ice floes with some interest but more anxiety. We had had, since midnight, a light SW. wind, but at 10 a. m. there came a perfect calm. At 11 a. m., to our surprise, the pressure ceased, and the advancing ice stopped, and then receded until it left a water lane about 10 yards in width. Down this water lane from ENE. we saw steadily advancing a fearful procession of ice of all sizes and shapes, from huge blocks 100 tons in weight to jagged pieces of a couple of hundred weight, in the utmost confusion, shrieking and groaning as they were squeezed and ground against each other, and where the edge of the channel was not of a regular and accom-

LOSS OF THE STEAMER JEANNETTE. 333

modating shape conveniently breaking off a few tons here and there and shoving it along in front as a road-cleaner. The rate of progress of this confusion was about ½ mile an hour. It passed along without serious hindrance until it got in the bend of the channel on our quarter and then it occasionally jammed. At such times the pressure was tremendous; the smaller pieces passed readily enough but the large hummocks or broken floe pieces would bring up against our floe dock and cause it to hump up and crack and groan as if it was going to break in all directions. I momentarily expected such to happen and that the ship would be sent into this frightful stream of moving ice to battle as she could. For five hours this state of affairs continued, and then it ceased as suddenly as it had begun. The word "halt," passed along a line of troops, could not have been obeyed more quickly than our ice procession came to rest. Sounding soon after we found we were in 23 fathoms, though it is not easy to make the additional depth of 5 fathoms account for the sudden stoppage in the ice movement. At this time, and many times subsequently, I was inclined to attribute the ice movements to tidal action, particularly as they occurred at or about the times of new and full moon, but the impossibility of measuring the tides in our circumstances made this supposition nothing more than a guess. Some long resisting mass of ice had given way, and the movement continued until the pressure was relieved and equilibrium restored. The probability of a recurrence of these movements made me anxious as to the future. Drifting with the ice would not perhaps be very bad, but the catching of the ship on some impediment or her inability to make turns as sharp as might be demanded would assuredly expose her to be crushed or overridden by the ice masses following her. So far as was possible preparations had been made for disaster. Packed sledges were in readiness, travelling gear at hand, dogs kept inboard, and in an emergency we could have promptly taken to the ice; but whether we would have been any better off was very doubtful.

The next day, the 8th, we passed in quiet. On the 9th the ice got under way again, and moved along for a short time without giving us any trouble. Our soundings had again decreased to 18 fathoms. On the 10th, in 17½ fathoms, the ice movement again began, and continued several hours. If it were not for the danger to the ship the watching of this ponderous procession would have been an enjoyable thing. But our ice dock was slowly giving away before the pressure and grinding of these large masses along its side; already the hundred yards between us and the moving ice stream had been reduced to a hundred feet, and the cracking and humping up remainder gave proof that it was only a question of time to reduce it to as many inches. The 11th of November was a day of much anxiety and care. At 6 a. m. the trembling and creaking of the ship gave notice that our ice procession had resumed its march. Going out on what little was left of our level ice alongside we were confronted by a fearful spectacle. The pressures and movements of the previous days were feeble in comparison to what was now going on. Large blocks 25 feet in length, 7 feet in thickness, and in breadth from 6 to 20 feet, were rearing up on end as they advanced, crushing smaller pieces to small lumps, or, toppling over, breaking themselves in all kinds of shapes and sizes, and all this with the most horrible noises, such as can hardly be described. The rumbling of a railway train in a tunnel, the shrieks of a thousand steam-whistles, the crash of a falling house, all combined, would make the nearest approach to the noise which deafened us for four and a half hours. Every few moments a stoppage would occur, some piece having caught under or against our floe, groans and shrieks would arise from the struggling mass, our little foothold would bend and dome up, the long tables of heavy ice in the moving stream would rear their heads in the air, while adding their pressure to the conflict, when, crash, something gives way, another yard of our dock has gone, and the march is resumed. A little of this goes a great way in disturbing one's calmness, and we were not improved by finding that a break had occurred in the ice across our bows, and that a projecting floe berg from the main stream was forcing its way like a wedge to cut a channel along our port side, and, in again connecting itsself with the main stream, cut us off from all connection with that hitherto quiet ice and hurl us along too. Under these circumstances sleeping or rest of any kind was hardly attainable, and it required but very little time for us to repair to the deck at each fresh movement. At 4.15 a. m., Nov. 12th, the ice got under way again along the whole line. The flowing ice stream at our side, close as it was, now failed to attract our entire attention, because of the more serious advance occurring right ahead of us. The projecting floe berg of yesterday having crossed our bow, seemed to have given up the attempt to cut a lane along our port side, and devoted itself to ripping up the small remainder of our ice dock ahead of us, and sweeping us and it out of the way at the same time. Behind this floe berg was a confused mass of piled-up ice, pushing and shoving it into and against our dock wall, the whole bearing down toward our stem as fast as a man could walk. On it came piling up large blocks in front of it, while the ship shook, jarred, and quivered at each surge of the ice. All hands had been called, and stood ready, but there was really nothing to be done. There was no place to go, and nothing to trust to but the possibility of our ship holding together after falling into the tumbling procession. (At this time, as at many others, I had reason to remark the calmness and firmness of every officer and man. No tremor of excitement, no symptom of alarm was apparent; simply facing the inevitable, there was nothing but watching and waiting for developments.) Some of us were standing on the roof of the house covering the forward part of the spar-deck, as commanding the best view of the surroundings. Suddenly the advancing mass seemed to gather greater velocity. It appeared to make one surge of great length, and was already under our head-booms. Instinctively we grasped the fore shrouds to keep our places when the crash came, for that the next moment would see us crushed or whirled along in the ice stream I did not doubt. But at that moment the advance stopped, the pressure ceased, and not a sound was to be heard. For two hours and a quarter had our suspense lasted, and as it was before dawn, with no moon, these hours had seemed ages. Darkness added much to the horror of the situation, which a temperature of 15° did not mitigate. The day passed without any further movement, though from our continued expectation the anxiety was not diminished. I used to compare our existence in those times to living over a powder-mill to which a train had been laid and fired, while we were simply awaiting the inevitable explosion, and such, I think, was the general feeling. Our days were becoming shorter and shorter, about 4 hours sunlight and as many hours twilight falling to our share. For 16 hours, when we had no moon, we were shrouded in darkness, and under these conditions the ice jammings and uncanny noises were intensified to our senses. What we could see we had less dread of, though we could not avert it; but to be surrounded by perils that we could not see was terribly wearing. The next morning, the 13th, at 2 o'clock, a loud crack under the ship startled us again; but beyond a small opening under the stern, which indicated that our ice dock had split in a line with the keel, we saw no occasion for alarm. The watching and waiting again commenced. Throughout the day everything remained quiet, and toward midnight we were settling down for some rest, when, with a few slight snaps, to our utter astonishment all the ice against the port side of the ship moved easily away to the N., and in 20 minutes we had 150 feet wide of water between us and the side of the dock which had held us so long. So quietly was it done that four of our dogs sleeping alongside were carried away without their being awakened, and before we could make an effort to get them on board ship. There was not a breath of wind at the time, and the ice and snow wall which we had built against our sides for warmth slid away into the darkness without a sound. What few possessions remained on the ice dock were now removed to the ship, the boats got ready for lowering, as much of the running rigging cleared away as could be got at, and before daylight we were in readiness for any kind of a move, whether with sleds, boats, or the ship itself. Lat. 71° 51′, long. 177° 20′ W. As soon as dawn came we saw our ice wall had stopped about 500 yards to the northward, and that ice 4 inches thick had formed over the water between it and ourselves. We were not able to send for our dogs, however, until the following day, for the ice intervening was opening in places, and small pieces of ice commenced drifting through the lane, as if forerunners of large masses to follow. That these larger masses would come sooner or later I was convinced, and that we should have trouble before long I had no doubt. With but a slight hold on one side on ice which probably extended down to our keel, but little pressure would be necessary to send us adrift. Though we might secure the ship to this floe piece by an ice anchor, it was questionable whether in case of renewed pressure it would not immediately be swept away into the running stream, with ourselves attached to it, in which case its room would be preferable to its company; and therefore I concluded to remain passive and wait for results. This rapidly freezing lane of water of 500 yards in width extended ENE. and WSW., but for only a short distance, soon narrowing and finally becoming a mere crack in the heavy floe ice. In the afternoon of the 15th a SE. gale set in, which continued during the 16th and 17th, with some very heavy squalls. It had the effect of raising the temperature, however, above zero, which was comforting to some extent. On the 16th the ice ahead of us got under way again, and bore down on us slowly but without damage, for fortunately the remaining side of our dock had a strong projecting tongue which withstood and caromed off the large pieces, causing them to float past us without injury. A small basin astern received the pieces, and by the time our lane alongside was filled up and the floe-bergs were beginning to rear their heads above the rail the pressure ceased. We were again completely surrounded, but in the most dreary manner. Such a confused mass of ice has to be seen to be understood. The awful procession which in passing along to starboard of us had come to a halt had its counterpart on our port side, and while the great ice tables on the one hand towered above us to prevent our egress, the huge blocks on the other clearly indicated "no thoroughfare" in this direction either.

Such was our condition on the 16th of November when the sun left us for the winter. As an astronomical fact we knew he was above our horizon on that date, though hidden by the clouds. We had really seen the last of him on the 15th. From this time to the 24th we had a constant succession of nips and pressures at all hours, with all winds, and at all temperatures. Accounts of them would be but endless repetition. Our ship groaned and trembled at the unequal conflict, while her frame cracked, her deck arched up, and flattened out actually as we walked over it, and the air was made hideous by the noises of ice grinding which I have tried heretofore to describe. Finally the ice on our port side tried to come on board of us, breaking through our light bulwark planking without difficulty. During this time we were kept at the extent of possible mental tension, never relaxed; for while the jamming and pressing were going on we were anxiously waiting for its cessation, and in the lulls we were anticipating a more severe recurrence. Our soundings varied from 22 to 27 fathoms, our drift being greater or less according to the force of the wind, and as a rule leeward in direction.

On the 24th, at 5 a. m., we had a more serious disturbance than usual. Pressure under the bow indicated the advance of an old enemy. While the ice was piled alongside in places higher than our rail, that under the bow was in blocks up to our billet-head, and a long tongue, just clear of our cutwater, was plowing away in the ice on our starboard side, prying us off in the most workmanlike manner. There seemed no good reason why that plowing tongue should have been shunted off from its original direction, for it had advanced originally in line with our keel, but such was the case, and it was preferable to having its force exerted to separate the ship and sandwich itself between. The ship groaned and creaked more dolefully than ever. Bound down by these clinging masses, she could not rise to pressure, and for a moment it was simply a question of relative strength and endurance. Suddenly the more loosely-packed ice in the lane on our port side yielded, the tongue gave a fresh lunge, the ship's stern rose, the floe split, and the ship righted, floating on an even keel in a narrow canal, which slowly widened as the ice opened until we had a space nearly equal to the length of the ship. Here we floated during that night, sometimes resting against one side and sometimes against the other, according as the wind, blowing with a velocity of 25 miles an hour, acted on us, and shoaling our water from 22 to 18 fathoms.

The 25th of November, 1879, was a day we shall long remember. Early in the morning the canal closed, nipping the ship severely, and, pinching down under her, heeled her over to starboard, starting our bulwark planking in several places. In an hour or so the pressure was relieved, and the ship righted again, while the ice opened as before, leaving us in a lane of water about 150 feet wide and perhaps twice as long. Towards 5 p. m. we commenced to move astern, a mass of ice ahead of us bearing down at the same time. A bright moonlight enabled us to see our surroundings, and to be prepared for them as they occurred; although there was really nothing that could be done. Having been at last sent into the path of the ice torrent, we could only await its arrival and witness its effect. We now observed that the lane led into a small lake, about 2 miles distant to the east, which lake had suddenly appeared in what had been heavily-packed ice, and the set of the moving ice was clearly in that direction. Just then the stern of the ship touched an angular floe piece, her head payed around as prettily as if she were casting under jibs, and at the moment we got before the light wind then blowing the long dreaded ice procession overtook us, surrounded us, jammed under us, and carried us along as helplessly as a feather is borne on a swiftly-flowing river. I cannot adequately describe the horrid din that this moving mass of screeching, grinding, and groaning ice created, added to, as it was, by creaking timbers as we lurched and reeled along. To make oneself heard it would have been necessary to shout, but as all our attention was fully occupied in looking toward the lake before mentioned, and calculating the chances of the ship reaching it and yet floating, no such effort was required. All hands were on deck and grouped upon the deck-house roof and poop while we were running this gauntlet. The half hour that it required to traverse the two miles was a long one, and just before its expiration we had more cause for uneasiness than ever. To our unpleasant surprise the ice stream, instead of flowing into the lake, seemed to jam somewhere before us in the canal and commenced its ugly trick of piling up great masses as we had seen before. Our movement began to decrease, the masses around us to thicken, the screams and groans to multiply, the creaking of the timbers to grow louder, until finally, with one tremendous crash, the barrier was broken and we were shot out into the lake with sufficient velocity to carry us across it and jam us into some thin ice on its further edge, where we remained.

We now found ourselves relieved from all immediate anxiety. Our position was a quiet one, and as ice commenced to form on the water surrounding us we hoped to freeze in solidly for the winter that was already long since begun. No signs of any movement appeared around us, and the distant ice gorge seemed to have come to a rest after we had been forced out of it. Hardly had we had time to congratulate ourselves upon our escape when a SE. gale sprung up, and blew for four days with velocities ranging between 25 and 40 miles. We drifted rapidly to the northwest, increasing the depth of water from 21 to 26 fathoms. At temperatures sometimes a little above zero and sometimes a little below it, ice formed around us to the thickness of twelve inches, and this held us, though the heavy squalls that shook the ship from truck to keelson seemed strong enough to drive us through it. From our rapid drift to the NW. I inferred some large water space in that direction, into which the ice was driving, and I feared some further trouble should this water space become filled and the ice, continuing its movement, pile up in tables in our vicinity. On the 29th November, the last day of the gale, something of the kind seemed about to happen, for our lake commenced to close, the ice being ripped up around us and forced to windward in overriding blocks. As we lay broadside to the movement we had its full force directed against our frame. The ice on our port or weather side being thick and tough, offered a sure resistance to our movement in that direction, and consequently we had to take the full brunt of the coming ice on our starboard or lee side. At first there was no reason for alarm; ice of only one foot in thickness was nothing to us. This broke in blocks, climbing up our side and falling back on the level floe; but out in the lake the floes cracked and overrode each other in advancing and formed blocks sometimes two, sometimes three, and sometimes four feet in thickness, and in all shapes and at all angles. These, jamming the broken ice already alongside, lifted it, and their surfaces adding to the thickness and increasing the momentum of the battering ram now at work. Ice piled up our sides, lodging and hanging above the bends, holding the ship down by its weight and preventing her rising under pressure, the frames snapped and complained, the deck planks humped up as we had seen them do before, and trembled under our feet. These pressures and uncertainties would last half an hour at a time, until it seemed as if wood and iron must collapse, when, to our relief, the floe on the port side would arch up and break and the few feet of space it afforded give us a breathing spell before we brought up against the hard ice, and the advancing tables took us in hand again and pushed us on for another nip. This lasted for eight hours, and at its conclusion we were as tightly nipped and wedged in on all sides as if held in a vise. (Nov. 30th, planet Venus clearly visible at noon. Beginning of fine auroræ.)

Dec. 2nd, lime-juice issue commenced. From this time to the 11th December we continued without any change, the tight grip in which the ice held the ship being neither diminished or increased. How it could very well have increased without crushing her sides in it was impossible to say. Accordingly we lived in a weary suspense, standing by for a disaster at any moment, grateful each morning that we were no worse off than the night before, but anxious about what might occur before another morning came. As a rule everybody kept dressed at all hours, with his outside furs close at hand; provisions, clothing, arms and ammunition were stored on deck ready for instant removal to the ice; sledges, dogs, harness, and traveling gear kept in convenient places; boats prepared for rapid lowering; in fine, all preparations were made for being turned out of our ship and driven to the floe and for the dreary time that would have followed. The sameness and monotony of such a life finally began to seem worse than our previous experiences; for somehow there was a dangerous excitement about them that warmed one's blood and gave him a sensation of activity, while waiting for delayed peril was cold and spiritless work. On the 11th December, however, we seemed to be promised a renewal of the old ice-gorge business. A crack was found in the heavy floe across our bows, and running parallel with our port side, quite close to, which in a few hours opened to a width of 6 feet. The ice immediately surrounding the ship showing no signs of separating, we had opportunity to witness a fine panorama, the whole ice country except ourselves moving along deliberately 200 yards to the NE., presenting all varieties and shapes of heavy floes in so doing. We had a chance to measure the amount of direct freezing since Nov. 25th, and found it twenty inches. When the ice had moved this 200 yards it came to a stop, the six feet of water narrowed as the floe edges closed on one another, and in a short time everything had resumed its ordinary quiet, having given us a new specimen of ice scenery to look at. While seeking a cause for this strange occurrence we noticed scud flying rapidly from SW., and other indications of the gale, which soon burst on us, reaching quickly a velocity of 40 miles an hour. Soundings in 32 fathoms, and a lively drift indicated to NE.

With these conditions our winter wore along. Occasional openings in the ice showed us that at no time could we expect a perfect state of rest, and frequent jars and shakings of the ship from ice pressures near to as well as at some little distance kept us in the state of mental tension before alluded to. At such times the place of the ice movement at a distance could be determined by the peculiar noises emitted, and its approach toward the ship or its motion in another direction be estimated. Occasionally the noises were of the combined shriek, groan, and crash which I have attempted to describe, but more frequently the noise was similar to that produced by the paddle-wheels of a steamer beating the water at moderate speed. If the line of pressure advanced the noises were of course more distinct; and if it was receding from us the paddle-like beatings would so regularly grow fainter that it was difficult to believe that a steamer was not there.

As the cold increased we were at first frequently startled by the snapping and starting of our metal bolts and fastenings and the iron frames of the cabin. This was easily explained by the contraction of the metal and its consequent separation from the wood, and the novelty soon wore off. We were fortunately favored during our first winter by having but little wind, which made our low temperatures much more endurable. By a moderate use of fuel we were able to keep our living apartments at a comfortable temperature, 50° Fah. Owing to this fact, and the precautions that had been taken to line the cabin throughout with felt between the planking and ceiling, to cover the poop deck with three layers of thick canvas, and particularly to provide a condensing chamber by shutting off the after part of the cabin for that purpose, we had none of the damp and dripping so common to previous Arctic ships, but enjoyed at all times a perfectly dry, warm, and pleasant apartment for general use and comfort. The rooms occupied by the executive officer and myself being in the forward part of the cabin had their forward ends more exposed to the open air, the front of the cabin being protected only by a tent awning over the quarter deck. On these cold surfaces moisture condensed and promptly froze, and its removal before thawing set in was easily accomplished. The sleeping apartments of the other officers were in the ward-room, but this being under the cabin was protected from contact with the outside air above, and by our snow walls as well as a felt lining radiation of heat was prevented. At first a fire was allowed in the ward-room, but the officers found it made the place too warm for comfortable and healthy sleeping, and it was discontinued. Such slight condensation as there was in these rooms in these quarters occurred almost entirely on the forward bulkheads of the two forward rooms, but as it was not objectionable so long as it froze, and could be easily removed before it would thaw, it was no serious matter. The greater part of the moisture condensed in the after store-room just forward of the ward-room, and as it did not attempt to melt during the winter its removal was deferred until the spring when the holds and store-rooms were broken out for restowing, and the ice was then dug out and carried away.

On the berth deck, during the first winter, we were not so fortunate, but we were so far able to profit by our experience as to make arrangements which secured perfect warmth and dryness and proper ventilation during the second winter. Before leaving the navy-yard at Mare Island I had caused to be constructed a wooden house which extended from the foremast to within [blank] feet of the bridge, resting upon the rail at either side, making a covered enclosure of [blank] feet in length, [blank] feet in breadth, and [blank] feet in height. This house only covered the berth deck in part, however, and though the remainder was protected by a tent awning over it, and covered with old mattresses, and snow to a depth of one foot, it still was cold enough to form a condenser for all moisture given off, and permitted a drip and dampness which was very uncomfortable to the berth deck in general and to the berths in particular. By suspending rubber blankets over the upper row of berths the trouble was mitigated, and by careful attention to the airing and drying of the mattresses each day during the out-door exercise of the crew, any ill effect was prevented. This deck-house served during our first winter as a place for our distilling apparatus, for washing and scrubbing clothes, for a workshop, for the storage of packed knapsacks and travelling gear, for general muster, for exercise in inclement weather, for amusements, until finally our provisions had to be hastily hoisted up into it to enable us to get at and control the disaster which overtook us.

In preparation for the second winter the deck-house was remodelled and made to cover the entire berth-deck by carrying it forward to the bows and terminating it aft at [blank] feet abaft the foremast. This made a perfect protection and serving as a condensing chamber for the berth deck also prevented a deposit on the berth-deck beams; second, a dryness and general comfort in the men's quarters that I think has not been equaled, and I am sure has not been excelled, in previous Arctic expeditions.

As a matter of course a regular routine of daily occupations had been established upon our original besetment in the ice, and several unusual sanitary arrangements were put in operation, as well with a view to the most economical use of fuel, consistent with health and comfort; 50° Fahrenheit was fixed as the regulation temperature for cabin and berth-deck. While the sun was away from us every officer and man was required to leave the ship for exercise, hunting, or amusement, as he might elect, daily, from 11 a. m. to 1 p. m.; and during these hours the living quarters were thrown open and ventilated thoroughly. So long as the sun was absent and the temperature above $-30°$ this outdoor exposure was made obligatory; upon the return of the sun, and at temperature at and below $-30°$, it was made optional. In extreme cases, also, when in strong winds and heavy snow drifts, exposure and exercise would seem more detrimental than beneficial, even at temperatures above $-30°$, option was permitted; but under all circumstances and at all temperatures the opening and ventilation of living quarters during those hours were rigidly attended to.

And so our winter progressed satisfactorily under the circumstances. Our drift was in all directions, depending on the direction and force of the winds. In no case did it seem to indicate any current, nor was any unusual difference of temperature to be detected in our observations of the water at different depths. The surface water when first exposed had a temperature of 29 uniformly, and the waters at the bottom 30°.

The amount of our daylight steadily diminished until Dec. 22d, at which time the very first faint gleam of coming light was noticed, at 8.40 a. m., and at 3.40 p. m. we were again in total darkness. At noon we were able to determine that the twilight was stronger than the moonlight then existing by the fact that our shadows were faintly cast on the ice in the first instance and not at all in the second. At the arrival of Christmas, and upon the incoming of the New Year, we were able to enjoy as much good cheer as our bountiful supplies afforded. Extensive additions were made to our usual bills of fare, general cheerfulness prevailed, we were all in good health and spirits, and in fine saw out the old year and welcomed in the new with undiminished zeal and unabated confidence in the ultimate accomplishments of something worthy of the American Artic expedition. As January, 1880, wore along, we were frequently startled by ominous jars and the unpleasant sound of moving ice, and openings began to occur in unpleasant proximity to the ship. As these openings closed again with greater or less force, large or small ridges of broken floe pieces were piled up on their edges, suggesting too disagreeably our previous experiences. At one time we were entirely surrounded by such a confused wall, and the dimensions of the enclosed space so steadily diminished that we could almost calculate the time that should elapse before we would be reached. On the 15th another ice disturbance occured, openings about 8 feet in width occuring from 20 to 100 feet distant. By these, we were left in the center of a small island of ice, whose thickness, 40 inches, would not prove much of a protection when the closing in occured. The next day only sufficient pressure was exerted to bring the edges together, and then it ceased, to our great satisfaction, for the necessity of being exposed to the outside temperature made our watching a disagreeable task. On this day mercury froze in our thermometer at —42°, though it remained liquid long enough to record —44½, when it yielded and became solid likewise. These temperatures were comfortable, however, compared to those of the next day, when a spirit thermometer registered —51°, which being corrected by comparison with standard gives a temperature of [blank].

The 19th of January was a day of disaster. At 1.30 a. m. I was startled by a loud cracking of the ship's frame, indicating that we were again under pressure. I at once repaired to the deck, but seeing nothing amiss, I went out on the ice to look for a cause. Everything was perfectly quiet, and I inferred that the noise must have been occasioned by the drawing of a metal fastining by contraction under the intense cold. After waiting an hour for further developments, nothing happening, I turned in. The wind was then from north, with from 5 to 8 miles velocity per hour. At 7.45 a. m. the wind suddenly shifted to WNW., the ice began to move and grind, and the ship was felt to be receiving great pressure. Our situation relative to the moving ice appears below.

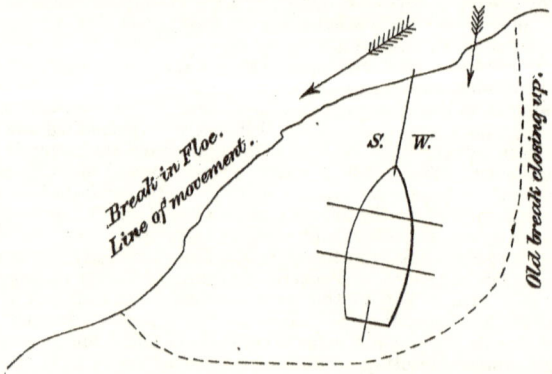

The line of ice movement appeared to be at the break, across the bows (which occurred Dec. 11th and afterwards closed), but it seemed to have a double direction; for while moving along slowly in the direction indicated by the large arrow it also advanced on us in the direction indicated by the short arrow. In consequence, the edges of the advancing ice piled up in large blocks under our bows, and, the pressure continuing, a great longitudinal strain was brought on the ship; and this, added to the transverse strain, made our wrenching and jaming a matter of some seriousness. As we had withstood greater transverse pressure without injury, no especial alarm was felt, and when finally the floe between our port side and the line of break buckled up and broke in long cracks, and the pressure ceased, we congratulated ourselves on one more lucky escape.

We therefore resumed our ordinary routine duties without further delay, among which the daily serving out of fuel made a visit to the fire-rooms come in at an opportune moment. Walter Sharvel (coal-heaver) heard upon entering the engine-room a noise as of running water in the bilge, and promptly returned to the deck to report it. An immediate examination revealed that in some of the strains of the morning we had sprung a leak. Water was found flowing in through the bow filling in two streams of an inch diameter each, 18 inches already stood in the fore peak, 24 inches in the storeroom just abaft it, 36 inches in the fore hold, and though but little time had elapsed since the first discovery, the water had risen above the floor plates in the fire-room. The forward deck pumps were at once rigged and manned, and I ordered steam to be raised in one boiler to drive our steam-pumps. One watch of men was assigned to pump, while the other, led by Lieut. Chipp, the ex. officer, at once set to work to break out and get on deck all our endangered provisions. Everything proceeded with the utmost dispatch and with perfect order and discipline. Not a sound or action indicated the slightest excitement, both officers and men being as cool and self-possessed as if performing a very ordinary evolution under the most favorable circumstances of a quiet harbor and temperate climate. The ship's books and papers were collected, travelling medicines, brandy, &c. To our great satisfaction, however, we found that the pumps held their own against the leak, and as the forward pumps were protected, as well as the men working them, by being within the deck-house, we had no reason to fear the freezing of the one or the consequences of exposure to the other. The getting of steam was no easy matter, the temperature of the Arctic regions presenting many obstacles. While the temperature of the open air was —50° that of the fire-room was —29°, and handling or preparing iron-work was no easy undertaking. All the sea-cocks being frozen fast in their seats, the boiler could not be run up in the ordinary manner, and it had to be filled through the manholes from above, by buckets of water dipped from the fast freezing bilge. This was necessarily a slow and trying operation under the circumstances, and much time also was consumed in preparing the pumps for receiving steam. It was only by the indomitable energy of Mr. Melville and the entire self-sacrifice of and devotion of the engineer's force that in $4\frac{1}{2}$ hours we had the steam-pumps ready to work and could afford a breathing spell to our hand pumpers forward. We had, as soon as possible, closed the gate of the forward water-tight compartment to keep away the danger of the water rising above the furnaces in the fire-room, and when the steam-pump was ready for work these gates were opened again and the water allowed to flow aft. Owing probably to the freezing of the limbers the water did not come aft readily, but such as did come was forced up through fire hose to the spar deck and so through a scupper to the ice outside, until the hose froze, when alternate pumping and thawing had to be resorted to. Fortunately this involved no serious consequences in the fire-room, for as the steam-pump's suction was on the port side and the ship was heeled $2\frac{1}{2}$° to starboard the water had to rise until it flowed over the keelson before being pumped out, and in the intervals of waiting the spar-deck hose could be thawed. The freezing or other stoppage of the limbers under the coal bunkers allowed the water to bank up, however, and accumulated so much forward that we now had to man the deck-pumps again and keep them going. Our provisions had all been removed, and, thanks to the unflagging energy of Lieut. Chipp, Mr. Cole, and the men employed, our loss was much less than we had had reason to fear. Subsequent examination showed that the amount of ruined provisions was as follows: 300 lbs. beans, 100 lbs. flour, 650 lbs. oatmeal, 200 lbs. cornmeal, 100 lbs. coffee, and 36 gallons vinegar. A comparative trifle when the quantity endangered is taken into account. Meanwhile efforts were being made to get at and stop the leak. Mr. Dunbar, ice pilot, with the two Alaskans, Alexy and Aniguin, set to work at the herculean task of digging away the masses of ice piled up under our head booms, in order to get down to the stem in a search for the injury. This they were unable to accomplish, for after they had dug away a large quantity without reaching any sign of damage, the water from beneath broke through the intervening layer of ice and rapidly filled the excavation already made, freezing almost as fast as it flowed. From within also, ineffectual efforts were being made. Regardless of the water below the freezing point, the discomfort and the exposure, Wm. Nindemann went down into the fore peak and standing there with the flowing water above his knees, stuffed oakum and tallow into every nook and crany from which water was forcing its way. As fast as one inlet was stopped another appeared, but finally, when the entire bow filling was so effectually stuffed with oakum and tallow as to allow but small streams to trickle through, the water burst through the seams of the ceiling on each side and accumulated as before.

Without any positive means of knowing how much injury the ship had received, it seemed probable that in the great longitudinal strain her fore foot had been broken off or turned aside, starting the garboard strakes. If this was really the case our condition was a serious one. Hand pumping as a steady work would soon exhaust our crew, and steam pumping would involve such an expenditure of fuel as no ship could withstand with any chance of prosecuting an Arctic exploration to a successful termination. The amount of water coming into the ship was about 4,000 gallons per hour, and it required both steam and manual labor to keep that under control. Having cleared of stores the fore-peak store room and fore hold, we could estimate closely as to whether we gained on the water or otherwise. But though we prevented it from gaining a greater depth than 3 feet, it was impossible to say how much more would rush in were the ice to open and let the ship down to her bearings in the water, an event which was not improbable at any moment.

Fortunately one of the steam-pumps in the engine-room could be dismounted and removed, and upon Mr. Melville's suggestion it was determined to carry this pump forward, place it over the foward store-room, and by connecting it with lengths of piping to the main boiler and a suction to the water below, pump directly and continuously by steam forward instead of intermittently aft. By this time midnight had arrived, and the men were well fatigued with their 13 hours of continuous labor. One watch, therefore, was piped below, had hot coffee and a ration of brandy administered to all hands, and the other watch set to work to shift the pump just mentioned. Pending the quiet state of the ice, the officers were allowed to seek some rest, the executive officer, chief engineer, and myself alone excepted. I am sure that the executive officer and chief engineer obtained no rest for several days, so great was the demand on their presence and services, and that they did not break down utterly under the strain was a matter of surprise. The services of all other officers were ready at all times, but from the peculiar nature of the work they could not replace or otherwise relieve those much overburdened gentlemen.

Whatever watch was on deck, John Cole, Alfred Sweetman, and Wm. Nindemann seemed to belong to it, and for some days these three men were as untiring in their labor and as unwilling to seek rest as if there were no such thing as physical exhaustion. The remainder of the men worked unflaggingly at the pumps while on deck, or in spells of pumping, in moving provisions aft, and showed throughout such cheerfulness and utter disregard of personal exposure and discomfort as entitle them to the highest praise. The amount of rest they obtained was necessarily small, for not only were they constantly disturbed by the noise incidental to the work in hand of rigging new pumping gear, but also when the work was completed the incessant clanging and clanking of the steam-pump made sleep impossible short of extreme exhaustion. The berth-deck, at first lumbered up by provisions and stores of all kinds, was afterward steadily wet and uncomfortable. And yet, with such wretched surroundings, with the possibility of being turned out of house and home at any moment and forced to encamp on the ice, with their strength taxed to the utmost to keep the leak from mastering us, these men worked on with a zeal and cheerfulness as unimpaired as if such incidents were matters of choice rather than necessity. The engineer's force was constantly occupied. Dismounting, removing, and remounting our steam-pump, running a line of steam-piping, driving a second pump in the engine-room, and keeping steam on a boiler, thawing hose, etc., kept them at the extreme of their strength, and for several days I question very much whether any body of men had greater demands made upon them.

The next day, the 20th, we found that the running water had either thawed the frozen limbers or freed them of other obstructions, and such a quantity now ran aft to the engine-room as to leave less work for the hand pumpers forward. By the morning of the 21st we had completed the connections to the auxiliary steam-pump moved to the berth-deck, and set it in operation. The two steam pumps now kept such good pace with the leak that we were able to give some reasonable amount of rest to our nearly exhausted crew. Exception must be made of Alfred Sweetman and Wm. Nindemann. After cutting out some of the ceiling above and below the bilge strokes, the one commenced the building of a heavy oak bulkhead across the fore peak (by which we hoped to confine the water to a small compartment, unless it overflowed the berth-deck) and the other, by driving plugs in all holes, and ramming ashes, cinders, oakum, plaster, tallow, felt, and white lead down among the frames and between the ceiling and planking, present all kinds of obstruction to the entrance of the water. Sometimes all day, sometimes all night, and sometimes both, from Jan'y 19 to Feb'y 4th, did these two men, separately or together, stand down in the fore peak, the water flowing around them nearly to their knees, working faithfully until their work was accomplished, and the good results of their work were evident in the gradually reduced amount of water coming into the ship and our ability to control the leak without such a ruinous expenditure of fuel as had been necessary theretofore. It is for these reasons that I have had the honor to recommend these two men to you for medals of honor, as a recognition of heroic conduct and devotion to duty under the most trying circumstances.

Ice movements and pressures were quite frequent during these days of our trouble, but so long as no further injury was sustained by the ship no great importance was attached to them. We were too much occupied with what trouble we had to attend to any prospective danger.

The intense cold continued, and added to our difficulties by freezing the water in our fore hold, and threatening to choke up our limbers and pump suctions. We certainly had ice enough to contend with outside without having it inside as well. On the 22d, only enough water would flow aft into the engine-room to feed the main boiler. Upon digging out our fire-hole alongside, to resume our interrupted daily soundings, we found that the floe immediately surrounding the ship had been under run by another effectually preventing access to the water beneath. Further examination showed that the under running floe had passed under the ship as far aft as the mainmast, lifting her out of her bed 2 inches forward, and it is probable that, prevented by the clinging ice on her sides from lifting her entirely, the strain had continued until her fore foot was broken and turned aside.

On the 23d January careful computation of the work done by the pumps showed that the amount of our leak was 3,663 gallons per hour, and yet we had seemingly gained on the leak. The amount of fuel necessary to keep steam to work the two pumps was so great as to become a very serious affair, for apart from wanting it for continuing our voyage should we ever be released, it was all we had to depend on for distilling, heating, and cooking. The importance of economical expenditure had always impressed itself on us, and when we saw such large inroads made on our coal it was with considerable misgiving. So soon, however, as we found we had actually controlled the leak, or rather had held our own against it, arrangements were begun for more economical steam-pumping than the use of a main boiler permitted, and thanks to the skill and untiring energy of Mr. Melville and the labor of his department we were eminently successful. A small 2-horse power Baxter engine and boiler had been procured in New York to drive a machine for giving electric light, and owing to the non-performance of the machine the boiler and engine had been applied to the distilling of water for drinking and cooking purposes. This was now geared to the pump brake of the forward hand bilge pump and set to work, performing well, and so relieving the steam-pumps below as to diminish largely the coal expenditure, which had averaged 1,500 lbs. a day for pumping alone, and was now reduced to 1,200 lbs. per diem. The boiler and engine belonging to our steam cutter were removed to the engine room, and a gearing devised by Mr. Melville whereby it was made to work a bilge pump attached to the main engine, and thus, as we had succeeded in thawing its delivery pipe in the ship's side, force water directly overboard instead of through freezing hose on deck in the open air. This also being made successful reduced our fuel expenditure 200 lbs. more, making a total saving by this ingenuity and practical skill of the chief engineer of 500 lbs. of coal a day. These things required much time in their preparation and much labor in constructing parts of the gearing; and it was not until the 13 February, that we were able to have fires under the main boiler with the knowledge that our auxiliary steam pumping apparatus would do the work of holding the water in check. By this time the labor of S. & N.* in ramming of oakum, tallow, plaster, ashes, cinders, &c., had brought about the desired result. The amount of water coming into the ship had been reduced from 4,000 gallons to 1,650 gallons an hour. and the coal expenditure from 1,500 lbs. to 400 lbs. a day, and though we had to deplore the expenditure of 14 tons of coal, valuable beyond price, we were consoled by the reflection that our condition might have been much worse. Though our men were relieved from the seeming endless strain of pumping by hand, they were none the less fully occupied. Our provisions, which now cumbered up the entire spardeck, had to be stowed somewhere to make moving about possible, and should an emergency arise have the ship under control. The only place offering was the coal bunker, and as a change to pumping the scarcely less fatiguing labor of shifting coal succeeded. Space necessary being made the greater part of our deck load was passed below into the bunkers, reserving on deck a quantity convenient for housing out on the ice in the event of such being required in the future.

From this time forward we lived in a state of anxious suspense, never knowing what moment we might have fresh trouble from ice pressures or increased pumping by being let down to our bearings in the water.

On the 26th January the sun reappeared, after an absence of 71 days, and we had the satisfaction now of seeing what we were about instead of groping around by artificial light. Its effect upon us mentally was very great, tending to mitigate the anxiety which had been ours when darkness added so much to the dangers surroundings us. Daylight steadily increased, and enabled us to prolong our excursions from the ship and witness the prodigious mounds and barriers of ice created during the pressures and movements of the winter. Our escapes from so many dangers seemed miraculous. Within half a mile in any direction such a scene of wreckage might be encountered as to convince us, had the ship been there, her fate had been certain. That which on November

---

*Sweetman and Nindemann.—J. A.

25th had been a large lake was now so reduced in area as to seem insignificant, and bordered as it was by ridges of broken floe pieces to a height of 40 and 50 feet, warranted the delusion that our ship had been dropped within it from the clouds. (Very feeble, remodel much of this stuff.)

So occupied were we in our efforts to control the leak and arrange more economical pumping apparatus that frequently the ship was nipped and squeezed so gradually and quietly as to escape our notice. On such occasions the fact was made known by the jamming of doors in their casings, preventing opening; and the release from pressure was indicated by a return to the usual facility. Apart from the inconvenience we attached no importance to these pressures. How much or how little the ice moved was of interest to us only as it might affect the leak, and we had an infallible gauge in the depth of water steadily in the ship. Soundings were taken inside of the ship now as well as outside, as before, and experience soon constructed a variation line of the proper rise and fall of this new Arctic stream to compare with our number of pump strokes.

The surgeon's examination of our physical condition about this time as showing the effect of the winter upon us. But beyond our being somewhat bleached by the absence of the sunlight there was no cause for remark, and it was a matter of congratulation that we had passed through our first Arctic winter trial with such happy results.

Our difficulties before the 14th February (when we hauled fires under the main boiler) were considerable. After Sweetman and Nindemann had filled up such spaces below among the frames and between the ceiling and planking as could be reached, they came up on the berth deck, and crawling under the lower tier of berths cut out small pieces of ceiling there and pushed and rammed ashes, oakum, and plaster, &c., on the masses already below and so filled up every nook and cranny. Still the water flowed; no matter how much stuff was rammed down, water seemed able to get along somehow, and it led to the belief that so much of our outside planking had been ripped aside as to let our ashes, &c., drop direct to the sea beneath. Occasionally we seemed to stop the water, but in a few moments it would burst out through the ceiling further aft. This rather deadened our hope of the extra bulkhead proving sufficient ultimately, for inasmuch as I would not weaken the ship by cutting the bilge strakes to allow the bulkhead to go out to the planking and rest against a frame on each side, the mere obstruction offered would not be a great assistance. Our idea originally was to make this bulkhead so strong that we could let the space forward of it fill with water and carry it there as in a small water-tight compartment; and should we get under way again stanchion down the berth deck to prevent it springing up by pressure and motion of the mass of water beneath. But if, as we now found, water forced its way along among the frames and through the flooring alongside the keelson abaft the bulkhead, of what use would the

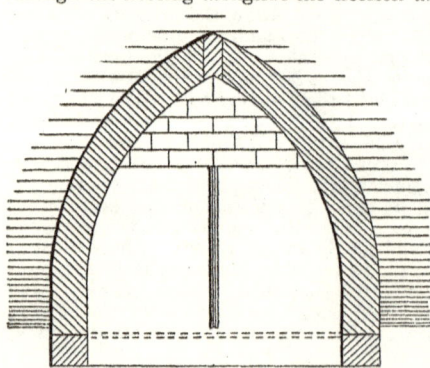

bulkhead be at all? And so I was sadly perplexed. Again, the fore foot being broken and the planking turned aside was merely a supposition. The keel might be broken for many feet and the garboards wrenched open as far as our fore hold, and the water which we were trying to stop on the sides might have originally entered from the line of the keel; for upon cutting away some of the heavy flooring alongside of the keelson forward, jets of water shot up and were only stopped by driving plugs. Unless, therefore, we could unite all the materials rammed down in the interspaces into a water-tight cement, and so prevent the ingress of water, all the bulkheads in the world that could be built in our fore peak would not prevent water from flowing aft. Again, the gates of the original water-tight bulkhead were found somewhat troublesome. The gates were constructed in a peculiar manner. The gate had a spindle attached to it, having a screw thread cut in its upper end. Through the spar deck extended an iron rod, with a socket at its lower end, in which a screw thread was also cut to fit the thread on the spindle. The opening and closing was therefore effected by turning this upper rod, no matter what depth of water was in the ship. On the 9th of February, therefore, when we suspected that these gates were not shut tight, because water flowed aft so readily, we tore up the flooring in the ice-gear hold to examine. The port gate was shut tight, but the starboard one was about half open. An accumulation of rust and dirt in the socket of the spar deck rod prevented the screw thread from biting that on the spindle, and we might turn this upper rod until the day of doom without either entirely opening or entirely closing the gate. However, the difficulty being overcome we got the gate shut, and to our disgust found that enough water still leaked aft into the fire-room to necessitate the working of the Sewell pump 15 minutes every hour. This was another argument in favor of the water finding its way between the planking and ceiling among the frames, despite the attempted fillings and cementing of plaster, oakum, &c. On the 12th February we had another proof that water-tight bulkheads were not a safeguard against being flooded out of house and home, and we accidentally found it out through the stupidity of one of our firemen, Boyd. The work imposed on the Baxter boiler in driving the hand bilge pump forward was so great, or rather so constant, that in order to prevent it choking up with salt it was necessary to blow it out dry once in every 12 hours, hauling fires, of course, and when the boiler is again filled lighting fresh ones. On this occasion the blowpipe was frozen, though Boyd neither knew it nor took the trouble to look before blowing out. Much more time was therefore required to empty the boiler, for in these latitudes a frozen pipe does not thaw readily, even with steam employed as the agent. The building of the new fire and the getting of steam again were so much delayed in consequence that 30 inches of water had accumulated just forward of the water-tight bulkhead. Nindemann still ramming in oakum and ashes, no matter what depth of water he stood in, whether to his waist or to his ankles, heard a noise as of water overflowing and falling; and going abaft the bulkhead determined that the water, having risen above the line of cement, &c., forward of the bulkhead, was simply falling into the clear pocket abaft it, and so flowing easily into the fire-room. This was another evidence of how much depended on our ashes and plaster filling, and whether that would prove effective depended, of course, how much of the ship's frame was exposed to the sea by the tearing away of the garboards and outside planking. Our bow filling, put in at the Mare Island yard, was also a source of uneasiness instead of a comfort and reliance. Theoretically, this was designed to make just so much solid bow to the vessel that stem or fore foot might be sliced off and yet leave a water-proof surface; but practically, it was, of course, limited by the same difficulties that came in with our bulkheads in the fore peak. For, since the filling extended only to the ceiling of the bows, it could not control the spaces between this and the bow planking, though from the calked close-timbering and deadwood one might reasonably hope for a practically solid and tight mass in that locality. At all events this extra filling was seemingly (from diagrams shown me, for I was not there at the time it was built) an additional strength and defense. Imagine, therefore, my disgust when on going to the scene of action on the memorable morning of January 19th I saw the water pouring out of the seams of this "solid filling," with no more hindrance than could have been offered by the meshes of a sieve. Theoretically, the filling was water-tight; practically, it leaked. I made up my mind quickly that no dependence was to be placed on filling bulkhead or cement should we get down to our bearings again in open water, and that something must be provided in anticipation of such an event. As soon, therefore, as men could be spared from the more pressing work then in hand, and sufficient space could be cleared away in the deck-house, I directed Chipp to have a spare topsail well thrummed, intending to get that under the bows when the time came, and trusting to that to keep out more water than could be controlled by our pumping power. Such of our hemp hawsers as were required for the purpose were therefore cut up and the making of this large thrum mat begun on the [blank] and finished on the [blank] of [blank].

Before being quite sure about his auxiliary pumps, Melville proposed removing the bridge wall of the steam-cutter's furnace and placing 16-inch grate bars instead of the 9-inch grate bars near them. Our fear with the present arrangement is that we could not generate steam enough to answer the demands of the pump, and more grate-surface removed that fear. When the change was made, away went everything beautifully; and so on February 13th the fires under the main boiler were hauled, the boiler blown out, all pipes drained to prevent freezing, and the terrible drain on our coal bunkers brought to an end. Our leak amounted at that date to about 1,600 gallons an hour, and to get rid of this water we had to keep the Baxter running the hand bilge-pump, as well as the steam-cutter's rig to the engine pump all the time.

On the 15th February we made the unpleasant discovery that water was flowing over the berth deck from under the berths. Some of the fillings between frames had cemented as we had hoped, but in preventing passage of water below had forced it to seek an outlet above (our berth deck being still below the water level). This we managed to overcome by boring holes through the deck, letting the water flow down into the fore peak, and in order to prevent it running out on the berth deck a coaming was built in front of the berths. Sweetman again indefatigably resumed the cementing business, and remained stretched under the berths for hours at a time, ramming down Arctic concrete, *i. e.*, ashes, oakum, plaster, felt, &c.

The pumping arrangements were working nicey, but we were having the results offered to our contemplation. The spar-deck bilge pump had its delivery necessarily through a scupper to the outside, and in the temperatures we were having (our average for February —39°) froze almost immediately on reaching the open air. We were in consequence piling up ice alongside very rapidly, and adding so much more weight to what was holding the ship down. The heavier it became the lower it would sink in the water, and as it was clinging closely to the ship would increase the pressure of the water against her bottom, and perhaps add to the leak. However, we could not help it, for men could not safely be exposed continually to low temperatures; such as we were having, and our only means of remedying the evil were to dig down till we came to water to discharge into, or to dig up and carry away our pumpings as fast as they froze, both clearly impracticable. To prevent our scuppers and hose from freezing we built an ice roof over its running discharge, protecting it from the outside air.

A great amount of discomfort was experienced by the men during all this time from the constant dampness of the berth-deck, and that they preserved their health under the circumstances was as wonderful as their cheerfulness and uncomplaining endurance was praiseworthy. For months everything was damp and wet. The deck-house, which would otherwise have been a sheltered and dry place, was now sloppy and uncomfortable in the extreme, the Baxter boiler keeping everything thawed without drying, and the leaks from the pump hose supplying a never ceasing amount of water. To reach the berth-deck one had to pass through the deck-house, and much moisture was thus tracked below. The streams of water flowing into the ship under and sometimes on the berth-deck kept it damp, and as the moisture condensed on the colder beams overhead a steady drip ensued on the forward and after ends, which made the discomfort complete.

Our Chinese cook and steward are as impassible and impenetrable in this cold weather as if we were enjoying a tropical spring. Seemingly emotionless, all weathers, all circumstances are alike to them; living by themselves in the cook-house they hold no communion generally with their fellow-man, but are nevertheless cheerful and contented with each other's society, singing songs or playing cards in the evening, day after day, with no concern for the future and no care for the past. Having constructed a drum by securing a seal skin to the head of an empty butter-keg, they beat away for hours at a time with the utmost enjoyment. Cold has no terrors for them. Bare headed, arms uncovered to the elbow, they walk out to the ash heap and back without hesitation. They will, for instance, wash dishes in hot water and immediately go out to a temperature of —45 and —50 to throw the water away, and they never catch a cold, get frost bitten, or have even chapped hands. When the steward was sick with a bilious attack for a few days the cook did the work of both, and when afterwards the cook had a slight attack, the steward took his turn of working double tides. All the ice commotion never disturbed their equanimity; the accident to the ship did not seem to bother them at all. They evidently are not going to be surprised by anything that turns up. The galley and the galley-house are models of neatness and cleanliness, and for good, quiet, and able servants give me Chinese from now henceforth. One peculiarity which they have is curious. Whatever they are told to do is generally found done in their own way. Directions, explanations, and informations are received quietly and respectfully, but though you think you are having your ideas carried out, somehow you find things so different as to be sure that the Chinaman has had his way after all. Generally I give up without protest, because I am sensible that their ideas are the best; but sometimes I have to insist on my own way. They do not understand why I give the men the same things to eat that the officers have, and they seem clearly of the opinion that I am ruining the crew by indulgence. Mince pies at X-mas for the berth deck seemed to them the crowning indulgence, and they gave me up apparently as irreclaimable. Only twice did I see anything like excitement show itself in them. Once was when the cook, having requested a rifle to go out to shoot seals, returned with it shortly after somewhat out of sorts. While waiting for the seals to rise he had doubtless rested the muzzle of his rifle in the snow, for when he had occasion to fire the piece burst, tearing the barrel to ribbons. I don't think he went shooting any more. The second time was on August, 1880, when three bears were approaching the ship together. He then was so anxious that we should get them that he was afraid to speak aloud lest the bears should hear him, and his usual calmness deserted him when he began to gesticulate and whisper the startling intelligence. However, we did not get the prize, though we wounded two of the three. We had a third Chinaman, Ah Sing, but he was so worthless from sea-sickness and natural stupidity that I discharged him at St. Michael's and sent him back in the Fanny A. Hyde. His countrymen thought but little of him, the steward saying with great contempt, "He only fifteen-dollar boy; what you expect for fifteen dollar"?

The two Alaskans, Alexy and Aniguin, were excellent men and throve wonderfully well. Occasionally they thought "plenty" about St. Michael's, being a little homesick, but generally they were bright and happy. They learned considerable of the English language, and always managed to very cleverly express their meanings when puzzled for an exact word. They were naturally and intuitively the most polite men I have met outside of civilization, and would even compare favorably with some choice ones within it. Upon meeting an officer they promptly saluted by touching the cap and tendered a "Good morning." If anything was said or done for them their "thank you" was immediately given. If one said "thank you" to them they were quick with "you are welcome." And all this in a manly, straightforward way, with no cringing or lip-service.

On March 1st we had our coldest weather, the temperature at midnight being —57.5 Fah. The snow, however, had commenced to melt on the ship's side, and at noon of that day I saw a trickling down from the seams. As a measure of the power of the sun's rays on our ship, I had a black-bulb thermometer attached to our planking on the port quarter, and got readings subsequently as follows:

March 2d, noon, open air, —47; B. B. on ship's side, +32.
      Midnight "   —46; " " " "   " +20.

First difference = 79° at noon, second difference = 66° at midnight; showing that 13° was caused by the sun at noon, and the remaining 66° was simply heat radiated through the ship's side from the stoves and our own heat from within.

(Work this up for a number of days and get mean result.)

A curious fact was brought to light on the 3d of March. An order having been given that anything found upon the ice in the course of daily excursions should be brought to the ship, one of the men brought in some shells and a piece of drift-wood. He says he first saw the wood in December, but, attaching no value to it, had not brought it in then; but he also saw at that time the print of two moccasins on the snow near the wood and but a single set. As these were not made by any of our ship's company, it is probable that the single block of ice bearing these prints and the wood had come from some Siberian river.

On the 4th March, having so cleared away and moved aft the coal as to get a sight of the ceiling, we made the unpleasant discovery that the ceiling had been crushed in some of our numerous squeezes. The athwart-ship thrust-beam placed on the coal-bunkers was so strongly trussed as to resist any doubling-up tendency, and the ends had been literally forced into the six-inch Oregon pine ceiling to the depth of half an inch, while the heads of the metal bolts forward and abaft of this transverse beam were ⅜ of an inch from the wood. In this part of the ship the frames were entirely new, the planking also new, the elm doubling newly fastened, and the six-inch ceiling and transverse beam were additions to her strength, and without being a solid block the ship was, in my opinion, as strong as wood and metal could make her. Nineteen inches of wood backed by such heavy trussing was surely a considerable protection; but I am convinced that twice that thickness would have afforded no more effectual resistance than an egg in a vise if we had been caught and squeezed in some of the pressures that occurred in our neighborhood.

By the 6th March we had manufactured so much ice by our steady pumping through the scuppers that it stood level with our rail on the starboard side nearly the whole length of the ship, sloping gently away until it merged with the floe level. By dint of great care and slow progress we now managed to cut a hole down to the sea beneath us to get a direct discharge. The difficulty of working with picks and bars in temperatures between —40° and —50° were enormous. Edges crumbled away like so much glass and points broke off as if made of wood; and such slow and cautious movement was necessary as nearly to freeze men before any result could be obtained. A piece of walrus liver frozen at this temperature stripped the edge off a razor as if it had been made of plaster. On the 9th March, the temperature having risen to —21° at one time, we set to work and dug a trench 4 feet in width all along the port side down to our doubling, thereby relieving the ship of so much holding-down weight. On the 10th we went to work on the starboard side, a much more difficult task, for the ice was of such a close character as to be much like flint. The water pumped out from the ship froze so uniformly as to leave no interstices, and pick-axes had nothing like the expected effect. Six hours were required to dig 25 feet in length, 4 feet in width, and about 4 feet in depth. So closely did the ice cling to the ship's form that not only was every seam shown, but in many cases the exact fibre of the elm doubling was imprinted in the surrounding mass.

On the 12th March we were astonished by a rise in temperature to —0°.3. This enabled us to make good progress in digging the ship out, and we were now at work away under the bows in furtherance of a plan to get at the fore foot. This was to dig away the surface blocks, and reaching the main floe to dig until about a foot remained intervening. Then in our ordinary low temperature ice would quickly form beneath, and we might go on until we had got down to a good depth. By the 23d our plan of digging after intervals of freezing had so far succeeded that we had got down to 6½ feet draft mark, but that night, unfortunately, the pressure of the water beneath was too great and it burst through the bottom of our pit, flooding it, the 10 ft. 10 ins. draft mark, necessitating an abandonment of the thing altogether, for we were now getting too high temperature to hope for such heavy freezing again.

We then set to work to dig away the ice in order to get a look at the stern-post and propeller, but in spite of the utmost care we only succeeded in reaching the top of the propeller frame when the water beneath broke through and flooded the pit. As deep as we got no injury could be detected.

Our time and attention were so entirely occupied with pumping water and trying to save coal that our lives during this time seemed to be devoted to nothing short of pumping dry the Arctic Ocean with the least possible expenditure of fuel. It may be that I am dwelling too long and too minutely on these subjects, but our efforts were so unremitting, our results so satisfactory, as to deserve somewhat more than a passing mention. I say *our* efforts and *our* results, though in fact these were made possible by the skill and ingenuity of Mr. Melville, who hardly completed one labor-saving as well as fuel-saving arrangement before he was engaged designing another. The evident hardening of the cement, &c., among the frames had so far reduced the amount of our leak, and the frequency with which the temperature rose to zero so lessened the discomfort of outside exposure, that we were able by the 7th of April to make a change in our pumping arrangements. The forward hand bilge pump not in use was taken up and placed within the fire-room hatch with its suction in the bilge; and the Baxter engine & boiler being removed to the engine room were connected by gearing to the brake of this pump. Upon opening all flood-gates the water rushed aft freely, and was readily got rid of by this new steam-pump, in fact too readily, for pauses ensuing our hose delivery froze and this intermittent pumping had to be discontinued and the flood-gates closed. Upon making the attempt to do much of the pumping by hand we found pumping for 20 minutes every hour would hold the water in check forward, and that the steam-cutter's boiler would drive the main engine bilge pump sufficiently fast to take care of such water as filtered aft through the bulk-heads; and therefore to our great satisfaction we were able to still further reduce our coal expenditure, keeping it at the reasonable amount of 220 lbs. a day for pumping and distilling.

I mention these items minutely to show how carefully our fuel was husbanded and how every pound was made to do its work before it was allowed to become ashes. I presume no one would have expected us to do hand pumping altogether, though it would of course have been more economical of fuel. The result in a short time would have been the complete exhaustion of our strength; and then if some further mishap had overtaken us, and we had been obliged to abandon our ship, we would have been in no condition for the long 200 miles of sledge dragging that separated us from the Siberian coast. Coals were more precious here than anywhere, it is true, because not to be replaced; but human life was of far greater value. Our usual monthly medical examination showed us to be in good health and vigor thus far, and made me doubly careful to serve the same general excellence.

By the 7th April we had 18 hours sunlight daily, and even in the faintest of the six hours twilight we had light enough to navigate the ship were we only free. Long, sinuous lanes of water were to be seen here and there from aloft, but nothing of importance came to view. The occasional openings in the floes were caused by the ice in motion with different velocities before the wind or from some offered obstruction here and there. No one opening was more than a few miles in length or a few yards in width, and consequently of no use to us save as fishing grounds for seals, and for this reason they were faithfully watched.

There was one more manner in which pumping might be done that had not been resorted to, and this was by a windmill, and Mr. Melville so promptly devoted himself to the plans, and Alfred Sweetman so zealously and intelligently carried out the construction that ere long we had mounted on board ship a windmill that kept up the pumping as finely as heart could wish. Moreover, to utilize this new auxiliary in light breezes as well as in fresh winds, Mr. Melville designed and his force constructed a pump of boiler-tubes and placed it beside the bilge pump already in the fire-room hatch. When, therefore, the wind was too light to enable the windmill to work the large pump it was connected to the smaller boiler-tube pump, and thus we were able as soon as the temperature became at all reasonable to keep a steady stream of water flowing out of the ship, relieving greatly and very often altogether the strain of doing such work by hand. The windmill was at first made with sheeting sails for facility of reefing, but not presenting a sufficiently flat surface, Lieut. Chipp recommended that tin be substituted, which was done with good effect; and in fact so perfect had our labor-saving appliances now become that the leak by decreasing seemed disposed to abandon the losing contest.

April 9th first bird of the year appeared—a raven lights on the ice near the ship; we fail to get him as a trophy.

15th, two snow-buntings, flying from sd., pause near ship and proceed NNW., where there is a suspicious appearance of land.

16th. Temperature reaches +12°; only 1 inch of ice forms sounding sole.

17th. Remove forecastle tent awning. Curious fact observed—mercury in artificial horizon "sea-saws" without blurring image; ice moved by swell. 60 lbs. fresh potatoes each week.

Dec. 6th to April 17th, daily issue of lime juice. From April 17th to ——— 3 days per week—Tu., Thur., & Sat.

From ——— to 2 days per week, Tu. & Fri.

18th. Comparison of American and English pemmican.

April 18th. Ice wasting on the surface; surface hummocks greatly reduced; possibly 1 mile an hour could be made with sleds; frequent openings occur; steam arising in jets or puffs.

19th. Remark excellence of salt beef. Our process of packing it in snow and soaking it in the fire hole softens and freshens it; potato salad.

21st. Raven seen close to; suspicious look of land north.

22d. Small, dull-colored sand bird comes from S. E.; flies west. Appearance of open water on horizon all around; probably long narrow lanes; much water-sky from some causes.

24th. Ice found to have wasted 8 inches from original thickness.

25th. Loosening of ice in N. W. inferred; lat. in 72° 55′; drifting regularly before S. E. winds and deepening water. Almost steady fall of light snow during whole of month; not enough for drinking purposes; softens as soon as falls.

26th. Lat. 72° 56′; soundings suddenly decrease from 44½ to 31.

27th. Temperature rises in middle of day to +25 (+21° at mid.)

28th. Snow soft and walking extremely bad; one flounders suddenly above his knees in rifts; shock of slip and labor of hauling legs out very wearing.

29th. A gull flies by, bound west.

30th. Much fog, occasioned by openings in the ice; thermometer reaches +29¼°; 20 ducks (about) seen flying west; removed cabin porch.

May 1st. Beautiful bright day. Temp. 27°.5 to 29°.8; fire allowed to die out during afternoon; all hands sunning themselves; sunburned to a brilliant red; bundle of spare sails opened; perfect condition; poop all winter; air clothing, bedding, and awnings; sun rise 0h. 55m. a. m.; remains above horrizon at midnight first time; temperature begins to fall as soon as sun passes prime outside, and reaches 1½° at midnight; amount of leak found to be only 300 gallons per hour; a kittiwake (Risso tridactylus) flies over ship W. to E.

2nd. Curious feature in connection with liquid binnacle compasses. As the temperature falls each night (sometimes below 10°) the needles are drawn to the right several degrees, and as the temperature increases in the morning, they gradually go back again, resuming a normal position, when the temperature is, say, 15° and over. As these compasses (Ritchie liquid 7½ in.) have not needles delicate enough to indicate similar variations, and as no such movement in azimuth is made by the ship, can the occurrence be attributed to the effect of temperature on the mixture of glycerine and alcohol in which the cards float?

4th. Water-sky frequent; light snow flurries common; difficulties in being sure that no snow water is drunk.

7th. Air filled with snow dust, causing brilliant parhelion of bright red and orange color.

9th. Berth-deck again dry and comfortable.

10th & 11th. Sameness and monotony.

13th. Appearance of ice field at 200 yards; broken pieces hove up; bad travelling, sinking to one's breast without warning; flock of birds fly from E. to W.

May 14th. Ice found to have gained 5 inches in thickness since April 24th.

15th. Blocks of floe edge found reared up in air 15 and 20 ft.; ice exerts a deadening effect on wind seemingly.

16th. All pumping done by wind-mill; disagreeable smell to the bilge water, though bilges are bright and clean; decaying animalculæ, (?) or chemical decomposition of saline constituents.(?)

17th. Carpenters make keel-runners for boats.

19th. Coal expenditure for all purposes, including pumping and distilling, 400 lbs; go out to examine ice in neighborhood; two miles N. E. of the ship strike a lane of young ice; follow it to the westward for about three miles, and could go further if desired. The young ice covers an opening which was about 200 hundred yards in width in some places, and 500 yards in others. Along the middle runs a vein of water about a foot wide. Occasionally pools and lanes are met, the rippling of the water being pleasant to eyes as well as to the ears. On each side of the young ice the heavy old ice stands piled up in irregular masses, 20 and 30 feet in height, where pressures had occurred. A month ago there was no opening. The thickest single floe is eight feet. Some seemingly fifteen feet in thickness are found to be two floes cemented together. General appearance, looking across country, very hilly and broken.

20th. Snow goggles unpleasant but beneficial; more or less complaint about eyes feeling scorched and sore; but I am inclined to think that they occasionally remove the goggles when away from the ship. Dunbar the only one who had serious scorch.

21st. Removed quarter deck awning; large flock of wild geese (?) fly from S. E. to N. W.

22nd. Hard time getting 425 lbs. bear ham through rough ice; Melville, Aniguin, myself, and eighteen dogs to do the work.

24th. Three little streams of water found running into shaft alley on st'b'd side; thawing of accumulated ice between frames. (?)

25th. Hopes for the future, because we have made as much to the N. W. this month as we made in previous eight months' imprisonment.

26th. Forty-two miles to the N. W. in five days; signs of thawing and wasting; all black substance, such as ashes, sink rapidly into the ice; wind has blown all snow away to drift, and leaves bare ice exposed to the sun's rays. B. B.* Near port side at noon $= +72°$; white bulb do. $= +70°$; at 2 p. m. open air $= +30°$, first time since October 10th.

27th. No fire in cabin and berth-deck between 9 a. m. and 5 p. m.; pump completed; steam now only for distilling 35 gallons water; the suspicious leak in the shaft alley lessens; belief that it arises from thawing of ice among frames; very heavy water-sky, except due north, all day.

28th. Much gloomy and dull weather this month; fine snow falling at some time every day.

29th. Sleet and snow; thermometer $= 32°.2$ at 4 p. m.; ice becoming soft and sloppy.

30th. Supposition that we may eventually describe curve

Thermom. 35° at noon; ice all sloppy; water running from it in all directions.

31st. Preparing to dismount deck-house.

June 1st. Resumed the hauling of the dredge; thick fogs; frequent falls of light snow.

2nd. Fine *summer* day! NW. gale and snow-storm; temp. 25° to 33°; 34 fathoms, deepening a little; although the surface of the floe is soft and mushy, and we can see it waste away, and though the water is all around our ditch, the ice at the sounding hole (100 yds. on stbd. qr.) is yet 48 inches thick. That waste does occur to the surface of the floe is evident, not only by the sinking of ashes and dirt, but by the reappearance of things long since buried; great delight of the dogs thereat.

3rd. Hypothesis as to direction of ice movement eventually.

4th. Doctor Ambler's report anent Nelse Iverson; dismantling deck-house since 1st; unpacking loaded sleds, and rearranging deck load of provisions.

5th. Readiness with which we change our drift with shifts of wind assumed to indicate general looseness of the ice; much water-sky in various directions.

6th. Rain; temperature $= 33°$.

7th. Scraping ship's side in readiness for painting; discontinued fires permanently for summer in cabin and on b. deck; temp. 23° to 28°.

10th. SE. gale; frequent snow.

11th. Thick fog or impenetrable snow.

12th. These are I think our gloomiest days; not alone because of the unpleasant weather, but because of continued disappointment, day after day; sun soon at his greatest northing.

14th. General reflections upon physical condition of cabin party; all sorts of weather in one day—sometimes a little blue sky, oftener overcast, a little fog, a little snow, and some squalls. Going to the southward generally this month.

15th. From aloft we can see ponds here and there at long intervals.

17th. Observe well-defined comet in N. W.

18th. Monotony very depressing; over nine months have we been held fast and drifted here and there at the will of the wind. So long as the temperature gave no chance for a change no one expected it, and we cheerfully accepted the inevitable. When, during the month of May, we steadily drifted to the nd. and wd., we were nearly as well pleased as if we had had a lane to move the ship along in, for we were *advancing*. Since the 4th inst. we have been as steadily going back, and to-day we are very nearly in the same latitude we reached a month ago, and about fifteen miles west of our old track, going on backward in our flight. Here, then, so far as we can judge, is a month lost, and

---

*Black bulb thermometer.—J. A.

worse than lost, for we have got into shallower water (21 fms.), where but little wave action can or will take place to break up the field which surrounds us. Water-sky in abundance indicates some ponds, if not larger openings, though as they change positions daily, no very considerable opening can have occurred. In our immediate vicinity, where the water pumped from the ship froze over the old ice, the crust is thawing and forming ponds. This makes our walking uncertain, for without warning one is apt to break through, and be in water over his knees. By the wasting of the ice the ship is more uncovered, and within a day or two we have noticed that she has come up, cradle and all, about four inches, as indicated by the falling of the water level on her doubling.

Every day Mr. Dunbar and the men are out on the hunt, and occasionally a seal is brought in, in tow of the dogs, as a result. All bears seem to have disappeared, not a single track having been seen for some days. They evidently have gone to the land, where the breeding season of birds affords them more attractive food than seal meat at rare intervals.

20th. Newcomb, while out to-day, found a dozen mosquitoes, and brought them carefully to the ship. They were found on the snow, lying dull and sluggish, as if blown a long distance by the wind. Daily average coal expenditure = 185 lbs, cooking and distilling.

21st. Quite a long description of daily monotonous existence.

22d. Third Ross' gull captured.

23d. Twenty-seven seals on hand. The supply of granulated ice being difficult of access, on account of the sloppy condition of our surroundings making bad sledding, we now fill our tank with the water drawn from the pools. (This has a sp. gr. of 1.0005 to 1.001, and its use for a limited time may be permitted.)

Remarked that all revolving storm centres pass to sd. of us. Dogs troubled by heat; at 32° Fahr. we are merely comfortable.

June 24th. Rain.

25th. One more Ross' gull, 9 seals; temp. 37°.5 at 3 p. m.

27th. From the crow's nest we can see that we are in the center of an ice island, a lane of water in some places ¼ mile wide, seemingly at a distance of mile; beyond, however, in all directions ice to the horizon.

28th. Mr. Dunbar started out with the dinghy on a sled to go ducking in the lane of water 1 mile N. W. of the ship. He came back about 4 p. m. with 13 ducks, and informed me that he had followed the lane (which he thought was north) for nearly 15 miles without coming to its end, it being in places ¾ of a mile wide. The ice on each side was very old and heavy, 5 and 6 feet out of water, and so deep under water that he could not see the bottom of it. I began to look upon this as an avenue of escape, and ran over in my mind how I could get the ship through the mile of intervening ice into the lane and push on for something; but at midnight the lane commenced to close.

Supposed leak in the shaft alley stopped altogether; the ice right around us wasting very fast; ship and cradle still rising; the surface of the floe is dotted here and there with small lakes, which enable us to readily get water for our tank, and also present so many excellent laundries for washing clothes. But at midnight the temperature has fallen to 27°.7, and now at the end of June we have *ice* forming on the surface of our ponds.

30th. 50 miles S. x E. of where we were on June 1st.

July 1st. Commence a new month with bright, pleasant weather; temperature varying from 33 to 38°.

2d. Temperature rises to 46.04 (the highest it got all summer).

3d. The amount of water finding its way into the fore peak has become very small within the last week or two, just a small stream running over the "floors;" but to-day even that small amount has ceased, and the fore peak and flour room are both as dry as a bone. The amount of water lodging in the fire-room bilge is correspondingly small. We have been accustomed to let about 5 inches accumulate, in order to have a convenient feed for our distilling apparatus, running the wind-mill or pumping by hand when that depth has been exceeded. The light airs and calms of the past day or two have necessitated the use of the Qr. Dk. bilge pump, and I have remarked that a dozen strokes or so each hour caused it to "suck." The melting of the surface-ice around us has so much decreased the mass of ice surrounding the ship that the cradle has been buoyed up by the water, bringing the ship into it. The decrease of the leak is pleasant enough, though of course I can assign no positive reason for it. The change from 3,663 gallons per hour to a dozen strokes of a hand bilge pump is too remarkable to be mentioned casually. The change has been a gradual one also. The settling down and hardening of the oatmeal, white lead, oakum, &c., among the frames may have caused a partial barrier to the water and the raising of the ship and ice out of the water, and thus diminishing the height of the waterhead may have so decreased the pressure as to make that barrier effectual. As no water flows into the fore peak this seems to follow naturally, and the small accumulation in the fire-room may proceed from some other source yet undiscovered. While it continues small it will occasion no inconvenience. We are unable to get under the coal-bunkers, because of the 56-odd tons of coal there, and it is of course impracticable to move this quantity while daily hoping for a breaking up of the ice and the resumption of our voyage. Our daily expenditure of fuel now amounts to 170 lbs. (110 lbs. galley, 60 lbs. distilling); but to-day by test the Dr. finds the granulated surface wasted ice contains only 2 grains chlaime per gallon, and we shall in two days save the 60 lbs. used in distilling. The little ponds in our neighborhood has been freezing every night at midnight with the temperature 30 and 31°, thus indicating the comparative freshness of the water. Our dogs drink freely from these ponds. Upwards of 40 seals on hand.

4th. Thick fog; penetrating mist; temp. 28½ to 36°.

5th. Celebrated July 4th. Thick fog and searching mist; flags all covered with frost-brine when hauled down.

6th. Hunting parties returning have circumnavigated our island, about 2½ miles in diameter, with narrow canal running all around it.

7th. Nowhere in my life have I experienced such a perfect *silence* as prevails in these icy wastes when the wind dies away. It is positively maddening. After 10 p. m., when all noise ceases on board ship and the dogs are dozing away on ash heaps and dirty spots around her, if one stands a little apart and looks at the surroundings he feels inclined to believe that no life exists but his own. On such occasions I go a little distance off and ruminate over our past and wonder as to our future; but to-night the silence was so painful as to force me back to the cabin, where human beings might be seen and their voices heard.

The running of the melted ice over the floes in long lanes has made regular sluice-ways, through which the water runs to find the sea level. Our old sounding hole, about 100 yards on our stb'd quarter, offers an inlet to the sea, and several streams have scored a way, or had a way made for them. This running water has wasted away the ice beneath until at the edges of the hole it is but two feet thick and covered by six inches of water, swirling about like a maelstrohm. Looking through this hole is like looking into some black cavern. Thick fog; some rain, and much mist.

8th. Mr. Dunbar having reported seeing some very thick ice was directed to carry a measuring line, with hook attached. He finds ice 10½ feet thick, and some 14⅜ feet thick. I am satisfied that 8 feet is the maximum thickness of ice found at *temperatures such as we have had*, and any greater thickness is formed by snow deposit or by overriding floes, seemingly one piece because of interfreezing.

9th. Loose sails, first time in 10 months; perfect condition.

10th. Day of steady rain and fog, and to our sensation more disagreeable than the coldest weather of winter. Temperature ranges between 32° and 35°. Dampness seems to pierce to the marrow; dry cold seldom heeded.

July 11th. Since the distilling has ceased we light a wood fire in the galley every evening to boil the tea water. Our empty barrels and boxes have quite accumulated largely, and we have quite a supply to haul on for accidental fires instead of using coal.

13th. We seem to be coming up slowly, ice and all, as indicated by the gradual falling of the water-level on our hull. Our usual heel of 5° to starboard is also increasing slightly. In order to get an idea of the correct thickness of the ice in our neighborhood (in case subsequent emergency should make it advisable to dig or saw out a dock or basin if possible and make an effort to drag the ship into it) I direct borings to be made in the floe, and Chipp obtained the following results:

	Below water.	Total.
Thickness of the ice under the stern,	= 5 feet 4 inches.	= 5 ft. 8 inches.
" " " 50 feet astern,	= 4 " 3 "	= 4 " 7 "
" " " 100 " "	= 5 " 0 "	= 5 " 4 "
" " " 150 " "	= 5 " 0 "	= 5 " 4 "

The ice as a general thing has *its* surface 4 inches *above* surface of the water. The ship is held firmly by a cradle of ice. From the mainmast forward there is a second floe piece, which shoved under the first floe on January 19th.

Walked out about 2½ miles to the S. E., where there has been an opening affording seal shooting. In a straight line the distance is about 1¼ miles, but owing to intervening small ponds many detours are necessary. These ponds, though formed by surface thawing, are knee deep, and sometimes too wide to jump across. Arrived at the open water, I found it nearly closed, about 6 feet in width remaining. Near this was considerable dirty ice, with shells and smooth pebbles, showing that it has been on the bottom or has rubbed along the land; or, query? is it refuse matter left on it by a walrus? (We know that the tusks of the walrus are the means by which the animal digs up shell-fish from the bottom, and it may be that tearing up a lump of the bottom in quest of food he brings the whole mouthful to the surface ice to overhaul it more comfortably.

Though not pertinent to this case, I am reminded here of the ducks who take in ballast to facilitate diving, and eject it for more convenient flying.) Near by we found a log, heavy from water soaking, but sound and fresh at the fractured end.

15th. Rain, mist, and thick fog. We feel this damp cold very much.

16th. Mist and fog; temperature 31° to 32°. This seems to be the time for seals to shed their coats, for all our captures are made while the seal is out of the water getting rid of his old hair by rubbing on the ice.

17. Much fog-mist and rain; and in the afternoon *snow*.

18th. This kind of life is most discouraging. If we were only drifting *towards* our goal we would be somewhat content; but, alas! we are steadily drifting away from it; as, if in our enforced idleness we were accomplishing anything for the good of science or human nature, it would be a comfort. But instead of either we are simply burning coal to cook food to consume day after day. Over 10 months of this imprisonment have we had, and in fact I can hardly assign any reason why it should not last any multiple of 10 months more. Currents there are none, except such as are created locally and temporarily by a wind, see-saw, jiggy-jiggy, northwest, with a S. E. wind, and then S. E. with a N. W. wind. The surface water shows no increase of temperature that is not due to the air, and the bottom water has a temperature of 30°. Fog-mist and snow; temp. 29°.5 to 33°.

19th. When one is tempted to feel blue of late, the sun, which under ordinary circumstances induces cheerfulness, rather adds to our disgust. For, as observations of that luminary determine our position, we are informed on each occasion how far we have gone backward; or, in other words, how much nearer we are to the South Pole instead of the North Pole. In the last 3 days we have gone 13½ miles S.xW., though we have been having W. and N. W. winds. Job is recorded to have had many trials and tribulations, which he bore with wonderful patience, but so far as is known he was never caught in pack ice, and drifted S.xW. with W. winds. However, his may have been an anteglacial period.

The ship is in the center of an irregularly-shaped island, about 3 miles in diameter, and which is separated from the neighboring ice by a lane ¼ of a mile in width. I am satisfied that most of this island is of one winter's ice growth, formed over the lake into which we were squeezed last November. The remainder, however (chiefly the borders), is ice of great thickness, perhaps 40 feet; the surfaces 3 feet above the water in level places; and, as frequently hummocks 40 feet in height are seen, the adjacent country may be called a rolling continuation of hills and dales, interspersed with jagged masses of broken floe edge, full of snow pits, and studded into ponds, as easy to travel over as to go through a city over the house tops.

20th. Fog-mist and rain; temp. 31° to 35° (backward summer).

21st. I can safely say that I did not feel one half as uncomfortable during the winter, with a temperature of —30°, as I do now at a temperature of 30°.

22d. Started to see more of our ice island. I succeeded, however, in getting around from west to north only, the traveling being very rough indeed. Arriving at "north," I found the lane of water closing up, the five-foot (one season's) ice piling up in huge slabs on some very old and heavy ice. The sight and sound quite carried me back to our experience during the winter. As the soft state of the surfaces rendered the "*high scream*" impossible, there was not much terror inspired; but one could not help being impressed with the tremendous force with which these blocks were crashed along, reared up, and tumbled over, and the silent grinning "surge" with which the force continued when one would suppose it counteracted and ended. Here I was ready to turn back, having been out 3 hours, and being wet through from wading and being dragged through ponds too wide to go around without immensely increasing the distance.

A truly wretched day; squally, rainy, snowy, & what not. At 6 a. m. Chipp required 7 letters to record the state of the weather, viz, o. c. m. q. p. r. s., which shows it must have been somewhat mixed. Temp. bet. 31° and 33°.

The wasting of the ice cradle allows the ship to settle, and our leak slightly increases. On the 15th our leak was 205 gallons per diem, and to-day it is 271 gallons per diem.

23d. Fog-mist, and a little snow; temp. between 29°.5 and 31°. Are we to have no summer at all?

26th. An unfortunate accident. Alexy had been out shooting, and brought back for his examination a Remington cartridge which had failed to explode. Sitting down quietly, and without being observed, he placed the cartridge between the thumb and finger of his left hand, while he picked away at the fulminate cap with his knife in his right hand. Suddenly the cartridge exploded, and, without detaching the bullet, the shell flew out into ragged edges, which cut Alexey's hand sadly, besides burning it with the powder. He was at once a sadly demoralized native, the shock affecting him considerably.

Temperature 33° by noon, 28°.5 at midnight, and this is the height of summer. Reflections on past and present.

27th. Snow falls nearly all day; temp. between 26° and 30°.

28th. Temp. rises from 29°.4 to 34°. During afternoon light snow fell steadily, and at 11 p. m. both rain and hail. For a summer day the weather was of course "perfectly lovely."

31st. Ther. 30° to 32°, mist-rain, snow, and wind squalls. If this month is a sample of July weather here generally, I do not want to see any more of it.

August 1st. Sad opening for the last month of summer. Snow, rain, fog, mist; thermomter 30°.2 to 33°.5 to 28°. Surface of all ponds and streams freezes, of course.

2d. Our humdrum existence is occasionally varied by finding shells, pieces of sponge, or bits of wood on the ice. These are being uncovered by the gradual melting of the snow and ice, and of course we cannot say how long they may have remained there, or how they came there originally. In the absence of facts, theories are as various as they are incongruous. Shells may be ascribed to drift, to being brought up from the bottom by grounding and turning floes, or to being rejected by walruses in feeding.

3d. Southerly winds; temp. 25°.5 to 34°.5 to 33°.2. Between 5 and 8 p. m. a strong odor of burning brush-wood filled the air, and was noticed by everybody except myself, and I had such a cold in the head as to lose sense of smell. From 6 to 10 p. m. a decided haze was apparent, but whether the haze and the odor of burning brush-wood can be connected in any way remains for future investigation. Ice seems to be compact again in all directions.

4th. Some rain & some snow, we have, of course. It is a poor summer day in this part of the world when we have not either or both.

8th. Another week has come and gone, and leaves our situation unchanged. What chance there is for a change may be inferred from to-day's temperature, 23° to 31°.5.

9th. Refreshing and soul-inspiring temperature, 21° to 31°. Fog and light snow, varied by fog and hail.

11th. Leak increasing from 8½ galls. per hour, July 15th, to 46¼ gallons per hour.

13th. *Sunset* 10h. 20m. On the 6th inst., by our lat. and his declination the sun was really below our horizon at midnight, but fogs were so regularly prevailing as to hide him about that time. To-night, however, we have clear weather, and can realize the fact that the sun at midnight is to us a thing of the past.

15th. Our mild weather (31°.5 to 34°) continues, and so does the fog. It is surprising to see how fog cuts away the ice. The feeble sun of June 21st did not do one half as much execution as the fog did to-day. The ice seems actually rotting away. The surface is soft and spongy, and fully honey-combed, though of course ice varying from 2 to 20 feet in thickness yet remains to stop us. The ship is yet held affectionately by ice gripping her nearly down to her keel, and heeling her over 7½° to stbd. Here and there on either beam, holes varying in diameter from 1 to 6 feet extend down through the ice; and at a distance of ½ mile on the stbd beam and 1 mile on the port beam there is a narrow lane of water, which serves to make our immediate vicinity an island. So that if we could get to this lane we might have the pleasure of sailing around a circle, were we not crushed by the ice coming together; for beyond the lane in any given direction is ice of the cheerful and consoling thickness of 20 to 40 feet.

16th. To-day I virtually decided that our chance of getting free this summer was gone, though as it never came it seems strange to speak of it as gone. In accordance with my plan for the deck-house during the coming winter, Sweetman commenced altering the frames and stanchions of that edifice.

17th. And so day by day our glorious summer is passing away, and we are accomplishing nothing. It is painful beyond expression to go around the ice in the morning and see no change since the night before, and to look the last thing at night at the same things we saw in the morning. And this has continued nearly a year. High as the temperature now is (34°–29°.7), with foggy weather a daily occurrence, we are yet held fast, seeing only ponds here and there, two and three feet deep, and occasionally having a hole through to the sea beneath. Is this always a dead sea? Does the ice never find an outlet? Surely it must go somewhere, for, as the thawing in three months by no means equals the freezing in nine months, it would require but a few years to make a solid choking up of this Arctic Ocean. The ice does not go out through Behring's Strait, for all or nearly all ice met in Behring's Sea is formed in that locality. It has no regular set in any direction, north, east, or west, as far as I can judge, but it slowly surges in obedience to wind pressure, and grinds back again to an equilibrium when the pressure ceases. Are there any tides in this ocean? Drifting about as we do, no tidal measurements are possible, of course. When last fall and winter we had our greatest pressure, at new and full moon, their regular recurrence seemed to indicate that tidal action existed. But now the moon creates nothing. Full moon or new moon, last quarter or first quarter, the ice seems immoveable as a rock. We are of course farther north now than we were last winter, and may have got beyond the Siberian tides, and be still south of the tides mentioned as flowing and ebbing through McClure Strait. Our water temperature and soundings taken daily give no encouragement. The surface has generally a temperature of 34°, due of course to its exposure to the sun and its capacity for absorbing and retaining heat. Two fathoms below the surface the temperature is 31°, and at the bottom 30°. At a temperature but 7½° above the freezing point of sea water, the lower ice cannot melt rapidly. On the surface the sun's rays or the cutting fog or the warmer water at the edges makes a wasted and rotten material, but under water the ice has apparently the same flinty hardness it had during midwinter; and it is of such irregular and varying thickness that no idea can be formed of its age or origin. We know that last November, when we were squeezed out of the heavy ice into our present location, we came into open water, a lake, so to speak. By careful measurements we know that ice has formed over this lake to a thickness of 5 feet 4 inches by February 4th; after which time its thickness could no longer be accurately measured because of underriding floes, though it is reasonable to suppose 7 feet not in excess. On the 13th July that ice was 5 feet in thickness, and to-day (August 17th) it is 3 feet 5 inches thick. Either we have had our summer or are yet to have it. The latter seems absurd at this late date. If we have had our summer, 3 feet 7 inches may be taken as the amount of one season's thaw, and the remaining 3 feet 5 inches will form a basis for next winter. Already our little ponds have frozen during the night and remain frozen until noon of the next day. This much being said of thin ice right around us, how are we to discuss ice which is 12 feet, 22 feet, 24 feet, 30 feet, and even 40 feet in thickness? We see daily ice which has been piled up in confused masses 24 feet above the surface of the water, and can only guess as to its thickness below. We drop a lead down to a projecting tongue 12 feet thus: 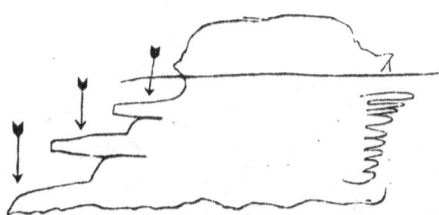 and think we have the thickness of that floe at all events; but, lo! a little further and we see a second projecting tongue, or perhaps a third thus:

and we sometimes get 22 feet in this way, making 46 feet in all without being certain that we have got to the lowest layer of the mass which we have climbed over. Really and truly I believe no such ice exists elsewhere; but whether it is a paleocrystic sea or not is a moot question.

17th. A marvellous temperature, 31° to 40°, leads us to hope for something after all. An unfortunate accident occurred to-day. H. H. Kaack (sea.), while passing along the berth-deck fell and broke the elbow-joint of his right arm. Beyond the long time (six weeks or so) necessary for a union to form between the broken bones and the continued contemplation of one more incapable in case of disaster to the ship, there is no serious consequence to be feared.

22d. Close quarters with a bear.

24th. But a short time since and we were revelling in the enjoyment of a sun above the horizon the whole 24 hours, and to-night a lantern was necessary at midnight to read the anemometer. For about 2 weeks we have had the cabin lamp lighted at 9 p. m. Our daily hunting parties are coming back empty handed. Seals enough are seen and shot, but they sink almost at once and are lost. This seems, as I have somewhere before remarked, to be the season for shedding coats, and there would appear to be a connection between the shedding and loss of fat. Under ordinary circumstances the seal when shot is buoyant enough to float until his carcase can be reached by a kayak; but now the moment the skin is punctured down pussy goes.

All reports seem to agree in pronouncing the ice in a wasted and disintegrated condition, needing only a fresh blow to send it into blocks and pieces. Fog, mist, and occasional drizzling rain; temp., 31.5° to 35.5°.

25th. I have been anxious to have a sight of our propeller to know whether any injury was sustained during our numerous ice squeezes and jammings. The ice surrounding the ship's stern had a thickness of 9 feet in some places, and its surface was about 2 feet under water. Sawing it seemed a herculean task, while blasting it with torpedoes might injure the ship. However, sawing was resorted to and successfully managed by Lieut. Chipp. When we had cleared away the large blocks the screw was triced up, and to our great satisfaction found as perfect as the day it was attached to the shaft. Satisfied that its being in place added greatly to strengthen the stern-post, it was again lowered to its seat.

In sawing the ice work was carried on on both sides, and when the heavy floes were nearly sawn through they broke by reason of the upward pressure of the water, and came bumping up to the surface. So much of the ship as was abaft the mainmast being thus released from its icy cradle, the following results ensued:

(Log.) "The ship immediately went down in the water 7 inches aft, and came up forward $\frac{1}{2}$ inch, the water level being now at a height of 7 feet 2 inches on the stern and 13 feet 9$\frac{1}{4}$ inches on the rudder-post. The heel is now 8$\frac{3}{4}$° to starboard, having been increased only $\frac{1}{4}$° by the change in immersion. The ship is yet firmly held by ice, which extends from the main rigging on the port side around the bows and to the after part of the fore rigging on the starboard side, and which, where possible to measure, is found to have a thickness of 10 feet 11 inches. It probably extends under the keel, forming a cradle; and though it would perhaps be possible to haul the ship astern into a small pool of clear water, it is not attempted for fear of increasing the facility with which water might enter through the damaged stern, and so require additional labor, or even steam pumping, to keep the ship free. Without a single lead of water in any direction, accessible to the ship, her being navigated is impossible, and there would be nothing gained by her being floated into a small lake."

Crimson snow; meteoric iron (?).

29th. Temp., 34°–28°.2; ice forming over all ponds again, remaining until noon of the following day.

The outlook from the crow's-nest is dreary enough: ice, ice, ice; in the little basin or valley in which we are numerous rivelets and pond holes may be seen, but beyond what *was* our encircling mountain ridge 20 to 40 feet high but *is* a ragged mass of confused chunks, there is a seemingly endless ice desert with a black pool here and there, but no leads, no channels, no avenues of advance or retreat.

30th. At midnight Jupiter and Saturn visible; birds flying south, 34°–26°.5.

31st. The last day of summer, 37°.2 to 25°.2, and ice $\frac{3}{4}$ of an inch over all ponds. Faint aurora visible at 11.15 p. m.

September 1st. At last we are on an even keel. This morning at 9.35 the ship suddenly righted, and moved astern about 2 feet. It was done very quietly and without shock except to a dog which was on the gang plank, and was suddenly tumbled to the ice below. New ice had formed around our fore part to the thickness of nearly an inch and the cracking and breaking of this sheet was the only accompaniment to our movement. One or two large chunks of ice rose to the surface from below on the port side and then all was still. By previous orders, at the first movement Sweetman ran down in the fore peek, and closed the opening in the extra bulk-head built last January. I feared that our taking water again would largely increase, but we found for the time no difference. The water level on the ship was at the height of 8 feet 4 inches on the stem and 13 feet 5$\frac{1}{4}$ inches on the rudder post. Believing that the ship was fairly afloat (her stern being 16 inches from the groove in which it had been resting) we carried an ice-claw to the floe astern and planted it on our port quarter, and then bending a hawser to it we tried to heave the ship astern with the capstan. To my surprise, beyond swinging her bow a little to starboard, perhaps a point, the ship was immovable. Thinking the ice on either bow was holding her, we took the ice-claw more nearly astern and hove again until we parted the hawser. Upon examining the ice around the bows the ship seemed clear, but upon probing with a stick we struck ice at a depth of 7 feet 4 inches. Evidently, then, keel and forefoot were yet held in a cradle. Desiring to get a little away from the heavy floe which had damaged us last winter, a large hawser was now brought into use, and we hove and hove without effect. An ice-saw, worked by a rope from the fore-yard-arm, was then set at work to cut through 11 feet thickness of ice in the manner shown on page 355.

After we had cut through 6 feet longitudinally we found that more water was coming into the ship than usual, and fearing to make a bad matter even worse if we continued to saw, the order was given to "belay everything," and no further attempt to float the ship was made on this occasion.

A computation of the amount of the leak, based on the area of the pump and the number of strokes, gives a result of 114$\frac{1}{4}$ gallons of water per hour, and we had only 46$\frac{1}{4}$ gallons per hour on August 11th. Hence our efforts to float the ship have increased the leak about 2$\frac{1}{2}$ times.

The comfort of being on an even keel is very great. No longer is moving about awkward and inconvenient; no longer do our plates, &c., show a tendency to slide away from us, and no longer do we have to mount high in the air to get on board ship from the ice.

Temperature rises from 24° to 36°.5; but during the afternoon we have an impenetrable fog.

2nd. A cheerless day. The usual fog in the forenoon, and from noon to midnight an almost steady fall of very thin snow. In one day we seem to have jumped into winter. All our lakes and rivulets are covered with ice an inch in thickness, and that in turn being covered by snow the general outlook is as cold and comfortless as possible. Numerous flocks of phalaropes flying to S. W. from N. E.

5th. One year in the ice, and only 150 miles to the nd. & wd. of where we entered it. If a time ever comes when I can sit down quietly, free from the mental strain I am now undergoing, I dare say I shall be able to describe in some coherent style my thoughts

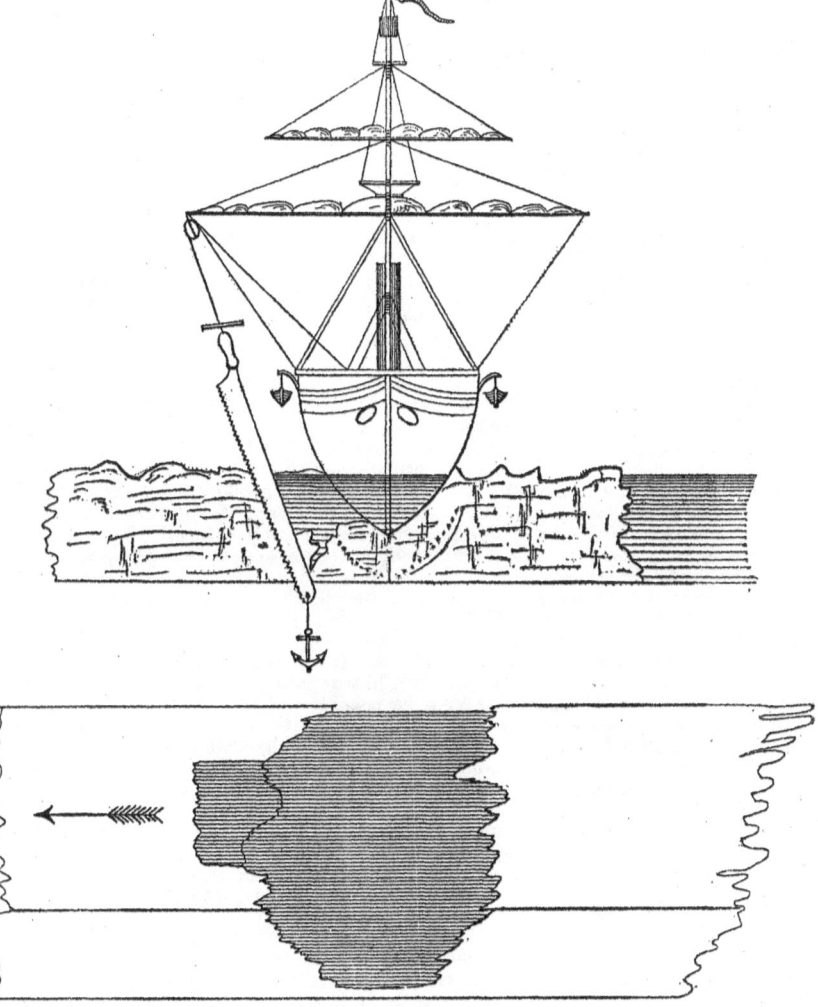

and feelings. But at this moment I have neither power nor inclination to mention them at any length. Anxiety, disappointment, difficulties, troubles, are all so inseparably mixed that I am unable to select any one for a beginning.

6th. 27° to 17°; refreshingly low temperature. Is this Indian summer? If so, what is Indian winter?

Splitting and cracking of the new ice in the lanes and ponds, caused by the wind bringing the heavy floes together, brings to our mind our experience of last winter, and prepares us for the contemplation of what is before us this winter.

7th. The deck-house and preparations for closing it in occupy our time and attention, and it is finally concluded by the 14th. This new arrangement of deck-house was a decided success over the experience of last winter. In the first place, as it covered the entire berth-deck there was none of the deposit of beads of moisture on the beams to drip into the berths. Next, the temperature of the berth-deck could be kept at a comfortable height, with due regard to ventilation; and last, the absence of fire in the deck-house ensured a tolerably dry footing within that edifice. The drawing shows the general arrangement.* The berth-deck sky-light was now always off, and a trap cut in the roof of the deck-house over it supplied fresh air and let out foul, as the case might be. The berth-deck stove-pipe passing upward gave some little heat within the deck-house, and the galley-room stove-pipe likewise passing upward added to it. The heat ascended from the berth-deck through the sky-light hole, and through the fire-hatch, and so relieved the deck-house from considerable cold, though not enough to prevent condensation and freezing. Except in extraordinary rises of temperature of the open air, no melting took place within, and there was generally neither slop nor drip.

This new arrangement necessarily threw the cook-house out in the cold, but we built porches to it on either side and padded its forward end with the felt which had been of no use in the deck-house the previous winter. At first, as cold weather set in, the moisture formed back of the steward's and cook's berths, and was troublesome by dripping down on the mattresses. But this was overcome by building pockets behind them, and occasionally removing the ice.

15th. A regular stormy day of wind and snow—NW., 16 to 26 miles an hour. Clouds of snow whirled through the air. Drifts, into which one might flounder to his waist, were as common as water holes used to be a month ago, and between them bare places of ice were as smooth as glass by the friction of the snow-blast, caused heels to fly up without warning or avoidance. Looking to windward was a sheer impossibility. Even the dogs, usually so indifferent to weather, were utterly disgusted, and after vainly seeking a shelter under the ship's side, or to leeward of a barrel, fairly gave it up and lay down anywhere and allowed themselves to be snowed in. Mounds here and there showed for a time where a dog was, but after a while these became undistinguishable, and a smothered howl now and then, as we ploughed along, was the first evidence we had of the presence of a dog.

Fires lighted; temperature 19°.5 to 9°.5. We stood the cold until noon, and then I was forced to order fires lighted. Got up all our pemmican into the deck-house.

19th. Cole's and Lee's rooms acting as condensers; Chipp suggests stove for galley-room. Adopted, *nem. con.* Sure to be necessary before long to keep pump from freezing, and to avoid freezing lime juice, &c., in store-room.

And so we prepare for our second winter in the pack. In some respects we are better prepared for it than for our first, though no preparation can be complete or effectual for such a life. We are tolerably certain of being quite as comfortable aft, and we are sure that the men will be more comfortable forward. If we are to have the same anxiety and trouble this winter that we had last we must bear it patiently, for we can neither avoid nor prevent it; and as far as getting ready for possible disaster, I think we have neglected nothing. Our experience of last winter showed us that our St. Michael's sledges were not fitted to drag the heavy weights necessary in case of abandonment, and none of them would have carried a boat. New and heavier sleds were then built, as well as especial sleds to carry our two dingheys; so that we are now much better off in that respect. But the wisdom of keeping sleds loaded on board ship is not clear to my mind, for in case of emergency I question our ability to get these loaded sleds to the ice without serious injury, even if the men had time to get them out one after the other. And again, if loaded sleds were placed on the ice now there is no assurance that in the first break up of the ice we would not lose them. I became convinced that whichever of the two plans I followed the first emergency would cause me to wish it had been the other one, and so I decided to do neither, but to fall back upon the following: Some sleds were put out on the ice with our Oomiak, which had been considerably reduced in size, and our boat sleds, with one dinghey, were placed on top of the deck-house, ready for shoving off. Our other boats were kept at the davits ready for lowering. Upon quarter-deck provisions of all kinds were stored, but most largely of those which our emergency would require, and the pemmican was conveniently stored in the deck-house. In the deck-house were also stored the knapsacks, travelling stoves, and dog harness, and the sleeping bags and tents were in the after store-room. With a detailed station bill, the duties of collecting the various articles at one place at short notice are provided for, and we can do nothing more than wait. Our method of procedure will, of course, be regulated by cir-

---

*No drawing attached. J. A.

cumstances, but we shall stick to the ship as long as she sticks to us, and when she leaves us we must strike out for ourselves.

I dislike naturally to dwell on the idea of abandonment of the ship. We have come through so much that it gives me hopes of surviving more. As long as enough of the ship remains to shelter us, sticking by that fragment is preferable to camping on ice; and I can conceive of no greater "forlorn hope" than an attempt to reach Siberia (say 240 miles distant) over the ice that surrounds us, and with a winter's cold sapping one's life at every step. Of course if we were to lose our ship we would make the effort to get there, but our chances of success would be extremely problematical.

* * * * * * *

I am very much afraid that our expenditure of fuel this winter will be much greater than that of last winter. We are now coming to much fine dust stuff (Nanaimo coal), which burns like powder, and requires a large quantity to generate enough heat. Last winter we had much anthracite coal among our daily issue, and that lasted longer and did better work.

20th. There is no doubt in my mind of the superiority of wooden houses and porches to tent awnings and hatch-covers; and the benefit to be gained compensates doubly, I am sure, for the inconvenience and lumbering up of the deck while making the passage from port to winter quarters. If I could have known before sailing from San Francisco all that I have learned during the past year, I think I could have brought about a more comfortable cruise and have saved myself much mental annoyance.

22nd. The early part of the day was marked by the lowest temperature ($+0.5$) so far in the month. But I shall not be surprised to find it much lower before September, 1880, is a thing of the past. In fact I have ceased being surprised at anything. This kind of life begets a careless kind of feeling as to what may happen, and a lazy belief that time is of no value whatever. Knowing that our surroundings to-day are the same as those of yesterday, we see no reason for anticipating a change to-morrow. With certain duties assigned for certain hours we move along mechanically, satisfied that we can do no more, and naturally unwilling to do less. Deriving our motive power from the food we eat, we perform the operations of breakfast, dinner, and supper as a duty rather than an enjoyment. With even a liberal variety of food we know exactly what we are going to eat and how much, and when we are going to eat it, and hence we have no novelty of anticipation. Eating, sleeping, and performing duties which are as regular as time and as invariable as the succession of one day to another, no calculation is necessary and no one heeds the arrival or departure of a new day or a new week. A prisoner in a jail has an advantage over us; for knowing his sentence, he can fix the day of his release; while we know "neither the day nor the hour."

24th. It is well worthy of mention that during the whole of the summer and spring, in all the leads and opening, we have seen no white whales. In the fall of 1879, after our besetment, whenever we made excursions to the large leads in our neighborhood it was not uncommon to see a white whale blow. Mr. Dunbar, whose experience gives weight to his opinion, argues from the facts that now we are far removed from the open sea. White whales, he says, never, unless chased, go far enough into a pack to jeopardize their easy return to the open water. White walrus and seals, on the other hand, will enter the pack readily and get from hole to hole by diving and swimming beneath, where there is no surface connection.

Oct. 5th, $+9°.5$ to $-14°$; grinding of ice to the eastward.

6th. Banking up snow against ship's side.

7th. The days are so much alike that we almost lose track of them, or rather fail to notice the date. Man is but a superior kind of machine, after all. Set him going and keep him wound up by feeding him, and he can run monotonously, like a clock. At least *we* do, and I do not suppose we are exceptional creatures.

9th. A dull, gloomy day, enough to make a man blue in enduring it. Dull, leaden-gray sky, no sun, and that exasperatingly light fall of snow, which is neither one thing or another.

Oct. 16. The hunting parties on going out this morning found an opening in the ice about 2 miles SE. and E. from the ship, and extending in disconnected ponds for a short distance. Where the ice had come together large ridges of piled-up slabs, 7 and 8 feet thick, rose to heights of 30 and 40 feet. As this occurred since yesterday, the pressure and upheaval must have taken place during the night. At this spot, just before 6 p. m. to-day, the whole ice ocean seemed to be alive, for it was grinding, cracking, and piling up at a prodigious rate. During the evening various cracks and snaps were heard around the ship, and occasionally we had a slight jar. Cracks here and there were found in our surrounding ice, but nothing serious occurred, though our cares and anxieties may be said to have received an increasing stimulus.

20th. Brisk E. S. E. wind, 18 to 21 miles, raises the temperature from $-2°$ to $+14°.5$, and an almost steady fall of fine snow, which, being driven along the surface of the ice takes up enough salt to become unfit for use. I do not notice that I am more sensitive to cold this winter than last, though it is an accepted theory that the second winter tells more severely upon the human form. With temperature such as we have to-day, I find the air soft and mild, and were it not that my hands break out with chillblains and old frost-bites, I should not hesitate to go without gloves. In the cabin, at a temperature of 50°, I am often too warm, and when by accident the temperature is allowed to run up to 60° I am positively uncomfortable.

21st. The regular monotony is disturbed by the stupendous discovery of a fox track.

24th. There is a considerable amount of doubt thrown on all observations taken during such cold weather as we experience in an Arctic winter. Sextants were never designed to be submitted to such contraction as they now undergo in use, and there is no way to allow for or remedy the change produced in the length of the arc. The greater the cold the greater the contraction, of course; but that gives no index error. A sextant very carefully adjusted to-day, and then having an index correction of —30″, was found after a short exposure to have an index correction of —4′, apparently; but how much the arc was actually shortened it would be impossible to say. The mercury on the index and horizon glasses cracks and splits. For a long time I have been trying to get some satisfactory lunars to check our chronometers, but they all gave such ridiculous results and differed so widely that I have despaired of getting anything reliable. If our zenith telescope is powerful enough we may be able to get some satisfactory results from eclipses of Jupiter's satellites.

27th. As the winter grows on and daylight fades, our anxieties are renewed. At the time of our perpetual day, when we hoped and prayed for a breaking up of the ice, so that we might make an effort to redeem ourselves, not a sound and not a motion were experienced. But now, at a time when the breaking up of the ice can produce nothing but disaster, so far as human judgment can foretell, we seem to be promised enough of it. This morning at daylight a crack or lane 6 feet in width was discovered on our port beam, about 500 yards distant. At 11.30 the ship received a considerable jar, causing the lamp chimneys and shades to rattle and ring, and the surrounding ice seemed to get a motion like a lift and a shove.

28th. Nothing occurred to-day, but we remain suspicious of the ice, and consider it is only taking a rest or preparing for greater efforts.

30th. Crackling of ice and noises of grinding commenced just after midnight, under the stem and on each quarter, and lasted until 3 a. m., and then paused until 3 p. m., when they recommenced. A narrow lane of water is found about a mile ahead of the ship.

31st. With this day ends the month; uneventful, and, so far as any results obtained are concerned, a clear waste of life. It is hard to feel satisfied even with our being still alive. *That*, after all, seems such a negative kind of thing—a living with no purpose, an existence without present tangible benefit, a mechanical supplying the system with food and clothing, in order to keep the human engine running. I have often wondered if a horse driving a saw-mill had any mental queries as to why he tramped over his endless plank, and what on earth there was accomplished by his so doing. The saw was generally out of his sight; he perceived no work done by it; he never changed his position relatively; he walked on and on without advancing a yard, and ended his day's work in identically the same place at which he began it, and as far as equine judgement could forecast would do the same thing the next day and any other day thereafter. If that horse had reasoning faculties, I pity him and appreciate now his thoughts and feelings. We are individually in that horse's position. We perceive no saw; we can detect nothing accomplished; we move on without advancing; we shall do to-morrow what we have done to-day, and what we did yesterday; and we fill up with oats, so to speak, merely that our saw-mill may not have to suspend sawing. This kind of life is worse than Mr. Mantalini and his mangle. With him life was "one demnition grind," with us it is one demnition blank.

The ice is already two feet thick, direct freezing since August 31st.

November 1st. Commenced winter routine, and though the sun has not yet left us I consider it well to resume to-day the usual two hours' exercise so long as the temperature remains above —30°.

3d. The monthly medical examination having been resumed on the 1st, the Doctor handed in his report to-day. Except in several especial cases, nothing is found to be wrong with us except a general want of tone, and a less vigor than at the same time last year. As this is exactly what would result for our life of enforced monotony and prolonged absence from land, there is no need for surprise. Generally we *feel* strong and well, but have, as a rule, lost flesh. The small difference of temperature during the summer months, compared with our spring and autumn cold weather, and the short time that such difference continued, have not been enough to allow us to spring back or rebound to anything like a normal condition; and we are again called upon to endure cold weather before we have had a decent chance to recover from our former trial. No doubt we shall be able to put in this winter as safely as last winter, so far as our health is concerned, so long as we have the ship for our home. But if we are turned out on the ice by disaster, we will not be as well able to stand the exposure as we were at this time a year ago.

The condition of our living quarters, as far as warmth and dryness go, is all that could be asked, and more than anybody else's experience has shown. Ventilation of the berth-deck is fairly secured by our present mode, and were it not for two things I could say the same of the cabin. Our first trouble aft is with our lamps. Last winter, while we had kerosene, we had light without smoke, but now we have to fall back upon Mare Island oil, and Walton's lamps, and we have great difficulty. The oil is poor, does not flow readily, and easily chokes the tubes. They cannot be cleaned often enough and the light soon grows dim. Turning up the wicks makes a tremendous smoke, and turning them down kills the light. We shall therefore resort to candles. Our second trouble is with odors from the stove. Much coal was carried on deck from St. Michael's, and 40 dogs lived on top of this coal, and their contributions to it have not added to its good qualities. Sea-sickness affected them with a general looseness, and the results were as inseparable from the coal then as now, and occasionally on throwing in our stoves a fresh supply of fuel we get a distilled dog fragrance of a peculiar kind.

5th. Cold snap to-day —28°, with an 18 mile N. W. wind, gave us warning by little stings, as our noses froze, to be prepared for winter. Ice ⅛ mile north of the ship opens to 200 yards width, and numerous cracklings and jars of the ship kept us more or less anxious all day.

6th. The sun left us to-day for his long absence of 91 days. (By extraordinary refraction it was raised above our horizon on the 9th and 10th, however, making 87 days between actual disappearance and reappearance.) The temperature got down to —33°, and the ice commenced its horrid screeching and grinding at some little distance, as if in celebration.

7th. It is idle to go on speaking longer of the coming and going of weeks; it is record enough when I mention the coming and going of months. On the first Sunday in the month the Articles of War are read with all the seriousness that would prevail in a frigate. The clause providing that "all offenses committed on shore shall be punished in the same manner as if they had been committed at sea," is read with as much impressiveness as if we were in a port, full of sailor temptations, instead of being in a howling wilderness of ice. I think many of us look back to "a shore" as some memory of our childhood, or of a previous existence in another sphere. That this world should be anything but pack ice is a tax upon even extraordinary credulity.

After muster we tumbled out on the ice. It was all there, fortunately, for with our pleasant (!) temperature it *might* have melted. During the forenoon a crack opened in the ice between the ship and the thermometer stand. This is the way it acted last year. Are we going to have the same old story, or worse?

14th. At 1.30 a. m. we were startled by a severe shock to the ship, shaking her as if she were sliding down an inclined plane and then suddenly brought up. No signs of disturbance were visible in the ice, and nobody forward had noticed any shock. But as soon as daylight enough appeared, after breakfast, it was discovered that the lead 1 mile ahead of the ship and the lead ⅛ mile astern were both open, the latter to the width of 100 yards. No doubt the rupture of these two fields produced the shock to the ship.

16th. Bar. rises since the 14th from 29″.50 to 31″.08 at 9 a. m., at which time the moon fulls, and temperature steadily rises from —30° to +8°.5 by the 17th, when we had a stiff easterly gale, 17 to 35 miles an hour, which blew the surface snow in blinding clouds and banked it up against the ship and even on board. So firmly did it pack these masses that the walking was like going up hills and down dales, and as one could not keep his eyes open long enough to pick his way many tumbles ensued unexpectedly. Bar. fell with wonderful rapidity from 30″.77 to 30″.10.

20th. Stars visible at 9 a. m.

28th. I am satisfied that we are affected by the length of time elapsed since we have set foot on shore. Like the old saying, "Dogs need grass occasionally," may be quoted as a proverb, "Man needs land once in a while." Excepting the small party that landed at Koliutchin Bay, none of us have set a foot on the land in nearly 15 months, and our sensations now are somewhat dulled when we try to realize what it was like. According to my idea we have become receivers of magnetism without proper earths to let it escape. Our rest is broken and unnatural. It is not an unusual thing for those of us who retire at 10 p. m. to lie awake until 3 a. m., and I, who *cannot* go to bed until after midnight, and *do* not as a rule retire until after 1 a. m., rarely fall asleep until 3.30. We all wake up again at short intervals afterwards, and no one sleeps after 9 a. m. Each morning we are dull and heavy, having no feeling of rest obtained, and a kind of leth argy clings to us until we get out for our daily walking exercise, from 11 to 1. From that time forward we are in our normal condition, having no especial desire for sleep, and yet feeling somewhat out of sorts for want of it.

December 1st. Our leak, for some unknown reason, has increased, being now 119 gallons per hour, or 2,856 gallons per day. However, it is no great matter, for we do not mind the short spell each hour that the pumps require.

2nd. The medical examination shows that our condition is improved over that of last month. We are so accustomed to the cold for the second time that we have forgotten that we ever had warmer weather, and experience no sense of uncomfortable change. Besides, a dry cold is less felt than a damp warmth (comparitively speaking), and we have less sense of personal discomfort at —30° than we have had at +30°, with fog, mist, or rain.

5th. A rapid fall of temperature from +19° to —29°. Found a crack in the ice 300 yards east in the forenoon, and when it closed in the evening the grinding and groaning were horribly suggestive of our last winter's experience.

6th. *Capella, and other 1st mag. stars, clearly visible at noon.

9th. Several heavy knocks and thumps under the stern, as if we were skimming over and striking blocks of ice under water.

11th. Temp., from —19° to —39°. Frequently during the day we were startled by loud reports, like the firing of heavy guns, and the ship was considerably jarred by them. I can only account for these noises by supposing them to be caused by the splitting of heavy ice floes when contraction sets in at such low temperature.

15th. Temp., —48°.

16th. Ditto for temperature. Numerous shakes and jars, as though we were passing over submerged ice-cakes. One of these jars lifted the ship somewhat and set my lamp swinging.

23rd. The ice on the road to the bear trap is cracked and broken in many places and undergoing great pressure.

24th. Minstrel entertainment.

25th. Christmas.

31st. Minstrels and ringing in the New Year in lat. 73° 48′ N. and longitude 177° 32′ E. During the past 16 months we have drifted 1,300 miles, far enough, if it had been in a straight line, to carry us to and beyond the pole, but we are yet only 220 miles NW. of where we were first beset. We have suffered injury, and danger has often confronted us; we have been squeezed and jammed, tossed and tumbled, have pumped a leaking ship for a year—but we are not yet daunted, and are as ready to dare everything as we ever were. And we face the New Year firmly hoping to do something worthy of ourselves, of Bennett's enterprise, and of the flag above us.

A true copy.

SAM. C. LEMLY,
Master U. S. Navy & Judge Advocate.

REPORT OF TRIP TO HENRIETTA ISLAND—CHIEF ENGINEER GEORGE W. MELVILLE, U. S. N.

U. S. ARCTIC SHIP JEANNETTE,
Arctic Ocean, June 6th, 1881.

SIR: In accordance with your written instructions and orders of May 31, 1881, I have the honor to report as follows:

A party, consisting of myself, Mr. Wm. Dunbar, ice pilot; W. C. F. Nindemann, sea.; H. H. Erichsen, sea.; J. H. Bartlett, 1st class fireman, and Walter Sharvell, coal heaver, with sixteen (16) dogs, and seven days' provisions; ten gallons of water, two (2) gallons of alcohol for cooking; small boat, sled, tent, and camp equipage, instruments, &c., &c., with properly prepared medicine case and written instructions for use.

I proceeded with all possible speed direct for the island, deviating only on account of bad going and open lanes of water. During our first day's journey I dismounted the boat four times and ferried over the water dogs and gear. We also had to unlash and carry our gear four times through bad places that were impassable otherwise, besides cutting a road nearly all the way, never having one hundred (100) yards of straight going at any time this day. Finally camped at seven (7) p. m., about four (4) miles distant from the ship, weather O. C. S., temp., 20°.

Wednesday, June 1st. On this day we were out at six (6) a. m., and underway by seven

(7) a. m. Got a bearing of the ship; also of the island. We passed through a terribly rough country, cutting roads and building up bridges. We saw no floe pieces at all; the ice was all brash hummock and jammed up masses, and all alive (*i. e.*, all in motion). After cutting through fifteen yards of road we advanced but five (5) yards on our course. We skirted along lanes of water (this day), running from NE. to SW., but not large enough to work a ship in. We worked twelve (12) hours and fifty (50) minutes (this day), and advanced about four (4) miles. About midday we cut through a large mass of glacier ice, fresh and sweet to the taste, and entirely different in appearance and cohesive structure from the surrounding masses of salt ice. Owing to its location, N. 43°, W. mag. of Jeannette Island, I concluded it had been discharged from a glacier on that island, and took the usual drift of the pack NW.

We lost sight of the ship about four (4) p. m. By seven (7) p. m. the dogs were so tired that we could not keep them up, some of them taking refuge under the sled. I forced this distance and extra labor to find a floe piece to camp on. We were so tired that neither men nor dogs ate all their supper. We camped at eight (8) hours and fifty minutes, and got a sounding in thirty-five (35) fathoms of water; slight drift S. W.

Thursday, June 2nd.—This morning we were out by five (5) and underway by six (6). Had some bad cutting and bridging to do at first, but afterward struck a good floe piece, and by seven (7) considered we had made good one and one-half (1½) miles. The land stood out bold and clear, and we all felt that we were almost there; but we struck immediately after into a bad hummocky floe, full of snow-drift, and deep, hard going, the sled sinking through to the cross-bars and sticking fast on every side. We struggled on until half past ten a. m. (10.30), when I saw in others, and felt in my own bones that our labor was being lost. I unloaded my sled and advanced light until eleven (11) a. m.; then dismounted my boat and sent back and brought up the gear, and by twelve-thirty (12.30) p. m., had loaded up boat and gear again and had hot soup. Advanced with sled and boat until one-thirty (1.30) p. m., when I found that the pack between us and the island was so broken up it was impossible to advance with the boat and gear, and if I was going to make the land at all I must have my boat, provisions, and most of my gear in as safe a place as possible in the moving pack. I therefore dismounted my boat in the center of a large floe piece and set up a signal staff on the highest hummock in the vicinity. I took the sled, dogs, camp equipage, instrument boxes, arms, one day's provision for men and dogs. We estimated the island as two (2) miles distant. Started at two (2) p. m., and passed through from four to six miles of broken and quickly moving pack ice, through which we could never have hauled our boat uninjured. We landed at five-thirty (5.30) p. m. In accordance with instructions, I was the first person to land. I then called my party on shore, in their presence unfurled our colors, and in the name of the Great Jehovah and the President of the United States I declared it a part of the territory of the United States, and in accordance with your instructions named it "Henrietta Island." We were very tired, and got into our beds very early.

Friday, June 3rd.—In the morning we were out by four (4), supposing we had had a good night's sleep, but sore in bones and muscle. I commenced a hurried survey of the N. western end of the island (S. E. end being almost inaccessible), the distance and uncertainty of the position of my boat and provisions accelerating my movements and increasing my anxiety.

I found the island to be a barren rock, fissured and riven by time and the action of heat and cold. The bold, black cape facing N. E. is without doubt volcanic. The upheaval is from E. to W., lines and layers of separation dipping to the W. at an angle of 30°. The face of the bold headland is black with age, stained in great patches of iron and spongy masses of black and red rock, resembling the refuse of a blast furnace. The island is traversed by two ridges, running in a N. E. and S. W. direction. The highest ridge, or the backbone, as it might be called, begins at a black headland 1,200 feet in height and is lost to view under the ice cap surmounting the whole island. The lower ridge commences at a knoll on the N. W. face, and after a slight depression rises to a considerable height in the S. W., where it fades away at a distance of eight miles.

There are five bold headlands on the N. E. face of the island. First, the bold black headland, 1,200 feet high, near which we landed. Next Cairn Point, 600 feet high, where the cairn, record, and pike staff are placed. Next the extreme N. point of the land, which shuts in a valley lying between the shore beyond and the center ridge of the island; and, finally, the large double headland beyond the valley to the S. W. There is also a slight depression or valley between Cairn Point and the backbone of the island, making back from the double headland. All this portion of the island is light-colored trap rock, slate, and shale.

The whole island is covered with a permanent ice cap, 250 to 300 feet high, above the back bone, and the large opening which we thought on board ship was a bay on the N. E. side of the island is a constantly discharging glacier; in fact, the whole N. E. face is continually discharging ice. Some of the slabs or pieces that had fallen on the ice floe from the edge of the main ice cap gave, when measured, 48 feet thickness of ice and 4 feet of thickness of snow, where it lay in the sea. How much more it measured before it fell I could not tell. There are five small glaciers discharging between headlands on this coast or face, beside the continual discharge all along the upper edge of the island, crawling down from the main ridge. There is a high ridge of broken glacier ice between the base of the island and the floe where the floe ice and glacier droppings are continually at war. I think there is no permanent ice foot attached to this side of the island, as the main pack continually grinding along carries off all discharges from the island. I found the glacier in 2.5 miles N. E. of the island. There was a slight growth of moss or black mould in the crevices of the rock. All that we gathered was picked out of the small crevices with a pencil point and knife blade. No fossil or animal remains of any kind were found. There were no broaches on which drift-wood could rest, and consequently we found none. No signs of bears, foxes, hares, or lemmings were seen, and no birds except dovekies, which were numerous in the rocky cliffs.

From the top of the island the ice fields could be seen for many miles away to the N. W., inshore of which was a large space of open water, extending toward and disappearing under the brow of the cliffs. The pack was much broken and fissured with lanes of water toward the N. W.; as far as the eye could see. The whole pack in all directions, from this outlook, was one jumbled up mass, and all in motion, lanes and leads continually changing. No seals or walrus or game of any kind was seen during our absence from the ship, eight dovekies being the extent of our game bag.

In the morning I prepared the record, set up the cairn and pike staff on Cairn Point; took bearings of all prominent headlands and points; made sketches for the accompanying chart of the island and profile of the land. The ship was plainly visible from the top of Cairn Point. My anxiety for boat, provisions, and equipment left on the ice, nothing of which was visible from the mountain tops, accelerated my movements, and by eight a. m. was underway, heading for the ship and keeping a lookout for our pike-staff signal. We could not follow our outward track, because it had broken so badly and had shifted so much. We sighted our signal about (10.30) ten-thirty a. m., and found our boat by one-thirty (1.30) p. m. and camped down for a rest, much relieved at our good fortune in finding our boat and gear intact.

Saturday, June 4th.—We were all out at 12.30, mounted our boat, stowed our gear, and were under way by 2.30 a. m., followed our old track back toward the ship for a couple of miles, the traveling being heavy on account of the deep snow and crust. Finally our track was lost in a general smashup of the floe, and we had laborious, hard traveling, with a cruel wind and snow storm from the N. W. We had a bad upset, which stove the port side of the boat, but not badly. My zeal to get my boat in toward the island on the day before got the better of my judgment, and it was in getting her back out of the scrape that she was damaged. Heading for the ship on a good large floe piece, but terribly heavy hauling on account of the snow and crust breaking through, making long detours to avoid ferrying over the water, after going S. W. to get N. E., by noon of this day saw the ship bearing N. E. The large block signal was a grand good mark for us when not shut in by snow squalls. By 1.30 p. m. we were so tired we could go no farther, and camped down. The pack is much more broken than it was on our inward journey, *i. e.*, we had longer distances to make to avoid open water. This was a hard day's journey for men and dogs, as it took all the strength of both while moving, and when we set fast or came to hummocks it took a breaking strain to haul through. All of this extra work comes on the men, for dogs will not haul in concert until the load is started. We hauled our sled all day long, down on the cross-bars, making three tracks in the snow, one for each runner and a center one for the boat's keel. We were all in our bags by four p. m.

Sunday, June 5th.—In the morning we were out by one thirty (1.30) a. m., and had the ship in plain sight three and a half ($3\frac{1}{2}$) miles distant. We were under way by two-thirty (2.30), knowing we would dine on board ship. We found large lanes of open water running N. E. and S. W., and skirted along one for two and a half ($2\frac{1}{2}$) miles, hoping for a crossing without the labor of ferrying. This lane of water set from the ship toward the island about five (5) miles, varying in width from one hundred yards to a half mile ($\frac{1}{2}$). By 6 a. m., found a jam in the lead, with the whole mass in motion, and in our haste to cross the moving mass, when within one mile of the ship, we had a bad upset and broke the runner of the sled. I unshipped the boat, divided the load, repaired the sled, put the boat and portion of the gear in a safe position, and started the sled and dogs with four men and half the weight in to the ship for another sled. By nine (9) a. m. new sled and gang of men arrived from the ship, and before ten (10) a. m. all arrived on board, none the worse for wear than usually falls to the lot of laboring mortals.

In regard to the men and equipment I desire nothing superior, to travel any distance.

Beyond the final breaking of the sleigh, a slight injury to the side of the boat, and the breaking of one snow-knife we had no accidents. All of our gear and equipments returned in good order. In amunition we expended one (1) Remington cartridge and twelve (12) gun cartridges.

Mr. Dunbar suffered badly from snow blindness after noon on the third (3) day, and had to be cared for from the morning of the fourth day until our arrival on board. Erichsen and Nindemann had bad cramps in the stomach after coming to the evenings of the fourth and fifth (4 & 5) days; gave each 2 oz. brandy, 15 drops tinct. opii, 5 drops extract capsicum. None of us slept well; no one could eat the food allowance; it would have lasted for twelve days, or more ; the alcohol was barely sufficient, and had we been compelled to melt snow or ice for water on our way toward the island it would not have been enough.

Our tent being white the glare within hurt our eyes. I think had it been dyed black or blue (not painted) we would have slept better. Two boat chisels should be added to the equipment of the boats, made like two-inch socket chisels, fitted on the end of short pike staffs (4 or 5 feet); the ends of the tent poles should be socket chisels. We found boarding pikes good ice picks in cutting roads, but not strong enough. Two light ice pick axes should be added to the sled equipment. Two small black or blue dungaree flags should go in the boats as signals in finding gear left behind or guides ahead. Two additional flat runners should be fitted underneath the bearers of the sleds, extending from the forward cross-bearer to the after bearer, and turning upward at both ends, tipped with iron and fastened to each of the cross-bearers. These staves or runners should be about six inches wide, to give a good bearing on top of the snow should the sled at any time sink so deep. Oak hogshead or pipe staves will give a correct idea of the dimensions. These should be set six inches apart, and the boat's keel should set between the upturned ends fore and aft. This would give room for padding at the upturned ends of the staves and prevent side riding of the boat without racking the keel. The bilge chock should run fore and aft the sled, secured by lashings to top rail and cross-bars, for a small boat extending across three of the bearers with a slight camber inward. In clinker-built boats it should be fitted to the projecting stakes. The fore and after ends of these chocks should be sharpened to pass through snow easily. It is astonishing to see what a hold the uprights of a McClintock sled take to snow or crust on top of snow. Athwart-ship chocks have the same objection. In fore and aft chocks, if they come well out and up on the boat's bilge, the boat is more firmly seated, it supports and protects the boat's bilge, and in rousing down the lashings the strain is more in a vertical direction without the outward rocking motion tending to burst the boat open. The boat's keel should also rest on the cross-bars.

Most of the sleeping-bags are too large. The bottoms should be made of reindeer skin, for the side next the ice is always cold; the tops of lighter material. They should be shaped nearly as the frustrums of two cones meeting at their bases. At the shoulders an elliptical piece should be set in at head and foot. Ellipse at foot 12″x16″; at head 10″x12″. This reduces the weight, makes the bag warmer, gives room enough for a man of 200 lbs. weight. It should have a shoulder circumference of 50″ to 60″, and made the neat length of the man, as he will involuntarily draw his feet up a little.

All of which is respectfully submitted.

Very respectfully,

GEO. W. MELVILLE,
P. A. Engi., U. S. N.

To Lieutenant GEORGE W. DE LONG, U. S. Navy,
Commanding Arctic Steamer Jeannette.

A true copy.

SAM. C. LEMLY,
Master U. S. Navy & Judge Advocate.

48TH CONGRESS, } SENATE. { EX. DOC.
2d Session. No. 48.

MESSAGE

FROM THE

PRESIDENT OF THE UNITED STATES,

TRANSMITTING

Communication from the Secretary of the Navy relative to the services extended in Russia to the survivors of the Steamer Jeannette Expedition.

JANUARY 28, 1885.—Read and referred to the Committee on Foreign Relations and ordered to be printed.

EXECUTIVE MANSION,
January 27, 1885.

To the Senate and House of Representatives:

I have the honor to transmit communications from the Secretary of the Navy recommending certain action by the Government in recognition of the services, official and personal, extended in Russia to the survivors of the Arctic Exploring steamer Jeannette and to the search parties subsequently sent to Siberia.

The authority of Congress is requested for extending the specific rewards mentioned in the paper accompanying one of the communications of the Secretary. The suggestion concerning the thanks of Congress is also submitted for consideration.

CHESTER A. ARTHUR.

NAVY DEPARTMENT,
Washington, January 10, 1885.

SIR: In view of the great services and the sympathy extended in Russia to the survivors of the Arctic Exploring steamer Jeannette, and to the search parties, subsequently sent to Siberia, it seems fitting that the Congress of the United States should tender to the Government and people of Russia an official expression of its thanks; and, further, that those officials and inhabitants of Siberia who directly and materially aided the surviving officers and men of the Jeannette and the officers of the search parties should receive such additional evidences of the appreciation of this Government as may be appropriate.

I have, therefore, the honor to recommend that the thanks of Congress be tendered to the Government and people of Russia; that the persons designated in the paper accompanying this communication be given the specific rewards set opposite their names, and that Congress be requested to make such special appropriation as may be necessary to carry these recommendations into effect.

I have the honor to be, sir, very respectfully,
WM. E. CHANDLER,
Secretary of the Navy.

The PRESIDENT.

RECOGNITION OF SERVICES EXTENDED BY RUSSIAN OFFICIALS AND OTHERS TO THE SURVIVORS OF THE ARCTIC EXPLORING STEAMER JEANNETTE AND TO THE OFFICERS OF THE SEARCH PARTIES.

SPECIAL REWARDS.

OFFICIALS.

Maj. Gen. George Tchernaieff, governor of Yakutsk, Russian Siberia: Sword, and letter from the President of the United States.
Ispravnick Kasharoffski, } Gold watch and silver medal.
Ispravnick Ipatieff,
Cossack-Subaltern Baieshoff: Silver medal, sporting rifle, and a gragratuity of $200.
Cossack-Subaltern Kalinkin: Silver medal, and a gratuity of $200.
Cossack Ivan Bozhedomoff: A gratuity of $100.

INHABITANTS OF IRKUTSK.

Mr. Stepanoff: Gold watch.
Mr. A. A. Thornan: Gratuity of $300.
Mr. Charles Lee: Gold watch.
Constantin Bobokoff: Silver medal.
Jaokin Grombeck: Silver medal.

NATIVES OF THE DISTRICT OF YAKUTSK.

Vassili Bobrowsky: Large silver medal and $500.
Ivan Androsoff: Medium silver medal.
Constantin Mohoploff: Medium silver medal.
Peter Arrara: Medium silver medal.
Slipsof Verbenie: Medium silver medal.
Alexei Atkasoff: Medium silver medal.
Nicolai Diakonoff: Medium silver medal.
Michael: Small silver medal.
Abanashi Bobrowsky: Small silver medal.
Maxim Stepenoff: Small silver medal.
Toros Savin: Small silver medal.
———— Korani: Small silver medal.

And to each of these 1 small-bore muzzle-loading sporting rifle, 500 rounds of ammunition, 1,000 percussion-caps, powder-flask, bullet-pouch, bullet-mold, cleaner, nipper, fine ax, waist-belt, sheath-knife, flint and steel, 2 pairs scissors, 100 glover's needles, 5 pounds of white and 5 pounds black linen thread, 20 yards navy flannel, 20 yards calico, 5 pounds tea, 10 pounds tobacco, and 5 pounds horse-hair for nets.

CRIMINAL EXILES IN DISTRICT OF YAKUTSK.

Kusma Eremioff (Russian): Two hundred and fifty dollars.
Yafim Kopoloff (Russian): One hundred dollars.
Feodore Serroroff (Yakut): One hundred dollars.

For general distribution among the natives of the villages of Kitach, Zemovialach, and Arrui a quantity of tea, tobacco, beads, flannel, calico, thread, needles, glover's needles, lead, and horse hair for nets, to be distributed by the headmen, and excluding those Yakuti specifically rewarded as above; the quantity should be ample for about three hundred people which is the estimated number that should benefit by this bounty.

NAVY DEPARTMENT,
Washington, January 10, 1885.

SIR: As it seems fitting that the important and valuable services, official and personal, extended in Russia to the survivors of the Arctic Exploring steamer Jeannette and to the search parties subsequently sent to Siberia should receive appropriate official recognition, I have the honor to recommend that your thanks be tendered the following named persons, all of whom, as specifically set forth in the reports made to this Department, materially aided the surviving officers and men of the Jeannette and the officers of the search parties:

Governor-General, Lieutenant-General Anuchin (Irkutsk).
Governor-General, Lieutenant-General Kalpokoffsky (Omsk).
Governor, Major-General Tchernaieff (Yakutsk).
Governor, Major-General Nassovich (Irkutsk).
Governor, Conseiller d' Etat Mertsalof (Tomsk).
Governor of Petropaulovsk.
General Peter Civer (Irkutsk).
Consul of France M. Edmond de Lagreué (Moscow).
Medical Director R. Kapello (Yakutsk).
Count Emil Ahlfeldt Laurwigen (St. Petersburgh).

As valuable services were also extended by Dr. R. Byelie and Mr. E. Leon, political exiles in Siberia, to the officers and men referred to, I shall, with your approval, tender them the thanks of this Department.

I have the honor to be, sir, very respectfully,
WM. E. CHANDLER,
Secretary of the Navy.

The PRESIDENT.

www.ingramcontent.com/pod-product-compliance
Lightning Source LLC
Chambersburg PA
CBHW032016230426
43671CB00005B/97